פְּנִינֵי רְנָה

Peninei Rena

Shemos I (Shemos-Bo)
Simcha Millman

Available on amazon.com

Cover Design: R' Dov Shmuel Tanchum Acoca
copyright © 2021 Simcha Millman
All rights reserved.
ISBN: 9798839912458

בס"ד

Congregation Knesseth Israel
698 Union Road
New Hempstead, NY 10977

Rav Chaim Schabes, Rav.

ר"ח סיון תשפ"א

My dear friend, Reb Simcha Millman שיחי' לאורך ימים טובים, with his compilation of the דברי תורה that he is presenting herein, has taught us many lessons.

The first one is the importance and חשיבות of the Shabbos table. Delectable food and melodious זמירות, are an integral part of the spirit of Shabbos, however, the centrality of the discussion of Torah topics, is really a part that at times is gives a secondary place, and Rabbi Millman is teaching us, how important and relevant this specific part is in our beautiful gathering around the Shabbos table.

The second point, not any less significant, is that, for a project to be successful, the key ingredient is preparation. Reb Simcha שליט"א, presents in front of us, the labor of getting ready and bringing up engaging and interesting conversation, that will surely bring in the inquisitive curiosity from all the members of the family, not just to hear a דבר תורה being said, but rather, pulling and sharing everyone's involvement in the דבר ה'.

Lastly, Rabbi Millman has done the leg work for us. He spent hours doing research, finding the many answers to thought provoking questions, and wants to share them with us. On the one hand, he is not giving us the benefit of doing all the preparation that he did, but on the other hand, many of us don't have the time or resources to put together a work as the one he has produced. For all of the above, we would like to be מחזיק טוב, and wish him continuous ברכה and הצלחה in all his work, together with his family in good health, and be זוכה to greet משיח צדקנו במהרה בימינו.

R. Chaim Schabes.

Foreword	i
Shemos	1
Why Does Sefer Shemos Begin With "And?"	1
Why Does the Posuk Need to Tell Us That Yosef Was in Egypt?	11
How Rav Leizer Gordon Proved That the Midrash Which Says That the Bnei Yisroel Had Six Children in Each Pregnancy in Egypt Is True and Not an Exaggeration.	17
Why Did the Bnei Yisroel Have to Go Into Exile?	24
What Did the Midwives Mean When They Described the Jewish Women as חָיוֹת, Which Literally Means Wild Animals?	32
What Good Is the Posuk Referring to That Hashem Did for the Midwives?	38
What Kind of Houses Were Made for the Midwives as a Reward for Fearing Hashem?	51
Why Doesn't the Torah Tell Us the Names of Moshe's Parents Initially?	60
What Did Yocheved See About Moshe "That He Was Good?"	71
What Is Meant by the Phrase הַלְהָרְגֵנִי אַתָּה אֹמֵר (Do You Say to Kill Me)?	79
Why Did Yisro's Daughters Refer to Moshe as an Egyptian Man?	85
The Beis HaLevi's Explanation of a Hard to Understand Shemos Raba	98
How Was a Sign for an Event That Would Only Happen in the Future a Proof Now to Moshe That Hashem Sent Him?	102
How Was Saying the Words פָּקֹד פָּקַדְתִּי a Proof That Moshe Was the Redeemer?	109
How Could Moshe Say the Bnei Yisroel Will Not Listen to Him After Hashem Promised They Would?	117
Why Did Hashem Want to Put Moshe to Death at the Inn?	129
Vaera	145
The Malbim's Explanation of How Moshe's Level of Prophesy Changed at the Beginning of Parshas Vaera.	145
What Does Shortness of Breath Mean and Why Did It Cause the Bnei Yisroel Not to Listen to Moshe?	150
How Could Moshe Conclude Pharaoh Would Not Listen to Him Based on the Bnei Yisroel Not Listening?	158
What Did Hashem Command Moshe and Aharon When the Torah Does Not Explicitly Tell Us?	167
Why Does the Torah Only List the Lineage of the Tribes of Reuven, Shimon, and Levi and Not the Rest of the Tribes?	176
Why Does the Torah Tell Us How Long Levi Lived and Not the Rest of the Tribes?	182
What Is Meant by Moshe Being Appointed a Lord Over Pharaoh?	186
Why Does the Posuk Tell Us How Old Moshe and Aharon Were When They Came to Pharaoh?	191
Why Does the Torah Mention Aharon Before Moshe?	195
Why Don't We Have Sorcerers in Our Times?	205
What Was the Reason for the Particular Order and Kinds of Plagues for the Ten Plagues?	212
Where Did the Egyptian Sorcerers Get Water From to Turn Into Blood If There Was Blood Throughout Egypt?	217
Why Did Moshe Need to Daven by Crying Out in the Plague of Frogs?	224

- Why Couldn't the Sorcerers Make Lice?..231
- Why Did Pharoah's Heart Become Hardened After Seeing That Not Even Till One of the Livestock of the Bnei Yisroel Died During the Plague of Pestilence?...............................240
- Since Hashem Hardened Pharoah's Heart, How Could Hashem Punish Him for Not Listening to Moshe?..247

Bo...257

- Why Would Hashem Hardening Pharaoh's Heart Be a Reason to Go to Pharaoh?............257
- Why Did Moshe Turn Before He Went Out From Before Pharaoh in the Plague of Locusts?..263
- Why Would "a Festival of Hashem to Us" Cause the Bnei Yisroel a Need to Bring Their Young Children and Cattle?..267
- What Did Pharaoh Mean When He Said "Evil" Is Before Your Faces?...........................278
- What Does "for All the Bnei Yisroel There Was Light in Their Dwellings" Come to Include?..282
- Why Was Hashem Concerned About What Avrohom Would Say About Fulfilling the Promise of Leaving Egypt With Riches?...287
- Why Do We Need to Know That No Dog Barked During the Plague of Killing of the Firstborns?...301
- Why Did the Korban Pesach Have to Be Specifically a Lamb?..308
- Why Was It Necessary to Take and Inspect the Korban Pesach Four Days Before Using It?..316
- Since Killing the Firstborn Was Done by Hashem Why Did the Bnei Yisroel Have to Worry About the Destroying Angel?...322
- Why Does One Posuk Mention Putting the Blood on the Lintel and Then on the Doorposts While Another Says to Do the Opposite?..332
- Why Does the Torah Add the Words כֵּן עָשׂוּ (So They Did), a Seemingly Superfluous Phrase?..341
- Why Is the Donkey the Only Non-Kosher Animal That Needs to Be Redeemed?...........347
- Why Is Tefillin Put on the Weaker Arm?..354

Foreword

When our children were young, my wife, Malka, and I decided that to increase our children's knowledge, understanding, and desire for Chumash; we would have a "question of the week" each Shabbos. The majority of the questions were well-known questions for which an answer could be found in typical Meforshim like Rashi, and we encouraged the children to find and supply answers for them. Of course, the depth of the Torah is endless, and even simple answers can be analyzed and understood in depth. To be honest, along with coming up with the question, I had to explore and compile as many answers to the question as I could, to know whether any particular answer of the children was valid. We did not necessarily each Shabbos cover all the answers that I found, but we tried to at least explore some answers in-depth to enhance the children's appreciation of both the answers they had found and other answers to the question.

After a number of years of doing this, I decided to compile and write up these answers so that others could also increase their knowledge, understanding, and desire of the Torah, Hashem's blueprint of the world. The Sefer contains about ten to fifteen questions per Parsha (many of them obvious or famous questions) and an in-depth analysis and interweaving about how the relevant Gemorahs, Medroshim, and Meforshim approach and answer these questions. When appropriate, I have taken the liberty of supplementing answers which do not fully answer the question with comments of other Meforshim even if the comments were not written for the original answer. In some cases, I have used comments a Meforesh writes even though the Meforesh did not comment in order to answer the particular question we are dealing with. In other cases, I choose to modify the answer a Meforesh offers, so it is easier for me to understand and explain. In this way, I attempt to find the fullest possible answers and analysis to the questions. The Sefer should hopefully be suited for a person who wishes to grasp and appreciate the wide spectrum of approaches to answer many fundamental questions on Chumash and are unable or does not have the resources or time to do it on their own. I have attempted to reference all sources cited to make it easier for the reader to look up the source, if desired. When appropriate, I have inserted introductions to the question, some rather lengthy, to give a bit more background and appreciation for the question and answers.

Mishlay (3:15) describes the Torah's wisdom as יְקָרָה הִיא מִפְּנִינִים וְכָל חֲפָצֶיךָ לֹא יִשְׁווּ בָהּ (it is more precious than pearls, and all your desirable things cannot be compared to it). The Malbim explains that pearls are precious because they are not found on the part of the earth that mankind dwells on

Foreword

but rather are found in the water. In a similar way, the Torah's wisdom is not found in man's intellect, but rather it is found in the heavens and is part of the wisdom of Hashem. Therefore, the Torah's wisdom is more precious than pearls since the heavens are further from man than is the earth's water. The second half of the Posuk tells us that even though one must give up the physical body's pleasures, desires, and wants to acquire the Torah's wisdom, it is worth it since "all your desirable things cannot be compared to it." I think that the easiest way to see that the Torah's wisdom is separate from a person's intellect is by noting that the Gemorah in Pesachim 66b says that if a person wise in Torah wisdom becomes angry, his Torah wisdom deserts him. Rav Chaim Shmulevitz (5733:23) explains that, unlike other wisdom, Torah wisdom only resides in a person who has refined character traits. Therefore, when a person displays the bad character trait of becoming angry, his Torah wisdom abandons him. This is as opposed to other wisdom that has over time resided and remained in both Gentiles and Jews whose character traits were reprehensible.

The Gemorah in Horayos 13a and the Bamidbar Raba (6:1) derive another dictum from the phrase, יְקָרָה הִיא מִפְּנִינִים. They say that a person with Torah wisdom is more precious than the Kohen Godol, who is the only person allowed to enter the inner of inner of the Beis Hamikdosh (the holy of holies). It is even true if the person with Torah wisdom is a Mamzer and has little genetic importance. A practical case where this dictum is applicable is where both the person with Torah wisdom and the Kohen Godol have been captured and are being held for ransom. If limited funds are available, one should redeem the person with Torah wisdom before one redeems the Kohen Godol. The Maharsha in Yuma 72a explains that the Tzitz the Kohen Godol wore had pearls in it, and that is how we know that Torah wisdom is more precious than a Kohen Godol. We note that the Tosfos Yom Tov on the Mishna in Horayos says that the Kohen Godol we are talking about is someone ignorant in Torah wisdom. This occurred during the era of the second Beis Hamikdosh, where in many cases, the Kohen Godol bought the position for money since he wanted the honor.

The Shir HaShirim Raba (1:4) says that the Bnei Yisroel are called with ten different expressions of happiness. One of these expressions of happiness is רִנָה. רִנָה is perhaps best translated as "joyous songs." Tehillim (126:5) says, הַזֹּרְעִים בְּדִמְעָה בְּרִנָּה יִקְצֹרוּ (Those who sow with tears will reap with **joyous song**). The joyous song is most typically sung by the Bnei Yisroel about and for Hashem. When building the first Beis Hamikdosh, Shlomo HaMelech davens in Sefer Melachim I (8:28) that Hashem should be, לִשְׁמֹעַ אֶל הָרִנָּה וְאֶל הַתְּפִלָּה (hearken to the joyous song and to the prayer). The Gemorah in Brochos 6a derives from this Posuk that in a place of joyous song, a Shul, davening should be offered. Rashi explains that the reason a Shul is called a place of joyous song is that the people there sing Hashem's praises in a melodious and pleasant voice.

I named this Sefer פְּנִינֵי רִנָה in memory of my daughter Perel (the Yiddish word for pearl) Rena ע"ה. Even when she was sick, she continued to praise Hashem with joyous song. We can appreciate this from the following article that was written and published by my wife, Malka, on her Shloshim.

Perel Rena Millman A"H
16 of Cheshvan 5748– 19 of Elul 5766

Foreword

My daughter, Perel Rena, suffered for five years from Systemic Juvenile Rheumatoid Arthritis. This disease is relatively rare, affecting a couple of hundred children per million, and can be debilitating but is not typically fatal. Unfortunately, she was niftar suddenly at the age of eighteen. Reflecting on her life and knowing that parents are given a touch of nevuah when they name their children, I can now see in retrospect how her name encompassed the essence of the brief life Hashem gave her.

Perel in Yiddish means pearl. A pearl is formed inside an oyster from an irritation caused by a single grain of sand. The oyster takes that irritant and makes it into something beautiful - a lustrous pearl, just like Perel Rena took her illness and created for herself something more than beautiful, and she did it with joy - Rena. The most common comment from the people who came to be menachem avel was that Perel Rena was always smiling. Almost no one knew she was sick, and that's what Perel Rena wanted. She didn't want to be the object of pity or attention. It was the power of her Rena that attracted those around her. People who saw her in shul, on the street, in school, all talked about her smile. Perel Rena was indeed– a pearl of joy.

Perel Rena set amazing goals for herself. Her email address said it all: PReMed117@att.net. She was sure her initials fitting right in was hashgacha, proving she was meant to be a rheumatologist. If the residency proved to be too demanding, then she would have settled instead for medical research in rheumatology as Perel Rena was determined from the age of sixteen to help others and perhaps even cure those with similar medical issues. Most of all, what she would have liked was to become an MD/PhD – no small goal for anyone.

With such lofty objectives, Perel Rena always recognized the value of time and felt she needed to utilize her time to the utmost. Perel Rena was sixteen when she started her first year at Touro. Starting so young was not an excuse to take it easy, though. Instead, she even went to college over the next two summers. Her last summer, she worked on a research project for the chief of pediatric rheumatology. Other "free" time was spent studying for her GRE's for graduate school. In other words, time was never free for Perel Rena. She used every minute to the utmost.

Perel Rena also spent a sizable portion of her busy schedule doing chesed. For Perel Rena, saying that chesed begins in the home was more than just a nice platitude. Given the limits of a weakened immune system, it was often the only reliable place she could accomplish chesed on a regular basis. The chesed Perel Rena was able to do in her own house was incredible. Using her talents in graphic design, she was able to undertake countless projects, one of the more important ones being for the shul's No Talking During Davening campaign – a campaign created by her father as a zechus for a refuah shelaimah for her. Perel Rena took care of the multiple monthly lists of members, posters, award certificates, etc. . . . all right from home.

Her chesed for the home was also exemplary. Her sisters could go to her for anything from help in school work, to help with clothes, or their hair, or packing school lunch. The meals she often planned and implemented were always superior, as Perel Rena never did anything halfway. The platters she baked and sent out of the house for a neighbor's simcha were always something special and done because she knew it was something that should be done. – to share in others' simchos.

Foreword

Realizing she was in a unique position to do chesed on a taanis because she wasn't zocheh to fast the past two years, Perel Rena did much for others, like creating elaborate post taanis menus, often with her good friend. Last Yom Kippur, since she couldn't fast, she decided to help a neighbor with small children during the long time it takes to eat Pochus MeKeshiur. She had worked out plans for what chesed she wanted to do for the Yom Kippur she wasn't zocheh to live to see as well, though what she wanted most of all was to be zocheh to fast once again.

Perel Rena never did things halfway or just to get by, despite the many opportunities she could have had to do just that. One example is how she gave 20% masser. Ten percent is often hard enough for many, but by her, she wanted to give the most she was allowed. Perel Rena also never used her illness as an excuse to do things halfway or just to get by. When she first fell ill, she missed almost half the ninth-grade year. The school was very understanding and told her she did not have to worry about what she missed. Even at age thirteen, Perel Rena was not going to accept that. She insisted on taking every midterm, one at a time, studying for an entire semester's worth of material on her own, even though she had daily fevers at that time, averaging 103 degrees. Not only did she come away with A's but with an attitude that would be with her for the next five years, the attitude that she was not going to take advantage in any way of being sick. And she stuck to her principles, as a college administrator attested when coming to be menachem avel. He told us how all students fill out index cards when they come to Touro. When they come to his office for one reason or another, he writes on their card any issues they might have brought up. Feeling sure that Perel Rena must have alluded at one time or another to her illness, he had checked Perel Rena's card before coming to be menachem avel– it was blank. Perel Rena had no complaints.

Perel Rena had no complaints since she had a knack for seeing the good in what others might view as bad. There was one long period during her first year at Touro when she would go in Monday through Thursday. Typically, during that period, she would get a fever every Thursday night of about 103 o. It would last through Shabbos morning. She was able to view this fever as a tremendous chesed because it occurred on weekends, so she didn't miss school, which was so important to her.

Perel Rena was considered exceptional even by the office of her pediatric rheumatologist. The work she did there on the research project her last summer, was accomplished in a typical fashion for her, above and beyond what was expected from a summer student. Perel Rena was considered an exceptional patient as well. When the office asked her for advice on how to get the teens they see to take their medicines since teenagers are chronically lax about taking their medications, Perel Rena had no advice. "How could they not want to take their medicine so they could get better?" she wondered.

In a world where we hear so often that attitude is everything, how Perel Rena felt about her own matzav after five years of illness became clear when one day within the last year, I needed to know the password on her computer. "What am I?" she asked. "I don't know," I told her, wondering exactly where her question was supposed to take me. "Winner," she said, "and now you won't

Foreword

forget it." And I didn't.

Perel Rena was able to maintain her positive attitude over the years because she had a remarkable sense of humor. When it was time to give herself her injections, which were as many as three to four a morning over her last summer, Perel Rena took the injections out of the refrigerator at breakfast. (Room temperature helped to slightly ease the burning sensation, which she compared to the feeling of rubbing alcohol on a raw wound.) She would finish breakfast and then cheerfully announce, "Okay, I'm going to shoot myself." And off she'd go for self-inflicted pain while we were all left smiling.

Besides for her injections, which she never complained about, Perel Rena took too many pills a day to count, big ones, little ones, individually packaged pills that were difficult to open . . . The only one she ever complained about and actually shuddered over when she took was a treif pill we had asked a shailah about. Every time she took it, she told me how much she disliked it. Not for any other pill had her very essence balked like it did for this one, which after much pleading was switched to another medication, not a dose too soon for her.

Despite the constant fevers, the ups and downs with her health over the years, the hospitalizations a couple of times a year, and the often overwhelming health concerns, Perel Rena was able to live, for the most part, a very "normal" life. In fact, very few people were even aware that Perel Rena had a chronic illness, not friends, not neighbors, not classmates, nor teachers, and that is exactly how she wanted it. Though Perel Rena strived so hard to be "normal" in every aspect of the word, the amazing heights she rose to in eighteen years of living up to her name was certainly anything but what would be our definition of normal, while for Perel Rena, she was being exactly that – perfectly normal – for her.

תהא נשמתה צרורה בצרור החיים

I would like to thank and give Hakoras HaTov to my wife, Malka, and to our children Bracha Chaya, Perel Rena ע״ה, Chaim Ozer, Yehudis Ester, Leah Menucha, and Yocheved Rus for encouraging me to do the "question of the week" each week. I would also like to thank and give Hakoras HaTov to Rav Schabes, Shlita, and Rav Dovid Moskovitz, Shlita of Boston, for reading and providing helpful, useful, and practical comments on this Sefer. I would also like to thank and give Hakoras HaTov to Rav Yosef Meir Kantor Zatzal, with whom I discussed some of these answers on our way to and from his nightly Amud Yomi Shiur, which I attended for over twenty years. His opinion that doing the "question of the week" was much better than testing the children on what they had learned the previous week gave me Chizuk to continue the project. Many thanks are due to my son-in-law Dovi Acoca נ״י for designing the beautiful cover for this Sefer. Most of all, I would like to thank and give Hakoras HaTov to HaKodosh Boruch Hu for continuously giving me the strength and desire to do this project.

Shemos

Why Does Sefer Shemos Begin With "And?"

וְאֵלֶּה שְׁמוֹת בְּנֵי יִשְׂרָאֵל הַבָּאִים מִצְרָיְמָה אֵת יַעֲקֹב אִישׁ וּבֵיתוֹ בָּאוּ (א:א) Shemos (1:1) And these are the names of the Bnei Yisroel who came to Egypt; with Yaakov, man and his household came.

Why does Sefer Shemos begin with "And?"

Rabeinu Bechay points out that Sefer Devorim starts with the Hebrew word אֵלֶּה (these) and does not say וְאֵלֶּה (and these) in contrast to how Sefer Shemos begins. We should add that, in fact, besides for Shemos and Devorim, other Parshios in the Chumash begin with the Hebrew word אֵלֶּה: Noach, Pekuday, and Maasai, while some begin with the Hebrew word וְאֵלֶּה: Toldos, and Mishpotim.

The Midrash Tanchuma on Shemos (3) says that before Yaakov went down to Egypt, he married off even the youngest of the people coming down to Egypt as the Torah says in our Posuk, "man and his household came." The Eitz Yosef quotes a Yepheh Toar that Yaakov knew he needed 70 people to come down to Egypt to match the 70 angel officers who are designated for each of the 70 nations. One could only be counted as one of the 70 if one was married since a single person is considered as missing half of his body. The Chizkuni and Kli Yakor say that the reason Yaakov married off even small children was that Yaakov knew that the Egyptians were morally corrupt, and therefore, he didn't want his descendants to be influenced by or to marry Egyptians.

The Shemos Raba (1:6) points out that the order in which the names of the tribes are mentioned is different in different places in Chumash. For example, by our Pesukim, the tribes are mentioned in the order of first the children of Leah and Rochel and then the children of the maidservants Bilhah and Zilpah. The Yepheh Toar says that we also find this order in the beginning of Sefer Bamidbar when the Nesiim (princes) of the tribes are designated to assist in the counting of the Bnei Yisroel. However, in Parshas Vayigash, before they went down to Egypt, the counting has first the sons of Leah, then the sons of her maidservant Zilpah, then the sons of Rochel, and finally the sons of her maidservant Bilhah. When Yaakov gives the Brochos to the Bnei Yisroel before he is Niftar, he first gives the Brochos to Leah's sons, followed by the sons of the maidservants and then by the sons of Rochel. Several times in Sefer Bamidbar, the Bnei Yisroel are listed in the order they encamped around the Mishkan. When the spies are sent out in the beginning of Parshas Shelach, a completely different order of Reuven, Shimon, Yehuda, Yisochar, Ephraim, Binyamin, Zevulon, Menashe, Don, Asher, Naftali, and Gad is used. The Shemos Raba says that the reason for these differing orders is so one should not denigrate the sons of the maidservants since sometimes they are listed before

Shemos

some of the sons of Yaakov's wives. The order also depended on the event they were being mentioned for since some events required different tribes to lead the event, and therefore, they are listed first. The Yepheh Toar says that most times, the order chosen is obvious, and for the other times, he references a Ramban in Parshas Vayigash (46:18).

The Ramban says that typically the Bnei Yisroel are listed, first the sons of Yaakov's wives and then the sons of the maidservants. However, in Parshas Vayigash, the order is different since the Torah counts by order of how many of the seventy people each wife or maidservant had. In Parshas Shelach, when the spies are sent out, the Ramban in Bamidbar (13:4) says that the Torah orders them according to who was the most honorable. These are examples of what the Shemos Raba means when it says "that it depended on the event they were being mentioned for, since some events required different tribes to lead the event and therefore, they are listed first."

The Malbim, in his Sefer Eretz Chemdah, says that the Zohar explains the reason Hashem chose to exile the Bnei Yisroel in Egypt was to prevent the Bnei Yisroel from intermingling with the Goyim, which would prevent them from being redeemed. It would seem that the Zohar he is referring to is on Shemos 15a. The redemption was in the merit that they did not change their names and that they did not intermarry with the Goyim. Therefore, Hashem chose a nation who despised even eating bread with the Bnei Yisroel as Beraishis (43:32) says, "because the Egyptians could not eat food with the Hebrews, because it is an abomination to the Egyptians." In addition, Hashem chose the Egyptians, who were the epitome of immorality, so that the Bnei Yisroel would be disgusted from intermingling with them. That is why our Posuk stresses that the people kept both their Hebrew names and kept "man and his household" by not intermingling with the households of the Egyptians.

Vayigash (46:4) says, "I (Hashem) will go down with you (Yaakov) to Egypt, and I will also bring you up." Pirkei D'Rabi Eliezer (39) explains how this prophecy was fulfilled. If one carefully counts the people coming down to Egypt, one finds that there were only 69 people who are mentioned, as Rashi in Beraishis (46:15) points out. Though there are many explanations about who the 70th was, the Pirkei D'Rabi Eliezer says that the 70th "person" was Hashem. In a similar way, the Pirkei D'Rabi Eliezer says that the Bnei Yisroel were one person short of the 600,000 people needed to be redeemed from Egypt. Here also, the Pirkei D'Rabi Eliezer says that Hashem joined with the count to give a count of exactly six hundred thousand. Only with the numerical inclusion of Hashem did the Bnei Yisroel have the required amount of people to go down to and be redeemed from Egypt.

1) The Shemos Raba (30:3) in the beginning of Parshas Mishpotim presents an answer to our question. In truth, the Torah many times introduces a topic with either the word אֵלֶּה or the word וְאֵלֶּה. The Maharzav on Beraishis Raba (12:1) explains that when one uses the word אֵלֶּה (these) or the word וְאֵלֶּה (and these), it is like a person who points his finger at an object that he made and says that what I made is beautiful and deserves to be praised. In the case of the Torah, it is as if the Torah is pointing with its figurative finger at the object and saying this object is fit to be praised. Many times in the Torah, when the Torah uses the word אֵלֶּה or וְאֵלֶּה, the Midrashim will explain the difference between these two words. For example, in our case, the Shemos Raba (1:2) and the Midrash Tanchuma in Shemos (2) says that wherever the Torah begins a topic with the word, וְאֵלֶּה

Shemos

the Torah is adding on another praise about this topic that was previously discussed. For example, says the Midrash Tanchuma, Sefer Shemos begins with וְאֵלֶּה (And these) to add on more praise to the names of the Bnei Yisroel who came to Egypt. When the Torah begins a topic with the word אֵלֶּה, it does so to praise this object to the exclusion of some aspect about this topic that was previously discussed.

In Parshas Mishpotim, the Shemos Raba (30:3), Midrash Tanchuma on Mishpotim (3), and Mechilta discuss why Mishpotim begins with וְאֵלֶּה and not אֵלֶּה. The Shemos Raba presents and explains in many cases why the Torah used either of these two words. It quotes Beraishis (2:4) which says, אֵלֶּה תוֹלְדוֹת הַשָּׁמַיִם וְהָאָרֶץ בְּהִבָּרְאָם (These are the generations of the heavens and the earth when they were created). The Nezer HaKodesh references the Pirkei D'Rabi Eliezer (3), which says that previously Hashem had made many worlds and had destroyed them. However, "these" (this Heaven and Earth) are the distinguished creation and will not be destroyed like the previous creations. We should point out that the Pirkei D'Rabi Eliezer says that Hashem did not actually create these worlds; Hashem just thought about creating them and calculated that they would not last.

The Shemos Raba also cites the beginning of Parshas Noach (6:9) where it says, אֵלֶּה תּוֹלְדֹת נֹחַ נֹחַ אִישׁ צַדִּיק תָּמִים (These are the generations of Noach, Noach was a righteous man). By using the word אֵלֶּה, the Torah is saying that only these generations of Noach are the distinguished generations. This generation, as opposed to the previous generations who were so corrupt that Hashem had to bring a flood to the world and destroy them. Another example is Beraishis (25:12) which says, וְאֵלֶּה תֹּלְדֹת יִשְׁמָעֵאל בֶּן אַבְרָהָם אֲשֶׁר יָלְדָה הָגָר הַמִּצְרִית שִׁפְחַת שָׂרָה לְאַבְרָהָם (And these are the generations of Yishmael the son of Avrohom, whom Hagar the Egyptian, the maidservant of Sorah, bore to Avrohom). The use of וְאֵלֶּה is similar to our Posuk, which also uses the word וְאֵלֶּה. In this case, even though Yishmael was important enough for Hashem to figuratively point a finger at them, he was no more distinguished than the six other sons which Avrohom had with Keturah, which are mentioned a few Pesukim earlier in Beraishis (25:2).

The Shemos Raba now presents an example which, at first glance, would seem to violate the general principle that when the Posuk uses the term וְאֵלֶּה, it does so to say that these are not more distinguished than the previous ones mentioned. Almost immediately following previous Posuk about Yishmael, it says in Beraishis (25:19) וְאֵלֶּה תּוֹלְדֹת יִצְחָק בֶּן אַבְרָהָם (And these are the generations of Yitzchak the son of Avrohom). Following our general principle, because the Torah used the terminology of וְאֵלֶּה, we would say that the generations of Yitzchak are also distinguished just like the generations of Yishmael, but not more distinguished. The problem would be that this does not make sense since the generations of Yitzchak included the righteous Yaakov, while the generations of Yishmael were all wicked people. The Shemos Raba says that "the generations of Yitzchak" are referring only to Esav and not Yaakov. Therefore, it makes sense to use the term וְאֵלֶּה to say that Esav was distinguished, but he was no more distinguished than the descendants of Yishmael, all of whom were wicked people. The way we know that the generation of Yitzchak is only referring to some of his descendants (just Esav) is because the Hebrew word for generation תֹּלְדֹת used in the Posuk is missing a "Vav" and is not written with two "Vavs" as the Posuk we quoted before from Beraishis (2:4), אֵלֶּה תוֹלְדוֹת.

Shemos

The Shemos Raba next considers Beraishis (37:2) towards the beginning of Parshas Vayeshev, which says, אֵלֶּה תֹּלְדוֹת יַעֲקֹב (These are the generations of Yaakov). This Posuk follows the lineage of all the leaders of Esav. By using the term אֵלֶּה and not וְאֵלֶּה, the Torah is saying that the generations that descended from Yaakov are distinguished since they are righteous as opposed to the generations that descended from Esav who were all wicked. The Shemos Raba considers Bamidbar (3:1), which says, וְאֵלֶּה תּוֹלְדֹת אַהֲרֹן וּמֹשֶׁה (And these are the generations of Aharon and Moshe). The Gemorah in Sanhedrin 19b points out that even though the Torah says the generations of Aharon and Moshe, it only lists the children of Aharon. From this Posuk, the Gemorah derives that someone who teaches someone else Torah (like Moshe did to Aharon's children) is equivalent to having given birth to them. Since we are only talking about Aharon's descendants, the Shemos Raba explains that the Torah uses the word וְאֵלֶּה to tell us that all Aharon's children were distinguished. Though the Torah says right after that two sons of Aharon, Nadav and Avihu, died because they brought foreign fire on the Mizbeach, they were nonetheless just as distinguished as Aharon's other two surviving sons.

The Shemos Raba, which is found at the beginning of Parshas Mishpotim, now considers the Posuk at the beginning of Parshas Mishpotim, which says וְאֵלֶּה הַמִּשְׁפָּטִים אֲשֶׁר תָּשִׂים לִפְנֵיהֶם (And these are the laws that you shall set before them). The Gemorah in Sanhedrin 56b says that when the Bnei Yisroel were in Moroh, right after they crossed the Red Sea, they were first given the logical laws to study. Now, in the beginning of Parshas Mishpotim, they are again given the logical laws (Mishpotim). By beginning Parshas Mishpotim with the word וְאֵלֶּה, the Torah is telling us that both the laws given in Moroh in addition to the laws given here at Mount Sinai were both distinguished, and the laws here did not supersede or conflict with those given in Moroh.

We have on purpose left out one other case, and that is our Posuk at the beginning of Parshas Shemos, which begins with וְאֵלֶּה. The Shemos Raba explains that the names here are also distinguished in addition to the first time that they are mentioned in Parshas Vayigash (46:8) when they went down to Egypt. The Eitz Yosef explains that just like when they first went down to Egypt, everyone was righteous and distinguished throughout their entire lives in Egypt (which was the majority of their life-span); they all remained righteous as when they first went down to Egypt.

2) The Shemos Raba (1:5) and Midrash Tanchuma in Shemos (3) answer our question similarly. We have already discussed in the first answer that when the Torah uses the word וְאֵלֶּה, it comes to add another mark of distinction to what was previously mentioned. They say that just like the Torah told us the meaning of all the brothers' names when they were born, each name was in addition distinguished by being prophecies to the redemption from Egypt and the full redemption at the time of Moshiach. The Yismach Moshe points out that the reason Shemos (1:5) emphasized that seventy people came down to Egypt was to point out that the merit of Yaakov and his sons coming down to Egypt would be a merit for redemption from both Egypt and when we were scattered amongst the 70 nations of the world

For example, Reuven's name was a prophecy to Hashem choosing Moshe to redeem the Bnei Yisroel from Egypt as is introduced in Shemos (3:7) וַיֹּאמֶר ה' **רָאֹה רָאִיתִי** אֶת עֳנִי עַמִּי אֲשֶׁר בְּמִצְרָיִם וְאֶת

Shemos

צַעֲקָתָם שָׁמַעְתִּי מִפְּנֵי נֹגְשָׂיו כִּי יָדַעְתִּי אֶת מַכְאֹבָיו (And Hashem said, "I have surely seen the affliction of My people who are in Egypt, and I have heard their cry because of their slave drivers, for I know their pains."). With regard to Shimon, it was a prophecy to the Posuk that the Bnei Yisroel first became fit to be redeemed when the Torah says in Shemos (2:24) וַיִּשְׁמַע אֱלֹקִים אֶת נַאֲקָתָם (Hashem heard their cry). With regard to Levi, the Shemos Raba and Midrash Tanchuma differ on which Pesukim about redemption their names were a prophecy for. We will choose to follow the Midrash Tanchuma, which lists Pesukim for all the names of the tribes. Levi is a prophecy for Zechariah (2:15) which describes that at the time of Moshiach וְנִלְווּ גוֹיִם רַבִּים אֶל ה' בַּיּוֹם הַהוּא (And many nations shall join Hashem on that day). Yehuda is a prophecy to the Posuk about the time of Moshiach in Sefer Yeshayahu (12:1): וְאָמַרְתָּ בַּיּוֹם הַהוּא **אוֹדְךָ** ה' כִּי אָנַפְתָּ בִּי יָשֹׁב אַפְּךָ וּתְנַחֲמֵנִי (And you shall say on that day (the day of redemption), "I will thank You, Hashem, for I made you angry with me (and sent you into exile); may Your wrath turn away and may You comfort me."). Yisochar is a prophecy to when Rochel will cry for the Bnei Yisroel when they are exiled to Babylonia, telling her that there will be a reward for her crying in the time of Moshiach when Sefer Yirmiyahu (31:15) says, כִּי יֵשׁ **שָׂכָר** לִפְעֻלָּתֵךְ נְאֻם ה' וְשָׁבוּ מֵאֶרֶץ אוֹיֵב (for there is a reward for your action, says Hashem, and they shall come back from the land of the enemy). Zevulon is a prophecy to Sefer Melachim I (8:13) where Shlomo, after building the Beis Hamikdosh, proclaims that once built the place of the Beis Hamikdosh will be forever when he says, בָּנֹה בָנִיתִי בֵּית **זְבֻל** לָךְ מָכוֹן לְשִׁבְתְּךָ עוֹלָמִים ("I have surely built You (Hashem) a house to dwell in; a settled place for You to dwell in forever."). Binyamin is a prophecy to when Yeshayahu prophesizes that Hashem will punish the Goyim for the shame they made to Tzion by totally destroying it down to its base and swears in Sefer Yeshayahu (62:8) נִשְׁבַּע ה' **בִּימִינוֹ** וּבִזְרוֹעַ עֻזּוֹ אִם אֶתֵּן אֶת דְּגָנֵךְ עוֹד מַאֲכָל לְאֹיְבַיִךְ וְאִם יִשְׁתּוּ בְנֵי נֵכָר תִּירוֹשֵׁךְ אֲשֶׁר יָגַעַתְּ בּוֹ (Hashem swore by His right hand and by the arm of His strength; I will no longer give your grain to your enemies, and foreigners shall no longer drink your wine for which you have toiled). Dan is a prophecy to the redemption from Egypt where it says in Shemos (15:14) וְגַם אֶת הַגּוֹי אֲשֶׁר יַעֲבֹדוּ **דָּן** אָנֹכִי וְאַחֲרֵי כֵן יֵצְאוּ בִּרְכֻשׁ גָּדוֹל (And also the nation that they will serve will I (Hashem) judge, and afterwards they will go forth with great possessions. The Midrash Tanchuma says that Naftali is a prophecy to Shir HaShirim (4:11) נֹפֶת **תִּטֹּפְנָה** שִׂפְתוֹתַיִךְ כַּלָּה דְּבַשׁ וְחָלָב תַּחַת לְשׁוֹנֵךְ וְרֵיחַ שַׂלְמֹתַיִךְ כְּרֵיחַ לְבָנוֹן (The words of your lips are sweet as if they drip flowing honey, O bride; honey and milk are under your tongue, and the fragrance of your garments is like the fragrance of Lebanon). The Shir HaShirim Raba (4:11) says that this Posuk refers to the fact that there were either 600,000 or 1,200,000 thousand prophets who prophesized during the days of Eliyahu when Prophecy was very prevalent. The reason we don't have any record of the vast majority of these prophecies is that they were prophecies for events and people at that time and did not have any messages for future generations. At the time of Moshiach, Hashem will reveal these prophecies, and this is what "The words of your lips are sweet as if they drip flowing honey" means, which will happen at the time of Moshiach. The Midrash Tanchuma says that Gad is a prophecy to the Mon that fell in the desert and signified the redemption from Egypt about which Bamidbar (11:7) says, וְהַמָּן כִּזְרַע **גַּד** הוּא וְעֵינוֹ כְּעֵין הַבְּדֹלַח (Now the Mon was like coriander seed, and its appearance was like the appearance of crystal). Asher is a prophecy to Malachi (3:12) which describes what happens after Hashem will send King Moshiach and says, וְאִשְּׁרוּ אֶתְכֶם כָּל הַגּוֹיִם כִּי תִהְיוּ אַתֶּם אֶרֶץ חֵפֶץ (And then all the nations shall praise you, for you shall be a desirable land). Finally, Yosef is a prophecy to Sefer Yeshayahu (11:11) which speaks about what will happen at the time that Moshiach will come and the people in exile will be returned as it says, וְהָיָה בַּיּוֹם הַהוּא **יוֹסִיף**

Shemos

וְהָיָה בַּיּוֹם הַהוּא יוֹסִיף אֲדֹנָי שֵׁנִית יָדוֹ לִקְנוֹת אֶת שְׁאָר עַמּוֹ אֲשֶׁר יִשָּׁאֵר מֵאַשּׁוּר וּמִמִּצְרַיִם וּמִפַּתְרוֹס וּמִכּוּשׁ וּמֵעֵילָם וּמִשִּׁנְעָר וּמֵחֲמָת וּמֵאִיֵּי הַיָּם (And it shall come to pass that on that day, Hashem shall continue to apply His hand a second time to acquire the rest of His people, that will remain from Assyria and from Egypt and from Pathros and from Cush and from Elam and from Shinor and from Chamas and from the islands of the sea).

Bamidbar (4:32), when referring to the vessels used in the Mishkan, says וּבְשֵׁמֹת תִּפְקְדוּ אֶת כְּלֵי מִשְׁמֶרֶת מַשָּׂאָם (You shall designate by name the vessels assigned to them (the Levite family of Merari) for their burden). The Sforno, at the beginning of Parshas Pekuday, says that not just the main vessels used in the Mishkan (the Aron, Shulchan, Menorah, and Mizbeach) but also each auxiliary vessel was important enough to be called by its specific name and not as a general category of vessels. In a similar way, the Sforno at the beginning of Shemos says that the reason our Posuk says, "And these are the names," is to point out that each of the tribes was important enough to be referenced by name. Rav Gifter, in his Sefer Pirkei Torah, writes that the name of the people mentioned in the Torah reflects their inner makeup. This was the case the first time the names of the tribes are mentioned in Parshas Vayigash (46:8). Rav Gifter says that the Shemos Raba and Midrash Tanchuma in this answer are telling us that in addition, their names also reflected the fact that while they lived in Egypt, they guided the Bnei Yisroel and planted the seeds to turn exile into redemption both for the redemption from Egypt and for the redemption at the time of Moshiach. The Maor VaShemesh says that the brothers davened for the redemption while they were still alive, and this is what the Midrashim mean when they say that the tribes' names now symbolized the redemption. These prayers were held for years until the time of the redemption, and at that point, the merit of their prayers allowed the Bnei Yisroel to be redeemed from Egypt.

The Vayikra Raba (32:5) says that the Bnei Yisroel were redeemed from Egypt since they kept their Hebrew names, kept their Hebrew language, did not speak Loshon Horah, and that they were not immoral. The Kli Yakor points out that had they either changed their Hebrew names or did not keep their Hebrew language, then the names of the tribes which only in Hebrew prophesize on the redemption would no longer have been a merit for them to be redeemed from Egypt.

3) The Shemos Raba (1:3) and Midrash Lekach Tov present another answer to our question. They say that the Bnei Yisroel are compared to the stars of the Heaven. Tehillim (147:4) says, מוֹנֶה מִסְפָּר לַכּוֹכָבִים לְכֻלָּם שֵׁמוֹת יִקְרָא (He (Hashem) counts the number of the stars; He calls them all by name). At the Bris Bain HaBesorim, Hashem says to Avrohom in Beraishis (15:5), "Please look heavenward and count the stars, if you are able to count them." And He (Hashem) said to him, "So will be your seed." Since the Bnei Yisroel are compared to stars, Hashem counted them all by name both when the Bnei Yisroel went down to Egypt and now when they died. The Yismach Yisroel references the Gemorah in Beitzah 3b, which says that an item that is counted is so important that it cannot be nullified no matter how much more of something else is mixed with it. For example, if one part of a counted item that is forbidden to eat becomes mixed up with one thousand times more of an item that is permissible to eat, the mixture is not permitted to be eaten. By the fact that Hashem counts each member of the Bnei Yisroel shows that Hashem considers each member of the Bnei Yisroel to be important. Rav Elchonon in Kovetz Parshios explains that each person has a special mission in this world, and therefore each person is named and counted. Since the Torah wants to emphasize

Shemos

that the tribes are being counted a second time, the Torah begins Sefer Shemos with "and." Not only does Hashem count and name the stars, but Hashem also counts and names all heavenly bodies when he takes them out (they become visible) as Sefer Yeshayahu (40:26) says, הַמּוֹצִיא בְמִסְפָּר צְבָאָם לְכֻלָּם בְּשֵׁם יִקְרָא (Hashem takes out their host by number; all of them He calls by name). The Maharal, in Gur Aryeh, says that the second part of the Posuk "all of them He calls by name" is referring to when they are put away (become invisible) since one calls "someone" when one wants them to come back (and be put away). Therefore, the Chizkuni and Mizrachi explain that counting and naming the Bnei Yisroel when they go down to Egypt and when they die is similar to Hashem counting and naming the stars. The Maharal says that the twelve tribes are also similar to stars in that there are twelve Mazalos (constellations of the Zodiac) and that in the same way a constellation includes many stars, so each tribe included many important people. The Kli Yakor explains that righteous people are like stars, which only shine brightly at night. Only after a person has been Niftar can we be sure and say that the person shone brightly and was righteous and did not stray from the path of righteousness. This is what Koheles means in Koheles (4:2) "And I praise the dead who have already died, more than the living who are still alive." Rav Gifter, in his Sefer Pirkei Torah, points out that the reason that the tribes were counted when they were Niftar is because they were now ready to begin the second phase of their "lives" in Olom HaBa. The Toldos Yitzchak takes this a step further and says that the reason that righteous people are compared to stars is because even after their time in this world is finished, their essence or Neshama remains alive. This is akin to stars who, even though they are not seen during the day, are still very much in existence. In fact, righteous people are more complete after they are Niftar than when they are still alive. Using what we have previously quoted from the Kli Yakor, the simplest way to explain this concept is that only after the person is Niftar can we be sure how righteous the person was since a person always has free choice. The Tzedah LeDerech says that the idea that righteous people are always in existence, even after their time in this world is finished, is what Daniyel (12:3) means when it says, "and those who bring the multitudes to righteousness are like the stars forever and ever."

Rav Yaakov Kaminetsky points out that we see in Yosef's dream that Yaakov was the sun, and the tribes were the stars. Only when the sun sets are the stars seen in their full glory. Here also, after Yaakov was Niftar, the light emanating from the tribes lit up the increasing darkening Egyptian exile. This added light is why the tribes are counted again since this much-needed light after Yaakov was Niftar was an added praise for the tribes. In fact, the Shemos Raba (1:8) and Seder Olam (3) say the slavery did not begin until after all the twelve tribes had been Niftar. Until then, these "stars" prevented the slavery from beginning. Rav Yaakov explains the 400 years of slavery officially began when Yitzchak was born. As long as the twelve tribes felt that their land was Eretz Yisroel and had the desire to return there, this fact alone was enough for Hashem to consider it as if they were in slavery without bringing any conditions of slavery from the Egyptians. However, when the next generation began feeling as if Egypt was their homeland, the conditions of slavery began.

4) The Yalkut Shimoni is the source of the answer Rashi presents to our question and presents the following Moshul. There was once a King that built his capital city, and it collapsed. He then rebuilt it, and it collapsed again. He rebuilt it a third time and made sure to reinforce the building, and this time it remained standing. The King was very pleased and always mentioned the city. Similarly,

Shemos

when Hashem was building the Bnei Yisroel, Avrohom had Yishmael and the sons of Keturah while Yitzchak had Esav. The Bnei Yisroel could not be built because of Yishmael and Esav. When Yaakov had twelve pillars upon which the Bnei Yisroel could be built, and they all remained righteous, Hashem was happy and kept mentioning them. This love for the Bnei Yisroel is why Hashem mentioned their names both when they went down to Egypt and when they were Niftar. Since the Torah wants to emphasize that they are being counted a second time, the Torah begins Sefer Shemos with "And." Rabeinu Bechay says that Hashem loves the Bnei Yisroel so much that in one Posuk in the Torah, the name "Bnei Yisroel" is mentioned five times. This Posuk is in Bamidbar (8:19), which says, וָאֶתְּנָה אֶת הַלְוִיִּם נְתֻנִים לְאַהֲרֹן וּלְבָנָיו מִתּוֹךְ בְּנֵי יִשְׂרָאֵל לַעֲבֹד אֶת עֲבֹדַת בְּנֵי יִשְׂרָאֵל בְּאֹהֶל מוֹעֵד וּלְכַפֵּר עַל בְּנֵי יִשְׂרָאֵל וְלֹא יִהְיֶה בִּבְנֵי יִשְׂרָאֵל נֶגֶף בְּגֶשֶׁת בְּנֵי יִשְׂרָאֵל אֶל הַקֹּדֶשׁ.

5) The Eben Ezra and Chizkuni answer our question similarly. The Eben Ezra and Chizkuni say that Sefer Shemos begins with "And" since the Torah wanted to connect to the subject in the last Pesukim of Sefer Beraishis. Beraishis (50:23) says, "Yosef saw children of a third generation born to Ephraim; also the sons of Machir the son of Menashe were born on Yosef's knees." Since that Posuk speaks about how the 70 people multiplied, it is connected to our Pesukim, which also speaks of the Bnei Yisroel multiplying. The Rashbam says that the reason our Posuk repeated the fact that only 70 people came down to Egypt is because the Torah wanted to highlight the fact recorded in Shemos (1:7) "The Bnei Yisroel were fruitful and swarmed and increased and became very, very strong, and the land became filled with them," until they numbered 600,000 men from age twenty and up when they went out of Egypt. By repeating that the Bnei Yisroel only numbered 70 when they came down to Egypt, the increase in numbers is much more remarkable.

6) The Ramban and Rabeinu Bechay answer our question similarly. They say that the Torah wanted to come back to the topic of the Bnei Yisroel coming down to Egypt for exile and connect this Posuk to the similar Posuk in Parshas Vayigash (46:8), which says, "And these are the names of the Bnei Yisroel who were coming to Egypt: Yaakov and his sons, Yaakov's firstborn was Reuven." By doing this, the Posuk is designating Sefer Shemos as the Sefer that covers the entire topic of the exile in Egypt, beginning when Yaakov and his sons came down to Egypt and culminating with the complete physical and spiritual redemption of the Bnei Yisroel when Hashem's Shechinah came to rest in the Mishkan. The Ramban says that we also find in another place an example where the same Posuk is repeated so that the Sefer talks about a complete epoch in history. The two volumes of Divrei HaYomim cover the history of mankind from creation all the way up to the time that Hashem put the idea into Koresh's heart to allow and aid the building of the second Beis Hamikdosh. Divrei HaYomim ends with the Pesukim וּבִשְׁנַת אַחַת לְכוֹרֶשׁ מֶלֶךְ פָּרַס לִכְלוֹת דְּבַר ה' בְּפִי יִרְמְיָהוּ הֵעִיר ה' אֶת רוּחַ כּוֹרֶשׁ מֶלֶךְ פָּרַס וַיַּעֲבֶר קוֹל בְּכָל מַלְכוּתוֹ וְגַם בְּמִכְתָּב לֵאמֹר. כֹּה אָמַר כּוֹרֶשׁ מֶלֶךְ פָּרַס כָּל מַמְלְכוֹת הָאָרֶץ נָתַן לִי ה' אֱלֹקֵי הַשָּׁמַיִם וְהוּא פָקַד עָלַי לִבְנוֹת לוֹ בַיִת בִּירוּשָׁלַיִם אֲשֶׁר בִּיהוּדָה מִי בָכֶם מִכָּל עַמּוֹ ה' אֱלֹקָיו עִמּוֹ וְיָעַל (And in the first year of Koresh, King of Persia, at the completion of the word of Hashem in the mouth of Yirmiyahu, Hashem aroused the spirit of Koresh the King of Persia, and he issued a proclamation throughout all his kingdom, and put it also in writing, saying: "So said Koresh the King of Persia: All the kingdoms of the earth has Hashem G-d of the heavens delivered to me, and He commanded me to build Him a House in Yerushalayim, which is in Yehuda. Who among you is of all His people, may Hashem his G-d be with him, and he may ascend."). Ezra, who wrote Divrei HaYomim, begins his own Sefer

Shemos

Ezra from the time that Divrei HaYomim ends till he was Niftar. Therefore, Ezra starts Sefer Ezra with the same Pesukim that he ended Divrei HaYomim with. These are the first two Pesukim in Sefer Ezra: וּבִשְׁנַת אַחַת לְכוֹרֶשׁ מֶלֶךְ פָּרַס לִכְלוֹת דְּבַר ה' מִפִּי יִרְמְיָה הֵעִיר ה' אֶת רוּחַ כֹּרֶשׁ מֶלֶךְ פָּרַס וַיַּעֲבֶר קוֹל בְּכָל מַלְכוּתוֹ וְגַם בְּמִכְתָּב לֵאמֹר. כֹּה אָמַר כֹּרֶשׁ מֶלֶךְ פָּרַס כֹּל מַמְלְכוֹת הָאָרֶץ נָתַן לִי ה' אֱלֹקֵי הַשָּׁמָיִם וְהוּא פָקַד עָלַי לִבְנוֹת לוֹ בַיִת בִּירוּשָׁלַם אֲשֶׁר בִּיהוּדָה. According to the Ramban and Rabeinu Bechay, the reason the Torah begins Sefer Shemos with "And" is because the Posuk in Vayigash begins with "And," and the Torah wanted to quote the same Posuk to establish the epoch of Sefer Shemos.

7) The Daas Zekanim, Kli Yakor, and Oznayim LeTorah answer our question similarly. The Shemos Raba (1:8) and Seder Olam (3) say the slavery did not begin until after all the twelve tribes had been Niftar. At that time, the Egyptians enacted special taxes on the Bnei Yisroel. The Shemos Raba (1:6) says that with these special taxes, it felt as if the Bnei Yisroel just now came to Egypt and were now being treated as foreigners. That is why our Posuk literally says, "And these are the names of the Bnei Yisroel who are coming to Egypt." The Kli Yakor explains that the reason our Posuk begins with "and" is to connect it to the last Posuk in Sefer Beraishis, which says, "And Yosef died at the age of one hundred ten years, and they embalmed him, and he was placed into the coffin in Egypt." Yosef's death, along with that of his brothers, changed the attitude of the Egyptians towards the Bnei Yisroel, and they now started enslaving them.

8) The Ohr HaChaim HaKodosh also presents an answer to our question. He says that beginning Sefer Shemos with "and" teaches us that Yaakov's sons were righteous just like Avrohom, Yitzchak, and Yaakov, who take up the bulk of the topics in Sefer Beraishis.

9) The Ohr HaChaim presents another answer to our question. The Midrash Tanchuma in Shemos (4) says that the 400-year exile began when Yitzchak was born. It derives this from Beraishis (15:13), which says, "And He (Hashem) said to Avrohom, "You shall surely know that your seed will be strangers in a land that is not theirs." Being "strangers in a land that is not theirs" only starts from when Avrohom has seed. Though Avrohom did have Yishmael thirteen years before Yitzchak, since the exile in Egypt had nothing to do with Yishmael, the exile starts from the seed (Yitzchak), which is relevant to the Egyptian exile. The "And" at the beginning of Shemos tells us that just like the generations who were in Egypt were in exile; their fathers, all the way back to when Yitzchak was born, were also in exile and also count in the 400-year exile.

10) The Ohr HaChaim presents another answer to our question. After Yaakov and Esav met in the beginning of Parshas Vayishlach, they went their separate ways. Beraishis (36:6) says, "And Esav took his wives, his sons, and his daughters and all the people of his household, and his cattle and all his animals and all his property that he had acquired in the land of Canaan, and he went to another land, because of his brother Yaakov." The Beraishis Raba (82:13) says that the reason Esav left Eretz Yisroel was because he did not want to have anything to do with the 400-year exile that Avrohom prophesized about. In contrast, says the Ohr HaChaim, Yaakov and his sons accepted Hashem's decree of the exile upon themselves. As proof, he quotes the end of our Posuk, which says, "man and his household came." Had they not willingly accepted the exile in Egypt, they would not have uprooted their houses and households in Eretz Yisroel and would only have temporarily

Shemos

moved to Egypt because of the hunger. The reason the Torah lists the names of Yaakov's sons in the beginning of Shemos, even though we already knew from the Pesukim in Vayigash who came down, was to count and detail the people who willingly accepted Hashem's decree of the exile. Therefore, the reason for beginning Sefer Shemos with "And" was to say that the Bnei Yisroel were counted again to show that they were still willing to accept Hashem's decree of the exile.

11) The Maor VaShemesh also ponders our question. In Parshas Vayigash, Hashem promised in Beraishis (46:4), "I (Hashem) will go down with you (Yaakov) to Egypt." In fact, there is a Gemorah in Megilah 29a, which says that Hashem's Shechinah went to any place where the Bnei Yisroel went into exile. The Gemorah says that an example of this is the exile of Egypt where Sefer Shmuel I (2:27) says, "And a man of G-d came to Eli, and he said to him: 'So said Hashem: "Didn't I appear to the house of your father, when they were in Egypt, enslaved to the house of Pharaoh?"'" Based on a Zohar at the beginning of Sefer Shemos 2b, the Maor VaShemesh explains that Hashem came immediately down with Yaakov when Yaakov went to Egypt. However, since the slavery had not begun yet, Hashem's entourage of angels did not accompany Hashem at that point. However, when the slavery began, Hashem was joined by hundreds of thousands of angels to be with the Bnei Yisroel in the Egyptian exile. The reason Sefer Shemos begins with וְאֵלֶּה is because the Torah is adding on another praise about this topic that was previously discussed, as we had previously quoted from the Shemos Raba. More concretely, in our case, previously, when Yaakov and his family came down, only Hashem came with them. Now, since the slavery was starting, Hashem's entire entourage of angels came to join Hashem and the Bnei Yisroel in Egypt.

12) The Sefas Emes (5644) also presents an answer to our question. The reason Sefer Shemos begins with וְאֵלֶּה is because the Torah is adding on another praise about this topic that was previously discussed, as we had previously quoted from the Shemos Raba. He says that even though the tribes were in Egypt, they still felt like they were spiritually in Eretz Yisroel. The tribes knew that the reason they and their descendants went down to Egypt was to publicize the fact that Hashem runs the world when the Bnei Yisroel were redeemed from Egypt. For example, when the splitting of the Red Sea took place, the Mechilta on Shemos (14:21) says that Hashem put it into nature that all water in the world split, and therefore all the world saw that Hashem runs the world. The first Mechilta in Parshas Yisro says that when the Torah was given, the entire world was shaking. The Gentiles were so frightened that Hashem was going to destroy the world that they ran to Bilam to find out what was going on. Bilam informed them that Hashem was not destroying the world but rather was giving the Torah to the Bnei Yisroel.

13) The Yismach Moshe quotes the Kosnos Ohr for another answer to our question. At the end of Sefer Beraishis, Yosef tells his brothers, "I am going to die; Hashem will surely remember you and take you up out of this land to the land that He swore to Avrohom, to Yitzchak, and to Yaakov." Yosef continues in the next Posuk and makes the Bnei Yisroel swear, "Hashem will surely remember you, and you shall take up my bones out of here." Therefore, we see that the bones of Yosef and all the brothers were going to be brought up from Egypt to Eretz Yisroel. Sefer Yirmiyahu (2:7) says, "and you came and contaminated My (Hashem's) land, and made My heritage an abomination." The Zohar in Parshas Vayechi 226a says that this Posuk refers to someone who is

Shemos

Niftar outside of Eretz Yisroel, and his body is buried in Eretz Yisroel. This Posuk does not apply to Yaakov since Hashem's Shechinah clung to Yaakov when he went down to Egypt and when he was brought up to be buried in Eretz Yisroel. By comparing the brothers to stars as the Shemos Raba (1:3) and Midrash Lekach Tov say, the brothers were also fit to be buried in Eretz Yisroel even though they were Niftar in Egypt. That is why the Pesukim in the beginning of Shemos only mention Yaakov's sons and not the rest of the 70 people since only they were fit to be buried in Eretz Yisroel. Therefore the "Vav" at the beginning of Parshas Shemos connects Yosef and his brothers being buried in Eretz Yisroel to their importance here in Parshas Shemos, thereby showing why they were fit to be buried in Eretz Yisroel.

Why Does the Posuk Need to Tell Us That Yosef Was in Egypt?

(א:ה) וַיְהִי כָּל נֶפֶשׁ יֹצְאֵי יֶרֶךְ יַעֲקֹב שִׁבְעִים נָפֶשׁ וְיוֹסֵף הָיָה בְמִצְרָיִם Beraishis (1:5) Now all those descended from Yaakov were seventy souls, and Yosef was in Egypt.

Why does the Torah need to tell us that Yosef was in Egypt?

Introduction
Rashi says that since Yosef and his sons were part of the 70 people, it is perplexing why the Torah would need to repeat something we already knew well, which was that Yosef was in Egypt.

The Midrash Lekach Tov says that even though there were 70 souls, the Torah describes them as שִׁבְעִים נָפֶשׁ (70 soul) using the singular for souls. The reason is that righteous people all have the same outlook, and they all serve the same G-d, Hashem. In contrast, Beraishis (36:6) says וַיִּקַּח עֵשָׂו אֶת נָשָׁיו וְאֶת בָּנָיו וְאֶת בְּנֹתָיו וְאֶת כָּל נַפְשׁוֹת בֵּיתוֹ (And Esav took his wives, his sons, and his daughters and all the souls of his household), and uses the plural souls to describe Esav's household. The Vayikra Raba (4:6) says that there were only six people in Esav's household; however, since all six people served a different idol, the term souls is used for Esav's household.

1) The Shemos Raba (1:7) and the Midrash Lekach Tov are the sources to the answer that the Chizkuni, Ralbag, Eben Ezra, and Ksav VeHakabola offer to our question. They say that the Torah is informing us that only by counting Yosef who was in Egypt does one get the sum total of 70 souls. The Chizkuni says that since Shemos (1:1) says, "And these are the names of the Bnei Yisroel who came to Egypt with Yaakov," our Posuk for accuracy says that Yosef did not come then, since he was already in Egypt. The Mizrachi says that this answer is considering our Posuk as if it was written וְיוֹסֵף שֶׁהָיָה בְמִצְרָיִם (and Yosef who was in Egypt). The Maharzav says that not only was Yosef necessary for the count of 70 people but also his two sons were part of the 70 souls. In fact, the Targum Yonason ben Uziel translates our Posuk as "Yosef and his sons were in Egypt" to explicitly say this.

The Gur Aryeh, Maskil LeDovid, and the Nitziv point out that according to this answer, that the Torah is including Yosef in the count of 70 souls, the phrase "Yosef was in Egypt" is out of place in our Posuk. Instead of saying, "Now all those descended from Yaakov were 70 souls, and Yosef was

Shemos

in Egypt," the Torah should have ostensibly said, "And Yosef was in Egypt, now all those descended from Yaakov were 70 souls."

The Gemorah in Baba Basra 123a says that if one counts the names of all those listed in Parshas Vayigash who went down to Egypt, including Yosef and his two sons who were already in Egypt, one only finds 69 people and not 70. In Devorim (25:3), when the Torah describes how many lashes are given to a person who deserves them, the Torah says, "He shall flog him with 40 lashes; he shall not exceed, lest he give him a much more severe flogging than these, and your brother will be degraded before your eyes." Based on the Mishna in Makos 22a, we Paskin that in actuality, one only gets 39 lashes and not 40. One might think that here also, the Torah was rounding from 69 to 70y. However, we cannot say this since the Pesukim also detailed how many of the 70 came from each of the mothers, Leah, Rochel, Bilhah, and Zilpah, and the numbers indeed add up to 70. The discrepancy arises if we count the number of people listed under Leah's descendants, we only get thirty-two and not thirty-three that the Posuk says there are, so the missing person would seem to be a descendant of Leah. The Ksav VeHakabola and Oznayim LeTorah say that the person who was not counted was Osnas, Yosef's wife and that there were, in fact, four people of the count of seventy already in Egypt.

The Pirkei D'Rabi Eliezer (38) and Meseches Sofrim (21:9) say that Dinah gave birth to a daughter from her relationship with Shechem. Yaakov took a metal plate, wrote Hashem's name on it, hung it on the daughter's shoulder, and sent her out of his house. The angel Michoel came, swooped her up, and brought her down to Egypt to the household of Potiphar. This daughter was known as Osnas, who eventually married Yosef in Egypt. Even though Beraishis (46:26) says that the count of seventy "excluded the wives of the sons of Yaakov," the Ksav VeHakabola says that Osnas is still counted. The Shemos Raba (80:11) says that when Shimon and Levi came to rescue Dinah from Shechem's palace, Dinah refused to go since she was embarrassed by what had happened to her. The only condition that caused her to leave was when Shimon took an oath that he would marry her. Before the Torah was given, it was permitted to marry one's sister, and because of these extraordinary circumstances, says the Matnos Kehunah, Shimon agreed to marry her. Despite the fact that Dinah was married to Shimon, says the Ksav VeHakabola, she was not excluded from the count of 70, which excluded the "wives of Yaakov's sons, since this exclusion only applied to those who were not a descendant of Yaakov. The Ksav VeHakabola and Oznayim LeTorah say that in a similar way that Dinah, Yaakov's daughter, was counted, Osnas, Yaakov's granddaughter, was also counted. Rashi on Beraishis (37:35) quotes two opinions of the Beraishis Raba (84:21) as to whom the brothers married. According to one opinion, the brothers all married their (twin) sisters. According to the second opinion, the brothers married Canaanite wives. We note that the Ksav VeHakabola and Oznayim LeTorah's explanation is consistent with the second opinion that the brothers married Canaanite wives. According to the first opinion that they married their twin sisters, we will need to say that all their wives (Yaakov's daughters) were Niftar before they went to Egypt except for Dinah and Osnas.

2) The Shemos Raba (1:7) is the source of the answer that Rashi presents to our question. Even though Yosef merited to become the King, he did not behave in a haughty behavior over his

Shemos

brothers. Just like Yosef was humble when he was a slave in Egypt, he continued to be humble when he became the King. The Maharzav and Maskil LeDovid say that the Midrash derived this from the fact that our Posuk says וְיוֹסֵף הָיָה בְמִצְרָיִם. The Beraishis Raba (30:8) and the Midrash Tanchuma in Shemos (13) say that wherever the Torah uses the Hebrew word הָיָה (was) in reference to a person like it does in our Posuk in reference to Yosef, it means that this person was the same during their entire life. The Maskil LeDovid states that even though Pharaoh changed Yosef's name to Tzofnas Paneach in Beraishis (41:45), Yosef kept using his name Yosef. He says that this is also implied by the phrase וְיוֹסֵף הָיָה בְמִצְרָיִם, telling us that Yosef and not Tzofnas Paneach was in Egypt. Even though Tzofnas Paneach (the explainer of things hidden from people's understanding) was a more prestigious name, Yosef did not use the name because of his humility.

The Abarbanel, Gur Aryeh, Nachalas Yaakov, and Maharshal, as quoted by the Tzedah LeDerech, all ponder the question of why Rashi ignored the first answer presented by the Shemos Raba, which is the simplest answer, and instead presented a more "Midrashic" answer. They all answer that since the first answer says that Yosef was part of the count of 70 people, Rashi was bothered by why the Torah didn't say Yosef and his sons were in Egypt since his two sons also were part of the 70 souls. In truth, points out the Tzedah LeDerech, the Torah also does not explicitly say with regard to all the other tribes that their sons were part of the counting. However, the Nachalas Yaakov and Tzedah LeDerech explain, the Torah does say "each man and his household came," which implies that with respect to the people who came to Egypt, members of the household are also counted. Since Yosef was not part of the group who came then to Egypt and therefore not included in "each man and his houschold came," Rashi was of the opinion that the Posuk should have listed Yosef's sons if the Posuk wants to tell us who the 70 souls were.

The Abarbanel and Rav Moshe Feinstein, in his Sefer Dorash Moshe, say that it seems out of place for the Torah to be telling us about Yosef's virtues at this point in time. As the Abarbanel says, it would seem more appropriate to tell us Yosef's virtues in Parshas Miketz or Vayigash when the Torah discusses Yosef's kingship or in Parshas Vayechi when the Torah discusses Yosef's Petirah. It is possible to answer this question based on something the Kli Yakor says. The Shemos Raba (1:3) and Midrash Lekach Tov say that the Bnei Yisroel are compared to the stars of heaven. The Kli Yakor extends these Midrashim to explain that righteous people are like stars, which only shine brightly at night. Only after a person has been Niftar can we be sure and say that the person shone brightly and was righteous and did not stray from the path of righteousness. The Kli Yakor says that this is what Koheles (4:2) means when it says, "And I praise the dead who have already died, more than the living who are still alive." Therefore, only now, when Yosef was Niftar, can we be sure of his total righteousness.

3) The Alshich HaKodosh also presents an answer to our question. Beraishis (45:28) quotes Yaakov as saying, "Enough! My son Yosef is still alive. I will go and see him before I die." From the Posuk, it would seem that Yaakov was planning to travel alone to Egypt to see Yosef and then return to Eretz Yisroel. That being the case, one can question why all 70 people and their wives went to Egypt, not to mention stayed there. The answer to that question is found in the phrase of our Posuk that "Yosef was in Egypt." The Gemorah in Shabbos 89b and the Shemos Raba (86:2) say that

Shemos

Yaakov was destined to be brought down to Egypt in chains of iron to begin the Egyptian exile. The Gemorah states that Yaakov's merit prevented him from going down to Egypt in this manner. The Shemos Raba (86:2) explains that Hashem was loathed to send his firstborn son Yaakov to Egypt in such an embarrassing manner. Rather Hashem decided to pull Yaakov's son, Yosef, to Egypt and make Yaakov follow him. When Yaakov decided to visit Yosef in Egypt, his sons refused to let him go alone and decided to come along with him to Egypt. Once Yaakov's sons decided to accompany Yaakov, the families also decided to come along. Therefore, not only was Yaakov spared from having to go to Egypt in chains of iron but also, all of Yaakov's family was spared from this in the merit of Yaakov. When our Posuk uses the phrase "Yosef was in Egypt," it is telling us how it came about that Yaakov and all 70 souls of his family were saved from coming to Egypt in "chains of iron." The fact that Yosef was in Egypt was also the reason that Yaakov decided to stay. Yosef sends the message to Yaakov in Beraishis (45:9-11) "Hashem has made me a lord over all the Egyptians. Come down to me, do not tarry. And you shall dwell in the land of Goshen, and you shall be near to me, you and your children and your grandchildren, and your flocks and your cattle and all that is yours. And I will sustain you there, for there are still five years of famine lest you become impoverished, you and your household and all that is yours." As the viceroy of Egypt, Yosef convinced Yaakov to stay, especially with the impending years of famine approaching.

4) The Abarbanel also ponders our question and says that the beginning Pesukim in Sefer Shemos are there to tell us who convinced Yaakov to come down to Egypt. The Torah tells us that it was Yaakov's eleven sons and, in addition, Yosef, who was in Egypt, who convinced Yaakov to come down to Egypt, despite the much lower level of holiness in Egypt as compared to Eretz Yisroel, where Yaakov lived. The reason Yosef is listed separately from the brothers is because they convinced Yaakov by accompanying Yaakov to Egypt, while Yosef convinced Yaakov because of already being in Egypt, not to mention being the viceroy of Egypt.

5) Rabeinu Bechay and the Toldos Yitzchak answer our question similarly. They say that the final redemption will be modeled after the redemption from Egypt. Similar to the 70 souls who went down to Egypt at the beginning of the exile, in the final redemption, Hashem will redeem us by making us victorious over all 70 nations of the world. Yosef is mentioned last to hint that there will be a descendant of Yosef, who will be the Moshiach ben Yosef, and he will redeem us by making us victorious over the 70 nations.

6) The Ksav Sofer also presents an answer to our question. He says that the beginning Pesukim in Sefer Shemos tell us how the 70 souls who came down to Egypt were as pristine many years after they came as they were when they originally came down to Egypt. The phrase "Yosef was in Egypt" tells us how the Bnei Yisroel stayed righteous during this early part of the Egyptian exile. As the ruler in Egypt, Yosef made sure that the Bnei Yisroel stayed separate from the Egyptians so that they would not pick up the influences of the Egyptian society. It was only after Yosef was Niftar that the Bnei Yisroel started to be influenced by the Egyptians.

7) The Malbim also ponders our question and writes that our Posuk is explaining why the Bnei Yisroel were considered important by the Egyptians. If there are a large number of important

Shemos

people, they lose their importance since there are so many of them, and they are not unique. However, the Bnei Yisroel, who were all important people, were only 70 souls, and therefore they were considered important and were respected by the Egyptians. That is what the first part of our Posuk is telling us by saying, "Now all those descended from Yaakov were seventy souls." The second reason that the Bnei Yisroel were important was because Yosef was in Egypt and was the viceroy of Egypt, making the other Bnei Yisroel brothers or nephews of the viceroy.

8) The Nitziv also ponders our question and has a very original way of how the 70 souls were counted. When introducing the count of the 70 souls who went down to Egypt in Parshas Vayigash, Beraishis (46:8-9) says, "And these are the names of the Bnei Yisroel who were coming to Egypt: Yaakov and his sons, Yaakov's firstborn was Reuven. And the sons of Reuven were Chanoch and Pallu, Chezron and Karmi." The Nitziv focuses on why it was necessary to add in the phrase "Yaakov's firstborn was Reuven," since, at first glance, this phrase adds in nothing to the count of the seventy souls. The Nitziv says that since Reuven was the firstborn and a firstborn gets two shares of inheritance, Reuven was counted as two people in the count of 70 people. With this approach, he answers a famous question which the Shemos Raba (94:9) ponders. Beraishis (46:15) tells us that the sum total of all the descendants of Leah was 33 people. However, if one counts the names, one finds only 32 people listed. The Nitziv says that since Reuven was the firstborn who counts as two people, therefore the total number is, in fact, 33 for the 32 people listed.

The Nitziv says that Reuven was only counted as two until they reached Egypt. However, in Egypt, where Yosef was the leader of all the brothers, Yosef is counted as two instead of Reuven. The Nitziv says that this is the purpose of why our Posuk says, "Now all those descended from Yaakov were seventy souls, and Yosef was in Egypt." The Torah is telling us that the number only became 70 in Egypt because Yosef was there and counted as two. He also points out that after Yosef was Niftar, the leadership position amongst the brothers went back to Reuven. As proof, he quotes a Bamidbar Raba (13:8), which relates that Reuven, Shimon, and Levi had leadership positions in Egypt. After Reuven was Niftar, Shimon took over the leadership position, and after Shimon was Niftar, Levi took it over.

Parenthetically, the Shemos Raba answers the number discrepancy in several different ways. One opinion is that Yocheved was born as they were entering the walls of Egypt, and she is the 70th person. Another opinion is that Yaakov was the 70th person. Another opinion is that Hashem's Shechinah completed the 70 persons. According to the way the Maharzav learns the Midrash, another opinion is that Chushim, the son of Dan, had a brother who was Niftar young but was the 70th person since he was alive at the counting of the 70 people. The Matnos Kehunah points out that this fact is hinted at in Beraishis (46:23) when the Torah says, "And the **sons** of Dan were Chushim" instead of the more grammatically correct "And the **son** of Dan was Chushim." The last opinion given by the Shemos Raba is that Serach, the daughter of Asher, completed the count of 70. Though Serach is counted by name, the Yepheh Toar says that she is counted as two since she was a righteous, wise woman and lived for over six hundred years until the days of Dovid HaMelech.

Shemos

9) The Pardes Yosef presents another answer to our question. The wives of the people who went down to Egypt are not counted, as Beraishis (46:26) says that the count of 70 excluded "the wives of the sons of Yaakov." The reason for this is that since man and wife are one unit, they are counted as one in the count of 70. Rashi on Beraishis (37:35) quotes one opinion of the Beraishis Raba (84:21) that the brothers all married their (twin) sisters. Since we know that Yosef, being that he was in Egypt, married Osnas, there would be one twin sister (or daughter of Yaakov) who was not married to a brother and, like Dinah, would have counted in the count of 70. Therefore, says the Pardes Yosef, the phrase "Yosef was in Egypt" implies to us who the 70th person going down to Egypt was, since only 69 people are mentioned. The only problem is that this answer is inconsistent with the Pirkei D'Rabi Eliezer (36), who says that everyone except Yosef and Dinah had a twin girl born with them so that they would each have whom to marry. Each brother, except Yosef, married a sister who had a different mother than he did.

10) Rav Moshe Feinstein, in his Sefer Dorash Moshe, also ponders our question. He answers that Rashi, based on the Shemos Raba (1:3) and Midrash Lekach Tov, says that the reason Yaakov's sons are counted again at the beginning of Parshas Shemos was that they were dear to Hashem like stars which Hashem counts when they rise and when they set. The reason Yaakov's sons were so dear was because of their righteousness. One might think that Yosef, being far away from Yaakov's influence for the majority of his early life in Egypt, was not as righteous. Therefore, the Torah tells us that Yosef was righteous and completely deserving of being counted when he was Niftar because of his righteousness. We can see that Yaakov's influence was so strong that it kept Yosef righteous even in Egypt. The Gemorah in Sotah 36b says that Yosef was seduced and ready to commit an immoral act with the wife of Potiphar. At that moment, the image of Yaakov came and appeared to Yosef in the window of the house.

11) The Oznayim LeTorah also presents an answer to our question. The Vayikra Raba (32:5) says that the Bnei Yisroel were redeemed from Egypt since they kept their Hebrew names, kept their Hebrew language, did not speak Loshon Horah, and that they were not immoral. The phrase "Yosef was in Egypt" tells us that not only did the rest of the brothers not change their names, but even Yosef, who was in Egypt and who received an Egyptian name of Tzofnas Paneach from Pharaoh, did not change his name. Even though Tzofnas Paneach meaning "the explainer of things hidden from people's understanding," was a very honorable name, Yosef instead chose to keep using his name Yosef. In fact, nowhere in the Torah does Yosef or anyone else refer to Yosef as Tzofnas Paneach.

12) The Oznayim LeTorah presents another answer to our question. The phrase "Yosef was in Egypt" is a prelude to the Pesukim following our Posuk when the Egyptians enslave everyone. The phrase "Yosef was in Egypt" reminds us that Yosef saved the country of Egypt from the terrible famine which would have devastated all of Egypt and, in fact, made Egypt enormously wealthy by gathering much of the riches of the region. Despite this fact, not only did the Egyptians enslave the people who came down to Egypt, but they also enslaved the sons of Yosef despite what Yosef did for the Egyptians.

Shemos

How Rav Leizer Gordon Proved That the Midrash Which Says That the Bnei Yisroel Had Six Children in Each Pregnancy in Egypt Is True and Not an Exaggeration.

Beraishis (1:7) וּבְנֵי יִשְׂרָאֵל פָּרוּ וַיִּשְׁרְצוּ וַיִּרְבּוּ וַיַּעַצְמוּ בִּמְאֹד מְאֹד וַתִּמָּלֵא הָאָרֶץ אֹתָם (א:ז) The Bnei Yisroel were fruitful and swarmed and increased and became very, very strong, and the land became filled with them.

How Rav Leizer Gordon proved that the Midrash, which says that the Bnei Yisroel had six children in each pregnancy in Egypt, is true and not an exaggeration.

Introduction
Rashi, based on the Shemos Raba (1:8) and Midrash Tanchuma on Shemos (5), says that based on this Posuk, six children were born in each pregnancy. The Matnos Kehunah says that the Shemos Raba derived this from the six descriptions of having many children (fruitful, swarmed, increased, became strong, became very, very strong, filled the land) in our Posuk. We note that the Midrash Lekach Tov, the Maharal in Gur Aryeh, and the Terumas HaDeshen, as quoted by the Tzedah LeDerech, say the six descriptions of having children are: fruitful, swarmed, increased, became strong, became very strong, became very, very strong). The Yalkut Shimoni on Shemos 162 is the source of the Nachalas Yaakov and Maskil LeDovid, who say that having six children is derived from the word וַיִּשְׁרְצוּ. The root of this Hebrew word is שֶׁרֶץ, which means a small, creepy animal. Of these Halachic class animals, the mouse is the one that reproduces the least for each pregnancy, and it has six mice in each pregnancy from which it derives that the Bnei Yisroel had six children per pregnancy. In Beraishis (1:28), Hashem blesses man with פְּרוּ וּרְבוּ (be fruitful and multiply). Based on that, says the Nachalas Yaakov, our Posuk should not have interrupted the words פָּרוּ and וַיִּרְבּוּ with the word וַיִּשְׁרְצוּ. The reason that the Posuk does do this is to highlight that the amount that they multiplied is derived from the word וַיִּשְׁרְצוּ.

The Maharal and Maskil LeDovid also ponder the reason why the Bnei Yisroel had exactly six children in each pregnancy as opposed to having five and seven or any other number, which would average out to six per pregnancy. They say that the number six is tied with the count of the Bnei Yisroel since they needed a count of 600,000 to be able to leave Egypt, indicating that the number of six people is an important number for the Bnei Yisroel to have. The Maharal also presents a second reason why the Bnei Yisroel had exactly six children in each pregnancy. Shemos (1:12) says, וְכַאֲשֶׁר יְעַנּוּ אֹתוֹ כֵּן יִרְבֶּה וְכֵן יִפְרֹץ (But as much as they would afflict them, so did they multiply and so did they gain strength). This implies, says the Maharal, that that the growth in population was directly related to how much the Egyptians afflicted us. The Shemos Raba (5:18) and the Midrash Tanchuma in Vaera (6) both say that the Bnei Yisroel had Megilos (scrolls), which talked about how Hashem would redeem us from Egypt that they would read every Shabbos. The reason they used to read them on Shabbos was because they had a day off from work on Shabbos. When Moshe first came to Pharaoh at the end of Parshas Shemos to ask Pharaoh to let the Bnei Yisroel leave Egypt, Pharaoh says in Shemos (5:9), "Let the labor fall heavy upon the men and let them work at it, and let them not talk about false matters." "Let them not talk about false matters" refers to reading these

Shemos

Megilos, and "Let the labor fall heavy upon the men" means that Pharaoh increased the Bnei Yisroel's affliction by making them also work on Shabbos. The Shemos Raba (1:28) says that when Moshe first went out of the palace and saw the burdens of the Bnei Yisroel, he went and convinced Pharaoh to allow the Bnei Yisroel a day off on Shabbos. Moshe argued to Pharaoh that the Bnei Yisroel would be more productive the rest of the week if only they had one day of vacation a week. The Tur in Orach Chaim 281 explains the meaning of the phrase that we say in the Shabbos morning Shemoneh Esreh יִשְׂמַח מֹשֶׁה בְּמַתְּנַת חֶלְקוֹ (Moshe rejoiced in the gift of his portion). He explains that Moshe was very happy that the day off he requested for the Bnei Yisroel in Egypt was the same day that Hashem commanded the Bnei Yisroel to keep Shabbos when the Torah was given. The Gemorah in Beitzah 16a says that Hashem told Moshe that He has a wonderful gift in his treasure house and the gift's name is Shabbos. That is what is meant, says the Tur, by the phrase that Moshe rejoiced in the gift (Shabbos) of his portion (which he chose for the Bnei Yisroel in Egypt). With the fact that the Bnei Yisroel had Shabbos off in Egypt, says the Maharal, the Bnei Yisroel were afflicted for six days of the week, and the growth in population was therefore defined by having six children in each pregnancy. The Tzedah LeDerech is not happy with either of the Maharal's explanations of why the Bnei Yisroel had six children in each pregnancy. Sefer Shmuel II (6:11) says, "And the Aron of Hashem dwelled in the house of Oved-Edom the Gittite three months; and Hashem blessed Oved-Edom, and all his household." The Gemorah in Brochos 63b says that the blessing Hashem gave to Oved-Edom was that his wife, his mother-in-law, and his eight daughters-in-law all had six children in one pregnancy. Since neither of Maharal's two explanations would be applicable to Oved-Edom, the Tzedah LeDerech does not understand why Oved-Edom's family would have exactly six children in each pregnancy.

The Oznayim LeTorah relates how once his father-in-law Rav Leizer Gordon, the Rosh Yeshiva of the Telshe Yeshiva in Europe, was approached by someone who told him that he had a hard time believing the truth of the Midrash, which relates that the Bnei Yisroel had six children in each pregnancy. It was obvious to this person that statistically, the Bnei Yisroel had a very high birthrate to increase from the 70 people who came down to Egypt to the 600,000 people who came out of Egypt just 210 years later. However, the person could not bring himself to believe that the Bnei Yisroel has six children in each pregnancy. It would seem that this person who approached Rav Gordon had a generic issue with believing Mamorei Chazal. Rav Gordon proceeded to prove undeniably from just the Pesukim in the Torah and some math that the Midrash was totally believable.

In Parshas Bamidbar, the firstborns of the Bnei Yisroel are counted as Bamidbar (3:40) says, "Hashem said to Moshe: Count every firstborn male aged one month and upward of the Bnei Yisroel, and take the number of their names." The reason the firstborns were counted was so that they could be redeemed by the corresponding people from the tribe of Levi. In Bamidbar (3:43) we are told, "The firstborn males aged one month and upward, according to the number of names, was twenty-two thousand, two hundred and seventy-three." We are also told in Bamidbar (1:45-46), "All the Bnei Yisroel were counted according to their fathers' houses, from twenty years and upward, all who were fit to go out to the army. The sum of all those who were counted: six hundred and three thousand, five hundred and fifty." We can't directly compare the two numbers since the

Shemos

firstborns were counted from age one month and up, while the Bnei Yisroel were counted from age twenty and up. As a quick rule of thumb, we will assume that the number of people from the Bnei Yisroel who were age thirty days until twenty years was the same as the number of people from age twenty and up. Using this rule of thumb, the number of Bnei Yisroel from age thirty days and up was about 1,200,000 people. Using the fact that only 22,273 of them were firstborns, we can calculate the average family size. The average family size was 1,200,000 divided by 22,273 or about 54 people.

We note that we have only included males in the above calculation. If we make the reasonable assumption that there were as many males as females, then we would get that there were twice the 22,273 firstborns or 44,546 total firstborns. Since we would also need to double the population of the total Bnei Yisroel from age thirty days and up, we would have 2,400,000 total people of the Bnei Yisroel. Dividing this number by the number of firstborns again gives the average family size as about 54 people.

Chapter 90 in Tehillim begins by telling us that it is a "prayer of Moshe," which implies that Moshe wrote this chapter. Tehillim (90:10) says, "The days of our years because of them are seventy years, and if with increase, eighty years," which informs us that typically people's lives averaged between seventy and eighty years. With this life span, it stands to reason that the women had, at most, ten pregnancies during their lifetimes. With an average family size of 54 people, this means that the number of children born in each pregnancy was approximately six, completely consistent with the Midrash Raba that the person coming to Rav Leizer Gordon did not believe. The Oznayim LeTorah concludes that this mathematical proof of the truth of the Shemos Raba is worth broadcasting to all Bnei Yisroel.

It is interesting to note that we can make a similar calculation to find out what the average size of the Leviyim's family was using the same method that Rav Leizer Gordon used. In Bamidbar (3:39) we are told, "The sum of the male Leviyim according to their families, from the age of one month and upward, counted by Moshe and Aharon according to the word of Hashem, was twenty-two thousand." However, Rashi, quoting from the Gemorah in Bechoros 5a, says that if we sum up the number of Leviyim from the three Leviyim families of Gershon, Kehas, and Merori, we find out that the total number of Leviyim from thirty days and up was, in fact, 22,300. Bamidbar (3:22) tells us that Gershon had 7,500, Bamidbar (3:28) tells us that Kehas had 8,600, and Bamidbar (3:34) tells us that Merori had 6,200. Adding these numbers together yields a sum total of 22,300. In fact, the Gemorah in Bechoros 5a says that a Roman minister (Kuntrukos) made this calculation and came to Rabban Yochanon Ben Zakai with this discrepancy of 300 between the actual sum total and the sum total given by the Torah. Rabban Yochanon Ben Zakai answered the Roman minister that the 300 Leviyim not included in the Torah's sum were firstborn Leviyim. Since they were both Leviyim and firstborns, they could not be used to redeem a firstborn from the non-Levite tribes, and therefore only 22,000 Leviyim were available to redeem the 22,273 firstborns from non-Levite tribes. The Torah in Parshas Bamidbar informs us how these extra 273 firstborns had to be identified and redeemed since there was no Levite to redeem them.

Shemos

Based on the Gemorah in Bechoros 5a, we know that there were 300 firstborn Leviyim out of 22,300 total Leviyim. Dividing these two numbers tells us that the average Levite family size was 74. Based on Rav Leizer Gordon's reasoning, the miracle of having six children in each pregnancy also occurred with the Leviyim. The Ramban points out that the total number of Leviyim is in a different class than the rest of the Bnei Yisroel. We have mentioned above that the number of Leviyim from age one month and up (including their firstborns) was 22,300. We are also told in Bamidbar (4:48) that there were 8,580 Leviyim from age thirty till age fifty. If we use the rough rule of thumb that there were as many people from one month till twenty years of age as there were from twenty and up, then there were only a little more than eleven thousand Leviyim from age twenty and up. The least amount of people in any of the other tribes is the tribe of Menashe, and in Bamidbar (1:35), we are told that they had 32,200 from age twenty and up. This implies that the number of Leviyim was far less than even half of the smallest of the other tribes of the Bnei Yisroel. The Ramban says that it is astonishing that the tribe which served Hashem in the Mishkan did not have the Brocha of being anywhere near as fruitful as any of the other tribes of the Bnei Yisroel. We have mentioned previously that Shemos (1:12) says: וְכַאֲשֶׁר יְעַנּוּ אֹתוֹ כֵּן יִרְבֶּה וְכֵן יִפְרֹץ (But as much as they would afflict them, so did they multiply and so did they gain strength). The Midrash Tanchuma on Vaera (6) says that the tribe of Levi was exempt from the very hard work in Egypt. Based on this, the Ramban answers that since the tribe of Levi was not afflicted with hard work, they did not multiply miraculously as the other tribes did with six children in each pregnancy, and therefore, their total numbers were low in comparison to the other tribes.

There are many answers given as to why the Leviyim were not afflicted with hard work. The Ramban says that it is and was a widespread custom to have religious leaders who were treated with respect. In the case of the Bnei Yisroel, this was the tribe of Levi, and respect demanded that they not be afflicted with hard work but allowed to continue teaching religion to the people. The Chizkuni says that when the Egyptians started enslaving the Bnei Yisroel, the Gemorah in Sotah 11b says that they started with a mild mouth. Rashi on the Gemorah explains that in the beginning, the Egyptians promised to handsomely pay the Jews proportionate to how much work they could do. Of course, many Jews were therefore enticed to work long and hard so that they could produce an enormous amount of work, expecting to be paid proportionately to their efforts. The Chizkuni says that the tribe of Levi when they heard this offer, refused to accept working for the Egyptians at all. The Midrash Tanchuma on Bamidbar (12) and the Beraishis Raba (100:2) both say that Yaakov told each of his sons, along with Ephraim and Menashe, to stand around and carry his casket in the same positions where the twelve tribes would surround the Mishkan while they were traveling in the desert. In addition, the Midrash Tanchuma says that Yaakov did not allow Yosef nor Levi to carry his casket from Egypt to Eretz Yisroel. The reason Yosef was not allowed was because, as King, it was below his dignity. The reason Levi was not permitted to carry Yaakov's casket was because he was destined to carry the Aron when they traveled in the desert, and it is incongruous for someone who carries the Aron of eternal life to carry an Aron with a dead person in it. The Daas Zekanim and Chizkuni say that since the Leviyim knew from Yaakov that they would be carrying the Aron of Hashem when they traveled in the desert, they did not want to degrade themselves by working for Pharaoh. Though the Egyptians started enslaving the Bnei Yisroel with a soft mouth and promised to pay them for their labor, the Egyptians soon enslaved the Bnei Yisroel and demanded that they

Shemos

continue working at the same output as when they thought they were being handsomely paid. Since the tribe of Levi had never participated in the "soft mouth" phase, they did not have to work in the slavery phase. The Chizkuni also presents a different reason the tribe of Levi was not afflicted with hard work. He says that there is a Midrash that says that Avrohom gave all his insights in Torah to Yitzchak. Yitzchak passed these down to Yaakov, who passed them down to Levi. Levi and the descendants of his tribe all made Yeshivos in Egypt. Since the Leviyim never did any manual labor and only taught and learned all day and night, they had no labor skills, and therefore the Egyptians did not enslave them. In Beraishis (47:22) we are told, "So Yosef made it a statute to this day concerning the farmland of Egypt for the one fifth. Only the farmland of the priests alone did not become Pharaoh's." Rav Sternbuch, in his Sefer Taam V'Daas on this Posuk, says that the reason Yosef did not tax the priests of Egypt was to set a precedence that when the Bnei Yisroel came to Egypt, their priests (the tribe of Levi) would not be taxed nor enslaved by Pharaoh. The Maskil LeDovid on Shemos (5:4) says that Pharaoh's daughter Basya asked for and was granted her wish that Moshe's tribe, Levi, should not be enslaved. The Maharal, in Gur Aryeh on Shemos (5:4), says that Pharaoh was hoping that if he didn't enslave the entire Bnei Yisroel and instead allowed one tribe to be free, the Egyptians would not fall under the decree of Beraishis (15:14) "And also the nation that they will serve will I judge." Therefore, he thought it wise not to enslave the tribe of Levi.

When we put together the calculation and conclusion of Rav Leizer Gordon with the words of the Ramban, we are left in a dilemma. The dilemma is more profound since it is based entirely on the numbers that the Torah presents to us. On the one hand, the Ramban shows us that the Leviyim were far less populous than any of the other tribes. On the other hand, applying Rav Leizer Gordon's analysis shows us that the average family size of the Leviyim was as big as and, in fact, even bigger than that of the Bnei Yisroel, which implies that they should be as populous as the other tribes.

It is possible that the answer to the dilemma is that the Leviyim only has such huge family sizes at the end of the enslavement and not during the bulk of the enslavement. When Moshe first came to Pharaoh and asked him to let the Bnei Yisroel go to the desert and serve Hashem for three days, Pharaoh became furious and ordered a huge increase in the amount of work and affliction. Pharaoh says in Shemos (5:8-9), "But the number of bricks they have been making yesterday and the day before yesterday you shall impose upon them; you shall not reduce it, for they are lax. Therefore, they cry out, saying, 'Let us go and sacrifice to our Hashem. Let the labor fall heavy upon the men and let them work at it, and let them not talk about false matters.'" We have previously shown that the Midrash Tanchuma says at this point, Pharaoh increased the Bnei Yisroel's affliction by making them work on Shabbos. Even though Pharaoh tells Moshe and Aharon in Shemos (4:4) "Go to your labors," Rashi says that he was telling Moshe and Aharon to go to their own work in their houses and stop putting ideas of freedom in the Bnei Yisroel's heads since the tribe of Levi did not participate in the hard labor. As proof that Moshe and Aharon were not enslaved, Rashi points out that Moshe and Aharon continued to many times go to Pharaoh, and if they had been enslaved with very hard work would not have been able to come at any time. The Tur, however, quotes an explanation that the Egyptians only enslaved people from nine years old until they were sixty.

Shemos

Being that Moshe and Aharon were 80 and 83 years old, respectively, the fact that they went in and out to Pharaoh is not proof that the Leviyim were not enslaved. The Ramban and this is especially explicit when the Tur quotes the Ramban, says that in the simple explanation of our Posuk, Pharaoh told Moshe and Aharon to join their brothers in the hard affliction and work of their fellow Bnei Yisroel. It is quite possible that in the same way, Pharaoh increased the Bnei Yisroel's affliction by making them work on Shabbos, he also increased the Bnei Yisroel's affliction by now having even the tribe of Levi work. Pharaoh justified this new decree by saying that the teachers of the Bnei Yisroel were responsible for these ideas about freedom. In fact, the Midrash Tanchuma explicitly says that Pharaoh blamed the idea of having these ideas of freedom on the tribe of Levi being free and therefore having the time to spread this message among the Bnei Yisroel.

The Abarbanel also writes that Pharaoh, at this point, assigned both Moshe and Aharon along with the entire tribe of Levi to be under the affliction of hard labor. The Malbim says that initially, after hearing Moshe's request, Pharaoh commanded Moshe, Aharon, and the entire tribe of Levi to be under the affliction of hard labor. However, Pharaoh soon changed his mind since he thought it would be even worse to have them working alongside the Bnei Yisroel all day and continue spreading the idea of going free from Egypt. Interestingly, the Ohr HaChaim says that the entire period of even harder affliction, which Pharaoh now decreed, only lasted for one day. Rabeinu Channanel, as quoted by Rabeinu Bechay, also says that it was only for one time that the Bnei Yisroel had to provide their own straw for making the bricks. The Ohr HaChaim on Shemos (6:6) says Hashem started the plague of blood only one day later and that once the plagues started, the Bnei Yisroel were no longer enslaved so harshly and only worked a bit for the Egyptians since they were still afraid of the Egyptians. The Ohr Yakor on the Orach Chaim ponders how this explanation of the Orach Chaim is consistent with the Gemorah in Rosh Hashana 11a, which says that the enslavement ended on Rosh Hashana, approximately six months before the Bnei Yisroel went out of Egypt. Tosfos on that Gemorah says that even though the Mishna in Idiyos (2:10) says that the Egyptians were judged for twelve months, it was only six months later, at Rosh Hashana, that the slavery stopped. The Ohr Yakor says that this is consistent with the Ohr HaChaim, who says that the Jews still worked a bit for the Egyptians since they were still afraid of the Egyptians. This period of working a little bit lasted until Rosh Hashana. The Tosfos Yom Tov on the Mishna in Idiyos says that the decree of having to also gather the straw which took place after Moshe first saw Pharaoh was in the month of Iyar. The Eyun Yaakov points out that being free from slavery on Rosh Hashana was similar to Yosef, who also was freed from prison on Rosh Hashana. We note that this Ohr HaChaim is not consistent with the Bamidbar Raba (11:2), which says, as explained by Rabeinu Bechay at the end of Parshas Shemos, that Moshe returned to Midyan for three months after first meeting Pharaoh and only then returned to Egypt. All in all, there are many opinions that the Leviyim were enslaved for at least a short time period, which, when applying Rav Leizer Gordon's theory to the Leviyim, would explain why at least the last generation of Leviyim had very big family sizes consistent with having six children in each pregnancy. Since the Leviyim, according to all opinions, were not enslaved during the entire time of slavery, this would also explain why their numbers were so low as compared to the other tribes.

Shemos

It is also possible that firstborn Leviyim disproportionally died in Egypt relative to non-firstborn children. Before the sin of the Golden Calf, a firstborn was the one who offered Korbanos to Hashem. It could very well be that firstborn Leviyim were especially suitable for offering Korbanos in Egypt since they were also members of the tribe of Levi who did not work for the Egyptians and therefore had much more time to study the Torah. In addition, the Bnei Yisroel could have known that eventually, the Leviyim would take the place of the firstborns, and therefore a firstborn Levi would be the best choice to offer Korbanos in Egypt. As proof of this hypothesis, Esav, when he sells his birthright to Yaakov, says in Beraishis (25:32): "Behold, I am going to die; so why do I need this birthright?" Rashi, on this Posuk, says that Esav knew that the position of firstborn serving Hashem was only temporary and would, in the future, be given to the Leviyim. Rashi also explains why Esav felt he was going to die from keeping the birthright. Bringing sacrifices has many prohibitions, punishments, and even death penalties involved with it. Rashi references the Gemorah in Sanhedrin 83a, which has a long list of prohibitions that cause the death penalty, such as those who do the service after having drunk wine, have long hair, did not wash their hands and feet, etc. Therefore, it is consistent that many Leviyim firstborns could have died in Egypt, and that is why there were so few firstborn Leviyim.

When Tzvi Rosenblum ז"ל heard the question of why there were so few Levite firstborns, he presented another explanation. The Ohr HaChaim HaKodosh on Bamidbar (3:39) has an alternative explanation to the Ramban as to why there was so few Leviyim relative to the other tribes. When Pharaoh made the decree that all Jewish baby boys were to be thrown into the Nile River, the Gemorah in Sotah 12a says that Amram, who at that time had fathered Miriam and Aharon, said, "we are working for nothing in attempting to have children." Therefore, Amram, who was the leader of the generation, went and divorced Yocheved. Seeing what the leader of the generation had done, all the Jewish men followed Amram's example and also went and divorced their wives. Amram's daughter Miriam said to him, "My father, your decree is even harsher than Pharaoh's decree since Pharaoh only decreed against the boys while you are also decreeing against the girls." Miriam convinced Amram to remarry Yocheved and even prophesized that they would give birth to Moshe, the savior of the Bnei Yisroel. The Ohr HaChaim says that though all the other tribes followed Amram's example and remarried their wives, many of the tribe of Levi did not remarry. The people of the tribe of Levi, since they were not enslaved, had a psychological problem in coming to grips with their children being thrown into the Nile. The enslaved Bnei Yisroel were so depressed from the immense hard work that they did not value their lives highly and were not extremely bothered with their children being thrown into the Nile River. Many of the Leviyim, however, who still had their dignity balked at remarrying and seeing their children thrown into the Nile River. On the basis of this Ohr HaChaim, Tzvi said that it is likely that the minority of Leviyim, who did remarry, took pity on the many Levite wives who were divorced and also married many of them. Having previously been married to other dignified Leviyim who were not enslaved, it would be logical that both husband and wife would be agreeable to such a marriage. Since all the subsequent children of these many wives would not be firstborns, it would make sense why the Leviyim had so few firstborns.

Shemos

Why Did the Bnei Yisroel Have to Go Into Exile?

Shemos (1:13) וַיַּעֲבִדוּ מִצְרַיִם אֶת בְּנֵי יִשְׂרָאֵל בְּפָרֶךְ (א:יג) So the Egyptians enslaved the Bnei Yisroel with back-breaking labor.

Why did the Bnei Yisroel have to go into exile?

Introduction
The Ramban on Beraishis (12:10) says that when Avrohom went down to Egypt when there was a hunger in Eretz Yisroel, Avrohom, without intention, sinned a great sin. His sin was that he put his righteous wife, Sorah, into the danger of being assaulted by Pharaoh out of fear that the Egyptians would kill him if they found out Sorah was his wife. Instead, Avrohom should have stayed in Eretz Yisroel and put his trust in Hashem that He would save him, Sorah, and everyone else who was with him from the hunger. Because of this unintentional sin, it was decreed on his children, the Bnei Yisroel, that they should go into exile under the hand of Pharaoh.

The Meam Loez at the end of Parshas Shemos says that this reason only applies to Avrohom himself and explains why Hashem told Avrohom the bad news that his children would be in slavery for 400 years. Had Avrohom not done a slight sin, Hashem would not have told this news to Avrohom. However, it is impossible that the reason for the exile would be for this slight sin of Avrohom either because such a small sin should not produce such a major punishment and perhaps, more importantly, one's children do not suffer because of the sins of their father, unless they continue the sins of their fathers. Therefore, we must find other reasons for why the Bnei Yisroel had to go into exile.

1) The Meam Loez at the end of Parshas Shemos compiled several answers to this question. One answer he says is that one of the "gifts," which the Bnei Yisroel only received after undergoing punishment, was the Torah. There are three reasons why a person does not accept upon themselves the yoke of the Torah. One reason is because the person either doesn't believe in Hashem or in the thirteen principles that the Rambam delineates in his Ani Maamin. Another reason is because the person is lax in toiling in Torah or in fulfilling the Mitzvos of the Torah since doing a Mitzvah properly requires effort and concentration, which the Yetzer Horah tries to convince the person not to do. This attitude leads to a person telling themselves even when a Mitzvah presents itself to them that it is too hard for them to do. Thirdly, the person could be so drawn to the pleasures of this physical world that the person would not forsake getting physical pleasure if doing the Mitzvah prevents him from this pleasure.

The Meam Loez says that if the Bnei Yisroel did not go into exile in Egypt, it would not have been possible to give the Bnei Yisroel the 613 Mitzvos. The reason for this is because they would have been used to enjoying the physical pleasures of life, and it would have been unlikely that they would accept and do the Mitzvos. Beraishis (1:31) says, "And there was evening, and there was morning on the sixth day." On no other of the days of creation does it say "the" before listing the number of the day. The Gemorah in Shabbos 88a says that we derive from this word "the" that the world was in limbo until the sixth day. The sixth day is the sixth day of Sivan, the day the Bnei Yisroel

Shemos

received the Torah. The world would only exist if the Bnei Yisroel agreed to accept the Torah since this was the whole purpose of the world's creation. Therefore, Hashem caused the Bnei Yisroel to go into the harsh exile in Egypt, where they would have to work constantly in all sorts of extremely hard labor. The Egyptians did not give them even a moment to rest. Therefore, when Hashem came to redeem the Bnei Yisroel from this exile, they were happy to willingly accept the yoke of the Torah and its 613 Mitzvos. They calculated that even though it is difficult to fulfill the Torah and it takes much effort to correctly observe even one Mitzvah, not to mention to learn all the intricacies in how to perform the Mitzvah, it was still better than the back-breaking labor in Egypt. The Shach at the beginning of Parshas Shemos also makes this point that otherwise, the Bnei Yisroel would not accept the yoke of doing all the Mitzvos. In addition, the exile in Egypt prepared them to eat only the very basic foods and not too much of even these foods. The Shemos Raba (1:12) says that Pharaoh decreed that the task-masters should force the Bnei Yisroel to finish up daily the amount of work the task-masters gave them. Pharaoh made sure that the daily allotment was so great that the Bnei Yisroel were forced by the task-masters to stay in the field the entire night and were not able to return to their houses at night. The task-masters argued that there was not enough time to go home and finish the allotment and that the Bnei Yisroel only had time to sleep a little bit in the field before starting the next day's allotment. Therefore, the Bnei Yisroel got used to being able to sleep anywhere and were used to only sleeping a little. The Braisah in the sixth chapter of Pirkei Avos (4) says: "this is the way of the Torah: Bread and salt you will eat, measured water you will drink, on the ground you will sleep, a life of suffering you will live, and in the Torah, you will labor. If you do this, Tehillim (128:2) says, 'You are fortunate, and it is good for you.' This means "You are fortunate" in this world, "and it is good for you" in the World to Come." The Bnei Yisroel's life in the exile of Egypt prepared them for a life of Torah and the acceptance of the 613 Mitzvos of the Torah, so the world could exist.

We mentioned previously that the Meam Loez says that in order to accept the Torah, one must believe in Hashem and in the thirteen principles that the Rambam delineates in his Ani Maamin. When the Bnei Yisroel saw all the plagues and miracles in Egypt, and at the Red Sea, without a doubt, they acquired belief in Hashem. He compares what happened to the Bnei Yisroel to what happens when one plants wheat or vegetables in the field, where only after the seed decays does the plant sprout out with new life and vigor. In a similar way, only after the pain and breaking down of the Bnei Yisroel in exile could the Bnei Yisroel arise as a nation ready to accept the holy Torah. He explains with this answer a puzzling part of the Bris Bain HaBesorim where Hashem tells Avrohom in Beraishis (15:14) וְגַם אֶת הַגּוֹי אֲשֶׁר יַעֲבֹדוּ דָּן אָנֹכִי וְאַחֲרֵי כֵן יֵצְאוּ בִּרְכֻשׁ גָּדוֹל (And also the nation that they will serve will I judge, and afterwards they will go forth with great possessions). He offers a Moshul to a person who is told that he will get a thousand lashes and afterward will get a reward of one thousand gold coins. The person will undoubtedly say that he has no interest in either the lashes or the gold coins. Moreover, it is difficult to understand how Hashem could pacify Avrohom with money by saying, don't worry about the fact that your children will be slaves for 400 years since they will get a monetary reward afterward. Only small children could be so gullible to accept such an offer. It is also hard to understand the use of the words בִּרְכֻשׁ גָּדוֹל (with a big possession) instead of saying with many or much possessions. Furthermore, even minimal wages for 600,000 people working for all these years would never add up to the amount they took with them when they left

Shemos

Egypt. I think the biggest proof of this is brought by the Gemorah in Sanhedrin 91a, which describes what happened when the Egyptians brought a court case to the court of Alexander the Great demanding that the Bnei Yisroel return all the money they took from Egypt. As proof of their claim, the Egyptians quoted Shemos (12:36), which says, "Hashem gave the people favor in the eyes of the Egyptians, and they lent them, and they emptied out Egypt." The Gemorah relates that there was a person called Geviha Ben Pesisa who asked permission from the Jewish elders to answer the claim of the Egyptians. Geviha Ben Pesisa argued that if the Egyptians won against him in the court case, one could say that the Egyptians won against a simple Jew, and if he won against them, one could say that the Torah taught to us by Moshe has defeated them. The Jewish elders gave him permission to answer the claim of the Egyptians. Geviha Ben Pesisa told the Egyptians that their entire claim is based on the Torah. Therefore, he said that he would refute their claim from the same Torah, which says only a few Pesukim later in Shemos (12:40), "And the habitation of the Bnei Yisroel, that they dwelled in Egypt, was four hundred and thirty years." Geviha Ben Pesisa asked the Egyptians to pay us wages for 600,000 men working for 430 years, which far exceeds the amount of money we borrowed from Egypt. In return, we will pay you for what we borrowed from Egypt. Alexander the Great then asked the Egyptians to counter Geviha Ben Pesisa's claim. The Egyptians pleaded to be given three days to prepare an answer, to which Alexander the Great agreed. When the Egyptians realized they did not have an answer, they abandoned all their fields and vineyards with their crops and ran away. The Gemorah tells us that it was the Shemitah year where we are forbidden to plant, and because of that, we had a big windfall of food in a year where food is typically difficult to get.

With the above being the case, it is hard to understand how Avrohom could be pacified with this reward. The Meam Loez explains that the reward Hashem promised Avrohom had nothing to do with gold or silver. Rather the great reward was the Torah, which the Bnei Yisroel could only receive after being purified through the years of slavery, as explained above. The reward of receiving the Torah completely pacified Avrohom, and that is why Avrohom did not have any arguments about the slavery.

The Nisivos Shalom, in his last essay on Parshas Vayechi, says that the exile in Egypt was to prepare and purify the Bnei Yisroel to be able to receive the Torah, similar to what the Meam Loez says. While in exile, the Bnei Yisroel sunk further and further into sin down to the 49th and next to last level of uncleanliness in Egypt. The exile in Egypt could not have been to purify the Bnei Yisroel from their sins since the 70 people of Yaakov and his family who went down to Egypt were all righteous. Had the exile been to purify the Bnei Yisroel from their sins, it would have had the opposite effect since the exile caused them many more sins. The Nisivos Shalom says that Yaakov was also pacified when he was told in Beraishis (46:3), "Do not be afraid of going down to Egypt, for there I will make you into a great nation." The great nation Hashem was referring to was a nation great in spirituality to receive the Torah and become the chosen people of Hashem, which they could only come to while going through the exile in Egypt.

With the above answer, we can understand a central part of the Hagadah of Pesach where "Rabban Gamliel was accustomed to say, Anyone who has not said these three things on Pesach has not

Shemos

fulfilled his obligation, and these are them: the Pesach sacrifice, matza, and morror." With regard to morror, we say, "This morror that we are eating, for the sake of what is it? For the sake to commemorate that the Egyptians embittered the lives of our ancestors in Egypt." The Plotsker, in his Hagadah Birchas HaShir, ponders the fact that the three things we mention, Pesach, matza, and morror, are ostensibly not listed in the correct chronological order. On the night before we left Egypt, we made the Pesach sacrifice, and on the next morning, the haste that Hashem took us out of Egypt did not allow enough time for our dough to rise. After we mention these, we mention morror and that it commemorated "that the Egyptians embittered the lives of our ancestors in Egypt." The embitterment of our lives took place well before we went out of Egypt and the miracles which the Pesach sacrifice and matza commemorate occurred. Moreover, we conclude this section of the Hagadah with, "Therefore we are obligated to thank, praise, laud, glorify, exalt, lavish, bless, raise high, and acclaim He who made all these miracles for our ancestors and for us." This implies that we also owe thanks to Hashem for the Egyptians embittering the lives of our ancestors in Egypt. The Plotsker offers a moshul to a Dr. who wanted to show off his abilities by offering to give a person some dreaded, painful disease and then cure the person completely. Akin to the Moshul of the Dr., we would ostensibly say that it would have been better had Hashem not had the Egyptians enslave and torture us as compared to having the enslavement and Hashem making a miracle and redeem us. With this answer to our question, we become aware that we need to thank Hashem for enslaving us and redeeming us since this was the only way it would be possible for us to receive and accept the Torah. This thought also explains why morror is mentioned after the Pesach sacrifice and matza. It is not the enslaving that we are focusing on but rather the fact that it led to us being able to receive the Torah, an event which occurred chronologically seven weeks after the time that the miracles of the Pesach sacrifice and matzo occurred.

2) The Abarbanel in his Sefer on the Hagadah called Zevach Pesach also presents an answer to our question. He says that Hashem brought the Bnei Yisroel into exile to do good for them and to make them exalted. It is known, that the purpose of this world is for its creator, Hashem, to be recognized, praised, and thanked for creating the world, as Sefer Yeshayahu (43:7) says, כֹּל הַנִּקְרָא בִשְׁמִי וְלִכְבוֹדִי בְּרָאתִיו יְצַרְתִּיו אַף עֲשִׂיתִיו (Everyone that is called by My name, and whom I created for My glory, I formed him, I also made him). During the lifetime of Odom's grandson, Enosh, the serving of idols was started. The practice became so widespread that only a few people remained that believed that there was one creator who created the world. Even among those few people, many of them believed that the creator had created the world but did not concern himself with how the world ran. The main country where all these heretical opinions were rampant was Egypt. When Avrohom began teaching the world true belief in Hashem, Hashem wanted to reward mankind by publicizing that Avrohom was correct. Hashem saw that the only way to do this was through wondrous signs in both the heavens and earth, which were against the laws of nature. The best way to accomplish this publicizing was to bring a nation to Egypt, the center of all heretical opinions, and then send a prophet to redeem this nation through wondrous miracles when the leader hardened his heart to refuse to allow the nation to be redeemed. The nation that was redeemed would also receive Hashem's Torah and, through it, publicize the beliefs of the Torah to all of mankind. Since Avrohom was the main teacher who taught the world true belief in Hashem, Hashem chose his descendants to be this nation to go down to Egypt, as a kindness to Avrohom. That is why Hashem,

Shemos

during the Bris Bain HaBesorim, told Avrohom that his descendants would be the ones to be slaves and then be redeemed so that true belief in Hashem would be known in all the world. Hashem told Avrohom that even though they would be enslaved, it would be for their eventual good.

The Abarbanel proves that this explanation is correct by noting that Avrohom did not react to the news that his children would be slaves by beseeching Hashem in prayer to annul this decree. "Is it possible that Avrohom would not say anything about his own children when Avrohom tries every argument possible to get the decree of the destruction of Sodom overturned?" In addition, in chapter 105 of Tehillim, Dovid HaMelech essentially describes what happened in the redemption from Egypt in a consistent way to this explanation that Hashem was rewarding the Bnei Yisroel. The first Posuk of chapter 105 begins with "Give thanks to Hashem, call out in His name; make His deeds known among the peoples." Tehillim (105:8-9) say: "He remembered His covenant forever, the word He had commanded to the thousandth generation, Which He had made with Avrohom." Tehillim (105:15-16) describe how Hashem orchestrated bringing the Bnei Yisroel to Egypt when it says: "He called a famine upon the land; He broke every staff of bread. He sent a man before them; Yosef was sold as a slave." Tehillim (105:25-27) say: "He turned their (the Egyptians) heart to hate His people, to plot against His servants. He sent Moshe, His servant, and Aharon, whom He chose. They placed upon them the words of His signs and His miracles in the land of Ham (Egypt)." The chapter concludes in Tehillim (105:42-45) with: "For He remembered His holy word with Avrohom, His servant. And He took out His people with joy, His chosen ones with joyful singing. And He gave them lands of nations, and they inherited the toil of kingdoms. In order that they keep His statutes and observe His laws. Hallelujah."

The Abarbanel compares what happened to the Bnei Yisroel to what happens to a cow when it is brought to the slaughterhouse. The ultimate purpose of bringing the cow to the slaughterhouse is for the cow to attain the highest level a cow can attain by becoming food for a human and by its flesh being incorporated into human flesh. The cow, however, resists and tries to fight its fate as much as possible. In a similar way, a person does not subjugate himself easily under the yoke of the Torah. Therefore, like the cow, the Bnei Yisroel did not go down to Egypt without resisting its fate as much as possible. Similar to the cow in the slaughterhouse, the Bnei Yisroel endured pain and even death to attain their ultimate purpose, which was gifted to them by Hashem, that of accepting the Torah.

3) The Shach at the beginning of Parshas Shemos presents another answer to our question. He says that just like Hashem tested Avrohom with ten tests to show the world how exalted Avrohom was and why Hashem chose him, similarly, Hashem tested Avrohom's children in Egypt to show the world why Hashem chose them. Though Avrohom has other descendants like the descendants of Yishmael and Esav, the slavery in Egypt showed how special the descendants of Yaakov were. This is the meaning of Devorim (4:20), which says: "But Hashem took you and brought you out of the iron crucible, out of Egypt, to be a people of His possession, as of this day."

4) The Meam Loez presents another answer to our question. Similar to the Abarbanel, he also says that the exile in Egypt was a kindness to the Bnei Yisroel. he also cites the difference between Avrohom's reaction to being given the news of the exile to Avrohom's reaction to being given the

Shemos

news that Sodom was going to be destroyed. He also says that Hashem rewarded Avrohom with his children being chosen to receive the Torah and spread the word of Hashem's existence to the whole world through the wonders of the redemption from Egypt. However, a problem arose while the Bnei Yisroel were in Egypt, and the problem was that they joined the Egyptians in worshipping idols. It was, therefore, necessary and due to Hashem's kindness that he had the Egyptians enslave and oppress the Bnei Yisroel under very harsh conditions in order to purify them from all of this spiritual uncleanness that now had become part of them. All this harsh slavery was needed to prepare us to believe in Hashem and in his ability to redeem us from even the most powerful empire of the world at that time.

5) The Meam Loez presents another answer to our question. He says that the exile and its afflictions were caused by the Bnei Yisroel, neglecting the Mitzvah of Bris Milah, the one Mitzvah, which Hashem had commanded Avrohom to be done to him and all his descendants. The Shemos Raba (19:5) says that all of the Bnei Yisroel stopped having a Bris Milah except for the tribe of Levi. This occurred shortly after Yosef was Niftar when the Bnei Yisroel decided to be like the Egyptians and not have a Bris Milah. The Egyptians also encouraged the Bnei Yisroel to not have a Bris Milah and be like them. As has happened unfortunately many times during the history of the Bnei Yisroel, the Bnei Yisroel trying to be like the Gentiles caused the Gentiles to begin hating the Bnei Yisroel and, in the case of Egypt, enslaving them. Since not performing the Bris Milah showed that the Bnei Yisroel did not want to serve Hashem and do His Mitzvos, Hashem caused the Egyptians, in a punishment measure for measure, to enslave the Bnei Yisroel instead. As further evidence that the enslavement was a measure for measure punishment, since the tribe of Levi continued to give their children a Bris Milah, they were not enslaved by the Egyptians.

6) The Abarbanel in his Sefer on the Hagadah called Zevach Pesach presents another answer to our question. He says that the exile and its afflictions were a punishment for the sin of the brothers throwing Yosef into a pit and then selling Yosef as a slave to Egypt. Since the brothers caused Yosef and his children to be in Egypt, it was appropriate that the brothers and their children should receive their punishment in Egypt. As a measure for measure punishment for selling Yosef as a slave, the Bnei Yisroel were made slaves to the Egyptians. Similarly, the measure for measure punishment for throwing Yosef into the pit was the Egyptians throwing the baby boys into the Nile River. In addition, the selling of Yosef occurred while they were pasturing sheep, and Yosef was sent by Yaakov to see the welfare of the sheep. As a measure for measure punishment, the brothers were forced to come down to Egypt since there was no grass for their sheep to pasture on in Eretz Yisroel as they told Pharaoh in Beraishis (47:4), "We have come to sojourn in the land, for your servants' flocks have no pasture, for the famine is severe in the land of Canaan. Now, please let your servants dwell in the land of Goshen." To have a measure for measure punishment, sheep played an important part. For example, the brothers shechted a sheep to fool Yaakov into thinking that Yosef was devoured by a wild animal, and Hashem made Yosef the ruler over the people who worshipped sheep. When the Bnei Yisroel's sin had been forgiven, and they were ready to leave Egypt, Hashem commanded them to slaughter a Korban Peach, which came from sheep. That is, they sinned with sheep, they were enslaved and oppressed by the people who worship sheep, and they were fully atoned for their sins by slaughtering a sheep for a Korban Pesach.

Shemos

The Abarbanel says that Yosef and his descendants were included in this exile because he spoke Loshon Horah about the brothers to Yaakov, which caused the brothers to hate Yosef and eventually to sell him. He says that Yaakov also was included in the exile because he aided the brothers' hatred of Yosef by making a coat of many colors for Yosef. Though Binyamin had no part in the selling of Yosef, since the selling of Yosef caused a decree against the Bnei Yisroel, Binyamin was also included in the decree. To help comprehend this concept, the Mechilta on Shemos (12:22) ponders why the Bnei Yisroel were prohibited from leaving their homes the night when the Egyptian firstborns were killed. The Mechilta derives from this prohibition a general rule that when permission is granted to the destroying angel to destroy, the angel does not differentiate between wicked and righteous people. This general rule is why Binyamin was included in the decree of exile.

The Abarbanel says that even though Yaakov and Yosef were punished by having to go into exile in Egypt, they were not punished as much as the brothers since they each were buried in Eretz Yisroel and not in Egypt. The Torah explicitly tells us in Beraishis Perek 50 how Yaakov was brought up for burial in Eretz Yisroel. The Torah also tells us in Shemos (13:19), "Moshe took Yosef's bones with him, for he (Yosef) had the Bnei Yisroel take an oath, saying, G-d will surely remember you, and you shall bring up my bones from here (Egypt) with you." In addition, Sefer Yehoshua (24:32) says, "And the bones of Yosef, which the Bnei Yisroel had brought up out of Egypt, they buried in Shechem, in the parcel of ground which Yaakov bought from the sons of Chamor the father of Shechem, for a hundred pieces of money; and they became the inheritance of the children of Yosef." However, since the Pesukim nowhere explicitly mention that the bodies of the rest of the brothers were either taken out of Egypt or were buried in Eretz Yisroel, the Abarbanel says that the bodies of the brothers were buried in Egypt as punishment for their sin of selling of Yosef. He does mention that Chazal in the Mechilta on Shemos (13:19) say that the Bnei Yisroel brought out the bodies of all the brothers from Egypt. The Mechilta derives this idea from the wording of that Posuk, which says that Yosef made the Bnei Yisroel swear that "you shall bring up my bones from here with you." The phrase "with you" implies that their bones were also brought out. However, the Abarbanel is of the opinion that this Chazal should not be taken at "face value" since otherwise, the Pesukim, especially in Yehoshua, would have told us that and perhaps where the brothers were buried.

The Abarbanel says that since the brothers were brought in exile to Egypt because of their sin, their children remained in exile. He compares this to the explanation of the Ralbag on Megilas Eichah (5:7), which says, "Our fathers have sinned and are no more, and we have borne their sins." The Ralbag explains that children can be born into a situation, like an exile, created by their parents, and will not be redeemed until either the children because of their good deeds, merit redemption, or because the time of the end of the decree has come. The Ten Commandments in Shemos (20:5) say, "You shall neither prostrate yourself before them nor worship them, for I, Hashem, your G-d, am a zealous G-d, Who visits the sins of the fathers upon the sons, upon the third and the fourth generation of those who hate Me." This idea that up to the fourth generation can be punished because of the sins of the parents resonates very well with how Hashem describes the end of the exile to Avrohom in Beraishis (15:16), which says, "And the fourth generation will return here (to

Shemos

Eretz Yisroel)." That is, the exile to Egypt brought on by the sin of the brothers extended till the fourth generation, consistent with the Posuk we have brought from the Ten Commandments. We see that Yehuda, who was involved with the sale of Yosef, had a child Peretz, who had a child Chetzron, who had a child Calev. The fourth-generation after Yehuda, Calev went into Eretz Yisroel.

The Abarbanel says that one should not question how Hashem told Avrohom about the exile into Egypt before the brothers sinned to cause the exile. We have other examples of Hashem talking about the results of the sin before the sin actually happened. For example, Shemos (23:20) says, "Behold, I am sending an angel before you to guard you on the way and to bring you to the place that I have prepared." Rashi, based on the Shemos Raba (32:3), says that the Torah is telling us the news that the Bnei Yisroel would in the future sin, and because of this, Hashem would send an angel to guard the Bnei Yisroel instead of Hashem guarding us himself. The sin would only occur later when the Bnei Yisroel made the Golden Calf, and therefore just like the news of the exile to Avrohom, Hashem is telling us about the results of the sin before the sin ever happened. Another example of telling about the results of the sin before the sin happened is in Devorim (31:16-17), which say, "And Hashem said to Moshe: Behold, you are about to lie with your forefathers, and this nation will rise up and stray after the deities of the nations of the land, into which they are coming. And they will forsake Me and violate My covenant which I made with them. And My fury will rage against them on that day, and I will abandon them and hide My face from them, and they will be consumed, and many evils and troubles will befall them, and they will say on that day, 'Is it not because our G-d is no longer among us, that these evils have befallen us?'"

The Abarbanel says that attributing the exile in Egypt to a sin of the Bnei Yisroel fits in very well with Beraishis (15:14), which says, וְגַם אֶת הַגּוֹי אֲשֶׁר יַעֲבֹדוּ דָּן אָנֹכִי וְאַחֲרֵי כֵן יֵצְאוּ בִּרְכֻשׁ גָּדוֹל (And also the nation that they will serve will I judge, and afterwards they will go forth with great possessions). This Posuk would be telling us that along with punishing the Bnei Yisroel for the sin of selling Yosef, Hashem will also punish the nation who the Bnei Yisroel will be enslaved by. If Hashem was not punishing the Bnei Yisroel, then the word וְגַם (and also) would seem to be superfluous.

The Abarbanel also explains what is meant in Beraishis (15:13), which says, "You shall surely know that your seed will be strangers in a land that is not theirs, and they will enslave them and oppress them, for four hundred years." Shemos (12:40) says, "And the habitation of the Bnei Yisroel, that they dwelled in Egypt, was four hundred and thirty years." The Abarbanel says that the end of the sin of selling Yosef occurred after four hundred years. At that time, the Prophet Yechezkel tells us that the Prophet of that time, who Chazal tell us was Aharon, says to the Bnei Yisroel in Sefer Yechezkel (20:6-8), "On that day I lifted up My hand to them to bring them out of the land of Egypt, to a land that I had sought out for them, flowing with milk and honey; it is the glory of all the lands. And I said to them: Every man cast away the despicable idols from before his eyes, and pollute not yourselves with the idols of Egypt; I am Hashem your G-d. But they rebelled against Me and would not consent to hearken to Me; they did not cast away, every man, the despicable idols from before their eyes, neither did they forsake the idols of Egypt; and I said to pour out My wrath over them, to give My anger full reign over them, in the midst of the land of Egypt." These Pesukim tells us that

Shemos

because of the sins of the generation of Bnei Yisroel in Egypt at that time; thirty years were added on the exile until the people started doing Teshuva as Shemos (2:23) tells us, "Now it came to pass in those many days that the king of Egypt died, and the Bnei Yisroel sighed from the labor, and they cried out, and their cry ascended to God from the labor."

The Meam Loez extends this reason of the Abarbanel by pointing out that the brothers caused Yaakov to suffer constantly and refuse to be consoled for 22 years without his beloved son Yosef. This was caused by ten of the twelve brothers since neither Yosef nor Binyamin had a part in causing this 22-year pain for Yaakov. Each brother was punished for 22 years of exile in Egypt, which would give a sum total of 220 years of exile. The Meam Loez says that one year of exile was subtracted from each of the brothers because of the pain they got by being buried in Egypt, as we have quoted from the Abarbanel previously. This leads to an exile of 210 years in Egypt, which is consistent with how many years the Bnei Yisroel spent in Egypt.

What Did the Midwives Mean When They Described the Jewish Women as חָיוֹת, Which Literally Means Wild Animals?

Shemos וַתֹּאמַרְןָ הַמְיַלְּדֹת אֶל פַּרְעֹה כִּי לֹא כַנָּשִׁים הַמִּצְרִיֹּת הָעִבְרִיֹּת כִּי חָיוֹת הֵנָּה בְּטֶרֶם תָּבוֹא אֲלֵהֶן הַמְיַלֶּדֶת וְיָלָדוּ (א:יט) (1:19) And the midwives said to Pharaoh, "Because the Hebrew women are not like the Egyptian women, for they are חָיוֹת; when the midwife has not yet come to them, they have already given birth."

What did the Midwives mean when they described the Jewish women as חָיוֹת, which literally means wild animals?

1) The Gemorah in Sotah 11b, the Shemos Raba (1:16), and Midrash Lekach Tov are the sources for the answer that Rashi presents to our question. They say that the midwives realized Pharaoh would question their excuse that the Jewish women are skilled as midwives since even midwives need another midwife when they give birth. Rather what they told Pharaoh was that the Jewish people are compared to wild animals who do not need any help from anyone when they are giving birth. For example, the tribe of Yehuda is compared to a lion, the tribe of Dan to a snake, the tribe of Naphtali to a deer, the tribe of Yisochar to a donkey, the tribe of Yosef to a bull, and the tribe of Binyamin to a wolf. With regard to all the rest of the tribes, all the Bnei Yisroel are compared to a lioness in Sefer Yechezkel (19:2). The Midwives proved that the Jewish women did not need any help giving birth by saying in our Posuk, "when the midwife has not yet come to them, they have already given birth."

The Eyun Yaakov on the Gemorah in Sotah 11b ponders the question of how Pharaoh could have believed that the Jewish women were like wild animals and not like humans with regard to not needing someone to help them give birth. Before we get to the Eyun Yaakov's answer, the Shemos Raba (1:12) says that Pharaoh made four decrees in different time periods of the slavery against the Bnei Yisroel. First, Pharaoh decreed that the task-masters should force the Bnei Yisroel to finish up daily the amount of work the task-masters gave them. Pharaoh made sure that the daily allotment was so great that the Bnei Yisroel were forced by the task-masters to stay in the field the entire night and were not able to return to their houses at night. The task-masters argued that there was not

Shemos

enough time to go home and finish the allotment and that the Bnei Yisroel only had time to sleep a little bit in the field before starting the next day's allotment. Pharaoh's real intention was to minimize the population of the Bnei Yisroel by not allowing them to return home at night.

Seeing what was happening, Hashem counteracted Pharaoh's plan, especially since Hashem needed to fulfill the promise He made to Avrohom in Beraishis (22:17) "That I (Hashem) will surely bless you (Avrohom), and I will greatly multiply your seed as the stars of the heavens and as the sand that is on the seashore." Instead, say the Gemorah and the Shemos Raba, the righteous Jewish women in that generation merited by their actions to redeem the Bnei Yisroel from Egypt and to destroy Pharaoh's plan. The Eyun Yaakov says that the way the righteous women brought the redemption is that through having many children, the Bnei Yisroel were able to complete the amount of hard work decreed upon them very quickly. When the Jewish women went to draw water for their husbands, Hashem caused that the water they drew to be composed of half water and half fish. The women then used the water and fish to bring two pots to their husbands, one of hot water and one of the fish. The women used the hot water for bathing their husbands and anointing them, along with feeding them the fish along with some water to drink, so that they could get back some of their strength after all their harsh labor that day. The Yepheh Toar says that they also used the hot water to warm up their bodies since they slept on the cold ground of the fields. Rashi on Shemos (38:8), based on the Midrash Tanchuma in Parshas Pekuday (9), elaborates that the women would then take out copper mirrors and use them to show both themselves and their husbands in the mirror. They would then entice the husband with words, saying, "I am more beautiful than you." In this way, the women became pregnant despite Pharaoh's evil decree of not allowing the husbands to come home at night.

The Gemorah and Shemos Raba continue and tell us what happened when it was time for the women to give birth. The Eitz Yosef says that since the women were also forced to work as slaves, not to mention that they had no money, they could not care for their new babies. Moreover, when later, Pharaoh decreed that all baby boys must get thrown into the Nile River, the women had little choice but to bring the babies to the fields instead. The women went out to the fields and gave birth under an apple tree. Hashem sent an angel who would clean the newborn babies and straighten them out, ensuring that they would be healthy. Both these things would have been done by a Midwife when the baby was born. As proof that this happened, the Gemorah quotes Sefer Yechezkel (15:4), which says, "And as for your birth, on the day you were born, your umbilical cord was not cut, neither were you washed with water for cleansing, nor were you salted, nor swaddled at all." The angel would then gather two round loaves, one of oil and one of honey. This is the meaning of Devorim (32:13), which says, "He (Hashem) let them suck honey from a stone, and oil from a flinty rock." The Maharsha on the Gemorah explains that since we don't ever find anywhere else that honey and oil were obtained from stones, the Gemorah is of the opinion that this Posuk describes what was given to the babies in Egypt.

The Gemorah and Shemos Raba relate that when the Egyptians found out that the babies were in the field, they attempted to murder them by bringing oxen and plowing the entire field. The Maharsha explains that even though the Egyptians saw how the children were surviving by a miracle, they were not in awe but rather ascribed it to sorcery as they ascribed a number of the first plagues of the ten plagues and were not impressed. Hashem made a miracle, and the babies were down into the ground until the Egyptians went away when the babies would come out like grass in a field. When the children grew up, they would come to their houses as flocks upon flocks. At the splitting of the

Shemos

Red Sea, it was these children who had grown up in the fields and seen Hashem constantly, that said in Shemos (15:2), "this is my Hashem, and I will beautify Him." The Midrash Tanchuma in Vaera (6) says that the tribe of Levi was exempt from the very hard work in Egypt. Based on this Midrash Tanchuma, the Eyun Yaakov points out that the reason Moshe wasn't saved in such a matter was because the tribe of Levi was not made to work on the fields. Therefore, this miracle of being born, raised, and taken care of in the fields did not apply to them.

The Shemos Raba (1:13) says that when Pharaoh saw that he was not getting the results he wanted from this decree, he made another (second) decree. This decree ordered the two Jewish Midwives to kill all Jewish baby boys. The Shemos Raba (1:18) says that when Pharaoh again did not get the results he wanted from this decree, he made a third decree, and Pharaoh ordered that all the male babies should be thrown into the Nile River. Since Pharaoh's astrologers told him that the redeemer of the Jews would be born that day but that they could not tell if he would be born from the Jews or the Egyptians, Pharaoh even extended the decree to include the Egyptians. For three months, Pharaoh's astrologers saw that the redeemer had not been caught, consistent with Shemos (2:2), which says that Yocheved was able to hide Moshe for three months. In these three months, the Yepheh Toar says that it is not clear whether the decree also remained on the Egyptians or just on the Bnei Yisroel. Rashi, on the Gemorah in Sotah 12a, says that it remained even on the Egyptians. The fourth and final decree occurred much later in time when Pharaoh made the slavery conditions much harsher by not giving the Bnei Yisroel straw to build the bricks with.

Parenthetically, the Maharal on the Gemorah in Sotah 12a ponders the question of why the astrologers couldn't see whether the redeemer was a Jew or Egyptian when they had the power even to know what day he was born on. The Maharal explains that since Moshe grew up in Pharaoh's house and was an adopted son of Pharaoh's daughter Basya, he could be considered as an Egyptian, as the Gemorah says in Megilah 13a that anyone who raises an orphan in their house is considered as raising their own child. Divrei HaYomim I (4:18) says that the sons of Basya, Pharaoh's daughter, were Yered, Avigdor, Soco, and Yehutiel. The Gemorah in Megilah 13a says that they were all different names of Moshe. Being that Moshe is considered by the Posuk as Basya's son, this fact caused the astrologers not to be able to tell if Moshe was Jewish or Egyptian.

We can now appreciate the answer the Eyun Yaakov in Sotah 11b offers to the question of how Pharaoh could have believed that the women were like wild animals and not like humans with regard to not needing someone to help them give birth. Pharaoh already was aware of the fact that the Jewish women were giving birth in the fields since Pharaoh had given the order to plow up these fields, which contained the Jewish babies. Therefore, Pharaoh was not surprised to find out that the Jewish women were like wild animals with regard to not needing someone to help them give birth.

2) Rashi, the Bechor Shor, the Abarbanel, and many years later, the Malbim answer our question similarly. They say that when they described the Jewish women as חָיוֹת, the Midwives meant that they were as skilled in the job of a Midwife as the professional Midwives themselves were. According to them, the word חָיוֹת means Midwife. As the Bechor Shor points out, Targum Onkelos similarly translates חָיוֹת as "they are knowledgeable." The Taz, in Divrei Dovid, and many years later, the Oznayim LeTorah ponder how this answers Pharaoh's complaint to the Midwives that they didn't follow his order and kill the Jewish baby boys. They explain that because the Jewish mothers were so skilled, they didn't call the Midwives right away but rather timed it so that the Midwives

Shemos

came after the birth and were only needed to cut the umbilical cord and to clean the baby. The Taz explains that this is in contrast to the Egyptian women who immediately called the Midwives when they first started feeling labor pain. Our Posuk says this explicitly when it concludes with the phrase, "when the midwife has not yet come to them, they have already given birth." Since the babies were already born before they arrived, the Midwives told Pharaoh that they didn't have a chance to follow Pharaoh's order and kill the Jewish baby boys, since otherwise, the mothers would immediately know that they had killed their babies who were previously alive. If the mothers knew that the Midwives killed their babies, there would be no way any other Jewish women would use the Midwives, and Pharaoh's plan for the Midwives to secretly kill the babies without the mothers knowing would not come to fruition. The Akeidah also says that the Jewish women gave birth themselves and only called the Midwives to cut the umbilical cord and clean the babies.

The Maskil LeDovid explains differently how the Midwives answered Pharaoh's complaint to them that they didn't follow his order and kill the Jewish baby boys. He says that because the Jewish women were themselves skilled as Midwives, they would call their friends or neighbors to help them give birth and would not need the services of the Midwives at all. I would think that even according to the Maskil LeDovid, the Midwives told Pharaoh that they would still call the Midwives but only for cutting the umbilical cord and cleaning the baby. Otherwise, it would be inconsistent with the end of our Posuk where it says, "when the midwife has not yet come to them, they have already given birth," which would imply that the Midwives were eventually called to the new mother, just not till after they had already given birth. The Gemorah in Sotah 11b says that when the Midwives gave their excuse to Pharaoh, Pharaoh replied that even if the Jewish women were skilled as midwives when a midwife gives birth, she calls another midwife to help her give birth. The Maskil LeDovid points out that his explanation gave the Midwives a good answer to Pharaoh's question since they did indeed call another midwife to help them give birth.

The Abarbanel is of the opinion that the Jewish mothers were not only skilled at giving birth themselves but were also skilled in cutting the umbilical cord and washing the baby. The Midwives told Pharaoh that they were never called by the Jewish mothers and therefore had no opportunity to follow Pharaoh's orders and kill the Jewish boys. When the Midwives told Pharaoh at the end of our Posuk, "when the midwife has not yet come to them, they have already given birth," they were telling Pharaoh that, therefore, they are never called by the Jewish mothers.

Rashi mentions this answer first before he presents the answer, which we presented as the first answer to our question. The reason he presents this answer second is because the first answer that the Jewish women give birth without the need of a Midwife in a similar manner to wild animals is more Midrashic and esoteric and is not the simplest answer to our question. Rashi on Beraishis (3:8) says, "but I (Rashi) have come only to teach the simple meaning of the Posuk and such Midrashim that clarifies the words of the verses, each word in its proper way." That being the case, the Mizrachi ponders why Rashi offered the second explanation, which is Midrashic, that the Jewish women give birth without the need of a Midwife in a similar manner to wild animals. He answers that according to the answer we are discussing, that the Midwives told Pharaoh the Jewish women were as skilled in the job of a Midwife as the professional Midwives themselves were, Rashi was bothered by the question of the Gemorah in Sotah 11b, that even skilled Midwives need another Midwife when they are giving birth themselves.

Shemos

3) The Midrash Lekach Tov, Rashbam, Ralbag, Eben Ezra, and Bechor Shor answer our question similarly. The Midrash Lekach Tov and Rashbam say that describing the Jewish women as חָיוֹת means that they are full of life and have a lot of life in themselves. The Midwives said that the Jewish women, even when they are giving birth, act with the dexterity, quickness, and full strength of a healthy non-pregnant woman. Because of this strength, says the Ralbag, they are able to give birth themselves. This is different than the last answer, which said that it was their skill as Midwives, which allowed them to give birth themselves.

4) The explanation of the Targum Yonason ben Uziel and Targum Yerushalmi of our Posuk also answers our question. They say that the Jewish women davened to Hashem for help giving birth, and Hashem answered their prayers, and they gave birth without any problems and without the need of a midwife. The Targum Yonason ben Uziel translates כִּי חָיוֹת הֵנָּה as "because they are astute." The Midwives explained to Pharaoh that the Jewish women were astute in realizing that when they put their full trust in Hashem and daven to Hashem, Hashem will answer their prayers and send their salvation.

5) The Bechor Shor, Toldos Yitzchak, and Ohr HaChaim answer our question similarly. They say the Midwives told Pharaoh that the Jewish women are astute, and because of their astuteness, they suspect that we might carry out your decree of killing the Jewish baby boys. Presumably, this explanation is based on the Targum Onkelos and Targum Yonason ben Uziel, who translate כִּי חָיוֹת הֵנָּה as "because they are astute." The midwives told Pharaoh that because of their astuteness, the Jewish women are careful to never call us. However, the Ohr HaChaim adds that the Midwives told Pharaoh that if a Jewish woman were to call them, they were prepared to carry our Pharaoh's decree. Furthermore, the Bechor Shor says that the Midwives pointed out to Pharaoh that previous to his decree, the Jewish women used to use them as Midwives, even though the Jewish women were midwives themselves since it is easier when another midwife helps even a midwife give birth. However, the Midwives told Pharaoh that now that the Jewish women suspect us, they are willing to give up the convenience of using a midwife since they are themselves midwives.

The Ohr HaChaim explains how the Midwives even answered why they brought food and water to the Jewish women instead of following Pharaoh's order and murdering the Jewish baby boys. The Midwives told Pharaoh that they indeed try to come, even without being called, to the Jewish women when it would be around the time for them to give birth. However, since the Jewish women were astute and suspected them, the Jewish women would tell the Midwives that their due date was later than it actually was. Therefore, by the time the Midwives got there, the Jewish women had already given birth. The Ohr HaChaim says that the Midwives explained to Pharaoh that the reason they brought gifts of food and water to the Jewish women was so that they could win the confidence of these women and thereby be able to carry out Pharaoh's decree. Despite this effort, the Midwives explained to Pharaoh that the Jewish women were too astute to be fooled by the gifts of food and water.

6) The Sforno also presents an answer to our question. He translates כִּי חָיוֹת הֵנָּה as "because they are midwives," similar to the second answer we have presented to our question. He says that since the Jewish women are skilled as midwives, they will immediately know if we do anything strange or even if we just speak of doing something strange. This will lead to the Jewish women not using us a second time and, more importantly, telling all their friends not to use us in the future. The Midwives

Shemos

told Pharaoh that even if they were successful once in carrying out Pharaoh's orders, no one in the future would call them, and therefore there was no point in even obeying Pharaoh's orders once since it was never Pharaoh's goal to only murder one or two Jewish baby boys.

7) The Midrash Lekach Tov and Ponim Yofos say that the Midwives told Pharaoh the Jewish women were so righteous that they were not included in the curse of Chava in Beraishis (3:16) "To the woman (Chava) He (Hashem) said, 'I shall surely increase your sorrow and your pregnancy; in pain, you shall bear children.'" The Gemorah in Sotah 12b proves that righteous Jewish women like Yocheved were not subject to the pain of childbirth. As proof, the Gemorah presents Shemos (2:1-2), which say, "A man of the house of Levi (Amram) went and married a daughter of Levi (Yocheved). The woman conceived and bore a son (Moshe), and when she saw him that he was good, she hid him for three months." The Gemorah is of the opinion that the reason Yocheved was able to hide Moshe for three months was because she was already three months pregnant with Moshe before she remarried Amram. That being the case, analyzes the Gemorah, why does the Posuk after Yocheved remarried say, "The woman conceived and bore a son," being that she conceived before she remarried. The Gemorah concludes that just like Yocheved had no pain when she conceived, she also had no pain when she gave birth. The Gemorah concludes that we may derive from here that righteous women of all generations were not affected by the curse of Chava to have pain during childbirth. Since the women did not have the pain of childbirth, the Midwives told Pharaoh, they were able to give birth on their own without the need of a midwife. The Ponim Yofos says that righteous people are called חַי. As proof, he cites the Gemorah in Brochos 18a, which says that righteous people, even after they have been Niftar, are still considered living. The Gemorah cites a Posuk about a person who was Niftar and was still called חַי. Therefore, righteous women would be referred to as חָיוֹת. When the Midwives described the Jewish women with the phrase כִּי חָיוֹת הֵנָּה, this should be translated that "they are righteous women."

Parenthetically we note that Rashi says that the reason Yocheved was able to hide Moshe for three months was because Moshe was born at the end of only six months of Yocheved's pregnancy with him. The Chizkuni points out that at first glance, this Rashi is at odds with the Gemorah we just mentioned that Yocheved was three months pregnant when she remarried Amram. He reconciles Rashi with the Gemorah by first saying that the Egyptians knew that a baby could be born after six months of pregnancy. Therefore, they started checking for babies six months after Amram and all the Bnei Yisroel decided to remarry despite Pharaoh's decree to kill the Jewish baby boys. Moshe was born after six months of pregnancy, but because Yocheved was pregnant for three months before she remarried, she was able to hide Moshe for three months before the Egyptians started checking for babies. Therefore, says the Chizkuni, Rashi is consistent with the Gemorah that Yocheved was pregnant for three months before remarrying Amram.

8) The Hegyona Shel Torah also ponders our question. He says that the phrase כִּי חָיוֹת הֵנָּה literally means that they are like wild animals. Wild animals are constantly fearful of being hunted. In a similar way, the Midwives told Pharaoh that by his decree, he had caused the Jewish women to be constantly in fear of being hunted. This fear increases their will to live and their will to make sure their children live. This fear also causes them to have the super-human strength to give birth on their own without a midwife since giving birth on their own avoids Pharaoh's decree that the Midwives should murder all the Jewish baby boys. Therefore, the Midwives told Pharaoh that

Shemos

because of his decree, the Jewish women were no longer using them, and they had no opportunity to carry out Pharaoh's decree.

What Good Is the Posuk Referring to That Hashem Did for the Midwives?

וַתֹּאמַרְןָ הַמְיַלְּדֹת אֶל פַּרְעֹה כִּי לֹא כַנָּשִׁים הַמִּצְרִיֹּת הָעִבְרִיֹּת כִּי חָיוֹת הֵנָּה בְּטֶרֶם תָּבוֹא אֲלֵהֶן הַמְיַלֶּדֶת וְיָלָדוּ. וַיֵּיטֶב אֱלֹקִים לַמְיַלְּדֹת וַיִּרֶב הָעָם וַיַּעַצְמוּ מְאֹד.(א:יט-כ) Shemos (1:19-20) And the Midwives said to Pharaoh, "Because the Hebrew women are not like the Egyptian women, for they are skilled as Midwives; when the midwife has not yet come to them, they have already given birth." G-d did good things for the Midwives, the people multiplied and became very strong.

To what good is the Posuk referring to that Hashem did for the Midwives?

Introduction
The Abarbanel says that Pharaoh used the Midwives so that he could secretly decrease the number of Jewish baby boys without embarrassing himself with a decree to the public. The reason this would have been an embarrassment was because even the Egyptians knew that it was wrong to murder and especially wrong to murder innocent children. In addition, Pharaoh was embarrassed to be killing people who were invited by the King to come to Egypt.

The Shemos Raba (1:14) ponders the question of why Pharaoh thought to use the Midwives for killing the Jewish boys being that he would have to take a chance that they would obey him instead of having his officers who obviously would obey him do it. It answers that Pharaoh was afraid of getting punished by Hashem if he or his officers did it themselves. The Yepheh Toar explains that in general, we have a Halachic principle that when a person appoints an emissary, whatever the emissary does is considered as if the person sending the emissary did it. However, if the person sends the emissary to do a sin, the emissary is supposed to not accept the mission or at least not carry out the sin, and if he does, the emissary is held responsible for doing the sin. For example, in our case, if the Midwives would, Chas VeShalom, had killed the baby boys, the sin of killing them would be on the Midwives since they are supposed to use their own intelligence not to do the sin. Therefore, Pharaoh calculated that having the Midwives kill the Jewish babies would save him from being punished for the killing.

The Shemos Raba (1:15) says that not only didn't the Midwives listen to Pharaoh and harm the Jewish boys, but rather they did everything they could to help them. For example, they would provide poor mothers with food and water so that they could revive themselves after giving birth and be able to nourish their new babies. Moreover, a certain percentage of births will result in babies born lame, blind, or having other birth defects. The Midwives davened to Hashem that no baby should have any birth defects so that no one would be able to say that they caused the birth defect and were participating in Pharaoh's decree. Hashem listened to their davening, and every baby was born without any birth defects. Even more so, some percentage of babies, or their mothers, especially at that time in history, were destined to die in the birthing process. The Midwives

Shemos

davened to Hashem with the same argument as above, and no baby or mother died of birthing complications. The Maharzav explains that the Shemos Raba derives the above from Shemos (1:17), which says, "The Midwives, however, feared Hashem; so they did not do as the king of Egypt had spoken to them, but they enabled the boys to live." The Maharzav says that the Torah is telling us that not only didn't the Midwives listen to Pharaoh, but they also did actions to "enable the boys to live." Parenthetically, the Ben Yehoyoda on the Gemorah in Sotah 11b ponders the question of why it was necessary to provide water when anyone could help themselves to water from the Nile River. He says that it wasn't plain water but rather water in which a special herb or medicine, which was beneficial to someone who had just given birth, was cooked.

The Gemorah in Sotah 11b and the Midrash Lekach Tov ponder who the Midwives were. They present two opinions. One opinion is that it was Yocheved and her daughter Miriam. The second opinion is that it was Yocheved and her daughter-in-law Elisheva, wife of Aharon. The Maharsha points out that only three women in the generation that went out of Egypt are mentioned by name, and these are Yocheved, Miriam, and Elisheva. Had it been anyone else, our Posuk would have told us their real name since we would not otherwise know who they were. The Maharsha also says that the reason for the opinion that it was Yocheved and her daughter-in-law Elisheva and not Miriam is because, at that point, Miriam would have been less than six years old, and it is unlikely that a girl so young would have been a midwife. The Seder Olam says that Miriam was 86 years old when she went out of Egypt. If we couple this to the fact that the Torah in Shemos (7:7) says that Moshe was 80 years old when he left Egypt and that the story of the Midwives took place before Moshe was born, we can see that Miriam was at most six years old at that time. Though Shemos (7:7) tells us that Aharon was 83 years old when he left Egypt or less than three years old at the time of the story of the Midwives, Elisheva could have been much older than Aharon so that she was an appropriate age to be a midwife at this time. Parenthetically, it seems that the Maharsha was not bothered by the issue that Aharon would have gotten married at the age of three. The Shemos Raba (1:18) says that the reason Pharaoh wanted to kill all the Jewish boys was because his astrologers told him that a savior was soon to be born to the Jews. The Eyun Yaakov ponders the question of why Pharaoh wasn't afraid that either of the Midwives would be the mother of this savior, and even if the Midwives killed all the Jewish boys for whom they were the midwife, the savior could still be born from them. He says that since the Shemos Raba (94:9) tells us that Yocheved was born just as they were entering the walls of Egypt, coupled with the fact that the Bnei Yisroel spent 210 years in Egypt means that she would have been 130 years old at the time of Moshe's birth. Pharaoh assumed that at this age, she was too old to give birth and that either Miriam or Elisheva was too young to give birth, and therefore Pharaoh did not have to worry about the Midwives giving birth to the savior of the Bnei Yisroel.

The Ponim Yofos ponders the question of how only two Midwives might have been needed for the births of all the Jewish women. He says that it is highly likely that there were more Midwives, both Jewish and perhaps also Egyptian. That being the case, he ponders the question of why Pharaoh only bothered these two Midwives with his decree of killing the Jewish baby boys. He points out that the Gemorah in Sanhedrin 57b says that it is considered as murder for a non-Jew to kill a fetus, while it is not considered as murder for a Jew to kill a fetus before the head of the fetus has emerged

Shemos

from its mother. Tosfos in Sanhedrin 59a says that it is nonetheless prohibited for a Jew to kill a fetus. The Melo HaRoim on this Gemorah ponders the question of whether it is considered as murder for a non-Jew to kill a fetus of any age or just a fetus that is in its ninth month. He says that the Gemorah and Rambam seem to imply that killing a fetus of any age is prohibited. Since the majority of fetuses survive, we can assume that a fetus of any age will survive.

The Shemos Raba (1:8) says that after Yosef was Niftar, the Bnei Yisroel stopped giving their sons a Bris Milah. The only exception was the tribe of Levi, as it says in the Sifrei on Bamidbar (9:5). The Ponim Yofos says that there may have been many Jewish Midwives; however, since everyone but the tribe of Levi stopped giving their children a Bris Milah in Egypt, they threw away the yoke of their Jewish forefathers by not giving their children a Bris Milah. That being the case, Pharaoh considered the rest of the Midwives as if they had the status of being non-Jews and, therefore, would be considered as murderers if they killed the Jewish fetuses. Therefore, Pharaoh only chose Yocheved and Miriam, who were of the tribe of Levi, to kill the Jewish boy fetuses right before they were born since they would not be murderers being that they were fully Jewish. This explanation also fits well with the Gemorah in Sotah 11b, which says that Pharaoh told the Midwives how to differentiate between a boy being born and a girl being born. Pharaoh said that if the fetus was coming out of the womb facing up, it was a girl, and if the fetus was facing down, it was a boy. Therefore, Pharaoh told the Midwives that they could know if the fetus was a boy or girl even before the fetus came out and murder all boys in a manner that they would not be classified as murderers.

The Ponim Yofos says that Pharaoh even tested the Midwives to ensure that they considered themselves as having the laws of Jews. The Gemorah in Sotah 11b says that Pharaoh demanded that the Midwives perform an immoral act with him. Though there was the danger that they could be killed for not accepting Pharaoh's demand, the Midwives refused Pharaoh's demand. The Gemorah says in Sanhedrin 74b that a non-Jew is not commanded to sanctify Hashem's name by allowing himself to be killed instead of committing the three cardinal sins. The Gemorah derives this Halacha from the case of Naamon, who was a great Aramean general who had Tzoraas (leprosy), as we are told in Sefer Melachim II, chapter 5. The Arameans kidnapped a young Jewish girl and made her a servant to the wife of Naamon. Seeing that Naamon was afflicted with Tzoraas, she suggested to her master that he should go to Elisha, who would cure him of his Tzoraas. Since he would need to make it politically correct to go to the Jews for help, Naamon went to his boss, the King of Aram, and told him what the young girl had suggested he do to be cured of Tzoraas. The Malbim explains that the King of Aram felt that the reason Naamon got leprosy was because he had killed Achav, the King of the Ten Tribes, who was the father of the present King of the Ten Tribes. The King sent the King of the Ten Tribes a letter along with a very nice present asking that he cure Naamon. The King of the Ten Tribes realized that he did not have the ability to cure Naamon, and he instead thought that the King of Aram wanted to invent an excuse to start a war with him since there was no way he could fulfill his request. Since the King of the Ten Tribes was afraid that he would lose such a war, he went into a state of mourning. When Elisha, the Prophet, heard about this, Elisha suggested that Naamon come to him and that he would cure him and create a big sanctification of Hashem's name. Subsequently, Naamon and his entourage came to Elisha, and instead of allowing him in, Elisha sent word that he should wash seven times in the Jordan River and

Shemos

be cured of his Tzoraas. Naamon was incensed with the way he was treated, and even more so with the simple advice he was given, and started making light of Elisha's advice by saying that the waters of the rivers in his home country were even better than the Jordan River. However, Naamon's servants advised and convinced Naamon to follow Elisha's advice, and he was cured. Naamon was elated, and he came back to Elisha, acknowledging that Hashem was the only true G-d and that he would now only believe in Hashem. However, Naamon had one problem which he details in Sefer Melachim II (5:18) when he says, "For this thing may Hashem forgive your servant; when my master comes to Bais-Rimmon to prostrate himself there, and he leans on my hand, and I will prostrate myself in Bais-Rimmon; when I bow in Bais-Rimmon, may Hashem forgive your servant for this thing." That is, Naamon would be forced to bow before the idol as he supported the King when the King bowed down to the idol. Elisha tells Naamon in the next Posuk, "Go in peace," which implies that since Naaman was a non-Jew, he was not obligated to sanctify Hashem's name by allowing himself to be killed for not bowing down to an idol. The Ponim Yofos says that had the Midwives been of the opinion that they were non-Jews, they would not have been obligated to risk their lives in not listening to Pharaoh to commit an immoral act with him. Since they risked their lives by not listening to Pharaoh, Pharaoh knew that they considered themselves to have all the laws of Jews and would therefore not be considered as murderers for killing the Jewish fetuses.

Despite the fact that they would not be murderers for killing a fetus, the Midwives refused to obey Pharoah's command and risked their lives. The Zohar at the beginning of Parshas Shemos 3b says that there is a great punishment that comes about from one who kills a fetus. It says that it would be better if such a person who would do such a thing would not be created since this person drives away the Shechinah from the Bnei Yisroel. In the merit that the Jews did not do such a thing even when there was a decree that all baby boys would be thrown into the Red Sea, they merited to be redeemed from the exile in Egypt.

1) The Shemos Raba (1:16) is the source of the answer that the Akeidah and the Nitziv present to our question. It says that the Midwives realized Pharaoh would question their excuse that the Jewish women are skilled as Midwives since even Midwives need another midwife when they give birth. Rather what they told Pharaoh was that the Jewish people are compared to wild animals who do not need any help from anyone when they are giving birth. For example, the tribe of Yehuda is compared to a lion, the tribe of Dan to a snake, the tribe of Naphtali to a deer, the tribe of Yisochar to a donkey, the tribe of Yosef to a bull, and the tribe of Binyamin to a wolf. With regard to all the rest of the tribes, all the Bnei Yisroel are compared to a lioness in Sefer Yechezkel (19:2). The good Hashem did for the Midwives is that Pharaoh accepted their excuse and did not do any harm to them.

The Midrash Lekach Tov says that the Midwives told Pharaoh that the Jewish women were so righteous that they were not included in the curse of Chava in Beraishis (3:16) "To the woman (Chava) He (Hashem) said, 'I shall surely increase your sorrow and your pregnancy; in pain, you shall bear children.'" The Gemorah in Sotah 12b proves that righteous Jewish women like Yocheved were not subject to the pain of childbirth. As proof, the Gemorah presents Shemos (2:1-2), which say, "A man of the house of Levi (Amram) went and married a daughter of Levi

Shemos

(Yocheved). The woman conceived and bore a son (Moshe), and when she saw him that he was good, she hid him for three months." The Gemorah is of the opinion that the reason Yocheved was able to hide Moshe for three months is because she was already three months pregnant with Moshe before she remarried Amram. That being the case, analyzes the Gemorah, why does the Posuk, after she remarried, say "The woman conceived and bore a son," being that she conceived before she remarried. The Gemorah concludes that just like Yocheved had no pain when she conceived, she also had no pain when she gave birth. The Gemorah concludes that we may derive from here that righteous women of all generations were not affected by the curse of Chava to have pain during childbirth. Since the women did not have the pain of childbirth, the Midwives told Pharaoh, they were able to give birth on their own without the need of a midwife. Parenthetically we note that Rashi says that the reason Yocheved was able to hide Moshe for three months is that Moshe was born at the end of only six months of Yocheved's pregnancy with him. The Chizkuni points out that at first glance, this Rashi is at odds with the Gemorah we just mentioned that Yocheved was three months pregnant when she remarried Amram. The Chizkuni reconciles Rashi with the Gemorah by first saying that the Egyptians knew that a baby could be born after six months of pregnancy. Therefore, they started checking for babies six months after Amram and all the Bnei Yisroel decided to remarry despite Pharoah's decree to kill the Jewish baby boys. Moshe was born after six months of pregnancy, but because Yocheved was pregnant for three months before she remarried, she was able to hide Moshe for three months before the Egyptians started checking for babies. Therefore, Rashi is consistent with the Gemorah that Yocheved was pregnant for three months before remarrying Amram.

We can appreciate the miracle Hashem did for the Midwives by making Pharaoh accept their excuse and not do any harm to them by examining what happened with a different King. The Midrash in Eichah (1:31) tells us that when Vespasian besieged Yerushalayim, he assigned four generals to destroy the four parts of Yerushalayim, including the Beis Hamikdosh. The western side was given to a general named Pangar. It was decreed in heaven that the Western Wall of the Beis Hamikdosh, which was closest to the holy of holies, would never be destroyed, and, of course, it is with that decree that the Western Wall remains standing till today. The Zohar at the beginning of Parshas Shemos 5b says that Hashem's Shechinah never removed itself from the western wall of the Beis Hamikdosh, which explains why it could not be destroyed. This decree caused Pangar not to destroy the Western Wall, and he was summoned by Vespasian, who demanded an explanation. Pangar answered Vespasian that "he swore that the only reason he left the Western wall was to glorify Vespasian's reputation." He explained that had he destroyed the Western wall, later generations would have no idea how great and militarily fortified Yerushalayim was. They might think that it was only a little town. With the remaining Western Wall intact, everyone could see how impressive Vespasian's victory was. Vespasian told Pangar that he had defended himself well, but since he failed to follow Vespasian's order, he was to climb to the top of a tower and throw himself off. "If you survive," said Vespasian, "I will let you live, and if you die, then you deserved the death penalty." Pangar threw himself off the tower and was killed since Rabban Yochanon ben Zakai had cursed him. Rabban Yochanon ben Zakai knew that in his heart, the real reason Pangar left the Western wall intact was as a memorial to commemorate the utter defeat of the Bnei Yisroel. Otherwise, says the Matnos Kehunah, he would have survived. We see from this story that even

Shemos

with such a good excuse, Pangar still was harmed by Vespasian, and it was a complete miracle that Hashem caused Pharaoh not to harm the Midwives at all.

The Akeidah says that someone who fears Hashem is also very careful not to transgress the commands of a normal king. Presumably, this is psychologically due to the fact that someone who makes himself subservient to Hashem, the King of Kings, would likely also be subservient to a mortal King. Mishlay (24:21) says this explicitly, "My son, fear Hashem and the king." Similarly, we have in Koheles (8:2), "I counsel you to obey the king's command and that in the manner of an oath to Hashem." Perhaps even more explicit is an episode that we are told about in Shmuel I (16:1-2). The Pesukim say, "And Hashem said to Shmuel, 'Until when are you mourning for Shaul when I have rejected him from reigning over Yisroel? Fill your horn with oil, and come, I shall send you to Yishai, from Beis Lechem, for I have seen for Myself a king among his sons.' And Shmuel said, 'How shall I go? For, if Shaul hears, he will kill me.' And Hashem said, 'You shall take a heifer with you,' and you shall say, 'I have come to slaughter (a sacrifice) to Hashem.'" We see from these Pesukim that even though Hashem sent Shmuel on a mission, Shmuel still had to fear that if Shaul found out, Shaul would kill him. The Akeidah says that the Midwives also feared what would happen if Pharaoh found out that they were not killing the Jewish boys as he had commanded them. Therefore, the Midwives stopped working as Midwives and instead focused on ensuring that the newborns and their mothers remained healthy. In that way, Pharaoh's command would not be applicable to them, and they would not have to fear Pharaoh killing them for disobeying his command. Consequently, when Pharaoh later questioned the Midwives as to why they did not carry out his command, the Midwives answered that they had given up on the profession of being Midwives since the Jewish women had no need for Midwives. They also told Pharaoh that if a Jewish woman were to call them to act as Midwives, they would definitely fulfill Pharaoh's command and kill the Jewish boys. Since they did nothing to violate Pharaoh's commandment, Pharaoh did not harm them.

2) The Shemos Raba (1:16) also presents another answer to our question. Since the midwife Shifra was Yocheved, the good Hashem did for her is that she was rewarded with a son, Moshe. When Moshe was born, Shemos (2:2) says, וַתֵּרֶא אֹתוֹ כִּי טוֹב הוּא (She (Yocheved) saw him (Moshe) that he was good). Rashi, whose source is the Gemorah in Sotah 12a and the Shemos Raba (1:20), says the "good" that Yocheved saw was that the entire house was filled with light after Moshe was born. The Gemorah in Sotah 12a says that the way we know that "good" is light is from Beraishis (1:4), which says, "And Hashem saw the light that it was good." In addition, Moshe received the Torah for the Bnei Yisroel, and the Torah is called a "good teaching" as Mishlay (4:2) says, כִּי לֶקַח טוֹב נָתַתִּי לָכֶם תּוֹרָתִי אַל תַּעֲזֹבוּ (For I gave you good teaching; forsake not My Torah). The Shemos Raba is of the opinion that the second midwife, Puah, was Miriam and the good Hashem did for her is that Hashem rewarded her with a great-grandson Betzalel who made an Aron for the Torah, which we have just shown is called "good." The Chasam Sofer ponders why Yocheved was rewarded by having a son, Moshe, who received the Torah itself, while Miriam was only rewarded with a son who made an Aron and Mishkan to house the Torah. He answers that since Miriam was very young, as we have shown in the introduction, all she could do was ably assist her mother, Yocheved, in doing everything a midwife has to do. Therefore, her great-grandson assisted the Torah in having a

Shemos

proper place to be in. Since Yocheved did the work itself, she was rewarded with a son, Moshe, who received the Torah itself.

3) The Midrash Lekach Tov is the source of the answer presented by the Ponim Yofos. It says that Hashem did good for the Midwives in this world but that Hashem left over the principle of their reward for the world to come. The Ponim Yofos quotes the Mishna in Kidushin 39b, which, with the explanation of Rashi, says that whoever performs a Mitzvah is rewarded with good in this world, his life is lengthened, and he inherits the world to come. The Ponim Yofos explains that this concept is similar to what Pirkei Avos (5:22) says, that the students of Avrohom Aveinu enjoy the fruits of their good deeds in this world and inherit the world to come. Just like Avrohom helped guests who came to him, the Midwives helped all the children and did not worry about the King doing bad to them. Because of this, the Midwives merited to be students of Avrohom through their good deeds for all the women and children that they helped and were rewarded with enjoying the fruits of their good deeds in this world and inheriting the world to come.

4) Rashi and the Eben Ezra answer our question similarly. They connect our Posuk with the next Posuk after ours, which says, "Now it took place when the Midwives feared Hashem, that He made houses for them." They say that the good which Hashem did for the Midwives was that He made them houses. Rashi, based on the Gemorah in Sotah 11b, says that the houses were not physical houses but rather houses of Kohanim, Leviyim, and Kings. The Daas Zekanim and Ohr HaChaim are troubled by the fact that according to this answer, there is a break of a whole Posuk between the Torah telling us that Hashem did good for the Midwives and telling us what the good was and therefore, they do not accept this answer. The Mizrachi, Gur Aryeh, and Tzedah LeDerech explain that Rashi is not saying that the only good Hashem did is that he made houses for the Midwives. The Toldos Yitzchak says that the Posuk after ours is telling us that because the Midwives feared Hashem and did not implement Pharaoh's plan, Pharaoh made houses for the Egyptians between each of the Jewish houses so that the Egyptians could know when a baby boy was born in one of the Jewish houses. Rashi disagrees and says that "he made them houses" refers to Hashem and not to Pharaoh and that this was one of the 'good things" that Hashem did for the Midwives.

The Ohr HaChaim says that according to Rashi, we can be of the opinion that the good which Hashem did was making houses for the Midwives and not have any problem with the intervening phrases in our Posuk and the next Posuk. The Gemorah in Sotah 11b and the Shemos Raba (1:15) says that not only didn't the Midwives listen to Pharaoh and harm the Jewish boys, but rather they did everything they could to help them. For example, they would provide poor mothers with food and water so that they could revive themselves after giving birth and be able to nourish their new babies. The Ohr HaChaim says that when our Posuk says, "the people multiplied and became very strong," it is telling us that Hashem provided the Midwives with enough funds so that they could continue providing food and water to the many new mothers and children. The next Posuk says that in addition to providing enough money for the Midwives to help the greatly expanding population of mothers/children, Hashem also provided a reward that went directly to the Midwives, and this was the fact that Hashem made them houses. Because the Pesukim are listing two good things that

Shemos

Hashem did for the Midwives, there is no break between our Posuk, which says that Hashem did good, and the two good things which Hashem did for them.

5) The Daas Zekanim, Chizkuni, Alshich, and Shach answer our question similarly. They say that the end of our Posuk, which says "the people multiplied and became very strong," is the good that Hashem did for the Midwives. When the Midwives told Pharaoh that the Jewish women, similar to animals, did not need the Midwives in order to give birth, Pharaoh thought that they were lying and had just invented this excuse. However, when Pharaoh saw that the Bnei Yisroel had a very large number of children, Pharaoh knew that it was not physically possible for two Midwives to have assisted in all these births. Therefore, Pharaoh was forced to conclude that since there were only two Jewish Midwives, the Midwives were not lying and that the Jewish women could give birth without the need of a Midwife.

6) The Alshich, Bechor Shor, Chizkuni, Maharil Diskin, Rav Hirsch, and Rav Gifter, in his Sefer Pirkei Torah, answer our question similarly. They say that not only did the Midwives have to worry about Pharaoh, but they also had to worry about the Bnei Yisroel. If any baby was stillborn, the Bnei Yisroel would suspect that the Midwives followed Pharaoh's orders, and Chas VeShalom killed the child. Even if a baby was born with a broken hand, foot, or similar physical issue which made them weak, the Bnei Yisroel would suspect the Midwives tried to kill the Jewish baby but were only able to break some of the baby's bones or weaken the baby. The good that Hashem did for the Midwives is said at the end of our Posuk when it says that the baby's "became very strong." All the Jewish babies were born very strong and healthy so that no one could even suspect that the Midwives did anything to obey Pharaoh's orders. Rav Gifter points out that it can be no more rewarding than seeing the good come out of one's actions, as it did in this case where the Midwives saw that everyone was born strong in their merit despite the typical number of stillborn and not fully physically healthy children that the laws of nature should have yielded.

7) The Ohr HaChaim, Chasam Sofer, and Rav Sternbuch, in his Sefer Taam V'Daas, answer our question similarly. The Mishna says in Pirkei Avos (4:2) that the reward of doing a Mitzvah is that Hashem gives the person the opportunity to do another Mitzvah. The Rav Bartenura on this Mishna explains that Hashem helps and arranges that the opportunity to do another Mitzvah will occur so that Hashem can give the person a reward for doing two Mitzvos and not just one. They answer that since the Midwives did such a great Mitzvah by endangering their own lives, Hashem arranged many times that they would get a chance to do this Mitzvah and reap much reward for their actions. They explain that this is what our Posuk tells us when it says Hashem did good by causing the people to "multiply greatly." The Ohr HaChaim also says that when Moshe and Aharon merited to become the leaders of the Bnei Yisroel, they were leading the nation that Miriam and Yocheved created by not obeying Pharaoh's orders and therefore were leading a nation that actually belonged to them.

8) The Toldos Yitzchak also presents an answer to our question and writes that the good Hashem did for the Midwives is the next phrase in our Posuk, which says, "the people multiplied." With so many more births and opportunities for work as a midwife, the Midwives got much income from

Shemos

their job as Midwives. The Tzedah LeDerech amplifies this idea by translating the last phrase in our Posuk (וַיַּעַצְמוּ מְאֹד) as referring to the Midwives saying that they became very rich instead of the more typical translation that they (the Bnei Yisroel) were very strong. As proof of this translation, he presents Beraishis (26:16), which says, וַיֹּאמֶר אֲבִימֶלֶךְ אֶל יִצְחָק לֵךְ מֵעִמָּנוּ כִּי עָצַמְתָּ מִמֶּנּוּ מְאֹד. The Ramban on this Posuk says that Avimelech told Yitzchak that even though I am King, I do not have in my home as many possessions as you (Yitzchak) do. Therefore, we see that the word עָצַמְתָּ can mean more powerful in riches, which is what the Midwives became.

The Yismach Moshe says that the Hebrew word וַיַּעַצְמוּ is a multifaceted word, which means that it became astonishingly very big, and what became big depends on the context. For example, at the beginning of Parshas Shemos, when the Torah tells us that the Bnei Yisroel became astonishingly big in terms of population number, Shemos (1:7) says וַיַּעַצְמוּ בִּמְאֹד מְאֹד. In Bamidbar (22:6), when Balak sees that the Bnei Yisroel are astonishingly strong, the Torah describes this with כִּי עָצוּם הוּא מִמֶּנִּי. As the Tzedah LeDerech says when Avimelech saw that Yitzchak was astonishingly rich, Beraishis (26:16) says וַיֹּאמֶר אֲבִימֶלֶךְ אֶל יִצְחָק לֵךְ מֵעִמָּנוּ כִּי עָצַמְתָּ מִמֶּנּוּ מְאֹד. When the Prophet Yoel says that righteous people who follow Hashem's word are astonishingly rich in merits and good deeds, Yoel (2:11) describes it with כִּי עָצוּם עֹשֵׂה דְבָרוֹ. The Yismach Moshe also says that the last phrase of our Posuk (וַיַּעַצְמוּ מְאֹד) refers to the Midwives and not to the Bnei Yisroel. As proof, the Yismach Moshe notes the seemingly strange grammar in the Hebrew phrase וַיִּרֶב הָעָם וַיַּעַצְמוּ מְאֹד. The first phrase, וַיִּרֶב הָעָם, is written in the singular that "the nation multiplied." The second part of the phrase וַיַּעַצְמוּ מְאֹד is written in the plural, which according to this answer, would translate as "they became rich." If this phrase was referring to the people, it should have used the singular tense "it (the nation) became rich."

The Gemorah in Sotah 11b says that the Midwives not only didn't listen to Pharaoh, who told them to kill the Jewish baby boys, but they also provided them with food and water. Rashi, on this Gemorah, explains that the Midwives hid the Jewish boys in their own houses and raised them. It would be typical that the more children the Midwives did this for, the poorer they would be for paying for all this support. However, exactly the opposite happened, and Hashem caused the Midwives to become astonishingly rich. According to the Yismach Moshe, our Posuk would be saying that "Hashem did good things for the Midwives, the people multiplied and (the Midwives) became very rich." In addition, the Posuk after ours, which says that "He made houses for them," means that "He (Hashem by making them astonishingly rich) made (many physical) houses for them (to house all the children they were raising)."

9) The Abarbanel also ponders our question and is of the opinion that the Midwives were Egyptian women. Otherwise, how could Pharaoh trust Jewish Midwives to kill children of their own nation? The Kli Yakor also says that some are of the opinion that they were Egyptian women. Furthermore, the Malbim says that according to the simple way of learning, they were Egyptian women. We can also derive that they were Egyptian from the Yalkut Shimoni in Yehoshua 9, which says that there were righteous women converts to Judaism: Hagar, Osnas (Yosef's wife), Tziporah (Moshe's wife), Shifra, Puah, Pharoah's daughter (Basya), Rochov, Rus, and Yael, the wife of Chever (who killed Sisra). By saying that they converted, this Yalkut Shimoni also answers the obvious question of

Shemos

why, if they were Egyptian, would the Midwives risk their lives to save the Jewish boys. Of course, as the Mogen Avrohom in his commentary Zeis Raanan on the Yalkut Shimoni says, this answer argues with the Gemorah in Sotah 11b, which says that the Midwives were Jewish.

The Abarbanel says that the good Hashem did for the Egyptian Midwives was that they became very rich from all the money that the Jews gratefully gave them for saving their Jewish sons and ignoring Pharoah's orders. The Posuk after ours says, "Now it took place when the Midwives feared Hashem, that He made houses for them." They were so rich that they are described as having houses full of all good things from all the riches that they received.

10) The Malbim also ponders our question and says that Pharaoh did not believe the excuse of the Midwives; and, in fact, wanted to harm them for not obeying his order. Nonetheless, Hashem did good to the Midwives by preventing Pharaoh from doing any harm to the Midwives. He explains that when Pharaoh saw that "the people multiplied," he realized that his previous plan of having the two Midwives kill the Jewish boys was no longer practical since there were so many children born that even if the two Midwives obeyed him, they would not significantly reduce the number of Jewish baby boys. Therefore, he ignored the two Midwives.

11) The Oznayim LeTorah and Rav Moshe Feinstein, is his Sever Dorash Moshe, answer our question similarly. They say that there can be no greater happiness for the Midwives that risked their lives so that more children would be born to the Bnei Yisroel than seeing their actions amplified by many births and the "the people multiplied." By risking their lives, they showed that children being born to the Bnei Yisroel was more important than their own lives; therefore, seeing many more children being born was the ultimate happiness for them. Therefore the "good" that Hashem did for the Midwives is said in the next phrase that "the people multiplied."

Rav Moshe further amplifies this point by saying that it is typical that someone who has to take care of a person with a sickness which forces the caregiver to work extremely hard for the sick person will not be pained so much if the sick person is Niftar, as long as the caregiver had no role in causing the sick person's death. He says that this is true even if the sick person is someone who he loves very much, like, for example, his parent. As long as the person cannot find a reason to blame himself for causing the death, it is perfectly normal and understandable for the person to be at least somewhat relieved. One may have expected that the Midwives would have reacted similarly. That is, if a child would have been born stillborn through no fault of the Midwives, we may have expected the Midwives to be relieved that they did not have to disobey Pharaoh's orders for this child. However, these Midwives were on such a lofty level that they would have been very much pained even if they had nothing to do with the child being born stillborn since all they cared about was another child being born to the Bnei Yisroel. The Pirkei D'Rabi Eliezer (39) says that the Bnei Yisroel were one person short of the 600,000 people needed to be redeemed from Egypt. He says that Hashem joined with the count to give a count of exactly 600,000. Given how important having 600,000 people was in allowing the Bnei Yisroel to be redeemed from Egypt, it is possible that having a child born stillborn would bring much pain to the Midwives.

Shemos

12) The Noam Elimelech also ponders our question and says that the highest level of serving Hashem is with the highest level of love for and fear of Hashem. These levels are achieved by a completely righteous person. The way to serve Hashem with the highest level of love is to be only interested in having the praises of Hashem sung by as many people as possible. The Midwives were on this level, and the "good" that they were rewarded with was that "the nation multiplied" so that because of the Midwives' efforts, there could be more people who would sing the praises of Hashem, and they could achieve this high level of love of Hashem in the merit of the Midwives actions.

The Midwives also achieved the highest level of fear of Hashem. With this level, the righteous person is able to cause the flow of needed blessings to this world so that the entire generation can benefit from it. We have mentioned previously that the Posuk after ours says, "Now it took place when the Midwives feared Hashem, that He made houses for them." Rashi, based on the Gemorah in Sotah 11b, says that the houses were not physical houses but rather houses of Kohanim, Leviyim, and kings. From this Posuk, we see that the reward to the Midwives for fearing Hashem was houses of Kohanim, Leviyim, and Kings. Though I will follow a similar idea as what the Noam Elimelech says, due to my limited understanding of how he explains this, I will instead choose to follow a different view of this reward. Rav Moshe Feinstein, in his Sefer Dorash Moshe, points out that the Midwives had such a high degree of fear of Hashem that they saved many lives which they were not obligated to. For example, they could have kept themselves out of danger from Pharaoh in many cases by choosing not to go to a woman in labor as long as it wasn't obvious that they were doing so to avoid carrying out Pharaoh's command. Despite this, the Midwives made every effort to not only go every time but also to do everything they could to help the mother and children live by also providing water and food when they went. Since the Midwives feared Hashem and knowing that Hashem knew their true intentions, fear of Hashem outweighed any fear of Pharaoh, so they had no thoughts about avoiding Pharaoh's command. As a reward for this fear of Hashem, Hashem gave them houses of Kohanim, Leviyim, and Kings. Kohanim and Leviyim, as the servants of Hashem in the Beis Hamikdosh, where Hashem's Shechinah rested, had to always have a fear of Hashem so that their service to Hashem was done completely correctly. Otherwise, they risked death as Bamidbar (18:3) says, "They (the Leviyim) shall keep your charge and the charge of the Tent, and they shall not approach the holy vessels or the Mizbeach (altar) so that neither they nor you will die." It is not surprising that when the Bnei Yisroel came up to Yerushalayim, Devorim (14:23) says that the purpose was "so that you may learn to fear Hashem, your G-d, all the days." A King also has to have the utmost fear of Hashem so that he does not err as Koheles (10:5) says, "There is an evil that I saw under the sun, like an error that goes forth from before the ruler (king)." The Torah tells this explicitly to the King in Devorim (17:19) when it says, "And it (the Sefer Torah that he writes) shall be with him, and he shall read it all the days of his life, so that he may learn to fear Hashem, his G-d, to keep all the words of this Torah and these statutes, to perform them." It was the total fear of Hashem, which the Midwives had, that merited them having houses of Kohanim, Leviyim, and Kings. Therefore, the great love and fear of Hashem that the Midwives had was rewarded in these two ways.

Shemos

13) The Yismach Moshe also ponders our question. As an introduction to his answer, he references the Gemorah in Baba Basra 10a, which says that giving Tzedakah is a great Mitzvah since it brings the redemption closer. The Gemorah proves this from Sefer Yeshayahu (56:1), which says, "So says Hashem, 'Keep justice and practice Tzedakah, for My salvation is near to come and My Tzedakah to be revealed.'" The Maharsha explains that the Posuk is telling us that the act of giving Tzedakah will bring the final redemption, and at that time, Hashem's acts of Tzedakah to us will occur in a revealed fashion as opposed to now when they are hidden. The Ben Yehoyoda on this Gemorah quotes his son, who says that the reason the Posuk also mentions "keep justice" is because the only Tzedakah which brings the redemption is that money which was justly acquired by the giver of Tzedakah. Therefore, the Posuk is telling us that justly acquired Tzedakah will bring the redemption near to come.

The Yismach Moshe ponders the question of why giving Tzedakah is such a great Mitzvah that it brings the final redemption closer. To explain this, he quotes a famous Gemorah in Shabbos 31a. The Gemorah tells us about a case where a convert came to Shammai and asked Shammai to convert him with the stipulation that he would teach him the entire Torah while the convert stood on one foot. Hearing this proposition, Shammai drove the person away with a stick he had in his hand, which is used for measuring a building. The convert then went to Hillel with the same request. Hillel said to him, "that which is hateful to you, do not do to your fellow person." Hillel concluded that this principle encompasses the entire Torah, and all the rest of the Torah is an explanation and elaboration and told the convert after conversion to go and start learning the explanation and elaboration. Parenthetically, the Kli Yakor on Vayikra (19:18) explains that Hillel told the convert the entire phrase of that Posuk, which says, "you shall love your neighbor as yourself. I am Hashem." The Kli Yakor says that "you shall love your neighbor as yourself" or "that which is hateful to you, do not do to your fellow person" encompasses all the Mitzvos which govern the relationship between two people. The second part of the phrase, "I am Hashem," is the guiding principle that governs all the Mitzvos between a person and Hashem. Therefore, the entire phrase encompasses the guiding principle for all the Mitzvos. Also, parenthetically, the Maharsha explains Shammai's response of driving the person away with a stick which is used for measuring a building. The convert wanted one foundational principle that the entire Torah was based on. Shammai, by showing him the measuring stick, was alluding to the fact that the Torah is like a building that needs a large base and foundation to stand on. If one puts a building on just a single pedestal, it will topple over immediately.

The Yismach Moshe ponders why the convert made such a strange request. He quotes and extends an idea which the Beis Shmuel presents to understand this request. Each Neshama has to fulfill all 613 Mitzvos of the Torah. If the Neshama does not fulfill all the Mitzvos, it is placed into another body or bodies until it has fulfilled all 613 Mitzvos. This convert was noble and serious about converting such that he wanted to make sure that he would be able to fulfill all 613 Mitzvos and not need for his Neshama to come back in a different body. We find precedence of referring to one time as one foot in the Torah. After Bilam hit his donkey three times, the angel says to Bilam in Bamidbar (22:32) עַל מָה הִכִּיתָ אֶת אֲתֹנְךָ זֶה שָׁלוֹשׁ רְגָלִים which literally means "why did you hit your she-donkey three feet," but which really means "why did you hit your she-donkey three times." The

Shemos

Beis Shmuel says that when Shammai heard this request, he drove the person away because it would be impossible for the convert to do those Mitzvos which only Kohanim can do, and other Mitzvos like Yibum (marrying the wife of a brother who dies childless) which are only applicable if such a case presents itself.

However, Hillel figured out a way how that convert, and for that matter, anyone else can fulfill all 613 Mitzvos of the Torah. The Beis Shmuel says that we have a concept that if one totally binds one's Neshama completely with all fellow Bnei Yisroel, then for him, all the Bnei Yisroel become one and the same entity. Being the same entity, every Mitzvah that someone does becomes his since he has made all the Bnei Yisroel one entity or body. Being one entity, it is just different parts of the same body doing a Mitzvah. Making all the Bnei Yisroel one entity is what Hillel was referring to when he advised the convert, "that which is hateful to you, do not do to your fellow person." The only thing left to explain after the words of the Beis Shmuel, says the Yismach Moshe, is what Hillel meant when he said, "all the rest of the Torah is an explanation and elaboration, which the convert after conversion should go and start learning the explanation and elaboration."

The Yismach Moshe says that even after one has made all of the Bnei Yisroel one entity by treating them exactly as he would treat himself, one still obviously needs to fulfill every possible Mitzvah that one can. One can only use the principle of being one entity for Mitzvos, where one has no possibility of fulfilling them. Also, one does not get a reward for his friend doing a Mitzvah. It is just that the person loses the designation of not fulfilling a certain Mitzvah that he has no possibility of doing. In addition, since the person did completely fulfill every Mitzvah that he had the possibility of doing, it implies that had he had the possibility of doing the Mitzvah he has no possibility of doing, he would have certainly done that Mitzvah. Therefore, his friend doing the Mitzvah can affect him and be considered as not lacking in doing that Mitzvah.

The Gemorah in Avodah Zara 5a says that Moshiach will not come until all the Neshomos, which are in the place called "Guf," are used up. Rashi explains that there is a storage place called "Guf," and from the beginning of time, all the Neshomos that will ever be needed in the future were placed there to be put into bodies that will be born over time. Based on this Gemorah, the Arizal explains that the quicker each Neshama fulfills all 613 Mitzvos and therefore no longer needs to return to a body in this world, the quicker Moshiach will come.

Based on the above reasoning, the Yismach Moshe proves why giving Tzedakah is such a great Mitzvah that it brings the final redemption closer since it causes the Mitzvos that the person who receives Tzedakah to be considered as if the giver of the Tzedakah did them. We have mentioned previously that Rashi on the Gemorah in Sotah 11b says that the Midwives hid the Jewish boys in their own houses and raised them, along with providing food and water for them. This act of Tzedakah caused all the Mitzvos that the Jewish boys eventually did during their lifetimes to be considered as if the Midwives did them. Therefore, when our Posuk says that the good Hashem did for the Midwives was that the people multiplied. The many people caused the Midwives to become very rich in Mitzvos and good deeds.

Shemos

What Kind of Houses Were Made for the Midwives as a Reward for Fearing Hashem?

Shemos (1:21) וַיְהִי כִּי יָרְאוּ הַמְיַלְּדֹת אֶת הָאֱלֹקִים וַיַּעַשׂ לָהֶם בָּתִּים (א:כא) Now it took place when the midwives feared Hashem, that He made houses for them.

What kind of houses were made for the Midwives as a reward for fearing Hashem?

Introduction
The Nitziv points out that it is not clear from the Posuk who it was who made the houses. From the flow of the Pesukim, it could either had been Hashem or Pharaoh. If it was Hashem who made the houses, it would have been as a reward for the midwives' fear of Hashem. If it was Pharaoh who made the houses, it was in preparation of his next decree which is detailed in the Posuk after ours, which says, "And Pharaoh commanded all his people, saying, 'Every son who is born you shall cast into the Nile, and every daughter you shall allow to live.'"

Our Posuk says וַיַּעַשׂ לָהֶם בָּתִּים (He made for them (plural male) houses) and not, at first sight, the more grammatical וַיַּעַשׂ לָהֶן בָּתִּים (He made for them (Midwives--plural female) houses). The Chizkuni, Rabeinu Bechay, and Abarbanel say that this is not unique. For example, in Beraishis (31:9), Yaakov, when speaking to his wives Rochel and Leah, says וַיַּצֵּל אֱלֹקִים אֶת מִקְנֵה אֲבִיכֶם וַיִּתֶּן לִי (Therefore, Hashem separated your (plural male and not plural female) father's livestock and gave it to me). Similarly, in Shemos (2:17), when the shepherds come and drive away Yisro's daughters from the well, the Torah says וַיָּבֹאוּ הָרֹעִים וַיְגָרְשׁוּם וַיָּקָם מֹשֶׁה וַיּוֹשִׁעָן וַיַּשְׁקְ אֶת צֹאנָם (But the shepherds came and drove them (plural male and not plural female) away; so Moshe arose and rescued them and watered their flocks).

The Meam Loez says that 130 years after the Bnei Yisroel came down to Egypt (or 80 years before they were redeemed from Egypt), Pharaoh had a bad dream. In the dream, Pharaoh was sitting on his throne, and when he looked up, he saw an elderly person standing before him and holding a scale/balance similar to what merchants use. The elderly man took all the officers and all the important Egyptian people and put them on one side of the balance. On the second side of the balance, the elderly person put a sheep. Pharaoh was astounded to see in his dream that the scale was perfectly balanced. The dream bothered Pharaoh so much that before dawn, Pharaoh summoned his wise men to tell them his dream and to ask for an interpretation. Bilam, one of Pharaoh's advisors, told Pharaoh that the dream foretold bad times for Egypt and that a bad calamity was going to befall Egypt. Bilam explained that a child would be born to the Bnei Yisroel, who would destroy all of Egypt, kill all the Egyptians, redeem the Bnei Yisroel out of your hands, and lead them out of Egypt. To combat this threat, Bilam advised Pharaoh to preempt this all from happening by finding a way to murder all the babies when they are born, before they grow up and pose a threat.

Along with Bilam, Pharaoh also called Yisro and Iyov to ask their interpretation of his dream. Yisro told Pharaoh that if only Pharaoh listened to his advice, everything would be fine. Yisro told Pharaoh not to do anything bad to the Bnei Yisroel since Hashem chose them in the past from

Shemos

amongst all the other nations of the world. Historically any King who had started up even a little with the Bnei Yisroel has caused the revenge of Hashem against them. It is known that when their grandfather Avrohom came down to Egypt, Pharaoh sent officers to take Sorah to his palace since Avrohom said that Sorah was his sister so that they would not murder him to take Sorah. After taking Sorah, Pharaoh and all the people in his palace were smitten with a terrible sickness that affected their entire body from their toes to their heads. Not until Pharaoh returned Sorah to Avrohom was Pharaoh cured. Avimelech had a similar experience to Pharaoh. In Avimelech's case, he was smitten with a unique plague that closed all openings in his body and even in the bodies of his animals. In addition, that night, an angel holding a drawn sword in his hand came to Avimelech and threatened to kill Avimelech for taking Sorah. Avimelech was forced to appease Avrohom with many presents so that Avrohom would forgive him, and the plague against Avimelech would stop. Avimelech had a similar experience with Yitzchak, who he drove out of his land and was punished with his trees and wells all drying up. Avimelech, along with his chief of the army Pichol, was also forced to come to Yitzchak and appease him, so Yitzchak would daven for him. Similar experiences happened with Yaakov, who was saved from the hands of Lavan, Esav, and many Kings who banded together to try and murder Yaakov after Shimon and Levi destroyed the city of Shechem. Yisro told Pharaoh that the bottom line was that he didn't know of any case when someone started up with the Bnei Yisroel and won the battle. Yisro also mentioned the friendship that the previous Pharaoh had with Yosef, such that Pharaoh installed Yosef as viceroy over the entire land of Egypt, being that Yosef saved Egypt from disaster during the years of famine. Yisro also mentioned that it was by invitation of Pharaoh that Yaakov and his entire family were brought down to Egypt, at which time the famine stopped in Yaakov's merit. Therefore, Yisro told Pharaoh that before it was too late, he should allow the Bnei Yisroel to go back to Eretz Yisroel, the land of their forefathers. Pharaoh was so incensed with Yisro's advice that Yisro was forced to flee to Midyan.

Pharaoh next asked for Iyov's advice. According to one version, Iyov told Pharaoh that he had no advice since Pharaoh was the King of the land, and no one should tell Pharaoh what to do. Another version had it that Iyov advised Pharaoh not to kill the Bnei Yisroel but rather to take away all their possessions and force them to do hard labor.

Bilam then told Pharaoh that the Bnei Yisroel are not afraid of being harmed by Pharaoh since whichever way he would choose to harm them, he would not be successful. Bilam told Pharaoh that if he wanted to consume them with fire, their grandfather Avrohom had already been thrown into a fiery furnace by Nimrod and emerged unscathed three days later. If Pharaoh wanted to kill them by the sword, their forefather Yitzchak was saved at the Akeidah even when he had a sword right at his throat. If you want to break and kill them with hard work, their father Yaakov shepherded the sheep of Lavan for twenty years through the heat of the day and the cold of the night and being forced to grab a nap on the cold ground at night. Despite this ordeal, Yaakov was still strong enough to be victorious over all the Kings of Canaan who came to fight him after Shimon and Levi killed all the men of Shechem. Therefore, Bilam suggested to Pharaoh that he come up with a unique way to murder the Bnei Yisroel, which had not been attempted in the past. More concretely, Bilam suggested that Pharaoh attempt to murder the Bnei Yisroel's children by throwing them into the

Shemos

water since this is a method that had not been tried before. Presumably, though the Meam Loez does not mention it, Bilam also told Pharaoh that he saw that the Jewish child who would be born to save the Bnei Yisroel would be killed with water as Rashi on the Posuk after ours quotes from the Gemorah in Sotah 12b, the Shemos Raba (1:18) and the Midrash Tanchuma in Vayakhel (4). The water the Egyptian sorcerers saw that would later kill Moshe was the water from the well of Miriam, which Moshe hit instead of speaking to. Pharaoh accepted this advice and instituted the evil decree of murdering the children of the Bnei Yisroel with water by having them thrown into the Nile River.

1) The Gemorah in Sotah 11b and the Shemos Raba (1:17) present an answer to our question. They quote the opinions of Rav and Shmuel, one of whom said that the houses were houses of Kings and the other of whom said that the houses were houses of Kohanim and Leviyim. The Gemorah and Shemos Raba conclude that the opinion which says houses of Kings means to say houses of Kings in addition to houses of Kohanim and Leviyim. According to this explanation, "he" who made houses was Hashem. The Yepheh Toar explains that houses refer to a special family, like the family of Kohanim. In Tehillim (115:10), which we say as a part of a full Hallel, the Posuk says בֵּית אַהֲרֹן בִּטְחוּ בַה׳ (the house of Aharon trusts in Hashem). Similarly, in Tehillim (135:19-20), which we say in the Shabbos morning davening, we mention the "house of Aharon" and the "house of the Leviyim," referring to all descendants of Aharon's family and Levi's family. We also find a house referring to a special family in Sefer Shmuel I (25:28). In that Posuk, Avigayil says to Dovid שָׂא נָא לְפֶשַׁע אֲמָתֶךָ כִּי עָשֹׂה יַעֲשֶׂה ה׳ לַאדֹנִי בַּיִת נֶאֱמָן כִּי מִלְחֲמוֹת ה׳ אֲדֹנִי נִלְחָם וְרָעָה לֹא תִמָּצֵא בְךָ מִיָּמֶיךָ (Forgive now your handmaid's transgression, for Hashem shall make for my lord a trustworthy house, for my lord fights the wars of Hashem. And let no evil be found in you all your days). Rashi, on that Posuk, explains that the "trustworthy house" was the establishment of the family dynasty of Kings. This expression of בַּיִת נֶאֱמָן is also used when a new couple is married to wish them that they establish a special family amongst the Bnei Yisroel.

The Maharsha and the Rif (Rav Yoshiyahu Pinto) on the Ain Yaakov explain that the Gemorah had a previous difference of opinions between the same Rav and Shmuel about who the Midwives that Pharaoh ordered to murder the Jewish baby boys were. According to one opinion, they were Yocheved and her daughter Miriam. According to this opinion, the houses were houses of Kohanim, Leviyim, and Kings. The houses of Kohanim and Leviyim were obtained by Yocheved, who had two sons Aharon and Moshe, who headed the houses of Kohanim and Leviyim. The houses of Kings were obtained by Miriam. The Gemorah in Sotah 11b and the Shemos Raba (1:17) prove that Dovid HaMelech was a direct descendant of Miriam. There is a second opinion between Rav and Shmuel that the Midwives were Yocheved and her future daughter-in-law Elisheva, wife of Aharon HaKohen. This opinion is consistent with the opinion we have quoted previously that the houses were houses of Kohanim and Leviyim. The house of Kohanim was a gift to both Yocheved through her son Aharon and Elisheva through her husband, Aharon. The house of Leviyim was a gift to Yocheved through her son Moshe.

The commentators on the Shemos Raba point out that there is an additional opinion found in Shemos Raba (48:4) about which houses and to whom they were given as gifts. We also find this opinion in the Midrash Tanchuma on Vayakhel (4). According to this opinion, houses of Kohanim

Shemos

and Kings were given to Yocheved. The house of Kohanim was given to Yocheved through Aharon HaKohen, and the house of Kings was given to Yocheved through Moshe, who was King over the Bnei Yisroel as it says in Devorim (33:4-5), "The Torah that Moshe commanded us is a legacy for the congregation of Yaakov. And He (Moshe) was King in Yeshurun, whenever the sum total of the people were gathered, and the tribes of Yisroel were together." According to this opinion, Miriam also got the house of Kings as Dovid HaMelech was her descendant. The Rashash explains that the reason this opinion does not want to say that the house of Leviyim descended from Moshe was that, unlike Aharon, Moshe was not the first of the tribe of Levi. The reason that the Gemorah in Sotah and the Shemos Raba say that the house of Leviyim descended from Moshe and not the house of Kings is that Moshe's children and descendants were not Kings, and therefore, it is difficult to give Moshe's family the label "house of Kings." Parenthetically the Rif on the Ain Yaakov says that the reason our Posuk says וַיַּעַשׂ לָהֶם בָּתִּים (He made for them (plural male) houses) and not the, at first sight, the more grammatical וַיַּעַשׂ לָהֶן בָּתִּים (He made for them (plural female) houses) is because the houses went to male descendants of the Midwives.

The Nefesh Yishai, as quoted by the Beshem Omro, ponders the question of how these gifts could have been inherited down to all future generations when the reward for doing a Mitzvah is a reward for the person themselves. He says that there is an exception to this rule, and the exception is anyone who does a Mitzvah while risking their life for doing the Mitzvah. An example of this is Pinchos, who risked his life to kill Zimri, the prince of the tribe of Shimon. Pinchos was rewarded that all his future descendants should be Kohanim. In a similar way, the Midwives risked their lives by ignoring the order of Pharaoh and therefore got a reward for all future generations.

The Ohr HaChaim says that the reward to the Midwives was measure for measure consistent with their actions. The Midwives risked their lives to save countless Jewish lives, and because of this, Moshe, Aharon, and Miriam merited to be the leaders of the Bnei Yisroel. In other words, he says that when Moshe, Aharon, and Miriam merited to become the leaders of the Bnei Yisroel, they were leading the nation that Miriam and Yocheved created by not obeying Pharaoh's orders and therefore were leading a nation which actually belonged to them. The Ralbag says that the biggest quality of a leader is how much the leader cares and does for the people that he leads. Since the Midwives risked their lives to care for the women and children, measure for measure, they were rewarded with having leaders since leaders most emulate these qualities of caring.

The Kli Yakor and Eyun Yaakov present another reason why the reward to the Midwives was measure for measure consistent with their actions. The Gemorah in Sotah 11b says that the Midwives not only didn't listen to Pharaoh, who told them to kill the Jewish baby boys, but they also provided them with food and water. Rashi, on this Gemorah, explains that the Midwives hid the Jewish boys in their own houses and raised them. As a reward for this, the Midwives were given houses of Kohanim and Leviyim. All the Bnei Yisroel have a Mitzvah to take off percentages of their crops and bring these foods to the Kohanim and Leviyim, measure for measure to the food that the Midwives provided the Bnei Yisroel. Though the Kli Yakor and Eyun Yaakov don't mention this, presumably, the same applies to the house of Kings that the Midwives were rewarded with. Especially in those days, the typical gifts one would send a King were (exotic) food items. For

Shemos

example, in Beraishis (43:11), Yaakov tells his children to go to the viceroy of Egypt and "take down to the man as a gift, a little balm, and a little honey, wax and lotus, pistachios and almonds." We note that the Ben Yehoyoda on the Gemorah in Sotah 11b ponders the question of why it was necessary to provide water when anyone could help themselves to water from the Nile River. He answers that it wasn't plain water that the Midwives provided but rather water in which a special herb or medicine which was beneficial to someone who had just given birth was cooked.

The Ben Yehoyoda on the Gemorah in Sotah 11b also presents a reason why the reward to the Midwives was measure for measure consistent with their actions. The Midwives risked their lives to save the Jewish baby boys. As a reward for this, they were given the house of Kohanim, Leviyim, and Kings, which are positions that are only applicable to boys. We can use an observation that the Alshich makes to reinforce what the Ben Yehoyoda says. He says that at first glance, our Posuk is grammatically incorrect when it says וַיַּעַשׂ לָהֶם בָּתִּים (and He (Hashem) made for them (plural males) houses). Since we are speaking about the Midwives, our Posuk should have said, "and He (Hashem) made for them (plural females) houses." He explains that since the houses of Kohanim, Leviyim, and Kings are positions only applicable to males, our Posuk is really saying, "And He (Hashem) made family positions for them (the male descendants of the Midwives) houses."

The Chofetz Chaim, in his Sefer Dovor BeIto (Chap. 19), presents another reason why the reward to the Midwives was measure for measure consistent with their actions. He says that since the midwives risked their lives to allow the children to live in addition to providing food and water for those who needed it, they were rewarded with houses that did the same thing. For example, Moshe and Aharon (the houses of Kohanim and Leviyim) saved the lives of the Bnei Yisroel. When the Bnei Yisroel sinned by making the Golden Calf as is described in Tehillim (106:20-23), Posuk (106:23) says, "He (Hashem) intended to destroy them and would have were it not that Moshe, His chosen one, stood before Him in the breach to return His wrath from destroying." Similarly, Aharon also saved the lives of the Bnei Yisroel as it says in Bamidbar (17:12-13) "Aharon took it (Ketores (incense)), just as Moshe had said, and he ran into the midst of the assembly, and behold, the plague had begun among the people. He placed the incense on it and atoned for the people. He stood between the dead and the living, and the plague ceased." Not only did Moshe and Aharon saved the lives of the Bnei Yisroel, but in addition, Moshe also provided food, the Mon, for the Bnei Yisroel to eat for the forty years that they were in the desert. Not to mention, our spiritual lives are dependent on studying the Torah, which Moshe received from Hashem to give to the Bnei Yisroel. We have already mentioned that the Gemorah in Sotah 11b and the Shemos Raba (1:17) prove that Dovid HaMelech was a direct descendant of Miriam. Dovid HaMelech's descendant, Moshiach, whose coming is the hope that our lives are dependent on, was a measure for measure reward for the lives of the Bnei Yisroel, which Miriam saved. Though the Chofetz Chaim does not say this, it would also seem that the resurrection of the dead, which occurs during the period of the coming of Moshiach, would be the measure for measure reward for Miriam saving the lives of the Bnei Yisroel. It also stands to reason that the great merit of providing water for all the Bnei Yisroel during the forty years that they were in the desert was a measure for measure reward to Miriam for providing water as a Midwife to the new mothers.

Shemos

Rav Moshe Feinstein, in his Sefer Dorash Moshe, also presents another reason why the reward to the Midwives was measure for measure consistent with their actions. He points out that the Midwives had such a high degree of fear of Hashem that they saved many lives which they were not obligated to. For example, they could have kept themselves out of danger from Pharaoh in many cases by choosing not to go to a woman in labor as long as it wasn't obvious that they were doing so to avoid carrying out Pharaoh's command. Despite this, the Midwives made every effort to not only go every time but also to do everything they could to help the mother and children live by also providing water and food when they went. Since the Midwives feared Hashem and knowing that Hashem knew their true intentions, fear of Hashem outweighed any fear of Pharaoh, so they had no thoughts about avoiding Pharaoh's command. As a reward for this fear of Hashem, Hashem gave them houses of Kohanim, Leviyim, and Kings. Kohanim and Leviyim, as the servants of Hashem in the Beis Hamikdosh, where Hashem's Shechinah rested, had to always have a fear of Hashem so that their service to Hashem was done completely correctly. Otherwise, they risked death as Bamidbar (18:3) says, "They (the Leviyim) shall keep your charge and the charge of the Tent, and they shall not approach the holy vessels or the Mizbeach so that neither they nor you will die." It is not surprising that when all the Bnei Yisroel came up to Yerushalayim three times a year, Devorim (14:23) says that the purpose was "so that you may learn to fear Hashem, your G-d, all the days." A King also has to have the utmost fear of Hashem so that he does not err as Koheles (10:5) says, "There is an evil that I saw under the sun, like an error that goes forth from before the ruler (King)." The Torah tells this explicitly to the King in Devorim (17:19) when it says, "And it (the Sefer Torah that he writes) shall be with him, and he shall read it all the days of his life, so that he may learn to fear Hashem, his G-d, to keep all the words of this Torah and these statutes, to perform them." It was the total fear of Hashem, which the Midwives had, that merited them having houses of Kohanim, Leviyim, and Kings. Therefore, the great love and fear of Hashem that the Midwives had was rewarded in these two ways.

Rav Sternbuch, in his Sefer Taam V'Daas, also presents a reason which he heard from Rav Yosef Soloveitchik from Yerushalayim, as to why the reward to the Midwives was measure for measure consistent with their actions. Rav Soloveitchik points out that since being born a Jew is dependent on whether one's mother is Jewish, even if Pharaoh had, Chas VeShalom, succeeded in killing all the Jewish baby boys, the Jewish nation would continue through the Jewish mothers. However, both being a Kohen or a Levi are dependent on one's father being a Kohen or Levi, and had Pharaoh, Chas VeShalom, succeeded, there would not be any Kohanim or Leviyim. Measure for measure for the Midwives thwarting Pharaoh's plan to kill the Jewish baby boys, the Midwives were rewarded with houses of Kohanim and Leviyim, which depended on having Jewish boys.

2) The Midrash HaGodol also presents an answer to our question and says that Pharaoh sent his emissaries to murder the Midwives for disobeying his orders. "He made houses for them" refers to Hashem protecting the Midwives from being found by Pharaoh's police, by Hashem covering the Midwives up from the police's view. Like a house providing protection from the elements, these "houses" provided protection from being seen by the Egyptian police.

Shemos

3) Rabeinu Bechay, the Toldos Yitzchak, the Tur, and the Tzedah LeDerech answer our question similarly. They say that it was Pharaoh who made the houses described in our Posuk. Since Pharaoh failed to get the Midwives to murder the Jewish boys, Pharaoh still wanted to make sure that all the Jewish baby boys were found, and therefore, he built houses between every Jewish house and settled Egyptian people in those houses so that the Bnei Yisroel could not hide their Jewish sons from being heard by the Egyptians.

This answer provides a good answer for a question my then ten-year-old daughter, Leah Menucha, asked me one Pesach at the Seder. We mention in the Hagadah the Posuk in Shemos (12:27) which says וַאֲמַרְתֶּם זֶבַח פֶּסַח הוּא לַה' אֲשֶׁר פָּסַח עַל בָּתֵּי בְנֵי יִשְׂרָאֵל בְּמִצְרַיִם בְּנָגְפּוֹ אֶת מִצְרַיִם וְאֶת בָּתֵּינוּ הִצִּיל וַיִּקֹּד הָעָם וַיִּשְׁתַּחֲווּ (you shall say, It is a Pesach sacrifice to Hashem, for He passed over the houses of the Bnei Yisroel in Egypt when He smote the Egyptians, and He saved our houses. And the people kneeled and prostrated themselves)." This Posuk implies that there was typically a house of Bnei Yisroel between two Egyptian houses, which is why Hashem had to skip over the houses of the Bnei Yisroel. In Shemos (9:26), the Torah says, "Only in the land of Goshen, where the Bnei Yisroel were, there was no hail." Or similarly in Shemos (8:18), "And I will separate on that day the land of Goshen, upon which My people stand, that there will be no mixture of noxious creatures there, in order that you know that I am Hashem in the midst of the earth." These Pesukim, at first glance, seem to say that Goshen was inhabited, at least primarily, by the Bnei Yisroel. Moreover, the Pirkei D'Rabi Eliezer (26) says that when Pharaoh kidnapped Sorah with the intention of marrying her, at the time, she and Avrohom came down to Egypt towards the beginning of Parshas Lech Lecha, as an incentive for marrying him, Pharaoh gave Sorah the land of Goshen. When Pharaoh found out that Sorah was married to Avrohom, the Pirkei D'Rabi Eliezer says that Pharaoh nonetheless said that she could keep the land of Goshen. Therefore, when Yaakov and his family came to Egypt, they were living on the land that Pharaoh had already previously given them. For this reason, says the Oznayim LeTorah, the Egyptians could have no complaints when Yosef gave this land to Yaakov and his family, Sorah's descendants. From the Pirkei D'Rabi Eliezer, it also sounds like only the Bnei Yisroel lived in Goshen. In fact, Rav Yaakov Kaminetsky, at the beginning of Parshas Vayechi, explicitly says that Yosef emptied the land of Goshen of all Egyptians so that the Bnei Yisroel could live in Goshen without any Egyptian influences. "That being the case," asked my daughter, "how were there Egyptian houses between Jewish houses as the Posuk we say in the Hagadah seems to tell us?" With this answer, we can say that from the time that the Bnei Yisroel came down to Egypt until this point in time, there were only Jewish houses in Goshen. Only now was an Egyptian house intentionally built between each Jewish house. All these Egyptian houses and neighbors make it easy to understand Shemos (3:22) speaking of when the Bnei Yisroel were leaving Egypt which says, "Each woman shall borrow from her neighbor and from the dweller in her house silver and gold objects and garments, and you shall put them on your sons and on your daughters, and you shall empty out Egypt." It would seem to me that these Egyptians who had lived for eighty years with the Bnei Yisroel since Moshe's birth and had firsthand witnessed Hashem saving them because of the Bnei Yisroel, likely made up the bulk of the Erev Rav that accompanied the Bnei Yisroel out of Egypt.

Shemos

All that is now left to understand, given that at the time of the ten plagues many Egyptians also lived in Goshen, is Shemos (9:26), which says, "Only in the land of Goshen, where the Bnei Yisroel were, there was no hail." Or similarly in Shemos (8:18), "And I will separate on that day the land of Goshen, upon which My people stand, that there will be no mixture of noxious creatures there, in order that you know that I am Hashem in the midst of the earth." Rav Schwab, in his Sefer Mayan Beis HaShoaivah, explains that indeed in those plagues, the Egyptians who also inhabited the land of Goshen were not affected by the plague in the merit of the Bnei Yisroel who lived in Goshen. Shemos (10:25) says, "But Moshe said, "You too shall give sacrifices and burnt offerings into our hands, and we will make them for Hashem our G-d." The Bnei Yisroel got these animals from the Egyptians who lived in Goshen and whose animals were spared because of the Bnei Yisroel living in Goshen. The animals of the rest of the Egyptians were destroyed during the ten plagues.

We have mentioned that Shemos (12:27) says, וַאֲמַרְתֶּם זֶבַח פֶּסַח הוּא לַה' אֲשֶׁר פָּסַח עַל בָּתֵּי בְנֵי יִשְׂרָאֵל בְּמִצְרַיִם בְּנָגְפּוֹ אֶת מִצְרַיִם וְאֶת בָּתֵּינוּ הִצִּיל וַיִּקֹּד הָעָם וַיִּשְׁתַּחֲווּ (you shall say, It is a Pesach sacrifice to Hashem, for He passed over the houses of the Bnei Yisroel in Egypt when He smote the Egyptians, and He saved our houses. And the people kneeled and prostrated themselves)." The Plotsker, in his Hagadah Birchas HaShir, ponders that the phrase וְאֶת בָּתֵּינוּ הִצִּיל (and He saved our houses) is ostensibly unnecessary since if Hashem passed over the houses of the Bnei Yisroel, it implies that the Bnei Yisroel's houses were saved. The Shemos Raba (18:2) says that those Egyptians who were afraid that Moshe's prophesy of the killing of the firstborn would take place brought their firstborn to stay in the house of a Jew and forced the Jews to let the firstborn stay. Given that the Bnei Yisroel had next-door Egyptian neighbors, as we have just seen, it was likely a very common occurrence that there was an Egyptian in most houses of the Bnei Yisroel. The phrase וְאֶת בָּתֵּינוּ הִצִּיל (and He saved our houses) is telling us that not only did Hashem jump over to smite the houses of the Egyptians but even in the houses of the Bnei Yisroel Hashem killed the Egyptian firstborns and saved us in our houses. Shemos (12:13) says, "And the blood will be for you for a sign upon the houses where you will be, and I will see the blood and skip over you, and there will be no plague to destroy you when I smite the people of the land of Egypt." The Mechilta on this Posuk says that because of doing the Mitzvah of putting the blood of the Korban Pesach on the lintel and doorposts, Hashem will kill the Egyptians inside the Bnei Yisroel's houses and skip over the Jews in the house. It says that obviously, Hashem did not need a sign to know which house was Egyptian and which house was Jewish. In summation, there was a double "Passover," one to skip the house of the Bnei Yisroel when the Egyptian firstborns were smitten and a second inside the houses of the Bnei Yisroel to skip over the Jews and only smite the Egyptian firstborns.

4) The Akeidah, Chizkuni, Abarbanel, and the Tur answer our question similarly. They say that Pharaoh ordered that the Midwives be forced to remain in a designated house and not allowed to go out so that the new mothers would be brought to these houses to give birth. The Abarbanel and Malbim explain that Pharaoh also stationed Egyptian officials in or outside these houses so that they would see, record, and follow home any women who came to consult with the Midwives before they gave birth or sent someone to tell the Midwives that they were giving birth. In addition, the Egyptian guards would know about the birth of the Jewish baby boys when/if the mother was

Shemos

brought to one of these houses. In that way, says the Malbim, the Egyptians would know every time the Midwives were contacted.

5) The Rashbam, Rabeinu Bechay, and Tur answer our question similarly. They say that not only did Pharaoh force the Midwives to use known and designated houses, but that Pharaoh also ordered them to never leave these houses so that they were under what we would term "house arrest." If any Jewish woman wanted to use their services as Midwives, they would have to come to this house of the Midwives.

6) The Bechor Shor and especially the commentator on it presents an answer to our question. He says that "He made houses for them" means that Hashem made these houses and that the term "houses" included the reward of having children. The commentator explains that typically women who do not have their own children, which lead to their own responsibilities in their own homes, become Midwives to help other women. The commentator says that as a reward for their actions, Hashem caused the Midwives to have children of their own. Assuming that the Midwives were Yocheved and Miriam, this explanation is not clear to me. Miriam's brother Aharon was born three years after Miriam and three years before Moshe. Even if Miriam was already old enough to help Yocheved and did not need to keep Yocheved busy with raising her, having Aharon at home did not seemingly put Yocheved into the class of people of women who did not have their own children. Since Yocheved had children before and after this episode, it is also not clear to me what the Bechor Shor means when he says the Midwives' reward was to have children. It is possible that the Bechor Shor is of the same opinion as the Abarbanel that Yocheved and Miriam were the leaders of the Midwives but that there were many more Midwives that they employed. Otherwise, says the Abarbanel, it is difficult to fathom how such a large nation as the Bnei Yisroel would only have two Midwives to service the entire population. It could be that this reward of children went to these many Midwives, who ostensibly originally took this job since they did not have children of their own.

7) The Abarbanel, Tur, and Rav Schwab, in his Sefer Mayan Beis HaShoaivah, answer our question similarly. They say that the phrase "He made houses for them" refers to Hashem making houses for the Bnei Yisroel. These houses were not necessarily physical houses but rather families. We see that the establishment of a family is called a house in Sefer Shmuel I (25:28), which we have reference previously and also in Sefer Shmuel II (7:11) when Hashem promises Dovid that "Hashem will make for you a house." The baby boys that were saved grew up and became leaders of the nation, and formed prominent families. The Tur points out that since the people of these families owed their lives to the Midwives, people also termed them the children of the Midwives.

8) The Mayanah Shel Torah quotes the Degel Machaneh Ephraim, who presents an answer to our question. He says that the Midwives became known as the "center of excellence" from whom to learn what true fear of Hashem means. "He made houses for them" means that Hashem caused that the Bnei Yisroel should hear about the Midwives and that these acts would inspire others to develop the character of fearing Hashem.

Shemos

9) The Maharil Diskin also ponders our question and writes that the houses Pharaoh made were houses all around the house of the Midwives. He explains that Pharaoh stationed his guards in these houses so that they could always know and follow the Midwives whenever they left their houses to see if they were going to help a woman giving birth. Pharaoh only stopped this practice when he extended the decree to throw baby boys into the Nile River to include both Egyptian and Jewish babies. This occurred right before Moshe was born and explains why the guards, if they lived around Yocheved's house, would not have heard about the fact that Moshe was born and have forced him to be immediately thrown into the Nile River.

10) The Ksav VeHakabola also presents an answer to our question. He says that despite the fact the Midwives did not follow Pharaoh's edict, Hashem put into Pharaoh's heart to do good for the Midwives and their households (houses). He says that when our Posuk says, "He made houses for them," it means that Pharaoh, because of Hashem's manipulating Pharaoh's heart, made their families important and distinguished by freeing them from taxes and from working as slaves. The Midrash Tanchuma on Vaera (6) says that the tribe of Levi was exempt from the very hard work in Egypt. Assuming that the Midwives were Yocheved and Miriam from the tribe of Levi, the family of the Midwives was freed from any labor at all, not just hard labor, in addition to any taxes. He says the reason our Posuk says וַיַּעַשׂ לָהֶם בָּתִּים (He made for them (plural male) houses) and not the at first sight more grammatical וַיַּעַשׂ לָהֶן בָּתִּים (He made for them (plural female) houses) is because the distinction of being free from taxes and work was something given to the male heads of their families.

11) The Yismach Moshe also ponders our question. Rashi, on the Gemorah in Sotah 11b, says that the Midwives hid many of the new baby boys in their own houses and raised them. When our Posuk says, "He made houses for them," it means that "He (Hashem) made (many physical) houses for them (to house all the children they were raising), by providing them with the financial wherewithal to be able to build all these houses."

Why Doesn't the Torah Tell Us the Names of Moshe's Parents Initially?

Shemos (2:1) וַיֵּלֶךְ אִישׁ מִבֵּית לֵוִי וַיִּקַּח אֶת בַּת לֵוִי (ב:א) A man of the house of Levi went and married a daughter of Levi.

Why didn't the Torah tell us the names of Moshe's parents?

Introduction
In Shemos (6:20), the Torah does say explicitly who Moshe's parents were when the Torah says, "Amram took Yocheved, his aunt, as his wife, and she bore him Aharon and Moshe, and the years of Amram's life were one hundred thirty-seven years."

The Maskil LeDovid says that it is typically embarrassing not to explicitly mention the names of people. In Bamidbar (13:30), after the spies delivered their denigrating report about Eretz Yisroel, the Torah says, "Calev silenced the people to hear about Moshe, and he said, 'We can surely go up

Shemos

and take possession of it (Eretz Yisroel), for we can indeed overcome it.'" The Gemorah in Sotah 35a tells us how Calev silenced the people. He noticed that when Yehoshua began to speak against the report that the ten spies brought, the people silenced Yehoshua. In fact, the Gemorah tells us that the people said, "let's not let this person with the cut off head speak to us." Rashi on the Gemorah explains that they were referring to the fact that Yehoshua did not have any sons to inherit his portion in Eretz Yisroel. The Maharsha ponders the fact that if we take the information that Yehoshua was Niftar at age 110 after spending 28 years in Eretz Yisroel, coupled with the fact that he spent 40 years in the desert, it means that he was only 42 years old at that time. That being the case, it would seem that Yehoshua had plenty of time to have sons and even grandsons by the time he was Niftar, to be able to inherit him.

The Eyun Yaakov presents an explanation which answers the Maharsha's question by adding in the explanation of the Aruch. The Aruch says that they were referring to the Yud, which Moshe added on to change Yehoshua's name from Hoshea to Yehoshua as Bamidbar (13:16) tells us, "and Moshe called Hoshea the son of Nun, Yehoshua." Beraishis (17:15) says, וַיֹּאמֶר אֱלֹקִים אֶל אַבְרָהָם שָׂרַי אִשְׁתְּךָ לֹא תִקְרָא אֶת שְׁמָהּ שָׂרָי כִּי שָׂרָה שְׁמָהּ (And Hashem said to Avraham, your wife Sarai-you shall not call her name Sarai, for Sarah is her name). Using the Hebrew spelling, Hashem removed the Yud from her name and replaced it with a Heh. Beraishis (17:5) says, וְלֹא יִקָּרֵא עוֹד אֶת שִׁמְךָ אַבְרָם וְהָיָה שִׁמְךָ אַבְרָהָם כִּי אַב הֲמוֹן גּוֹיִם נְתַתִּיךָ (And your name shall no longer be called Avram, but your name shall be Avraham, for I have made you the father of a multitude of nations). Using the Hebrew spelling, Hashem also added a Heh to Avrohom's name. The Yerushalmi in Sanhedrin (2:6) says that since the Gematria of Yud is ten and the Gematria of Heh is five, Hashem took the Yud from Sarah's name and split it into two Heh's, one Heh was put in Sarah's name and one Heh in Avrohom's name. The Yud came to Hashem and expressed its sorrow that it had been taken out of the name of our righteous Matriarch Sorah. Hashem consoled the Yud by telling it that previously, it was the last letter in the female name Sarai; in the future, it will be added as the first letter in a name of a man when Hoshea's name was changed from Hoshea to Yehoshua. The Eyun Yaakov explains that since the source of Yehoshua's letter Yud was from a female, Sarah, Yehoshua was not able to have any male children. This answers the Maharsha's question of how the people knew that Yehoshua would never have any boys even though he was only 42 years old at the time.

In Divrei HaYomim I (7:26-27), when discussing the lineage of Yehoshua, the Posuk says, "Ladan his son, Ammihud his son, Elishama his son. Nun his son, Yehoshua his son." Since the Posuk does not say who Yehoshua's son was, the Gemorah in Eruvin 63a derives that Yehoshua had no sons. There are several reasons given why it was ordained that Yehoshua should not have any sons. The Gemorah in Eruvin 63a says that anyone who Paskins a Halacha in front of his Rebbe goes to the grave without a child. As proof, the Gemorah presents the episode in Bamidbar (11:27-28), which say, "The lad ran and told Moshe, saying, 'Eldad and Medad are prophesying in the camp!' Yehoshua the son of Nun, Moshe's servant from his youth, answered and said, 'Moshe, my master, imprison them!'" We note that Rashi, on this Posuk, quotes one of the views of the Gemorah in Sanhedrin 17a that Eldad and Medad were prophesizing that Moshe will be Niftar and Yehoshua will lead the Bnei Yisroel into Eretz Yisroel. Though this prophecy was prophesizing good news for Yehoshua that he would be the next leader of the Bnei Yisroel, Yehoshua stood up for Moshe's

61

Shemos

honor and paskined that Moshe should imprison them. Though Yehoshua acted very nobly, paskining in front of his Rebbe caused Yehoshua to be punished with not having any sons.

The Gemorah in Eruvin 63b presents another reason why Yehoshua was punished with not having any sons. For the first 14 years (seven years spent conquering and seven spent dividing the land) that the Bnei Yisroel were in Eretz Yisroel, Rashi in Zevachim 112b says that they set up the Mishkan in a place called Gilgal, which was near Yericho. We can see this from Sefer Yehoshua (5:10), which says, "And the Bnei Yisroel encamped in Gilgal, and they made the Korban Pesach on the fourteenth day of the month at evening in the plains of Yericho. The Pesukim soon afterward in Sefer Yehoshua (5:13-14) say, "And it was when Yehoshua was in Yericho, that he lifted up his eyes and saw, and, behold, a man was standing opposite him with his sword drawn in his hand; and Yehoshua went to him, and said to him, Are you for us, or for our adversaries? And he said, No, but I am the captain of the host of Hashem; I have now come. And Yehoshua fell on his face to the earth and prostrated himself, and said to him, what does my lord say to his servant?" The Gemorah in Eruvin 63b explains what is meant in these Pesukim. The Gemorah says that the angel told Yehoshua that he had neglected to bring the daily afternoon sacrifice and that now that it is dark (wars in those days were only fought during the day), he had also neglected the study of Torah. Yehoshua asked the angel to clarify which sin caused the angel to come. The angel said, "I have now come," which meant that the angel came for the sin happening at that point during the night, which was the sin of not studying Torah. The Gemorah derives from Sefer Yehoshua (8:13) that Yehoshua corrected this mistake by delving into the depths of Torah at night. Both Rashi and Tosfos point out that the Posuk from which the Gemorah derives that Yehoshua spent all night delving into the depths of Torah occurred in a subsequent battle in a city called Ai. The Gemorah's point, though, is that at a later time, Yehoshua corrected the sin of not studying Torah during the night when in battle. The Gemorah proves tangentially what Yehoshua's sin was that caused him to not have any sons. When the Bnei Yisroel went to besiege Yericho, we can derive that the holy Aron was taken into battle as Sefer Yehoshua (6:4) says, "And seven Kohanim shall bear seven trumpets of rams' horns before the holy Aron, and on the seventh day you shall encircle the city seven times, and the Kohanim shall blow with the trumpets." When the angel came and told Yehoshua about the sin of not learning Torah that night, it can be implied that they instead were besieging Yericho at night. Therefore, they did not return the holy Aron to the Mishkan in Gilgal. The Gemorah says that we have an oral tradition that any time the holy Aron and the Shechinah are not resting in their proper places that the Bnei Yisroel are prohibited from having marital relations. Therefore. Yehoshua's mistake of continuing the siege of Yericho at night caused that the people had to abstain from marital relations. As a measure for measure punishment, Yehoshua was punished for this sin by not having any sons. The Ritvah on this Gemorah explains why the other two sins, not offering the daily afternoon sacrifice and not learning Torah at night, could not have resulted in Yehoshua being punished with the inability to have sons. Hashem punishes only measure for measure, and neither of these sins would then result in a punishment of not having sons.

The Chasam Sofer in Bamidbar (13:16) quotes the Gemorah in Sanhedrin 100a to present another reason why Yehoshua was punished with not having sons. The Gemorah in Sanhedrin 100a says that someone who calls his Rebbe by name is an apikoras (apostate). After hearing the prophecy of

Shemos

Eldad and Medad, the Posuk quotes Yehoshua, saying, 'Moshe, my master, imprison them!' In Shulchan Aruch, Yoreh Deah (242:15), it says that it is forbidden for a student to call his Rebbe by name, whether his Rebbe is alive or not. The Rema explains that it is permitted if the student attaches a title of respect to the name as, for example, "my teacher Moshe." The Shach further clarifies that the Rema is talking in a case when his Rebbe is not in his presence. However, in the presence of his Rebbe, he should call him only by title as, for example, using the term Rebbe. The Chasam Sofer explains that Yehoshua previously had the name Yehoshua as we see the first time he is mentioned in Shemos (17:9) when it says, "So Moshe said to Yehoshua, 'Pick men for us, and go out and fight against Amalek.'" When Yehoshua called Moshe by name in Bamidbar (11:28), as punishment, the Yud in front of Yehoshua's name was taken away, and he was called Hoshea. Subsequently, before sending him as one of the twelve spies in Bamidbar (13:16), Moshe saw that Hoshea would need some protection to save him from the other spies' influence, and therefore Moshe added back the Yud to his name. Moshe got this Yud from Sorah as the Yerushalmi in Sanhedrin (2:6), which we have quoted above explains. Because the Yud came from Sarah's previous name Sarai which was unable to have sons, Yehoshua was also unable to have sons. According to all three explanations of why Yehoshua was punished by not having sons, we can answer the Maharsha's question of how the people knew that Yehoshua would never have any boys even though he was only 42 years old at the time.

Parenthetically, the Nitziv, in his Sefer Meromay Sodeh, presents another explanation as to what the people meant when they termed Yehoshua a "person with the cut off head." We have mentioned previously that Eldad and Medad prophesized that "Moshe will be Niftar and Yehoshua will lead the Bnei Yisroel into Eretz Yisroel." The people termed Yehoshua a "person with a cut off head" to mean that Yehoshua was now a "head" or leader only over his own tribe of Ephraim. The people accused Yehoshua of only wanting to go to Eretz Yisroel so that he could become the leader of all of Klal Yisroel and not just a leader with "a cut off head." Therefore, the people completely discounted what Yehoshua said since they felt that it was just self-serving. The Ain Eliyahu also presents a similar explanation to the Nitziv as to why they discounted Yehoshua's testimony.

The Ben Yehoyoda presents an additional explanation as to what the people meant when they termed Yehoshua a "person with the cut off head." The Gemorah in Sanhedrin 92b tells us that members of the tribe of Ephraim went out thirty years too early from Egypt and were murdered by the Philistines. Since Yehoshua was the leader of the tribe of Ephraim, the people said that just like his ancestors left Egypt too early, so Yehoshua was trying to bring them into Eretz Yisroel too early. The people termed rushing before the time, and getting many people killed because of it, as a "cut off head."

Since Calev knew that the people would silence him, like they had Yehoshua, if he started off by fully backing Moshe, Calev began by saying, "Is this the only thing the son of Amram has done to us?" The Gemorah says that since Calev used the belittling phrase "son of Amram" instead of "Moshe," the people assumed that he was going to reinforce the report that they had heard from the ten spies which denigrated Moshe and his ability to bring them and conquer Eretz Yisroel. The people quieted down to hear Caleb's report, and therefore, he was able to continue with a report that

Shemos

fully backed Moshe and the ability of the people to conquer Eretz Yisroel. Therefore, we see, says the Maskil LeDovid, that not using one's name is belittling the person. However, in our Posuk, there is no reason to think that the Posuk is belittling Yocheved by not using her name and instead calling her "daughter of Levi." The Gemorah in Baba Basra 120a says that there could be another reason for Yocheved to be termed "daughter of Levi," and that would be if she was just a young girl and was only known because of her father, Levi. However, the Gemorah in Baba Basra 120a proves that Yocheved was born right when the Bnei Yisroel got to Egypt. Since Moshe was 80 years old when the Bnei Yisroel went out of Egypt and since the entire time the Bnei Yisroel spent in Egypt was 210 years yields that at that point, Yocheved was 130 years old, so she obviously was not a little girl. Rather the Gemorah in Baba Basra 120a says that at that point, Yocheved became like a young girl again, with her flesh becoming tender, her wrinkles were smoothed out, and her young girl beauty returned to her. This answers the question of why Yocheved is called "daughter of Levi" but does not answer the question of why her name and even more perplexing, Amram's name was not explicitly said in our Posuk.

Along with the Gemorah in Baba Basra 120a, the Gemorah in Sotah 12a gives us more details about this marriage of Amram and Yocheved. The Gemorah says that Amram was the leader of the generation. When Amram saw that the wicked Pharaoh decreed that every Jewish baby boy should be thrown into the Nile River, Amram said, "we are working for nothing in attempting to have children." Therefore, Amram went and divorced Yocheved. Seeing what the leader of the generation had done, all the Jewish men followed Amram's example and also went and divorced their wives. Amram's daughter Miriam said to him, "My father, your decree is even harsher than Pharaoh's decree." Miriam proceeded to cite three reasons why Amram's decree was harsher than Pharaoh's. We will follow the explanation of the Maharsha that the reason Miriam gave three reasons was because she was referring to Pharaoh's three decrees, which the Gemorah had mentioned previously and was showing that Amram's solution was harsher than each of Pharaoh's three decrees. Pharaoh initially decreed that the Midwives should kill the Jewish baby boys before they were born. To this decree, Miriam said that Amram's solution was harsher since his solution made sure neither boys nor girls were born, and Pharaoh's decree was to prevent boys from being born. Pharaoh next decreed that the children, once they were born, should be thrown into the Nile River, to which Miriam said that Pharaoh's decree only affected life in this world while Amram's decree also affected life in the world to come. With respect to Pharaoh's third decree that even the Egyptians should throw their babies into the Nile River, Miriam said that it was quite questionable if the Egyptians would go along with such a decree since Pharaoh was a wicked person. In contrast, everyone had followed Amram's decree completely and had divorced their wives since Amram was a righteous person and the leader of the generation. With this, the Gemorah explains another strange wording in our Posuk, which says, "A man of the house of Levi went" without explaining where he went. The Gemorah says that Amram did not physically go anywhere but rather that he followed and went after the advice of his daughter Miriam.

Amram realized that Miriam was correct, and he remarried Yocheved. However, before he remarried her, a miracle occurred that Yocheved returned to her youth, as we have discussed previously. The Eyun Yaakov quoting Rav Shapiro, says that had Yocheved not returned to her

Shemos

youth, the rest of the Bnei Yisroel would not have followed Amram's example. They would have said that the only reason Amram remarried Yocheved was that she was so old that he knew she would not have any more children, and he would not be affected by Pharaoh's decrees. When everyone saw how youthful Yocheved had become, they knew that Amram remarried her even though she was quite capable of having more children. Therefore, everyone followed his example and remarried their wives. The Eyun Yaakov says that there was also a practical reason why Yocheved's youth returned. The Egyptians also saw what had happened to Yocheved and were now ready to check if she had children from that point on. According to the Gemorah, Yocheved was already three months pregnant with Moshe before her youth returned. Therefore, Yocheved was able to hide Moshe for three months in her house without the Egyptians suspecting that she had a child.

The Gemorah in Sotah 12a, along with the Gemorah in Baba Basra 120a, ponder why our Posuk uses language, which gives the appearance that this was their first marriage. The Gemorah says that Amram made a wedding at which he sat Yocheved in an ornate chair that only brides of first marriages were sat in, at those times. The Ben Yehoyoda says that the reason Amram did this was to publicize the fact that Yocheved's youth had returned to her, and she was now as youthful as a typical first-time bride. The Gemorah also says that both Miriam and Aharon danced before the newlyweds. By the fact that the Gemorah says that only Miriam and Aharon danced at the wedding, it would seem that the Gemorah is of the same opinion as the Zohar 19a, towards the end of Parshas Shemos, which says that the wedding was a relatively private affair.

1) The Zohar 19a, towards the end of Parshas Shemos, presents an answer to our question. It says that Amram made this remarriage a private affair so that no one would know that Amram had remarried Yocheved and the Torah informs us that it was private by not mentioning either Amram or Yocheved by name. Rav Meir Bergman, in his Sefer Shaarei Orah II, ponders the question of how this Zohar is consistent with the Gemorah in Sotah 12a, which says that all the Bnei Yisroel remarried their wives following Amram's lead when he remarried Yocheved if the affair was so private. Rav Bergman concludes that the Bnei Yisroel only found out after the marriage that Amram had remarried Yocheved. Rav Bergman proves how private the remarriage was by the Gemorah, telling us that only Miriam and Aharon danced in front of the couple. The Alshich and Tzedah LeDerech present us with an additional reason why the remarriage was so private. Amram and Yocheved did not want anyone, especially the Egyptians, to be able to calculate, based on when they got remarried, how long she may have been pregnant for so that she could hide Moshe's birth.

2) The Zohar 19a, towards the end of Parshas Shemos, presents another answer to our question. It says that when our Posuk says וַיֵּלֶךְ אִישׁ (A man went), it is referring to the angel Gavriel who went and brought Yocheved back to Amram so that Amram should remarry her. Another opinion in the Zohar says that even if Amram himself went to remarry Yocheved, he only did it because this thought of action was put into his heart by Hashem. Either way, Amram was passive in what took place, and therefore even according to the opinion that he actually went to remarry Yocheved, it really wasn't Amram who was active in initiating the remarriage. Therefore, his name is not mentioned explicitly.

Shemos

The Zohar 11a presents us with another reason why Gavriel was actively involved in this remarriage. When the body of a righteous person is conceived, the angel Gavriel is in charge of getting the appropriate Neshama from Gan Eden for this body. Therefore, says this Zohar, "A man went," is referring to Gavriel going and getting the proper Neshama for Moshe.

We can bring a proof to the Zohar which says that when our Posuk says וַיֵּלֶךְ אִישׁ (A man went), it is referring to the angel Gavriel. Beraishis (37:15) says that when Yosef went to search for his brothers: "Then a man found him, and behold, he was straying in the field, and the man asked him, saying, 'What are you looking for?' And he said, 'I am looking for my brothers. Tell me now, where are they pasturing?'" The Midrash Tanchuma in Parshas Vayeshev (2) tells us that this "man" was the angel, Gavriel. As proof, it brings Daniyel (9:21), which says וְהָאִישׁ גַּבְרִיאֵל (and the man (angel) Gavriel).

3) The Ramban presents an answer to our question. We have mentioned previously that our Posuk used a strange wording when it says, "A man of the house of Levi went," without explaining where he went. He says that the Torah can use the expression וַיֵּלֶךְ (and he went) to describe someone who is inspired to do a new or not typical thing. For example, Beraishis (37:27) says, לְכוּ וְנִמְכְּרֶנּוּ לַיִּשְׁמְעֵאלִים, which the Ramban would translate as "let us be inspired to sell him (Yosef) to the Yishmaelim." In Sefer Yeshayahu (1:18), it says לְכוּ נָא וְנִוָּכְחָה, which he would translate as "let us be inspired and debate." Sefer Yirmiyahu (18:18) says לְכוּ וְנַכֵּהוּ בַלָּשׁוֹן, which he would translate as "let us be inspired to smite him with the tongue." In all these cases, the person is not necessarily going anywhere but is inspiring themselves or someone else to do some action. In our case, despite the fact that Pharaoh had made a decree that all Jewish boys were to be thrown into the Nile River, Moshe's father Amram decided to remarry Yocheved notwithstanding having recently divorced her because of Pharaoh's decree. It certainly took a good deal of inspiration to do such a thing. The Abarbanel is of a similar opinion as the Ramban. The Abarbanel and Nitziv say that the action of inspiration was the fact that Amram married his aunt Yocheved. Besides the fact that the Torah later prohibited such a marriage, it was not typical or sensible to marry one's aunt. Typically, one highly respects and fears one's aunt. However, as a result of the sin of eating from the Eitz HaDaas, typically the husband rules over the wife as Hashem tells Chava in Beraishis (3:16), "And to your husband will be your desire, and he will rule over you." Since ruling over one's aunt would not be typical or sensible, it required much inspiration for Amram to marry his aunt Yocheved.

The Ramban says that the reason our Posuk does not mention the names of Moshe's parents is because if it mentioned their names, the Posuk would also need to trace their lineage several generations till Levi, so we know who they were. At this point, the Posuk did not want to digress to discuss who Moshe's parents were and just wanted to tell us that the savior of the Bnei Yisroel was born. For that matter, points out the Abarbanel, the Posuk doesn't even tell us about the birth of Moshe's siblings, Aharon and Miriam, so it could be brief.

4) The Akeidah also presents an answer to our question. He says that at this point in time, Amram was not known as a leader of the tribe and was just a regular member of the tribe of Levi like

Shemos

everyone else. Only later, after Amram's sons Aharon and Moshe began prophesizing, did Amram become known as the leader of the tribe and, in fact, all of Klal Yisroel. Yocheved was also not a well-known person. That is why when Miriam called her to become Moshe's wet nurse for Basya, Basya thought that she was just a regular wet nurse. The Torah emphasizes that neither of them was well known by not calling them by name. The only problem with this explanation is that it is contrary to the Gemorah in Sotah 12a, which says that at this point in time, Amram was the leader of the generation. In addition, according to the Gemorah in Sotah 11b, Yocheved was one of the Midwives that Pharaoh himself appointed to carry out his decree of murdering the Jewish baby boys, so she was even well known to Pharaoh.

5) The Alshich HaKodosh also presents another answer to our question. Similar to the Ramban, he notes that our Posuk used a strange wording when it says, "A man of the house of Levi went," without explaining where he went. He quotes a Zohar on Beraishis 185a, in the middle of Parshas Vayeshev, which analyzes why Reuven threw Yosef into a pit full of snakes and scorpions as opposed to being dealt with by his brothers and how Beraishis (37:21) describes this as Reuven was trying to save Yosef. It explains that if one, Chas VeShalom, is thrown into a pit of snakes and scorpions, then if one is righteous or if one has enough merit from one's parents, it is likely that Hashem will save him. However, if one is put into the hands of one's enemy, no matter how righteous one is or how much merit one has from one's parents, it is unlikely that he will be saved. The Ohr HaChaim on that Posuk explains that a person, since he has freedom of choice, is able to kill even someone who does not deserve to die. Since Hashem has created this world on the premise that people have free will, it is only in extraordinary cases that Hashem intervenes to take away a person's free will and prevents that person from killing another. Animals, on the other hand, will not kill a person unless that person has been previously sentenced to death in the heavenly court. Therefore, there was a much greater chance of saving Yosef by throwing him into a pit filled with snakes and scorpions as opposed to allowing Yosef to remain under the hands of his brothers, who had decided to kill him. The Alshich applies this concept to our case. When Pharaoh had made a decree that the Midwives or Pharaoh's own policemen should murder the Jewish baby boys, Amram felt that it was better to divorce his wife and not risk having a Jewish baby boy. However, when Pharaoh's new decree of throwing the Jewish baby boys into the Nile River was enacted, Amram knew that there was a much better chance of being saved from the Nile River as opposed to being saved from people who were ordered to kill the Jewish baby boys. Therefore, once this new decree was announced, Amram went and remarried Yocheved.

The Alshich says that the reason Amram and Yocheved's names are not mentioned was because the Torah wanted to stress that Moshe's parents were old at that time. In the case of Yocheved, the Torah wants us to know that she was a daughter of Levi, and in the case of Amram, the Torah wanted us to know that he was from Levi's house, which the Alshich says means that he was a grandson of Levi. Despite their age, to show that Amram's calculation was correct, the Alshich says that Hashem made a miracle and returned Yocheved to her youthful appearance, so everyone would know that it was for the purpose of having more children that Amram remarried Yocheved.

Shemos

6) The Maharal, in his Sefer Gur Aryeh on Shemos (1:15), also ponders our question. He says that the reason the names of Moshe's parents were not mentioned until after Moshe was born was because Moshe was already prepared by Hashem to come and redeem the Bnei Yisroel from Egypt during the first seven days of the creation of the world. Different than with all other children where if their parents did not have this child, the child would never have been brought into this world; it was not the same with Moshe. Though Amram and Yocheved were the best parents to have Moshe, had they not had Moshe, Moshe would have been born from different parents. Had the Torah told us the names of Moshe's parents before he was born, we would have thought that it was only because of Moshe's parents that Moshe was brought into this world.

7) The Shach on the Torah presents a perhaps more esoteric answer to our question. He says that Hashem wanted to hide Moshe, the savior of the Bnei Yisroel, for as long as possible from the Satan so that the Satan would not bring any spiritual judgments on Moshe. Therefore, Hashem caused that he should be taken and brought up by the daughter of Pharaoh so that the Satan could not even imagine that such a person could be the savior of the Bnei Yisroel. Furthermore, Hashem caused that Moshe would then be sent to the house of Yisro, who had been a priest of idols and would even marry his daughter. From the Satan's perspective, it was to appear as impossible that the savior of the Bnei Yisroel could emerge from such a Tameh environment that he was in. It was only much later, after Moshe's return to Egypt, crowned as the savior of the Bnei Yisroel, that the Torah tells us who Moshe's illustrious parents were. The reason for this is that at this point, it was no longer needed to hide Moshe from the Satan and any havoc that he could play in thwarting Moshe from becoming the savior of the Bnei Yisroel.

8) Rav Hirsch also presents an answer to our question. The reason the Torah only says that both Moshe's parents were members of the tribe of Levi and not what their names were, was because their most important quality, in this case, was that they were members of the tribe of Levi. Throughout history, members of the tribe of Levi were those who consistently took action and acted with great courage in the face of adversity. For example, they took the lead when the Golden Calf was made in helping Moshe kill those who had made it. They fought with the Bnei Yisroel, who wanted to go back to Egypt after Aharon was Niftar and the clouds disappeared, as Rashi details in Bamidbar (26:13). They also had one of the tribe's members, Pinchos, as it says in Bamidbar (25:11), who "turned My (Hashem's) anger away from the Bnei Yisroel by his zealously avenging Me among them so that I did not destroy the Bnei Yisroel because of My zeal." We also find many years later that members of the tribe of Levi were the leaders in fighting the Greek oppression when the miracle of Chanukah took place. In our case, the Egyptians were cruelly and inhumanely making many decrees against the Bnei Yisroel, and it would take a member of the house of Levi to save and redeem the Bnei Yisroel from this oppression.

9) Rav Schwab, in his Sefer Mayan Beis HaShoaivah, also ponders our question. Similar to Rav Hirsch, Rav Schwab also says that the reason the Torah only says that both Moshe's parents were members of the tribe of Levi and not what their names were, was because their most important quality, in this case, was that they were members of the tribe of Levi. He says that in Egypt, only the tribe of Levi kept the Torah. As proof, he quotes the Shemos Raba (19:5), which says that the

Shemos

only tribe which kept the Mitzvah of Bris Milah, one of the few commandments they had at that time, was the tribe of Levi. The Bamidbar Raba (3:6) is even more explicit when it says that even though the Bnei Yisroel served idols in Egypt, the tribe of Levi kept to their service of Hashem and did not go astray. Therefore, only a member of the tribe of Levi was fit to bring the Bnei Yisroel back to the service of Hashem and redeem them from Egypt.

10) Rav Moshe Feinstein, in his Sefer Dorash Moshe on Shemos (6:11), also presents an answer to our question. Rav Moshe says that the only time the Torah mentions who Moshe's parents are is after Moshe is chosen to be the savior of the Bnei Yisroel. He says that the Torah is teaching parents a lesson on how one should act when one has the good fortune of being blessed with a child of enormous ability and desire for Torah values. A parent may wrongly think that there is no reason to constantly watch that child and make a special extra effort to learn Torah with the child. The parents assume that there is no need for this because of the child's capabilities and being born with a desire for Torah learning and values. Rather, one should be extra careful in such a situation to make sure that these abilities do not get channeled to other subjects and that the child, Chas VeShalom, drifts away from the Torah. He points to the Gemorah in Sukkah 52a, which says that the greater a person is in Torah learning, the greater is the Yetzer Horah of that person attempting to lead him astray. The story is told about the Vilna Gaon that one day, his students told him, "Rebbe, we wish we could have your Yetzer Hara." The worst thing your Yetzer Horah tells you is to stop learning for a few seconds, while ours tells us to stop learning for hours or days. The Vilna Gaon answered them, "Oh no, you don't." You don't know how strong my Yetzer Horah is. As proof, he cited this Gemorah in Sukkah 52a. Rav Chaim Shmulevitz, in his Sefer Sichos Musar (5733:26), explains that simply one might think that the greater the person is, the greater the person's ability will be to subdue the Yetzer Horah and therefore, Hashem makes the Yetzer Horah proportionately stronger. Making the Yetzer Horah proportionately stronger would make the chance that the Yetzer Horah is victorious and the ability of free choice equal for all people, no matter how great they are. However, this hypothesis is not true, and that the greater the person is, the Yetzer Horah for that person will be so strong as to make it more likely for the person to sin. As proof, he quotes the Gemorah's example in Sukkah 52a. The Gemorah says that Abaye once overheard a conversation between a certain man and a certain woman. The man told the woman that they should both get up very early the next morning and set out together on their way. Abaye decided that he would follow behind them to prevent them from doing a sin. Abaye followed behind them for several hours in a meadow until they reached a crossroads where they went off in different paths. Rashi explains that they were from different cities, and this was the point that they had to take different paths to get to their destination. Before they separated their paths, Abaye overheard them say that their paths lead far apart so that they can no longer travel together, but the company would have been pleasant had they been able to do so. Upon hearing this, Abaye said to himself that had he made the journey with that woman, he would have been unable to restrain himself from sinning with her. We see from this story that it was harder for the great Abaye to overcome his Yetzer Horah than it was for the traveler whom he followed since his Yetzer Horah was so strong that it was more likely for him to sin. This is also what the same Gemorah means when it describes the reaction at the end of days when the Yetzer Horah will be slaughtered and no longer have any power. The Gemorah says that the slaughtered Yetzer Horah will appear as a high mountain that can hardly be climbed to the righteous

people. To the wicked people, the Yetzer Horah will appear like a strand of hair that can easily be broken. The Gemorah says that the righteous people will cry and say, "How were we able to overcome such a high mountain?" The wicked people will cry and say, "How were we not able to overcome this strand of hair?" Based on the reaction to the Yetzer Horah as told to us by this Gemorah, Rav Chaim concludes that the Yetzer Horah of the righteous person is so great that the righteous person has a greater danger of sinning than a wicked person does.

Therefore, Rav Moshe concludes, only after Moshe is chosen as the savior of the Bnei Yisroel and prophet was it safe to say who his parents were. At that point, we could see that they had correctly raised Moshe so that he developed into the great person that he became.

11) Rav Meir Bergman, in his Sefer Shaarei Orah, also ponders our question. The Rambam in Hilchos Teshuva (5:2) says, "A person should not entertain the thesis held by the fools among the gentiles and the majority of the undeveloped among the Bnei Yisroel that, at the time of a man's creation, Hashem decrees whether the person will be righteous or wicked. This is untrue. Each person is fit to be righteous like Moshe Rabeinu or wicked, like Yorovam ben Nevot." Had the Torah mentioned the names of the illustrious parents of Moshe, we would have erroneously thought that Moshe could have only become who he was because of who his parents were. By not mentioning his parents, we are taught that the reason Moshe was as righteous as he was, was due to his own hard work in refining his character.

We note that the Oznayim LeTorah also says that the reason Moshe's parents were not mentioned is because it was not necessary for Moshe to have been born of such illustrious parents for him to have become who he was. However, he does narrow down quite a bit who Moshe's parents could have been. Though he says that anyone could have been the parents of a righteous person as Moshe, it was still necessary that his mother be willing to sacrifice her life for all of Klal Yisroel, similar to what Yocheved did, and that his father be great in Torah, good deeds and fear of Hashem, similar to how Amram was. We know that Amram was great in Torah and fear of Hashem since the Gemorah in Sotah 12b says that Amram was the Torah leader of the generation. The Gemorah in Baba Basra 17a says that Amram, the father of Moshe, was among the four people who were only Niftar because mankind ate from the Eitz HaDaas, and death was decreed to come to all members of mankind. Otherwise, they were so clean of sin that they were not fit to be Niftar. The other three were Binyamin, son of Yaakov Aveinu, Yishai father of Dovid HaMelech, and Kilav, son of Dovid HaMelech. The Maharal, in his explanation of this Gemorah, says that all four of these people only reached this level because of the combined merit of themselves and either their father or son. That is why all four people are mentioned with the name of either their father or son.

We can also obtain another proof of the stature of Amram by what the Rambam says in Hilchos Melachim (9:1). The Rambam says, "Six precepts were commanded to Odom: (1) the prohibition against worship of false gods; (2) the prohibition against cursing G-d; (3) the prohibition against murder; (4) the prohibition against incest and adultery; (5) the prohibition against theft; (6) the command to establish laws and courts of justice. Even though we have received all of these commandments from Moshe and, furthermore, they are concepts which one accepts as logical, it

Shemos

appears from the Torah's words that Odom was commanded concerning them. The prohibition against eating flesh from a living animal was added for Noach, as Beraishis (9:4) says, "Nevertheless, you may not eat flesh with its life, which is its blood." Therefore, there are seven commandments. These matters remained the same throughout the world until Avraham. When Avraham arose, in addition to these, he was commanded regarding circumcision. He also set up the Shacharis Davening. Yitzchak separated Maaser and set up an additional Davening (Mincha) before sunset. Yaakov added the prohibition against eating the Gid HaNosheh (sciatic nerve). He also set up the Maariv Davening. In Egypt, Amram was commanded regarding other Mitzvos. Ultimately, Moshe came, and the Torah was completed by him." We note that the Radvaz, on this Rambam, says that it is not clear what Mitzvos Amram was commanded. Nonetheless, we see from this Rambam the prominent position that Amram had in the chain of how our Mitzvos were given to us. Parenthetically, the Ragachover Gaon in his Sefer Tzofnas Paneach, as quoted by the Meorah Shel Torah, says that the Mitzvah that Amram added was the Mitzvah of getting married in the Halachic way that we do. According to the Oznayim LeTorah, it is not clear to me how many other candidates could have fulfilled the criteria he sets. The criteria are of the mother being willing to sacrifice her life for all of Klal Yisroel, similar to what Yocheved did, and that the father be great in Torah, good deeds and fear of Hashem, similar to how Amram was.

What Did Yocheved See About Moshe "That He Was Good?"

(ב:ב) וַתַּהַר הָאִשָּׁה וַתֵּלֶד בֵּן וַתֵּרֶא אֹתוֹ כִּי טוֹב הוּא וַתִּצְפְּנֵהוּ שְׁלֹשָׁה יְרָחִים Shemos (2:2) The woman conceived and bore a son, and she saw him that he was good, she hid him for three months.

What did Yocheved see about Moshe "that he was good?"

Introduction
The Rashbam, Ramban, Rabeinu Bechay, Toldos Yitzchak, Alshich, Gur Aryeh, the Maharsha on Sotah 12a, the Rashash on Shemos Raba (1:20), and Rav Hirsch all make the point that every mother sees her child as being good, and therefore has mercy on her child and protects the child from harm. That being the case, the whole phrase seems to be superfluous. The Rashbam points out that because of this fact, we cannot take our Posuk as telling us that Yocheved hid Moshe for three months only because she saw that he was good. We will later see that many Meforshim are of the opinion that Moshe was born after only six months of pregnancy. The Akeidah says that during these next three months, Yocheved pretended to the world that she was still pregnant. Presumably, she wore clothes to make it appear that she was still pregnant.

The Vayikra Raba (1:3) and the Yalkut Shimoni 428 say that Moshe had ten names: (1) Yered, (2) Chaver, (3) Yekusiel, (4) Avigdor, (5) Avi Socho, (6) Avi Zanuach, (7) Tuvia, (8) Shemiah, (9) Ben Evyasar, and (10) Moshe. The Yalkut Shimoni explains that Moshe got the name Yered, which typically means bringing down, since Moshe brought the Torah down from the heaven to the earth or because Moshe brought Hashem's Shechinah down from the heavens to the earth. Sometimes the Hebrew word Yered can mean he rules as King. For example, Tehillim (72:8) says, וְיֵרְדְּ מִיָּם עַד יָם וּמִנָּהָר עַד אַפְסֵי אָרֶץ (And may he reign from sea to sea, and from the river to the ends of the land).

Shemos

According to this translation, the name Yered would be referring to Moshe's rulership over the Bnei Yisroel. Moshe got the name Chaver (bring together) since he brought together Hashem's children to their father in heaven. Moshe got the name Yekusiel from the Hebrew word Kaveh or hope because he caused Hashem's children to put their faith in their father in heaven. The Yalkut Shimoni explains that Moshe got the name Avigdor or father of Gedor since many Rabbinic leaders established laws to prevent us from violating the Torah, and Moshe was the head of these Rabbinic leaders. Moshe got the name Avi Socho since the Hebrew word Socho means to see, and Moshe was the head of all seers or prophets. Moshe got the name Avi Zanuach from the Hebrew word Zoneach or rejection since Moshe was the head of all people who got the Bnei Yisroel to reject idols. Moshe got the name Tuviah from our Posuk. Moshe got the name Shemiah because Hashem listened to the davening of Moshe on behalf of all the Bnei Yisroel. Moshe got the name Ben Evyasar from the Hebrew word Vetar or forgive since he was the child that his father in heaven forgave through him for the making of the Golden Calf.

The Shemos Raba (1:24) tells us that Pharaoh's advisors saw through their sorcery that Moshe would die because of water. That is why they decreed that all boy babies should be thrown into the Nile River. Pharaoh's advisors did not know that the actual water that led to Moshe being Niftar was the water from the rock that Moshe hit instead of speaking to. Pharaoh's advisors saw through their sorcery that Moshe was thrown into water, and at that point, they canceled the decree since, as far as they knew, the water would kill Moshe. The Pirkei D'Rabi Eliezer 48 says that Pharaoh's daughter Basya was afflicted with leprosy, and this was the reason she went to bathe in the Nile River since it is therapeutic for leprosy. The Pirkei D'Rabi Eliezer says that when she stretched out her hands and touched Moshe's basket in the Nile River, she was immediately cured of her leprosy. Basya immediately concluded that the child was righteous, and that is why she saved him and adopted him. The Ponim Yofos says that Basya assumed that Moshe had just been born when she found him since he looked around the size of a normal baby born after nine months of pregnancy. Since it was now three months after Pharaoh's sorcerers had told Pharaoh that the Savior of the Jews had been born, neither she nor Pharaoh made the connection that he could possibly be the one who the sorcerers had been talking about.

The Gemorah in Brochos says that the day Moshe was saved was the sixth day of Sivan. The Gemorah says that we know that Moshe was born on the seventh day of Adar. Three months later is the sixth day of Sivan. The angels said before Hashem, "how can someone who in the future is supposed to receive the Torah on this day be smitten on this day?"

It is taken as a given by some Meforshim, for example, the Eyun Yaakov on the Gemorah in Sotah 12a, that Moshe was born on Shabbos. We will see later that some commentators are of the opinion that Moshe was already born circumcised. That being the case, all that would be needed at Moshe's Bris was to take a drop of blood from the place of the Bris Milah. However, the Eyun Yaakov uses the fact that Moshe was born on Shabbos to argue with an opinion that this Bris of taking a drop of blood was done on the eighth day, being that since it was Shabbos doing so would not have been permitted. The Yismach Moshe quotes a Gemorah in Shabbos 156a, which says that someone who is born on Shabbos will be Niftar on Shabbos. The Gemorah says that since some sort of permitted

Shemos

desecration of Shabbos had to occur when the person was born on Shabbos, it is fitting that the person would be Niftar on the holiest day of the week. The Maharsha explains that no matter how great a person is, if he is Niftar on Shabbos, it is forbidden to desecrate the Shabbos on behalf of the Niftar. This shows everyone the sanctity of Shabbos. Since the day of Shabbos had to be desecrated when the person was born, the person is "rewarded" by sanctifying Shabbos by being Niftar on Shabbos and showing everyone how Shabbos cannot be desecrated on his behalf. The Maharsha also makes the observation that we know that many people who are born on Shabbos are, in fact, not Niftar on Shabbos. The Maharsha says that only the most righteous people have the merit to be born and Niftar on Shabbos. Tosfos in Menochos 30a says that the reason we say the prayer Tzidkoscho in Mincha of Shabbos is because Moshe was Niftar at that time on Shabbos. Though there is some controversy on how Moshe could have written the parts of the Sefer Torah that describe what Moshe did on the last day of his life, many commentators are of the opinion that Moshe was Niftar on Shabbos as Tosfos writes. That being the case, says the Yismach Moshe, it would then follow that Moshe was also born on Shabbos.

1) The Gemorah in Sotah 12a and the Shemos Raba (1:20) present an answer to our question. They quote Rav Meir, who says that Moshe's name was Tov. Rav Meir takes our Posuk, which says טוֹב הוּא (he is good) literally. The Pirkei D'Rabi Eliezer 48 quotes this answer in the name of Rav Shimon. The Maharsha explains that Yocheved gave all her children names, which corresponded with what was happening in Egypt at that time. She called her oldest daughter Miriam because when she was born, the conditions of slavery became completely oppressive. The Shir HaShirim Raba (2:11) says that of the 210 years the Bnei Yisroel were in Egypt, the worst oppressive years were the last 86 years. The beginning of 86 years coincided with the birth of Miriam. The reason she was named Miriam is because Miriam means bitter and that was the time that Shemos (1:14) says, וַיְמָרְרוּ אֶת חַיֵּיהֶם בַּעֲבֹדָה קָשָׁה (And they (the Egyptians) embittered their lives with hard labor). The Maharsha says that Aharon was given his name from the Hebrew word for the river (יְאֹר) since when he was born, the decree of throwing the boy babies into the river was going to soon begin. However, when Moshe was born, despite the horrible oppression, Yocheved saw good since, through Moshe, good and redemption would be brought to the Bnei Yisroel. Therefore, says the Maharsha, she called Moshe, Tov (good). The Yepheh Toar points out that in Megilas Rus, the name of the closest relative and redeemer of Rus was Tov as Rus (3:13) says. Therefore, the name Tov is not an unheard-of name for a person.

The Gemorah in Nedorim 38a says that when Hashem commanded Moshe to carve the second Luchos to replace the first set of Luchos, which had been broken because of the sin of the Golden Calf, Hashem told Moshe that the words of the Torah would be only his and his descendants. The Maharsha and Maharal in Chidushay Agodos explain that even though all the Bnei Yisroel would be commanded in all 613 Mitzvos, they would not be given the right to derive how each commandment and its details can be derived. These principles are derived from the thirteen principles of Rabi Yishmael through the intense analysis (Pilpul) of the exact words and phraseology of the Torah. However, the Gemorah says that Moshe was Tov Ayin, which literally means a "good eye," but figuratively means a benevolent person, and Moshe shared this right of learning Pilpul with all the rest of the Bnei Yisroel. The Gemorah uses Mishlay (22:9) to describe Moshe טוֹב עַיִן הוּא יְבֹרָךְ כִּי נָתַן

Shemos

מַלַחְמוֹ לַדָּל (He who has a generous eye will be blessed, for he gave of his bread to the poor). The Rosh on the Gemorah explains that bread is an allusion to the Torah, our spiritual sustenance, which Moshe gave to the Bnei Yisroel, who were poor spiritually. The Eyun Yaakov on the Gemorah in Sotah 12b explains that naming Moshe, Tov was a prophecy to the benevolent act that Moshe would do with the Torah by giving its Pilpul to the Bnei Yisroel. The Yepheh Toar says that this prophesy also included the many times that Moshe stood up to protect the Bnei Yisroel from punishment in the desert, which also showed Moshe's benevolence to his fellow man. In addition, Bamidbar (12:3) tells us, "Now this man Moshe was exceedingly humble, more so than any person on the face of the earth." Moshe's humbleness also made him benevolent in his dealings with his fellow man.

2) The Gemorah in Sotah 12a and the Shemos Raba (1:20) present another answer to our question. The Gemorah quotes Rav Yehuda, and the Shemos Raba quotes Rav Yoshiyah, who say that Moshe's name was Tuvia. The Rashash and Eitz Yosef explain that this opinion opines that the name Tov is not a typical name for a person while the name Tuvia is found many times in Sefer Ezra. The Yepheh Toar and Maharzav say that Tuvia is a contraction of Tov and the name of Hashem. According to this answer, the phrase "that he was good" is to be taken literally, meaning that this was his name. Continuing on the theme of what he says for the name Tov, the Yepheh Toar says that Moshe was also Tov (good) to Hashem, being that Moshe was completely righteous and straight in his service of Hashem. The Maharsha says that we can find a hint to the name Tuvia in our Posuk when it says כִּי טוֹב הוּא (that he was good). If we take the letter before the word טוֹב (Yud) and the letter after the word טוֹב (Heh), we get the Yud and Heh to change the name Tov to Tuvia. It is interesting that in the list of Moshe's ten names, which we have mentioned previously from the Vayikra Raba and Yalkut Shimoni, the name Tuvia and not the name Tov as is mentioned in the Gemorah is listed. It is possible that the author of the list in the Midrash and the Yalkut Shimoni do not agree with the opinion of Rav Meir that Moshe was given the name Tov. It is also possible that the author of the list agrees with the explanation of the Rashash and Eitz Yosef above that Tov is not a typical name for a person.

3) The Gemorah in Sotah 12a and the Shemos Raba (1:20) present another answer to our question. The Gemorah quotes Rav Nechemia, and the Shemos Raba quotes Rav Yehuda, who say that the phrase in our Posuk "that he was good" means that Moshe was fit to be a prophet. The Yepheh Toar points out that not only was Moshe fit to be a prophet, but as Devorim (34:10) says, "And there was no other prophet who arose in Yisroel like Moshe, whom Hashem knew face to face," meaning that Moshe was the greatest prophet. The Maharsha points out that we do not find Yocheved listed as one of the seven women prophets detailed in Megilah 14a, so according to this answer, we may ponder how Yocheved knew that he was fit to be a prophet. Rashi, on the Gemorah in Sotah 12a, says that Yocheved saw this through a Holy Spirit. The Maharsha says that Yocheved knew it through her daughter Miriam who is one of the seven women prophets; as Shemos (15:20) says, "Miriam, the prophetess, Aaron's sister, took the drum in her hand, and all the women came out after her with drums and with dances." The Eitz Yosef, both on the Midrash and on the Ain Yaakov, says that Yocheved deduced Moshe's potential by the Mazal or star at the time he was born. The Gemorah in Nedorim 38a says that Hashem only rests his prophetic spirit on someone

Shemos

who is mighty, wealthy, wise, and humble. The star at the time Moshe was born showed that Moshe would have these qualities.

4) The Gemorah in Sotah 12a and the Shemos Raba (1:20) present another answer to our question. The Gemorah and Shemos Raba quote others who say that the phrase in our Posuk "that he was good" means that Moshe was born having a Bris Milah (circumcised). The last Devorim Raba on the Torah describes what happened when the Satan came to take away Moshe's life under the rule that every person is destined to die. Moshe argues that he was different than other people, and one of the arguments that Moshe attempted to use to show this was that he was born already having a Bris Milah. The Beraishis Raba (4:6) is the source to Rashi on Beraishis (1:7) who asks why the words כִּי טוֹב are not mentioned on the second day of creation. He answers that since the final configuration of where the water would be in the world was not set until the third day, it does not say כִּי טוֹב on the water until the third day. He says that in general, anything that is not completed cannot be described with the words כִּי טוֹב (it was good). The Yedei Moshe uses this concept to explain why it does not say כִּי טוֹב (It was good) to describe the creation of man. Since man is not created complete but needs a Bris Milah, the Torah does not use the words כִּי טוֹב to describe man. The Akeidah points out that this is to be contrasted to the creation of animals where the Torah does say כִּי טוֹב since animals are created complete and do not require any human acts to become complete. However, since Moshe was born with a Bris Milah, he was complete, and therefore our Posuk describes him as כִּי טוֹב. Parenthetically the Avos D'Rabi Noson (2:5) lists thirteen people who were born with a Bris Milah (1) Iyov, (2) Odom, (3) Odom's son Shes, (4) Noach, (5) Noach's son Shem, (6) Yaakov, (7) Yosef, (8) Moshe, (9) Bilam, (10) Shmuel, (11) Dovid, (12) Yirmiyahu, and (13) Zerubavel. The Eitz Yosef on the Shemos Raba says that, in general, very righteous people were born already complete with a Bris Milah. Rabeinu Bechay points out that people born with a Bris Milah are similar to Odom, who was created by Hashem with a Bris Milah. The Chizkuni says that the reason we say the Posuk הוֹדוּ לַה' כִּי טוֹב כִּי לְעוֹלָם חַסְדּוֹ right after the Bris Milah is performed is because we have just made the child complete so he can be described as כִּי טוֹב after having the Bris Milah.

5) The Gemorah in Sotah 12a and the Shemos Raba (1:20) are the source for the answer that Rashi presents to our question. They quote the Chachomim, who say that when Moshe was born, the house filled up with light. The Chachomim derived this from the fact that our Posuk describes Moshe as כִּי טוֹב while Beraishis (1:3) describes the light that was created as כִּי טוֹב. The Eitz Yosef, both on the Shemos Raba and on the Ain Yaakov, explains that since our Posuk says, "she saw him that he was good," it means that there was something that had to do with seeing. Light, which allows one to see with, fits that description very well.

The Maharzav explains what this light was by quoting a Zohar 31b on Beraishis, where it discusses the Ohr HaGanuz (light created on the first day of creation). It says that Hashem showed Odom this light, and Odom was able to see with it from one end of the world to the other end. When Hashem saw that there would be three wicked generations (the generation of Enosh who first started serving idols, the generation of the flood, and the generation of the tower of Bavel), Hashem hid the Ohr HaGanuz so that these wicked people should not be able to use it. Hashem gave this light to Moshe

Shemos

for the first three months from his birth. After three months, when Moshe was brought to Pharaoh, Hashem took away this light from Moshe, and Hashem returned it to Moshe on Mount Sinai when Moshe received the Torah. It was this light that Shemos (34:35) is referring to when it says, "Then the Bnei Yisroel would see Moshe's face, that the skin of Moshe's face had become radiant, and then Moshe would replace the covering over his face until he would come again to speak with Him (Hashem)." Parenthetically, the Oznayim LeTorah says that based on this Zohar, we can understand why Pharaoh didn't see this light and become suspicious that Moshe was the Savior of the Bnei Yisroel. It is also quite possible that Pharaoh did not see this light since it is a spiritual light to which only highly refined spiritually righteous people can see, which of course, excluded Pharaoh.

The Mizrachi ponders why no other mother, besides Yocheved, made a waterproof basket and put their child in the Nile River. The Mizrachi answers that because Yocheved saw the miracle of the house filling up with light after Moshe was born, she thought that a miracle would occur with Moshe, and he will remain alive. The Nachalas Yaakov quotes the Gemorah in Sotah 11b, which says that the reason Miriam was called Puah the Midwife was because she cried out with Holy Spirit and said that her mother is destined to have a son who will save the Bnei Yisroel. That being the case, he ponders why Yocheved would not have known that a miracle would occur with Moshe even without the sign of the house being filled up with light. He answers that had there not been the sign of the house filling up with light, Yocheved could have thought that Miriam's prophesy was referring to a later son who she would have. He proves this from the Gemorah in Sotah 13a, which says that when the house filled up with light, Miriam's father Amram stood up and kissed her on her head and said, "My daughter, your prophecy has been fulfilled." One can derive from this Gemorah that had the house not filled up with light, Amram would not have made this statement. Amram would not have made this statement either because he did not believe what Miriam said was true since she was not yet an established prophet or that even if he believed her, her prophecy could have been referring to a later child. The person who wrote notes on the Nachalas Yaakov says that there was an important reason why Yocheved came up with the idea of the waterproof basket. It was known that the reason Pharaoh decreed that all baby boys (including Egyptian boys) should be thrown into the Nile River on the day Moshe was born was because his astrologers saw that the Savior of the Bnei Yisroel had been born. Since the astrologers do not see in a clear vision, Yocheved correctly deduced that when Moshe would be put in the river (even though he was safe in the waterproof basket), the astrologers would think that he had been drowned in the river, and Pharaoh would annul his decree.

The Maharal, in Gur Aryeh, presents another reason why Yocheved hid Moshe as long as she could and then put him in a waterproof basket, different than all the other mothers. He says that the Egyptians decreed that anyone who hid a baby boy would be put to death. The Gemorah in Sotah 12a and the Shemos Raba (1:20) say that the Egyptians thought of a system where they were guaranteed to find any hidden Jewish baby boys. The Egyptians would go into every house where they had any suspicions that a Jewish baby could be hidden, bringing along with them an Egyptian baby. When they came into the house, they made the Egyptian baby cry so that the Jewish baby would hear him and also cry. Facing certain death since this method of the Egyptian baby was very reliable, the parents were allowed to kill the child to save their own lives, and therefore they did not

Shemos

hide their baby boys. However, when Yocheved saw the miracle of the house filling up with light, she knew that Hashem would make a miracle for Moshe to be saved. That is why she was not afraid to hide Moshe for as long as possible and then made him a waterproof basket.

The Oznayim LeTorah says that at least on a simple level, we find an example of this light in the Gemorah Brochos 5b. The Gemorah relates how Rabi Eliezer was slick, and Rav Yochanon came to visit him. Rav Yochanon saw that Rabi Eliezer was lying in a dark room. Rav Yochanon uncovered his arm, and light filled the room.

6) The Targum Yonason ben Uziel, Daas Zekanim, Rashbam, Akeidah, Bechor Shor, Chizkuni, Toldos Yitzchak, Tur, Ohr HaChaim, Shach, Ponim Yofos, and Malbim answer our question similarly. They say that Moshe was born after only six months of pregnancy. That being the case, Yocheved first thought that there might be issues with this premature baby, which, especially at that time in history, it was very rare that he would live. However, after thoroughly checking him, "she saw him that he was good" and that he was fully mature. The Rashbam says that both his hair and fingernails were those of a full-term baby. Since "she saw him that he was good," therefore, Yocheved decided to hide him, as opposed to what she would have done if there was no chance that he would live, where Yocheved would not have risked her life to hide him. The Shach also presents another reason why Yocheved hid Moshe. Since it was rare that such a premature baby would be so healthy and developed, Yocheved was afraid that someone might give him an Ayin Horah if they saw him. As proof to this explanation, the Tur and the Shach cite Sefer Yirmiyahu (44:17), which uses טוב to mean healthy when it says וַנִּשְׂבַּע לֶחֶם וַנִּהְיֶה טוֹבִים (and we were satiated with bread, and we were healthy).

7) The Eben Ezra, Ralbag, Chizkuni, and Sforno answer our question similarly. They say that וַתֵּרֶא אֹתוֹ כִּי טוֹב הוּא (she saw him that he was good) means that he was much more beautiful than any other baby she had ever seen. Parenthetically, since Yocheved was a midwife, she had seen many babies and was well qualified to make this assessment. The explanation of the Sforno and Eben Ezra is consistent with how the Pirkei D'Rabi Eliezer 48 describes Moshe when he was born as looking like an angel of Hashem. The Radal on the Pirkei D'Rabi Eliezer explains that this was a prophecy for later when Moshe would go up to heaven for forty days and forty nights and be with the angels.

The Chizkuni and Sforno say that translating כִּי טוֹב הוּא as "he was beautiful" is similar to Beraishis (6:2) וַיִּרְאוּ בְנֵי הָאֱלֹקִים אֶת בְּנוֹת הָאָדָם כִּי טֹבֹת הֵנָּה וַיִּקְחוּ לָהֶם נָשִׁים מִכֹּל אֲשֶׁר בָּחָרוּ (The sons of the nobles saw the daughters of man that they were beautiful, and they took for themselves wives from whomever they chose). Since Moshe was so outstandingly beautiful, Yocheved surmised that it was part of a larger plan of Hashem. The Sforno says that a beautiful appearance shows inner physical completeness, which would aid that person in becoming a prophet.

8) Rabeinu Bechay also ponders our question. Shemos (2:6) says, וַתִּפְתַּח וַתִּרְאֵהוּ אֶת הַיֶּלֶד (She (Basya) opened it (the basket), and she saw him (the child). The Gemorah in Sotah 12b and the Shemos Raba (1:24) say that the Torah should have said וַתֵּרֶא אֶת הַיֶּלֶד (and she saw the child) instead of וַתִּרְאֵהוּ אֶת הַיֶּלֶד (and she saw him the child). They say that the "him" in the Posuk means that she saw

Shemos

both Moshe and Hashem's Shechinah with Moshe in the basket. Rabeinu Bechay says that if Basya merited to see the Shechinah with Moshe, how much more so did Yocheved also merit to see the Shechinah with Moshe. Therefore, he says that in our Posuk, when it says וַתֵּרֶא אֹתוֹ כִּי טוֹב הוּא (she saw him that he was good), it means she saw Moshe was good since she saw the Shechinah was with him.

9) The Alshich HaKodosh also presents an answer to our question. He quotes the Gemorah in Menochos 53b, which quotes Rav Ezra who explained the teaching יבוא טוב ויקבל טוב מטוב לטובים (Let good come and receive good from good for those who are good). Rav Ezra explains who all the "goods" are in this phrase. He explains that יבוא טוב (Let good come) refers to Moshe as our Posuk says וַתֵּרֶא אֹתוֹ כִּי טוֹב הוּא (and she saw him that he was good). He explains the next phrase, ויקבל טוב (and receive good), refers to the Torah which is called good as it says in Mishlay (4:2) כִּי לֶקַח טוֹב נָתַתִּי לָכֶם תּוֹרָתִי אַל תַּעֲזֹבוּ (For I gave you good teaching; forsake not My Torah). He explains the next part of the phrase מטוב (from good) refers to Hashem as we say in Ashrei found in Tehillim (145:9) טוֹב ה' לַכֹּל וְרַחֲמָיו עַל כָּל מַעֲשָׂיו (Hashem is good to all, and His mercies are on all His works). Finally, the last part of the phrase לטובים (for those who are good) refers to the Bnei Yisroel as Tehillim (125:4) says, הֵיטִיבָה ה' לַטּוֹבִים וְלִישָׁרִים בְּלִבּוֹתָם (Be good, Hashem, to the good and to the upright in their hearts (Bnei Yisroel)). Putting this all together, the phrase יבוא טוב ויקבל טוב מטוב לטובים means "Let Moshe come and receive the Torah from Hashem for the Bnei Yisroel."

The Alshich explains that Yocheved realized that Moshe was not only going to be the Savior of the Bnei Yisroel, but he would also be the receiver of the Torah for the Bnei Yisroel. This is what our Posuk means when it says, "and she saw him that he was good." Therefore, she knew that the merit of the Torah would protect Moshe, and she would be able to hide him for the following three months until the sixth day of Sivan. On that day, Yocheved also knew Moshe would be saved, as the Shemos Raba (1:24) tells us that the angels said before Hashem, "how can someone who in the future is supposed to receive the Torah on this day be smitten on this day?"

10) Rav Hirsch and the Oznayim LeTorah answer our question similarly. They say that "and she saw him that he was good" means that she saw that he was a good baby who did not cry for no reason. Yocheved knew that as long as she satisfied Moshe's requirements as a baby, he would not cry, and therefore she could keep him hidden from the Egyptians.

11) The Nitziv also ponders our question. The Gemorah in Baba Basra 120a and the Beraishis Raba (94:9) tell us that Yocheved was born just as they were entering the walls of Egypt. Coupled with the fact that the Bnei Yisroel spent 210 years in Egypt and that Moshe was 80 years old when the Bnei Yisroel left Egypt means that Yocheved was 130 years old when she gave birth to Moshe. The Nitziv says that generally, children born to older people are weak or may have other physical problems. However, after examining Moshe, Yocheved saw that Moshe was completely and totally healthy. That is what our Posuk means when it says, "and she saw him that he was good." The fact that Moshe was so healthy is also the reason that Yocheved took the risk, despite the Egyptian's horrible decree, and "she hid him for three months."

Shemos

What Is Meant by the Phrase הַלְהָרְגֵנִי אַתָּה אֹמֵר (Do You Say to Kill Me)?

Shemos (2:13-14) וַיֵּצֵא בַּיּוֹם הַשֵּׁנִי וְהִנֵּה שְׁנֵי אֲנָשִׁים עִבְרִים נִצִּים וַיֹּאמֶר לָרָשָׁע לָמָּה תַכֶּה רֵעֶךָ. וַיֹּאמֶר מִי שָׂמְךָ לְאִישׁ שַׂר וְשֹׁפֵט עָלֵינוּ הַלְהָרְגֵנִי אַתָּה אֹמֵר כַּאֲשֶׁר הָרַגְתָּ אֶת הַמִּצְרִי וַיִּירָא מֹשֶׁה וַיֹּאמַר אָכֵן נוֹדַע הַדָּבָר (ב:יג-יד) He (Moshe) went out on the second day, and behold, two Hebrew men were quarreling, and he said to the wicked one, "Why are you going to strike your friend?" And he retorted, "Who made you a man, a prince, and a judge over us? Do you plan to slay me as you have slain the Egyptian?" Moshe became frightened and said, "Indeed, the matter has become known!"

What did the Jewish person mean by the phrase הַלְהָרְגֵנִי אַתָּה אֹמֵר (do you say to kill me)?

Introduction
Moshe said, "Why are you going to strike your friend?" The Shemos Raba (1:29) and Midrash Lekach Tov are the sources of Rashi, who derives from this phrase that the person had not yet hit his friend and had only raised his hand to hit his friend. Otherwise, Moshe would have asked him, "Why did you strike your friend?" Since the Posuk calls him a wicked person, the Gemorah in Sanhedrin 58b, the Shemos Raba, and Midrash Lekach Tov all say that this is the source of the statement of Chazal that someone who raises his hand to hit his friend is called a wicked person.

The Shemos Raba (1:30) and Midrash Tanchuma on Shemos (10) say that at first glance, it would have been more grammatically correct to say הַלְהָרְגֵנִי אַתָּה מְבַקֵּשׁ (do you seek to kill me) instead of הַלְהָרְגֵנִי אַתָּה אֹמֵר (do you say to kill me)? The Yalkut Shimoni says that it would have been more appropriate to say הַלְהָרְגֵנִי אַתָּה עֹשֶׂה (are you going to do something to kill me) instead of הַלְהָרְגֵנִי אַתָּה אֹמֵר (are you going to say something to kill me)? The Midrash Lekach Tov says that it would have been more appropriate to say הַלְהָרְגֵנִי אַתָּה חָפֵץ (do you want to kill me).

Rashi, based on the Shemos Raba (1:28) and the Midrash Lekach Tov, says that the Jew that was being hit was the husband of Shlomis bas Divri. The Shemos Raba (1:28) says that Shlomis bas Divri's husband was Dasan, the same Dasan, along with Avirom that rebelled against Moshe in the rebellion of Korach. The Egyptian taskmaster became attracted to Shlomis bas Divri, and to satisfy his desires, he awoke Dasan in the middle of the night and forced him to leave his house. The Egyptian then came in and replaced Dasan in bed with her to satisfy his desires. Since it was in the middle of the night, Shlomis bas Divri had no idea that it was the Egyptian and not her husband. Dasan later returned and figured out what had happened. When the Egyptian realized that he had figured out what had happened, the Egyptian began hitting Dasan without remorse. Parenthetically, the Yalkut Shimoni says that Dasan wanted to divorce his wife over this incident, and she went to her brother Avirom for help. The next day the two people arguing, according to the Shemos Raba (1:29), Targum Yonason ben Uziel, and Midrash Lekach Tov, were Dasan and Avirom, who were arguing about Dasan's plans to divorce Avirom's sister, Shlomis bas Divri.

The Jewish man scolded Moshe by saying, "Who made you a man, a prince, and a judge over us?" The Midrash Tanchuma and one opinion in the Shemos Raba say that at that point, Moshe was a bit under twenty years old. The Jewish man (Dasan) was telling Moshe that since Moshe was less than twenty years old, he did not yet qualify for having the title of "man" and therefore had no right to

Shemos

admonish him with the phrase "Why are you going to strike your friend?" The Shemos Raba has another opinion that Moshe was around forty years old at the time of this episode. That being the case, Dasan told Moshe that even if he was qualified to have the title of "man," he was still not qualified to be a prince or a judge over Dasan. The Maharzav explains that Dasan told Moshe that he and his brother-in-law Avirom were important people in Egypt.

We can figure out what made Dasan and Avirom important people if we look at a question that bothers the Maharil Diskin at the end of Parshas Shemos. In Shemos (14:3), the Posuk says וַיֹּאמֶר פַּרְעֹה לִבְנֵי יִשְׂרָאֵל נְבֻכִים הֵם בָּאָרֶץ סָגַר עֲלֵיהֶם הַמִּדְבָּר (literally: And Pharaoh said to the Bnei Yisroel They are trapped in the land. The desert has closed in upon them). Though most commentators, like Rashi, are of the opinion that this Posuk should be translated "And Pharaoh said about the Bnei Yisroel" and not "And Pharaoh said to the Bnei Yisroel" since the Bnei Yisroel had already left Egypt, the Targum Yonason ben Uziel says that two people of the Bnei Yisroel stayed behind when the rest of the Jews left Egypt, and they were Dasan and Avirom. According to the Targum Yonason ben Uziel, when that Posuk says, "And Pharaoh said to the Bnei Yisroel," the Bnei Yisroel are Dasan and Avirom. Pharaoh addressed them at that moment since they were the only two Jews who did not leave Egypt, despite seeing and living through ten plagues that Hashem brought to take the Bnei Yisroel out of Egypt. Being how wicked Dasan and Avirom were that they didn't even leave Egypt when everyone else left, the Maharil Diskin ponders how it was possible that they didn't die during the plague of darkness. Rashi on Shemos (10:22), quoting from the Shemos Raba (14:3), says that one of the reasons Hashem brought the plague of darkness was because there were wicked people in that generation who did not want to leave Egypt. These people deserved the heavenly death penalty before it was time for the Jews to leave Egypt. Since Hashem did not want the Egyptians to see these Jewish people being killed and conclude that the plagues were not just meant for them since even the Bnei Yisroel were dying, Hashem killed these wicked Jews when the Egyptians could not see what was happening due to the plague of darkness. The Maharil Diskin ponders why Dasan and Avirom were not killed at this time. He says that they did not die because they were part of the Jewish officers who were given the job of making sure that the Bnei Yisroel fulfilled their quotas of work every day. Shemos (5:14) says that after Pharaoh stopped giving the Bnei Yisroel straw for bricks, "And the officers of the Bnei Yisroel whom Pharaoh's taskmasters had appointed over them were beaten, saying, "Why have you not completed your quota to make bricks like the day before yesterday, neither yesterday nor today?" Since these officers, which included Dasan and Avirom, were beaten because of their protection of their fellow Jews, they merited not to be killed out during the plague of darkness. We can now appreciate what Dasan and Avirom meant when they told Moshe in our Posuk that as important people, Moshe had no right and was not qualified to be a prince or a judge over them and their actions.

The Shemos Raba says that Dasan and Avirom had another point to make when they told Moshe that he was not qualified to be a prince or a judge over them. They told Moshe that the reason he was acting like he could judge them was because he was pretending that he was a son of Basya, daughter of Pharaoh, or a member of the Egyptian royal family. Dasan and Avirom said that they knew that he was not Basya's son but rather Yocheved's son, and being a fellow Jew, he was not qualified to be a prince or a judge over them. The Maharzav points out that based on this, we see

Shemos

that Pharaoh thought that Moshe was Basya's son. Had Pharaoh known that Moshe was Jewish, he would have implemented his decree and murdered Moshe by throwing Moshe back into the Nile River. The Yalkut Shimoni says that when Dasan and Avirom came to Pharaoh to tattle on him, they first told Pharaoh that Moshe was after Pharaoh's kingly robes and crown. Upon hearing this, Pharaoh was calm and did not have any problem. They finally incensed Pharaoh when they said that Moshe, who you think is your daughter Basya's son, is really not hers. Upon finding out that Moshe was Jewish and that he had killed an Egyptian taskmaster, Pharaoh gave orders to kill Moshe. The Yalkut Shimoni says that had Dasan and Avirom not tattled on Moshe, no one else would have tattled on him.

The Yalkut Shimoni says that Dasan had a type of prophesy when he said to Moshe, "do you say to kill me." Eventually, in the desert at the time of Korach's rebellion, Dasan and Avirom were indeed killed by Moshe's words when Moshe said in Bamidbar (16:29-30), "If these men die as all men die and the fate of all men will be visited upon them, then Hashem has not sent me. But if Hashem creates a creation, and the earth opens its mouth and swallows them and all that is theirs, and they descend alive into the grave, you will know that these men have provoked Hashem."

1) The Shemos Raba (1:30), Midrash Tanchuma on Shemos (10), Midrash Lekach Tov, and Yalkut Shimoni are the source for the answer that Rashi presents to our question. In the previous Posuk to ours, the Torah tells us that Moshe killed the Egyptian taskmaster who had been hitting the Jewish person Dasan without remorse. We can derive from the phrase הַלְהָרְגֵנִי אַתָּה אֹמֵר (are you going to say something to kill me), instead of the at first glance more appropriate phrases we listed in the introduction, that Moshe killed the Egyptian taskmaster using the explicit name of Hashem (Shem Hamchfurosh).

The Ramban ponders the question of how Dasan knew that Moshe had killed the Egyptian using the Shem Hamehfurosh. He assumes that all Dasan saw was the Egyptian falling down dead, which could have meant that he died of natural causes like a heart attack. The only other thing that Dasan saw was that Moshe immediately buried the Egyptian. For all Dasan knew, Moshe only did this because he became afraid that someone might see the Egyptian dead and just assume that Moshe had something to do with his death. Though Shemos (2:12) does say וַיַּךְ אֶת הַמִּצְרִי (he (Moshe) hit the Egyptian), it does not necessarily mean that Moshe physically hit the Egyptian. In Sefer Melachim II (19:35), the Posuk says וַיְהִי בַּלַּיְלָה הַהוּא וַיֵּצֵא מַלְאַךְ ה' וַיַּךְ בְּמַחֲנֵה אַשּׁוּר מֵאָה שְׁמוֹנִים וַחֲמִשָּׁה אָלֶף וַיַּשְׁכִּימוּ בַבֹּקֶר וְהִנֵּה כֻלָּם פְּגָרִים מֵתִים (And it came to pass on that night that an angel of Hashem went out and hit one hundred eighty-five thousand of the camp of Assyria. And they arose in the morning, and behold, they were all dead corpses). Though this Posuk literally says that the angel hit the soldiers, it was not a physical hitting, as evidenced by the fact that those who remained alive and got up in the morning had no idea how all the soldiers died. In a similar fashion, though the Torah says that Moshe hit the Egyptian, it does not necessarily mean that it was a physical hitting.

The Maharal, in Gur Aryeh, answers the Ramban's question by pointing out that even if one kills using the Shem Hamehfurosh, one still has to at least do an action and physically hit his victim so that the use of the spiritual Shem Hamehfurosh would physically kill someone. As proof, the

Shemos

Maharal brings the episode of how Dovid killed Golyus, the giant. Sefer Shmuel I (17:45) says, "And Dovid said to the Philistine (Golyus), 'you come to me with sword, spear, and javelin, and I come to you with the Name of Hashem, the Lord of Hosts, the G-d of the armies of Yisroel which you have taunted." The Maharal says that since Dovid said that he came with "the Name of Hashem" it means that Dovid killed Golyus with the Shem Hamehfurosh. Despite killing Golyus with the Shem Hamehfurosh, Sefer Shmuel I (17:49) states, "And Dovid stretched his hand into the bag, and took a stone therefrom, and slung it, and he hit the Philistine (Golyus) in his forehead, and the stone sank into his forehead, and he fell on his face to the ground." Therefore, he concludes that even when using the Shem Hamehfurosh to kill someone, one must, in addition, do a physical action for the Shem Hamehfurosh to kill someone. He also says that the Red Sea was split with the Shem Hamehfurosh. Despite using the Shem Hamehfurosh, Moshe still did an action with his staff and hand to split the Red Sea as Shemos (14:21) says, "And Moshe stretched out his hand over the sea." Since Moshe had to physically hit the Egyptian though not with such force to kill him, and nonetheless, the Egyptian died, Dasan was able to figure out that he had been killed with the Shem Hamehfurosh.

The Nachalas Yaakov presents a simple answer to the Ramban's question of how Dasan knew that Moshe killed the Egyptian with the Shem Hamehfurosh. He says that there were no other Egyptians around, and since Moshe felt comfortable among the Jews, he said the Shem Hamehfurosh out loud. Alternatively, at that point, Moshe could not fathom that a Jew would tattle about him, and therefore he told the Jews who witnessed the killing of the Egyptian that he had killed him with the Shem Hamehfurosh. The Maskil LeDovid answers the Ramban's question by saying that Dasan figured out that Moshe had used the Shem Hamehfurosh since he noticed Moshe's lips moving and then saw the Egyptian fall immediately thereafter.

The Maskil LeDovid presents another answer to the Ramban's question. Rashi in Sukkah 45a explains the meaning of the phrase that we say during Hoshanos on Succos of אֲנִי וָהוֹ הוֹשִׁיעָה נָא. Rashi explains that there are three Pesukim, one after the other in Parshas Beshalach, all of whom have exactly seventy-two letters. The three Pesukim are found in Shemos (14:19-21). Rashi says that if you take a letter from the first Posuk, count how many letters from the beginning of the Posuk this letter is and then take the letter at the same count of letters from the end of the next Posuk and combine it with the letter at the same count of letters from the beginning of the third Posuk one will form one of the names of the Shem Hamehfurosh. Let us take a concrete example and combine the first letter of the first Posuk, the last letter of the second Posuk, with the first letter of the third Posuk. Looking at the Pesukim, one can see that this spells out וָהוֹ. A more complicated example is the 37th letter. The 37th letter of the first Posuk is the Aleph of the word מֵאַחֲרֵיהֶם, the 37th letter from the end of the second Posuk is the first Nun of the word הֶעָנָן, and the 37th letter of the third Posuk is the Yud of the word קָדִים. Together this spells the Hebrew word אֲנִי. According to Rashi, אֲנִי וָהוֹ הוֹשִׁיעָה נָא means that we are asking to be saved with the first and middle (thirty-seventh) name of the Shem Hamehfurosh. The Maskil LeDovid says that when Moshe confronted Dasan in our Pesukim, he said לָמָּה תַכֶּה רֵעֶךָ (why will you hit your friend). If we take the 8th letter of the first Posuk, we get the Chof of the word מַלְאַךְ, the 8th letter from the end of the second Posuk is the Heh of the word זֶה, and the 8th letter from the beginning of the third Posuk is the Sof of the word אֶת. Though not in the

Shemos

same order as they appear in the Pesukim, this spells out the Hebrew word תִכֶּה. The Maskil LeDovid explains that when Dasan heard Moshe use the word תִכֶּה, he became suspicious that Moshe was trying to use this Shem Hamehfurosh to kill him and guessed that he had used the same Shem Hamehfurosh to kill the Egyptian. The Megaleh Amukos, as quoted by the Yalkut Reuveni, also says that Moshe killed the Egyptian using the Shem Hamehfurosh of תִכֶּה.

The Mizrachi ponders the question of why Moshe didn't use the Shem Hamehfurosh to kill Dasan when he threatened to tattle to Pharaoh about what Moshe did to the Egyptian. The Maharal, in Gur Aryeh, and the Nachalas Yaakov answer that Moshe did not want to kill Dasan since he wasn't sure whether or not Dasan was bluffing in his threat to tattle to Pharaoh. The Abarbanel and Maskil LeDovid take it a step further and says that it wasn't logical that Dasan should tattle to Pharaoh since Moshe had saved him by killing the Egyptian and Dasan, therefore, owed Moshe a debt of gratitude. In addition, Moshe, at the end of our Posuk, says, "Indeed, the matter has become known!" The Maharal says that this implies that Dasan had already revealed what happened to other people so that even if Dasan was killed, it wouldn't solve the problem since it was still likely that Pharaoh would find out.

The Maskil LeDovid also answers the Mizrachi's question about why Moshe did not use the Shem Hamehfurosh to kill Dasan. He answers that since Dasan was Jewish, Moshe preferred for Hashem himself to take any action on Dasan, which Dasan deserved, and that therefore it wasn't up to him to decide to kill him with the Shem Hamehfurosh. He uses the expression found in the Gemorah in Baba Metzia 83b when the Gemorah says the one should let Hashem take action for a certain problem rather than taking matters into one's own hands יבוא בעל הכרם ויכלה את קוציו (let the owner of the vineyard come and destroy his thorns).

The Taz, in Divrei Dovid, says that Dasan rebuked Moshe for using the Shem Hamehfurosh. The Gemorah says in Kidushin 71a that among other qualities, one does not transmit the forty-two or seventy-two letter Shem Hamehfurosh to anyone younger than half a lifetime. The Gemorah in Sanhedrin 69b says that the midway point of a person's life is the age of 35. Rashi on the Gemorah says that this is derived from Tehillim (90:10) "The days of our years because of them are seventy years." The Eitz Yosef explains that the reason for being older than half a lifetime is because, in the first half of one's lifetime, one thinks more selfishly and may be led to misuse the Shem Hamehfurosh for one's selfish reasons. In addition to being older than 35 years old, the Shem Hamehfurosh was also only given to someone who does not get angry, does not become intoxicated, and does not insist on his due. In general, one must be mature enough not to use the Shem Hamehfurosh for one's own agenda. According to the opinion that Moshe was only twenty years old at this time, Dasan rebuked Moshe for using and knowing the Shem Hamehfurosh, also implying that he was wrongly and impermissibly using it for his own gain and agenda.

With the Gemorah in Kidushin 71a as background, we can better appreciate the answer the Eitz Yosef presents to the Mizrachi's question about why Moshe did not use the Shem Hamehfurosh to kill Dasan. He says that Moshe did not want to use the Shem Hamehfurosh for his own purposes of

Shemos

protecting himself. We have seen from the Gemorah in Kidushin 71a that it is wrong and impermissible to use the Shem Hamehfurosh for one's own gain and agenda.

2) The Rambam in Moreh Nevuchim (1:65) and the Eben Ezra on our Posuk answer our question similarly. They say that הַלְהָרְגֵנִי אַתָּה אֹמֵר can be translated as "are you thinking (wanting) to kill me." We find in other Pesukim that the Hebrew word אֹמֵר does not necessarily mean speaking but can also mean thinking. For example, Koheles (2:1) says אָמַרְתִּי אֲנִי בְּלִבִּי (I said (thought) to myself). Mishlay (23:33) says וְלִבְּךָ יְדַבֵּר תַּהְפֻּכוֹת (your heart will speak (think) confusedly). Tehillim (27:8) says לְךָ אָמַר לִבִּי (On Your behalf, my heart says (thinks)).

3) The Sforno, Abarbanel, and Malbim answer our question similarly. We have mentioned in the introduction that Dasan pointedly told Moshe that he was not an honorable person and had no right to act as "a man, a prince, and a judge" over Dasan and Avirom. The Malbim says that someone who wants to get involved with adjudicating a quarrel must be either "a man, a prince, or a judge." He explains that "a man" refers to someone who is highly respected in the eyes of all the people and who will be listened to because of this respect. "A prince" refers to someone who, because of his strength or the strength of the person who appointed him, will be listened to. "A judge" refers to someone who everyone has accepted to judge such cases and will be listened to because everyone has accepted to do this.

The Sforno, Abarbanel, and Malbim say that Dasan told Moshe that despite this fact, Moshe still chose to get involved in a quarrel that was "none of his business." Therefore, Dasan concluded that Moshe got involved because Moshe wanted to entice Dasan to get angry and start a fight with him so that Moshe could have an excuse for also killing Dasan. When Dasan said הַלְהָרְגֵנִי אַתָּה אֹמֵר, they say that Dasan was criticizing Moshe and claiming that he was "trying to use words to get Dasan angry at him." The Abarbanel says that Dasan could also have implied by using the words הַלְהָרְגֵנִי אַתָּה אֹמֵר that Moshe was enticing Avirom to kill Dasan just like Moshe had killed the Egyptian on the previous day.

4) The Akeidah and Ponim Yofos answer our question similarly. In Jewish law, there is a concept of what is called a Rodef. The Mishna says in Sanhedrin 73a that there are those whom we save from sinning at the cost of their lives. An example of this is someone running after another person to kill that person. Anyone is allowed and, in fact, encouraged to save the person being pursued through killing the pursuer if the pursuer has been warned to stop and refuses to do so. We note the allowance to kill the Rodef does not apply, in a case where lesser means, like wounding the pursuer, would prevent the innocent's murder. This allowance of Rodef only applies before the pursuer has killed the person he is pursuing. However, once the pursuer has committed the crime, it is only in the hands of Beis Din to judge the case and punish as it decides.

The Akeidah says that Dasan picked up on the fact that Moshe had used the future tense when he said לָמָּה תַכֶּה רֵעֶךָ (Why are you going to strike your friend?). Since Moshe was of the opinion that Dasan was going to strike his friend in the future, Moshe would be permitted to save Dasan's friend by even killing Dasan if that was the only option. According to the Akeidah with the words הַלְהָרְגֵנִי

Shemos

אַתָּה אֹמֵר Dasan was accusing Moshe of trying to find a Halachic excuse for killing him. The Ponim Yofos points out that our Posuk says וַיֵּצֵא בַּיּוֹם הַשֵּׁנִי וְהִנֵּה שְׁנֵי אֲנָשִׁים עִבְרִים נִצִּים (He (Moshe) went out on the second day, and behold, two Hebrew men were quarreling). He points out that the Hebrew word for quarreling used here is נִצִּים. In Shemos (21:22) וְכִי יִנָּצוּ אֲנָשִׁים וְנָגְפוּ אִשָּׁה הָרָה וְיָצְאוּ יְלָדֶיהָ וְלֹא יִהְיֶה אָסוֹן עָנוֹשׁ יֵעָנֵשׁ (And should men quarrel and hit a pregnant woman, and she miscarries but there is no fatality, he shall surely be punished). In that Posuk like ours, the same Hebrew word for quarreling is used. The Gemorah in Sanhedrin 74a says that the case involved a fight where they were trying to kill one another, especially since the next Posuk, Shemos (21:23), says, "But if there is a fatality, you shall give a life for a life." Since the same Hebrew for quarreling was used in our Posuk, we must also be talking about a case where Dasan and Avirom were trying to kill each other. In such a case, Moshe would have been totally justified and encouraged to stop Dasan from killing Avirom by killing Dasan, especially after Moshe had warned Dasan to stop when he said, "Why are you going to strike (kill) your friend?"

5) The Rashbam also ponders our question. He says that Dasan, by saying הַלְהָרְגֵנִי אַתָּה אֹמֵר (do you say to kill me) was rhetorically asking Moshe if Moshe was of the opinion that anyone who hit a Jew was deserving of being killed. Dasan pointed out that Moshe had killed the Egyptian on the previous day for hitting a Jew and now, according to Dasan's understanding, threatened to kill Dasan for hitting a fellow Jew, Avirom. Implied in Dasan's argument is that one is not deserving of being killed for just intending to hit and not kill his fellow Jew. Obviously, he does not agree with the opinion of the Ponim Yofos in the previous answer that Dasan was trying to kill Avirom.

Why Did Yisro's Daughters Refer to Moshe as an Egyptian Man?

וַתֹּאמַרְןָ אִישׁ מִצְרִי הִצִּילָנוּ מִיַּד הָרֹעִים וְגַם דָּלֹה דָלָה לָנוּ וַיַּשְׁקְ אֶת הַצֹּאן (ב:יט) Shemos (2:19) They (Yisro's daughters) replied, "An Egyptian man rescued us from the hands of the shepherds, and he also drew water for us and watered the flocks."

Why did Yisro's daughters refer to Moshe as an Egyptian man?

Introduction
The Midrash Tanchuma on Shemos (11) says that Egyptians have a distinctive appearance and that it was easy to see from Moshe's appearance that he "did not look Egyptian."

When describing the home that Moshe got refuge at, Shemos (2:16) says, "The priest of Midyan had seven daughters." The Shemos Raba (1:32) and Midrash Tanchuma on Shemos (11) ponder the question of how Hashem could have led Moshe to find refuge in the house of a priest of idols since Hashem hates idols. The Midrash Tanchuma puts it more succinctly by asking how it was possible to reward such a righteous person as Moshe by leading him to come to such a house. Being in such a house is especially troublesome since it led to Moshe marrying the daughter of a priest of idols. Previous to Moshe's coming, Yisro was a priest to idols and experienced the fact that they have no power. This caused him to become disgusted with the idols and instilled in himself a desire to repent from serving idols. Yisro called a meeting of the people of his city and announced to them

Shemos

that in light of the fact that he had served a number of years as the priest of the city, he now wanted to retire since he was getting old, and he suggested that they get a replacement for him. To underscore his request, Yisro took all the priestly vessels and handed them over to the city. The people of the city excommunicated him and agreed that no one should have anything to do with him, including not doing any work for him nor shepherding his sheep. The Eitz Yosef explains that the people of the city were not fooled and figured out that Yisro had become disgusted with serving idols since the job of being a priest is typically done by an elderly person, so that the excuse of retirement did not make sense. All the people Yisro tried to hire to shepherd his sheep, refused and therefore, Yisro was forced to have his daughters become his shepherds. The Eitz Yosef explains that such a job was not honorable for a woman to do, especially since it made it likely that she might find themselves in secluded fields where she could be attacked by men. The Eitz Yosef contrasts this situation to that of Rochel, who was the shepherd of Lavan's sheep. In the case of Rochel, as opposed to Yisro, her father Lavan was a very poor and unimportant person at that time. Being that he could not afford to hire a shepherd, he had to take the risk of using Rochel as his shepherd since, at that time, he did not have any sons.

Yisro's daughters would come early to get water for their sheep since they were afraid of the other shepherds. They would also come back later after all the shepherds had left for the day to get more water for the sheep. On the day Moshe came, the shepherds decided to immorally assault Yisro's daughters, and as they were trying to flee their attackers, Moshe heard their cry for help and saved them from their attackers. Another opinion I that the shepherds decided that day to drown Yisro's daughters, and when Moshe came, they had already thrown them into the water from where Moshe saved their lives by rescuing them from drowning.

The Shemos Raba (1:32) says that despite the fact that his daughters told Yisro that an Egyptian man had saved them, Yisro figured out that Moshe was Jewish. When Yisro's daughters described how Moshe had drawn water for all their sheep and that the water rose up to Moshe so that it would be much easier to draw, Yisro knew that such a miracle only happens to a Jewish person. The Shach on the Torah says that not only did Yisro know Moshe was Jewish, but he even had a very good idea of who he was. He says that Yisro knew Moshe wasn't an Egyptian since no Egyptian would save someone whom they did not know. Yisro was still advising Pharaoh when Pharaoh was informed that Moshe had saved a Jewish slave from being mercilessly beaten by an Egyptian by killing the Egyptian. Yisro calculated that only a person like Moshe would risk his life to save a stranger.

In the previous Posuk to ours, it says, "They (Yisro's daughters) came to their father Reuel, and he said, 'Why have you come so quickly today?'" The Shemos Raba (1:32) says that Reuel was Yisro. The reason Yisro got the name Reuel is that he became a "friend of Hashem." The Targum Yonason ben Uziel and the Ramban say that Reuel was the father of Yisro and that Yisro had two names, Yisro and Chovov. When he converted, he took the name Chovov. This is consistent with Bamidbar (10:29), which says, "Then Moshe said to Chovav the son of Reuel the Midyanite, Moshe's father-in-law." The Ramban says that Yisro's daughters went to Reuel because, at that point, Yisro was still working and was not around at the house. The only issue with this explanation is that Shemos (2:18) says, "They came to their father, Reuel." The Torah ostensibly should have

Shemos

said that they came to their grandfather Reuel, and in fact, the Targum Yonason ben Uziel translates the Posuk as "they came to their grandfather Reuel." The Ramban answers that a number of times in Tanach, a grandfather is called a father since many times a grandparent refers to their grandson as their son. One example is Beraishis (29:5), which says, "Do you know Lavan, the son of Nachor?" In reality, Besuel was Lavan's father, and Nachor was Lavan's grandfather.

The Shemos Raba is of the same opinion as the Mechilta at the beginning of Parshas Yisro, which says that Yisro had seven names: Yisro, Yeser, Chovov, Reuel, Chever, Potiel, and Kaini. The Ramban is of the same opinion as Rav Shimon Bar Yochai in the Sifrei on Bamidbar (10:29), who says Yisro had just two names, Yisro and Chovov.

Shemos (2:11) says, "Now it came to pass in those days that Moshe grew up and went out to his brothers and looked at their burdens." The Shemos Raba (1:30) presents two opinions on how old Moshe was at the time, Rav Yehuda's opinion is that he was twenty years old, and Rav Nechemia's opinion is that he was forty. Very shortly after going out to his brothers, Moshe was forced to flee Egypt after killing the Egyptian, and Shemos (7:7) says that Moshe returned to Egypt when he was eighty years old. According to either opinion of how old Moshe was, there are a number of years in Moshe's life for which the Torah does not give us any details of what happened to Moshe. The Yalkut Shimoni (168) fills in the details of what happened during those years.

The Yalkut Shimoni says that when Moshe started growing up in Pharaoh's palace, being that Pharaoh's daughter Basya treated Moshe like her son, the officers in Pharaoh's regime became afraid of Moshe. In particular, one of Pharaoh's chief advisors, Bilam, was very frightened when he heard a rumor that Moshe wanted to kill him. Previously, Pharaoh had called a meeting of his three chief advisors, Reuel (either Yisro's father or Yisro himself), Bilam, and Iyov. At this meeting, he asked for their advice on the situation described in Shemos (1:9), which says, "Behold, the people of the Bnei Yisroel are more numerous and stronger than we are." In contrast to what the Reuel and Iyov advised, Bilam advised murdering all the Jewish baby boys by forcing them to be thrown into the Nile River. Being the advisor of this plan, it is easy to understand how frightened for his life Bilam became when he heard the above rumor. Because of the rumor, Bilam and his two sons ran away from Egypt and settled in the land of Kush.

Also, around the time Moshe was forced to flee from Egypt, it was also the time that a great war broke out between Kush and some of the states around it. Kunkus, King of Kush, prepared for war and left Bilam in charge of the capital city while he went out to fight the rebellion. He gave Bilam the keys to the walled city so that no one would be able to enter the city. The Yalkut Shimoni parenthetically tells us that Bilam was none other than Lavan. While Kunkos was waging war, Bilam gathered the people of Kush and convinced them to rebel against Kunkos by not letting him back in the city when he returned from war. The people agreed to the plan, chose Bilam as their new King, and made his two sons royal officers. They also fortified the city as follows. They raised the height of two of the walls of the city enormously. On the third side, they dug many wells until the third side of the city had a gigantic moat in front of it. Finally, on the fourth side, they gathered many snakes such that it was impossible to get into the city from any of its four sides.

Shemos

When Kunkus returned from war and approached his city, he saw that the walls of the city had been raised. He thought to himself that while he was away, some surrounding King had tried to invade the city and that this forced the inhabitants of the city to raise the height of the walls to defend themselves. When Kunkus got closer to the city, he saw that the gates of the city were closed, and he called out to the people in charge of the gates to let him into the city. Bilam told the people in charge of the gates not to open them, and Kunkus tried to enter the gates by force and lost 130 soldiers. The next day Kunkus decided to enter the city from the side where there was the moat since at least the walls were lower on that side. He sent thirty chariots of troops, but they got trapped in the wells that were dug under the moat and drowned. Kunkus then decided to have his troops chop down trees and build ten rafts to get across the moat. However, when the rafts got near the wells, the water currents became ferocious, and all ten rafts sunk, drowning 200 people on the ten rafts. On the next day, they tried to invade the city on the fourth side when the snakes were. One hundred seventy additional troops were lost, and Kunkus gave up on the idea of returning to his city.

Seeing that he could not take the city by force, Kunkus instead decided to lay siege to the city. Around this time, Moshe comes after escaping Egypt and meets Kunkus, who is in the middle of besieging the city. The Yalkut Shimoni says that at this point, Moshe was eighteen years old. In addition, we are told that Kunkus besieged the city for nine years. During these nine years, Moshe became respected and loved by Kunkus' army, and he was appointed adviser to Kunkus. At the end of nine years, Kunkus got very sick and died on the seventh day of his illness. His army buried him opposite his former city on the side of the city facing Egypt. The army built a big monument over his grave and engraved his whole life story on the monument.

After they finished the monument, the army realized that it had a dilemma on what to do next. If they tried to invade the city, it was likely that they would suffer many casualties and would not be able to take the city. If they remained besieging the city and the countries who had previously fought Kunkus found out that Kunkus had died, they would come and surprise the army with an attack on them. The countries would not be afraid since they would know that they were leaderless. They would also no longer be afraid of Kunkus, being that he was no longer alive and able to lead them in war. Therefore, they decided to appoint a king so that they could continue the siege of the city until it fell and, in the meantime, have a leader to again make them a formidable army. They put together a stage from their clothes, brought up Moshe on the stage, and proclaimed him the King. In addition, they decided that they would give Moshe the wife of Kunkus to become Moshe's wife. The Yalkut Shimoni says that at that point, Moshe was 27 years old.

On the second day after his coronation, the army came to Moshe and asked for his advice on what to do in the future, being that they had besieged the city already for nine years, and it had been nine years since they saw their wives and family. Moshe told them that if they attacked the city, they would just be defeated as they had been previously, but that he had a different strategy. Moshe advised them to go to the forest and look for storks' nests. Moshe said, "take the baby storks and raise them while training them to follow your orders." The people listened to Moshe, and they

Shemos

gathered and raised many storks. One day, after the storks grew up, Moshe told them not to feed them for a couple of days so that they would be very hungry. On the third day, Moshe told them to put on their armor, take their horse and their stork and prepare to go to war against the side of the city where the snakes were. When the army got to where the snakes were, they had the storks go and eat all the snakes since they were very hungry, and their long neck and beaks made it possible for them to eat the snakes without the snakes being able to defend themselves. With the snakes gone, the army invaded the city, killed 1,100 people in the city without losing any men from the invading army, took over the city, and was able to be reunited with their wives and children.

When Bilam saw that the city had fallen, he and his two sons grabbed horses, escaped the city, and returned to Egypt. In the meantime, Moshe was installed as King of the city. At that point, they also gave Moshe, Kunkus' wife, to become his wife, but Moshe did not live with her since she was a Canaanite. Moshe feared Hashem, and he knew how Avrohom had commanded his servant Eliezer to make sure that Yitzchak did not marry a Canaanite, along with how Yitzchak had told Yaakov not to marry a Canaanite when he sent him off to Lavan's house. The Yalkut Shimoni relates how Moshe was very successful as King conquering Edom, Aram, and other surrounding kingdoms.

Moshe was King for 40 years. At one point in the 40th year, when Moshe sat on the throne with the queen (Kunkus' wife) on his side, Kunkus' wife complained to the officers that for 40 years, Moshe had never lived with her, and Moshe had never served any of the idols of Kush. She advised the officers to appoint her son Muncham who had been fathered by Kunkus but who had been a baby when Moshe was appointed King. She added that it would be far better for the people to serve one of their own, the son of a King, rather than serving a slave from Egypt. The officers thought about it till morning, and when they got up in the morning, they decided to listen to her advice and appoint Muncham as the King. However, the people were still afraid of Moshe, and they decided to give him many presents and make a big ceremony to honor him for all his years as King before sending him away.

Moshe was 67 years old when he was sent away from Kush. The Yalkut Shimoni says that Hashem orchestrated for Moshe to be removed as King of Kush since it was time to begin the process of redeeming the Bnei Yisroel from Egypt. Moshe decided to head towards Midyan since he was afraid to return to Egypt, being that Pharaoh wanted him killed. At this point, the episode with Yisro's daughters occurred. Subsequently, the Yalkut Shimoni says that Moshe came to Reuel and told him how he had escaped from Egypt and how he had been King over Kush for many years before being forcefully "retired from his job as King." Hearing this, Reuel decided to put Moshe into prison, feeling that by imprisoning Moshe, the people of Kush would be thankful to him. Reuel had Moshe imprisoned for ten years, during which time Reuel's daughter Tziporah had pity on Moshe and provided him with bread and water. At the end of ten years, Tziporah went to her father Reuel and said, "do you remember the Jewish man you put into prison ten years ago?" In those days, we should realize that prisons were deep pits in the ground, subjecting the prisoner to be at the mercy of both the weather and to all sorts of pests that could be found in a pit. Tziporah reminded her father that he had never provided any food to Moshe and challenged him to investigate what had become of him. Of course, her father Reuel had no idea that Tziporah had been providing food to

Shemos

Moshe for all those years, and therefore Reuel told Tziporah that he was sure that Moshe was dead. Tziporah persisted and reminded her father that he had heard that Hashem, the G-d of the Jews, has done many wondrous miracles for the Jews, including saving Avrohom from the fiery furnace in Uhr Kasdim. In addition, Hashem saved Yitzchak from being slaughtered at the Akeidah, along with Yaakov being saved from and winning his fight with the angel. Moreover, Moshe himself had been saved from being thrown in the Nile River and from being executed by Pharaoh. Reuel accepted Tziporah's challenge and went to the pit when he saw, to his astonishment Moshe standing and davening to Hashem. Reuel took Moshe out of the pit, gave him a haircut for the first time in ten years, gave him new proper clothes to wear, and fed him proper food. Soon after, Moshe went to the garden that was behind Reuel's house. Moshe again davened and thanked Hashem for the miracle of saving him during these ten years, and at the end of his davening, he saw a staff of Sapphire stuck into the ground of the garden. When Moshe got closer and observed the staff, he saw that Hashem's name was engraved on the staff. Moshe touched the staff, and it easily dislodged itself from the garden into Moshe's hand.

The Yalkut Shimoni explains that Hashem created this staff during creation and according to the Pirkei D'Rabi Eliezer 19 was one of the ten things created right before Shabbos. Odom had taken it with him when he was driven out of Gan Eden. The staff next went to Noach, who transferred it to his son Shem until it got transferred to Avrohom. Avrohom gave the staff to Yitzchak, who gave it to Yaakov before Yaakov left to go to Lavan's house. Yaakov took the staff down to Egypt and transferred it to Yosef. After Yosef was Niftar, the Egyptians entered Yosef's palace and took the staff. The staff ended up by Pharaoh's advisor Reuel. When Reuel left Egypt with his life in danger after advising Pharaoh not to do any harm to the Bnei Yisroel, who had done so many good things for the Egyptians during the rulership of Yosef, Reuel took the staff with him to Midyan. Reuel planted the staff in his garden and challenged all the officers that anyone who could remove the staff would get his daughter Tziporah as a wife. None of the officers were able to remove the staff from the ground until Moshe easily removed it. Reuel was astonished when he heard what Moshe had done, and he fulfilled his promise of giving Tziporah to Moshe as a wife. The Yalkut Shimoni says that Moshe was 77 years old when he was released from prison by Reuel. Tziporah followed in the path of our righteous ancestors Sorah, Rivka, Rochel, and Leah. Soon afterward, they had their first son Gershom, and three years later, when Moshe was 80 years old, they had their second son Eliezer.

1) The Shemos Raba (1:32) and Midrash Tanchuma on Shemos (11) answer our question similarly. The Egyptian man that Yisro's daughters were referring to was the Egyptian taskmaster, who Moshe killed for hitting the Jew in Shemos (2:11). They present a Moshul to a person who was bitten by a scorpion. The Yerushalmi in Brochos (5:1) says that if after the bite from the scorpion, the person can put the limb with the bite into water before the scorpion gets to water, then the person will live and the scorpion will die. Conversely, if the scorpion, unfortunately, gets to water first, then the scorpion will live, but the person will not live. The Yerushalmi tells the story of Rav Chanina ben Dosah, who was standing and davening Shemoneh Esreh, and in the meantime, a scorpion came and bit him. Despite being bitten, Rav Chanina ben Dosah did not interrupt his Shemoneh Esreh, and he remained standing in the same place. Afterward, they found the scorpion dead in its hole.

Shemos

Subsequently, his students asked him whether he felt the bite of the scorpion. He answered that he was so absorbed in his davening that he didn't feel the bite. Rav Yitzchak adds that Hashem created a spring of water under Rav Chanina ben Dosah's foot so that he would be saved by encountering the water before the scorpion did.

Getting back to the Moshul, after the person quickly ran to the river, he noticed a young child drowning and saved him. The young child profusely thanked the man for saving his life. The man responded that it was really the scorpion who had saved his life since had the scorpion not bitten him; he would not have been at the river at that time to save the child from drowning. Similarly, Moshe would never have been in Midyan to save Yisro's daughters had the Egyptian taskmaster not hit the Jew, causing Moshe to kill the Egyptian and forcing Moshe to run away to Midyan because of the death penalty he was under for killing the Egyptian. The Oznayim LeTorah ponders the question of why Moshe would reveal the fact that he was a fugitive to Yisro's daughters, who he had just met for the first time in his life. If we consider that the Yalkut Shimoni says that Yisro put Moshe in prison for ten years after finding out that he was a fugitive, this question becomes even more powerful. We may answer this question based on the Yepheh Toar, who says that Moshe told them this so that they would realize that Hashem orchestrated that Moshe be there to save them. Moshe did not want to take any undue credit on behalf of himself for being there. We may also answer the question from what the Meam Loez says. Moshe figured out, was told, or knew that Yisro had recently stopped serving idols and began serving Hashem. Moshe wanted to teach Yisro that Hashem orchestrates everything that happens in the world. In addition, Moshe pointed out that Hashem orchestrating that Moshe would be around at exactly the right time to save Yisro's daughters might well be his reward or perhaps one of his rewards for giving up the worshipping of idols. Rav Sternbuch, in his Sefer Taam V'Daas, says that when Moshe was forced to flee Egypt, he was despondent that he would be leaving his brothers and sisters, the Bnei Yisroel, behind. Now Moshe saw how Hashem had orchestrated all this so that he could save Yisro's daughters. He says that a person should always believe that there are no coincidences and everything is orchestrated from Hashem for our good. In the future, in the world to come, we will see how everything that happened to us was orchestrated by Hashem for our own good.

In his Sefer Shaarei Orah (2), Rav Meir Bergman ponders the question of why Moshe said that the source of his coming to Midyan was the Egyptian he killed instead of attributing his forced coming to Midyan to the two Jews who were fighting each other. These two Jews reported to Pharaoh that Moshe killed the Egyptian, instigating Pharaoh to issue a death warrant on Moshe. Moreover, given the caliber of the person that this Egyptian was, it would not seem warranted to attribute anything positive to him. Rashi, based on the Shemos Raba (1:28) and the Midrash Lekach Tov, says that the Jew that was being hit was the husband of Shlomis bas Divri. The Shemos Raba (1:28) says that Shlomis bas Divri's husband was Dasan, the same Dasan, along with Avirom that rebelled against Moshe in the rebellion of Korach. The Egyptian taskmaster became attracted to Shlomis bas Divri and to satisfy his desires, he awoke Dasan in the middle of the night and forced him to leave his house. The Egyptian then came in and replaced Dasan in bed with her to satisfy his desires. Since it was in the middle of the night, Shlomis bas Divri had no idea that it was the Egyptian and not her husband. Dasan later returned and figured out what had happened. When the Egyptian realized that

Shemos

he had figured out what had happened, the Egyptian began hitting Dasan without remorse. Parenthetically, the Yalkut Shimoni says that Dasan wanted to divorce his wife over this incident, and she went to her brother Avirom for help. The next day the two people arguing, according to the Shemos Raba (1:29), Targum Yonason ben Uziel, and Midrash Lekach Tov, were Dasan and Avirom, who were arguing about Dasan's plans to divorce Avirom's sister, Shlomis bas Divri. Rav Bergman says that it seems inappropriate to ascribe anything positive to such a person as that Egyptian.

Rav Bergman relates a story that he heard from his father-in-law, Rav Shach, which Rav Shach heard from the Brisker Rov. When the Yeshiva Rav Meir Shapiro had planned for Lublin had its dedication ceremony, including placing the cornerstone of the Yeshiva, a very rich person who had given much money for the Yeshiva was honored with placing the cornerstone. Afterward, the Boyaner Rebbe called over this person and told him that obviously giving such a large sum of money for the Yeshiva was a great Mitzvah. In addition, it was also quite a merit and a great honor for him to be honored with placing the cornerstone in front of so many people, many of whom of great prominence. In Pirkei Avos (4:2), we are taught that the reward of doing a Mitzvah is the opportunity to do another Mitzvah. "Therefore," said the Boyaner Rebbe, "I am sure that you previously did a great Mitzvah, with no one knowing that you did this Mitzvah and that you got the present honor as a reward for doing the first Mitzvah." "I am jealous of that first Mitzvah that you did," concluded the Boyaner Rebbe.

Rav Bergman explains that a similar event happened to Moshe when he came to Midyan. As we have remarked previously, Moshe saved the daughters of Yisro either from being immorally assaulted or from being drowned to death. Moshe showed even more kindness by subsequently watering their sheep. In addition, the daughters of Yisro had already accepted to follow in the ways of the Torah, even before Moshe got there, so saving them was quite a Mitzvah. Moshe explained to the daughters of Yisro how he had been given the merit of this great Mitzvah by Hashem, causing him to come to Midyan just at that moment. Shemos (2:12) tells us, "He turned this way and that way, and he saw that there was no man, so he (Moshe) struck the Egyptian and hid him in the sand." Similar to what the Boyaner Rebbe said, Moshe explained that it was the Mitzvah he did of killing the Egyptian who was mercilessly beating up Shlomis bas Divri's husband that was the merit. Therefore, Moshe wasn't saying that the cause of his coming to Midyan was the Egyptian man, but rather the cause was that he killed the Egyptian man.

Rav Bergman uses this approach to explain why Yisro, after hearing what happened, told his daughters in Shemos (2:20), "So where is he? Why have you left the man? Invite him, and let him eat bread." The Rus Raba (5:9) says that a poor man does more for the person who provides him than the provider does for the poor man. What the poor man is doing is enabling the provider to do kindness for the poor man. Using this principle, Yisro told his daughters that it would be quite appropriate to invite such a "doer of kindness" to their table so that he does kindness for them by gracing their table.

Shemos

2) The Shemos Raba (1:32) presents another answer to our question. It says that the reason Yisro's daughters called him an Egyptian was because he was wearing Egyptian clothes. This answer is consistent with the Nitziv, who says that Yisro's daughters knew that all the Bnei Yisroel did not change their Hebrew language nor their Jewish way of dressing. Presumably, they knew this from being told by their father, Yisro. Therefore, since he was not wearing Jewish clothes but rather Egyptian clothes, they concluded that he was Egyptian.

The Oznayim LeTorah says that these Egyptian clothes were the clothes Moshe wore as a prince in Egypt. The Midrash Lekach Tov on Shemos (6:6) says that the four merits that helped the Bnei Yisroel be redeemed from Egypt were that they kept speaking their language, they kept their Jewish style of clothes, they did not reveal the secret to the Egyptians that they were leaving Egypt permanently, and they did not stop giving a Bris Milah. The Oznayim LeTorah says that the reason Moshe did not wear Jewish clothes was that since Moshe was in the King's palace, he was required to wear Egyptian royal clothes and not Jewish clothes. He says that this is similar to the Gemorah in Baba Kama 83a, which says that there was a haircut style that the Greeks used, called Komi, which was prohibited since it was a distinctive haircut style used by idolaters. The Gemorah says that the Rabonon allowed Avtolmus ben Reuven to cut his hair in this style since he needed to be close to and intermingle with the Roman monarchy. Tosfos references a Gemorah in Meilah 17a, which says that there was an occasion when the Romans made a decree that the Jews should not keep Shabbos, do a Bris Milah, and observe the laws of family purity. The Gemorah says that Reuven ben Istrobli went and cut his hair in this Komi style so that they would not know that he was a Jew, and he went and sat together with the people who made the decree. He said to them, "If one has an enemy, does he want them to become rich or poor?" They answered, "To become poor." That being the case, "let the Jewish enemies not work on Shabbos so that they should become poor from losing the income from this day." In addition, Rashi on the Ain Yaakov explains that by giving them Shabbos off, they will make lavish meals and spend the income that they earned the rest of the days of the week. The Romans concluded that his argument was correct, and they annulled the decree against keeping Shabbos. He then said to them, "If one has an enemy, does he want him to be strong or weak?" They answered, "To be weak." That being the case, "let the Jews give a Bris Milah to their children and let them get weak because of the loss of blood." Rashi on the Ain Yaakov explains that the blood lost when they are babies will not return, and they will not be as strong as they would have been without a Bris Milah. They again concluded that his argument was correct, and they annulled the decree on Bris Milah. Finally, he said to them, "if one has an enemy, does he want them to be great in number or less in number?" They answered, "to be less in number." That being the case, "let the Jews observe the laws of family purity so that they will be less often with their wives." Yet again, they concluded that his argument was correct, and they annulled the decree on the laws of family purity. Tosfos in Baba Kama 83a says that the person who presented these arguments was Avtolmus ben Reuven and that he was allowed to cut his hair in the Komi style to save the Jews from these terrible decrees.

Rashi and the Aruch explain that this haircut style entailed shaving all hair forward of a line running from ear to ear over the top of the head. The hair on the back of that was left to grow long. The prohibition of following the practices used by idolaters is derived from Vayikra (18:3) "Like the

Shemos

practice of the land of Egypt, in which you dwelled, you shall not do, and like the practice of the land of Canaan, to which I am bringing you, you shall not do, and you shall not follow their statutes." The Rema in Yoreh Deah (178:1) explains that this prohibition does not apply to practices where there is a logical reason for it. For example, the practice that every professional Doctor wears a distinctive style of dress is logical so that one can identify that this person is a professional Doctor and will know to come to him in time of need. In addition, some practice done for honor or any other logical reason is permitted. As an example, the Rema presents the practice of burning all the possession of a King who has died to honor the dead King by not having his possessions used by someone else. The prohibition does apply either to practices that are done to promote immorality or to practices where there is no logical reason for why they are done.

The author of the Shulchan Aruch in Yoreh Deah (178:2) says that a person who is close to the King and must therefore wear Gentile garments is permitted to do so. The Beis Yosef on the Tur ponders how the Rabonon were able to permit a person close to the King to transgress a prohibition that the Torah prohibits. He says that they needed to permit it to save the Jews and, therefore, would only be permitted in such a circumstance. The Bach says that the Torah prohibition is only for a case where the Jew is following the Gentile practice because she/he wants to be like the Gentiles, which shows that the Jew agrees with their beliefs. But in a case where the only reason the Jew is following the Gentile practices is to not be embarrassed and "stick out like a sore thumb," there is no prohibition from the Torah to follow a Gentile practice, and the prohibition is Rabbinic. Since the prohibition is Rabbinic, these same Rabonon said that it is permitted for someone close to the King to wear Gentile clothes, and that is why Moshe was permitted to do so.

The Oznayim LeTorah assumes that the last event that happened in Moshe's life before coming to Midyan was escaping Pharaoh's execution squad, who were trying to execute him for killing the Egyptian. Though this would be at odds with the timeline of Moshe's life, which we have presented from the Yalkut Shimoni, it is consistent with how the Torah juxtaposes these two events. He quotes a Gemorah in Sanhedrin 92b, which teaches us that even when one is threatened with mortal danger, one should still maintain one's dignity. The Gemorah derives this from the fact that Chananyah, Mishael, and Azariah kept on the clothes of their high office even when they were thrown into the fiery furnace for not bowing down to Nebuchadnezzar's golden image. The Maharsha explains that by wearing one's dignified clothes in such a situation, one shows that one is not mourning from the judgment that Hashem has decreed but rather accepting Hashem's decree with love in a dignified manner.

Despite the fact that the daughters of Yisro came to the conclusion on their own that Moshe was an Egyptian, the Devorim Raba (2:8) says that Moshe was punished for not correcting this misconception and at least saying that he was from Eretz Yisroel. It says that Yosef, who publicized the fact that he was a Jew and was from Eretz Yisroel when (among other places) he says in Beraishis (40:15) "For I was stolen from the land of the Hebrews" merited to be buried in Eretz Yisroel. Moshe did not correct the daughters of Yisro and announce that he was Jewish and from Eretz Yisroel, which is why Moshe was not buried in Eretz Yisroel. The Oznayim LeTorah ponders the question of why Moshe was punished if ostensibly he was not present at the conversation when

Shemos

Yisro's daughter informed him that an Egyptian man saved them. He answers this question by quoting a Midrash that Moshe was outside the house and, in fact, heard what Yisro's daughters said and did not call out and correct them. The Eitz Yosef quotes a Sefer Chasidim (117) who also says that Moshe heard when Yisro's daughters said that an Egyptian man saved them and did not correct them. The Mekor Chesed on the Sefer Chasidim also says that the Midrash (VaYosha) says that Moshe was outside the house when he overheard Yisro's daughter saying this. We may use what the Matnos Kehunah on the Devorim Raba (2:8) says to answer the Oznayim LeTorah's question. He says that either before or after Moshe was brought into the house and they still treated him like he was an Egyptian, Moshe should have protested and said that he was Jewish and from Eretz Yisroel.

Rav Sternbuch, in his Sefer Taam V'Daas, increases Moshe's culpability by pointing out that Yisro was already at the point in his life where he held the Jews in high esteem. We can prove that Yisro held Jews in high esteem because otherwise, Moshe would have been ill-advised to ever tell Yisro that he was Jewish. Had Yisro not held Jews in high esteem, Moshe, as a person with a death sentence, should have been worried that Pharaoh's soldiers might come someday looking for him, and Yisro would hand him over. Based on this risk, we might ponder the question of how Moshe knew how highly Yisro esteemed Jews to risk his life by later telling Yisro that he was Jewish. We may answer this concern if we couple together the Midrash, which says that Moshe was outside, and the Shemos Raba (1:32), which says that despite the fact that his daughters told Yisro that an Egyptian man had saved them, Yisro figured out that Moshe was Jewish. When Yisro's daughters described how Moshe had drawn water for all their sheep and that the water rose up to Moshe to make drawing it easier, Yisro knew that such a miracle only happens to a Jewish person. As we have mentioned in the introduction, the Shach on the Torah says that not only did Yisro know that Moshe was Jewish, but he even had a very good idea about who he was. The Shach says that Yisro knew that Moshe wasn't an Egyptian since no Egyptians would save someone they did not know. With Moshe overhearing this conversation between Yisro and his daughters, it is no wonder that Moshe felt secure, eventually revealing to Yisro that he was Jewish.

The Oznayim LeTorah ponders another question about why it would seem more understandable that Yosef, as opposed to Moshe, would broadcast the fact that he was Jewish and from Eretz Yisroel. Yosef grew up in Eretz Yisroel, his entire family was in Eretz Yisroel at that point, he intended to return to his father, and at least his brother Binyamin in Eretz Yisroel was constantly in his thoughts, so it made sense that he would say that he was a Jew from Eretz Yisroel. For Moshe, who had never seen Eretz Yisroel in his life and all his family and friends were in Egypt, it made sense why he might not immediately protest when Yisro's daughters called him an Egyptian. We may use the Maharzav to answer this question who says that even in Egypt, the Jews were still identified as Jews as it says in Shemos (2:13) "He went out on the second day, and behold, two Hebrew men were quarreling."

The Oznayim LeTorah says that at first glance, it would also make more sense to hold Moshe accountable for not protesting that he was a Jew, as opposed to not protesting that he was from Eretz Yisroel. From the day Hashem told Avrohom during the Bris Bain HaBesorim that Eretz Yisroel would belong to his descendants, it was incumbent for his descendants to believe without any doubt that Eretz Yisroel is our land. Moreover, either Moshe soon told him or Yisro very quickly figured out that Moshe was a Jew, so revealing that Moshe was Jewish was soon rectified. However, we do not find anywhere that Moshe said that he was only temporarily living in Egypt and that he was awaiting every day to be redeemed and return to his land in Eretz Yisroel. Therefore, Moshe was punished by not being buried in his land. Eretz Yisroel has a unique characteristic in that it "feels" its embarrassment and is able to take retribution for its embarrassment. For example, Eretz Yisroel is the only land that must rest every seven years, just like a Jew is the only person who must rest every seven days. If Eretz Yisroel does not rest every seven years, it will take retribution for this as Vayikra (26:34) says, "Then, the land will be appeased regarding its sabbaticals. During all the days that it remains desolate while you are in the land of your enemies, the land will rest and thus appease its sabbaticals." In addition, if the land becomes embarrassed because of all the sins of its residents, it will be appeased as Vayikra (18:28) says, "And let the land not vomit you out for having defiled it, as it vomited out the nation that preceded you." When Yisro's daughters are glamorizing all the wonderful acts of kindness that he did for them, it is most imperative to say that he was a Jew from Eretz Yisroel. In that way, Eretz Yisroel becomes known as a land that contains the type of people who do kindness for others even when he had to risk injury at the hands of the shepherds who had attacked Yisro's daughters.

3) The Tur also presents an answer to our question. The Tur says that Moshe intentionally hid his identity and pretended to be an Egyptian since he was a fugitive from Egypt. Moshe did not want anyone to figure out who he was, less they return him back to the executioner in Egypt.

4) The Abarbanel and many years later, the Oznayim LeTorah answer our question similarly. They say that Moshe spoke Egyptian to the shepherds as he was chasing them away. This led Yisro's daughters to conclude that Moshe was Egyptian. The Abarbanel says that the Midyanim were afraid of the Egyptians since the Egyptians had invaded and taken over Midyan. Yisro's daughters concluded that this was why he was able to single-handedly defeat so many Midyanim shepherds and water their sheep since they were petrified of being punished by the Egyptian rulers. This explanation of the Abarbanel would also explain why Moshe would assume that they would understand Egyptian when he talked to them in Egyptian. The Oznayim LeTorah says that Moshe knew they would understand Egyptian because the Egyptian language became prevalent at that time in many countries because of Egypt's prominence among nations.

5) The Alshich HaKodosh also presents an answer to our question. He writes that this was the day after Yisro had retired from being the priest of Midyan and decided to serve Hashem and to no longer serve idols. As we have previously quoted from the Shemos Raba, the Midyanites figured out why Yisro was retiring and refused to have anything to do with him, including refusing to work for him as a shepherd. Yisro's daughters were pressed into service as shepherds and were understandably not so happy with this new job, especially since they knew how badly the other shepherds would now treat them. When they returned very early that day, at a time that neither Yisro nor his daughters expected to be back, Yisro told them that Hashem had rewarded them with having an easy time with the sheep and shepherds in the merit that Yisro had given up serving idols.

Shemos

Yisro's daughters told him that his assessment was incorrect. The only reason they were home early was that an Egyptian man, who ostensibly served idols as other Egyptians, saved them from being attacked by all the shepherds. The fact that he was able to do this single-handedly despite being vastly outnumbered proved that he must have used some sorcery and witchcraft of idols to succeed. An idolatrous Egyptian doing sorcery was the only plausible explanation Yisro's daughters could come up with to explain what had happened that day.

6) The Oznayim LeTorah also presents an answer to our question. The Yalkut Shimoni in Devorim (829) says that Moshe was very happy when he heard about the Halachos of a person who goes to an Oray Miklat (city of refuge) if the person kills someone without the intention to kill him. Since the person is not punished as a murderer, Moshe felt relieved since he killed the Egyptian without the intention to kill him. The Yalkut Shimoni in Shemos 167 also says a similar thing and compares Moshe's reaction to a person who eats a food knowing how the food tastes and therefore being happy that the Halachos of Oray Miklat exist.

We must ponder the question of why Moshe's killing of the Egyptian is considered unintentional. The Shemos Raba (1:30) says that Moshe killed the Egyptian using the explicit name of Hashem (Shem Hamehfurosh). Rashi in Sukkah 45a explains the meaning of the phrase that we say during Hoshanos on Succos of אֲנִי וָהוֹ הוֹשִׁיעָה נָא. Rashi explains that there are three Pesukim, one after the other in Parshas Beshalach, all of whom have exactly seventy-two letters. The three Pesukim are found in Shemos (14:19-21). Rashi says that if you take a letter from the first Posuk, count how many letters from the beginning of the Posuk this letter is and then take the letter at the same count of letters from the end of the next Posuk and combine it with the letter at the same count of letters from the beginning of the third Posuk one will form one of the names of the Shem Hamehfurosh. Let us take a concrete example and combine the first letter of the first Posuk, the last letter of the second Posuk, with the first letter of the third Posuk. Looking at the Pesukim, one can see that this spells out וָהוֹ. A more complicated example is the 37th letter. The 37th letter of the first Posuk is the Aleph of the word מֵאַחֲרֵיהֶם, the 37th letter from the end of the second Posuk is the first Nun of the word הֶעָנָן, and the 37th letter of the third Posuk is the Yud of the word קָדִים. Together this spells the Hebrew word אֲנִי. According to Rashi, אֲנִי וָהוֹ הוֹשִׁיעָה נָא means that we are asking to be saved with the first and middle (thirty-seventh) name of the Shem Hamehfurosh. The Maskil LeDovid says that when Moshe confronted Dasan in our Pesukim, he said לָמָּה תַכֶּה רֵעֶךָ (why will you hit your friend). If we take the 8th letter of the first Posuk, we get the Chof of the word מַלְאָךְ, the 8th letter from the end of the second Posuk is the Heh of the word זֶה, and the 8th letter from the beginning of the third Posuk is the Sof of the word אֶת. Though not in the same order as they appear in the Pesukim, this spells out the Hebrew word תַכֶּה. The Maskil LeDovid explains that when Dasan heard Moshe use the word תַכֶּה, he became suspicious that Moshe was trying to use this Shem Hamehfurosh to kill him and guessed that he had used the same Shem Hamehfurosh to kill the Egyptian. The Megaleh Amukos, as quoted by the Yalkut Reuveni, also says that Moshe killed the Egyptian using the Shem Hamehfurosh of תַכֶּה.

The Malbim quotes the Rambam in Hilchos Melachim (10:6), who says that a Gentile who hits a Jew is punished by heaven, and not through man, with death. By using the explicit name of Hashem to kill the Egyptian, Moshe was just the conduit for heaven to kill the Egyptian. That being the case, Moshe did not directly and intentionally kill the Egyptian and could avail himself with hiding in a city of refuge. The Yalkut Reuveni quotes a Kavonas HaAri, who also says that Moshe needed to go into exile in a city of refuge. The Oznayim LeTorah explains that Moshe going to Midyan was akin to going to a city of refuge. The Mishnah in Makos 12b says that someone who kills unintentionally and then goes to an Oray Miklat must humble himself and tell them that he killed someone if the people of the Oray Miklat want to honor him. Moshe followed this Halacha, and when the daughters of Yisro wanted to honor him for saving them, he was obligated to humble himself and tell them that he killed the Egyptian. The daughters of Yisro paraphrased Moshe's remarks and said that "the person who killed the Egyptian saved us."

The Beis HaLevi's Explanation of a Hard to Understand Shemos Raba

Shemos (3:1) וּמֹשֶׁה הָיָה רֹעֶה אֶת צֹאן יִתְרוֹ חֹתְנוֹ כֹּהֵן מִדְיָן וַיִּנְהַג אֶת הַצֹּאן אַחַר הַמִּדְבָּר וַיָּבֹא אֶל הַר הָאֱלֹקִים חֹרֵבָה (ג:א) Moshe was pasturing the flocks of Yisro, his father in law, the chief of Midyan, and he led the flocks after the free pastureland, and he came to the mountain of G-d, to Chorev.

The Shemos Raba (2:1) says that when Hashem appeared to Moshe in the mountain of G-d, Hashem told Moshe that the redemption from exile would show Hashem's traits of compassion and gracefulness (רחום וחנון). Hashem's trait of compassion will be shown on the Bnei Yisroel when Hashem makes it that they will not be affected by the plagues. Hashem's trait of gracefulness will be shown when Hashem puts the image of the gracefulness of the Bnei Yisroel into the minds of the Egyptians. This image will cause the Egyptians to lend the Bnei Yisroel many precious possessions right before they leave Egypt. The Yepheh Toar says that even though we know there were many Bnei Yisroel who refused to go out of Egypt and who Hashem killed in the plague of darkness, nonetheless, the Bnei Yisroel were not punished or affected by the plagues, which solely punished the Egyptians.

The Beis HaLevi on this Midrash ponders what connection there is between the Bnei Yisroel not being affected by the plagues and the Egyptians lending the Bnei Yisroel many precious possessions because the Bnei Yisroel found favor in their eyes.

The Beis HaLevi quotes the Shir HaShirim Raba (1:3), where Shlomo describes the Bnei Yisroel with the phrase לְרֵיחַ שְׁמָנֶיךָ טוֹבִים (Because of the fragrance of your goodly oils). It says that the Bnei Yisroel are like oil which does not mix with other liquids since the Bnei Yisroel do not mix with the Gentiles. The Beis HaLevi explains that Hashem gave the Torah to the Bnei Yisroel so that they would be separate from the Gentiles. If the Bnei Yisroel do try to get close and mix with the Gentiles, Hashem strengthens the division between the Bnei Yisroel and the Gentiles by putting hate into the heart of the Gentiles against the Bnei Yisroel. Indeed the Bnei Yisroel tried to break down the separation between them and the Egyptians, and therefore, Shemos (1:12) says, וַיָּקֻצוּ מִפְּנֵי בְּנֵי יִשְׂרָאֵל (Hashem caused the Bnei Yisroel to be disgusting in the eyes of the Egyptians). Had the Bnei Yisroel remained separate from the Egyptians as they were during the time Yaakov and Yosef were

Shemos

alive, the Egyptians would have loved and respected them as they had while Yaakov and Yosef were alive.

The Beis HaLevi quotes the Zohar 15a in Shemos. It says that Hashem wanted to keep the twelve tribes and their descendants from getting mixed up with the Gentiles. For this reason, Hashem took the brothers down to Egypt since the Egyptians were a brazen people who denigrated Jewish customs. Their disgust for Jews would prevent the Jews from intermarrying with them and mingling with them. In addition, the Egyptians despised both the male and female Jews and, therefore, would not capture the Jewish women so that the Bnei Yisroel could go out of Egypt a pure nation when the sins of the inhabitants of Eretz Yisroel was completed. The Beis HaLevi proves from this Zohar that being despised by the Gentiles keeps the Jews from intermingling with them, and that is why Hashem brought the Bnei Yisroel to exile in Egypt.

The Beis HaLevi quotes two Gemoros in Pesachim. The Gemorah in Pesachim 118b quotes part of Sefer Tehillim (68:31) בִּזַּר עַמִּים קְרָבוֹת יֶחְפָּצוּ (He (Hashem) scatters nations that desire קְרָבוֹת). Rashi, on this Posuk, says that nations refer to the Bnei Yisroel, which is composed of many tribes. The Gemorah, though this is not the simple translation of the Posuk, explains that this Posuk is telling us that the cause of the Bnei Yisroel being scattered among the nations of the world is the friendship (קְרָבוֹת) that the Bnei Yisroel desire to have with the other nations. Instead, as the Eitz Yosef quotes from the Iyei Hayom, Bilam praised the Bnei Yisroel in Bamidbar (23:9) הֶן עָם לְבָדָד יִשְׁכֹּן וּבַגּוֹיִם לֹא יִתְחַשָּׁב (they (Bnei Yisroel) are a nation that will dwell alone, and will not be reckoned among the nations). The Gemorah in Pesachim 87b quotes part of Sefer Shoftim (5:11) צִדְקֹת פִּרְזֹנוֹ בְּיִשְׂרָאֵל (they will talk about the righteous deeds (Hashem performed) for the open cities in Yisroel). The Gemorah says that this Posuk teaches us that Hashem performed a righteous deed with Yisroel in that he scattered us among the nations. The Gemorah explains this concept by quoting a story of an apostate trying to convince Rav Chanina that the Gentiles are better than the Jews. The apostate quotes Sefer Melachim I (11:16), which says, "For Yoav and all of Yisroel remained there for six months until he had killed every male in Edom." "As for us," said the apostate, "you Bnei Yisroel have been by us for many years, and we have not done anything to you." For completeness, we should mention the context of the story of Yoav, which the apostate conveniently did not mention, was that it was in the middle of a war that Yoav, Dovid's general, fought with the Edomites who had attacked the Bnei Yisroel many times. Rav Chanina said that one of his students, Rav Oshiya, would rebut the apostate. Rav Oshiya told the apostate that the only reason the Gentiles have not killed the Jews is because the Gentiles are in a dilemma on how to do it. Rav Oshiya explained that they couldn't, Chas VeShalom, kill out all the Jews because the Jews are scattered among many nations, and each nation has control over just some small portion of Jews. Rav Oshiya continued that if you decide to kill out only the Jews that are under your nation, this idea will not work since you will become known in the world as a ruthless and cruel nation. The Gemorah ends with the apostate confirming to Rav Oshiya that this is indeed the dilemma that they, the Gentiles, grapple with. By combining these two Gemoros in Pesachim, the Beis HaLevi concludes that Hashem has to scatter us among the nations because we are looking for friendship with the Gentiles. Looking for friendship with the Gentiles causes Hashem to make the Gentiles hate us, which Chas VeShalom,

Shemos

could lead to them trying to destroy us. By Hashem scattering us among the nations, Hashem prevents the Goyim from destroying us, as the apostate confirmed.

With the above as background, the Beis HaLevi explains the Shemos Raba about the connection between the Bnei Yisroel not being affected by the plagues and the Egyptian lending the Bnei Yisroel many precious possessions because the Bnei Yisroel found favor in their eyes. In addition, the Beis HaLevi explains why one would even contemplate the Bnei Yisroel being affected by the plagues, which were ostensibly for the good of the Bnei Yisroel so that the Egyptians would agree to send them out of Egypt.

We have previously quoted the Posuk where Bilam praises the Bnei Yisroel in Bamidbar (23:9) הֶן עָם לְבָדָד יִשְׁכֹּן וּבַגּוֹיִם לֹא יִתְחַשָּׁב (they (Bnei Yisroel) are a nation that will dwell alone, and will not be reckoned among the nations). The Beis HaLevi says that the Midrash on this Posuk says that since the Bnei Yisroel held themselves separate from the Egyptians with regard to their clothes and food, Hashem did not judge the Bnei Yisroel and the Egyptians together. The closest Midrash I could find to that is written in the Yalkut Shimoni Bamidbar (768), which says that in general, the Bnei Yisroel separate themselves from the other nations with regard to their clothes and food. Not only aren't the Bnei Yisroel and the other nations punished with the same punishment, but they are judged at a different time of day, with the Gentiles being judged at night while the Bnei Yisroel are judged during the day. The Yerushalmi in Rosh Hashana (1:3) says that the reason the Bnei Yisroel are judged by day is because that is when (especially before the invention of electricity) the Bnei Yisroel are occupied in doing Mitzvos. Therefore, their judgment will likely turn out better when they are judged during the day.

The Shemos Raba (11:2) says that the Bnei Yisroel were also fit to be punished during the plague of wild animals that invaded Egypt as the fourth of the ten plagues. The Maharzav and Toldos Noach say that this is derived from Shemos (8:19), which when describing the plague of wild animals, says וְשַׂמְתִּי פְדֻת בֵּין עַמִּי וּבֵין עַמֶּךָ (And I will make a redemption between My people and your (Pharaoh's) people). The use of the word "redemption" implies that the Bnei Yisroel were fit to be punished had Hashem not redeemed the punishment from the Bnei Yisroel and instead placed it on the Egyptians. The Yepheh Toar explains that since the wild animals came from far-off lands and were very mobile in comparison to the previous plagues, it would be natural that they would also go into Goshen and affect the Bnei Yisroel. In a similar way, explains the Beis HaLevi, if a wicked person gets punished with a contagious punishment, others can get affected by the spread of this contagious punishment. The only merit that protects the Bnei Yisroel from being affected by the contagious punishment is separating themselves from the Gentiles. This is what Dovid HaMelech is referring to in Tehillim when he says in Chapter (26:4-5), "I did not sit with dishonest men, neither did I go with hypocrites. I hated the congregation of the evildoers, and I did not sit with the wicked." Dovid HaMelech concludes in Sefer Tehillim (26:9), "Gather not my soul with sinners nor my life with men of blood," meaning that he asked for protection from any contagious punishment which might be meted out to the wicked people.

Shemos

Shemos (3:21-22) say, "And I will put this people's favor in the eyes of the Egyptians, and it will come to pass that when you go, you will not go empty-handed. Each woman shall borrow from her neighbor and from the dweller in her house silver and gold objects and garments, and you shall put them on your sons and on your daughters, and you shall empty out Egypt." Even in the times of the Beis HaLevi one hundred fifty or so years ago, they understood the dangers of putting on clothes from people infected with such contagious diseases as lice and boils as the Egyptians were. Moreover, they also understood that the people who would be most affected by these contagious diseases would be young children. He says that they also understood this many years before in Egypt and nonetheless outfitted their children with the clothes of the Egyptians.

Combining the above, the Beis HaLevi explains the Shemos Raba (2:1), which says that when Hashem appeared to Moshe in the mountain of G-d, Hashem told Moshe that the redemption from exile would show Hashem's traits of compassion and gracefulness (רַחוּם וְחַנּוּן). Hashem's trait of compassion will be shown on the Bnei Yisroel when Hashem makes it that they will not be affected by the plagues. Hashem's trait of gracefulness will be shown when Hashem puts the image of the gracefulness of the Bnei Yisroel into the minds of the Egyptians. This image will cause the Egyptians to lend the Bnei Yisroel many precious possessions right before they leave Egypt. Because of Hashem's trait of compassion, the Bnei Yisroel merited not to be affected even by the plagues, which could have been contagious. Knowing this, the Bnei Yisroel had no compunctions on even receiving clothes from the Egyptians which, according to the Mechilta on Shemos (12:35), were more expensive than the gold and silver that the Bnei Yisroel got from the Egyptians, despite the fact that the Egyptians had been punished with contagious diseases. The Maharal Diskin explains that the clothes were more expensive than the gold or silver because the clothes contained precious stones attached to the clothes.

The Beis HaLevi continues that the Bnei Yisroel merited not being infected with the contagious diseases of the Egyptians when they separated themselves from the Egyptians by doing the Mitzvah of Korban Pesach, which required that they first do a Bris Milah. Since the Korban Pesach required slaughtering a sheep, which was the deity of the Egyptians, this act separated the Bnei Yisroel from the Egyptians. In addition, doing a Bris Milah physically separated the Bnei Yisroel from the Egyptians. Shemos (12:13) says, "And the blood will be for you for a sign upon the houses where you will be, and I will see the blood and skip over you, and there will be no plague of destruction on you when I smite the people of the land of Egypt." Even though only the firstborn Egyptians died, their dead bodies caused contagious diseases that could harm others. Putting the blood on the doorposts signified that the inhabitants of the house had fulfilled the Mitzvah of Korban Pesach and, therefore, would not be harmed even by a contagious disease which could be caused through the firstborn Egyptians being killed.

It seems to me that with this approach, we can answer the Toldos Yitzchak's question of why before the Bnei Yisroel were given the Mitzvah of Korban Pesach, they were not told to ask for clothes from the Egyptians as it says in Shemos (11:2) "Please, speak into the ears of the people, and let them borrow, each man from his friend and each woman from her friend, silver vessels and golden vessels." Yet when the Bnei Yisroel left Egypt, the Bnei Yisroel also got clothes from the Egyptians

Shemos

as we are told in Shemos (12:35), "and the Bnei Yisroel did according to Moshe's order, and they borrowed from the Egyptians silver objects, golden objects, and garments." In addition, at the beginning of Moshe's mission to redeem the Bnei Yisroel, we have already mentioned that Moshe is told in Shemos (3:21-22) says "And I will put this people's favor in the eyes of the Egyptians, and it will come to pass that when you go, you will not go empty-handed. Each woman shall borrow from her neighbor and from the dweller in her house silver and gold objects and garments, and you shall put them on your sons and on your daughters, and you shall empty out Egypt." According to the explanation of the Beis HaLevi that we have presented, we can answer this question as follows. Before they had the Mitzvos to separate themselves from the Egyptians by making a Korban Pesach and performing a Bris Milah, the Bnei Yisroel would not be convinced to take the Egyptian garments since they would think that they were contagious. Therefore, in Shemos (11:2), which was before the Bnei Yisroel received the Mitzvah of Korban Pesach and Bris Milah, they were not told to ask for garments. Only later, after getting these Mitzvos, were they told to also ask for garments.

The Toldos Yitzchak has a different approach as to how the Bnei Yisroel received the precious clothes even though Moshe did not tell the Bnei Yisroel to ask for clothes. On the night of the killing of the firstborn, along with the commandment to eat the Korban Pesach, the Bnei Yisroel were also commanded in Shemos (12:22) וְאַתֶּם לֹא תֵצְאוּ אִישׁ מִפֶּתַח בֵּיתוֹ עַד בֹּקֶר (and you shall not go out, any man from the entrance of his house until morning). At midnight, the Egyptian firstborns were killed, and soon after, we are told in Shemos (12:33), "So the Egyptians took hold of the people to hasten to send them out of the land, for they said, 'We are all dead.'" The Bnei Yisroel remembered that they were commanded to ask the Egyptians for their gold and silver, and therefore they asked the Egyptians for it. Rashi quoting the Mechilta on Shemos (12:35), says that the Egyptians were so eager to get the Bnei Yisroel to hurry up and leave that instead of bringing them the specific article of gold and silver that the Bnei Yisroel asked for, they brought two of the same article. All of this was an attempt to get the Bnei Yisroel to leave since the Egyptians feared that soon all the Egyptians would die. The haste of the Egyptians left the Bnei Yisroel is a quandary since they still had a number of hours to go till morning, and they were commanded not to leave their house until morning. The Bnei Yisroel, says the Toldos Yitzchak, came up with an ingenious idea to stall for time. The Bnei Yisroel asked the Egyptians for their precious clothes. By asking for clothes, the Bnei Yisroel could stall the Egyptians because even if they did bring them clothes, the Bnei Yisroel could complain that the clothes needed to be adjusted to fit or needed a different color. This request caused the Egyptians to frantically run around trying to fulfill the specifications of the Bnei Yisroel for clothes. Because of their request for clothes, the Bnei Yisroel managed to stall the Egyptians until morning when they were allowed to leave their houses to go out of Egypt. Hashem predicted this ingenuity to Moshe when he told Moshe at the beginning of his mission that the Bnei Yisroel would ask for expensive clothes from the Egyptians.

How Was a Sign for an Event That Would Only Happen in the Future a Proof Now to Moshe That Hashem Sent Him?

Shemos (3:11-12) But Moshe וַיֹּאמֶר מֹשֶׁה אֶל הָאֱלֹקִים מִי אָנֹכִי כִּי אֵלֵךְ אֶל פַּרְעֹה וְכִי אוֹצִיא אֶת בְּנֵי יִשְׂרָאֵל מִמִּצְרָיִם. וַיֹּאמֶר כִּי אֶהְיֶה עִמָּךְ וְזֶה לְךָ הָאוֹת כִּי אָנֹכִי שְׁלַחְתִּיךָ בְּהוֹצִיאֲךָ אֶת הָעָם מִמִּצְרַיִם תַּעַבְדוּן אֶת הָאֱלֹהִים עַל הָהָר הַזֶּה (ג:יא-יב)

Shemos

said to G-d, "Who am I that I should go to Pharaoh, and that I should take the Bnei Yisroel out of Egypt?" And He said, "For I will be with you, and this is the sign for you that it was I Who sent you, when you take the people out of Egypt, you will worship G-d on this mountain."

At first glance, the Pesukim seem to say that Hashem answers Moshe that the sign that Hashem sent him would be "when you take the people out of Egypt, you will worship G-d on this mountain." That being the case, how was a sign for an event that would only happen in the future a proof now to Moshe that Hashem sent him? The Alshich says that, in general, a sign is something that occurs now and is used to prove that something in the future will occur. This sign is different at first glance in that Hashem said that he would prove that he will be with Moshe from an event that would only happen in the future.

Introduction
Rashi, on our Pesukim, says that Moshe asked two questions. Moshe's first question when he said, "Who am I that I should go to Pharaoh," was, how was he an important enough person to speak with Kings? Moshe's second question when he said "that I should take the Bnei Yisroel out of Egypt" was that even if he was an important enough person to speak with Kings, what merit do the Bnei Yisroel have that miracles should be made for them and they should be redeemed from Egypt?

We note that Rashi is somewhat different from how the Shemos Raba (3:4) explains Moshe's two questions. The Shemos Raba (3:4) on these Pesukim says that Moshe's first question when he said, "Who am I that I should go to Pharaoh" was how was he going to be able to go to a place of robbers and murderers? Moshe's second question when he said "that I should take the Bnei Yisroel out of Egypt" was that even if he would successfully go and survive in Egypt, what merit do the Bnei Yisroel have that they should be able to be redeemed from Egypt? The Yepheh Toar on this Shemos Raba ponders the question of how Moshe, who was always the advocate for the Bnei Yisroel, could ask what merit the Bnei Yisroel have that they should be able to be redeemed from Egypt. He answers that when Hashem told him in the previous Posuk, "So now come, and I will send you to Pharaoh, and take My people, the Bnei Yisroel, out of Egypt," Moshe interpreted that Hashem was telling him that he, because of his own merits, should take the Bnei Yisroel out of Egypt. Otherwise, thought Moshe, if Hashem was taking the Bnei Yisroel out, Hashem would have said, "So now come, and I will send you to Pharaoh, and I will take My people, the Bnei Yisroel, out of Egypt." That being the case, Moshe, in his humility, said that he didn't have the merit to take the Bnei Yisroel out, and therefore he asked what merit the Bnei Yisroel had to redeem themselves from Egypt.

1) Rashi answers that our whole question is not a question at all. This type of answer can be appreciated from a story about the Beis HaLevi and his son Rav Chaim Soloveitchik. At one time, the Beis HaLevi was asked to explain the difference in Torah learning between him and his phenomenal son. He explained that when someone comes to ask him a question in Torah study, he contemplates the question and gives an explanation to answer the question. "I am happy," "because I have provided a good answer to the question, and the person who asked the question is happy because he asked a good question." However, when someone asks a question to my son, Rav

Shemos

Chaim, he is so sharp in his Torah knowledge that he quickly shows how the question is not a question at all. The Beis HaLevi continued, "Rav Chaim is not happy because he didn't give an answer to a worthwhile question and the person who asked the question is not happy because he didn't ask a worthwhile question."

Rashi divides up the answer that Hashem gave Moshe by saying that when Hashem said, "For I will be with you, and this is the sign for you that it was I Who sent you," is the answer to Moshe's first question. "When you take the people out of Egypt, you will worship G-d on this mountain," is the answer to Moshe's second question. Therefore, worshipping Hashem on this mountain was not the sign that Hashem was giving Moshe that Hashem sent Moshe and our question is not a question. Rashi explains that Hashem was referring to the burning bush that Moshe had just seen as the sign for Moshe that Hashem sent him. In a similar way that the bush does not get consumed when it does the mission of Hashem, so also Moshe will not get consumed or harmed when he goes to Egypt and Pharaoh on Hashem's mission. In terms of what merit the Bnei Yisroel have to be redeemed from Egypt, Hashem told Moshe that the merit is that they will agree to receive the Torah on this mountain of Hashem. Parenthetically the Maor VaShemesh says that Moshe was not worried in his first question about being physically harmed. Rather Moshe was worried that he might become haughty if he redeemed the Bnei Yisroel from Egypt, and therefore it was better to remain humble and not be the redeemer. Hashem showed Moshe with the bush that it is possible to have Hashem's Shechinah rest in it and still remain a lowly bush.

The Chasam Sofer says that it is interesting that besides this Posuk, no other mention of the fact that being redeemed from Egypt was for the purpose of accepting the Torah was made during the time the Bnei Yisroel were in Egypt. Yet the Shemos Raba (29:3) says that the entire purpose of redeeming the Bnei Yisroel from Egypt was so that we should accept Hashem and his Torah. He explains that as long as the Bnei Yisroel were slaves, it would not be a great accomplishment for the Bnei Yisroel to accept the Torah since they would reason that accepting Torah and Mitzvos was better than being slaves in Egypt. Therefore, Hashem waited until the Bnei Yisroel were completely free before offering them the Torah, so that accepting the Torah and Mitzvos was a great accomplishment. Hashem tells Moshe in our Posuk that the Bnei Yisroel will agree to receive the Torah, and therefore they already have this merit while they are still slaves in Egypt, though they will not even be offered the Torah until they are free.

2) The Ponim Yofos and Ksav Sofer answer our question similarly. When Moshe questioned his worthiness to redeem the Bnei Yisroel by, among other things saying "how he was not an important enough person to speak with Kings," Hashem told Moshe that this was the best qualification for being worthy of being the redeemer of the Bnei Yisroel. Only a very humble person who remained humble even when put into a position of leadership was qualified to lead the Bnei Yisroel. Hashem told Moshe that this is the reason that he caused his Shechinah now to rest in a lowly thorn bush since a thorn bush has no reason for haughtiness. Hashem showed Moshe how important humility is to be chosen by Hashem from the fact that "when you take the people out of Egypt, you will worship G-d on this mountain." The Gemorah in Sotah 5a says that when Hashem gave the Torah, Hashem did not choose any of the great mountains or hills but rather chose the less lofty and therefore

Shemos

humble Mount Sinai upon which to give the Torah. Similarly, the Gemorah says that when Hashem first spoke with Moshe, Hashem did not choose to rest his Shechinah in any of the fine trees but rather in a lowly thorn bush. The Gemorah in Megilah 29a tells how the majestic mountains pushed to have the Torah given on them, only to be told that because of their haughtiness, they are blemished in comparison with Mount Sinai. In a similar way, says the Gemorah, a haughty person is a blemished person. Therefore, the sign which Hashem gave Moshe of "when you take the people out of Egypt, you will worship G-d on this mountain" was an explanation for why Moshe was extremely qualified to be the emissary of Hashem and redeem the Bnei Yisroel from Egypt.

3) The Ksav Sofer does not prefer to be of the opinion like Rashi that in our Posuk, the phrase "this is the sign for you that it was I Who sent you" has nothing to do with "when you take the people out of Egypt, you will worship G-d on this mountain." He quotes the Shemos Raba (3:4) in what Moshe was saying when he said to Hashem מִי אָנֹכִי כִּי אֵלֵךְ אֶל פַּרְעֹה. It gives a Moshul to a King who promised to give a county and a well-pedigreed maidservant to his daughter when he married her off. Instead, when she actually got married, he gave her an un-pedigreed maidservant. When Yaakov went down to Egypt, Hashem said to him in Beraishis (46:4) אָנֹכִי אֵרֵד עִמְּךָ מִצְרַיְמָה וְאָנֹכִי אַעַלְךָ גַם עָלֹה "I (Hashem) will go down with you to Egypt, and I will also bring you up." The Ksav Sofer says that when Hashem told Avrohom about the Bnei Yisroel going into slavery for 400 years, Hashem says in Beraishis (15:14) וְגַם אֶת הַגּוֹי אֲשֶׁר יַעֲבֹדוּ דָּן אָנֹכִי (And also the nation that they will serve will I (Hashem) judge." Both of these Pesukim say that Hashem himself will judge the Egyptian and will redeem the Bnei Yisroel from Egypt, by referencing the Hebrew word אָנֹכִי as referring to Hashem. Therefore, says the Ksav Sofer, similar to the Moshul brought down by the Shemos Raba, when Moshe said in our Posuk מִי אָנֹכִי he was asking why Hashem was not redeeming the Bnei Yisroel himself as Hashem had promised. Moshe calculated that the reason Hashem wasn't redeeming the Bnei Yisroel himself was either because the Bnei Yisroel did not have the merit to be redeemed or because they had not spent 400 years in exile as Hashem had told Avrohom that they would. If the Bnei Yisroel did not meet these requirements, then even if Hashem in his mercy was ready to redeem the Bnei Yisroel anyway, Hashem was not required to redeem them himself.

The Ksav Sofer says that Hashem answered Moshe that he was correct that the Bnei Yisroel have neither the merit on their own nor had they been enslaved for 400 years. Therefore, Hashem was not required to redeem the Bnei Yisroel himself. As proof of this, Hashem said in our Posuk, "when you take the people out of Egypt, you will worship G-d on this mountain." Hashem says in the first Posuk of the Aseres HaDibros (Ten commandments) in Shemos (20:2) that the Bnei Yisroel are required to serve Hashem since, "I am Hashem, your G-d, Who took you out of the land of Egypt, out of the house of bondage." The Ksav Sofer ponders the following case. A person was convicted by the King and was sentenced to a standard prison term with no accommodations for any mercy, and the person served this sentence completely. Subsequently, the King demanded that the person be his slave forever and for all future generations because of the person's original crime. Though, unfortunately, such cases have happened historically, the King's subsequent demand is completely unjustified. Yet, Hashem sentenced us to slavery in Egypt and, upon being redeemed, told us that we are required to serve Hashem forever since "I am Hashem, your G-d, Who took you out of the land of Egypt, out of the house of bondage." The only rational explanation for Hashem's demand is

Shemos

the fact that either the Bnei Yisroel did not have the merit to be redeemed or because they had not spent 400 years in exile, as Hashem had told Avrohom that they would. When Hashem answered Moshe, "For I will be with you, and this is the sign for you that it was I Who sent you, when you take the people out of Egypt, you will worship G-d on this mountain," Hashem was explaining to Moshe why Hashem had chosen Moshe to redeem the people and Hashem had not redeemed them himself. The sign or the proof that Moshe was correct that the Bnei Yisroel had neither the merit to be redeemed nor had spent the entire time in Egypt they were required to was the fact that Hashem would require us to serve Hashem after we were redeemed when we stood on the mountain of G-d, Mount Sinai. According to this explanation, the "sign" was not a sign for the future but rather an explanation for answering Moshe's question now.

4) The Ksav Sofer offers another explanation of our question. The Shemos Raba (2:6) says that when Hashem first spoke to Moshe at the burning bush, Moshe took five steps forward to speak with Hashem. The Ksav Sofer says that these five steps refer to different levels of rising to the level of receiving prophecy, which Moshe was not at prior to this point. Since Moshe knew that he was not prepared for prophecy, Moshe asked מִי אָנֹכִי (Who am I) to get to this level of prophecy. Moshe also asked what merit the Bnei Yisroel had to be redeemed from Egypt. Hashem answered that in a similar way that you didn't refine yourself to receive prophecy but nevertheless, because of need I gave you prophesy so also the Bnei Yisroel who are currently sunk deep in many levels of spiritual uncleanliness I will also raise in spirituality to the point that they will, "worship G-d on this mountain." Therefore, the fact that you currently experienced quickly being raised to become a prophet is a sign that you should believe that the Bnei Yisroel will quickly rise in spirituality to be on the spiritual level to serve Hashem on Mount Sinai. This answers our question since, according to this explanation, the sign is from something that already happened already.

5) The Ksav Sofer presents another answer to our question. We can appreciate this answer better if we consider something the Chasam Sofer writes. Tehillim (105:28), describes the ninth plague of darkness and says שָׁלַח חֹשֶׁךְ וַיַּחְשִׁךְ וְלֹא מָרוּ אֶת דְּבָרוֹ (He (Hashem) sent darkness, and it darkened, and they did not disobey His word). The question that many commentators deal with is what is meant and who is being referred to by, "they did not disobey His word." He says that during the plague of darkness, the Egyptians sat in mortal fear of their lives. Had the Bnei Yisroel wanted to, they could have killed them all since the Egyptians could not see anything. They could also have taken any money or possessions they wanted to, and even more so, they could have easily escaped Egypt by just walking out with no fear of the Egyptians being able to chase them. He quotes the Targum Yonason ben Uziel on Beraishis (50:25) וַיַּשְׁבַּע יוֹסֵף אֶת בְּנֵי יִשְׂרָאֵל לֵאמֹר פָּקֹד יִפְקֹד אֱלֹקִים אֶתְכֶם (And Yosef made the Bnei Yisroel swear, saying, "G-d will surely remember you). The oath Yosef made the Bnei Yisroel take was that they would not leave Egypt until the true redeemer came and said the words פָּקֹד פָּקַדְתִּי. It is the Bnei Yisroel being referred to by Sefer Tehillim (105:28) that "they did not disobey His word," and instead held fast to the oath that they had undertaken to not leave Egypt unless under the direction of the redeemer.

The Ksav Sofer says that the Bnei Yisroel at that time in Egypt were very bad and sinful in their relationship with Hashem. The only good quality they had was that they were not ungrateful people,

Shemos

a quality that they showed to the Egyptians by not harming them either physically or financially during the plague of darkness. Consistent with this idea, we are told in Devorim (23:8), "You shall not despise an Egyptian, for you were a sojourner in his land." We must be grateful that, at least in the beginning, during the time of Yosef, the Egyptians were very welcoming of us living in their land. When Moshe asked Hashem, "why Moshe should take the Bnei Yisroel out of Egypt and, "what merit do the Bnei Yisroel have that they should be able to be redeemed from Egypt?" Hashem told Moshe about the quality of the Bnei Yisroel for being grateful. Since they were a grateful people, they would not on their own escape from Egypt even during the plague of darkness and therefore needed a leader to redeem them. This is especially true according to what we have brought from the Chasam Sofer that the Bnei Yisroel took an oath to this effect. Hashem impressed Moshe about the importance of being grateful when Hashem told Moshe, "when you take the people out of Egypt, you will worship G-d on this mountain." Because of the Bnei Yisroel's character of gratefulness, they will be grateful to Hashem for taking them out of Egypt, and therefore they will accept Hashem's Torah and will keep it, in the very least out of gratefulness to Hashem. According to this answer, the sign of what would happen at the mountain of Hashem was proof of why the Bnei Yisroel's character was so important and was not a sign for an event that would happen in the future.

Parenthetically we should mention that this explanation of the Ksav Sofer is consistent with a different explanation of his, which is found at the end of Parshas Beshalach. The Mechilta is the source of Rashi's statement at the beginning of Parshas Yisro that Yisro came to join the Bnei Yisroel because he heard about Kriyas Yam Suf (the splitting of the Red Sea) and the war against Amalek. Many commentators ponder the question of why it was specifically only these two miracles that caused Yisro to join the Bnei Yisroel instead of the many other miracles like being fed with the miraculous Mon and being covered and protected by the clouds of glory. The Ksav Sofer says that Yisro was bothered by how well the Bnei Yisroel would receive him. Hearing these two events, Yisro concluded that the Bnei Yisroel excelled in being grateful people. Therefore, they would accept Yisro warmly since Yisro gave refuge to Moshe in Midyan when he was a fugitive from Pharaoh, and the Bnei Yisroel would be very grateful for this. The way Yisro derived that the Bnei Yisroel were grateful people is by contrasting their behavior at Kriyas Yam Suf with their behavior of fighting a war with Amalek. At Kriyas Yam Suf, they were encircled with the Egyptian army boasting 600 chariots to their rear as we are told in Shemos (14:7) along with mountains to their sides and the Red Sea in front of them. Since they were in desperation of being killed by Pharaoh's army with no other possible non-miraculous escape, the Bnei Yisroel should have at least tried to attack Pharaoh's army, being that with 600,000 men of fighting age, the Bnei Yisroel had 1,000 soldiers for every Egyptian chariot. Since Yisro also heard that the Bnei Yisroel fought a war soon after this with Amalek, this fact showed Yisro that the Bnei Yisroel were not afraid to go to war when necessary. Putting the reaction of the Bnei Yisroel to these two events together showed Yisro that the only reason they did not attack the Egyptians was because of their great character of gratefulness. This character was so strong that even under threat of death, they did not attack and fight with the Egyptians.

6) The Ksav Sofer presents another answer to our question. We have mentioned in a previous answer of the Ksav Sofer that Moshe, when he said מִי אָנֹכִי was questioning why Hashem did not

Shemos

redeem the Bnei Yisroel himself as Hashem had promised to Avrohom and Yaakov. He here says that in truth, Hashem did redeem the Bnei Yisroel himself since the final plague, which freed them, the killing of the firstborn was done only by Hashem, as we especially emphasize in the Hagadah, which we say on Pesach. That being the case, we can ponder why Hashem just didn't do this plague alone and why there was a need for Moshe to go to Pharaoh and to have the first nine plagues. He says that the sign of "when you (Moshe) take the people out of Egypt, you will worship G-d on this mountain" was given by Hashem to answer Moshe's question of why there was a need for Moshe and why Hashem didn't just do the plague of killing the firstborns.

The Ksav Sofer ponders why Hashem didn't use either Aharon or one of the seventy elders to redeem the Bnei Yisroel from Egypt instead of Moshe. He explains that if Hashem had chosen one of these people who were already leaders of the Bnei Yisroel, there would have been a big argument since each of these leaders had their own segment of the Bnei Yisroel who wanted this person as their leader. An argument like this would have been very detrimental to all of the Bnei Yisroel accepting the Torah, which Hashem told Moshe was going to happen soon after they came out of Egypt. Accepting the Torah was, in fact, the essential reason why the Bnei Yisroel needed to be redeemed, and more importantly, it was their world mission to accomplish. It would be very detrimental if an already established leader of the Bnei Yisroel received the Torah because those wanting a different leader would refuse to accept the Torah since their leader was not chosen to receive it. Therefore, Hashem told Moshe that they needed a new leader who was not at all established and supported by anybody to redeem the Bnei Yisroel from Egypt. Then if the Bnei Yisroel accepted Moshe as their leader, everyone would accept him and, more importantly, the Torah. The only big issue was how to get the Bnei Yisroel to accept the leadership of Moshe. It was only by showing the people through the help of Hashem how Moshe made miracle after miracle and delivered plague after plague on the Egyptians that Moshe was accepted unanimously as the leader. That is why, explained Hashem to Moshe, Hashem could not just do the plague of killing the firstborn, which Hashem himself did and redeem the Bnei Yisroel out of Egypt. According to this answer, the sign is also just an explanation of why Hashem was appointing Moshe as the redeemer.

7) The Ksav Sofer presents another answer to our question. We have quoted in the introduction Rashi's opinion that Moshe's first question when he said, "Who am I that I should go to Pharaoh" was how he was an important enough person to speak with Kings? In addition to not being important, Moshe also says in Shemos (4:10), "I am not a man of words, neither from yesterday nor from the day before yesterday, nor from the time You have spoken to Your servant, for I am heavy of mouth and heavy of tongue." Hashem answered Moshe in our Pesukim, "For I will be with you." The Ksav Sofer explains that because Moshe could not speak well when he got to Egypt, it became obvious to everyone that he was the emissary of Hashem for two reasons. Firstly, especially in those times, someone who could not speak well would not come to meet with the King. Even if the King would grant such a person an audience, the King would soon decide that it was below the King's honor to grant such an unfit for conversation person an audience and would severely punish such a person for insulting the King's dignity and honor. Only a true emissary of Hashem would go to Pharaoh even if he was unfit to speak well. In addition, it would be ludicrous for the Bnei Yisroel

Shemos

to think that such a person could sway and convince Pharaoh through his mastery of words, so when Moshe was successful, it was obvious to the Bnei Yisroel that he was Hashem's emissary.

The Droshas HaRan (Drosha 5) says that the reason Hashem chose Moshe, who was unfit to speak well, to give the Torah was so that no one should be able to say that Moshe, because of his oratory skills, convinced the Bnei Yisroel to accept all the Mitzvos. Rather because Moshe was unfit to speak well, everyone knew that the Bnei Yisroel only accepted the Torah because they all saw Hashem appear on Mount Sinai and give them the Torah. He says that this was the reason Hashem did not cure Moshe of his problem speaking. With this as background, the Ksav Sofer explains that in our Posuk, Hashem tells Moshe that he will ensure that the Bnei Yisroel will know that Moshe is Hashem's emissary by not curing him. In addition, there was another reason that Hashem did not want to cure Moshe of his speech problems. The sign or reason for this is, "when you take the people out of Egypt; you will worship G-d on this mountain," and Hashem wanted everyone to know that the people accepted the Torah solely because of their belief in Hashem who appeared to them on Mount Sinai.

8) Rav Sternbuch, in his Sefer Taam V'Daas, also presents an answer to our question. He says that Moshe wanted that the Bnei Yisroel to get a definitive proof of Hashem being the master of the world through the redemption from Egypt. The Rambam in Hilchos Yesodei HaTorah, Chapter 7, says that the Bnei Yisroel did not fully believe in Hashem because of the miracles and wonders that Moshe performed. He explains that whenever anyone's belief is based on miracles or wonders, the commitment of his heart has shortcomings because it is possible to perform a miracle through sorcery. He says that all the miracles which Moshe performed in the desert were not to prove his prophecy but rather because there was a need for that miracle at that time. An example of this is when Moshe split the sea to save the Bnei Yisroel from the Egyptians. True belief in Hashem only occurred when our own eyes and our own ears heard Hashem say to Moshe, go tell the Bnei Yisroel this and that. What made us believe in Hashem was what Devorim (5:4) says, "Face to face, Hashem spoke with you (Bnei Yisroel) at the mountain out of the midst of the fire." Rav Sternbuch uses this Rambam to explain what our Posuk means when it says, "this is the sign for you that it was I Who sent you, when you take the people out of Egypt, you will worship G-d on this mountain." Hashem told Moshe that the Bnei Yisroel would not receive a definitive proof of Hashem being the master of the world through the redemption from Egypt, despite all the signs and miracles Moshe will do for the Bnei Yisroel. Only the sign at Mount Sinai will give the Bnei Yisroel definitive proof in Hashem, something no other religion or nation can claim to have.

How Was Saying the Words פָּקֹד פָּקַדְתִּי a Proof That Moshe Was the Redeemer?

לֵךְ וְאָסַפְתָּ אֶת זִקְנֵי יִשְׂרָאֵל וְאָמַרְתָּ אֲלֵהֶם ה' אֱלֹקֵי אֲבֹתֵיכֶם נִרְאָה אֵלַי אֱלֹקֵי אַבְרָהָם יִצְחָק וְיַעֲקֹב לֵאמֹר פָּקֹד פָּקַדְתִּי אֶתְכֶם וְאֶת הֶעָשׂוּי לָכֶם בְּמִצְרָיִם (ג:טז) Shemos (3:16) Go and assemble the elders of Yisroel, and say to them, "Hashem, G-d of your forefathers has appeared to me, the G-d of Avrohom, Yitzchak, and Yaakov, saying, I have surely remembered you and what is being done to you in Egypt."

Shemos

How was saying the words פָּקֹד פָּקַדְתִּי a proof that Moshe was the redeemer? As the Ramban asks, "How did they know Moshe wasn't just saying the words that he heard the redeemer was supposed to say?"

The Midrash Tanchuma in Shemos (24) says that the sign of the redeemer was known by Avrohom and Yitzchak, who passed it down to Yaakov. Yaakov passed the sign to Yosef, who told them (ostensibly the Bnei Yisroel) that any redeemer who will come and say the words פָּקֹד פָּקַדְתִּי is the true redeemer.

Shemos (3:13) says, And Moshe said to Hashem, "Behold I come to the Bnei Yisroel, and I say to them, 'The G-d of your fathers has sent me to you,' and they say to me, 'What is His name?' what shall I say to them?" In the next Posuk, Hashem tells Moshe what name to use to show the Bnei Yisroel that he is the redeemer. The Rambam in Moreh Nevuchim (1:63) ponders how telling them this name of Hashem is any proof that Moshe was the redeemer. The Rambam says that either the Bnei Yisroel knew this name would be used to redeem the Bnei Yisroel beforehand or did not know it. If they did know it, then the same way they knew it would be the same way that Moshe knew it, and therefore what proof is it for Moshe to tell them this name of Hashem? If the Bnei Yisroel didn't know this name, then again, what proof is it if Moshe uses this name? We can apply this analysis of the Rambam similarly to Moshe proving to the Bnei Yisroel that he is the redeemer by saying the words פָּקֹד פָּקַדְתִּי.

The Maharal, in Gur Aryeh, explains why the sign was to essentially double over the words and say פָּקֹד פָּקַדְתִּי. He says that the word פָּקֹד (to remember) can either be used in a good or a bad context. For example, the Posuk used the word פָּקֹד for good when it says in Beraishis (21:1) וַה' פָּקַד אֶת שָׂרָה (And Hashem remembered Sorah [and she became pregnant with Yitzchak]). Shemos (34:7), uses the word פָּקֹד for bad when it says פֹּקֵד עֲוֹן אָבוֹת עַל בָּנִים וְעַל בְּנֵי בָנִים עַל שִׁלֵּשִׁים וְעַל רִבֵּעִים (He (Hashem) remembers the sins of parents on children and children's children, to the third and fourth generations). The Maharal says that the redemption from Egypt will involve both good and bad. Hashem will remember the Bnei Yisroel for good and redeem them from Egypt while remembering the Egyptians for bad and punishing them severely for their actions against the Bnei Yisroel.

The Oznayim LeTorah points out that for the exile in Egypt, not only were we given the number of years it would take but we were also given a sign to know who the true redeemer would be. In contrast, in the exile, which we currently find ourselves, we not only do not know how long the exile will be but we were also not given a sign to know who the true redeemer will be. It is no wonder that we have had several false redeemers during this exile. May the true redeemer come speedily in our days.

1) Pirkei D'Rabi Eliezer (48) and the Shemos Raba (5:13) present an answer to our question. They say that the sign that the redeemer would say פָּקֹד פָּקַדְתִּי was given to Avrohom. Avrohom gave over the sign to Yitzchak, Yitzchak to Yaakov, Yaakov to Yosef, Yosef to his brothers, and Asher gave the sign over to his daughter Serach. When Moshe and Aharon came and did the signs in front of them, the elders of the Bnei Yisroel went to Serach and told them that two people came (Moshe and

Shemos

Aharon) and did these signs in front of us. Serach told them these signs do not mean anything with regard to them being the true redeemers. They then told Serach that they (Moshe and Aharon) also said the words פָּקֹד פָּקַדְתִּי. Serach told them, "If they told you those words, then they are the true people who have come to redeem the Bnei Yisroel." This is what caused what Shemos (4:31) tells us, "And the people believed, and they heard that Hashem had remembered the Bnei Yisroel, and they kneeled and prostrated themselves."

When the Bnei Yisroel went down to Egypt, we know that Serach was alive as Beraishis (46:17) says, "And the sons of Asher were Yimnah, Yishvah, Yishvi, and Briah, and Serach, their sister; and the sons of Briah were Chever and Malkiel." When the Bnei Yisroel were counted in the 40th year in the desert, Bamidbar (26:46) says that Serach was still alive. Since the Bnei Yisroel also spent 210 in Egypt, that means that Serach was at least 250 years old in the 40th year of the Bnei Yisroel being in the desert.

The Beraishis Raba (94:9) tells us that Serach was alive during the times of Dovid HaMelech, which is approximately 400 years after the Bnei Yisroel came into Eretz Yisroel. The Gemorah in Sanhedrim 38a is the source of Rashi in Devorim (4:25), telling us that the Bnei Yisroel spent 850 years in Eretz Yisroel before the destruction of the first Beis Hamikdosh. Rashi on the Gemorah points out that Sefer Melachim I (6:1) says, "And it was in the four hundred and eightieth year after the departure of the Bnei Yisroel from Egypt, in the fourth year, in the month of Ziv, and the second month of Shlomo's reign over Israel, that he did (begin to) build the house of Hashem." Since the Bnei Yisroel spent forty years in the desert, the Posuk implies that the Bnei Yisroel started building the Beis Hamikdosh 440 years after they came to Eretz Yisroel. Since this was the fourth year of Shlomo's reign as King, and Shlomo took over the kingship after Dovid was Niftar implies that Dovid HaMelech was Niftar 436 years after the Bnei Yisroel came into Eretz Yisroel.

The Pesukim in Sefer Shmuel II, chapters 19 and 20, describe how Dovid returned to Yerushalayim after the revolt of Avshalom, Dovid's son, was defeated. Dovid had been forced to flee to the other side of the Jordan River during the revolution. Dovid's tribe of Yehuda accompanied Dovid across the Jordan River to return to Yerushalayim. After they crossed the Jordan River, a large delegation of all the other tribes of the Bnei Yisroel came to greet them to show that they also supported Dovid being King. A debate broke out over why only the tribe of Yehuda accompanied Dovid with the other tribes of the Bnei Yisroel, saying that they also wanted to take part in the honor. While this debate was going on in the process of Dovid's returning to Yerushalayim, a person called Sheva ben Bichri from the tribe of Binyamin said that since Dovid chose to go back with people of his own tribe, there was no reason for people of other tribes to support Dovid. This message resonated with the people of the other tribes, and Dovid knew that if he didn't kill Sheva ben Bichri immediately he would have an even bigger revolution on his hands than had happened during the time of Avshalom. With Dovid's general Yoav in pursuit, Sheva ben Bichri ran to the walled city of Avel in Beis Maaca to save himself. Not to be outdone, Yoav besieged the city and began erecting a large mound of dirt in front of the wall so that they could get into the city. When they were getting ready to enter the city, a wise woman from the city called out to Yoav and said that she wanted to speak with him. The wise woman pointed out to Yoav that had he first asked the people of the city of Avel to make

Shemos

peace with him, they would have made peace since the people of the city are supporters of Dovid. "This would be much better than your current plan to wipe out an entire city," argued the wise woman. Yoav answered the wise woman that "if you just give us Sheva ben Bichri, I will immediately end the siege of the city and leave." The wise woman went to the people of the city and convinced them to cut off Sheva ben Bichri's head, which they threw out to Yoav, prompting Yoav to leave and go back to Yerushalayim.

In describing herself to Yoav, the wise woman said in Sefer Melachim II (20:19): אָנֹכִי שְׁלֻמֵי אֱמוּנֵי יִשְׂרָאֵל. The simple translation of this phrase is: "I am of the city which is peaceful and faithful to Yisroel." The Beraishis Raba (94:9) says that this wise woman was Serach, the daughter of Asher. The reason she called herself שְׁלֻמֵי is because she completed the seventy people who went down to Egypt. It is of the opinion that the root of שְׁלֻמֵי is שָׁלֵם (complete). It says that Serach told Yoav that both he and his master Dovid were wrong in how they acted since the Torah says in Devorim (20:10), "When you approach a city to wage war against it, you shall propose peace to it." Seeing that the woman had talked to him in a haughty manner, Yoav asked her who she was. To this, she answered אָנֹכִי שְׁלֻמֵי אֱמוּנֵי יִשְׂרָאֵל, meaning, I am the one who completed the seventy people, and I am the one who completed the directive of one trustworthy person (Yosef) to another trustworthy person (Moshe). Serach taught the people a Halachic point, which they did not realize when they didn't immediately give Yoav, Sheva ben Bichri. Serach taught them that if there was a group of people who Gentiles came to and said that unless you give us one of your group, we will kill all of you, then they are not allowed to choose that one person from their group and give that person to the Gentiles. The reason is that the blood of the person they choose is not cheaper than any of the other people's blood. Instead, they must face the consequences of all of them getting killed. However, if the Gentiles specified the person (as in this case with Sheva ben Bichri), then they are allowed to hand over the person. It further clarifies that one can only give over this person if both they and the person are trapped inside the city such that they will all be killed if they don't hand over the person. However, if they are outside the city and the specified person is inside the city, then they are not allowed to hand over the specified person since it is quite possible that they will escape being they are not trapped in the city. Based on this Halachic argument, Serach convinced the people of the city to hand over Sheva ben Bichri to Yoav.

In the Beraishis Raba, we have just quoted, Serach describes herself as "I am the one who completed the directive of one trustworthy person (Yosef) to another trustworthy person (Moshe)." The Radal says that the reason Yosef is described as a trustworthy person is because Yosef brought all the money that he collected to Pharaoh as Beraishis (47:14) says, "And Yosef collected all the money that was found in the land of Egypt and in the land of Canaan with the grain that they were buying, and Yosef brought the money into Pharaoh's house." The Tanah D'Bay Eliyahu Raba (25) also says this about Yosef. With regard to Moshe, the Matnos Kehunah points out that the Torah itself testifies that Moshe was trustworthy, as Bamidbar (12:7) says, "he (Moshe) is faithful throughout My (Hashem's) house." Before Yosef was Niftar, Beraishis (50:25) says that he made the Bnei Yisroel swear that "you shall take up my bones out of here (Egypt)." The Maharzav and Matnos Kehunah both say that Serach completed this directive of Yosef by telling Moshe where Yosef was buried.

Shemos

Shemos (13:19) says, "Moshe took Yosef's bones with him, for he (Yosef) had made the Bnei Yisroel swear, saying, Hashem will surely remember you, and you shall bring up my bones from here with you." The Gemorah in Sotah 13a and the Mechilta on Shemos (13:19) tell us details of how Moshe found Yosef's bones right before they left Egypt. The Gemorah and Mechilta say that since Moshe knew that Serach was still alive, he went to her and asked her where Yosef was buried. Serach told Moshe that the Egyptians made a metal coffin for Yosef and put it into the Nile River so that the water of the Nile River would be blessed. Rashi on the Gemorah explains that it hardly rains in Egypt, and Egypt depends on the Nile River to overflow its banks to irrigate the crops. Rashi also explains that the Egyptians built channels in the ground to route the overflowing water so that the water would get to as many fields as possible. However, Moshe had a problem in that the metal coffin was sunk in the Nile River, so he had to figure out a way to get it. The Gemorah and Mechilta continue and says that Moshe stood on the banks of the Nile River where Serach showed him Yosef's coffin was put and announced, "Yosef, Yosef, the time about which Hashem swore that he would redeem the Jews has arrived and therefore the time for the fulfillment of the oath that you made the Bnei Yisroel swear has also arrived. If you show yourself now, then we will take you with us, and if not, we are absolved of your oath." The Gemorah and Mechilta say that Yosef's coffin immediately floated up to the surface of the Nile River.

The Gemorah and Mechilta also present Rav Noson's account of how Moshe found Yosef's bones. Rav Noson says that the Egyptians made an above-ground burial place where their Kings were buried together. Again, Moshe had no way of knowing where Yosef was buried since there was no signage. Standing near the graves, Moshe asked Yosef to identify himself using the same statement that the Gemorah and Mechilta previously said that Moshe used at the Nile River. Immediately after making the statement, Yosef's coffin started shaking so that Moshe could identify it. We note that the Shemos Raba (20:19) also brings these two versions of where Yosef was buried and says that Serach pointed these places out to Moshe.

The Devorim Raba (11:7) says that Moshe looked everywhere for three days and three nights to try and find Yosef's bones so that he could fulfill Yosef's oath. After three days and three nights, Serach saw Moshe and recognized that he was very tired from exhausting work. After Serach inquired of why Moshe looked so tired, Moshe informed her that he had been looking without success for three days and three nights for the bones of Yosef. Serach told Moshe to come with her, and she would show him where Yosef's bones were. She brought Moshe to a place along the banks of the Nile River and informed Moshe that this was the place where they made an extremely heavy coffin and sunk it into the Nile River. Serach told Moshe that the Egyptians did this to prevent the Bnei Yisroel from ever being redeemed from Egypt since they know of the oath that Yosef made the Bnei Yisroel swear to take his bones with them. The Devorim Raba says that Moshe told Yosef to use the merit of his good deeds, which he had done while alive, to daven that he be brought up from the depths of the Nile River and allow the Bnei Yisroel to be redeemed. Immediately after these words, Yosef's coffin began rising up to the surface of the Nile River. As a reward for Moshe spending all this time looking for Yosef's bones instead of joining with the Bnei Yisroel to gather riches before they left Egypt, Moshe was rewarded with Hashem himself burying Moshe.

Shemos

From the above discussion, we see that Serach lived for about 650 years. The Targum Yonason ben Uziel on Beraishis (46:17) says that because Serach was the one who informed Yaakov that Yosef was still alive and gave him back his life, Serach merited to be taken alive into Gan Eden (and only know life). The Braisah is Meseches Derech Eretz Zutah (1) says that only nine people in world history merited to be taken into Gan Eden while they were still alive, and one of the nine people was Serach, the daughter of Asher. The Braisah in Meseches Kallah (3) says that only seven people in world history merited to be taken into Gan Eden while they were still alive, and one of the seven people was Serach.

Tosfos in Sotah 13a ponders the question of why Moshe didn't ask either Mochir or Yair, both sons of Menashe, where Yosef was buried. Beraishis (50:23) tells us that even Mochir's sons were born while Yosef was still alive. In Bamidbar (32:40-41), we are told that both Mochir and Yair were alive in the fortieth year in the desert when Moshe gave them inheritance on the other side of the Jordan River. Therefore, they were obviously also alive forty years earlier when the Bnei Yisroel were being redeemed from Egypt. He answers that they had lost trust with the leaders of Yosef's family since they had previously miscalculated the time of redemption and a great tragedy occurred. The Gemorah in Sanhedrin 92b references Divrei HaYomim I (7:21), which says that the children of Ephraim went out of Egypt to Eretz Yisroel and were killed by the Philistines. Rashi explains that the reason they went out early is that they calculated that the 400 years of Egyptian exile prophesized by Avrohom began when the prophecy was given at the Bris Bain HaBesorim. In reality, the 400-year exile started with the birth of Yitzchak 30 years later. In addition, Tosfos quotes the Pirkei D'Rabi Eliezer (48), which we have quoted previously, which says that the secret phrase of the redeemer was given to Serach and not to Mochir and Yair. For both these reasons, Moshe chose to trust in and ask Serach where Yosef was buried. The Tosfos Shantz points out that according to the Devorim Raba (11:7), which says that Serach met Moshe after he tried for three days and nights to find Yosef on his own, the question of why Moshe didn't go to Mochir or Yair instead of Serach is not a question, since Moshe did not go to anybody.

We should also contemplate the greatness of Serach by the fact that the people immediately believed her that Moshe was the redeemer because he used the words פָּקֹד פָּקַדְתִּי and that she was entrusted with this sign. As we have mentioned previously, the nation endured a great tragedy only thirty years beforehand when the children of Ephraim left at the wrong time and were all killed by the Philistines. The Pesiktah Raba (15), along with the Radal on the Pirkei D'Rabi Eliezer, point out that the Bnei Yisroel now thought that since they had only been in Egypt for 210 years, that they had to wait until they were in Egypt for 400 years as Beraishis (15:13) says. Only the greatness of Serach and the sign that she had received persuaded them that now was the true time of the redemption.

2) The Shemos Raba (5:2) is the source of the answer which the Ramban presents to our question. It says that Moshe was only twelve years old when he was forced to leave Egypt. The Yepheh Toar and Matos Kehunah say that the Shemos Raba derived this from when the quarreling Jew (Dasan) said to Moshe in Shemos (2:14), "Who made you a man, a prince, and a judge over us?" Since

Shemos

Dasan accused Moshe of not even being a "man," which one only becomes when one turns thirteen, we can derive that Moshe was only twelve. The Shemos Raba ponders why Moshe had to be sent in exile out of Egypt at such an age and concludes that Hashem orchestrated this so that he would be too young to know the sign of פָּקֹד פָּקַדְתִּי.

Parenthetically this Shemos Raba is of the opinion that Yosef gave the sign to Levi, Levi to his son Kehas, and Kehas to his son Amram, and therefore these were the only people who knew the sign (and not Serach). In Bamidbar Raba (13:2), the Midrash tells us that when Odom sinned, Hashem's Shechinah distanced itself from this world up to the first heaven. When Kayin sinned by killing his brother Hevel, Hashem distanced himself further from this world by going up to the second heaven. When the generation of Enosh started serving idols for the first time in the world's existence, Hashem distanced himself to the third heaven. When the generation of the flood sinned, Hashem went to the fourth heaven. When the generation of the tower of Bavel sinned, Hashem distanced himself to the fifth heaven. When the people of Sidom sinned, Hashem went to the sixth heaven, and when the people of Egypt sinned with their immorality, Hashem went to the seventh heaven. It continues that seven righteous people then came and brought the Shechinah back to this world. Avrohom, Yitzchak, and Yaakov respectively brought the Shechinah down to the sixth, to the fifth, and to the fourth heaven. Levi brought the Shechinah down to the third heaven, and his son Kehas brought the Shechinah to the second heaven. Kehas' son Amrom brought the Shechinah down to the first heaven, and Amrom's son Moshe brought the Shechinah to this world where it rested in the Mishkan. From this Midrash, we see that Levi, Kehas, and Amrom were the righteous people of their respective generations, and it is not surprising that the Shemos Raba on our Pesukim says that the sign of פָּקֹד פָּקַדְתִּי was handed down to these righteous people. Since the sign was only handed down from one righteous person to the next, the Yepheh Toar explains that one had to be at least Bar Mitzvah to show that one had the righteousness to be given such a sign. The Maharzav says that the sign was only handed over privately when one was on one's death bed so that Amram, when Moshe was only twelve, would not yet have handed over the signs. I do not fully understand, according to the Maharzav, why Moshe had to go into exile when he was only twelve years old, since, according to the Maharzav, he would not have been given the sign until Amram was on his death bed.

3) The Ramban presents another answer to our question. He says that it was revealed through Yaakov's prophesy that no one would come and falsely claim to be the redeemer and only the true redeemer would say the words פָּקֹד פָּקַדְתִּי. The Maharal, in Gur Aryeh, vehemently argues with the Ramban's answer since such a prophecy would violate the principle of free will, which is given to everyone, thereby allowing someone to falsely claim that they are the redeemer if they so desired. The Maharal says that the concept of free will is the reason that Devorim (18:21) says that when a prophet comes, one will question, "How will we know the word that Hashem did not speak?" Otherwise, Hashem could just cause all prophets to speak the truth.

4) The Maharal, in Gur Aryeh, also presents an answer to our question. He says that the sign of saying the words פָּקֹד פָּקַדְתִּי was not proof that the person saying this was the true redeemer. All the sign did was cause the people to listen and take heed of what the person said, but it was not definitive proof. To prove this, he points out that after Hashem told Moshe to use the words פָּקֹד

Shemos

פָּקַדְתִּי in Shemos (3:16), He assures Moshe in Shemos (3:18) וְשָׁמְעוּ לְקֹלֶךָ (And they will listen to your voice). Despite this assurance, Moshe still says in Shemos (4:1) וְהֵן לֹא יַאֲמִינוּ לִי וְלֹא יִשְׁמְעוּ בְּקֹלִי כִּי יֹאמְרוּ לֹא נִרְאָה אֵלֶיךָ ה' (Behold they will not believe me, and they will not heed my voice, but they will say, "Hashem has not appeared to you").

If we combine a point that the Malbim makes with the answer of the Maharal, we may appreciate this answer even more. The Malbim observes that Hashem told Moshe וְשָׁמְעוּ לְקֹלֶךָ and despite this, Moshe says וְלֹא יִשְׁמְעוּ בְּקֹלִי. At first glance, it would seem that Moshe is, Chas VeShalom, contradicting Hashem with Hashem saying that they will "listen to your voice" and Moshe saying that they "will not listen to my voice." However, if we look closely, Hashem described the listening using the Hebrew letter Lamed when Hashem said וְשָׁמְעוּ לְקֹלֶךָ and Moshe used the letter Beis when he said וְלֹא יִשְׁמְעוּ בְּקֹלִי. The Malbim says that when one uses the letter Lamed and says וְשָׁמְעוּ לְקֹלֶךָ, one is saying that they will listen to what you have to say but will not necessarily believe what you say and/or do what you say. However, if one instead says וְשָׁמְעוּ בקולך, it means that not only will they listen, but they will also believe and/or do what you say. When Moshe said וְלֹא יִשְׁמְעוּ בְּקֹלִי, he is saying that the Bnei Yisroel will not believe what he has to say. Hashem says that פָּקֹד פָּקַדְתִּי will only cause the Bnei Yisroel to listen but not necessarily believe what Moshe is saying.

5) The Oznayim LeTorah also presents an answer to our question. He points out that the Hebrew word פָּקֹד can have two connotations. We have previously quoted Beraishis (21:1) וַה' פָּקַד אֶת שָׂרָה where the Hebrew word פָּקֹד means to remember. In Bamidbar (3:15), the Hebrew word פָּקֹד means to count as the Torah says פְּקֹד אֶת בְּנֵי לֵוִי לְבֵית אֲבֹתָם לְמִשְׁפְּחֹתָם (Count the children of Levi according to their fathers' house according to their families). He says that the sign of the words פָּקֹד פָּקַדְתִּי is that the redeemer of the Bnei Yisroel will tell them the exact number of the Bnei Yisroel in Egypt without the need of a census since Hashem will give the redeemer this number through prophecy. This is quite a certain sign that this was the true redeemer sent from Hashem. With this explanation, he answers the question of when a census was taken such that Shemos (12:37) could say, "The Bnei Yisroel journeyed from Rameses to Succos, about six hundred thousand on foot, the men, besides the young children." The Pirkei D'Rabi Eliezer (39) says that this was a very exact count since Hashem joined with the count to give a count of exactly 600,000. Only with the numerical inclusion of Hashem did the Bnei Yisroel have the required amount of people to be redeemed from Egypt. The redeemer telling the Bnei Yisroel the exact count of the Bnei Yisroel served another purpose. We have previously quoted the Pesiktah Raba (15), which says the Bnei Yisroel were afraid that since they had only been in Egypt for 210 years, that they had to wait until they were in Egypt for 400 years. By informing the Bnei Yisroel that their population had "exploded" from seventy people to 600,000 people in only 210 years, Moshe was also telling them that they could be redeemed early. The reason is that the vast number of the Bnei Yisroel had performed all the slavery that was decreed to be done in Egypt in a shorter amount of time.

We can appreciate this answer of the Oznayim LeTorah even more if we consider what the Malbim says in Sefer Shmuel II (24:1). He points out that there are four Hebrew words to describe counting, Sefirah, Meniah, Pekidah, and Nosoh. The Torah uses Sefirah when we count each object, one by one, such as in the days of Sefiras HaOmer, where we count each day that passes, day by day. That

Shemos

is why the Torah, when referring to Sefiras HaOmer, says in Vayikra (23:15) **וּסְפַרְתֶּם** לָכֶם מִמָּחֳרַת הַשַּׁבָּת מִיּוֹם הֲבִיאֲכֶם אֶת עֹמֶר הַתְּנוּפָה שֶׁבַע שַׁבָּתוֹת תְּמִימֹת תִּהְיֶינָה (And you shall count for yourselves, from the morrow of the rest day from the day you bring the Omer as a wave offering seven weeks; they shall be complete). The Torah uses Meniyah when we are counting to determine if we have, or still have, a certain number that we are looking for. When Hashem wants to make sure that all the stars that were there are still there, Sefer Tehillim (147:4) says, **מוֹנֶה** מִסְפָּר לַכּוֹכָבִים לְכֻלָּם שֵׁמוֹת יִקְרָא (He (Hashem) counts the number of the stars; He calls them all by name). As another example, we use the word Minyan to see if we have at least ten people. The Torah uses Pekidah if all we are interested in is the total count or bottom line, as an accountant would say. An example is when the total number of the Bnei Yisroel that were counted is given in Bamidbar (1:46) וַיִּהְיוּ כָּל **הַפְּקֻדִים** שֵׁשׁ מֵאוֹת אֶלֶף וּשְׁלֹשֶׁת אֲלָפִים וַחֲמֵשׁ מֵאוֹת וַחֲמִשִּׁים (The sum of all those who were counted: six hundred and three thousand, five hundred and fifty). Finally, the Torah uses the term Nosoh to count and assign people to a position or task of honor. For example, Parshas Nosoh begins with the Posuk **נָשֹׂא** אֶת רֹאשׁ בְּנֵי גֵרְשׁוֹן גַּם הֵם לְבֵית אֲבֹתָם לְמִשְׁפְּחֹתָם (Take a census of the sons of Gershon, of them too, following their fathers' houses, according to their families). With this understanding of the Malbim, the answer of the Oznayim LeTorah makes a lot of sense as to why the sign used the words פָּקֹד פָּקַדְתִּי to describe Moshe telling them the exact bottom line of how many people there were in the Bnei Yisroel at that time.

6) Rav Sternbuch, in his Sefer Taam V'Daas, also ponders our question. Similar to the Maharal, he says that using the words פָּקֹד פָּקַדְתִּי is not a sure sign that one is the redeemer. Rather using the words is like a "knock" on the heart of the Bnei Yisroel. Only if the person using the words is the true redeemer will Hashem cause the hearts of the Bnei Yisroel to truly believe the one who uses the words. In effect, Hashem will send the redeemer with an aura, which will cause the people to believe in him. He compares this to the first Posuk in Parshas Yisro, which says, "Now Moshe's father-in-law, Yisro, the priest of Midyan, heard all that Hashem had done for Moshe and for Yisroel, His people, that Hashem had taken Yisroel out of Egypt." Many people heard exactly the same thing Yisro heard, but only Yisro heard the news and was inspired to come and join the Bnei Yisroel.

How Could Moshe Say the Bnei Yisroel Will Not Listen to Him After Hashem Promised They Would?

Shemos (4:1) וַיַּעַן מֹשֶׁה וַיֹּאמֶר וְהֵן לֹא יַאֲמִינוּ לִי וְלֹא יִשְׁמְעוּ בְּקֹלִי כִּי יֹאמְרוּ לֹא נִרְאָה אֵלֶיךָ ה' (ד:א) Moshe answered and said, "Behold they will not believe me, and they will not heed my voice," but they will say, "Hashem has not appeared to you."

In Shemos (3:18) it says וְשָׁמְעוּ לְקֹלֶךָ וּבָאתָ אַתָּה וְזִקְנֵי יִשְׂרָאֵל אֶל מֶלֶךְ מִצְרַיִם וַאֲמַרְתֶּם אֵלָיו ה' אֱלֹקֵי הָעִבְרִיִּים נִקְרָה עָלֵינוּ וְעַתָּה נֵלֲכָה נָּא דֶּרֶךְ שְׁלֹשֶׁת יָמִים בַּמִּדְבָּר וְנִזְבְּחָה לַה' אֱלֹקֵינוּ (And they will hearken to your (Moshe's) voice, and you shall come, you and the elders of Yisroel, to the King of Egypt, and you shall say to him, "Hashem, G-d of the Hebrews has happened upon us, and now, let us go for a three days' journey in the desert and offer up sacrifices to Hashem, our G-d." This Posuk would seem to indicate that Hashem promised Moshe that they would listen to Moshe. How then could Moshe

Shemos

later in the same prophesy with Hashem say in our Shemos (4:1), "Behold they will not believe me, and they will not heed my voice?"

Introduction

The Gemorah in Shabbos 97a quotes Raish Lokesh, who says החושד בכשרים - לוקה בגופו (one who suspects innocent people is punished by being punished in his body). The proof is from our Posuk where Moshe says וְהֵן לֹא יַאֲמִינוּ לִי (and they will not believe me). Hashem answered Moshe that the Bnei Yisroel are believers who are the children of believers, while Moshe will ultimately fail to believe. The Gemorah explains that we know the Bnei Yisroel did believe Moshe as Shemos (4:31) says, וַיַּאֲמֵן הָעָם וַיִּשְׁמְעוּ כִּי פָקַד ה' אֶת בְּנֵי יִשְׂרָאֵל וְכִי רָאָה אֶת עָנְיָם וַיִּקְּדוּ וַיִּשְׁתַּחֲווּ (And the people believed, and they heard that Hashem had remembered the Bnei Yisroel, and they kneeled and prostrated themselves). The Gemorah says that we also know the Bnei Yisroel are children of believers because it says about Avrohom in Beraishis (15:6): וְהֶאֱמִן בַּה' (And he believed in Hashem). However, the Gemorah says that Moshe will fail to believe as Bamidbar (20:12) says, וַיֹּאמֶר ה' אֶל מֹשֶׁה וְאֶל אַהֲרֹן יַעַן לֹא הֶאֱמַנְתֶּם בִּי לְהַקְדִּישֵׁנִי לְעֵינֵי בְּנֵי יִשְׂרָאֵל (Hashem said to Moshe and Aharon, "Since you did not have belief in Me to sanctify Me in the eyes of the Bnei Yisroel"). The Gemorah continues and explains how we know that Moshe was punished in his body for this sin. Shemos (4:6) says וַיֹּאמֶר ה' לוֹ עוֹד הָבֵא נָא יָדְךָ בְּחֵיקֶךָ וַיָּבֵא יָדוֹ בְּחֵיקוֹ וַיּוֹצִאָהּ וְהִנֵּה יָדוֹ מְצֹרַעַת כַּשָּׁלֶג (And Hashem said further to him (Moshe), "Now put your hand into your bosom," and he put his hand into his bosom, and he took it out, and behold, his hand was leprous like snow).

The Chasam Sofer on this Gemorah explains the severity of the punishment of someone who suspects innocent people. The Vayikra Raba (17:4) tells us that Hashem, being merciful, first punishes one's possessions before punishing one's body. It proves this by showing that this was the way that Iyov was punished. For all other sins, Hashem being merciful first punishes one's possessions before putting a punishment on one's body. The reason for this is because Hashem judges the person favorably that the person will do Teshuva when the person sees his possessions being punished. Since the point of a punishment is so that the person does Teshuva, this person will have a chance to atone for his sin and do Teshuva without his body being punished. However, someone who suspects innocent people and does not judge them favorably is not worthy for Hashem to judge favorably that the person will do Teshuva. If the person is suspected that he will not do Teshuva, then there is no reason to punish his possessions, which will typically be handed down to his inheritors, who may well be righteous. Therefore, such a person is punished in his body. The Chasam Sofer compares this to the case of an informer where we Paskin in Shulchan Aruch, Choshen Mishpot (388:13) that one is prohibited from directly destroying his property since it is possible that the informer will have righteous children who will inherit him. This Halacha about his property is in contrast to the Halacha that we can even kill an informer who is on his way to inform if we can only prevent his plan by killing him.

In Devorim (31:14), Hashem tells Moshe הֵן קָרְבוּ יָמֶיךָ לָמוּת קְרָא אֶת יְהוֹשֻׁעַ וְהִתְיַצְּבוּ בְּאֹהֶל מוֹעֵד וַאֲצַוֶּנּוּ (Behold, your days are approaching for you to die. Call Yehoshua and stand in the Tent of Meeting, and I will inspire him). The Devorim Raba (9:6) ponders the question of why the decree that Moshe should die was communicated to him using the word הֵן (behold). It explains the answer by using a

Shemos

Moshul to someone who honored the King by bringing him a present of a sharp sword. Instead of graciously accepting the present, the King told his officers to cut off the head of the person using the sharp sword he had brought as a present. Upon hearing this, the person protested and said to the King, "My master, the King, are you going to use the present I brought for your honor to cut off my head?" In our case, Moshe protested that he had used the word הֵן (behold) for Hashem's honor when he said in Devorim (10:14) הֵן לַה' אֱלֹקֶיךָ הַשָּׁמַיִם וּשְׁמֵי הַשָּׁמַיִם הָאָרֶץ וְכָל אֲשֶׁר בָּהּ (Behold, to Hashem, your G-d, belong the heavens and the heavens of the heavens, the earth, and all that is on it). Moshe said to Hashem, "Is Hashem going to use the same word that I used for praising Hashem to decree my death to me." Hashem told Moshe, "A bad neighbor sees things coming into his neighbor but not things coming out." Hashem told Moshe, "Don't you remember that when I sent you to redeem the Bnei Yisroel from Egypt, you said (in our Posuk) וְהֵן לֹא יַאֲמִינוּ לִי. The Maharzav explains that a bad neighbor can see much merchandise coming to his neighbor's house and be very jealous of his neighbor. However, this jealousy is completely misplaced since the bad neighbor keeps a "blind eye" and does not see that all the merchandise is really owned by someone else who picks up all the merchandise. The Maharzav says that the jealously can also be completely misplaced if the bad neighbor keeps a "blind eye" to the overwhelming expenses his neighbor must pay for all the merchandise. Similarly, Hashem told Moshe that he had chosen a Posuk when he had said something good about Hashem using the word הֵן (behold) but had forgotten the time when he had used the word הֵן (behold) to say something bad about the Bnei Yisroel.

Rav Sternbuch, in his Sefer Taam V'Daas on this Posuk, says that the word הֵן (behold) was very disturbing to Moshe since it implied that Moshe's death was both obvious that it should happen and something not possible to change. He explains that Moshe was disturbed by being treated worse than a typical person who does not know when he will be Niftar. Since the person does not know, the person can always hope that even if it has been decreed that he should die, his sin may be forgiven, and his decree may be softened so that he remains among the living. The Gemorah in Brochos 10a tells how Hashem sent the Prophet Yeshayahu with the prophecy to tell King Chizkiyahu to give his final instructions to his household, for he would soon die both in this world and in the world to come. After Chizkiyahu asked Yeshayahu why he had received such a horrible decree, he told him that it was because he did not attempt to have any children. Chizkiyahu explained that he did not attempt to have children because he saw through his holy spirit that he would have children who will do evil. He said that he decided that it is better not to attempt to have children rather than having such children. Yeshayahu answered him that he had no business mixing into the plans of Hashem and that he had to just fulfill the commandment that Hashem gave him and all mankind to attempt to be fruitful and multiply (פְּרוּ וּרְבוּ). What Hashem then decides to do is Hashem's decision. Admitting to his error, Chizkiyahu asked Yeshayahu for permission to marry his daughter, reasoning that perhaps both their merits will be enough to have children who will not do evil. Yeshayahu told him that it was too late for this since a decree of death on Chizkiyahu had already been issued. Hearing this, he told Yeshayahu to end his prophecy and leave the palace. He said that he had the following tradition and teaching from his father's house that even if a sharp sword is already on one's neck and nothing additional is needed to kill him, one should not refrain from davening for mercy from Hashem. Chizkiyahu immediately proceeded to turn to the wall and daven to Hashem.

Shemos

Sefer Yeshayahu (38:3-5) say, "And Chizkiyahu wept profusely. And the word of Hashem came to Yeshayahu, saying, Go and say to Chizkiyahu, 'So has Hashem G-d of your father Dovid said, I have heard your prayer; I have seen your tears. Behold, I will add fifteen years to your life.'" Rav Sternbuch explains according to this Shemos Raba, Hashem told Moshe that he had used the word הֵן (behold) to describe how the Bnei Yisroel would not believe. Using the word הֵן (behold) means that it is both obvious that it will happen and something not possible to be any different. The Gemorah says in Baba Kama 50a that Hashem judges those that are close to him (the most righteous people) concerning sins, which are only as wide as the width of a hair. The Toras Chaim on this Gemorah ponders why Hashem is so exacting with righteous people and why they should be treated any differently than wicked people or even people who are not completely righteous.

As an introduction to his point, the Toras Chaim points to one of the first Rashis in Chumash where Rashi ponders why the name of Hashem, אֱלֹקִים is used as the one who created the world. Rashi, based on combining together the Beraishis Raba (14:1) with the Beraishis Raba (12:15) and the Shemos Raba (30:13), says that Hashem first wanted to create the world so that it would be under the rules of judgment, but realized that the world could not exist under these rules. Therefore, Hashem changed the system so that the world would be run under the rules of mercy with some of the rules of judgment. That is why later Beraishis (2:4) says that Hashem (mercy) Elokim (judgment) made the heaven and the earth. The Toras Chaim explains that completely righteous people are judged under the pure rule of judgment, which does not grant even a hair's breadth of leeway when one has sinned. Since even a mortal King will meet out very serious punishments to anyone who even hints of rebelling, how much more so should the punishment be for someone who sins and rebels against the King of all Kings. Therefore, Moshe was punished with Hashem using the word הֵן (behold) to tell him that he was being treated worse than a typical person who does not know when he will be Niftar. The Eitz Yosef on Menochos 29b quotes the Beer Mayim Chaim on the Torah, who uses this concept to explain a difficult Gemorah in Menochos 29b. The Gemorah says that when Moshe came up to the heavens to get the Torah, he found Hashem putting crowns on some of the letters of the Torah. Moshe questioned whether anyone was holding back Hashem from giving the Torah as it is. Hashem told Moshe that after many generations, there would be a Rabi Akiva who will learn heaps and heaps of Halachos from every crown. The Gemorah tells us that Moshe first asked to see Rabi Akiva and Moshe sat in on one of Rabi Akiva's Shiurim. After hearing the amazing Shiur, Moshe requested to see Rabi Akiva's reward in this world. Moshe was shown the Romans raking Rabi Akiva's body with iron combs pulling out so much flesh that they sold it at the meat market. Moshe asked Hashem to explain how this was the reward for so much Torah. Hashem told Moshe to be quiet and ask no more questions since Hashem said that this is part of Hashem's greater plan. The Beer Mayim Chaim explains that a spiritual giant like Rabi Akiva was judged with strict judgment, similar to how Moshe was being judged in this case.

1) The Shemos Raba (3:12) presents an answer to our question. It writes that at that time, Moshe did not speak properly since Hashem had told him previously in Shemos (3:18) וְשָׁמְעוּ לְקֹלֶךָ (and they will listen to your voice). Because Moshe spoke improperly, Hashem gave him signs to do to prove that he was the savior of the Bnei Yisroel. The Maharzav explains that had Moshe not spoken

Shemos

improperly, Moshe would have been able to convince the people with his words alone and without needing signs. Now that Moshe spoke improperly and needed signs, the Shemos Raba explains how the signs themselves would show that Moshe had acted improperly. The first sign Moshe was given was that of the staff turning into a snake. Hashem asks Moshe מַזֶּה בְיָדֶךָ (what is in your hand). The word מַזֶּה is not a real word but a word which is pronounced as two words מַה זֶּה and written as one word. The Shemos Raba, according to the Maharzav, explains that the word מַזֶּה was written this way since, without vowels (like the Torah is written), it could be read as מִזֶּה, which means "from this." According to this reading, Hashem was telling Moshe that he deserved to be hit with "from this which is in your hand." The sign itself, which was to turn his staff into a snake and then back to a staff, also had a message for Moshe. Moshe did a similar action as the snake did when it talked Loshon Horah against its creator, and therefore he got a sign involving a snake. The Beraishis Raba (19:4) says that the snake told Chava that Hashem had only been able to create the world because he ate from the Eitz HaDaas. The snake added on that the only reason Hashem told Chava not to eat from the Eitz HaDaas is because He is, Chas VeShalom, jealous that Chava will be like him and create other worlds. The Shemos Raba says that this is why Moshe ran away when his staff turned into a snake since, says the Eitz Yosef, he was afraid that the snake would bite him. The Yepheh Toar explains that had Hashem not wanted to send this message to Moshe, Hashem could have just told Moshe what the sign would be similar to the third sign where Moshe did not at that time turn water into blood. Finally, the third sign that Moshe got was that he was going to turn the water into blood. This was also a message to Moshe that through water, his own blood and life would be taken away when he hit the rock instead of speaking to it to give forth its water. The Maharzav explains that Moshe got angry with the people for asking for water, calling them rebels, and hit the rock because Moshe felt they did not fully believe in both Hashem and him.

Parenthetically the Shemos Raba explains that the sign of the snake was also a message to Pharaoh. In Sefer Yechezkel (29:3), Hashem says to Yechezkel, "Speak and you shall say; So says Hashem, G-d: Behold I am upon you, O Pharaoh, king of Egypt, the great crocodile that lies down in the midst of its rivers, who said, 'My river is my own, and I made it myself.'" The Shemos Raba says that a crocodile is synonymous with a snake as Sefer Yeshayahu (27:1) says, "On that day, Hashem shall visit with His hard and great and strong sword on Livyason the serpent, and upon Livyason the crooked serpent and He shall slay the crocodile that is in the sea." The sign foretold that before Moshe walked into Pharaoh's Palace, Pharaoh was squirming around like a snake saying all the things he was going to do. All Moshe had to do was walk into the palace and figuratively put his hand on Pharaoh, and the snake Pharaoh turned quiet and motionless as a stick.

The Ain Eliyahu on the Gemorah in Shabbos 97a says that when Moshe declares in our Posuk, "Behold they will not believe me, and they will not heed my voice," Moshe was saying that even the elders of the Bnei Yisroel, not to mention the Bnei Yisroel themselves, would not believe nor heed Moshe's voice. The Meam Loez explains that the reason the elders listened to Moshe was because they had received the tradition that the savior of the Bnei Yisroel would say the words פָּקֹד פָּקַדְתִּי and indeed, those were the words that Moshe said to them. Since the rest of the people did not have this tradition, they were not as readily convinced. Being that Moshe should have known that the elders

Shemos

would believe him, Moshe is punished in his body for suspecting innocent people, like the elders, would not listen.

2) The Rambam in Hilchos Yesodai HaTorah (8:1-2) also presents an answer to our question. He says that on Mount Sinai, all the Bnei Yisroel saw and heard Hashem speaking to Moshe and telling him to tell the Bnei Yisroel this and that. This was an irrefutable proof that Moshe's was a true prophet as Hashem tells Moshe in Shemos (19:9), "Behold, I am coming to you in the thickness of the cloud, in order that the people hear when I speak to you, and they will also believe in you forever." The Rambam explains that this Posuk shows that until that point on Mount Sinai, the people's belief in Moshe was a belief that still left them with questions and doubts about Moshe. He says that Moshe knew that at the point of the beginning of Moshe's prophesy in our Posuk, even if the people believed him, it would be a belief that still left them with questions and doubts about Moshe and whether they could know for sure that he was true. This would even be the case if Hashem were to give Moshe signs to prove to the Bnei Yisroel that he was a prophet. In fact, Hashem already told Moshe in Shemos (3:12), "For I will be with you, and this is the sign for you that it was I Who sent you. When you take the people out of Egypt, you will worship G-d on this mountain." He explains that only when they "worship G-d on this mountain (Mount Sinai)" was Hashem telling Moshe that the people will completely believe in Hashem. The Rambam and Eben Ezra on our Posuk say that when Moshe says in our Posuk, "Behold they will not believe me, and they will not heed my voice," Moshe was saying that even though Hashem had told him and he believed that the Bnei Yisroel would listen to his voice initially, they could still have lingering doubts about Moshe.

3) The Eben Ezra, Chizkuni, and Abarbanel answer our question similarly. They say that when Hashem previously said, "And they will hearken to your (Moshe's) voice, and you shall come, you and the elders of Yisroel, to the King of Egypt," Hashem only said that the elders would listen to Moshe, but Hashem did not say that the rest of the people would listen to Moshe. In our Posuk, when Moshe says, "Behold they will not believe me, and they will not heed my voice," Moshe was referring to the rest of the people. We have mentioned previously that the Meam Loez explains the reason the elders listened to Moshe was because they had received the tradition that the savior of the Bnei Yisroel would say the words פָּקֹד פָּקַדְתִּי and indeed, those were the words that Moshe said to them. Since the rest of the people did not have this tradition, they were not as readily convinced.

4) The Ramban also presents an answer to our question. He writes that when Hashem declared in Shemos (3:18), "And they will hearken to your (Moshe's) voice," this was not a promise, but rather it was a statement that it is fitting and logical that they "should hearken to your voice." He compares this to Bamidbar (14:13-14) after the spies return with their bad report about Eretz Yisroel, and Moshe is speaking to Hashem to try and moderate the punishment that Hashem is contemplating punishing the Bnei Yisroel. The Torah there says, "But the Egyptians will hear that You (Hashem) have brought this nation out from its midst with great power. They will say about the inhabitants of this land, who have heard that You, Hashem, are in the midst of this people; that You, Hashem, appear to them eye to eye and that Your cloud rests over them." The Ramban says that Moshe was saying in these Pesukim that it would be fitting and logical for the Egyptians to say

Shemos

this. Similarly, in Shemos (7:17), where Hashem says to Pharaoh through Moshe, "With this, you will know that I am Hashem," it also means that it is fitting and logical for them to know this. He even says that in Shemos (4:8) where after having Moshe do the two signs, Hashem says that for the third sign, "And it will come to pass, that if they do not believe you, and they do not heed the voice of the first sign, they will believe the voice of the last sign," Hashem is not guaranteeing that they will listen to the third sign. Rather, Hashem is saying that it is fit and logical that they will listen to the third sign. Therefore, in our Posuk, Moshe is asking Hashem as to what happens if the people, out of their own free will, do not do what is fit and logical and do not listen to Moshe's message from Hashem.

5) The Ramban, Sforno, Abarbanel, and Ohr HaChaim answer our question similarly. They say that when Hashem stated in Shemos (3:18), "And they will hearken to your (Moshe's) voice," it was a promise that they would listen and come along with Moshe and Aharon to Pharaoh. They would then hear, as it states in Shemos (3:18), Moshe tell Pharaoh, "Hashem G-d of the Hebrews has happened upon us, and now, let us go for a three days' journey in the desert and offer up sacrifices to Hashem, our G-d." However, in addition to promising Moshe that the people will listen to come along, Hashem also told Moshe in the next Posuk, "However, I know that the King of Egypt will not permit you to go." Therefore, what Moshe meant in our Posuk when he said, "Behold they will not believe me, and they will not heed my voice," but they will say, "Hashem has not appeared to you." is referring to after hearing Pharaoh's refusal. Moshe was afraid that the people would say that had Hashem really appeared to you and told you to say this to Pharaoh, Pharaoh would not have refused your request.

6) The Abarbanel also presents another answer to our question. He says that Moshe was confident the people would heed what he said when he told them that they would be redeemed from Egypt since they all knew that Hashem had made a treaty (the Bris Bain HaBesorim) that Hashem would take the Bnei Yisroel out of this slavery. However, in our Posuk, when Moshe says, "Behold they will not believe me, and they will not heed my voice," but they will say, "Hashem has not appeared to you." Moshe expresses doubt whether the people will believe that Hashem himself had appeared to him and appointed him as the savior of the Bnei Yisroel. Instead, Moshe was worried that they might think that some intermediary, like a star, influenced Moshe to say that he was the savior of the Bnei Yisroel, and they will not believe that Hashem Himself came in prophesy to Moshe. Therefore, Moshe was in no way showing any disbelief in what Hashem told him in Posuk (3:18) "And they will hearken to your (Moshe's) voice." The Ralbag answers our question similarly to the Abarbanel.

7) The Ohr HaChaim HaKodosh also presents another answer to our question. The Gemorah in Nedorim 38a says that Hashem only rests his prophetic spirit on someone who is mighty, wealthy, wise, and humble. The Maharsha explains that the Prophet must be mighty and wealthy because these are qualities the common person gives respect to, and therefore it will help him gain respect even of the common person. The Rambam says in Hilchos Yesodai HaTorah (7:1) that "it is one of the basic tenents of our religion to know that Hashem grants prophesy to people." He continues that "the Prophet must be great in wisdom, mighty in character, who is never overcome by his natural

Shemos

inclinations in any regard. Instead, with his mind, he overcomes his natural inclinations at all times. He must also possess a very broad and accurate mental capacity. A person who is full of all these qualities and is physically sound is fit for prophecy." The Kesef Mishna ponders why the Rambam does not list the same qualities as the Gemorah in Nedorim 38a lists. He says that the Rosh on the Gemorah in Nedorim 38a says that these qualities are only required for a prophet who has prophecy on a steady basis. The Kesef Mishna says that the qualities listed by the Rambam apply to someone who just temporarily becomes a prophet. The Ohr HaChaim says that Moshe, because of his humility, felt that he was not on a high enough level to be a prophet for Hashem, even to be a temporary prophet. When Moshe says in our Posuk, "Behold they will not believe me, and they will not heed my voice," but they will say, "Hashem has not appeared to you," Moshe is saying that the people will never believe that such a lowly person as himself could ever have even temporary prophecy. With regard to being a temporary prophet, Moshe accessed himself that he was not "great in wisdom" as the Rambam requires of a prophet. In addition, the Rambam says that the temporary Prophet must be "physically sound." Moshe said that because it was difficult for him to speak, he did not qualify even as a temporary prophet. Moreover, as the savior of the Bnei Yisroel, he would need to be a steady prophet, and for that, one of the conditions is that he needed to be rich. At that point, as a shepherd of Yisro, Moshe was quite poor. In fact, the Gemorah in Nedorim 38a says that Moshe only became rich later from the fragments of the precious stones used to make the Luchos as Shemos (34:1) says, "Hew for yourself two stone tablets like the first ones." The Gemorah says that since the Posuk says "for yourself," we derive that the fragments from the hewing were given to Moshe, and that is how Moshe became rich. Therefore, Moshe concluded that if the people asked the elders of the Bnei Yisroel whether Moshe had the qualities to be their savior, the elders would say that he did not.

8) The Dubna Magid, in his Sefer Ohel Yaakov, also ponders our question. He references a Gemorah in Brochos 59a. The Gemorah relates how Rav Katina was walking along the road and came across the house of a sorcerer who did sorcery using the bones of a dead person. When Rav Katina got to this house, he felt an earthquake. Rav Katina asked, "does the sorcerer know how such an earthquake happens." The sorcerer shouted and said, "Katina, Katina, why shouldn't I know? When Hashem remembers that his children are in pain amongst the nations of the world, Hashem sheds two tears in the Great Sea (Mediterranean Sea). This sound is heard from one end of the world to the other, and that is what an earthquake is." Rav Katina replied, "The sorcerer is a fraud, and his words are false." Rav Katina said that if the sorcerer were correct, we would feel two earthquakes, one from each of the two tears. Parenthetically the Gemorah says that there were, in fact, two earthquakes, but that the reason Rav Katina did not admit this to the sorcerer was so that the whole world would not make the mistake of following the sorcerer. The Gemorah also proceeds to give other explanations for the source of earthquakes.

The Dubna Magid focuses on the statement of Rav Katina, "The sorcerer is a fraud, and his words are false," which at first glance seems repetitive. He explains that speaking falsely can come under two categories. For example, a person could say that he saw a lion on the way. One possibility is that the person never saw a lion at all on the way, and the person knows that he was lying when he said that he saw a lion on the way. The second possibility is that he saw a different animal like a

Shemos

dog and mistakenly thought the other animal was a lion. In this case, the person thinks that he is telling the truth, though, in reality, what he is saying is false and never happened. Similarly, in the case of the Gemorah, Rav Katina realized that the sorcerer did not believe the words that he was saying. He also did not believe that the Bnei Yisroel are important enough to cause Hashem to shed two tears when Hashem sees the Bnei Yisroel in pain amongst the nations of the world. The only reason the sorcerer said this was to con Rav Katina by telling Rav Katina what he wanted to hear. Therefore, Rav Katina said that the sorcerer is a fraud and con artist. In addition, Rav Katina said that even if the sorcerer believed what he was saying, what he was saying was false since it didn't explain the physical phenomena of the one earthquake that happened. The Dubna Magid says that Rav Saadia Gaon writes that false prophecy also has these two categories. One category of a false prophet is someone who pretends he got a prophecy when in reality, he never got one. This Prophet knows that what he is saying is false. The second category is a prophet who did indeed get a prophecy but does not understand correctly what the prophecy is telling him. The Yerios HaOhel, in his commentary on the Dubna Magid's Sefer, says that these two types of false prophecies are what Yechezkel prophesizes to the false prophets in Sefer Yechezkel (13:7) "Have you not prophesied vain prophecy, and spoken false divination; yet you say, 'The word of Hashem, while I did not speak."

The Dubna Magid quotes the Gemorah in Sanhedrin 89a, which brings Tzidkiyah ben Kenaanah as the example of one who prophesizes that which he did not hear. Yehoshofot, King of Yehuda, joined with Achav, the wicked King of the Ten Tribes, to attack Aram. Before attacking, Yehoshofot requested that a prophet be first consulted. Achav gathered 400 prophets, each of whom advised him that he should attack Aram and would be successful. In addition, Sefer Melachim I (22:11) says, "And Tzidkiyah son of Kenaanah made himself iron horns, and he said, 'So said Hashem, 'With these shall you gore the Arameans until you destroy them completely.'" The Gemorah gives us some background about what Tzidkiyah ben Kenaanah did wrong. In Sefer Melachim I, Chapter 21, we are told that Achav, in addition to his main palace in Shomron, also had another recreational palace in a city called Yizrael. There was a person Novos who owned a vineyard right next to this recreational palace of King Achav, and King Achav wanted the vineyard so he could turn it into a garden or meadow. Tosfos in Sanhedrin 20b says that Achav wanted to turn it into a place where he would put his idol. Anyway, Achav offered Novos to either swap the vineyard for another vineyard elsewhere or to sell it to him. Novos told Achav in Sefer Melachim I (21:3), "Hashem forbid me to give the inheritance of my forefathers to you." The Malbim explains that Novos was sending a message to King Achav about how careless he was with his spiritual inheritance of Hashem from his forefathers, being that he forsook the inheritance to serve idols. Failing to reach a deal with Novos, Achav returned to his palace and told his wife, Queen Ezevel, about why he was so distraught. Queen Ezevel advised King Achav not to be upset and promised to take care of the situation for him. Queen Ezevel issued a royal letter to the leaders of the city of Yizrael about how Novos had embarrassed both the King and his idol and told them to put Novos to death using two false witnesses. The leaders complied with this request and put Novos to death. With Novos dead, Queen Ezevel told King Achav to take over the property.

Shemos

The Gemorah describes what went on in heaven as a result of this episode. The Gemorah bases itself on Sefer Melachim I (22:20-22), which say, "And Hashem said, 'Who will entice Achav so that he will go up and fall in Ramos-Gilad?' One said in this manner, and another one said in that manner. And a certain spirit came forth and stood before Hashem and said, 'I will entice him,' and Hashem said to him 'How?' And he said, 'I will go forth, and I will be a lying spirit in the mouth of all his prophets.' And Hashem said, 'You will entice, and you will prevail. Go forth and do so.'" The Gemorah explains that this spirit was the spirit of Novos. The spirit then went forth and put prophesy into the mouths of the 400 prophets, including Tzidkiyah ben Kenaanah, to send Achav into battle against Aram, falsely telling him that he would be victorious when in fact, he was killed in war. Being that the spirit of Novos gave this false prophecy to Tzidkiyah ben Kenaanah, the Gemorah ponders how Tzidkiyah ben Kenaanah could be held accountable for giving over this false prophecy. The Gemorah answers that he should have figured out that the prophecy was false. His knowledge should have been based on the principle that one prophetic signal could come to many prophets, but no two prophets relate the prophecy that they have seen with the same words.

The Rambam in Hilchos Yesodai HaTorah (7:3) says that a prophet sees a metaphoric image. Immediately, the interpretation of the imagery is put into his heart, and he knows its meaning. Therefore, each Prophet will use his own words to describe the interpretation. The Gemorah says that in the case of Achav, all 400 prophets used exactly the same words to describe the prophecy, which should have clued Tzidkiyah ben Kenaanah that his prophecy was false. The Gemorah ponders how we can know for sure that Tzidkiyah ben Kenaanah knew of this principle. The Gemorah answers that he should have figured it out from King Yehoshofot of Yehuda, who, after hearing the prophecies of these 400 prophets, says in Sefer Melachim I (22:7), "Is there no other prophet of Hashem here from whom we may inquire?" The Gemorah relates how, when King Yehoshofot said this, King Achav questioned how he could want another prophet after hearing the prophecies of 400 prophets. King Yehoshofot told him that he had a tradition from his grandfather's house that two prophets do not relate the prophecy that they have seen using the same words, and therefore all 400 prophets were false.

Based on the above, the Dubna Magid explains what Moshe means in our Posuk when he says, "Behold they will not believe me, and they will not heed my voice," but they will say, "Hashem has not appeared to you." Firstly, Moshe says that the Bnei Yisroel will not believe me because they will think that I made up the prophecy. Secondly, even if they will believe me, they will say that I was fooled like Tzidkiyah ben Kenaanah and got my prophecy from an unholy source like a spirit trying to trick me into delivering a false prophecy. Since this was a reasonable doubt on Moshe's part, Hashem gave Moshe signs to prove that his prophecy came from Hashem and not from an unholy source. For simplicity, I will choose not to follow exactly what the Dubna Magid says to prove this, but rather use what the Shemos Raba, which we have examined above in the first answer, says. The Shemos Raba (3:12) says that all three signs showed that Moshe had accused the Bnei Yisroel falsely and that the Bnei Yisroel would indeed believe Moshe's prophecy. Only Hashem, who loves the Bnei Yisroel and who defends them against anyone, even Moshe, who speaks falsely against them, would punish for this. An unholy source, says the Dubna Magid, would never defend

Shemos

the Bnei Yisroel, and therefore the three signs proved that Moshe's prophecy was from Hashem and not an unholy source.

9) The Malbim and Rav Gifter, in his Sefer Pirkei Torah, answer our question similarly. The Malbim notes that Hashem told Moshe in Shemos (3:18) וְשָׁמְעוּ לְקֹלֶךָ (they will listen to your voice). In our Posuk, Moshe questions whether the Bnei Yisroel יִשְׁמְעוּ בְּקֹלִי (will listen in my voice). He explains that the one different Hebrew letter leads to a vast difference between these two expressions. Listening "into" someone's voice implies that the person will accept what he has heard and will follow what he was told. That is what Moshe in our Posuk says that he is unsure whether the Bnei Yisroel will do. Listening "to" someone's voice implies fully hearing everything the person has to say and then making a decision whether he will do what he was told. It does not necessarily mean that the person will follow what he has heard, and that is what Hashem told Moshe the Bnei Yisroel would do. Therefore, say the Malbim and Rav Gifter, Moshe was not at all contradicting Hashem's words when he expressed doubt whether the Bnei Yisroel would follow what Moshe asked them to do.

According to the Malbim and Rav Gifter, we can ponder the question that based on the above, Moshe would be justified in expressing doubt whether the Bnei Yisroel would follow what Moshe asked them to do. However, as we have explained previously, Moshe used a word וְהֵן, which expressed that he was certain that the Bnei Yisroel would not listen to him. The Ksav VeHakabola says that the word וְהֵן can also mean "if," and that is how he translates it in our Posuk. An example of when the word וְהֵן means "if" is in Sefer Yirmiyahu (2:10) where it says וּרְאוּ הֵן הָיְתָה כָּזֹאת (and see if there was any such thing). Rashi on that Posuk says that the word וְהֵן in that Posuk means "if." It would be easier to understand if the Malbim and Rav Gifter would also translate the word וְהֵן as "if" in our Posuk.

The Malbim also explains why the Bnei Yisroel would have a problem following what Moshe told them. He says that a prophet who comes for the first time and needs to prove to the people that he is a true prophet can do it in either two ways. The first way is to prophesize a good event that will happen very soon, and when the event happens, it will affirm that he is a true prophet. It has to be a good event because a bad event does not necessarily have to occur. Secondly, the Prophet can show wondrous miracles that run against the natural laws of the physical world, and this will also show that he is a true prophet sent by Hashem, who is not bound by the laws of nature. Given that until this point, Hashem had not given Moshe any wondrous miracles against the laws of nature to do, Moshe thought that he would be proving that he is a true prophet by prophesizing that he will tell Pharaoh to let the Bnei Yisroel leave Egypt, and that will happen very soon. However, Hashem just told him in Shemos (3:19) that Pharaoh would not let the Bnei Yisroel leave Egypt after Moshe requested that he do that. For this reason, Moshe was left with no way to prove that he was a true prophet and, therefore, correctly doubted the Bnei Yisroel would listen to him. Therefore, Hashem gave Moshe three wondrous miracles that went against the laws of nature to prove that Moshe was indeed a true prophet.

Shemos

10) The Koznitzer Magid, in his Sefer Avodas Yisroel, also presents an answer to our question. The Yalkut Shimoni (240) in Parshas Beshalach says that the Bnei Yisroel were redeemed from Egypt in the merit of their belief in Hashem as Shemos (4:31) relates, "And the people believed, and they heard that Hashem had remembered the Bnei Yisroel, and they kneeled and prostrated themselves." In Moshe's analysis, if the Bnei Yisroel were redeemed from Egypt in the merit of their belief in Hashem, then in order for this to be a merit, it was necessary that they believed in Hashem from their own free will. If it was done with their own free will, analyzed Moshe, then there is a chance that they will choose not to believe. According to this analysis of Moshe, when Hashem said in Shemos (3:18), "And they will listen to your (Moshe's) voice," it had to be that the Bnei Yisroel had a choice in whether to listen and therefore, it was possible that they would not listen. That is what Moshe means in our Posuk when he says, "Behold they will not believe me, and they will not heed my voice." The Koznitzer Magid explains that Moshe's analysis was flawed. He says that there is a master plan for the world, and despite this, each person has free will to do what they choose since Hashem has many ways to ensure that the master plan comes about. Hashem told Moshe that the master plan had it that the Bnei Yisroel would be redeemed from Egypt in the merit of their belief in Hashem, and therefore they will indeed "listen to your voice." However, the master plan in no way took away the free will of each individual to choose whether to believe in Hashem.

11) The Sefas Emes (5663 and 5666) also ponders our question. He says that both the exile and redemption from Egypt were blueprints for all future exiles and redemptions. That is why, it is a Mitzvah to mention the redemption from Egypt every day. Even though it wasn't an issue for the redemption from Egypt since Hashem promised Moshe that they would believe in him, Moshe wanted to ensure that if in a future redemption the people did not fully believe, this would not prevent the redemption from taking place. The Sefas Emes references his time period where there was a lack of belief by many, and of course, it is even truer in our time. Despite our lack of full belief in Hashem and the final redemption, may Hashem bring it speedily in our days.

12) The Oznayim LeTorah also presents an answer to our question. He writes that great people will listen and obey what an ordinary person says if the ordinary person is quoting even greater people than they. For example, in Beraishis (16:2), Sorah tells Avrohom הִנֵּה נָא עֲצָרַנִי ה' מִלֶּדֶת בֹּא נָא אֶל שִׁפְחָתִי אוּלַי אִבָּנֶה מִמֶּנָּה וַיִּשְׁמַע אַבְרָם לְקוֹל שָׂרָי ("Behold now, Hashem has restrained me from bearing children; please come to my handmaid; perhaps I will be built up from her." And Avram listened to Sarai's voice). The Beraishis Raba (45:2) says that Avrohom listened to the Holy Spirit that was in Sorah when she spoke. This Posuk describes listening to the Holy Spirit of Sorah as לְקוֹל שָׂרָי, the same expression that Hashem used in Shemos (3:18) when Hashem told Moshe that the Bnei Yisroel would listen to him. Therefore, Moshe understood that the people would only listen to him if they believed that Moshe was speaking to them in the name of Hashem. However, Hashem never promised Moshe that the people would for sure believe that Moshe was speaking to them in the name of Hashem. In our Posuk, Moshe says וְלֹא יִשְׁמְעוּ בְּקֹלִי (they will not listen to me speaking as an ordinary person). Due to his humbleness, Moshe felt that there was not a chance that the Bnei Yisroel would listen to him if they felt that he was speaking to them himself as opposed to speaking to them in the name of Hashem. For this reason, Hashem gave Moshe three signs to prove to the Bnei Yisroel that Moshe was speaking in the name of Hashem. Therefore, Moshe fully believed

Shemos

Hashem's previous promise that if the people knew he was speaking in the name of Hashem, they would believe him. Moshe's belief in no way contradicts his saying if the people felt that he was speaking to them himself, they would not believe him.

Why Did Hashem Want to Put Moshe to Death at the Inn?

Shemos (4:24) וַיְהִי בַדֶּרֶךְ בַּמָּלוֹן וַיִּפְגְּשֵׁהוּ ה' וַיְבַקֵּשׁ הֲמִיתוֹ (ד:כד) Now he (Moshe) was on the way, in an inn, that Hashem met him and sought to put him to death.

Why did Hashem want to put Moshe to death at the inn?

Introduction
In Shemos (4:19), Hashem tells Moshe, "Go, return to Egypt, for all the people who sought your life have died." The next Posuk tells us, "So Moshe took his wife and his sons, mounted them upon the donkey, and he returned to the land of Egypt." The Abarbanel explains that only after hearing from Hashem that "all the people who sought your life have died" did Moshe decide to bring his sons and wife along. Otherwise, it would have been too dangerous for them. Coming along with his family and especially with very young children showed the Bnei Yisroel that Moshe was confident in his own prophecy. Building confidence in the Bnei Yisroel was important since we see how tentative their belief in Moshe was when Pharaoh did not immediately free the Bnei Yisroel.

The Vayikra Raba (1:5) analyzes Shemos (3:10) which says וְעַתָּה לְכָה וְאֶשְׁלָחֲךָ אֶל פַּרְעֹה וְהוֹצֵא אֶת עַמִּי בְנֵי יִשְׂרָאֵל מִמִּצְרָיִם (So now go, and I (Hashem) will send you (Moshe) to Pharaoh, and take My people, the Bnei Yisroel, out of Egypt). It says that the reason there is a Heh at the end of the word לְכָה is to tell Moshe that if he doesn't redeem the Bnei Yisroel from Egypt, no one else will redeem them. The Matnos Kehunah explains that instead of using the strange word לְכָה to mean "go" the Posuk should have used the same and typical word (לֵךְ) as is used in Shemos (3:16) לֵךְ וְאָסַפְתָּ אֶת זִקְנֵי יִשְׂרָאֵל (Go and assemble the elders of Israel). The reason the Torah added on a Heh at the end of the word לֵךְ is so that the reading of the word would be the same as the word לְךָ (to you). If we used the Hebrew word לְךָ instead of לְכָה, our Posuk would be translated as "only to you (Moshe) is the mission of going to Pharaoh and taking the Bnei Yisroel out of Egypt. The Lev Eliyahu ponders the question of how Hashem could want to put Moshe to death at the inn when Hashem already revealed that only Moshe could redeem the Bnei Yisroel from Egypt. If Moshe was Chas VeShalom killed, how would the Bnei Yisroel be redeemed from Egypt? What would become of what is said in Shemos (3:7-8), "And Hashem said, "I have surely seen the affliction of My people who are in Egypt, and I have heard their cry because of their slave drivers, for I know their pains. I have descended to rescue them from the hands of the Egyptians and to bring them up from that land, to a good and spacious land, to a land flowing with milk and honey?"

The Lev Eliyahu quotes the Yerushalmi in Makos (2:6), where wisdom is figuratively asked what the punishment of someone who sins is. Wisdom answers, quoting Mishlay (13:21), חַטָּאִים תְּרַדֵּף רָעָה (Evil will pursue the sinners). The Gemorah then figuratively asks prophesy what the punishment of someone who sins is. Prophesy answers, quoting Sefer Yechezkel (18:4), הַנֶּפֶשׁ הַחֹטֵאת הִיא תָמוּת (the

Shemos

soul that sins, it shall die). The Gemorah then figuratively asks Hashem what the punishment of someone who sins is. Hashem answers that the person should do Teshuva, and he will be forgiven. The Pnei Moshe on the Gemorah explains that according to the letter of the law, Wisdom and Prophesy are correct that one must be punished if one sins. However, in his infinite mercy, Hashem does not judge with the letter of the law and permits one to be forgiven if one does proper Teshuva.

The Gemorah in Baba Kama 50a says that Hashem is very careful with the actions of the most righteous people and will punish them on sins, which are only a hair breath. The Toras Chaim ponders why Hashem is so exacting with righteous people and why they should be treated any differently than wicked people or even people who are not completely righteous. As an introduction to his point, he points to one of the first Rashis in Chumash where Rashi ponders why the name of Hashem, אֱלֹקִים is used as the one who created the world. Rashi, based on combining together the Shemos Raba (14:1) with the Shemos Raba (12:15) and the Shemos Raba (30:13), says that Hashem first wanted to create the world so that it would be under the rules of judgment, but realized that the world could not exist under these rules. Therefore, Hashem changed the system so that the world would be run under the rules of mercy with some of the rules of judgment. That is why a later Posuk, Beraishis (2:4), says that Hashem (mercy) Elokim (judgment) made the Heaven and the earth. The Toras Chaim explains that completely righteous people are judged under the pure rule of judgment, which does not grant even a hair's breadth of leeway when one has sinned. Since a mortal King will meet out very serious punishments to anyone who even hints of rebelling, how much more so should the punishment be for someone who sins and rebels against the King of all Kings. That is why Moshe, Aharon, Aharon's two sons, and similar people were punished for even the slightest infraction against Hashem. That being the case, Moshe is judged under the rule of judgment, for which the Yerushalmi in Makos (2:6) already told us what happens to a person who sins if the person is judged under the rule of judgment as both Wisdom and Prophecy say. Therefore, if Moshe did even the slightest sin, he is punished severely despite the fact that there are other ramifications like how the Bnei Yisroel will get redeemed from Egypt. The Lev Eliyahu says that this is just how Hashem set up the system in the world, and that is that a very righteous person is punished severely. Since this rule is set, it cannot be undone by side issues. How Hashem redeems the Bnei Yisroel under these circumstances is Hashem's problem to work out.

The Oznayim LeTorah also ponders the Lev Eliyahu's question concerning how the Bnei Yisroel would be redeemed if Moshe was killed, given that only he was able to redeem the Bnei Yisroel. He answers that only Moshe could redeem the Bnei Yisroel in the miraculous way that he did. However, a much less qualified leader doing much fewer miracles than Moshe could still take the Bnei Yisroel out of Egypt.

The Gemorah in Nedorim 31b and the Shemos Raba (5:8) say that this punishment was because of some lack of zealousness in performing the Mitzvah of Bris Milah. The Gemorah in Nedorim 32a and the Shemos Raba tell us how it was made clear to Tziporah that this was the problem. The Shemos Raba says that an angel came and swallowed up Moshe from his head all the way down to where his Bris Milah was. The Gemorah says that in addition, a second angel came and swallowed up Moshe from his feet all the way up to the place of his Bris Milah, so only the place of Moshe's

Shemos

Bris Milah was not swallowed. Parenthetically, the Gemorah says that the names of the angels were אַף (anger) and חֵמָה (wrath). It was now clear to Tziporah what the problem was, so the next Posuk, Shemos (4:25) says, "So Tziporah took a sharp stone and severed her son's foreskin and cast it to his feet, and she said, 'For you are a bridegroom of blood to me.'"

The Ain Eliyahu on the Gemorah ponders how the Gemorah knew that the names of the angels were אַף (anger) and חֵמָה (wrath). He says that the commentators ponder why it was that Moshe would be sentenced to death for not being zealous in giving his son a Bris Milah. If Moshe had, Chas VeShalom, decided not to give Eliezer a Bris Milah at all; he would have transgressed not fulfilling a positive Mitzvah for which there is no death penalty to the father. The Gemorah in Menochos 41a tells of an angel meeting Rav Katina and the angel criticized him for, among other things, wearing a woolen garment with rounded corners. A rounded corner garment is exempt from Tzitzis since it does not have corners. Since this was the garment he was wearing, he was not fulfilling the positive commandment of wearing Tzitzis. Rav Katina was taken aback by this criticism and asked the angel, "since when does the heavenly court punish for the failure to fulfill a positive Mitzvah?" The Anaf Yosef explains that it is enough of a punishment that the person is forfeiting the enormous heavenly reward of fulfilling the positive Mitzvah. The angel replied that at a time when there is Heavenly wrath in the world, Heaven does punish for not fulfilling a positive Mitzvah. Parenthetically, Tosfos points out that Rav Katina was specifically referring to Tzitzis, where there is no obligation to buy a four-cornered garment if he does not have one. For positive Mitzvos, which one is required to fulfill like Sukkah or Lulav and Esrog, not only does Heaven punish for not fulfilling them, but even a human court is authorized to beat a person until he fulfills these positive Mitzvos. The Maharsha explains that in a time of wrath, it is incumbent on righteous people like Rav Katina to do as many Mitzvos as possible in order to protect the people of their generation from being punished. The Eyun Yaakov on the Gemorah in Menochos explains that this is why Moshe was punished at the inn. When Moshe argues with Hashem whether he was the correct candidate to redeem the Bnei Yisroel, Shemos (4:14) says, "And Hashem's wrath was kindled against Moshe," which shows that there was wrath in the world at this time. He quotes a Yalkut Reuveni on our Posuk, who says that Hashem's wrath remained kindled against Moshe from that point on, especially when he got to the inn. Because there was wrath against Moshe, the two angels אַף (anger) and חֵמָה (wrath) attacked Moshe in the inn, since he did not immediately fulfill a positive commandment of Bris Milah. The Ain Eliyahu explains that there was wrath in the world for a different reason. The Shemos Raba (19:5) says that all of the Bnei Yisroel stopped having a Bris Milah except for the tribe of Levi. The wrath against the rest of the Bnei Yisroel was bad enough, but if Moshe, who was a part of the tribe of Levi, also was not doing a Bris Milah, there was even more wrath specifically directed to Moshe. That is how the Gemorah knew that specifically, these two angels אַף (anger) and חֵמָה (wrath) attacked Moshe in the inn. Parenthetically we should mention that although a Bris Milah is "only" a positive Mitzvah, the Tur, in his introduction to Yoreh Deah, Hilchos Milah (260), says that it is a stronger positive Mitzvah than all other positive Mitzvos. The reason is that if the father does not give his son a Bris Milah, then after the son becomes Bar Mitzvah, he is obligated himself to receive a Bris Milah, and if he does not, he is punished with the punishment of Kores. In addition, Bris Milah is called thirteen times in the Torah,

Shemos

a treaty between Hashem and the Bnei Yisroel. Finally, Avrohom was not called complete until he took a Bris Milah.

The Oznayim LeTorah says that what happened to Moshe was also a precedent to what was going to happen when the Bnei Yisroel were going out of Egypt. We have previously explained that the Shemos Raba (19:5) says that all of the Bnei Yisroel stopped having a Bris Milah except for the tribe of Levi. Before the Bnei Yisroel went out of Egypt, Hashem was looking for a merit to allow the Bnei Yisroel to be redeemed. Hashem told Moshe to tell the Bnei Yisroel to take a Bris Milah so they would have this merit. However, many of the Bnei Yisroel refused to get a Bris Milah. Hashem then commanded the Bnei Yisroel to bring a Korban Pesach with the stipulation that one had to have a Bris Milah in order to eat from it. Hashem then used the winds to carry the smell of Moshe's Korban Pesach through Gan Eden and then throughout Egypt. This smell was so irresistible that the people came to Moshe to beg him for a piece of his Korban Pesach. Moshe told them that only those with a Bris Milah could eat of the Korban Pesach and because the smell was so irresistible, the people agreed to immediately take a Bris Milah. The Midrash concludes that the blood of the Bris Milah intermingled with the blood of the Korban Pesach as Sefer Yechezkel (16:6) says, "And I (Hashem) passed by you (Bnei Yisroel) and saw you downtrodden with your blood, and I said to you, 'With your blood, live,' and I said to you, 'With your blood, live.'" The reason the Navi repeats the phrase "With your blood, live" is because there was blood from two sources, the Bris Milah and the Korban Pesach. The Oznayim LeTorah says that when Moshe was trying to convince the Bnei Yisroel to have a Bris Milah, he also told the Bnei Yisroel what happened to him in our Posuk because of some lack of zealousness in performing a Bris Milah. Since Moshe was in the middle of traveling to Egypt when the episode in our Posuk occurred, the Bnei Yisroel knew that Hashem would also hold them accountable for not having a Bris Milah even though they would need to travel out of Egypt almost immediately after their Bris Milah.

Beraishis (44:3) says, "The morning became light, and the men (Yosef's brothers) were sent on their way, they and their donkeys." The Gemorah in Pesachim 2a derives from this Posuk that it is preferable to travel during the daylight hours. The Oznayim LeTorah says that we can see from this incident that Moshe followed this principle of Chazal and stopped at the inn before it became dark. Otherwise, since we do not perform a Bris Milah at night, the fact that there was time for Moshe to do the Bris Milah implied that it was still light when Moshe got to the inn.

Rav Sternbuch, in his Sefer Taam V'Daas, says that we can see from this episode that one cannot "bribe" Hashem by arguing that since Moshe was going back to Egypt to redeem the Bnei Yisroel, he would be forgiven if he didn't do a different Mitzvah, like Bris Milah. Rather a person must always remember that he is obligated in all the Mitzvos even when he is doing the greatest Mitzvos, like saving the Bnei Yisroel. Moreover, Rav Simcha Zizzel from Kelm, in his Sefer Ohr Rav Simcha Zizzel, says that even if one gets so preoccupied in doing a great Mitzvah that he forgets to do a standard Mitzvah like davening, one is still held accountable for this lapse. He explains that the main idea of doing a Mitzvah is doing what Hashem wants us to do. If the person does not do a standard Mitzvah, which is what Hashem wants us to do, then the person completely weakens the impact of the great Mitzvah he is doing since he is not completely doing what Hashem wants. He

Shemos

concludes that, in his opinion, Moshe, on his own, would never have come to this lack of zealousness. Hashem just wanted Moshe to serve as an example to the Bnei Yisroel so that they would realize the responsibility they have in fulfilling what Hashem wants when they got the Torah soon after coming out of Egypt.

We will first consider those answers, which say that it was the Bris Milah of Moshe's second son Eliezer which caused the events described in our Posuk. The Shemos Raba (5:8) is the source of Rashi on our Posuk, who says our Posuk is discussing the Bris Milah of Eliezer. The Maharzav explains how the Shemos Raba knew that it was Eliezer. We know from the explicit Pesukim at the beginning of Parshas Yisro that Eliezer was Moshe's second son. The Devorim Raba (11:10) says that from the time Hashem spoke to Moshe at the burning bush, Moshe no longer lived with his wife, Tziporah. Since the burning bush episode took place before the episode at the inn in our Posuk, the fact that Moshe no longer lived with Tziporah implies that no child could have been younger than the child whose Bris Milah we are talking about at the inn. Therefore, the Shemos Raba is of the opinion we must be speaking about the Bris Milah of Moshe's youngest child, Eliezer.

1) The Gemorah in Nedorim 31b and the Mechilta on Shemos (18:3) are the sources to the answer, which Rashi presents to our question. The Gemorah quotes Rabi Yehoshua ben Korcha, who derives from this incident that the Mitzvah of Bris Milah is so great that all the merits Moshe had were not enough to save him when he had a lack of zealousness for doing a Bris Milah. Rav Yossi says that one cannot say that Moshe, Chas VeShalom, had a lack of zealousness in whether to do the Bris Milah. The Gemorah says that Moshe made the following calculation. If he gave Eliezer the Bris Milah now and left Midyan immediately to go to Egypt, it would be a danger to the child for a few days. The Gemorah quotes Beraishis (34:25) when Shimon and Levi attacked the city of Shechem. The Torah there says, "Now it came to pass on the third day (after their Bris Milah), when they (the inhabitants of Shechem) were in pain, that Yaakov's two sons, Shimon and Levi, Dinah's brothers, each took his sword, and they came upon the city with confidence, and they killed every male." Moshe's other alternative was to give Eliezer a Bris Milah and then wait three days before traveling. This alternative is also problematic since Hashem commanded him to go and return to Egypt immediately. Therefore, Moshe calculated that when Hashem commanded him to immediately return to Egypt, the commandment also took into account that he would need to not give Eliezer a Bris Milah before departing to Egypt. That being the case, Rav Yossi ponders why Moshe was punished at the inn. He answers that when Moshe got to the inn, he became involved in matters of lodging at the inn. The Yerushalmi in Nedorim (3:9) says that the way we know that Moshe became involved in matters of lodging at the inn is because our Posuk says וַיְהִי בַדֶּרֶךְ בַּמָּלוֹן (Now he (Moshe) was on the way, in an inn). The Korban HaEidah on the Yerushalmi explains that these words tell us that immediately after Moshe was on his way, he was in the inn. That is, Moshe went immediately from the way to matters of the inn.

The Ran and the Rosh on the Gemorah in Nedorim, the Rosh's son, the Tur in his Sefer on Chumash, the Mizrachi, and the Korban HaEidah on the Yerushalmi explain that the inn was not far away from Egypt. That being the case, it would not have been a danger to Eliezer to have the Bris

Shemos

Milah and travel the short distance to Egypt either because the distance was short or because the greatest danger occurs on the third day of the Bris Milah, by which time Eliezer would already be in Egypt. It would then seem that Moshe was ready to give Eliezer the Bris Milah at the inn, but instead of immediately giving Eliezer the Bris, Moshe first became involved in matters of lodging at the inn. Rav Sternbuch, in his Sefer Taam V'Daas, explains why Moshe was punished because of this. He writes that if Moshe was too involved with the commandment of going back to Egypt to give his son a Bris, then Moshe should have been too involved with the commandment of going back to Egypt to become involved with matters of lodging at the inn. Put another way, if Moshe now had time to become involved with matters of lodging at the inn, Moshe now had time to give Eliezer a Bris Milah. In general, we derive an important principle from what happened to Moshe. For example, a person cannot claim that he does not have the time to learn Torah if he had the time to do other less important things. A person cannot claim that he does not have the money to give Tzedakah if he had the money to buy unnecessary items. The Beis HaLevi in Parshas Vayigash says that this was exactly the way that Yosef completely refuted Yehuda's argument on why Yosef should free Binyamin. Yehuda argued that Yosef (who they didn't know was Yosef at that time) should have mercy on Yaakov since Yaakov would be extremely pained and might die when he found out that Binyamin was not returning to him. According to the Beis HaLevi, Yosef refuted this argument when he said in Beraishis (45:3), "I am Yosef. Is my father still alive?" When Yosef said, "Is my father still alive?" he was not asking a question, being that they had already told Yosef that Yaakov was alive. Rather he was making a statement of how it was possible that Yaakov could be alive after having been subjected to so much pain of thinking that Yosef was dead for 22 years. If Yehuda really believed his argument, implied Yosef, how could he not worry about Yaakov's pain when he took away Yosef from Yaakov? Therefore, Yosef showed a direct contradiction to Yehuda's argument from his own previous action with Yosef. This is what the Midrash on that Posuk means when it says that Hashem will come on the day of judgment and rebuke everyone according to what they are. Hashem will show that every excuse for a sin is contradicted by the person's own previous actions, as in the examples that we quoted from Rav Sternbuch above.

The Shitah Mekubetzes on the Gemorah in Nedorim ponders the following question. We know that giving a Bris Milah on the eighth day supersedes the Mitzvah of not desecrating the Shabbos if the eighth day falls out on Shabbos. The Yerushalmi (3:9) immediately preceding the part which discusses our Posuk proves that observing Shabbos is so great that it measures as much as observing all the other Mitzvos. The Shitah Mekubetzes puts these two facts together and ponders why we shouldn't conclude that doing the Bris Milah should have superseded the Mitzvah of going to Egypt. He answers that Moshe calculated that if Hashem wanted him to first do the Bris Milah before going to Egypt, then Hashem would not have told him to go to Egypt until after he had done the Bris Milah and had given Eliezer three days to recuperate from the Bris Milah.

Vayikra (18:5) says, "You shall observe My statutes and My ordinances, which a man shall do and live by them. I am Hashem." The Gemorah in Yuma 85b derives from the phrase "and live by them" that a person should not die for them. That is, the saving of a life overrides doing a Mitzvah. In fact, Rashi on that Gemorah explains that even if doing the Mitzvah would lead to a possibility of death, it would also override doing a Mitzvah. For example, we are to desecrate the Shabbos

Shemos

because of the possibility of saving someone's life. It is only this principle that would tell us that Moshe was not obligated to do the Mitzvah of Bris Milah on his son while fulfilling the commandment of going to Egypt since there would be the possibility that his son would die from the danger of traveling. The Mizrachi ponders the following question. This new principle was only given when the Torah was given. Since it was the period of time before the Torah was given, this principle should not be applicable yet, and that being the case, how was Moshe permitted to not give his son a Bris Milah? He answers that even before the Torah was given, it was still logical that it was better to give up doing one Mitzvah for being able to do all the other Mitzvos for the rest of his life. The Shitah Mekubetzes on the Gemorah in Nedorim and the Yedei Moshe also answer similarly to the Mizrachi. According to the Mizrachi, it would seem that the added principle after the Torah was given is that one should give up doing the one Mitzvah even for just the possibility that it might endanger one's life. The Maharal, in Gur Aryeh, says that the Mizrachi's answer to his question is so obvious that his question is not even a question.

The Eyun Yaakov also presents an answer to the Mizrachi's question. Even though the Mitzvah of "and live by them" that a person should not die for them was not yet given, it was already given to Avrohom that a child has their Bris Milah on the eighth day after they are born, as opposed to immediately after they are born. The reason for waiting is in order for the child to get healthier after its birth so that there are no medical complications. That is why if there are any medical complications, the Bris Milah is delayed until after the child fully recovers so that the Bris Milah should not cause any medical problems. That being the case, the idea that one avoids the Bris Milah causing medical complications was always a concept with regard to Bris Milah even before the Torah was given. The Eyun Yaakov points out that there is, in fact, a case where one gives a Bris Milah even immediately after a child is born. In Shulchan Aruch, Yoreh Deah (267), the laws of servants are discussed. More concretely, the ramifications of the Halacha of one who buys a Gentile slave needing to give the servant a Bris Milah are discussed. The Shulchan Aruch says that there are cases when one gives the servant a Bris Milah on the eighth day and a case when one can give the servant a Bris Milah as early as the first day after they are born. If one buys a female servant who is pregnant and she gives birth, then the child has a Bris Milah on the eighth day. The reason for this Halacha is because the Jew owns the female servant and, by extension, the child when it is born, and anything the Jew owns has a Bris Milah on the eighth day. If one buys the child of the female servant, then the child is given a Bris Milah right away so that if the child is bought when it is one day old, then it gets a Bris Milah on that day since every male that a Jew owns must have a Bris Milah. Therefore, we see that it is even possible to give a valid Bris Milah to a one-day-old child. The Eyun Yaakov says that the only reason we must, in general, wait until the child is eight days old is because the Torah was concerned that the Bris Milah should not lead to medical complications. Therefore, Moshe already knew before the Torah was given that a Bris Milah should not be given if it causes medical complications. Parenthetically the Eyun Yaakov says that since the Torah was not as concerned about the servant, he is allowed to have a Bris Milah when he is one day old.

The Ben Yehoyoda presents a couple of answers he and his son gave to the Mizrachi's question. Firstly, he says that in our case, Moshe was only not doing a Mitzvah as opposed to actively violating a Mitzvah not to do something like the case of desecrating Shabbos for danger. He is of

Shemos

the opinion that not doing a Mitzvah because it is dangerous would be a logical conclusion even before the Torah was given. The Yedei Moshe also answers similarly to the Ben Yehoyoda. Secondly, the Ben Yehoyoda says that since Moshe always intended to eventually give his son a Bris Milah when they got to Egypt, it is logical that one can delay doing a Mitzvah because of danger.

2) The Eben Ezra, Akeidah, and Ralbag present an answer to our question. The Eben Ezra says that the Jews of that time had a tradition that was handed down which said that a child should not have a Bris Milah on the eighth day either if the child was sick or if the child was traveling, and those transporting the child were unable to stop for three days. Moshe considered and applied the second part of this tradition to his own case since he was unable to stop for three days, being that he was an emissary of Hashem to take the Bnei Yisroel out of Egypt. However, the Eben Ezra, Akeidah, and Ralbag say that this was all based on one assumption: Moshe's family had to travel with him to Egypt. The Ralbag says that Moshe made the assumption that if the Bnei Yisroel saw him coming to Egypt without his family, they would think he did this since he was not so confident that he would redeem the Bnei Yisroel. Hashem sent an angel that came in the form of a snake to show Moshe about the big mistake that he made in his reasoning of taking his family along and thereby delaying Eliezer's Bris Milah from taking place.

3) The Daas Zekanim and Maskil LeDovid answer our question similarly. The Daas Zekanim is troubled by the question that when Eliezer had his Bris Milah at the inn, Moshe was in the same predicament that he had been in Midyan in needing to now wait three days for Eliezer to recover, thereby delaying Hashem's commandment to go to Egypt. Shemos (4:27) says, "Hashem said to Aharon, "Go toward Moshe, to the desert." So he went and met him on the mount of G-d, and he kissed him." Rashi in Parshas Yisro on Shemos (18:2) quotes the Mechilta on this Posuk, which tells us about the conversation between Moshe and Aharon when they met. Aharon said to Moshe, "Who are these?" Moshe replied, "This is my wife, whom I married in Midyan, and these are my sons." "And where are you taking them?" Aharon asked. "To Egypt," Moshe replied. Aharon retorted, "We are suffering with the first ones, and you come to add to them?" At that point, Moshe said to Tziporah, "Go home to your father." Tziporah took her two sons and went away. The Daas Zekanim and Maskil LeDovid say that the episode at the inn occurred after Aharon had this conversation with Moshe. In fact, the Maskil LeDovid says that it happened immediately after the conversation with Aharon. Therefore, since Tziporah was now returning to Midyan, there was no issue for her to wait at the inn for three days before going back to Midyan. Though we may be troubled that the Torah tells us about the episode at the inn before the meeting between Moshe and Aharon, the Daas Zekanim and Maskil LeDovid are not troubled by this and are of the opinion that the Torah is not in chronological order. According to them, the Torah does not record what happened in chronological order, even in a case such as ours, where what happened at the inn would have been much easier to understand in chronological order according to their answer. The Nachalas Yaakov is troubled by the fact that the Mechilta, which Rashi quotes, says explicitly that after the conversation with Aharon, Moshe immediately sent Tziporah and her sons, home. It seems to me that as the Maskil LeDovid says, we must say, according to this answer, that Aharon met

Shemos

Moshe immediately before what happened at the inn, and Tziporah did not yet have a chance to go home before the angel came and swallowed Moshe.

4) The Tur also presents an answer to our question. He says that Moshe was under the impression that the Bnei Yisroel would very soon be redeemed from Egypt. That being the case, and since the inn was not very far from Egypt, Moshe and Tziporah planned that Tziporah would remain in the inn with the children until the Bnei Yisroel were redeemed from Egypt and then accompany them from the inn. It is possible that part of this decision was based on Moshe not wanting to take the risk of his family being enslaved or persecuted if they were to enter Egypt. That being the case, Moshe was obligated to give Eliezer a Bris Milah immediately. Moshe was then punished because he first became involved in matters of lodging at the inn.

5) The Ponim Yofos and Maskil LeDovid argue with the Rosh, Tur, Ran, Mizrachi, and Korban HaEidah on the Yerushalmi's assertion in the first answer that this inn was close to Egypt and that is why Moshe could have performed the Bris Milah at the inn. A few Pesukim after our Posuk in Shemos (4:27), the Torah says, "Hashem said to Aharon, 'Go toward Moshe, to the desert.' So he went and met him on the mount of G-d, and he kissed him." The Ponim Yofos says that the "mount of G-d" refers to Mount Saini. A proof for this can be seen from the Ramban on Shemos (18:1) who says that we find in Shemos (18:5) "Now Moshe's father-in-law, Yisro, and his (Moshe's) sons and his wife came to Moshe, to the desert where he was encamped, to the mountain of G-d." The Ramban proves that the Bnei Yisroel were at that time on Mount Sinai so that Mount Sinai is synonymous with "mount of G-d." Since Mount Sinai is many stops away from Egypt, as the Pesukim say in Parshas Masei, this indicates that Moshe was still far away from Egypt. According to the Ponim Yofos, we are still left with the question of why Moshe was punished for not giving a Bris Milah at the inn and not punished when he originally left Midyan. Moshe's calculation, given in the Gemorah Nedorim 31b, that if he gave Eliezer the Bris Milah now and travel, it will be a danger to the child for a few days was as valid now as it was when Moshe left Midyan. He says that when Moshe left Midyan, it was before Eliezer was eight days old, and he was not yet halachically able to give Eliezer a Bris Milah. Moshe, therefore, needed to take Eliezer and, of course, his mother Tziporah along on the way to Egypt since if he left them in Midyan, there would be no one to give Eliezer a Bris Milah. Now when they got to the inn, Eliezer was already at or past eight days old. Therefore, Moshe could give Eliezer a Bris Milah at the inn, and Tziporah and Eliezer could stay at the inn to recover from the Bris Milah. However, "Hashem met him and sought to put him to death" since Moshe became involved in matters of lodging at the inn, instead of immediately doing the Bris Milah.

6) The Rif (Rav Yoshiyahu Pinto) on the Ain Yaakov also ponders our question. Like the Ponim Yofos, he is also of the opinion that the inn was far away from Egypt, and in fact, he is of the opinion that it is the first inn that they visited on the way back to Egypt. The Rif says that Moshe fulfilled Hashem's command to go back to Egypt by leaving Yisro's house and heading toward Egypt. Therefore, there was no problem of giving Eliezer a Bris Milah at the first inn and then waiting three days until Eliezer recovered. Even if they subsequently continued on their journey to Egypt, Moshe had already fulfilled the command of going back to Egypt.

Shemos

7) The Abarbanel and the Malbim also present an answer to our question. They say that Moshe had to be constantly ready to receive further prophecies from Hashem so that he could get all the necessary instructions for redeeming the Bnei Yisroel from Egypt. That being the case, Moshe had to always be thinking about spiritual matters and about his mission. However, when Moshe got to the inn, he was not on the spiritual level to receive prophecy since he first busied himself with the physical matters of setting up to sleep at the inn. When our Posuk says וַיִּפְגְּשֵׁהוּ ה' וַיְבַקֵּשׁ הֲמִיתוֹ (Hashem met him (Moshe) and sought to put him to death), they say that Hashem meeting Moshe meant that Hashem wanted to give him more prophecy about his mission in Egypt. Since Moshe was not on the spiritual level to receive this prophecy, he was almost killed by Hashem appearing to him when he was not on the correct level for this. The Abarbanel says that when Tziporah saw that Moshe was in danger of dying, she quickly assessed that this could be due to either one or two of the following causes. Either Moshe should have given Eliezer a Bris Milah immediately at the inn, or he should not have brought his family along so that it would be easier for Moshe to remain on a high spiritual level to attain prophecy. For the first possibility, Tziporah immediately gave Eliezer a Bris Milah, and for the second possibility, she announced to Moshe that she was going to return to Midyan with the two small children immediately after Eliezer recovered from his Bris Milah.

8) The Toldos Yitzchak and Meshech Chochmah answer our question similarly. Similar to what the Abarbanel says in the introduction, they say that Moshe decided to bring his wife and small children so that the Bnei Yisroel would have confidence in him that he would redeem the Bnei Yisroel from Egypt. Moshe reasoned that if he didn't bring his family along, the people would say that Moshe himself was not even confident about his mission and therefore wanted to make it easy for him to quickly and easily return to Midyan if his mission failed. The Chizkuni and Rashbam both say that Moshe should instead have given Eliezer a Bris Milah in Midyan and then hurried on his way to Egypt to fulfill the mission of redeeming the Bnei Yisroel from Egypt. They say that Hashem wanted to kill Moshe at the inn because he had to go slowly and worry about physical issues of sleeping at the inn because of his family instead of fulfilling Hashem's command with alacrity and zealousness. The Meshech Chochmah also says that Moshe was punished for bringing his family along. The Toldos Yitzchak says that Moshe could have performed the Bris in Midyan, and after Eliezer recovered, he could have summoned his family to join him in Egypt. However, because of his humility, Moshe did not feel that it was right to ask his father-in-law Yisro to bring his family to him in Egypt, being that it would have been too dangerous for his wife and small children to travel alone. The only other option would have been for Moshe to hire a driver to bring them to him, but since Moshe did not have any money, he could not do this either. Therefore, Moshe decided to bring them along with him, which led to the issues at the inn. Parenthetically, the Toldos Yitzchak says that Moshe was so poor that he only had one donkey (which was cheaper than a horse) to take his entire family to Egypt. Since Tziporah had just given birth, he put her holding Eliezer on the donkey and had Gershom sit in the back of Tziporah and hold on to her while Moshe walked along with the donkey.

The Toldos Yitzchak says that there was another reason why Moshe did not give a Bris Milah to Eliezer in Midyan and go immediately to redeem the Bnei Yisroel from Egypt. Tziporah, though

Shemos

she wasn't Jewish yet, allowed Moshe to give a Bris Milah to their oldest son Gershom, reasoning that he should have a Bris Milah as his father had. However, when she saw that Gershom had medical difficulties after the Bris Milah and she saw how much Gershom cried after getting his Bris Milah, she did not allow Moshe to give a Bris Milah to their second son Eliezer. Moshe, should not have listened to her and should have given Eliezer a Bris Milah whether or not Tziporah allowed it. That is why Hashem wanted to kill Moshe at the inn. Seeing how the snake swallowed up Moshe, as we have mentioned in the introduction, Tziporah realized that not having a Bris Milah was the cause of what was happening to Moshe, and she immediately took a shark rock to give Eliezer a Bris Milah. Shemos (4:25) says, "So Tziporah took a sharp stone and severed her son's foreskin and touched it to his feet." He says that "touched it to his feet" is referring to the sharp rock. Tziporah was so much in a hurry and frenzy that she not only cut off Eliezer's foreskin but also partially cut the foot of Eliezer.

9) The Shach also ponders our question. Shemos (4:20) says, "So Moshe took his wife and his sons, mounted them upon the donkey, and he returned to the land of Egypt." We have mentioned previously that one donkey does not really have enough room to seat Tziporah and her two children. He says that the reason Moshe only used one donkey was because he wanted to hint to Tziporah that she should remain behind in Midyan while he went to Egypt to redeem the Bnei Yisroel, as Aharon eventually convinced her to do. However, Moshe feared that if he told this directly to Tziporah, she would not want to listen since she preferred to go along and remain with her husband. Moshe also thought that Tziporah would be afraid that Moshe might go to Egypt to find another wife, this one from his own family who were in Egypt. Therefore, Moshe could only hint this to Tziporah. He says that what happened in the inn was Hashem showing Tziporah that it was preferable that she didn't go along, since without his family accompanying him, Moshe could travel much more quickly to Egypt and have much more time to deal with the Bnei Yisroel, who were extremely oppressed and in need of being consoled. The Shach says that the incident at the inn happened at the first inn they came to on the first day of their travels. They also soon met Aharon who reinforced this message, and Aharon plus the incident at the inn convinced Tziporah to go back to Midyan.

10) The Chasam Sofer also presents an answer to our question. He says that by the time Moshe got to the inn, it was already past the eighth day from when Eliezer had been born. Since it was no longer a Bris Milah done on time on the eighth day, Moshe calculated that it would be better to delay the Bris Milah even further. We have mentioned in the introduction that the vast majority of the Bnei Yisroel did not have a Bris Milah in Egypt and that they would all have a Bris Milah right before they left Egypt. Moshe calculated that it would be better to delay Eliezer's Bris Milah until the Bnei Yisroel left Egypt so that he would participate in doing the Bris Milah along with many others of the Bnei Yisroel. Moshe, at that point, was under the impression that the redemption would be relatively imminent after he got to Egypt. That being the case, he was not afraid that something might, Chas VeShalom, happen to Eliezer such that Eliezer might die before getting his Bris Milah. However, at the inn, Hashem showed Moshe that his calculation was wrong since no one can know when one's end might come. Even Moshe, who, as we showed in the introduction, Hashem had told, was the only person able to redeem the Bnei Yisroel from Egypt, was in danger of

Shemos

dying at the inn before he even got to Egypt. How much more so did Moshe have to be careful with Eliezer who had no such guarantee on life?

11) The Chasam Sofer also presents a second answer to our question. He says that had the Gemorah in Nedorim not said that Moshe was punished for occupying himself with issues of the inn before giving Eliezer a Bris Milah, he would have given an entirely different reason for Moshe's punishment. Shemos (4:18) says, "Moshe went and returned to Yisro, his father-in-law, and he said to him, 'Let me go now and return to my brothers who are in Egypt, and let me see whether they are still alive.' So Yisro said to Moshe, 'Go in peace.'" He derives from this Posuk that Moshe did not tell Yisro that Hashem had told him that he was the one chosen to redeem the Bnei Yisroel from Egypt, and that is why he was going back to Egypt. He extends this concept to include Tziporah, also not knowing about Moshe's mission. Presumably, he would be of the opinion that Moshe was much too humble to reveal to his father-in-law and even to his wife that Hashem had specifically chosen Moshe as the only person worthy of redeeming the Bnei Yisroel from Egypt. That being the case, both Yisro and especially Tziporah were unable to fathom why Moshe would think that visiting his family was more important than giving his son a Bris Milah. In fact, this caused a Chilul Hashem that both Yisro and Tziporah, based on their knowledge, would think that Moshe was forsaking a Mitzvah of Bris Milah for visiting his family. He quotes the Gemorah in Yuma 86a, which says that if someone has the sin of Chilul Hashem, it is such a grave sin that neither Teshuva, Yom Kippur, nor suffering punishment alone is powerful enough to even just protect the person from a full punishment. Rather only the combination of Teshuva, Yom Kippur, and suffering punishment is able to protect the person from a full punishment and is only forgiven fully when the person is Niftar. The Gemorah proves this from Sefer Yeshayahu (22:14), which says, "And it was revealed in My ears, Hashem of Hosts; that this sin shall not be atoned for you until you die." Rashi on the Gemorah explains that this Posuk shows that there is a sin that is only atoned for on death. Since Chilul Hashem is the gravest sin, the Gemorah concludes that this Posuk must be talking about the punishment for Chilul Hashem. The Chasam Sofer concludes that Tziporah only much later, when she and her father heard about all the miracles with which Hashem through Moshe had caused the Bnei Yisroel to be redeemed from Egypt, found out the real reason Moshe went back to Egypt. She thought that the only reason Hashem wanted to kill Moshe was because Moshe had put visiting his family before doing the Mitzvah of Bris Milah. For this loss of respect for Moshe, says the Chasam Sofer, Tziporah had no compunctions leaving Moshe and going back to her father in Midyan.

12) Rav Meir Bergman, in his Sefer Shaarei Orah, also ponders our question. The whole purpose of going out of Egypt was so that they could receive the Torah on Mount Sinai. Beraishis (1:31) says, "And there was evening, and there was morning on the sixth day." Different than all the other days of creation, the Torah uses the word "the" before "sixth day." Rashi, the Kli Yakor, and some commentators in explaining the Gemorah in Shabbos 88a all say that the world was in limbo until the sixth day. The sixth day is the sixth day of Sivan, the day the Bnei Yisroel received the Torah. The world would only exist if the Bnei Yisroel agreed to accept the Torah. The Zohar in Parshas Terumah 170b says that when the Bnei Yisroel came to the Red Sea, Hashem wanted to split the sea. The angel, who is in charge of Egypt, named Rahav, came and asked for justice. Rahav said, Master

Shemos

of the World, why do you want to punish the Egyptians and split the sea for the Bnei Yisroel. Both the Egyptians and the Bnei Yisroel are wicked, and Hashem's ways are of justice and truth. The Egyptians serve idols, and the Bnei Yisroel serve idols. The Egyptians are immoral, and the Bnei Yisroel are immoral. The Egyptians are murderers, and the Bnei Yisroel are murderers. In that situation, says the Zohar, it was difficult for Hashem since Rahav did have a point, yet the Bnei Yisroel were right up to the banks of the Red Sea with the Egyptians right in back of them. It says that at the time of the morning watch, Hashem took into account the merit of Avrohom, who got up early on the morning watch to fulfill the command of Hashem to bring Yitzchak to the Akeidah. Rav Bergman explains that the extra merit of Avrohom was the fact that he was enthusiastic and zealous to do Hashem's Mitzvos, and that is why he got up early. Since this zealousness is what saved the Bnei Yisroel and destroyed the Egyptians, the Bnei Yisroel needed a leader who would imbue zealousness and enthusiasm into doing the Mitzvos that the Bnei Yisroel received on Mount Sinai. This would justify the fact that Hashem split the Red Sea and saved the Bnei Yisroel. When Moshe did not show this enthusiasm for the Mitzvah of Bris Milah in our Posuk, our Posuk says, "Hashem met him and sought to put him to death." The reason for this punishment is that Moshe was not showing the enthusiasm Hashem would need for doing justice by splitting the Sea despite Rahav's argument, in the merit of Avrohom's and the Bnei Yisroel's enthusiasm for doing Mitzvos. The Ralbag on our Posuk also mentions the fact that as leader of the Bnei Yisroel, he needed to teach the Bnei Yisroel enthusiasm for Mitzvos.

13) We will now present an answer that assumes that Moshe's first child Gershom got the Bris Milah at the inn. The Targum Yonason ben Uziel and the Yalkut Shimoni (169) say that the reason Hashem wanted to kill Moshe was because his son Gershom did not have a Bris Milah because his father-in-law Yisro did not allow him to give Gershom a Bris Milah. The Targum Yonason ben Uziel concludes by saying that Eliezer did have a Bris Milah because of the deal Moshe and Yisro made. The Mechilta on Shemos (18:3) in Parshas Yisro provides us with more details of the deal between Moshe and Yisro. When Moshe asked Yisro for permission to marry his daughter Tziporah, Yisro gave his permission on one condition. Yisro asked that Moshe's first son should be brought up and trained to worship idols while any subsequent sons could be brought up to serve Hashem. Moshe agreed, and Yisro forced Moshe to take an oath on this agreement. The Mechilta says that this is the meaning of Shemos (2:21) וַיּוֹאֶל מֹשֶׁה לָשֶׁבֶת אֶת הָאִישׁ וַיִּתֵּן אֶת צִפֹּרָה בִתּוֹ לְמֹשֶׁה. According to the Mechilta, the root of the Hebrew word וַיּוֹאֶל means to take an oath. As an example, we find this usage in Beraishis (26:28) when Avimelech says to Yitzchak תְּהִי נָא אָלָה בֵּינוֹתֵינוּ בֵּינֵינוּ וּבֵינֶךָ וְנִכְרְתָה בְרִית עִמָּךְ (Let there now be an oath between us, between ourselves and you, and let us form a covenant with you). The Baal HaTurim on Shemos (18:3) says that when Tziporah realized that Moshe was going to be killed for this, she absolved Moshe of this oath by performing the Bris Milah on Gershom. The Baal HaTurim points out that this oath to Yisro had ramifications for Moshe. Sefer Shoftim (18:30) says, וַיָּקִימוּ לָהֶם בְּנֵי דָן אֶת הַפָּסֶל וִיהוֹנָתָן בֶּן גֵּרְשֹׁם בֶּן מְנַשֶּׁה הוּא וּבָנָיו הָיוּ כֹהֲנִים לְשֵׁבֶט הַדָּנִי עַד יוֹם גְּלוֹת הָאָרֶץ (And the children of Dan set up for themselves the graven image. And Yonason, the son of Gershom, the son of Menashe, both he and his sons were priests to the tribe of the Danites until the day of the exile of the land). In that Posuk, the Hebrew word מְנַשֶּׁה is written with the Nun hanging above the rest of the word so that if we ignore the Nun, we instead of מְנַשֶּׁה get the name מֹשֶׁה. The Gemorah in Baba Basra 109b says that, in fact, this is referring to Moshe

141

Shemos

Rabeinu. The Gemorah, as explained by the Rashbam, says that the reason the name מְנַשֶּׁה is ascribed to Moshe is because his grandson followed in the path of Menashe, the son of Chizkiyahu who was notorious for serving idols. The Baal HaTurim says that Moshe's grandson being a priest for idols was a result of this oath, which Moshe took for Yisro.

In his Sefer Pirkei Torah, Rav Gifter explains more about this oath and how Moshe agreed to it. He says that Yisro demanded that Moshe marry Tziporah without converting her until she had her first son. Rav Gifter explains that since Yisro did not have any sons, he wanted one grandson to be in place of a son for him. The Ramban on Beraishis (26:5) says that Avrohom, Yitzchak, and Yaakov only kept the Mitzvos when they were in Eretz Yisroel. The Ramban alludes to a Sifrei quoted by Rashi on the second paragraph of Kriyas Shema in Devorim (11:18), which says that the reason for doing Mitzvos even after going in exile is to keep ourselves used to doing Mitzvos when we return to Eretz Yisroel. One can imply from this Sifrei that had there not been this reason of remaining fresh in the performance of these Mitzvos, there would be no obligation to keep them outside of Eretz Yisroel, and therefore our forefathers only meticulously kept the Mitzvos in Eretz Yisroel. Therefore, says Rav Gifter, according to the Ramban, there would not be a problem with Moshe entering into such an agreement with Yisro. The Ohr HaChaim on Beraishis (26:5) says that in some small number of cases, our forefathers calculated that there would be such a gain in doing something which the Torah would later prohibit, that the gain overrode the loss in reward from not keeping that particular Mitzvah. An example of this was Yaakov marrying two sisters. This opinion is typically quoted as the competing answer to the Ramban's line of reasoning. Therefore, even according to this opinion, Moshe seemed to calculate that the gain of marrying Tziporah outweighed Gershom not being Jewish, and therefore, Moshe entered into this deal with Yisro. He explains that when Yisro agreed that Moshe and his family, including Gershom, could go to Egypt, this showed that Yisro had nullified his oath since Gershom was no longer going to be with Yisro. With the oath nullified, Moshe should have immediately started Gershom's conversion process, including giving him a Bris Milah, and Moshe is punished for not giving it at the first opportunity. Parenthetically, the Meshech Chochmah explains with the above oath why Gershom and Eliezer got their names. At the beginning of Parshas Yisro, Shemos (18:3) says that the older son Gershom got his name "because he (Moshe) said, 'I was a stranger in a foreign land.'" Shemos (18:4) says that the younger son Eliezer got his name because "The G-d of my father came to my aid and rescued me from Pharaoh's sword." Since Moshe was rescued from Pharaoh's sword before he left Egypt, this happened chronologically before Moshe became a stranger in a foreign land. Therefore, it would have made much more sense if Moshe would have named his sons according to the chronological order of events so that the oldest son would have been called Eliezer and not Gershom. The Meshech Chochmah explains that since Gershom was not converted when he was born, Moshe did not want to name him with a name that contained "The G-d of my father," and therefore, he was not named Eliezer.

14) The Ksav VeHakabola answers our question in a very unique way, which answers many of the questions posed in the above introduction and previous answers. He says that when our Posuk says וַיְבַקֵּשׁ הֲמִיתוֹ (sought to put him to death), it is not referring to Hashem but Moshe wanting to put himself to death! This explanation immediately answers the question of how Hashem could want to

Shemos

kill Moshe after telling him that only Moshe was able to take the Bnei Yisroel out of Egypt. He argues for his explanation since it is not appropriate to ascribe to Hashem that He wants to put someone to death. Rather Sefer Yechezkel (33:11) says, "Say to them: As I live, says Hashem, G-d, I do not wish for the death of the wicked, but for the wicked to repent of his way so that he may live. Repent, repent of your evil ways, for why should you die, O house of Yisroel!" The Ksav VeHakabola says that if Hashem does not wish for even the wicked to die, how much more so does Hashem not wish for his servant Moshe to die. He says that after Moshe realized that Hashem was punishing him for his sin, Moshe concluded that if he was wicked in the eyes of Hashem, then he had no reason to continue living. He says that Moshe has a similar response to Hashem after Moshe questioned Hashem's ability to provide enough meat for the Bnei Yisroel in the desert when the Bnei Yisroel complained about not having meat to eat. In Bamidbar (11:15), Moshe says to Hashem, "please kill me if I have found favor in Your eyes so that I do not see my misfortune."

Vaera

The Malbim's Explanation of How Moshe's Level of Prophesy Changed at the Beginning of Parshas Vaera.

וַיְדַבֵּר אֱלֹקִים אֶל מֹשֶׁה וַיֹּאמֶר אֵלָיו אֲנִי ה' (ו:ב) Shemos (6:2) G-d spoke to Moshe, and He said to him, "I am Hashem."

We present the Malbim's explanation of how Moshe's level of prophecy changed at the beginning of Parshas Vaera.

The previous Posuk to ours says וַיֹּאמֶר ה' אֶל מֹשֶׁה עַתָּה תִרְאֶה אֲשֶׁר אֶעֱשֶׂה לְפַרְעֹה כִּי בְיָד חֲזָקָה יְשַׁלְּחֵם וּבְיָד חֲזָקָה יְגָרְשֵׁם מֵאַרְצוֹ (And Hashem said to Moshe, "Now you will see what I will do to Pharaoh, for with a mighty hand he will send them out, and with a mighty hand he will drive them out of his land.") Until now, says the Malbim, when Hashem had spoken to Moshe, Hashem had always used the word וַיֹּאמֶר, and now for the first time the Torah describes Hashem's speaking to Moshe with the Hebrew word וַיְדַבֵּר. From this point in the Torah and onwards we will many times see the Posuk וַיְדַבֵּר ה' אֶל מֹשֶׁה לֵּאמֹר (And Hashem spoke to Moshe saying).

At the beginning of Vayikra, he explains the difference between the Hebrew word וַיְדַבֵּר (and he spoke) and the Hebrew word וַיֹּאמֶר (and he said). He quotes the Radak who says that the Hebrew word וַיֹּאמֶר is used when one person is talking to someone else, and the word וַיֹּאמֶר will always be followed by who is being spoken to. The Hebrew word וַיְדַבֵּר can be used to describe the characteristic of speaking as Megilas Ester (1:22) says, לִהְיוֹת כָּל אִישׁ שֹׂרֵר בְּבֵיתוֹ **וּמְדַבֵּר** כִּלְשׁוֹן עַמּוֹ (that every man dominate in his household and **speak** according to the language of his nationality), and in that case, does not need to say who is being spoken to. In fact, וַיְדַבֵּר is the general characteristic of the art of speech and under this category comes different ways of speaking an example of which is וַיְצַו (and he commanded) as in Beraishis (28:6) וַיְצַו עָלָיו לֵאמֹר לֹא תִקַּח אִשָּׁה מִבְּנוֹת כְּנָעַן (He (Yitzchak) commanded him (Yaakov), saying, "You shall not take a wife of the daughters of Canaan."). Another example is וַיַּגֵּד (and he told) as in Beraishis (29:12) וַיַּגֵּד יַעֲקֹב לְרָחֵל כִּי אֲחִי אָבִיהָ הוּא וְכִי בֶן רִבְקָה הוּא וַתָּרָץ וַתַּגֵּד לְאָבִיהָ (And Yaakov told Rochel that he was her father's kinsman and that he was Rivka's son, and she ran and told her father). Another example is וַיֹּאמֶר (and he said) as in Beraishis (3:1) וַיֹּאמֶר אֶל הָאִשָּׁה אַף כִּי אָמַר אֱלֹהִים לֹא תֹאכְלוּ מִכֹּל עֵץ הַגָּן (and it (the snake) said to the woman (Chava), "Did G-d indeed say, 'You shall not eat of any of the trees of the garden?'" Another example is וַיְסַפֵּר (and he told) as in Shemos (18:8) וַיְסַפֵּר מֹשֶׁה לְחֹתְנוֹ אֵת כָּל אֲשֶׁר עָשָׂה ה' לְפַרְעֹה וּלְמִצְרַיִם

Vaera

עַל אוֹדֹת יִשְׂרָאֵל אֵת כָּל הַתְּלָאָה אֲשֶׁר מְצָאַתַם בַּדֶּרֶךְ וַיַּצִּלֵם ה' (Moshe told his father-in-law about all that Hashem had done to Pharaoh and to the Egyptians on account of Yisroel, and about all the hardships that had befallen them on the way, and that Hashem had saved them.). Another example is וַיִּשְׁאַל (and he asked) as in Beraishis (32:30) וַיִּשְׁאַל יַעֲקֹב וַיֹּאמֶר הַגִּידָה נָּא שְׁמֶךָ (And Yaakov asked (the angel) and said, "Now tell me your name"). Yet another example is וַיַּעַן (and he answered) as in Beraishis (18:27) וַיַּעַן אַבְרָהָם וַיֹּאמַר (And Avrohom answered and said). As opposed to וַיֹּאמֶר (and he said) where the Torah tells us what was said, the Torah when it uses וַיְדַבֵּר (and he spoke) does not necessarily need to tell us what the person spoke of. For example, in Beraishis (42:24) it says וַיִּסֹּב מֵעֲלֵיהֶם וַיֵּבְךְּ וַיָּשָׁב אֲלֵהֶם וַיְדַבֵּר אֲלֵהֶם וַיִּקַּח מֵאִתָּם אֶת שִׁמְעוֹן וַיֶּאֱסֹר אֹתוֹ לְעֵינֵיהֶם (And he (Yosef) turned away from them and wept, then returned to them (the brothers) and spoke to them; and he took Shimon from among them and imprisoned him before their eyes). In this Posuk, we are not told what Yosef said to his brothers before taking Shimon. Similarly, we find וַיְדַבֵּר used for permission to speak in Beraishis (24:33) וַיּוּשַׂם לְפָנָיו לֶאֱכֹל וַיֹּאמֶר לֹא אֹכַל עַד אִם דִּבַּרְתִּי דְּבָרָי וַיֹּאמֶר דַּבֵּר (And food was set before him (Eliezer) to eat, but he said, "I will not eat until I have spoken my words." And he (Lavan) said, "Speak").

It is therefore common to find the Torah first use the term וַיְדַבֵּר (and he spoke) and then use the term וַיֹּאמֶר (and he said) to tell us what the actual words used were. For example, Beraishis (19:14) says, וַיֵּצֵא לוֹט וַיְדַבֵּר אֶל חֲתָנָיו לֹקְחֵי בְנֹתָיו וַיֹּאמֶר קוּמוּ צְּאוּ מִן הַמָּקוֹם הַזֶּה כִּי מַשְׁחִית ה' אֶת הָעִיר וַיְהִי כִמְצַחֵק בְּעֵינֵי חֲתָנָיו (So Lot went forth and spoke to his sons-in-law, the suitors of his daughters, and he said, "Arise, go forth from this place, for Hashem is destroying the city," but he seemed like a comedian in the eyes of his sons-in-law). That is, Lot also spoke other things with his sons-in-law, but the words important for us to know is "Arise, go forth from this place, for Hashem is destroying the city." Similarly, is the very common Posuk וַיְדַבֵּר ה' אֶל מֹשֶׁה לֵּאמֹר (and Hashem spoke to Moshe saying). This Posuk tells us that first Hashem told Moshe about all the Halachos including all their specific laws along with everything any future person would derive in whatever topic that was going to be presented to the Bnei Yisroel (וַיְדַבֵּר). Then Hashem told Moshe exactly what to write in the Torah about this topic (לֵּאמֹר).

I think we can understand a bit more about how this worked from what the Ohr HaChaim writes on Vayikra (13:34). He ponders two statements of the Gemorah, which at first glance seem to be contradictory. The Gemorah in Megilah 19b derives from a Posuk that Hashem showed Moshe the fine interpretations of the Torah, the fine Rabbinic interpretations, and what the Sages would innovate in the future. Rashi explains that the fine interpretations of the Torah are what Halachos are included when the Torah says "also" and "with" and what Halachos are excluded when the Torah says "only or "but." Rashi explains that the fine Rabbinic interpretations are what the later Sages inferred from the Mishna. The Yerushalmi Peah similarly says that Moshe was told everything that an old or learned student would rule before his Rabbi, such that if someone said some Halacha was new, he would be told that the Halacha had been around for all time. On the flip side, there is a Gemorah in Menochos 29b, which says that when Moshe went to heaven to receive the Torah, he found Hashem sitting and attaching crowns on top of some of the letters of the Torah. Moshe asked Hashem, "Who is holding Hashem back from giving the Torah as it is." Rashi explains that the letters were already written and that at this point, Hashem was attaching crowns to

146

Vaera

some of them. Hashem answered Moshe, "There is one man who is destined to exist at the end of many generations whose name is Akiva ben Yosef, and he will derive heaps and heaps of Halachos from the crowns. Moshe then said, "Master of the universe, please show him to me." Hashem told Moshe to turn around. Upon turning around, Moshe saw that he was in Rabi Akiva's class. Moshe walked to the back of the eighth row of students and sat down. As he listened to the discussion, Moshe was not able to understand what they were saying and became disheartened. At one point in the discussion, the students asked Rabi Akiva for the source of what he was saying. Rabi Akiva answered that the source is a Halacha transmitted to Moshe at Mount Sinai. Upon hearing this, Moshe was relieved. At first glance, the Gemorah, which says that Moshe was told by Hashem everything the Sages would innovate in the future, is in contradiction to this Gemorah that says Moshe could not understand what Rabi Akiva was discussing. The Ohr HaChaim explains that Hashem told Moshe all the Halachos of both the written and oral Torah that would be innovated for all future generations. In addition, Hashem made hints of all these Halachos in the written Torah. However, Hashem told Moshe neither all the hints nor how one could derive all the Halachos from the hints in the written Torah. That is the job of all the Torah Sages for all future generations. Therefore, Moshe knew all the Halachos that Rabi Akiva was presenting to his students; he was just not familiar with how Rabi Akiva was explaining how to derive these Halachos from the hints in the written Torah. This approach explains what the Bamidbar Raba (19:6) means when it says that things that were not revealed to Moshe were revealed to Rabi Akiva and his fellow Rabbis. Going back to the Malbim, when the Torah many times introduces a topic with the Posuk וַיְדַבֵּר ה' אֶל מֹשֶׁה לֵּאמֹר included in וַיְדַבֵּר is all the Halachos of both the written and oral Torah that would be innovated for all future generations for this topic. Included in the word לֵּאמֹר is how to exactly write the written Torah so that all the hints necessary to derive all the Halachos are present in the written Torah.

With this approach, says the Malbim, we can understand a Gemorah Yerushalmi in Sanhedrin (4:2), which says that had the Torah been given cut up into pieces, it would not have a foot to stand on and exist. Rather, and as an example, continues the Gemorah, because of the Posuk וַיְדַבֵּר ה' אֶל מֹשֶׁה לֵּאמֹר we derive many Halachos from Shemos (23:2) which says, לֹא תִהְיֶה אַחֲרֵי רַבִּים לְרָעֹת וְלֹא תַעֲנֶה עַל רִב לִנְטֹת אַחֲרֵי רַבִּים לְהַטֹּת (You shall not follow the majority for evil, and you shall not respond concerning a lawsuit to follow many to pervert justice). There is also a similar Midrash Shochar Tov 12 to this Gemorah. The Ridvaz on this Gemorah references how Rashi explains the above Posuk in his explanation on Chumash. According to the simple meaning Rashi says, the Posuk would be taken as one concept. The phrase "You shall not follow the majority for evil" means: If you see wicked people perverting justice, do not say, "Since they are many, I will follow them." The rest of the Posuk, "you shall not respond concerning a lawsuit to follow many to pervert justice," means: if the litigant asks you about that corrupted judgment, do not answer him concerning the lawsuit with an answer that follows those many to pervert the judgment from its true ruling. Rather tell the judgment as it is, and let the neck iron (punishment for perverting justice) hang on the neck of the many. According to the simple explanation, the entire Posuk is talking about not following or aiding wicked people who pervert justice. However, the Gemorah derives many Halachic concepts from this Posuk by dividing it up into phrases and by examining how the Posuk is written. According to the Gemorah in Sanhedrin 2a, the phrase "You shall not follow the majority for evil" means: we may not decide unfavorably for the defendant (for evil) by a majority created by one

Vaera

judge for capital crimes. For example, if we have a Beis Din (court) with 23 judges and 12 of the judges decide that the person is guilty while 11 decide that the person is innocent, then despite the majority ruling that the person is guilty, the person is declared innocent. However, the beginning part of the Posuk, which tells us not to follow the majority, would seemingly conflict with the last phrase of the Posuk, which says to follow the majority. To resolve this conflict, the Gemorah says that there is a majority after whom you do decide the verdict. If a majority of at least two judges decide the person is guilty, then the person is declared guilty. In addition, since the first part of the Posuk says that we don't go after a majority for evil, this implies that for the good of the defendant (to declare him innocent), a majority of one is enough. We also need to consider the inner phrase of the Posuk: וְלֹא תַעֲנֶה עַל רֵב לִנְטֹת (which literally means that one should not answer a quarrel to follow). The Gemorah in Sanhedrin 36a points out that the Hebrew word רֵב is written, missing a Yud for the middle letter. Without the Yud, the Hebrew word רֵב can be read as רַב or master. The Gemorah says that this phrase comes to tell us that in capital cases, one starts from the opinion of the most junior member of the court and proceeds by increasing seniority such that only at the end is the senior member of the court asked for his opinion. In this way, no judge will face the temptation of accepting the opinion of a more senior member of the court and will honestly give his opinion. The gist of the above is that the Posuk can be divided into three separate phrases from which many pertinent Halachos can be derived. This is what the Yerushalmi means that because of the Posuk וַיְדַבֵּר ה' אֶל מֹשֶׁה לֵאמֹר we are able to derive many Halachos from this Posuk. The word לֵאמֹר (saying) tells us that Hashem told Moshe exactly how to write each word and how to phrase each phrase along with giving Moshe orally all the Halachos, as implied in the word וַיְדַבֵּר. This arrangement allows us to figure out where these Halachos are hinted at in the written Torah.

The Vayikra Raba (1:14) says that all other prophets saw their prophecies through a piece of glass that was cloudy, while Moshe saw his prophecy through a piece of glass that was clear. The Yepheh Toar explains that all other prophets had prophecies in which they saw images alluding to their prophecy while Moshe got direct words and not images. A prime example of how this worked for other prophets is found in Sefer Yirmiyahu (1:11-12) which says, וַיְהִי דְבַר ה' אֵלַי לֵאמֹר מָה אַתָּה רֹאֶה יִרְמְיָהוּ וָאֹמַר מַקֵּל שָׁקֵד אֲנִי רֹאֶה. וַיֹּאמֶר ה' אֵלַי הֵיטַבְתָּ לִרְאוֹת כִּי שֹׁקֵד אֲנִי עַל דְּבָרִי לַעֲשֹׂתוֹ (And the word of Hashem came to me, saying: What do you see, Yirmiyahu? And I said, "I see a rod of an almond tree." And Hashem said to me; You have seen well, for I hasten My word to accomplish it.). Rashi on the Posuk explains that Yirmiyahu was shown an almond tree since an almond tree is the first tree to flower, and therefore it symbolized that the results of the prophecy (which we will soon see) would quickly occur. Similarly, we find another example of how prophesy worked for Yirmiyahu in the following Pesukim (1:13-14): וַיְהִי דְבַר ה' אֵלַי שֵׁנִית לֵאמֹר מָה אַתָּה רֹאֶה וָאֹמַר סִיר נָפוּחַ אֲנִי רֹאֶה וּפָנָיו מִפְּנֵי צָפוֹנָה. וַיֹּאמֶר ה' אֵלָי מִצָּפוֹן תִּפָּתַח הָרָעָה עַל כָּל יֹשְׁבֵי הָאָרֶץ (And the word of Hashem came to me a second time, saying: What do you see? And I said, "I see a bubbling pot whose foam is toward the north." And Hashem said to me; From the north, the misfortune will break forth upon all the inhabitants of the land.). This prophecy prophesized that the Babylonians would soon invade and capture the Bnei Yisroel and bring about the end of the first Beis Hamikdosh.

The Gemorah in Yevomos 49b says that all the other prophets saw their prophesies through an Asparklaria Sheainah Meirah (a piece of glass that does not let light through) while Moshe saw his

Vaera

prophecy through an Asparklaria HaMeirah (a piece of glass that does allow light through). The Malbim in Bamidbar (12:6) says that we can understand this Gemorah based on how the Pesukim describe Moshe and other prophets in Bamidbar, Chapter 12. Bamidbar (12:6) says, וַיֹּאמֶר שִׁמְעוּ נָא דְבָרַי אִם יִהְיֶה נְבִיאֲכֶם ה' בַּמַּרְאָה אֵלָיו אֶתְוַדָּע בַּחֲלוֹם אֲדַבֶּר בּוֹ (He (Hashem) said, "Please listen to My words. If there be prophets among you, Hashem will make Myself known to him in a vision; I will speak to him in a dream."). With regard to Moshe, Bamidbar (12:7-8) say, פֶּה. לֹא כֵן עַבְדִּי מֹשֶׁה בְּכָל בֵּיתִי נֶאֱמָן הוּא. אֶל פֶּה אֲדַבֶּר בּוֹ וּמַרְאֶה וְלֹא בְחִידֹת וּתְמֻנַת ה' יַבִּיט וּמַדּוּעַ לֹא יְרֵאתֶם לְדַבֵּר בְּעַבְדִּי בְמֹשֶׁה (Not so is My servant Moshe; he is faithful throughout My house. With him, I speak mouth to mouth, in a vision and not in riddles, and he beholds the image of Hashem. So why were you not afraid to speak against My servant Moshe?). There is a fundamental difference in the word used in these Pesukim to describe a vision for other prophets מַרְאָה as opposed to the word used by Moshe מַרְאֶה. A מַרְאָה is a mirror, while a מַרְאֶה is a plain piece of glass without the silvered back coating of a mirror. In a mirror, one sees a reflection of one's own image, and one is not able to see what is on the other side of the mirror, while a plain clear piece of glass allows one to view everything that is happening in the back of the glass. Other prophets, who have a vision through a mirror, see their prophesy in terms of objects on their side of the mirror, i.e., objects in this world, as we saw above in the prophecy of Yirmiyahu. Moshe did not see his prophecy in terms of objects or pictures but rather saw "the image of Hashem," which allowed him to receive his prophecy directly in words and being exactly shown what and how to write the words in the Torah.

Based on the above discussion, it should come as no surprise that the Posuk וַיְדַבֵּר ה' אֶל מֹשֶׁה לֵּאמֹר is pretty unique to Moshe. In Sefer Yehoshua, we find an exception where Sefer Yehoshua (20:1) says, וַיְדַבֵּר ה' אֶל יְהוֹשֻׁעַ לֵאמֹר. In the following Pesukim laws about the cities of refuge where one who murdered unintentionally takes refuge are discussed. Within these Pesukim, says the Malbim on the Posuk in Yehoshua, the Gemorah derives Halachos about these cities which are not found in the Torah. For example, in Makos 10b, the Gemorah derives the Halacha that a city of refuge where the majority of the residents are themselves murderers cannot serve as a city of refuge. The Gemorah derives this from Sefer Yehoshua (20:4), which says, "And he shall flee to one of those cities, and he shall stand at the entrance of the gate of the city, and shall declare his cause in the ears of the elders of that city, they shall take him into the city to them, and give him a place, and he shall dwell among them." The Gemorah says that the Posuk describes the murderer as "declaring his cause in the ears of the elders of that city" which would not be an apt description if "his cause" (that he murdered) is the same as their cause (they also are murderers). For this one topic, Yehoshua had a direct prophesy, like Moshe did, and was told all the Halachos about this topic and exactly how to write it. The Vilna Gaon on Sefer Yehoshua (20:1) also says that the reason it begins with וַיְדַבֵּר ה' אֶל יְהוֹשֻׁעַ לֵאמֹר is that it is a continuation of the topic in the Torah about cities of refuge.

The Gemorah in Makos 11a explains what Sefer Yehoshua (24:26) means when it says וַיִּכְתֹּב יְהוֹשֻׁעַ אֶת הַדְּבָרִים הָאֵלֶּה בְּסֵפֶר תּוֹרַת אֱלֹקִים (And Yehoshua wrote these words in the book of the laws of G-d). One opinion of the Gemorah is that the Posuk is referring to what Yehoshua wrote about the cities of refuge for an unintentional murder in Chapter 20 of Sefer Yehoshua. The Gemorah says that since the topic of cities of refuge are "words of Torah" by writing them in his Sefer Yehoshua, he is recording more Halachos about this topic, and therefore they are "words in the book of the laws of G-d."

In truth, says the Malbim, there is one other place in Nach where we do have a similar Posuk to וַיְדַבֵּר ה' אֶל מֹשֶׁה לֵּאמֹר. Divrei HaYomim I (21:9) says, וַיְדַבֵּר ה' אֶל גָּד חֹזֵה דָוִיד לֵאמֹר (And Hashem spoke to Gad, David's prophet, saying). He shows that when this same episode is described in Sefer Shmuel II, Chapter 24, it can be implied that this prophecy was said through an angel and was hence not the same as a prophecy of Moshe. It seems to me that since this Posuk about a prophecy of the prophet Gad is not followed by laws, one would not be led to say that it was similar to the prophecy of Moshe in the laws of the Torah. Only in the case of Yehoshua that we have discussed, was their laws given after a similar Posuk to וַיְדַבֵּר ה' אֶל מֹשֶׁה לֵּאמֹר, and therefore we have seen that these laws indeed do have the same characteristic as laws in the Torah. In the Torah we have Beraishis (8:15) וַיְדַבֵּר אֱלֹקִים אֶל נֹחַ לֵאמֹר. The Vayikra Raba (1:9) says that since Noach was Hashem's animal caregiver in the ark, there was no embarrassment in Hashem speaking to Noach directly (in words and not in pictures).

What Does Shortness of Breath Mean and Why Did It Cause the Bnei Yisroel Not to Listen to Moshe?

וַיְדַבֵּר מֹשֶׁה כֵּן אֶל בְּנֵי יִשְׂרָאֵל וְלֹא שָׁמְעוּ אֶל מֹשֶׁה מִקֹּצֶר רוּחַ וּמֵעֲבֹדָה קָשָׁה (ו:ט) Shemos (6:9) Moshe spoke thus (about the redemption from Egypt) to the Bnei Yisroel, but they did not hearken to Moshe because of their shortness of breath and because of their hard labor.

What does shortness of breath mean in this context, and why did it cause the Bnei Yisroel not to listen to Moshe.

Introduction
Rav Elchonon Wasserman in Kovetz Parshios is quoted as many times hearing from the saintly Chofetz Chaim that what will happen in our last exile before Moshiach comes will mirror what happened in our first exile in Egypt. As proof for this concept, he would quote Micha (7:15), which is talking about our final redemption, and says, "As in the days of your exodus from the land of Egypt, I will show him wonders (at the time of the final redemption)." We will be so fatigued by the harshness of our troubles that we will not even have the strength to accept the news of the coming redemption mirroring the Bnei Yisroel in Egypt.

1) The Shemos Raba (6:5) and the Mechilta on Shemos (12:6) answer our question similarly. They both ponder how it is possible that someone would speak to someone about their freedom, and they would not listen. It is especially troublesome in a case like ours where the one speaking has the capability to follow through on providing freedom. Rather, they both say that "shortness of breath" refers to the fact that the Bnei Yisroel were serving idols and that serving idols caused them not to want the freedom that was dependent on their giving up serving idols. The Maharzav says that "their shortness of breath and hard labor" means "their breath or thoughts on belief in G-d and the hard decision to give up the labor of serving idols." The Yepheh Toar points out that originally

Vaera

when Moshe told the Bnei Yisroel that he was going to redeem them, Moshe did not mention that part of the redemption was that they had to give up serving idols. A few Pesukim earlier Hashem told Moshe in Shemos (6:7) "And I will take you to Me as a people and I will be a G-d to you, and you will know that I am Hashem your G-d." Only now did the Bnei Yisroel find out that the redemption included giving up idols and serving Hashem. The Mechilta explains that what happened at this point in history is explained in Sefer Yechezkel (20:6-8) "On that day I lifted up My (Hashem's) hand to them to bring them out of the land of Egypt, to a land that I had sought out for them, flowing with milk and honey; it is the glory of all the lands. And I said to them: Every man cast away the despicable idols from before his eyes, and pollute not yourselves with the idols of Egypt; I am Hashem your G-d. But they rebelled against Me and would not consent to hearken to Me; they did not cast away, every man, the despicable idols from before their eyes, neither did they forsake the idols of Egypt; and I said to pour out My wrath over them, to give My anger full reign over them, in the midst of the land of Egypt. But I did, for the sake of My Name so that it should not be desecrated before the eyes of the nations in whose midst they were, before whose eyes I made Myself known to them, to bring them out of the land of Egypt." As the Mechilta explains, even if the Bnei Yisroel had the merit of doing other Mitzvos, serving idols is such a grave sin that no other Mitzvah or combination of Mitzvos can balance the demerit that worshipping idols brings.

A couple of Pesukim after ours, Moshe says the following to Hashem "Behold, the Bnei Yisroel did not hearken to me. How then will Pharaoh hearken to me, seeing that I am of closed lips?" The Beraishis Raba (92:7) says that this is one of the ten Kal VeChomers (a logical conclusion that if the easier thing (in our case the Bnei Yisroel not hearkening to Moshe) yields such a conclusion, it is logical to think that the harder thing (in our case Pharaoh not hearkening to Moshe) will also yield this same conclusion) that are listed in the Torah. Many commentators ponder the question of whether our Kal VeChomer makes logical sense since our Posuk tells us that the reason the Bnei Yisroel did not hearken to Moshe was because of their shortness of breath and because of their hard labor, and therefore it is not logical to conclude that Pharaoh who did not have these issues would not hearken to Moshe. The Maharzav and the Maharif point out that according to this answer, the Kal VeChomer makes complete logical sense. Both the Bnei Yisroel and Pharaoh did not hearken to Moshe because of "shortness of breath and hard labor," which means a problem with their belief in Hashem. Therefore, if even the Bnei Yisroel, who were Moshe's brethren, did not hearken to Moshe, it is logical to conclude that Pharaoh will also not hearken to Moshe.

2) Rashi presents an answer to our question. Rashi says that someone who cannot take deep or even normal breaths but only short ones is called מִקֹּצֶר רוּחַ (short of breath). The Maharal, in Gur Aryeh, explains that they were so worried about the enormous workloads that the Egyptians had placed on them that they could not take a normal breath and could not concentrate enough to hear what Moshe was saying. He also explains that וּמֵעֲבֹדָה קָשָׁה means that they were much too weak to be able to do the work that they were given by the Egyptians which was so hard relative to the strength that they had. Since they were constantly thinking about this overwhelming work, they could not listen to Moshe.

Vaera

The Mizrachi and Maharal explain the Kal VeChomer that Moshe said, "Behold, the Bnei Yisroel did not hearken to me. How then will Pharaoh hearken to me, seeing that I am of closed lips?" They say that this Kal VeChomer means that if the Bnei Yisroel for whom the news of their redemption is for their good did not listen to me, how then will Pharaoh for whom the news is for his bad listen to me? The Maharal says that despite the fact that the Bnei Yisroel did not listen because of their shortness of breath and hard work, this is much less of a reason not to listen than the news of redemption being for their bad as it was for Pharaoh. The Mizrachi says that Moshe was not aware that it could be impossible for the Bnei Yisroel to receive news of their redemption and not listen to it because of their shortness of breath and hard work. Moshe just attributed it to his lack of good communication, being that he was one of "closed lips." The Maskil LeDovid says that we can see that Moshe only attributed it to his "closed lips" because this is what Moshe mentions as the reason the Bnei Yisroel did not listen to him when he makes the Kal VeChomer.

3) The Bechor Shor, Nitziv, Rav Hirsch, and the Oznayim LeTorah answer our question similarly and say that קֹצֶר רוּחַ means lack of patience. The Bnei Yisroel were so enslaved that they did not even have a second for themselves, having barely a chance to eat and sleep, and therefore they could not even think about the long description and philosophy of redemption that Moshe presented them when he did as commanded "Therefore, say to the Bnei Yisroel, 'I am Hashem, and I will take you out from under the burdens of the Egyptians, and I will save you from their labor, and I will redeem you with an outstretched arm and with great judgments. And I will take you to Me as a people.'" Moshe explained to the Bnei Yisroel in detail that Hashem used four descriptions of redemption, "I will take you out," "I will save you," "I will redeem you," and "I will take you," and what these four descriptions of redemption meant. This answer is similar to what the Meshech Chochmah says that the Bnei Yisroel had no time to think about the future and could just think about the present and were only interested in hearing that they would not have to work anymore.

4) The Chizkuni also ponders our question. He writes that the Bnei Yisroel were afraid to listen to Moshe because of what happened the last time between Moshe and Pharaoh. After Moshe had asked Pharaoh to let the Bnei Yisroel go and serve Hashem in the desert for three days, Pharaoh says in Shemos (5:7-8), "You (the taskmasters) shall not continue to give stubble to the people to make the bricks like yesterday and the day before yesterday. Let them go and gather stubble for themselves. But the number of bricks they have been making yesterday and the day before yesterday you shall impose upon them; you shall not reduce it, for they are lax. Therefore, they cry out, saying, 'Let us go and sacrifice to our G-d.'" מִקֹּצֶר רוּחַ וּמֵעֲבֹדָה קָשָׁה is referring to the shortness of breath and hard work the Bnei Yisroel just got from Pharaoh as a "reward" for listening to Moshe previously.

5) The Ramban also ponders our question. He says that the Bnei Yisroel were afraid that if they did listen to Moshe, the Egyptians would kill them. He references Shemos (5:21), which says, "And they (the officers of the Bnei Yisroel) said to them (Moshe and Aharon), "May Hashem look upon you and judge, for you have brought us into foul odor in the eyes of Pharaoh and in the eyes of his servants, to place a sword into their hands to kill us." This fear is what our Posuk means when it

Vaera

says that they didn't listen to Moshe, מִקֹּצֶר רוּחַ. He says that וּמֵעֲבֹדָה קָשָׁה means the oppressive work the taskmasters placed upon them which did not even give them time to think.

6) The Sforno also presents an answer to our question and says that מִקֹּצֶר רוּחַ means that the Bnei Yisroel did not fully believe in Hashem at this time. In his commentary on the Sforno, Rav Cooperman explains that when Moshe initially came to the Bnei Yisroel and told them that Hashem was redeeming them from Egypt, the Bnei Yisroel fully believed that Hashem would redeem them. We see this in Shemos (4:31) "And the people believed, and they heard that Hashem had remembered the Bnei Yisroel and that He saw their affliction, and they kneeled and prostrated themselves." However, after Moshe went to Pharaoh and the Bnei Yisroel saw how not only did Pharaoh not grant Moshe's request but also made the work conditions much worse the Bnei Yisroel's belief in Hashem began to wane. Our Posuk does tell us that had the Bnei Yisroel not been subjugated to the וּמֵעֲבֹדָה קָשָׁה (hard work) which they just received from Pharaoh as a result of Moshe's request; their belief would have been enough to accept what Moshe now said that the redemption was coming. However, the hard work did not allow them to think about and believe in what Moshe was saying.

7) The Ralbag also ponders our question and writes that מִקֹּצֶר רוּחַ (shortness of breath) is not referring to the Bnei Yisroel but rather to Moshe. Since Moshe was speaking directly to the Bnei Yisroel, the Bnei Yisroel had a difficult time fully understanding what Moshe was saying, being that Moshe's oration skills were lacking. Moshe was aware of this problem, and that is why he describes himself in Shemos (6:12) "I am of closed lips." It would seem that Moshe's "closed lips" led to him speaking with "shortness of breath."

8) The Abarbanel also presents an answer to our question. He says that מִקֹּצֶר רוּחַ (short of breath) is a psychological reason, like what Rashi says, that the Bnei Yisroel were so worried about the enormous amount of work that they could not even breathe normally and concentrate enough to hear what Moshe was saying. וּמֵעֲבֹדָה קָשָׁה is a physical reason that their workload was so hard and time consuming that the Bnei Yisroel did not even have the time to listen to what Moshe was telling them.

9) The Ohr HaChaim also presents an answer to our question. He writes that the learning of Torah broadens the heart of a person and that the opposite of a broad heart is a קֹצֶר רוּחַ. Therefore, the reason they did not listen is that they had not yet studied Torah, and they, therefore, did not have the broadness of heart/mind to accept what Moshe was saying. We have explained previously that many Meforshim have an issue with the Kal VeChomer that Moshe made when he said, "Behold, the Bnei Yisroel did not hearken to me. How then will Pharaoh hearken to me, seeing that I am of closed lips?" The problem with the Kal VeChomer is that our Posuk tells us why the Bnei Yisroel did not listen to Moshe, and therefore Pharaoh who did not have this issue might well hearken to Moshe. The Ohr HaChaim says that Moshe did not figure out that the Bnei Yisroel did not have a broad heart because they had not studied Torah, and therefore, according to Moshe's understanding, this Kal VeChomer was completely logical.

Vaera

10) The Noam Elimelech presents a perhaps slightly esoteric answer to our question. He says that the opposite of קֹצֶר רוּחַ (literally short spirit) is someone with a long spirit. Someone with a long spirit has a very lofty Neshama, which, if the person chooses to listen to his Neshama, the person knows that he needs to serve Hashem with many different types of services. In fact, his entire lifespan will not be enough to serve Hashem in all the many different types of services. The opposite of such a person, a קֹצֶר רוּחַ, is someone who thinks that whatever he does is sufficient for serving Hashem. The Bnei Yisroel had a short spirit and therefore felt that they were serving Hashem quite sufficiently. Consequently, they felt that if their service to Hashem did not bring the redemption, they saw no possibility that Moshe could bring the redemption either. Therefore, they did not listen to Moshe when he spoke about the redemption.

We have explained previously that many Meforshim have an issue with the Kal VeChomer that Moshe made when he said, "Behold, the Bnei Yisroel did not hearken to me. How then will Pharaoh hearken to me, seeing that I am of closed lips?" The Noam Elimelech says that Moshe, due to his humbleness, did not contemplate that the reason the Bnei Yisroel did not listen was because of a problem of their having a short spirit. Moshe could only ascribe their not listening to a problem in himself conveying the message of the redemption, and therefore Moshe truthfully said the Kal VeChomer.

11) The son of the Nodeh BeYehudah presents an answer to our question. The Shir HaShirim Raba on Shir HaShirim (2:8) says that when Moshe came to the Bnei Yisroel and told them that they would be redeemed during this month of Nisan, the Bnei Yisroel told Moshe that it was not possible. Their reasoning was that Hashem had told Avrohom that the Bnei Yisroel would be enslaved for 400 years. Since the Bnei Yisroel has only been in Egypt for 210 years, it was way before the time to be redeemed. Moshe answered that since Hashem wanted the Bnei Yisroel to be redeemed, Hashem would not worry about this calculation.

With this answer of the Nodeh BeYehudah's son, we can better understand something that the Midrash Lekach Tov says on our Posuk. Shemos (12:40) says, "And the habitation of the Bnei Yisroel, that they dwelled in Egypt, was four hundred and thirty years." On this question, it ponders the fact that Hashem told Avrohom in the Bris Bain HaBesorim, Beraishis (15:13) "And He (Hashem) said to Avrom, 'You shall surely know that your seed will be strangers in a land that is not theirs, and they will enslave them and oppress them, for four hundred years.'" The Midrash Lekach Tov says that if we count from the time Yitzchak was born (consistent with the Posuk saying "your seed"), it was 400 years after Yitzchak's birth that the Bnei Yisroel went out of Egypt. However, if we count from the Bris Bain HaBesorim (which took place 30 years before Yitzchak was born), then the Bnei Yisroel went out of Egypt 430 thirty years later.

The Midrash Lekach Tov on our Posuk points out that the Gematria of the Hebrew word מְקֻצָּר is 430. The Rabeinu Bechay, Toldos Yitzchak and Baal HaTurim all quote this. Combining this with the Shir HaShirim Raba that the Nodeh BeYehudah's son quotes, we can say that the reason the Bnei Yisroel did not listen to Moshe was that they had only been in Egypt for 210 years and therefore were far from the 430 years (מְקֻצָּר) of the exile to Egypt. We should also keep in mind that

Vaera

the Gemorah in Sanhedrin 92b references Divrei HaYomim I (7:21) that children of Ephraim went out of Egypt to Eretz Yisroel 30 years previously and were killed by the Philistines. Rashi on the Gemorah explains that the reason they went out early is that they calculated that the 400 years of Egyptian exile prophesized by Avrohom began at the time the prophecy was given at the Bris Bain HaBesorim when in reality, the 400-year exile started with the birth of Yitzchak, 30 years later. Realizing the great tragedy which had occurred to the children of Ephraim 30 years earlier, it is understandable that the Bnei Yisroel were not ready to go out of Egypt until they were sure that the correct calculation of the time in Egyptian exile had been made.

With this answer, the Nodeh BeYehudah's son explains the Kal VeChomer Moshe makes to Hashem, "Behold, the Bnei Yisroel did not hearken to me. How then will Pharaoh hearken to me, seeing that I am of closed lips?" We have previously said that many commentators ponder the question of whether our Kal VeChomer makes logical sense since our Posuk tells us that the reason the Bnei Yisroel did not hearken to Moshe was because of their shortness of breath and because of their hard labor, and therefore it is not logical to conclude that Pharaoh who did not have these issues would not hearken to Moshe. According to him, Moshe was saying, "Behold, the Bnei Yisroel did not hearken to me (because they did not believe that the 400 or 430 years were up). How then will Pharaoh hearken to me (since Pharaoh will also say that the 400 years are not up) being that I am of closed lips?"

12) The Pardes Yosef also presents an answer to our question. We have mentioned previously that the Bnei Yisrocl only stayed for 210 years in exile as opposed to the 400 years that Hashem had told Avrohom that his children would be in exile. He says that there are two reasons brought by Chazal as to why the exile in Egypt was abbreviated. Firstly, Chazal tell us that the Bnei Yisroel were on the 49th and last level of Tumah in Egypt, and if they had stayed in Egypt any longer, they would have fallen to the 50th level of Tumah for which there would be no hope of redemption. Parenthetically the Shach on Shemos (12:7) says the redemption from Egypt is mentioned 49 times in the Torah. This number of times is to hint to us that the Bnei Yisroel were only redeemed from Egypt since they did not fall to the 50th level of Tumah.

The Beis HaLevi, in Pashas Bo, explains that had the Bnei Yisroel fallen to the 50th level of Tumah, no remnant of holiness which they inherited from the forefathers Avrohom, Yitzchak, and Yaakov would have remained with them. Therefore, they would have no spiritual connection to the forefathers. Hashem had promised Avrohom in Beraishis (15:13) "You shall surely know that your seed will be strangers in a land that is not theirs, and they will enslave them and oppress them, for four hundred years." On the 50th level of Tumah, the Bnei Yisroel would no longer have been called Avrohom's seed any more than Esav, or Yishmael's children are considered as Avrohom's seed. This is the simplest way of understanding what is said over in the name of the Arizal that if the Bnei Yisroel would have waited any longer in Egypt, they would have entered the 50th level of Tumah and would never have been redeemed. This is also what we mean in the Hagadah when we say in the paragraph of Avodim HaYenu, "if Hashem had not taken us out of Egypt, we, our children, and our grandchildren would have been enslaved to the Egyptians. Had we fallen to the 50th level of

Vaera

Tumah, we would have been just like the Egyptians, and there would have never been a point in time where it would make any sense to redeem us from Egypt.

It is interesting to see what did happen to two people who stayed behind in Egypt when the Bnei Yisroel left. After leaving Egypt, Shemos (14:3) literally says, "And Pharaoh will say to the Bnei Yisroel, they are trapped in the land. The desert has closed in upon them." The only problem with this literal translation is that ostensibly the Bnei Yisroel had already left Egypt and no longer were there for Pharaoh to speak to. Therefore, Rashi and most commentators are of the opinion that the Posuk needs instead to not be translated literally but rather is saying what Pharaoh would be saying about the Bnei Yisroel. However, the Targum Yonason ben Uziel says that the Torah tells us that Pharaoh will speak to Dasan and Avirom who had remained in Egypt when all the rest of the Bnei Yisroel went out of Egypt. We know that despite seeing countless miracles and having Hashem reveal himself to the Bnei Yisroel at Mount Sinai, Dasan and Avirom would not listen or accept anything that Moshe said. When Moshe told the Bnei Yisroel that on Shabbos, unlike all the other days of the week, no Mon would fall, Dasan and Avirom went out anyway to gather Mon even though there was none to gather. In the rebellion of Korach, Dasan and Avirom tell Moshe in Bamidbar (16:13-14) after being asked to come to Moshe, "Is it not enough that you have brought us out of a land flowing with milk and honey to kill us in the desert, that you should also exercise authority over us? You have not even brought us to a land flowing with milk and honey, nor have you given us an inheritance of fields and vineyards. Even if you gouge out the eyes of those men, we will not go up." Dasan and Avirom refer to Egypt as a land flowing of milk and honey and blatantly ignore the fact that it was the sin of the spies which caused the Bnei Yisroel to be killed in the desert. Dasan and Avirom, who had remained in Egypt and had fallen to the 50th level of Tumah, are no longer affected by all the spirituality that the Bnei Yisroel saw in the desert. Had we remained in Egypt, we would also, Chas VeShalom, had behaved like Dasan and Avirom, and there would not have been any reason to redeem us from Egypt. The Maharil Diskin at the end of Parshas Shemos ponders the question of why Dasan and Avirom did not die in the plague of darkness together with all the many Bnei Yisroel who did not want to be redeemed from Egypt. He answers that Dasan and Avirom were saved from death in Egypt because they were part of the Jewish officers who were beaten up for not forcing the Jews to meet the impossible quota of bricks after the Egyptians no longer gave the Bnei Yisroel the straw to make the bricks.

The Pardes Yosef says that מִקֹּצֶר רוּחַ means that the Bnei Yisroel were short of spirituality, so much so that they were almost on the 50th level of Tumah. Therefore, they did not listen to Moshe. The second reason, says the Pardes Yosef, that the Bnei Yisroel only remained in Egypt for 210 and not 400 years was that the work was so hard that they did as much work in 210 years as a normal person would do in 400 years. That is what our Posuk means when it says that they also did not listen to Moshe because of וּמֵעֲבֹדָה קָשָׁה (severity of work). We can perhaps understand this concept better if we examine what the Pirkei D'Rabi Eliezer (48) says. Similar to the Midrash Lekach Tov we have quoted previously, it ponders how we can understand Shemos (12:40) which says, "And the habitation of the Bnei Yisroel, that they dwelled in Egypt, was four hundred and thirty years." This Posuk seems to contradict the fact that Hashem told Avrohom in the Bris Bain HaBesorim, Beraishis (15:13) "And He (Hashem) said to Avrom, 'You shall surely know that your seed will be

Vaera

strangers in a land that is not theirs, and they will enslave them and oppress them, for four hundred years.'" As we have mentioned previously, starting from the time Yaakov and his family came down to Egypt, the Bnei Yisroel were in Egypt for 210 years. The Pirkei D'Rabi Eliezer says that five years prior to that, Yosef's two sons Menashe and Ephraim, were born. The Radal on the Pirkei D'Rabi Eliezer says that it would seem that both Yosef's sons were born in the same calendar year since otherwise it would have said that Yosef's oldest son was born five years before Yaakov came down to Egypt. Both Ephraim and Menashe are counted as part of the twelve tribes. Therefore, says the Radal, we count the start of when the Bnei Yisroel were in Egypt from the time Menashe and Ephraim were born. His is as opposed to when Yosef came down 17 years earlier since Ephraim and Menashe and not Yosef are counted as part of the 12 tribes. Counting from when Ephraim and Menashe were born yields that the Bnei Yisroel were in Egypt for 215 years. The Pirkei D'Rabi Eliezer says that since the Egyptians overworked the Bnei Yisroel by making them work both by day and by night, it is counted as if the Bnei Yisroel were in Egypt for double 215 years or 430 years. That is what Shemos (12:40) means when it says, "And the habitation of the Bnei Yisroel, that they dwelled in Egypt, was four hundred and thirty years." When Hashem told Avrohom in the Bris Bain HaBesorim, Beraishis (15:13) "And He (Hashem) said to Avrom, 'You shall surely know that your seed will be strangers in a land that is not theirs, and they will enslave them and oppress them, for four hundred years,'" it is referring to the total physical years from when Avrohom's seed, Yitzchak, was born. The Pardes Yosef says that the Bnei Yisroel did not accept either of the two reasons brought by Chazal as to why the exile in Egypt was abbreviated and that they were not ready to go out of Egypt, and therefore they did not listen to Moshe.

12) Rav Yaakov Kaminetsky, in his Sefer Emes LeYaakov, also ponders our question. The Shemos Raba (5:18) and the Midrash Tanchuma in Vaera (6) both say that the Bnei Yisroel had Megilos (scrolls), which talked about how Hashem would redeem them from Egypt that they would read every Shabbos. The Shemos Raba says that they used to read them on Shabbos because they had a day off from work on Shabbos. When Moshe first came to Pharaoh at the end of Parshas Shemos to ask him to let the Bnei Yisroel leave Egypt, Pharaoh says in Shemos (5:9) "Let the labor fall heavy upon the men and let them work at it, and let them not talk about false matters." "Let them not talk about false matters" refers to reading these Megilos, and "Let the labor fall heavy upon the men" means that Pharaoh increased the Bnei Yisroel's affliction by making them also work on Shabbos. The Shemos Raba (1:28) says that when Moshe first went out of the palace and saw the burdens of the Bnei Yisroel, he went and convinced Pharaoh to allow the Bnei Yisroel a day off on Shabbos. Moshe argued to Pharaoh that the Bnei Yisroel would be more productive the rest of the week if only they had one day of vacation a week. The Tur in Orach Chaim 281 explains the meaning of the phrase that we say in the Shabbos morning Shemoneh Esreh יִשְׂמַח מֹשֶׁה בְּמַתְּנַת חֶלְקוֹ (Moshe rejoiced in the gift of his portion). He explains that Moshe was very happy that the day off he requested for the Bnei Yisroel in Egypt was the same day that Hashem commanded the Bnei Yisroel to keep Shabbos when the Torah was given. He points out that in Beitzah 16a, the Gemorah says that Hashem told Moshe that He has a wonderful gift in his treasure house and the gift's name is Shabbos. That is what is meant by the phrase that Moshe rejoiced in the gift (Shabbos) of his portion (which he chose for the Bnei Yisroel in Egypt).

Vaera

Rav Yaakov says that the Bnei Yisroel thought that when Moshe went to Pharaoh and told him to let the people leave Egypt and serve Hashem for three days in the desert that Pharaoh would immediately listen. Not only did Pharaoh not listen, but he also took away the one day a week that the Bnei Yisroel had used to think about the redemption. These events caused the Bnei Yisroel to become despondent and completely give up on the idea of being redeemed. Therefore, מִקֹּצֶר רוּחַ וּמֵעֲבֹדָה קָשָׁה means that the Bnei Yisroel did not listen to Moshe because of their despondency of ever being redeemed and because of the hard work of having to work all seven days of the week.

How Could Moshe Conclude Pharaoh Would Not Listen to Him Based on the Bnei Yisroel Not Listening?

Shemos (6:12) וַיְדַבֵּר מֹשֶׁה לִפְנֵי ה' לֵאמֹר הֵן בְּנֵי יִשְׂרָאֵל לֹא שָׁמְעוּ אֵלַי וְאֵיךְ יִשְׁמָעֵנִי פַרְעֹה וַאֲנִי עֲרַל שְׂפָתָיִם (ו:יב) But Moshe spoke before Hashem, saying, "Behold, the Bnei Yisroel did not hearken to me. How then will Pharaoh hearken to me, seeing that I am of closed lips?"

Shemos (6:9) already said the reason the Bnei Yisroel did not listen to Moshe was "because of their shortness of breath and because of their hard labor." That being the case, how could Moshe conclude that Pharaoh would not listen to him based on the fact that the Bnei Yisroel did not listen to him, since Pharaoh did not have either "shortness of breath or hard labor?"

Introduction
The Beraishis Raba (92:7) says that this is one of the ten Kal VeChomers (a logical conclusion that if the easier thing, in our case the Bnei Yisroel hearkening to Moshe, yields such a conclusion it is logical to think that the harder thing, in our case Pharaoh hearkening to Moshe will also yield this same conclusion) that are listed in the Torah.

There can be two categories of answers to a question. We can appreciate the two categories from a story about the Beis HaLevi and his son Rav Chaim Soloveichik. At one time, the Beis HaLevi was asked to explain the difference in Torah learning between him and his phenomenal son. He explained that when someone comes to ask him a question in Torah study, he contemplates the question and gives an explanation to answer the question. "I am happy because I have provided a good answer to the question, and the person who asked the question is happy because he asked a good question." However, when someone asks a question to my son, Rav Chaim, he is so sharp in his Torah knowledge that he quickly shows how the question is not a question at all. The Beis HaLevi continued, "He is not happy because he didn't give an answer to a worthwhile question and the person who asked the question is not happy because he didn't ask a worthwhile question."

1) We will first examine answers from the category of answers that our question is not a question. The Daas Zekanim, Chizkuni, and Mizrachi present such an answer to our question. They say that Moshe was not aware that it could be impossible for the Bnei Yisroel to receive news of their redemption and not listen to it because of their shortness of breath and hard work. Moshe just attributed it to his lack of good communication, being that he was one of "closed lips." The Maskil LeDovid says that we can see that Moshe only attributed it to his "closed lips" because this is what

Vaera

Moshe mentions as the reason the Bnei Yisroel did not listen to him when he makes the Kal VeChomer. Therefore, the Torah is recording what Moshe said from his perspective where he had no idea about the Bnei Yisroel's not listening to him "because of their shortness of breath and because of their hard labor." Without this knowledge, Moshe was completed justified to conclude that Pharaoh would also not listen to him.

2) The Maharzav and the Maharif answer our question similarly. The Shemos Raba (6:5) and the Mechilta on Shemos (12:6) ponder how it is possible that someone would speak to someone about their freedom, and they would not listen. It is especially troublesome in a case like ours where the one speaking has the capability to follow through on providing freedom. Rather, they both say that "shortness of breath" refers to the fact that the Bnei Yisroel were serving idols and that serving idols caused them not to want the freedom that was dependent on their giving up serving idols. The Maharzav says that "their shortness of breath and hard labor" means "their breath or thoughts on belief in G-d and the hard decision to give up the labor of serving idols." The Yepheh Toar points out that originally when Moshe told the Bnei Yisroel that he was going to redeem them, Moshe did not mention that part of the redemption was that they had to give up serving idols. A few Pesukim earlier Hashem told Moshe in Shemos (6:7) "And I will take you to Me as a people and I will be a G-d to you, and you will know that I am Hashem your G-d." Only now did the Bnei Yisroel find out that the redemption included giving up idols and serving Hashem. The Mechilta explains that what happened at this point in history is explained in Sefer Yechezkel (20:6-8) "On that day I lifted up My (Hashem's) hand to them to bring them out of the land of Egypt, to a land that I had sought out for them, flowing with milk and honey; it is the glory of all the lands. And I said to them: Every man cast away the despicable idols from before his eyes, and pollute not yourselves with the idols of Egypt; I am Hashem your G-d. But they rebelled against Me and would not consent to hearken to Me; they did not cast away, every man, the despicable idols from before their eyes, neither did they forsake the idols of Egypt; and I said to pour out My wrath over them, to give My anger full reign over them, in the midst of the land of Egypt. But I did, for the sake of My Name so that it should not be desecrated before the eyes of the nations in whose midst they were, before whose eyes I made Myself known to them, to bring them out of the land of Egypt." As the Mechilta explains, even if the Bnei Yisroel had the merit of doing other Mitzvos, serving idols is such a grave sin that no other Mitzvah or combination of Mitzvos can balance the demerit that worshipping idols brings.

The Maharzav and Maharif point out that according to this answer, the Kal VeChomer makes complete logical sense. Both the Bnei Yisroel and Pharaoh did not hearken to Moshe because of "shortness of breath and hard labor," which means a problem with their belief in Hashem. Therefore, if even the Bnei Yisroel, who were Moshe's brethren, did not hearken to Moshe, it is logical to conclude that Pharaoh will also not hearken to Moshe.

3) The Yismach Moshe also ponders our question. Before we cite the Gemorah that he quotes, we should give an introduction so that we can better understand it. The Rambam in Hilchos Chanukah (3:12-13) tells us how Hallel was recited in the old days. The Shliach Tzibur would recite each phrase of Hallel, and the congregation would answer the word Hallelukah to each phrase. In the entire Hallel, the congregation would say the word Hallelukah 123 times. The Rambam also says

Vaera

that in addition to the 123 times of saying the word Hallelukah, the congregation would also repeat the first phrase of each chapter of Hallel. The Yismach Moshe quotes the Gemorah in Rosh Hashana 27a, which says for both the saying of Hallel and hearing the reading of the Megilah, even if ten people read it simultaneously, one can fulfill one's obligation. The Gemorah says that the reason is that these readings are dear to the person listening to them, and therefore he will concentrate and hear each word from the particular person he is listening to. Rashi explains that these particular readings are so dear because they are read infrequently, and they are novel to the person listening.

The Yismach Moshe says that a similar phenomenon occurs when someone who is hard of speech speaks. If what the listener is saying is dear to the people he is talking to, then they will concentrate and understand what he is saying. Despite the fact that what Moshe was saying should have been dear to the Bnei Yisroel, they did not concentrate on understanding him "because of their shortness of breath and because of their hard labor." Therefore, said Moshe, it is logical that Pharaoh will not concentrate on hearing what Moshe had to say since what he had to say was not only not dear to Pharaoh but was, in fact, something Pharaoh hated to hear.

4) The Ksav Sofer and Yismach Moshe present another answer to our question. The Yismach Moshe says that Moshe calculated that there are two possibilities in what will happen when he speaks to Pharaoh and asks him to let the Bnei Yisroel go free. Either Pharaoh will listen to Moshe and agree to his request, or Pharaoh will not listen and instead will get angry and make the slavery conditions of the Bnei Yisroel even worse as he had done the first time Moshe met with him. Moshe certainly did not want to cause the slavery conditions to be worse for the Bnei Yisroel, and therefore he decided that the smartest thing to do was to first see how the Bnei Yisroel would receive the prophecy Hashem had told him to tell the Bnei Yisroel. Otherwise, it is difficult to fathom why Hashem wanted Moshe to first speak to the Bnei Yisroel since it wasn't in their hands to be freed from slavery. Rather, say the Ksav Sofer and Yismach Moshe, Moshe felt that Hashem was looking for the Bnei Yisroel to have merits to be redeemed. This is the reason that Hashem told him to tell the Bnei Yisroel in Shemos (6:7) "And I will take you to Me as a people, and I will be a G-d to you, and you will know that I am Hashem your God, Who has brought you out from under the burdens of the Egyptians." Moshe thought that the Bnei Yisroel would listen to him and accept Hashem and, in fact, accept the Torah and that this merit would cause Pharaoh to let the Bnei Yisroel leave Egypt. However, the Bnei Yisroel did not listen to Moshe, and Moshe felt that this lack of merit would cause Pharaoh not to listen to him and rather make the slavery conditions worse as he had done previously. That is what Moshe meant when he said in our Posuk, "Behold, the Bnei Yisroel did not hearken to me. How then will Pharaoh hearken to me, seeing that I am of closed lips?" Rather than making a Kal VeChomer, Moshe was instead just making a cause and effect statement that Bnei Yisroel not getting merits for whatever reason would cause Pharaoh not to listen and accept what Moshe told him. The Ksav Sofer explains that since Hashem can look into the future and see the Bnei Yisroel accepting the Torah, this merit will, in fact, retroactively help the Bnei Yisroel be redeemed from Egypt.

Vaera

5) The Yismach Moshe at the beginning of Parshas Bo presents another answer to our question. The Yalkut Shimoni on Sefer Yona (549) explains why Yona did not want to obey Hashem and travel to Nineveh to tell them to do Teshuva and prevent their city from being destroyed. It says that Yona was afraid the people of Nineveh would listen to him and do Teshuva and that this action would be a bad reflection on the Jews for the times that they did not do Teshuva despite being admonished by a prophet to do Teshuva. The Yismach Moshe says that Moshe was afraid that in contrast to the Bnei Yisroel not listening to him, Pharaoh would listen, and if that happened, Moshe would be of "closed lips." Since Moshe had already complained to Hashem of being "heavy of mouth and heavy of tongue" in Shemos (4:10) and Hashem had responded in the next Posuk, it is difficult to say that Moshe reopened this subject now. Rather, in our Posuk, Moshe was saying that he would be left with nothing to say (closed lips) to defend the Bnei Yisroel if Pharaoh were to listen. Because of this possibility, Moshe was hesitant to go to Pharaoh. Hashem answered this fear in Shemos (7:4) by saying, "But I will harden Pharaoh's heart, and I will increase My signs and My wonders in the land of Egypt," so that Moshe need not worry that Pharaoh would listen to him.

6) The Noam Elimelech also presents an answer to our question. The Noam Elimelech says that in general, if one speaks heartfelt words and words of integrity, they will be listened to by the person who hears them. There are two things that prevent these words from being listened to: (1) if the listener is in a depressed state and (2) if the listener is a jokester or other non-serious person. Both these conditions also depend on the person who is delivering the message. If the person delivering the message is a totally righteous person, then even if the listener is in a depressed state, the listener will nonetheless accept the message. However, if the person is a jokester or other non-serious person, it will not be accepted even if the message comes from a totally righteous person. Moshe felt that the reason the Bnei Yisroel did not listen to him was that he was not totally righteous, and therefore his message could not get across to the Bnei Yisroel since they were depressed. Therefore, it is a logical assumption that Pharaoh, who is a non-serious person with regard to listening to messages from Hashem, will certainly not listen to Moshe.

7) We will now look at answers which assume our question of the Bnei Yisroel having a reason, "shortness of breath and hard labor" not to listen to Moshe would not make it logical that Pharaoh who did not have this reason would also not listen. The Tur presents an answer to our question. When Moshe first came to Pharaoh asking him to let the Bnei Yisroel go, he answered in Shemos (5:7-8), "You shall not continue to give stubble to the people to make the bricks like yesterday and the day before yesterday. Let them go and gather stubble for themselves. But the number of bricks they have been making yesterday and the day before yesterday you shall impose upon them; you shall not reduce it, for they are lax. Therefore, they cry out, saying, 'Let us go and sacrifice to our G-d.'" The Tur says that Pharaoh found out that the Bnei Yisroel did not want to listen to Moshe because they were afraid that Pharaoh would again increase their workload as he had done previously. Since Pharaoh knew the Bnei Yisroel did not want to listen to Moshe when he talked to them about their leaving Egypt, Pharaoh had no reason to listen to Moshe when he asked him to allow the Bnei Yisroel to leave Egypt. Pharaoh could reply to Moshe, "Why should I allow them to leave if they do not want to go out themselves?" According to this answer, when the Torah says the Bnei Yisroel didn't listen to Moshe because of "hard labor," the Torah is referring to their fear of

Vaera

getting even harder labor than they already had. Therefore, the result of Pharaoh not listening is a logical extension of the Bnei Yisroel not listening.

8) The Taz, in his Sefer Divrei Dovid, and the Levush on Rashi answer our question similarly. They point out that Moshe concludes his statement in our Posuk by saying Pharaoh will not listen to him, "seeing that I am of closed lips." Since it is disrespectful to choose someone who cannot speak well to be the emissary to the King, Moshe felt that Pharaoh would take affront to him being chosen as an emissary and would not even begin listening to what he had to say. As the Levush says, one would have to exert much effort listening and deciphering what Moshe was saying, and Pharaoh as King would refuse to make this effort. Though it is true the Bnei Yisroel did not listen to Moshe "because of their shortness of breath and because of their hard labor," Moshe says that this reason paled in comparison to the affront Pharaoh would take with such an emissary as he. According to this answer, Moshe is saying that if the Bnei Yisroel, who it would not be such an affront for someone who cannot speak well, did not listen to Moshe, then Pharaoh for whom it is a big affront will certainly not listen.

Parenthetically the Droshos HaRan (Drosha 5) says the reason Hashem chose Moshe, who was unfit to speak well, to give the Torah was so that no one should be able to say that Moshe convinced the Bnei Yisroel to accept all the Mitzvos because of his oratory skills. Rather because Moshe was unfit to speak well, everyone knew that the Bnei Yisroel only accepted the Torah because they all saw Hashem appear on Mount Sinai and give them the Torah. The Ran says that this was the reason Hashem did not cure Moshe of his speaking problem.

9) The Daas Zekanim, Mizrachi, and Maharal, in his Sefer Gur Aryeh, answer our question similarly. They say our Kal VeChomer means that if the Bnei Yisroel for whom the news of their redemption is for their good did not listen to me, how then will Pharaoh for whom the news is for his bad, listen to me? The Maharal says that despite the Torah saying the Bnei Yisroel did not listen because of their shortness of breath and hard work, this is much less of a reason not to listen than the news of redemption being for their bad as it was for Pharaoh. As the Daas Zekanim says, and we have mentioned previously from the Mechilta on Shemos (12:6), it is hard to fathom how it is possible Moshe would speak to the Bnei Yisroel about their freedom and they would not listen.

Rav Meir Bergman quotes an essay of Rav Chaim Shmulevitz in Sichos Musar (Essay 27, 5731) to show how strongly a person desires to be free. The Gemorah in Gittin 45a tells us about Rav Elish, who unfortunately was captured and put in jail. One day, he found himself sitting next to someone who understood bird language. It seems from the story that this person was a Gentile. A raven came and said something. He turned to the man and asked him what the raven said. The man answered that the raven said, "Elish, escape. Elish, escape." Rav Elish said that a raven is a liar, and one cannot trust what he says. The Maharsha explains that he was referring to the raven that Noach tried to send from the ark. As Rashi explains on Beraishis (8:7), the raven refused to listen to Noach and go on the mission that he sent it out for. Soon a dove came by and also said something. He asked the man what the dove said. The man answered that the dove said, "Elish, escape. Elish, escape." Rav Elish said that the Bnei Yisroel are compared to a dove; it would seem that this is a

Vaera

sign that a miracle will happen to me, and I will be able to escape. The Maharsha explains that the dove did listen to Noach and go on the mission that he sent him. However, Rav Elish was also worried that the person could have been lying about what the dove really said. Therefore, he reasoned that since the Bnei Yisroel are compared to a dove, Hashem would not have sent a dove unless the news was true. The Gemorah concludes that a miracle happened to Rav Elish, and he escaped and was transported to the other side of the river so that the guards could not catch him. The person who understood bird language also escaped, but he was caught and executed.

Rav Chaim quotes Rav Akiva Eiger, who writes in Gilyan HaShas on this Gemorah that the Aruch in his Sefer proves from this Gemorah that Rav Elish understood bird talk. However, Rav Akiva Eiger says that the Seder HaDoros questions the Aruch's interpretation since this Gemorah seems to be saying that he did not understand bird talk. Rav Chaim explains that had Rav Elish not known bird talk, he would not have believed the other person, especially in such a life-threatening situation. Rather, Rav Elish heard and understood what the raven and dove had said. However, he was afraid that his mind was just playing tricks on him, and his ears were just hearing what his heart wanted him to hear after being in captivity without hope of freedom. To verify that the raven and dove had actually said such a thing, he consulted the other person. Only when the other person confirmed that the raven and dove had actually said such a thing did he know that his mind was not playing tricks on him. This is how the Aruch knows from this Gemorah that Rav Elish understood bird talk. We see from this Gemorah, says Rav Meir Bergman, that a person who so desires to have his freedom can have his mind make up things that never happened so that the person could dream that he was getting his freedom.

Rav Chaim says that we find a similar example with Bilam. When the Moabite officers first come to Bilam, Hashem appears to him at night and tells him in Bamidbar (22:12), "You shall not go with them (Moabite officers)! You shall not curse the people (Bnei Yisroel) because they are blessed." Bilam gets up the next morning and tells the Moabite officers in Bamidbar (22:13), "Return to your country, for Hashem has refused to let me go with you." Bilam, however, stressed to these officers that the reason Hashem was not letting him go with them was that they were not important enough officers for a person of his stature to go with. As proof that this was what Bilam stressed to the officers after the officers return to Balak with his message, it says in Bamidbar (22:15), "So Balak continued to send dignitaries, more and higher in rank than these." In essence, Bilam reinterpreted Hashem's commandment in a manner consistent with what he wanted to hear.

Rav Meir Bergman says that the Bnei Yisroel had every reason to listen to Moshe when he spoke about their freedom since this is what they wanted to hear. If despite this, they did not listen to Moshe, it is logical to conclude that Pharaoh, who did not want to hear what Moshe was going to tell him, would not listen to him.

10) The Maharal, in his Sefer Gur Aryeh, presents another answer to our question. He says that Moshe argued that there were two reasons Pharaoh did not listen: (1) it was for his bad and (2) it was an affront for someone who could not speak well to be sent to speak to Pharaoh. The Bnei Yisroel only had one reason not to listen to Moshe, and that was "because of their shortness of

Vaera

breath and because of their hard labor." Since Pharaoh had more reasons not to listen, it is a logical conclusion that if the Bnei Yisroel did not listen, Pharaoh also would not listen.

11) The Abarbanel also presents an answer to our question. He writes that we know the Bnei Yisroel believed in Moshe as Shemos (4:31) says, "And the people believed, and they heard that Hashem had remembered the Bnei Yisroel and that He saw their affliction, and they kneeled and prostrated themselves." Despite believing in Moshe, the Bnei Yisroel had a reason not to listen to Moshe "because of their shortness of breath and hard work." Pharaoh had two reasons not to listen to Moshe: (1) unlike the Bnei Yisroel, he did not believe that Hashem was going to redeem the Bnei Yisroel, and (2) Moshe had a difficult time speaking. Therefore, since the Bnei Yisroel did not listen to Moshe, it is a logical conclusion that Pharaoh would not listen to Moshe.

12) The Ohr HaChaim also ponders our question. Like the Abarbanel in the previous answer, he says the Bnei Yisroel believed in Hashem while Pharaoh denied any belief in Hashem when he said in Shemos (5:2), "Who is Hashem that I should heed His voice to let Israel out? I do not know Hashem, neither will I let Yisroel out." In addition, the Bnei Yisroel had a reason to listen to Moshe since he was talking about a topic (redemption) that was for their good. In contrast, Moshe was telling Pharaoh something which was bad for Pharaoh. These two reasons versus the one reason the Bnei Yisroel had for not listening to Moshe makes it a logical conclusion that Pharaoh would not listen to Moshe.

13) As quoted in the Nodeh BeYehuda on the Torah, the son of the Nodeh BeYehuda also ponders our question. The Shir HaShirim Raba on Shir HaShirim (2:8) says that when Moshe came to the Bnei Yisroel and told them that they would be redeemed during this month of Nisan, the Bnei Yisroel told Moshe that it was not possible. Their reasoning was that Hashem had told Avrohom that the Bnei Yisroel would be enslaved for 400 years. Since the Bnei Yisroel has only been in Egypt for 210 years, it was way before the time to be redeemed. Moshe answered that since Hashem wanted the Bnei Yisroel to be redeemed, Hashem would not worry about this calculation.

We should also keep in mind that the Gemorah in Sanhedrin 92b references Divrei HaYomim I (7:21) that children of Ephraim went out of Egypt to Eretz Yisroel 30 years previously and were killed by the Philistines. Rashi on the Gemorah explains that the reason they went out early is that they calculated that the 400 years of Egyptian exile prophesized by Avrohom began at the time the prophecy was given at the Bris Bain HaBesorim when in reality, the 400-year exile started with the birth of Yitzchak, 30 years later. Realizing the great tragedy which had occurred to the children of Ephraim 30 years earlier, it is understandable that the Bnei Yisroel were not ready to go out of Egypt until they were sure that the correct calculation of the time in Egyptian exile had been made.

According to the Nodeh BeYehudah's son, Moshe was saying, "Behold, the Bnei Yisroel did not hearken to me (because they did not believe that the 400 or 430 years were up). It is then logical to ask how then will Pharaoh hearken to me (since Pharaoh will also say that the 400 years are not up) being that I am of closed lips?"

Vaera

14) The Ksav Sofer and Hegyona Shel Torah answer our question similarly. The Hegyona Shel Torah says that a person who is drowning will even grab hold of a far-fetched chance to be saved, like grabbing onto a piece of straw. Therefore, it is very surprising the Bnei Yisroel did not grab onto Moshe's promise to redeem them, which would seemingly have been a much more likely possibility than the drowning person grabbing onto a piece of straw. The Ksav Sofer says that someone who is promised a great reward after doing much hard work will have a much easier time accepting doing the hard work since they look forward to the reward. Therefore, it is also very surprising that after Moshe told them about their freedom and about getting their own land of Eretz Yisroel, the Bnei Yisroel did not listen to Moshe. Rather, the Bnei Yisroel were so oppressed that they fell into a great depression and gave up all hope of being redeemed or even of trying to be redeemed. Even with the promise of their own land, says the Ksav Sofer, it was meaningless to them since they could not imagine themselves fighting and conquering a land. Consequently, they made no effort to grab onto Moshe's promise to redeem them.

Pharaoh was aware the Bnei Yisroel made no effort to grab onto Moshe's promise to redeem them. Since it is not possible to redeem someone who does not want to be redeemed and is not clamoring to get his freedom, Pharaoh had no reason to worry about fulfilling or even listening to Moshe's demand to let the Bnei Yisroel go free. Therefore, it is a logical extension that if the Bnei Yisroel made no effort to grab onto Moshe's promise to redeem them, Pharaoh would not even listen to Moshe's demand to grant the Bnei Yisroel their freedom. As the Hegyona Shel Torah says, no master will free his slave if the slave makes no effort and shows no desire to be free. The Ksav Sofer also explains why Moshe added on the phrase "I am of closed lips." The only even remote possibility of getting a response from such depressed people is if one is a master orator and can stir up the people with meaningful and masterful words. Since Moshe knew that this was not the case, there did not seem to be any possibility of the Bnei Yisroel wanting to go out of Egypt.

15) The Ksav Sofer also presents another answer to our question. Pharaoh was familiar with the concept that there will come a time when the Bnei Yisroel will be redeemed from Egypt. He was also probably familiar with Hashem telling Avrohom in the Bris Bain HaBesorim that the Bnei Yisroel would be enslaved for 400 years. In addition, the Shemos Raba (1:18) says even Pharoah's own astrologers told Pharaoh that a savior would be born to the Jews, which prompted Pharaoh to try and kill all the Jewish boys. However, when Hashem sent Moshe to Pharaoh, he instructed him to just tell Pharaoh to allow the Bnei Yisroel to go to the desert for a few days to worship Hashem as Shemos (5:3) "Now let us go on a three-day journey in the desert and sacrifice to Hashem our G-d, lest He strike us with a plague or with the sword." The concept of allowing the Bnei Yisroel to go into the desert for a few days to sacrifice to Hashem was not something that Pharaoh was familiar with. Therefore, Pharaoh dismissed it out of hand over a fear of the Bnei Yisroel, using this as an opportunity to escape and never return to Egypt. In addition, Pharaoh increased the severity of the slavery as a punishment for presenting such a request to him.

The Ksav Sofer says that Moshe's Kal VeChomer began with the fact that even though he told the Bnei Yisroel about being fully redeemed from Egypt, the Bnei Yisroel still did not listen to Moshe despite the fact they had a tradition that they would be redeemed from Egypt. Based on the Bnei

Vaera

Yisroel not listening, it is a logical conclusion that Pharaoh would not listen to a request for spending a few days in the desert to serve Hashem since he had a tradition that the Bnei Yisroel would eventually be completely redeemed from Egypt.

Parenthetically, the Ksav Sofer discusses why Hashem chose to ask Pharaoh for the Bnei Yisroel to spend a few days in the desert instead of asking for them to be fully redeemed. He says that the reason for this request was to help harden Pharaoh's heart so that he would not listen to the request and thereby be punished with the ten plagues. The Beis HaLevi says that the reason for this request was to show how wicked and cruel Pharaoh was. Pharaoh did not allow even this short vacation, even though it might allow the Bnei Yisroel to work more productively when they got back. At the end of Parshas Shemos, he says the reason Pharaoh would not accept such a request was that it involved strengthening the Bnei Yisroel's belief in Hashem by serving Hashem for three days in the desert. The whole reason the Egyptians enslaved us was so they could decrease our religiosity. The Yalkut Shimoni (268) at the end of Parshas Beshalach tells us that the Bnei Yisroel had one main Mitzvah, doing a Bris Milah, which they kept in Egypt being that it had been given to and handed down from Avrohom. The Egyptians seeing that it was their main Mitzvah went to the Bnei Yisroel and told them to give up the Mitzvah of Bris Milah, thereby becoming similar to the Egyptians, and as a reward, the Egyptians promised to make the slavery work lighter. The Gemorah in Sotah 11b and the Midrash Tanchuma in Vayetze (9) say the Egyptians made the men do women's work like kneading and baking bread, and the women do men's work like chopping wood. The Beis HaLevi says that if the Egyptians were interested in getting more work out of the Bnei Yisroel, they would have given the men and women work they were accustomed to do. Instead, the Egyptians did not do this since they were not interested in the work but rather in using the work to cause the Bnei Yisroel to be less religious. Finally, he says that this was the message Hashem sent Pharaoh when Hashem had Aharon's stick turn into a snake. The Gemorah in Tanis 8a says that a lion claws its prey and then eats it, and similarly, a wolf tears its prey and eats it. However, a snake bites but does not get any pleasure or benefit from biting its prey. In a similar way, Pharoah's enslavement of the Bnei Yisroel was like a snake with regard to the fact that he was not interested in their work. Parenthetically, the Gemorah says that at the end of days, the other animals will ask the snake why it bites even though it has no pleasure. The snake will answer that it is behaving like a person who maligns others by speaking Loshon Horah even though the person who is doing the maligning may do the maligning without getting any advantage for themselves. By asking Pharaoh to just allow the Bnei Yisroel three days in the desert, Hashem was proving Pharoah's real reason for keeping the Bnei Yisroel enslaved. By asking to go to the desert without bringing along the necessary provisions, it would be impossible to escape and not come back to Egypt since there were no provisions to be found in the desert, so Pharaoh could not even refuse the request on the grounds that the Bnei Yisroel would not return.

16) Rav Schwab, in his Sefer Mayan Beis HaShoaivah, also presents an answer to our question. The Midrash Tanchuma in Vaera (6) says that the tribe of Levi was exempt from the very hard work in Egypt. In addition, the Bamidbar Raba (13:8) says that the tribes of Reuven, Shimon, and Levi did not serve idols in Egypt as opposed to all the other tribes. That being the case, it was completely perplexing to Moshe why at least the tribe of Levi did not listen to Moshe, since they were neither

Vaera

under hard work nor were worshipping idols, so they would seemingly have no reason not to listen to Moshe. He says it was this part of the Bnei Yisroel (the Leviyim) that Moshe was referring to when he says in our Posuk, "Behold, the Bnei Yisroel did not hearken to me. How then will Pharaoh hearken to me, seeing that I am of closed lips?" Given that even this part of the Bnei Yisroel did not listen, argued Moshe, it proves that it is my closed lips that prevent people from listening to me. Therefore, it is a logical conclusion that Pharaoh will also not listen to me.

What Did Hashem Command Moshe and Aharon When the Torah Does Not Explicitly Tell Us?

וַיְדַבֵּר ה' אֶל מֹשֶׁה וְאֶל אַהֲרֹן וַיְצַוֵּם אֶל בְּנֵי יִשְׂרָאֵל וְאֶל פַּרְעֹה מֶלֶךְ מִצְרָיִם לְהוֹצִיא אֶת בְּנֵי יִשְׂרָאֵל מֵאֶרֶץ מִצְרָיִם (ו:יג)

Shemos (6:13) Hashem spoke to Moshe and to Aharon, and He commanded them concerning the Bnei Yisroel and concerning Pharaoh, the King of Egypt, to let the Bnei Yisroel out of the land of Egypt.

At first glance, the Torah does not detail what it was that Hashem commanded Moshe and Aharon concerning the Bnei Yisroel and concerning Pharaoh. What did Hashem command Moshe and Aharon?

1) The Yerushalmi in Rosh Hashana (3:5) presents an answer to our question and says that Hashem commanded Moshe and Aharon to tell the Bnei Yisroel about the topic of sending one's Jewish servant free as is detailed in the first Pesukim in Parshas Mishpotim. A Jewish servant can serve for at most six years for his master. After that, unless the Jewish servant wants to remain with his master, the servant must be set free. The Korban HaEidah on the Yerushalmi explains that part of Hashem commanding about this topic was the promise that in the merit of observing this Mitzvah, the Bnei Yisroel would be redeemed from Egypt. The Yerushalmi continues that this is consistent with the opinion of Rav Hilah, who says that the reason the Bnei Yisroel were exiled from Eretz Yisroel at the time of the destruction of the first Beis Hamikdosh was that they did not keep the Mitzvah of sending their Jewish servants free. He references the Pesukim in Sefer Yirmiyahu Chapter 34. Towards the end of the first Beis Hamikdosh, the armies of the Babylonians under Nevuchadnetzar were attacking Yerushalayim. Yirmiyahu prophesizes to King Tzidkiyahu that Nevuchadnetzar would capture Yerushalayim, along with taking Tzidkiyahu captive. The Malbim explains that many of the poor Jews were being held as Jewish slaves by the richer Jews and officers at that time. Tzidkiyahu was afraid that they would escape from their masters and join the enemy Babylonians so that they would be free. Therefore, Tzidkiyahu made a treaty that all Jewish slaves would be granted their freedom and that they would be free for the rest of their lives. Tzidkiyahu did not tell the rich Jews and officers about the new treaty, but when they found out, they also agreed to abide by the new treaty. Not a long time later, the rich Jews and officers regretted their decision and forcibly went and captured the former slaves and enslaved them again. Yirmiyahu relates the following prophecy in Sefer Yirmiyahu (34:13-14), which says, "So says Hashem G-d of Yisroel; I made a treaty with your fathers on the day that I brought them forth out of the land of Egypt, out of the house of slaves, saying: 'At the end of seven years you shall let go every man his brother Jew who has been sold to you, and when he has served you for six years you shall let him go

Vaera

free from you.'" In Sefer Yirmiyahu (34:20-22), Yirmiyahu continues that as punishment for forcibly re-enslaving their fellow Jews after granting them their freedom, "I will deliver them into the hands of their enemies and into the hands of those who seek their lives, and their dead bodies shall become food for the birds of the heavens and for the beasts of the earth. And Tzidkiyahu, King of Yehuda, and his princes I will deliver into the hands of their enemies and into the hands of those who seek their lives, and into the hands of the army of the King of Babylon who have gone up away from you. Behold I command, says Hashem, and I will return them to this city, and they shall fight against it and capture it, and burn it with fire, and the cities of Yehuda I will make desolate without an inhabitant." Since Sefer Yirmiyahu says that the treaty to not enslave a Jewish servant for more to six years was described as "I made a treaty with your fathers on the day that I brought them forth out of the land of Egypt," the Yerushalmi derives that this must have been done at the commandment given in our Posuk.

Rav Chaim Shmulevitz in Parshas Bo (5731) ponders why the Mitzvah of sending a Jewish servant free after working a maximum of six years would be the first commandment to the Bnei Yisroel in Egypt. The Chinuch quotes the Gemorah in Arachin 29a, which says that the laws of a Jewish servant are only applicable when the laws of Yovel are applicable, which did not happen till after the Bnei Yisroel went into Eretz Yisroel. That being the case, Rav Chaim is perplexed at why the Bnei Yisroel were given as their first Mitzvah a Mitzvah that would not be applicable to them for many years. It would seem that it would have been sufficient to wait until the Torah was given to command the Bnei Yisroel about the laws of a Jewish servant. He answers that the Bnei Yisroel would be most sensitive to the laws of a Jewish servant at the time that they themselves were being redeemed from slavery. This is a similar concept to what Shemos (23:9) says, "And you shall not oppress a stranger, for you know the feelings of the stranger since you were strangers in the land of Egypt." A person is most sensitive to something when it happens, and afterward, his feeling cools down. Had Hashem waited till the giving of the Torah to first tell the Bnei Yisroel about the laws of a Jewish slave, their feelings on the subject would have been cooled off. Since it was such an obvious concept to the Bnei Yisroel when they left Egypt, the Bnei Yisroel are expected for all future generations to strongly uphold this law. That is why the Bnei Yisroel were given such a severe punishment of exile when they ignored this law at the time of Tzidkiyahu at the end of the first Beis Hamikdosh.

Rav Chaim presents an example of this concept from the Gemorah in Sanhedrin 20a. The Gemorah in Sanhedrin 19b-20a discusses Dovid HaMelech's wives. When Shaul was King, the giant Golyus taunted the Bnei Yisroel's army to have someone come out and fight him. The Bnei Yisroel were so despondent at the prospect of being able to fight Golyus that Shaul offered in Sefer Shmuel I (17:25) "And it will be, that the man who will kill him, the King (Shaul) will enrich him with great riches, and he will give him his daughter, and he will make his father's house free in Yisroel." The Gemorah tells us how Shaul reneged from giving both his oldest daughter (Meirav) and his daughter Michal as a wife to Dovid. After Dovid had killed Golyus, he was appointed to Shaul's army. Shaul became very jealous of Dovid when the people started saying that Dovid was a much greater warrior than Shaul. After reneging on giving Dovid his oldest daughter in marriage, Shaul promised to give Michal in marriage to Dovid as long as Dovid fulfilled one condition. Sefer Shmuel I

Vaera

(18:25) says, "And Shaul said, 'So shall you say to Dovid, The King has no desire in a dowry, but in one hundred foreskins of Philistines, to avenge himself upon the King's enemies.' But Shaul thought to make David fall by the hand of the Philistines." Because of his jealousy of Dovid, Shaul had no desire to fulfill this promise but rather wanted to use this promise to set up Dovid to be killed by the Philistines. Dovid successfully brought the one hundred foreskins of the Philistines to Shaul. However, Shaul kept wanting to kill Dovid as Sefer Shmuel I (19:11-12) says, "And Shaul sent messengers to Dovid's house to guard him and to put him to death in the morning, and Michal his wife told Dovid, saying, 'If you do not flee for your life tonight, tomorrow you will be put to death!'" Later in Sefer Shmuel I (25:44), it says, "And Shaul had given his daughter, Michal, wife of Dovid, to Palti ben Laish, who was from Gallim." The Gemorah explains that Shaul was of the opinion that there was a Halachic loophole that prevented Dovid's marriage to Michal from taking place.

However, Palti ben Laish, like Dovid, was of the opinion that Michal was married to Dovid. The Gemorah in Sanhedrin 19b explains how Palti ben Laish prevented himself from sinning with Michal. He took a sword, stuck it between their two beds, and proclaimed that whoever does this act (of having relations with Michal) should be stabbed with this sword. Rav Chaim asks the perhaps obvious question of how the sword could prevent him from sinning with Michal since, just like he put it there, he could easily remove it. Rather, he explains that the sword served as a reminder that in the beginning, Palti was so overcome with righteousness and holiness that he stuck the sword in the ground. When he saw the sword at a future date, even if he cooled down from his righteousness and holiness, it reminded him of how proper he had been, and that thought prevented him from sinning. Similarly, the Bnei Yisroel got the Mitzvah of a Jewish slave immediately when they came out of Egypt, had complete enthusiasm for keeping this Mitzvah since they were sensitive to how being enslaved felt should for all future generations keep them from violating this Mitzvah. That is why they were punished so severely with exile and destruction when they did not keep this Mitzvah. Rav Chaim concludes that many times in our lives, we are overcome with a feeling of righteousness and holiness to do a Mitzvah or not do an Aveirah. The important thing is to always remember that moment and use that remembrance to spur us on to keep doing that Mitzvah or not doing that Aveirah.

The Meshech Chochmah explains how the Mitzvahs involved with a Jewish slave were applicable even at the point that the Bnei Yisroel were leaving Egypt. He references the Bamidbar Raba (13:8), which ponders why in the beginning of Parshas Vaera, only the lineage of the three tribes of Reuven, Shimon, and Levi are mentioned. It relates that Reuven, Shimon, and Levi had leadership positions in Egypt. After Reuven was Niftar, Shimon took over the leadership position, and after Shimon was Niftar, Levi took it over. The Meshech Chochmah postulates that when the tribes of Reuven, Shimon, and Levi were in leadership positions, they took Jewish slaves who were sold to them by the Egyptians. Instead of being slaves to the Egyptians, these Jewish slaves were slaves to the Jews in leadership positions. There was a reason why it was ordained that the tribes of Reuven, Shimon, and Levi were not fully enslaved by the Egyptians. Since, as opposed to all the other tribes, Yaakov did not give these three tribes a blessing, these tribes may have felt like they were not such an integral part of the Bnei Yisroel. We know that because of the very harsh conditions of the

Vaera

Egyptian slavery, the Bnei Yisroel sunk down to the 49th and next to the last level of Tumah and were almost as Tameh as the Egyptians. It would have been possible that the tribes of Reuven, Shimon, and Levi would have sunk even further into Tumah and have become completely intermingled with the Egyptians, Chas VeShalom, since they felt that they were not as blessed as the other tribes. Therefore, Hashem did not enslave these three tribes.

It is also possible, says the Meshech Chochmah, that there was another scenario for how some of the Jews owned Jewish slaves. The Midrash Tanchuma on Vaera (6) says that the tribe of Levi was exempt from the very hard work in Egypt. That being the case, it is possible that they bought and employed Jewish slaves. Therefore, in our Posuk, which says, "Hashem commanded them concerning the Bnei Yisroel and concerning Pharaoh," it was the same commandment, to free the Jewish slaves, that was given to the Bnei Yisroel as it was to Pharaoh.

2) The Shemos Raba (7:3) and Sifrei in Parshas Behalosecha on Bamidbar (11:12) are the sources to one of the answers which Rashi presents to answer our question. They say that Hashem told Moshe that the Bnei Yisroel are people who refuse to listen, who have tempers, and who are very bothersome. Hashem commanded Moshe and Aharon to accept the Bnei Yisroel despite these traits. They should even accept the scenario that the Bnei Yisroel will want to curse them and stone them. The Eben Ezra quoting Rav Yeshayahu, says that the commandment was that Moshe and Aharon should not get angry against the Bnei Yisroel even if they do not listen to them. The Nachalas Yaakov explains the reason Hashem commanded Moshe and Aharon now about this is that Moshe seemed bothered when he said in the Posuk prior to ours, "Behold, the Bnei Yisroel did not hearken to me. How then will Pharaoh hearken to me, seeing that I am of closed lips?"

The Yalkut Shimoni in Bamidbar (664) says that Hashem was very specific in this commandment of how to treat the Bnei Yisroel despite the fact that the Bnei Yisroel were very bothersome to Moshe and Aharon. It says that Hashem commanded Moshe and Aharon in our Posuk to never call the Bnei Yisroel rebellious no matter how badly they behave. In Bamidbar (20:10), after the Bnei Yisroel bitterly complained about their lack of water after Miriam was Niftar, the Torah says, "Moshe and Aharon assembled the congregation in front of the rock, and he said to them, 'Now listen, you rebels, can we draw water for you from this rock?'" Hashem told Moshe and Aharon that since they did not keep the commandment given to them in our Posuk, they lost the right to live and lead the Bnei Yisroel into Eretz Yisroel.

The Oznayim LeTorah says that there is a hint in the Torah to this explanation. Immediately after our Posuk, the lineage of the tribes of Reuven, Shimon, and Levi are listed. We have examined in depth elsewhere how many Meforshim answer the question of why the lineage of only these three tribes is given at this point. After commanding Moshe and Aharon to accept the Bnei Yisroel despite the above traits, Hashem listed the tribes which would be the leaders of all the rebellions against Moshe and Aharon in the desert. The tribe of Reuven would produce Dasan and Avirom, who constantly rebelled against Moshe and Aharon until they were killed in the rebellion of Korach. The tribe of Shimon produced Zimri, who rebelled against Moshe after Bilam sent the daughters of

Vaera

Moav to sin with the Bnei Yisroel at the end of Parshas Balak. The tribe of Levi produced Korach, who would rebel against Moshe and Aharon.

In a similar way, the Shemos Raba tells us what Hashem commanded Moshe and Aharon with respect to Pharaoh. Similar to the command about the Bnei Yisroel, Hashem told Moshe and Aharon to give respect to Pharaoh as a King despite the fact that he was going to be punished. As the Shach on the Torah explains, since Pharaoh is a King, obviously Hashem wanted Pharaoh to be King. Mishlay (21:1) says, "A King's heart is like rivulets of water in Hashem's hand; wherever He wishes, He turns it," and therefore Pharoah's actions are not necessarily his own free will. In his Sefer Mayan Beis HaShoaivah, Rav Schwab also says a similar thought to that of the Shach. That being the case, Moshe and Aharon were commanded not to disrespect Pharaoh because of his actions. The Shemos Raba highlights an example of how Moshe and Aharon did this. When describing what would happen on the night of Pesach when all the Egyptian firstborn were killed, Shemos (11:8) says, "And all these servants of yours (Pharoah's) will come down to me and prostrate themselves to me, saying, 'Go out, you and all the people who are at your feet,' and afterwards I will go out." In actuality, Pharaoh himself, and not his servants went to find Moshe and Aharon as Shemos (12:30-31) says, "And Pharaoh arose at night, he and all his servants and all the Egyptians, and there was a great outcry in Egypt, for there was no house in which no one was dead. So he called for Moshe and Aharon at night, and he said, 'Get up and get out from among my people, both you, as well as the Bnei Yisroel, and go, worship Hashem as you have spoken.'" However, because of respect to Pharaoh, Moshe and Aharon did not tell Pharaoh that he would break the laws of decorum for a King and go himself looking for Moshe and Aharon. The Mizrachi and Maharal, in Gur Aryeh, say that in addition to Hashem telling Moshe and Aharon to be gentle with the Bnei Yisroel despite their harsh characteristics, Hashem also told them to be gentle with Pharaoh even if he got angry with them.

Rashi on Beraishis (48:2), quoting the Midrash Tanchuma in Vayechi (6), says that the reason Yaakov summoned all his strength to sit up for Yosef was that one must show respect to a King. That being the case, says the Maskil LeDovid, this obligation of showing respect to a King should already have been known to Moshe and Aharon. He answers that Moshe and Aharon could have thought that Pharaoh was different and did not need to be shown respect since Hashem told them in Shemos (7:1), "Hashem said to Moshe, 'See! I have made you a lord over Pharaoh, and Aharon, your brother, will be your speaker.'"

3) The Shemos Raba (7:3) offers another answer to our question. Before we can fully appreciate this answer, we must note that the Hebrew word used for commanded in our Posuk is וַיְצַוֵּם. The Maharzav explains that in Aramaic, this word means to "join in partnership" or to "be together in company with." For example, the Gemorah in Sukkah 52a uses this Aramaic word when two people were parting ways because they lived in different cities and said that the company would have been pleasant had they been able to do so. Though it is an Aramaic word, the Maharzav shows that the Torah can also use this word to mean to "join in partnership" or to "be together in company with." He quotes the Beraishis Raba on Beraishis (49:29), describing what Yaakov said to his sons right before he was Niftar. The Torah says וַיְצַו אוֹתָם וַיֹּאמֶר אֲלֵהֶם אֲנִי נֶאֱסָף אֶל עַמִּי קִבְרוּ אֹתִי אֶל אֲבֹתָי אֶל הַמְּעָרָה

171

Vaera

אֲשֶׁר בִּשְׂדֵה עֶפְרוֹן הַחִתִּי (And he (Yaakov) commanded them and said to them, "I will be brought in to my people; bury me with my fathers, in the cave that is in the field of Ephron the Hittite"). The Beraishis Raba explains that Yaakov said to his sons that if their deeds were righteous, they would merit to have Yaakov join with them even after he was Niftar. If not, Yaakov would stay together with his forefathers in the Meoras HaMachpaylah. The Maharzav on that Midrash explains that this Beraishis Raba is using the Aramaic translation of וַיְצַו as meaning "joining" to explain Yaakov talking about whether he would be joining the Bnei Yisroel after he was Niftar.

With this introduction, we can better understand the answer that the Shemos Raba on our Posuk presents to our question. It says that Hashem was telling Moshe and Aharon to join with the leaders of the tribes of the Bnei Yisroel in order to take them out of Egypt. This is the explanation of why our Posuk is juxtaposed to the next Posuk which says אֵלֶּה רָאשֵׁי בֵית אֲבֹתָם (These (the names that follow) are the heads of the fathers' houses). The Yepheh Toar explains that Hashem told Moshe and Aharon to join forces with the leaders of the Bnei Yisroel so that they can share the "burden" of redeeming the Bnei Yisroel.

4) The Shemos Raba (7:4) presents another answer to our question. It paints a Moshul of a King who had a field. The King had both fruit trees and non-fruit trees planted in the field. His servants questioned the King as to why he had planted non-fruit trees in his field. The King answered, "just like I need fruit trees, I also need non-fruit trees, since if I didn't have non-fruit trees, where would I get the wood to build bathhouses and furnaces?" In a similar fashion, just like the praise of Hashem comes from souls of the righteous people (the fruit trees) in Gan Eden; similarly, the praise of Hashem comes from the souls of the wicked people (non-fruit trees) in Gehenom.

The Eitz Yosef explains that this Shemos Raba is of the opinion that Hashem was asking Moshe and Aharon to give honor to both the Bnei Yisroel and to Pharaoh since both of them will sanctify Hashem's name. Though it is easy to understand how the Bnei Yisroel will sanctify Hashem's name, even Pharaoh, who is wicked, will also praise and sanctify Hashem's name when he says in Shemos (9:27) when trying to get the hail to stop, "I have sinned this time. Hashem is the righteous One, and I and my people are the guilty ones." The Yepheh Toar ponders the question that the Vayikra Raba (16:4), quoting Rav Levi, says that Hashem does not like the praise of wicked people. The Yepheh Toar answers that Rav Levi is talking about a wicked person who is saying the praise of Hashem and the wonders that Hashem does. Since this wicked person, despite saying this, nonetheless sins, one cannot trust what the wicked person says, and therefore his praise is worthless. In our case, where the wicked Pharaoh admits that he deserved the punishment that he was getting and was correctly judged, this is proper praise of Hashem since he is showing remorse for his sins.

5) Rashi answers our question in what he terms the simple way. He says that Hashem commanded Moshe and Aharon to say two different things, one to the Bnei Yisroel and the other to Pharaoh. Moshe and Aharon were commanded to tell the Bnei Yisroel that they were going out of Egypt. They were commanded to tell Pharaoh to let the Bnei Yisroel go out of Egypt and that if he didn't, he would be punished with afflictions.

Vaera

The Maskil LeDovid ponders the question of why Rashi presents this simple answer after he first presents the Midrashic answer that we have examined in our second answer to our question. In general, Rashi always presents the simple answer before he presents a Midrashic answer. The Maskil LeDovid says that the reason is that Rashi was bothered by two issues with the simple answer, and therefore he did not present it as his first answer. The first issue is that Moshe had already told the Bnei Yisroel that they were going out of Egypt, so there was no new command to the Bnei Yisroel in our Posuk. The second issue is that many Pesukim later in Shemos (7:2) Hashem commands Moshe and Aharon to tell Pharaoh to let the Bnei Yisroel leave Egypt, when the Posuk says, "You shall speak all that I command you, and Aharon, your brother, shall speak to Pharaoh, that he let the Bnei Yisroel out of his land." Therefore, according to the simple answer, the commandment in our Posuk would seem superfluous.

6) The Midrash Lekach Tov is the source to Rabeinu Bechay and the Baal HaTurim, who answer our question similarly. It says that Hashem told Moshe and Aharon to warn the Bnei Yisroel that they should not serve idols. Rabeinu Bechay says that we see that the Hebrew word צַו (command) refers to a command to serve idols in Sefer Hoshea (5:11) עָשׁוּק אֶפְרַיִם רְצוּץ מִשְׁפָּט כִּי הוֹאִיל הָלַךְ אַחֲרֵי צָו (Ephraim is plundered, broken by judgment, because he desired and followed a command). The Metzudos Dovid says that this was the command of Yorovam ben Nevot, who built golden calves and commanded the ten tribes to worship them instead of worshipping Hashem. The tribe of Ephraim willingly fully listened to this command of Yorovam ben Nevot, and this Posuk describes their punishment. We know the Bnei Yisroel served idols in Egypt as the Prophet Yechezkel tells us when he says that the Prophet of that time, who Chazal tell us was Aharon, says to the Bnei Yisroel in Sefer Yechezkel (20:6-8) "On that day I lifted up My hand to them to bring them out of the land of Egypt, to a land that I had sought out for them, flowing with milk and honey; it is the glory of all the lands. And I said to them: Every man cast away the despicable idols from before his eyes, and pollute not yourselves with the idols of Egypt; I am Hashem your G-d. But they rebelled against Me and would not consent to hearken to Me; they did not cast away, every man, the despicable idols from before their eyes, neither did they forsake the idols of Egypt; and I said to pour out My wrath over them, to give My anger full reign over them, in the midst of the land of Egypt."

The Shach on the Torah points out that this Midrash Lekach Tov can be connected to our second answer that Hashem told Moshe to disregard how bothersome and troublesome the Bnei Yisroel will be. He says Hashem told Moshe that just like Hashem was overlooking and not getting angry with the fact that the Bnei Yisroel were serving idols in order to redeem them from Egypt similarly, Moshe and Aharon should overlook the fact that the Bnei Yisroel may be bothersome and troublesome and not get angry with them.

7) The Sforno also presents an answer to our question and says that the Hebrew word וַיְצַוֵּם can also be translated as being appointed to a position as a prince or ruler. For example, in Bamidbar (27:19) Hashem commands Moshe to take Yehoshua וְהַעֲמַדְתָּ אֹתוֹ לִפְנֵי אֶלְעָזָר הַכֹּהֵן וְלִפְנֵי כָּל הָעֵדָה וְצִוִּיתָה אֹתוֹ לְעֵינֵיהֶם. Consistent with the Sforno, the Ramban on that Posuk says that the simplest translation of that Posuk would be "And you shall present him before Elazar the Kohen and before the entire congregation, and you shall appoint him as (the next) leader in their presence." Similarly, in Sefer

Vaera

Shmuel I (13:14) after Shaul errs, Shmuel tells him **וַיְצַוֵּהוּ ה'** לוֹ אִישׁ כִּלְבָבוֹ בִּקֵּשׁ ה' לוֹ תָקוּם לֹא מַמְלַכְתְּךָ וְעַתָּה לְנָגִיד עַל עַמּוֹ כִּי לֹא שָׁמַרְתָּ אֵת אֲשֶׁר צִוְּךָ ה' ("But now, your Kingdom shall not continue; Hashem has sought for Himself a man after His heart, and Hashem **has appointed him** to be a ruler over His people, for you have not kept that which Hashem commanded you"). Another example of the root of the Hebrew word וַיְצֻוֵּם translated as being appointed is found in Sefer Shmuel II (7:11) when Noson the Prophet tells Dovid HaMelech וּלְמִן הַיּוֹם אֲשֶׁר **צִוִּיתִי** שֹׁפְטִים עַל עַמִּי יִשְׂרָאֵל וַהֲנִיחֹתִי לְךָ מִכָּל אֹיְבֶיךָ וְהִגִּיד לְךָ ה' כִּי בַיִת יַעֲשֶׂה לְּךָ ה' (And even from the day that I **appointed** judges to be over my people Yisroel; and I will give you rest from all your enemies. And Hashem has told you that Hashem will make for you a house).

The Sforno says that in our Posuk, Moshe and Aharon are appointed as officers over the Bnei Yisroel and officers over Pharaoh. In the case of Pharaoh, the appointment was to facilitate the Bnei Yisroel being redeemed from Egypt. The Ohr HaChaim is of a similar opinion as the Sforno that the Hebrew word וַיְצֻוֵּם can also be translated as being appointed to a position as a prince or ruler. He says that Moshe and Aharon were appointed Kings over the Bnei Yisroel and over Pharaoh. This appointment as a King gave Moshe and Aharon the right to force the Bnei Yisroel to leave Egypt even if they refused and to force Pharaoh to listen even if he had no desire to listen to Moshe and Aharon. With this explanation, we can understand the juxtaposition of our Posuk to the previous Posuk, which says, "But Moshe spoke before Hashem, saying, 'Behold, the Bnei Yisroel did not hearken to me. How then will Pharaoh hearken to me, seeing that I am of closed lips?'" Now that in our Posuk Hashem appointed Moshe and Aharon as Kings over the Bnei Yisroel and Pharaoh, they could force both the Bnei Yisroel and Pharaoh to listen to them, which answered Moshe's complaint in the previous Posuk. With this approach, he also answers the juxtaposition of our Posuk to the next set of Pesukim, which present the genealogy of Moshe and Aharon. A Jewish King must have a genealogy that traces itself back to Yaakov. The Ohr Yakor is his commentary on the Ohr HaChaim cites a Rambam in Hilchos Melachim (1:4), which says that we do not appoint a King whose lineage stems from converts even from many previous generations. Rather we appoint a King whose mother has a complete Jewish lineage. Therefore, the next set of Pesukim trace the genealogy of Moshe and Aharon back to Yaakov to show us that Moshe and Aharon were appropriate for the title of being made Kings over the Bnei Yisroel. Parenthetically we should mention that the Kesef Mishna points out that the Rambam means either the mother or father must have a complete Jewish lineage. Shlomo HaMelech had a son Rechavom who took over as the next King after Shlomo. His mother was Naama, who was a convert of the Ammonites. Only because of the lineage of Rechavom's father, Shlomo was Rechavom fit to be a King over the Bnei Yisroel. We note that the Gevuras Yitzchak is somewhat perplexed as to how Aharon was considered a King. Only about Moshe does Devorim (33:5) say, "And He was King in Yeshurun."

8) The Akeidah also ponders our question and writes that when the Torah uses the term וַיְצֻוֵּם (and He commanded), it does not necessarily mean a verbal commandment. Rather it can also mean Hashem is putting in the "heart" or desires of someone or something to do a certain action. For example, in Sefer Melachim I (17:4), Hashem tells the Prophet Eliyahu וְהָיָה מֵהַנַּחַל תִּשְׁתֶּה וְאֶת הָעֹרְבִים צִוִּיתִי לְכַלְכֶּלְךָ שָׁם (And it shall be from the brook you shall drink and I have commanded the ravens to feed you there). Obviously, Hashem did not verbally command the ravens but rather put it in their

Vaera

heart to bring food for Eliyahu. Similarly, in our Posuk, Hashem commanded means that Hashem put charm, respect, and fear of Moshe and Aharon in the hearts of the Bnei Yisroel and in the heart of Pharaoh.

The Berditchever Rebbe, in his Sefer Kedushas Levi, explains that there are two types of righteous people who give rebuke. One type of righteous person can cause just through who he is and what he says even wicked people to turn to the correct path and serve Hashem. This type of righteous person does not have to explain or bring proofs to what he says nor have any special oratory skills. Rather his simple words on their own make an impression on people and immediately enter their hearts. The second type of righteous person must first bring convincing and well-put arguments for people to follow what he says. In the previous Posuk to ours, Moshe says to Hashem, "How then will Pharaoh hearken to me, seeing that I am of closed lips?" In our Posuk, Hashem tells Moshe that being a convincing and articulate speaker is not required for this mission to Pharaoh since Hashem has put in his heart that Pharaoh should listen to him just like the first type of righteous person is listened to.

9) The Chizkuni, Ralbag, Alshich, Abarbanel, and Malbim answer our question similarly. They say that Hashem commanded Moshe and Aharon to together speak both to the Bnei Yisroel and to Pharaoh. The Yalkut Reuveni also answers our question in this way. The Alshich explains that both originally when Hashem first spoke to Moshe and also in the previous Posuk to ours, Moshe had told Hashem that he was not qualified for the mission of redeeming the Bnei Yisroel from Egypt. That is why our Posuk, where Hashem commands Moshe and Aharon to jointly speak to both the Bnei Yisroel and Pharaoh, is juxtaposed to the previous Posuk when Moshe says to Hashem, "Behold, the Bnei Yisroel did not hearken to me. How then will Pharaoh hearken to me, seeing that I am of closed lips?" The Alshich, Abarbanel, and Malbim all point out that until our Posuk, only Moshe and not Aharon was appointed to speak to Pharaoh and convince him to free the Bnei Yisroel. We note that the Ralbag and many years later the Nitziv point out that having Aharon and Moshe speak to the Bnei Yisroel was only in effect while the Bnei Yisroel were in Egypt. Afterward, Hashem would communicate through Moshe alone to tell the Bnei Yisroel everything which Hashem told him.

10) The Abarbanel also presents another answer to our question. He says that this command wasn't to Moshe or Aharon but was rather commanded to the Bnei Yisroel and to Pharaoh regarding Moshe and Aharon. When our Posuk says, וַיְצַוֵּם אֶל בְּנֵי יִשְׂרָאֵל וְאֶל פַּרְעֹה מֶלֶךְ מִצְרָיִם the Abarbanel translates this literally that "Hashem commanded to the Bnei Yisroel and to Pharaoh" instead of translating it as we have above "Hashem commanded concerning the Bnei Yisroel and concerning Pharaoh." The commandment to the Bnei Yisroel was that they should listen to Moshe and Aharon and give them proper respect. Similarly, Hashem commanded Pharaoh that he should respect Moshe and Aharon and give them a chance to say what Hashem commanded them to say to him without belittling them and without granting them an audience. As a result of finding out that Pharaoh respected Moshe and Aharon, the Bnei Yisroel would be more receptive to hearing Moshe and Aharon's words.

Vaera

11) Rav Hirsch also ponders our question and says that Hashem commanded Moshe and Aharon to accept Hashem's mission for them as a commandment and thereby be zealous in carrying out this mission. Included in this commandment was for Moshe and Aharon to stop making calculations about whether they were fit for this mission as Moshe had done in the Posuk previous to ours when he said to Hashem, "Behold, the Bnei Yisroel did not hearken to me. How then will Pharaoh hearken to me, seeing that I am of closed lips?" Until this point, when Hashem had told Moshe and Aharon about the mission to redeem the Bnei Yisroel, Hashem never commanded them to undertake this mission.

12) The Hegyona Shel Torah also presents an answer to our question. In the previous Posuk to ours, Moshe says to Hashem, "Behold, the Bnei Yisroel did not hearken to me. How then will Pharaoh hearken to me, seeing that I am of closed lips?" Many commentators say that Moshe's logical proof Pharoah would not listen to him, known in Hebrew as a Kal VeChomer, is not a good logical argument. A few Pesukim previous to this Shemos (6:9) tells us that there was a reason that the Bnei Yisroel did not listen to Moshe when the Torah says "they (Bnei Yisroel) did not hearken to Moshe because of shortness of breath and because of hard labor." Since Pharaoh did not have these issues, it does not logically follow that Pharaoh would also not listen to Moshe. Both the Shemos Raba and Mechilta ponder how it is possible that someone would speak to someone about their freedom, and they would not listen. It is especially troublesome in a case like ours where the one who is being quoted (Hashem) has the capability to follow through on providing freedom. The Hegyona Shel Torah says that the Bnei Yisroel not listening proves that the Bnei Yisroel were so depressed that they had completely given up on the idea of ever being redeemed from Egypt. That being the case, Pharaoh would not listen to Moshe and Aharon to free the Bnei Yisroel since he would say that even the Bnei Yisroel themselves do not want to be redeemed. Therefore, in our Posuk, Hashem commanded Aharon and Moshe to tell the Bnei Yisroel that their attitude and depression were preventing their redemption since Pharaoh would use their attitude as an excuse to not free them. As the Hegyona Shel Torah says, "which master would not grant his servant's desire to remain their servant?"

Why Does the Torah Only List the Lineage of the Tribes of Reuven, Shimon, and Levi and Not the Rest of the Tribes?

אֵלֶּה רָאשֵׁי בֵית אֲבֹתָם בְּנֵי רְאוּבֵן בְּכֹר יִשְׂרָאֵל חֲנוֹךְ וּפַלּוּא חֶצְרוֹן וְכַרְמִי אֵלֶּה מִשְׁפְּחֹת רְאוּבֵן. וּבְנֵי שִׁמְעוֹן יְמוּאֵל וְיָמִין וְאֹהַד וְיָכִין וְצֹחַר וְשָׁאוּל בֶּן הַכְּנַעֲנִית אֵלֶּה מִשְׁפְּחֹת שִׁמְעוֹן. וְאֵלֶּה שְׁמוֹת בְּנֵי לֵוִי לְתֹלְדֹתָם גֵּרְשׁוֹן וּקְהָת וּמְרָרִי וּשְׁנֵי חַיֵּי לֵוִי שֶׁבַע וּשְׁלֹשִׁים וּמְאַת שָׁנָה. (ו:יד-טז) Shemos (6:14-16) These are the heads of the fathers' houses: The sons of Reuven, Yisroel's firstborn: Chanoch, Pallu, Chetzron, and Karmi, these are the families of Reuven. And the sons of Shimon: Yemuel and Yamin and Ohad and Yachin and Tzohar and Shaul, the son of the Canaanitess, these are the families of Shimon. And these are the names of Levi's sons after their generations: Gershon, Kehas, and Merari, and the years of Levi's life were one hundred thirty-seven years.

Why does the Torah only list the heads of the houses of the tribes of Reuven, Shimon, and Levi and not the rest of the tribes?

Vaera

Introduction

The Tzedah LeDerech ponders the question of why the lineage of Moshe and Aharon are presented here and not when Moshe and Aharon first spoke to Pharaoh in Shemos (5:1). He answers that since Pharaoh not only refused to listen to Moshe and Aharon when they first came to him but also made the slavery harsher, the Bnei Yisroel began to doubt whether Moshe and Aharon were appropriate for this mission as Shemos (5:20-21) says "They met Moshe and Aharon standing before them when they came out from Pharaoh's presence. And they said to them, 'May Hashem look upon you and judge, for you have brought us into foul odor in the eyes of Pharaoh and in the eyes of his servants, to place a sword into their hands to kill us.'" Therefore, before Moshe and Aharon went again to Pharaoh, the Torah tells us their lineage to stress that they were the appropriate people for this mission.

1) The Bamidbar Raba (13:8), Shir HaShirim Raba (4:7), Rashi, from the Peskita Raba, and the Rashbam, from the Mechilta, answer our question similarly. The Bamidbar Raba and Shir HaShirim Raba say that the Shir HaShirim (4:7) כֻּלָּךְ יָפָה רַעְיָתִי וּמוּם אֵין בָּךְ (You are all fair, my beloved, and there is no blemish in you) is referring to the twelve tribes. They question how this is possible since Yaakov in Parshas Vayechi gives rebuke to Reuven, Shimon, and Levi about their past sins. They answer that despite rebuking Reuven, Shimon, and Levi, Yaakov also blessed all the twelve tribes as it says at the end of the blessings of Yaakov in Beraishis (49:28) "All these are the twelve tribes of Yisroel, and this is what their father spoke to them and blessed them; each man, according to his blessing, he blessed them." Since Yaakov initially rebuked Reuven, Shimon, and Levi, they are mentioned by themselves in our Pesukim to compensate for Yaakov rebuking them. By mentioning only these three tribes now, the Torah shows that they are just as important tribes as the other tribes. Therefore, all the tribes are included when Shir HaShirim says, "You are all fair, my beloved, and there is no blemish in you."

2) The Bamidbar Raba (13:8) and Shir HaShirim Raba (4:7) present another answer to our question. Mishlay (15:31) says אֹזֶן שֹׁמַעַת תּוֹכַחַת חַיִּים בְּקֶרֶב חֲכָמִים תָּלִין (The ear that listens to reproof of life shall lodge among the wise). They say that when Yaakov rebuked Reuven, Shimon, and Levi, they accepted the rebuke, and therefore as Mishlay implies, they "shall lodge among the wise." The reward to "lodge among the wise" happens in our Pesukim when they are mentioned along with Moshe and Aharon when our Pesukim want to tell us their lineage.

3) The Bamidbar Raba (13:8) and Shir HaShirim Raba (4:7) present another answer to our question. They say that all the rest of the tribes besides Reuven, Shimon, and Levi worshipped idols in Egypt. That is why they alone merited to be named in our Pesukim.

4) The Bamidbar Raba (13:8) and Shir HaShirim Raba (4:7) present another answer to our question. They say that Reuven, Shimon, and Levi took leadership positions in Egypt while the rest of the tribes did not. Reuven first took a position of leadership in Egypt. Presumably, this was after Yosef was Niftar. After Reuven was Niftar, this position was given to Shimon, and after he was Niftar, it was given to Levi. After Levi was Niftar, they wanted to give this position to Yehuda, and a

Vaera

heavenly voice came out and said not to give Yehuda a leadership position at this time and to wait until the time of the Kingship of Dovid. The Eitz Yosef says that these Midrashim are not consistent with the Seder Olam (which Rashi also quotes on our Pesukim), which says that Levi lived the longest of all the tribes and was the last of the twelve brothers to be Niftar. According to this Seder Olam, it would not have been possible for Yehuda to be offered the leadership position after Levi was Niftar. It seems to me that it is possible to make the Midrash consistent with the Seder Olam by saying that the leadership position was offered to Yehuda's son, who took his place after Yehuda was Niftar.

5) The Bamidbar Raba (13:8) and Shir HaShirim Raba (4:7) present another answer to our question. They say that only these three tribes kept their pedigree in Egypt. The Yepheh Kol on the Shir HaShirim Raba explains that though the other tribes were careful not to intermarry with the Egyptians, these three tribes were careful not to marry someone from a family which did not have as distinguished a pedigree as they did. The Yedei Moshe on both Midrashim offers another interpretation about this answer. We have seen in the previous answer that these three tribes took positions of leadership among the Bnei Yisroel. Because of these positions of leadership, these three tribes were not enslaved by the Egyptians. Rashi on Bamidbar (26:5), based on the Shir HaShirim Raba (4:12), says that the Gentiles were mocking the Bnei Yisroel when they counted all the people from each father's house in Parshas Pinchos. The Gentiles argued that since the Egyptians controlled the bodies of the Bnei Yisroel by enslaving them, they also had free reign over their wives whenever they wanted. Hashem testified to the fact that this was not true and that the husbands were all the fathers of their children. The Yedei Moshe says that the Gentiles did not mock these three tribes of Reuven, Shimon, and Levi since they were not enslaved. Therefore, there were no questions, even from the mocking gentiles, about the pedigrees of these three tribes, and therefore their pedigrees are listed separately in our Pesukim.

6) Rashi on our Posuk presents an answer to our question. He says that since the Torah wanted to describe the lineage of Moshe and Aharon, this necessitated listing all the descendants of Levi. Since the Torah had to describe this lineage anyway, the Torah went back further in lineage and started from the tribe of Reuven, the firstborn of Yaakov. The Torah stopped when it finished describing Moshe and Aharon's lineage.

7) The Sforno, Gur Aryeh, Abarbanel, Kli Yakor, Alshich, Malbim. and Oznayim LeTorah answer our question similarly. Rashi on Beraishis (37:1) quotes a Beraishis Raba (39:10) and a Midrash Tanchuma on Vayeshev (1) to explain the concept found a number of times in the Torah where the Torah quickly lists a number of people in a few Pesukim and then spends a number of Pesukim describing one person. They present a Moshul to a King who lost a very precious pearl in a pile of dirt and pebbles. The King ordered all his servants to take sieves and sieve all the dirt and pebbles looking for the pearl. It took a number of piles to sieve through, but eventually, they were successful in finding the pearl and a great celebration ensued. The King discarded all the dirt and pebbles and only focused on the pearl that he had found. In a similar way, the Torah spent some Pesukim examining (sieving) the people in the generations after Noach until the proper person (the pearl) was found. Once Hashem found the appropriate person Hashem did not return to discussing

Vaera

all the people who were not chosen and were discarded but rather spent many Pesukim focusing solely on the life and actions of the pearl, Avrohom. Another example is at the end of Parshas Vayishlach, where all the descendants of Esav are quickly examined until the Torah focuses exclusively on Yaakov and his sons (the pearl).

Similarly, in our Pesukim, the Sforno, Gur Aryeh, Abarbanel, Kli Yakor, Alshich, Malbim, and Oznayim LeTorah all say that the Hashem was searching for a leader to redeem the Bnei Yisroel from Egypt. Since Reuven was the firstborn and it would have been appropriate for the leader to come from his tribe, Hashem first started searching in the tribe of Reuven. When this was unsuccessful, Hashem began searching in the tribe of Shimon. When the search in the tribe of Shimon was unsuccessful, Hashem began searching in the tribe of Levi until Hashem found the pearls, Moshe and Aharon, that were the appropriate leaders to redeem the Bnei Yisroel. As the Abarbanel says, this way of searching showed that Hashem did not play favorites by starting to choose from the tribe of Levi, but rather He was only interested in finding the appropriate candidate, no matter what tribe they were from.

The Sforno ponders the question of why the Torah only mentions the sons of Reuven and Shimon and not their descendants, while for Levi, the Torah mentions not only the sons but also their descendants. In our Pesukim, the Torah introduces the lineage of Reuven and Shimon by saying, "these are the heads of the fathers' houses," while the lineage of Levi is introduced with the phrase "And these are the names of Levi's sons after their generations." He says that only the names that the Torah mentions were appropriate to be the redeemer of the Bnei Yisroel. In the case of Reuven and Shimon, this only included their sons who came down with Yaakov to Egypt and were influenced by Reuven and Shimon. However, though the sons of Reuven and Shimon were appropriate people to redeem the Bnei Yisroel, they could not be chosen since they had been Niftar. We can understand this Sforno based on what he wrote in the beginning of Parshas Shemos when the names of the sons of Yaakov are listed. Bamidbar (4:32), when referring to the vessels used in the Mishkan says וּבְשֵׁמֹת תִּפְקְדוּ אֶת כְּלֵי מִשְׁמֶרֶת מַשָּׂאָם (You shall designate by name the vessels assigned to them (the Levite family of Merari) for their burden). At the beginning of Parshas Pekuday, he says that not just the main vessels used in the Mishkan (the Aron, Shulchan, Menorah, and Mizbeach) but each auxiliary vessel was important enough to be called by its specific name and not as a general category of vessels. In a similar way, at the beginning of Shemos, he says that the reason our Posuk says, "And these are the names," is to point out that each of the tribes was important enough to be referenced by name. Similarly, in our Pesukim, with respect to the tribes of Reuven and Shimon, only their sons were important enough to be mentioned by name.

Therefore, the Sforno is of the opinion that the people referenced by name in our Pesukim were referenced by name since they were appropriate to be chosen to redeem the Bnei Yisroel from Egypt. He says that the reason the Torah records how long Levi, his son Kehas, and his grandson Amram lived was to show why in the tribe of Levi there were people appropriate to redeem the Bnei Yisroel who were descendants of Levi's sons, as opposed to descendants of Reuven and Shimon's sons. Since Levi and his son Kehas lived a long life, they were able to take part in bringing up Amram in a manner that he was an appropriate person to redeem the Bnei Yisroel. Because of this

Vaera

proper upbringing of Amram, Amram was able to raise Moshe, Aharon, and Miriam so that they also would be the appropriate leaders to redeem the Bnei Yisroel from Egypt. Rav Hirsch says that with the long life spans of Amram and his father Kehas, neither Kehas nor Amram had been dead a long time when Moshe and Aharon assumed their leadership positions to redeem the Bnei Yisroel from Egypt. Not only that, says the Sforno, but with the help of his wife Elisheva, who was the sister of the leader of Yehuda, Aharon raised four sons such that they were appropriate to be the Kohanim. We note that the Oznayim LeTorah presents a different reason for naming all the different people in the tribe of Levi. He says that since we would meet them later on in the Torah, it was, therefore, appropriate to list their lineage so we would know who they were.

The Targum Yonason ben Uziel on Shemos (6:16) says that not only did Levi live till 137 years but that he also saw and was alive when Moshe and Aharon, the saviors of the Bnei Yisroel, were born. The Perush Yonason on this Targum says that this is hard to fathom. We know that the entire time from when Yaakov and his family came down to Egypt until the redemption spanned 210 years. We also are told in Shemos (7:7) that Moshe was 80 years old and Aharon 83 when they spoke to Pharaoh. That means that Moshe was born 130 years after Yaakov and his family came done to Egypt. We are also told in the Torah that Yosef was 30 years old when he became the viceroy in Egypt. Yaakov and his family came down two years into the years of famine which had followed the seven years of plenty, meaning that Yosef was 39 years old when Yaakov and his family came down to Egypt. The Perush Yonason assumes that Levi was four years older than Yosef, which is what the Sifsei Chachomim says on Shemos (6:16) though as we will see that the calculation for Levi being alive when Moshe was born will not work even if Yosef and Levi were the same age. Anyway, if Levi was 43 years old when he came to Egypt and lived for 137 years implies that he was in Egypt for 94 years. Above, we have shown that Moshe was only born when the Bnei Yisroel had been in Egypt for 130 years so that Moshe was born 36 years after Levi had been Niftar. Therefore, the Perush Yonason says that the Targum Yonason ben Uziel saying that Levi was alive when Moshe and Aharon were born is problematic. The only possible explanation I have seen, which is very novel, is that when the Torah says that Levi lived for 137 years, it means that the 137 years is the amount of time that Levi lived in Egypt. Since we have previously said that Levi was 43 years old when he came down to Egypt, it would imply that Levi was 180 years old when he was Niftar. Since Levi's grandfather, Yitzchak was Niftar at 180 years; it is not unimaginable that Levi could live to 180 years. If we accept this novel interpretation, Moshe would have been seven years old when Levi was Niftar. The Shemos Raba (1:8) and Seder Olam (3) (which Rashi quotes on Shemos (6:16)) say that there was no slavery as long as one of Yaakov's sons was still alive. If we combine this with the Shir HaShirim Raba (2:11), which says that the bitterest part of the exile began when Miriam was born six years before Moshe was born, then this would be inconsistent with this novel explanation that Levi lived for 180 years.

Rav Hirsch says that the naming of all the different people of the tribe of Levi served a different purpose. He says that our Pesukim introduce a mission which has never been accomplished before or after Moshe and Aharon, and therefore the Torah had to make sure to tell us that they were completely human, born of other humans whose relationship to them the Torah details. I quote Rabbi Levy, his grandson, in his translation of Rav Hirsch into English. "We know well enough

Vaera

how, in later times, a Jew whose genealogical table was not available, and because it was not available, and because he brought the world a few sparks of light borrowed from Moshe, became to be considered by nations as begotten of G-d, and to doubt his divinity became a capital crime. Our Moshe was a man, remained a man, and is to remain a man." Therefore, the Torah tells us that when Hashem spoke to Moshe in Egypt, people knew his parents, grandparents, uncles, aunts, and all his cousins, who all knew that Moshe was a human being.

Rav Hirsch also points out that the fact that Hashem carefully "sifted" through the tribes of Reuven and Shimon until settling on the tribe of Levi and subsequently Moshe and Aharon also served a different purpose. It was to show that Hashem only chooses to grant prophecy to someone exalted who had refined themselves to be able to receive prophecy. In other religions, again quoting Rabbi Levy, "A man could be known as a complete idiot today and tomorrow proclaim the word of G-d. The spirit of G-d could suddenly descend upon an ignorant, uneducated person and lo! He can speak in seventy languages, which phenomenon is not without alleged instance in imaginary or pretended prophets in other circles: and then the more ignorant, the more uneducated the prophet of today was yesterday, the greater the proof of the divinity of the Call that worked this change." Instead, the Gemorah in Nedorim 38a says that Hashem only rests his prophetic spirit on someone who is mighty, wealthy, wise, and humble. Therefore, Hashem does not choose weaklings, people dependent on others for support, or simpletons to be a prophet. Consequently, Hashem had to carefully "sift" to find the people, Moshe and Aharon, suitable for this mission.

8) The Ramban and Rabcinu Bechay answer our question similarly. They say that if the Torah only started the lineage of Moshe and Aharon from the tribe of Levi and did not mention Reuven or Shimon, it would appear that Levi would have taken over the position of firstborn because of the honor of Moshe and Aharon being from his tribe. Therefore, the Torah first mentions Reuven and Shimon so that we would not make this mistake.

9) The Kli Yakor also presents an answer to our question. The Gemorah in Shabbos 88a says that when the Torah was given, there were many things that came in threes. The Torah is composed of three parts, Torah, Neviim, and Kesuvim. The Torah was given to the Bnei Yisroel, who are composed of three types of people, Kohanim, Leviyim, and Yisroelim. The Torah was given through Moshe, who was the third child born to his parents, after Miriam and Aharon. The Torah was given after three days of the Bnei Yisroel preparing (the Sheloshes Yemay HaGbolah) and was given on the third month of the year (Sivan). Rabeinu Nisim on the Gemorah points out that there are other things that come in three for Moshe and the Bnei Yisroel. We have three forefathers (Avrohom, Yitzchak, and Yaakov). Moshe was from the third tribe, Levi (after Reuven and Shimon). Both the names of Levi and Moshe, when spelled in Hebrew, have three letters. Yocheved was able to hide Moshe for three months. Rabeinu Nisim also quotes the Midrash Tanchuma in Yisro (10), which has more examples of sets of three. We daven three times a day. When we say Kedushah, we say Kodosh three times. The Kli Yakor says that by enumerating Reuven and Shimon before Levi, the Torah wanted to show how Levi also fits this pattern of three. Not only was Levi the third tribe after Reuven and Shimon, but he also had three sons, as opposed to

Vaera

Reuven, who had four and Shimon who had five, and therefore choosing the tribe of Levi was very appropriate for the receiver of the Torah, Moshe, to hail from.

Why Does the Torah Tell Us How Long Levi Lived and Not the Rest of the Tribes?

וּבְנֵי שִׁמְעוֹן יְמוּאֵל וְיָמִין וְאֹהַד וְיָכִין וְצֹחַר וְשָׁאוּל בֶּן הַכְּנַעֲנִית אֵלֶּה מִשְׁפְּחֹת שִׁמְעוֹן. וְאֵלֶּה שְׁמוֹת בְּנֵי לֵוִי לְתֹלְדֹתָם גֵּרְשׁוֹן וּקְהָת וּמְרָרִי וּשְׁנֵי חַיֵּי לֵוִי שֶׁבַע וּשְׁלֹשִׁים וּמְאַת שָׁנָה (ו:טו-טז) Shemos (6:15-16) And the sons of Shimon: Yemuel and Yamin and Ochad and Yachin and Tzohar and Shaul, the son of the Canaanites, these are the families of Shimon. And these are the names of Levi's sons after their generations: Gershon, Kehas, and Merari, and the years of Levi's life were one hundred thirty-seven years.

Besides Yosef at the end of Parshas Vayechi, why does the Torah tell us how long Levi lived and not the rest of the tribes?

Introduction
Rashi says that if we add together the years of Levi, his son Kehas, his grandson Amram, and his great-grandson Moshe, all of whose ages are the only ones listed by the Torah in our Pesukim, we will be forced to conclude that the Bnei Yisroel did not spend 400 years in Egypt. Rather when Avrohom was told in Beraishis (15:13), "You shall surely know that your seed will be strangers in a land that is not theirs, and they will enslave them and oppress them, for 400 years" the 400 years began with the birth of Yitzchak. Kehas is one of the seventy people mentioned who went down to Egypt. If we add together Kehas' lifetime (133 years) with Amram's lifetime (137 years) and the 80 years Moshe was old when the Bnei Yisroel were redeemed from Egypt, we only get the sum of 350 years, so the 400 years could not possibly have been just in Egypt. Even the 350-year calculation is assuming that Kehas and Amram were Niftar on the day their son was born, which is highly unlikely.

The Maskil LeDovid brings proof that the lifetimes of Levi, Kehas, and Amram are only mentioned to prove this point. When the Torah mentions how long a person lived, it always says either וַיִּהְיוּ חַיֵּי or וְאֵלֶּה יְמֵי. For example, Beraishis (23:1) says וַיִּהְיוּ חַיֵּי שָׂרָה מֵאָה שָׁנָה וְעֶשְׂרִים שָׁנָה וְשֶׁבַע שָׁנִים (And the life of Sarah was one hundred years and twenty years and seven years). Beraishis (47:28) says וַיְהִי יְמֵי יַעֲקֹב שְׁנֵי חַיָּיו שֶׁבַע שָׁנִים וְאַרְבָּעִים וּמְאַת שָׁנָה (and Yaakov's days, the years of his life, were a hundred and forty-seven years). In Beraishis (25:7) the Torah mentions how long Avrohom lived with the words וְאֵלֶּה יְמֵי when the Torah says וְאֵלֶּה יְמֵי שְׁנֵי חַיֵּי אַבְרָהָם אֲשֶׁר חָי מְאַת שָׁנָה וְשִׁבְעִים שָׁנָה וְחָמֵשׁ שָׁנִים (And these are the days of the years of Avraham's life that he lived: one hundred years and seventy years and five years). However, when listing the years of Levi, Kehas, and Amram, the Posuk uses a different phraseology and says וּשְׁנֵי חַיֵּי (and the years of the life were). "Years of life" is the active part of the phrase, which emphasizes the number of years each lived, instead of emphasizing the name of the person who lived this number of years.

1) The Midrash Lekach Tov and Rashi answer our question similarly. They say that listing how long Levi lived tells us how many years the enslavement in Egypt was because as long as any of the

Vaera

twelve tribes were alive, the slavery did not begin. They prove this by noting that Shemos (1:6) says, "Now Yosef died, as well as all his brothers," and subsequently Shemos (1:8) says, "A new King arose over Egypt, who did not know about Yosef. The Midrash Lekach Tov says that Levi went down to Egypt when he was 43 years old since he was born three years after Yaakov married Leah. Yosef was born seven years after Yaakov married Leah as per the following calculation. The Gemorah in Brochos 60a and the Midrash Tanchuma in Parshas Vayetze (8) say that when Leah was pregnant with Dinah (her seventh pregnancy), she made the following calculation. She prophetically knew that Yaakov was destined to have twelve sons. Since she had already given birth to six sons and both Bilhah and Zilpah had already given birth to two sons each, only two sons were left to be born to Yaakov. "If the baby I am pregnant with is a boy," said Leah to Hashem, then my sister Rochel will not even have as many sons as either of the two maidservants, Bilhah or Zilpah." Therefore, she requested from Hashem that the child she was pregnant with would be a girl even though it was going to be a boy and named her Dinah since she passed judgment over her that she should be a girl. Implied, in this statement, is the fact that Yosef had not yet been born when Leah was pregnant with Dinah. This is consistent with the Pirkei D'Rabi Eliezer (36), who says that within seven years, Yaakov had twenty-two children since Leah had children after only seven months of pregnancy. To get to the total of twenty-two children, everyone except Yosef and Dinah had a twin girl born with them so that they would each have whom to marry. Each brother, except Yosef, married a sister who had a different mother than he did.

From the above, Levi was four years older than Yosef. Beraishis (41:46) says, "And Yosef was thirty years old when he stood before Pharaoh, the king of Egypt." Seven years of plenty followed by two years of famine ensued before Yaakov came down to Egypt, as Yosef tells his brothers after revealing himself to them in Beraishis (45:6), "for already two years of famine have passed in the midst of the land." That made Yosef 39 years old and Levi 43 years old. Since Levi was Niftar when he was 137 years old, it implies that he lived 94 years in Egypt. Being that the entire time the Bnei Yisroel spent in Egypt was 210 years and that the slavery did not start as long as any of the brothers were alive implies that the slavery lasted for 116 years.

The Gemorah in Baba Basra 121b says that a chain of seven people saw everyone who ever lived. Odom was alive when Metsushelach was born; Metsushelach saw Shem, Shem saw Yaakov, Yaakov saw Amram, Amram saw Achiya HaShiloni, Achiya HaShiloni saw Eliyahu HaNovi, and Eliyahu HaNovi is still alive. The Midrash Lekach Tov says that since Yaakov saw Amram, and Amram was not one of the 70 people coming down to Egypt, implies that Amram was born during the 17 years that Yaakov lived in Egypt as Beraishis (47:28) tells us when it says, "And Yaakov lived in the land of Egypt for seventeen years." The Torah tells us that Moshe was 80 years old when the Bnei Yisroel left Egypt, and the Torah also tells us that Amram was 137 years old when he was Niftar. The sum of their total life in Egypt is 217 years. We also know that the Bnei Yisroel spent two hundred and ten years in Egypt. Even if Amram was born immediately before Yaakov was Niftar, Moshe would have been at most 24 years old when Amram was Niftar.

The fact that the Gemorah says that Amram was alive when Achiya HaShiloni was born implies that Achiya HaShiloni was one of the people who came out of Egypt. At the time of leaving Egypt, the

Vaera

least age he could have been for Amram to have seen him is Moshe's age at the time of leaving Egypt (80) minus the most Moshe could have been when Amram was Niftar (24) or 56 years old. The Gemorah in Baba Basra 121b ponders how it was possible for Achiya HaShiloni to be able to go into Eretz Yisroel since there was a decree that anyone over age 20 who went out of Egypt was Niftar before they could go into Eretz Yisroel due to the punishment for the rebellion of the spies. The Gemorah presents two answers to this question. Firstly, the Gemorah says that Achiya HaShiloni was from the tribe of Levi who did not participate in the rebellion of the spies nor in the rebellion of making the Golden Calf, and therefore anyone from the tribe of Levi was not included in the decree of not going into Eretz Yisroel. The Rashbam says that we see that Achiya was a Levi in Divrei HaYomim I (26:20) where the Posuk says "And the Leviyim: Achiya over the treasuries of the House of G-d and to the treasuries of the holy things." Secondly, the Gemorah says that we also find at least two people (Yair and Mochir, the sons of Menashe) who were not from the tribe of Levi but did make it into Eretz Yisroel. The Gemorah quotes a Braisah, which says that these two sons of Menashe were born when Yaakov was still alive, and they did not die until after the Bnei Yisroel entered into Eretz Yisroel. The Gemorah explains that Yair and Mochir, sons of Menashe, did not die in the desert because the decree only applied to people from age 20 to age 60 in the desert. Yair and Mochir, having been alive when Yaakov was still alive during the first seventeen years of the exile in Egypt, imply that they were at least 210 minus 17 or 193 years old when they left Egypt. This is well about the maximum age of 60 years old not to be included in the decree of those who died in the desert. Similarly, we have calculated that Achiya HaShiloni was at least 56 years old when the Bnei Yisroel left Egypt. The maximum Achiya HaShiloni could have been was 80 years old, so that if he was 61 or older at the time of the redemption from Egypt, he also, like Yair and Mochir, would not have been under the decree of dying in the desert. We should mention that the third category of people not affected by the decree of dying in the desert were the women who had no part in the decree of the spies or in the sin of the Golden Calf.

Parenthetically we know that Achiya HaShiloni was alive more than 400 years after the Bnei Yisroel entered Eretz Yisroel. Sefer Melachim I (11:29-31) say, "And it came to be at that time when Yorovam had left Yerushalayim, that Achiya, HaShiloni, the prophet, found him on the way, and he was wearing a new garment, and the two of them were alone in the field. And Achiya grasped the new garment that was upon him and tore it into twelve pieces. And he said to Yorovam, Take for yourself ten pieces, for so has Hashem, the G-d of Yisroel, said, 'I shall tear the kingdom out of Shlomo's hands, and I shall give you the ten tribes.'" Shlomo HaMelech lived more than 400 years after the Bnei Yisroel entered Eretz Yisroel. Later on, when Yorovam sinned, his son became very sick, and his wife went to visit Achiya HaShiloni to find a cure for her son. Sefer Melachim I (14:4-5) say, "And Yorovam's wife did so, and she arose and went to Shilo and came to the house of Achiya; Achiya could not see for his eyes were still because of his advanced age. Now Hashem had said to Achiya, 'Behold the wife of Yorovam is coming to ask of you concerning her son as he is sick; you shall speak to her thus and thus.'" Achiya HaShiloni being alive in those times was how he was alive when Eliyahu HaNovi was alive since Eliyahu also lived at that point in history.

The Rashbam and Tosfos on the Gemorah in Baba Basra 121b point out that the author of the Braisah who mentions these seven people whose lifetimes spanned all of history is not of the

Vaera

opinion that Pinchos, son of Elazar and grandson of Aharon the Kohen, was the same person as Eliyahu HaNovi. Had he been of the opinion that they were the same person, then either Moshe or Aharon could have been substituted for Achiya HaShiloni, since, as opposed to Achiya HaShiloni, who is not mentioned in the Torah, the Torah tells us that both Moshe and Aharon were alive when Pinchos was alive. Even better, if he had been of the opinion that Pinchos and Eliyahu HaNovi are the same person, then Amram and Achiya HaShiloni could have been replaced with either Yair or Mochir, son of Menashe who both saw Yaakov and saw Pinchos. In this way, only six people would have been needed to span history. Tosfos also points out that the author of the Braisah could not have been of the opinion that Serach, like Eliyahu, lived forever. The Targum Yonason ben Uziel on Beraishis (46:17) says that because Serach was the one who informed Yaakov that Yosef was still alive and gave him back his life, Serach merited to be taken alive into Gan Eden (and only know life). Otherwise, the list of people who spanned history could have substituted Serach for Amram, Achiya HaShiloni, and Pinchos and would only be five people.

The Taz, in his Sefer Divrei Dovid, ponders why Rashi says that Levi lived the longest when it seems that Ephraim lived longer than Levi. Divrei HaYomim I (7:20-22) say, "And the sons of Ephraim: Shuselach, and Vered his son, and Sachas his son, and Eladah his son, and Sachas his son. And Zavad his son, and Shuselach his son, and Ezer, and Elad, and the men of Gas, the natives of the land (Philistines), killed them because they came down to take their cattle. And Ephraim, their father, mourned for them many days, and his brothers came to console him." The Gemorah in Sanhedrin 92b references these Pesukim in Divrei HaYomim I and explains that children of Ephraim went out of Egypt to Eretz Yisroel and were killed by the Philistines. Rashi explains the reason they went out early is that they calculated that the 400 years of Egyptian exile prophesized by Avrohom began at the time the prophesy was given at the Bris Bain HaBesorim when in reality, the 400-year exile started with the birth of Yitzchak, 30 years later. Since the Posuk says that Ephraim mourned for them, this implies, says the Taz, that Ephraim was alive 30 years before the end of the Egyptian exile. Since Ephraim was born several years before Yaakov came down to Egypt and the Egyptian exile was 210 years long implies that Ephraim lived till past 180 years which is much older than Levi. The Taz says that Ephraim did not really live till that point but that he saw in prophesy what was going to happen to his children, and Ephraim mourned what would happen in the future. One of the proofs he presents is that the Posuk says, "And Ephraim their father mourned for them many days." This Posuk is reminiscent of Beraishis (37:34), which says, "and he (Yaakov) mourned for his son (Yosef) many days." With regard to Yaakov, the Beraishis Raba (84:21) is the source for the answer that Rashi and the Rabeinu Bechay offer that one can only be comforted for someone who is dead but cannot be comforted for someone who is still alive. The Gemorah in Pesachim 54b says that a special decree was made on a person who was Niftar such that the pain of his passing should be slowly forgotten. Therefore, explain Rashi and the Rabeinu Bechay, since Yosef was still alive, this decree was not applicable, and Yaakov's pain on Yosef's "passing" did not decrease over time. Similarly with Ephraim, says the Taz, since the event did not happen yet and his descendants were not really dead yet, Ephraim could not be comforted for many days.

The Maskil LeDovid says that we can be of the opinion that Ephraim lived till 30 years before the redemption from Egypt and still be consistent with the fact that Levi lived the longest of the

Vaera

brothers. Even though Ephraim and Menashe replaced Yosef in the count of the tribes, they were still not real sons of Yaakov. The Midrash Lekach Tov and Rashi say that listing how long Levi lived tells us how many years the enslavement in Egypt was because as long as any of the twelve tribes were alive, the slavery did not begin. They are only referring to the actual sons of Yaakov and not his grandson Ephraim.

2) The Rashbam, Ramban, Akeidah, Abarbanel, and Malbim all answer our question similarly. They all compare the listing of Levi's years to which people the Torah singles out in Sefer Beraishis to inform us how long they lived. In Sefer Beraishis, the Torah only tells us how long the important people, like Avrohom, Yitzchak, Yaakov, and Yosef, lived. In other places, the Torah tells us the number of years the leader of the generation lived as it does in the ten generations from Odom till Noach and the ten generations from Noach till Avrohom. Similarly, Levi (and for that matter Kehas and Amram) was an important person from whom the King and prophet of the Bnei Yisroel descended, and therefore the years of his lifetime are mentioned. For proof of this concept, the Akeidah, Abarbanel, and Malbim all point to Tehillim (37:18) which says יוֹדֵעַ ה' יְמֵי תְמִימִם (Hashem knows the days of the complete and perfect). Obviously, this Posuk does not mean that Hashem, Chas VeShalom, only knows the days of the complete and perfect people since Hashem knows the days of everyone. Rather Hashem only makes known to others, through the Torah, the days of the complete and perfect people.

3) The Sforno also presents an answer to our question. He says the reason the Torah records how long Levi, his son Kehas, and his grandson Amram lived was to show why in the tribe of Levi there were people appropriate to redeem the Bnei Yisroel who were descendants of Levi's sons, as opposed to descendants of Reuven and Shimon's sons. Since Levi and his son Kehas lived a long life, they were able to take part in bringing up Amram in a manner that he was an appropriate person to redeem the Bnei Yisroel. Because of this proper upbringing of Amram, Amram was able to raise Moshe, Aharon, and Miriam to be the appropriate leaders to redeem the Bnei Yisroel from Egypt.

4) The Eben Ezra and Ramban answer our question similarly. They say that the reason the Torah records how long Levi lived, as opposed to the rest of the tribes, is to give honor to Moshe and Aharon, who descended from Levi. The Eben Ezra says that this is the same reason the Torah records how long Moshe and Aharon's father (Amram) and grandfather (Kehas) lived.

What Is Meant by Moshe Being Appointed a Lord Over Pharaoh?

Shemos (7:1) וַיֹּאמֶר ה' אֶל מֹשֶׁה רְאֵה נְתַתִּיךָ אֱלֹקִים לְפַרְעֹה וְאַהֲרֹן אָחִיךָ יִהְיֶה נְבִיאֶךָ (ז:א) Hashem said to Moshe, "See! I have made you a lord over Pharaoh, and Aharon, your brother, will be your prophet."

What is meant by Moshe being appointed a lord over Pharaoh?

Introduction
The Bamidbar Raba (14:6) and the Yalkut Shimoni on our Posuk point out that Hashem two Pesukim (6:29) earlier said to Moshe, "I am Hashem. Speak to Pharaoh everything that I speak to

Vaera

you." They say that Hashem was warning Moshe that even though he was making him a lord over Pharaoh, he should remember that he also had a lord over him, Hashem. Therefore, Hashem was warning Moshe not to get haughty about being called a lord since he was only a lord over one person, Pharaoh. The Bamidbar Raba compares this statement to a similar statement from Pharaoh to Yosef when he made him a lord over Egypt. Pharaoh says in Beraishis (41:44), "I am Pharaoh, and besides you, no one may lift his hand or his foot in the entire land of Egypt." By saying, "I am Pharaoh," he was telling Yosef that even though he was being made a lord over all of Egypt such that no one could do anything with him, he should always remember that he must still fear Pharaoh, who is his King.

1) The Shemos Raba (8:3) and Midrash Tanchuma in Vaera (9) present an answer to our question. They say that it means to go and take payment from the Egyptians. They take the Hebrew word for Pharaoh and note that it means to take payment. Therefore, they say that when our Posuk uses the word Pharaoh, it is not referring to the person Pharaoh but to taking payment. The Maharzav explains that they are bothered by the fact that our Posuk seems to be in contradiction to Shemos (4:16) where Hashem tells Moshe about Aharon וְדִבֶּר הוּא לְךָ אֶל הָעָם וְהָיָה הוּא יִהְיֶה לְךָ לְפֶה וְאַתָּה תִּהְיֶה לוֹ לֵאלֹהִים (And he (Aharon) will speak for you (Moshe) to the people, and it will be that he will be your speaker, and you will be his lord). In that Posuk, it seems that Moshe will be the lord to Aharon, while in our Posuk, if we are referring to the person Pharaoh, then it seems that Moshe will be the lord to Pharaoh. Therefore, they write that we are not referring to the person Pharaoh in our Posuk, and we can reconcile the two Pesukim by Moshe being the lord over Aharon. The Shemos Raba (3:16) explains that Moshe being a lord over Aharon means that Aharon will fear Moshe even though he is Moshe's older brother.

The Midrashim continue with Moshe asking Hashem how he should take payment from the Egyptians. Hashem answers that Moshe should take the stick which had the acronyms of the ten plagues written on them, and use this staff to perform the ten plagues. This is the conclusion of when Hashem previously told Moshe that he would be a lord over Aharon as Shemos (4:17) says, "And you shall take this staff in your hand, with which you shall perform the signs." This is another proof, says the Maharzav, that our Pesukim and those in Shemos (4:17) are talking about the same topic of Moshe being the lord over Aharon.

The Bechor Shor says that the Hebrew word אֱלֹקִים can mean a judge. When referring to monetary disagreements, Shemos (22:8) says עַל כָּל דְּבַר פֶּשַׁע עַל שׁוֹר עַל חֲמוֹר עַל שֶׂה עַל שַׂלְמָה עַל כָּל אֲבֵדָה אֲשֶׁר יֹאמַר כִּי הוּא זֶה עַד הָאֱלֹהִים יָבֹא דְּבַר שְׁנֵיהֶם אֲשֶׁר יַרְשִׁיעֻן אֱלֹהִים יְשַׁלֵּם שְׁנַיִם לְרֵעֵהוּ (For any sinful word, for a bull, for a donkey, for a lamb, for a garment, for any lost article, concerning which he will say that this is it, the pleas of both parties shall come to the **judges**, and whoever the **judges** declare guilty shall pay twofold to his neighbor. Both Rashi and the Chizkuni also say that making Moshe a lord means to be a judge to punish Pharaoh for his sins. The one who wrote notes on the Chizkuni references what he says on Shemos (32:1) when the people thinking that Moshe was late in coming down from Mount Sinai tell Aharon קוּם עֲשֵׂה לָנוּ אֱלֹהִים אֲשֶׁר יֵלְכוּ לְפָנֵינוּ כִּי זֶה מֹשֶׁה הָאִישׁ אֲשֶׁר הֶעֱלָנוּ מֵאֶרֶץ מִצְרַיִם לֹא יָדַעְנוּ מֶה הָיָה לוֹ (Get Up! Make us gods that will go before us, because this man Moshe, who brought us up from the land of Egypt we don't know what has become of him). The Chizkuni is of the opinion

Vaera

that when the people said to Aharon עֲשֵׂה לָנוּ אֱלֹהִים they did not ask him to make an idol but rather asked him to appoint for them a judge and leader since אֱלֹהִים can be translated as a judge. He says that we cannot say that Aharon was asked to make an idol, and this is what he made since otherwise, having done such a grave sin, how could he and his descendants bring atonement for the Bnei Yisroel? In addition, if Aharon had, Chas VeShalom, made an idol, he would have been killed with all the others who served the Golden Calf as an idol. Moreover, the only sin the Torah ever mentions about Aharon is being involved with hitting the rock instead of speaking to it. Aharon decided that he did not want to appoint anyone to be a judge and leader over the Bnei Yisroel as they requested, since when Moshe returned, this person might not want to give up his position of authority. He also did not want to take the position for himself since he did not want Moshe to have any despondency when he would come down and find him leading the Bnei Yisroel. Instead, he decided to delay the Bnei Yisroel's request to appoint a leader by getting them involved with making a Golden Calf to occupy themselves until Moshe came down.

Avrohom was promised at the Bris Bain HaBesorim in Beraishis (15:14) "And also the nation that they will serve will I judge." The Brisker Rov (Rav Velvel Soleveichick) says that the purpose of the ten plagues was not to force Pharaoh to send the Bnei Yisroel out of Egypt but rather to fulfill Hashem's promise to Avrohom to judge the Egyptians. Therefore, Moshe was commanded in our Posuk to bring judgment onto the Egyptians. The Mishna in Ediyus (2:10) says that there were five groups of people who were/are judged for 12 months: (1) the generation of the flood, (2) Iyov, (3) the Egyptians after enslaving the Jews, (4) Gog and Mogog, (5) wicked people who spend the 12 months after their deaths in Gehenom. The Brisker Rov says that just like wicked people are punished for 12 months in Gehenom, so too were the wicked Egyptian punished for 12 months in Egypt.

Rabeinu Bechay on Shemos (10:5) explains how the 12 months are calculated. He says that Hashem appeared to Moshe at the burning bush on the 15th day of Nisan. Exactly a year later, on the 15th day of Nisan, the Bnei Yisroel went out of Egypt. Hashem spent seven days convincing Moshe to accept the mission of taking the Bnei Yisroel out of Egypt. Rabeinu Bechay says that these seven days correspond to the seven days of Pesach in the following year, which culminated with the Egyptians being drowned at the Red Sea. After the 21st of Nisan, Moshe went back to Midyan to obtain permission from Yisro to go to Egypt. Moshe had taken an oath to Yisro that he and his family would not leave Midyan without Yisro's permission, as the Gemorah in Nedorim 65a says. Therefore, Hashem told Moshe to first return to Midyan to get permission to go to Egypt. Moshe then went to Egypt and subsequently went to Pharaoh to ask Pharaoh to free the Bnei Yisroel. Pharaoh instead made the workload heavier by making the Bnei Yisroel gather their own straw for making bricks. This situation of the heavier workload went on for three months until the first plague, blood, came in the month of Av. On Shemos (5:22), he quotes a Shir HaShirim Raba (2:9), which says that after first speaking with Pharaoh and having Pharaoh increase the work, Moshe did not go to Pharaoh for another three months. Shemos (7:25) tells us that the plague of blood lasted for seven days and the Shemos Raba (9:12) on this Posuk says that Moshe warned Pharaoh for 24 days before the plague came. Therefore, the entire plague lasted a month. The next seven plagues came at the beginning of each of the subsequent months, which calculates that the eighth plague,

Vaera

locusts, occurred at the beginning of the Hebrew month of Adar. The ninth plague, darkness, took place on Rosh Chodesh Nisan, and it was followed by the last plague, the killing of the firstborn on the 15th day of Nisan when the Bnei Yisroel went out of Egypt. When at the burning bush Hashem said in Shemos (3:20) "And I will stretch forth My hand and smite the Egyptians with all My miracles that I will wreak in their midst, and afterwards he (Pharaoh) will send you out" the Egyptians punishment had been set and the one-year period of punishments had begun.

2) The Shemos Raba (8:1) and the Midrash Tanchuma on Vaera (9) answer our question similarly. Pharaoh pretended to be a G-d when he is quoted in Sefer Yechezkel (29:3) "Pharaoh, King of Egypt, the great crocodile that lies down in the midst of its rivers, who said, 'My river (Nile) is my own, and I made it myself.'" Now Hashem commanded Moshe to show that he was greater than Pharaoh so that Pharaoh should realize that Moshe more aptly fits the description of being a G-d than he did. The Yalkut Shimoni 180 explains that Hashem used the name אֱלֹקִים when Hashem created the world as the first Posuk in the Torah says בְּרֵאשִׁית בָּרָא אֱלֹקִים אֵת הַשָּׁמַיִם וְאֵת הָאָרֶץ (In the beginning אֱלֹקִים created the heavens and the earth. With this same name of אֱלֹקִים Hashem made Moshe, a lord over Pharaoh. The Yepheh Toar explains that just like in creating the world, Hashem did wondrous acts; in a similar way, Hashem will do wondrous acts (the ten plagues) when Hashem takes the Bnei Yisroel out of Egypt. Since Pharaoh will be powerless to stop these plagues, he can only conclude that Hashem, through his servant Moshe, is more powerful than he. The Yalkut Shimoni 181 says that Hashem also changed Moshe and Aharon's appearance so that when they came to meet Pharaoh, they looked like angels causing much fear in Pharaoh.

3) The Shemos Raba (8:2) and the Midrash Tanchuma on Vaera (9) present another answer to our question. We have mentioned in the previous answer that Pharaoh pretended to be a G-d. When Hashem told Moshe he was making him a lord over Pharaoh, Hashem was saying that through Moshe, Hashem will show the world that Pharaoh is nothing. After the ten plagues and after Pharoah's remaining army was killed in the Red Sea, Pharaoh was left being a ruler of what had previously been the strongest country in the world and what was now a country in shambles.

4) The Targum Yonason ben Uziel also presents an answer to our question. He says that Hashem was telling Moshe he had no more reason to be afraid of Pharaoh since Hashem had now made Moshe a lord over Pharaoh. Being a lord over Pharaoh meant that Pharaoh would now be afraid of Moshe. Rav Hirsch explains that an idol worshipper's main idea of a deity is the fearsome power of the deity over him. He says that after all the wonders that Moshe did, it would not be surprising if Pharaoh fell down at Moshe's feet and worshipped him as a G-d.

5) The Eben Ezra and the Toras HaRambam answer our question similarly. They say that נְתַתִּיךָ אֱלֹקִים לְפַרְעֹה means that Hashem appointed Moshe as an angel for Pharaoh. In the notes on the Toras HaRambam, the editor says that Rav Avrohom, the Rambam's son, heard orally from the Rambam that it means as an angel in our Posuk. On its simplest level, we have mentioned earlier that the Yalkut Shimoni 181 says that Hashem changed Moshe and Aharon's appearance so that when they came to meet Pharaoh, they looked like angels causing much fear in Pharaoh. However, the Eben Ezra and Toras HaRambam take the concept of being an angel to a deeper level. They say that

Vaera

Aharon, who was appointed as a prophet with regard to Pharaoh, was to receive his prophecy through an angel, who in this case was Moshe. That is, Moshe was not going to speak directly to Pharaoh, and instead, he would give his commands to Aharon, who would relay them to Pharaoh.

The Abarbanel, Tur, and Malbim answer our question slightly differently than the Eben Ezra and Toras HaRambam. They say that Moshe will not only be like an angel but rather will be like a G-d who commands and holds the people responsible for following his instructions. A G-d does not speak to the people but rather uses a prophet to communicate with the people. The Nitziv points out that in the previous Posuk Moshe said that he was not a good speaker and was instead of closed lips and therefore it would be better not to send him on this mission as he says in Shemos (6:30) "Behold, I am of closed lips; so how will Pharaoh hearken to me?" Hashem fulfilled Moshe's request and told Moshe that he would no longer speak to Pharaoh directly. However, the reason for Pharaoh not speaking directly to Moshe had nothing to do with the way Moshe presented it that Pharaoh would consider him unworthy of speaking with because of his speech problems. Rather Pharaoh will consider Moshe as a G-d and be so afraid of Moshe that he will realize that he is not fit to speak directly to Moshe but rather can only speak to him through Aharon, the intermediary. The Shach says that there was another reason why Hashem arranged that Pharaoh did not speak to Moshe. Moshe was going to speak directly with Hashem, and it was inappropriate that the same mouth which spoke with Hashem should also speak with the wicked Pharaoh. He says that we can learn the concept of maintaining a pure mouth from the Yerushalmi in Brochos (1:2), which quotes Rav Shimon Bar Yochai saying that had he been alive at the time of the giving of the Torah, he would have requested to have two mouths. One mouth just for Torah, and the other mouth for all other needs.

The Abarbanel says that Hashem gave Moshe full permission to command or make any demands of Pharaoh that he wanted as if he were a G-d. Although he does not specify if or when Moshe used this ability, one of the times when this did seem to be used was during the plague of frogs when Pharaoh begged Moshe to remove the plague. Moshe says to Pharaoh in Shemos (8:5), "Glorify yourself over me. For when shall I entreat for you, for your servants, and for your people, to destroy the frogs from you and from your houses, that they should remain only in the Nile River?" Moshe made this offer to let Pharaoh choose the end time of the plague of frogs on his own since Hashem never told Moshe to make such a statement.

6) The Alshich also presents an answer to our question. We have mentioned previously that our Posuk seems to be in contradiction to Shemos (4:16) where Hashem tells Moshe about Aharon וְדִבֶּר הוּא לְךָ אֶל הָעָם וְהָיָה הוּא יִהְיֶה לְּךָ לְפֶה וְאַתָּה תִּהְיֶה לּוֹ לֵאלֹהִים (And he (Aharon) will speak for you (Moshe) to the people, and it will be that he will be your speaker, and you will be his lord). In that Posuk, it seems that Moshe will be the lord to Aharon, while in our Posuk, it seems that Moshe will be the lord to Pharaoh. The Alshich explains that in the previous Posuk, Moshe complained that he was not a good speaker and was instead of closed lips, and therefore it would be better not to send him on this mission. This is what he says in Shemos (6:30) "Behold, I am of closed lips; so how will Pharaoh hearken to me?" Because of these complaints, Hashem changed the mission from Moshe being a lord onto Aharon to Moshe being a lord onto Pharaoh. Though he does not exactly explain

Vaera

what changed, presumably being a lord onto Aharon meant that he would command and hold Aharon responsible for following his instructions. Now Aharon would be a prophet and passively transmit Moshe's message to Pharaoh. In addition, Moshe would be elevated to the position of being a lord over Pharaoh and would directly command Pharaoh what to do. This was necessary since Hashem knew Pharaoh would, on many occasions, refuse to listen to Moshe. Had Moshe been acting as the emissary of Hashem, then it would be an embarrassment to Hashem that Pharaoh refused to listen since someone who doesn't listen to an emissary also embarrasses the one who sent him. With Moshe no longer being the emissary of Hashem but rather a lord over Pharaoh, it meant that when/if Pharaoh refused to listen to Moshe, he was just embarrassing Moshe.

7) The Chupas Eliyahu, as quoted by the Meam Loez, also ponders our question. He says that every nation, besides the Bnei Yisroel, has an angel who is in charge of the nation. The angel is tasked with channeling life and sustenance to his nation. Hashem told Moshe that he had put Moshe in charge of the angel of Egypt so that all life and sustenance will be channeled through Moshe to the angel and then to the Egyptians. With this arrangement, Moshe no longer had to have any fear of Pharaoh since Pharaoh will be dependent, through his angel, on Moshe. In essence, since Egypt's angel boss was previously Hashem, Moshe is now taking Hashem's place with respect to Pharoah's/Egypt's angel. It is possible that this is what the Rabeinu Bechay means when he says that Moshe no longer had to worry about Pharaoh since Moshe was placed as the boss over him.

Why Does the Posuk Tell Us How Old Moshe and Aharon Were When They Came to Pharaoh?

Shemos (7:7) וּמֹשֶׁה בֶּן שְׁמֹנִים שָׁנָה וְאַהֲרֹן בֶּן שָׁלֹשׁ וּשְׁמֹנִים שָׁנָה בְּדַבְּרָם אֶל פַּרְעֹה (ז:ז) And Moshe was eighty years old, and Aharon was eighty-three years old when they spoke to Pharaoh.

Why does the Torah tell us how old Moshe and Aharon were when they came to Pharaoh?

Introduction
The Chasam Sofer points out that the Torah could have told us at any point during the redemption how old Moshe and Aharon were. Therefore, we can ponder why the Torah ties in, telling us their ages with their coming to Pharaoh.

1) We can infer an answer to our question from what Rashi says on Shemos (6:18). He says that we can calculate from the information given to us in the Torah that the Bnei Yisroel could not have spent the entire 400 years of exile in Egypt. Rather when Hashem told Avrohom in Beraishis (15:13), "You shall surely know that your seed will be strangers in a land that is not theirs, and they will enslave them and oppress them, for four hundred years," the 400 years began from the birth of Yitzchak. Rashi points out that Kehas (Moshe's grandfather) was one of the 70 people who went down to Egypt, as the Torah tells us in Beraishis (46:11). In Shemos (6:18), we are told that Kehas lived for a total of 133 years. We are told in Shemos (6:20) that Moshe's father Amram lived for a total of 137 years. Our Posuk tells us that Moshe was 80 years old when the Bnei Yisroel went out of Egypt. If we add together the years of Kehas, Amram, and the 80 years of Moshe, we get a sum

Vaera

total of 350 years, which is the maximum amount of time the Bnei Yisroel could have been in Egypt, showing that the full 400 years were not spent in Egypt. Of course, the calculation of 350 years is making the unreasonable assumption that Kehas was just born when he came down to Egypt and that there was no overlap in the lives of both Amram and his father Kehas, and also of Moshe and his father, Amram. The actual correct figure is that the Bnei Yisroel spent 210 years in Egypt. According to this answer, we can say that the only reason Aharon's age is also mentioned is that it would be awkward to mention Moshe's age and not Aharon's. We note that this answer does not answer the Chasam Sofer's question of why the Torah ties in, telling us Moshe and Aharon's ages with their coming to Pharaoh.

2) The Sforno also presents an answer to our question and says that 70 years old was an old age in Moshe's times. Chapter 90 in Tehillim begins with תְּפִלָּה לְמֹשֶׁה (A prayer of Moshe), which implies that Dovid HaMelech when he wrote Sefer Tehillim, incorporated a prayer which Moshe wrote into Tehillim. In that Chapter, Tehillim (90:10) says יְמֵי שְׁנוֹתֵינוּ בָּהֶם שִׁבְעִים שָׁנָה (a typical life span is seventy years). The Sforno says that despite the fact that both Moshe and Aharon were old, they nonetheless displayed much energy both here and throughout the 40 years that the Bnei Yisroel were in the desert, to do the will of Hashem.

3) The Eben Ezra also presents an answer to our question and says that Moshe and Aharon are the only examples in Tanach of prophets who, once they got old continuing to prophesize. He continues that Moshe and Aharon were unique in that Hashem spoke to them and received the Torah from Hashem. All other prophets either prophesized the future or rebuked the people about the present.

4) The Abarbanel also ponders our question. He writes that it is not appropriate to send young people for a meeting with the King since they are impetuous, especially about such important matters as asking for freedom. Rather one must send older people who are thoughtful and have acquired wisdom with age for such a mission to speak to the King. Even more so, when we consider how many times Pharaoh reneged on his promises to Moshe and berated Moshe, it was necessary to send a wise old man in charge of his emotions for this mission. By telling us Moshe and Aharon's ages, the Torah is underscoring how Hashem made sure to send the appropriate people on this mission to Pharaoh.

5) The Alshich HaKodosh also presents an answer to our question. At the beginning of this topic, in Shemos (7:1-2) Hashem tells Moshe that: רְאֵה נְתַתִּיךָ אֱלֹהִים לְפַרְעֹה וְאַהֲרֹן אָחִיךָ יִהְיֶה נְבִיאֶךָ. אַתָּה תְדַבֵּר אֵת כָּל אֲשֶׁר אֲצַוֶּךָּ וְאַהֲרֹן אָחִיךָ יְדַבֵּר אֶל פַּרְעֹה וְשִׁלַּח אֶת בְּנֵי יִשְׂרָאֵל מֵאַרְצוֹ ("See! I have made you a lord over Pharaoh, and Aharon, your brother, will be your speaker. You shall speak all that I command you, and Aaron, your brother, shall speak to Pharaoh, that he let the Bnei Yisroel out of his land."). Therefore, Moshe was given the major role of being the "lord over Pharaoh" while Aharon was given the more minor role of telling Pharaoh what the "lord" Moshe has said to him. The previous Posuk to ours says, "Moshe and Aharon did; as Hashem commanded them, so they did." The Torah is telling us that despite Aharon's diminished role, Aharon faithfully followed the role that Hashem had given him. By telling us that Aharon was three years older than Moshe in our Posuk, the Torah is telling

Vaera

us why it was such a great deed that Aharon took the lesser role to his younger brother without any qualms.

6) The Ksav Sofer also ponders our question. He references the previous Posuk to ours, which says, "Moshe and Aharon did; as Hashem commanded them, so they did." That is, the Torah is telling us that neither Moshe nor Aharon had any self-centered reasons, like wanting the honor of the office, for following Hashem's command. Rather they did it solely because this was Hashem's command. We have mentioned previously that during Moshe's era, the typical person lived till 70 years old. Being that both Moshe and Aharon were well past that age, their desire for honor was no longer applicable. Therefore, the Torah tells us Moshe and Aharon's ages to underscore the fact that they were not seeking honor when they accepted the position to redeem the Bnei Yisroel from Egypt.

7) The Ksav Sofer presents another answer to our question. In this answer, he also says that the Torah is proving to us that Moshe and Aharon did not accept the position they were given because of their desire for honor. The Torah in Parshas Shemos already related to us that Moshe many times refused to accept the position of redeeming the Bnei Yisroel from Egypt. Therefore, it would not be reasonable nor logical to think that Moshe wanted the position because of his desire for honor. Had Moshe desired honor, Moshe would not have kept refusing to accept the position. Our Posuk proves to us that Aharon also did not accept the position because he desired honor since it wasn't so honorable to be subservient to his younger brother Moshe. Therefore, the Torah has to tell us Moshe and Aharon's ages so that we know that Aharon also only accepted the position since it was the command of Hashem and not for his own honor.

8) The Malbim also presents an answer to our question. He says that by telling us how old Moshe and Aharon were, the Torah is telling us that despite the fact Moshe and Aharon were old for people of their time, they nonetheless followed Hashem's instructions completely faithfully. Though it is not clear what he precisely means by this statement, it seems to me that he is saying that because they were old, Moshe and Aharon could have taken the attitude that they could figure out for themselves what the proper way to relate to Pharaoh was. Our Posuk and the Posuk previous to it is telling us that despite being old, Moshe and Aharon meticulously followed everything that Hashem told them to do.

9) The Oznayim LeTorah and Taam V'Daas answer our question similarly. It is customary in the secular world for someone who gets old to retire from their position and "take it easy." However, the Torah is teaching us in this Posuk that this should not be the attitude and custom of the elders and leaders of the Bnei Yisroel. With elders and leaders of the Bnei Yisroel, the older they get, the more meticulous they get with respect to refining their character and the more insights they can derive from their study of the Torah.

We can perhaps appreciate this concept better if we examine the Gemorah in Baba Metzia 87a, which says that Avrohom davened that a person's body should show the signs of getting older. The Maharal, in his explanation of the Gemorah in Baba Metzia 87a, and the Nisivos, in Nachalas Yaakov, explain the reason for the change that Avrohom davened for. From the time that a person is

Vaera

born, his Neshama can grow and become more powerful through doing Mitzvos and good deeds. As we grow older, our physical capabilities become weaker. However, with regard to knowledge capabilities, the last Mishna in Meseches Kinim says that people unlearned in Torah, the older they get, the less capable their knowledge capability gets. However, the older they get for those learned in Torah, the more their knowledge becomes keener. They explain that the weaker the physical body gets, the more ability the spiritual Neshama has to grow stronger.

The Maharal says that Avrohom realized that spiritual prowess was missing in his generation, and that is why it was so difficult to recognize Hashem. To improve this situation and allow spirituality to grow stronger, Avrohom davened to Hashem for the diminishment of the power of the physical. The Nisivos also points out that until Avrohom's time, everyone thought that the older a person got, the less important the person was. Therefore, Avrohom davened that the body's prowess should decrease, and it should be evident that at least for those learned in Torah, the older they get, the more their knowledge becomes keener.

We have already mentioned that Moshe and Aharon were old relative to the other people of their generation. By telling us how old they were when they began their mission of redeeming the Bnei Yisroel from Egypt, the Torah is telling us that these older people were the ideal candidates to choose to lead the Bnei Yisroel out of exile. Their age gave them a more refined character and more insights into how to do this. As the Oznayim LeTorah says, the accomplishments Moshe and Aharon made by leading the Bnei Yisroel out of Egypt and by receiving the Torah are testament against the secular thinking that Moshe and Aharon should have retired and "taken it easy" at their age and certainly should not have been appointed to new positions.

10) Rav Schwab, in his Sefer Mayan Beis HaShoaivah, also presents an answer to our question. Both Moshe and Aharon standing before Pharaoh were the biggest proof that all of Pharaoh's ideas for stopping the Bnei Yisroel were fruitless. Eighty years before, when Moshe was born, Pharaoh made the decree that every baby boy who was born should be thrown into the river. Even though Pharaoh's astrologers saw the exact day that Moshe, the savior of the Bnei Yisroel, was born, Pharaoh could not prevent Moshe from being the savior. With regard to Aharon, he quotes the Aruch who writes about Aharon that in the chronicles of Moshe it is written that when Aharon was born, Pharaoh began the decree of trying to kill all Jewish boys either directly or by throwing them into the Nile River. This decree would seem to correspond to the decree Pharaoh made for the midwives to kill the Jewish baby boys. According to this answer, it would seem that somehow Pharaoh found out exactly how old Moshe and Aharon were at the time they came to him so that Pharaoh knew that his plans were thwarted. This was a manifestation of Mishlay (19:21) which says, רַבּוֹת מַחֲשָׁבוֹת בְּלֶב אִישׁ וַעֲצַת ה' הִיא תָקוּם (There are many thoughts in a man's heart, but Hashem's plan, that shall stand).

Vaera

Why Does the Torah Mention Aharon Before Moshe?

Shemos (7:26) הוּא אַהֲרֹן וּמֹשֶׁה אֲשֶׁר אָמַר ה' לָהֶם הוֹצִיאוּ אֶת בְּנֵי יִשְׂרָאֵל מֵאֶרֶץ מִצְרַיִם עַל צִבְאֹתָם (ז:כו) That is Aharon and Moshe, to whom Hashem said, "Take the Bnei Yisroel out of the land of Egypt with their legions."

Why did the Torah mention Aharon before Moshe?

Introduction
The Noam Elimelech ponders how it was possible for such holy people like Moshe and Aharon, who were so holy that Hashem appeared to them many times, to be able to speak to such an unholy person as Pharaoh. Shemos (4:16) says, "And he (Aharon) will speak for you (Moshe) to the people, and it will be that he will be your speaker, and you will be his leader." The Noam Elimelech answers that since Moshe and Aharon are the speaker and leader respectively, it means that they could both loudly talk to each other in front of Pharaoh, and Pharaoh would hear what they were saying without either Moshe or Aharon speaking directly to Pharaoh.

1) The Mechilta on Shemos (12:1), the Tosefta on Krisus (4:7), the Mishna in Krisus 28a, the Beraishis Raba (1:15), and the Shir HaShirim Raba (4:5) are the sources for the answer which Rashi and the Ohr HaChaim present to our question. They say that there are places in the Torah when Aharon is mentioned before Moshe, and there are other places where Moshe is mentioned before Aharon. This way of mentioning them informs us that Moshe and Aharon were equal. The Mechilta says that in general, when the Torah mentions two names together, the first name is the more important person. However, when sometimes one is mentioned first, and other times the other is mentioned first, the Torah is informing us that they are both of equal stature. As an example, the Mechilta, Tosefta, and Beraishis Raba quote the first Posuk in Beraishis "In the beginning of G-d's creation of the heavens and the earth." This Posuk lists Heaven before earth. However, in Beraishis (2:4), the Torah says, "on the day that Hashem, G-d made earth and Heaven." Since in this Posuk, earth is listed before Heaven implies that Heaven and earth are of equal importance. Another example they offer is Shemos (3:6), "And He (Hashem) said, "I am the G-d of your father, the G-d of Avrohom, the G-d of Yitzchak, and the G-d of Yaakov." This Posuk lists our forefathers as Avrohom, Yitzchak, and Yaakov implying that Avrohom is the most important. In Vayikra (26:42) the Torah says "and I will remember My covenant with Yaakov, and also My covenant with Yitzchak, and also My covenant with Avrohom I will remember. And I will remember the Land." Since in this Posuk, our forefathers are listed in the opposite order from the Posuk we have previously quoted implies that all our forefathers are equal. Another example the Mechilta, Tosefta, Beraishis Raba, and the Mishna in Krisus 28a present is Shemos (20:12) which says, "Honor your father and your mother." This Posuk would imply that one's father is more important than one's mother. In Vayikra (19:3), the Torah says, "Every man shall fear his mother and his father." Since they are listed in the opposite order in this Posuk, it implies that one's father and one's mother are equal. The Beraishis Raba and Tosefta present Bamidbar (14:6), which says, "Yehoshua the son of Nun and Calev the son of Yephuneh, who were among those who had scouted the land, tore their clothes." This Posuk implies that Yehoshua was greater than Caleb. However, Bamidbar (14:30) says, "You (Bnei Yisroel) shall not come into the Land concerning which I raised My hand that you

Vaera

would settle in it, except Calev the son of Yephuneh and Yehoshua the son of Nun." Since they are listed in the opposite order, this implies that Yehoshua and Calev are equal. The Mishna in Krisus 28a offers an example of a Korban, which can be brought either from a lamb or from a goat. For example, Shemos (12:5), talking about a Korban Pesach, says, "You shall have a perfect male lamb in its first year; you may take it either from the sheep or from the goats. For a Korban Pesach, sheep are mentioned before goats as Korbanos in the Torah, and one might think that a sheep is preferable to a goat. With regard to a Korban Chatos, Vayikra (4:28) says, "if his sin that he committed is made known to him, he shall bring his sacrifice: an unblemished female goat, for his sin that he committed." Several Pesukim later, Vayikra (4:32) says, "If he brings a sheep for his sin offering, he shall bring an unblemished female." Since, in this case, a goat is mentioned before a sheep, this implies that for a Korban, which can be brought from either a sheep or a goat, there is no preference between the two animals. With regard to birds as Korbanos, the Mishna in Krisus, and the Beraishis Raba say that in the vast majority of cases, turtle doves are mentioned before young doves, and one might think that turtle doves are preferable. An example of this is Vayikra (1:14) which says, "And if his sacrifice to Hashem, is a burnt offering from birds, he shall bring it from turtle doves or from young doves." However, Vayikra (12:6), talking about the topic of a woman who gave birth, the Torah says, "And when the days of her purification have been completed, whether for a son or for a daughter, she shall bring a sheep in its first year as a burnt offering, and a young dove or a turtle dove as a sin offering, to the entrance of the Tent of Meeting, to the Kohen." This teaches us that there is no preference with regard to a Korban regarding whether a turtle dove or a young dove is brought.

The Tosefta says that in all the cases that it quotes, the second Posuk quoted is the only time that the opposite order is used. In fact, the only case, says the Maharzav on the Beraishis Raba, where the order frequently is either way, is that of the Heaven and the earth. Applying this rule to our case would say that our Posuk is the only time that Aharon is mentioned before Moshe. The Tur on our Posuk presents two other Pesukim where Aharon is mentioned first. Bamidbar (3:1-2) says, "These are the descendants of Moshe and Aharon on the day that Hashem spoke to Moshe at Mount Sinai. These are the names of the sons of Aharon: Nadav the firstborn Avihu, Elazar, and Itamar." Another example is Shemos (6:20) "Amram took Yocheved, his aunt, as his wife, and she bore him Aharon and Moshe, and the years of Amram's life were one hundred thirty-seven years." He explains that these Pesukim are mentioning the births and family of Aharon and Moshe and therefore list Aharon first because he was older than Moshe. However, as the Tosefta says, our Posuk is the only Posuk not listing the genealogy of Moshe and Aharon, which mentions Aharon before Moshe. The Kli Yakor explains that the reason the Torah chose to show that Moshe and Aharon were equal by mentioning Aharon first in our Posuk is that our Pesukim are part of the section of the Torah, which give us the background as to who Moshe and Aharon were.

Devorim (34:10) says, "And there was no other prophet who arose in Yisroel like Moshe, whom Hashem knew face to face." This Posuk implies that there was no greater prophet than Moshe, meaning that Moshe was greater in prophecy than Aharon. The Ponim Yofos, the Shelah, as quoted by the Ksav Sofer, and the Maskil LeDovid all say that at this point where the Bnei Yisroel are going out of Egypt, Moshe and Aharon were equal. However, after the Bnei Yisroel left Egypt,

Vaera

Moshe surpassed Aharon, and they were no longer equal. For example, when the Torah was given on Mount Sinai, Moshe is told in Devorim (5:27-28), "Go say to them (Bnei Yisroel), 'Return to your tents.' But as for you (Moshe), stand here with Me, and I will speak to you all the commandments, the statutes, and the ordinances which you will teach them, that they may do them in the Land which I give them to possess." Since only Moshe and not Aharon was commanded to "stand here with Me" we may derive that Moshe was greater than Aharon, at the time the Torah was given.

The Gemorah in Nedorim 38a says that Hashem only rests his prophetic spirit on someone who is mighty, wealthy, wise, and humble. The Maharsha explains that the reason he must be mighty and wealthy is that these are qualities the common person gives respect to, and therefore it will help him gain respect even of the common person. The Ksav Sofer uses this concept of the Gemorah to explain how Moshe was equal to Aharon in Egypt and became greater than Aharon after the Bnei Yisroel left Egypt. Bamidbar (12:3) says, "Now this man Moshe was exceedingly humble, more so than any person on the face of the earth." If we consider the Gemorah we have quoted, which says that humility is necessary for prophetic spirit and consider the Posuk we have just quoted says that Moshe was the humblest person ever, we may derive that consequently, Moshe's humility was the cause of his being the greatest in prophecy in all of Yisroel. He says that Moshe's humility could not be detected until Moshe was sent to speak to Pharaoh, one of the greatest Kings of the world. Being that Moshe, before he went to Pharaoh, was a simple person, no one expected that he would have anything to be haughty about. Only after Moshe remained humble even after speaking to Pharaoh could anyone detect that he was a humble person. Moshe's stature grew when he became leader of the Bnei Yisroel, performed all the miraculous actions of taking the Bnei Yisroel out of Egypt, and finally had Hashem appear to him on Mount Sinai. Despite this, Moshe remained the humblest person ever in Yisroel, causing his level of prophecy and greatness to grow. That is why Moshe became steadily greater than Aharon when the Bnei Yisroel left Egypt. Before they first went to Pharaoh, since Aharon had already prophesized previously and was known to the Bnei Yisroel as a prophet, not to mention being three years older than Moshe, at this point Aharon may have been greater than Moshe in prophecy.

If at the time before they spoke to Pharaoh, Aharon was equal or perhaps even greater than Moshe, the Ksav Sofer ponders the question of why Hashem did not choose Aharon as the redeemer of the Bnei Yisroel from Egypt. He answers that Hashem did not want to appear in prophesy in the spiritually impure Land of Egypt any more often than was absolutely necessary. Therefore, Hashem chose to give the prophecy of redemption to Moshe, who was in Midyan, and not to Aharon, who was in Egypt.

The Ksav Sofer offers another explanation as to how Moshe and Aharon could be equal and yet be consistent with the Posuk, which says, "And there was no other prophet who arose in Yisroel like Moshe, whom Hashem knew face to face." He explains that both Moshe and Aharon were equal in their ability to have prophecy. However, since Aharon lived his entire life in Egypt, he had two big issues which curtailed his ability to have prophecy. Firstly witnessing firsthand the horrible slavery left Aharon in a sad state of mind. In Melachim II, Chapter 3, Elisha the prophet is asked to find out

Vaera

from Hashem through prophecy whether the armies of the King of the Ten Tribes, the King of Yehuda, and the King of Edom will be victorious in battle against the Moabites. Though angry with the request because of how the King of the Ten Tribes had treated Hashem and his Prophets, Elisha agrees to do this for the sake of the King of Yehuda. However, because of his anger, Elisha requests a musician to transform him into a happy mood in order to have a prophetic vision. Thus we see that in order to be able to receive prophecy, one must be in a joyous frame of mind. Needing to be in a happy state of mind for prophecy is one of the issues that Aharon faced in Egypt. The second issue Aharon faced, which we have mentioned previously, is that because of all the Tumah in Egypt, Hashem did not want to give prophecy any more than was absolutely necessary in Egypt. On the other hand, Moshe in Midyan not only didn't have either of these two issues that Aharon had in Egypt but in addition, as a shepherd, he had plenty of time to devote to working on himself spiritually without people disturbing him. Because of all these factors and despite the fact that that they were born with equal ability to have prophecy, Moshe rose in prophecy to become much greater than Aharon. However, since it was only because of the respective circumstances that they found themselves in during their lifetimes, Hashem considered it as if they were both equal in prophecy.

In his Sefer Dorash Moshe, Rav Moshe Feinstein presents two other explanations as to how Moshe and Aharon could be equal and yet be consistent with the Posuk, which says, "And there was no other prophet who arose in Yisroel like Moshe, whom Hashem knew face to face." Firstly, Aharon was also a part of the mission to redeem the Bnei Yisroel from Egypt. Despite the fact that Moshe was greater, it was still necessary to also have Aharon for this mission, and therefore, they were both integral parts of this mission. When a bigger or stronger person is not able to do something by himself and needs a weaker person to aid him to get something done, they share in any profits from their joint venture. Similarly, in our case, even though Moshe was greater since he needed Aharon for this mission, Aharon shares equally in the mission.

Secondly, says Rav Moshe, even though Moshe was greater than Aharon, Aharon, for his entire life, completely did all that Hashem wanted him to as best as he could possibly do. Though Moshe was greater than Aharon, Moshe consequently had more that was expected of him to accomplish during his life. However, since both Moshe and Aharon did everything that was expected of them, they are considered equal by Hashem. Rav Moshe uses this concept to explain an interesting Gemorah in Baba Base 10b. The Gemorah says that Rav Yosef, the son of Rav Yehoshua, became very ill and became unconscious. He eventually regained consciousness, but during the time he was unconscious, his Neshama temporarily left his body and went to Heaven. After regaining consciousness, his father, Rav Yehoshua, asked him what he had seen in the next world. Rav Yosef told his father that he had seen an upside-down world, those that in this world were at the top were at the bottom in the next world, and those that were at the bottom in this world were at the top in the world to come. Rashi on the Gemorah explains that those that were in this world at the top refers to those wealthy people who, because of their wealth, were given the utmost of honor in this world. Similarly, Rashi explains that those that were at the bottom of this world refer to those poor people who were disrespected in this world. The Gemorah continues that Rav Yehoshua corrected his son and said that he had not seen an upside-down world in the next world but rather a correct and clear

Vaera

world. The Maharal, in his explanation of this Gemorah, says that since the rich people got honor for a completely materialistic and physical reason, being there is no materialism in the world to come, there will be no reason to give them any honor. The poor people, who have accustomed themselves to having little if any materialism in this world, will be honored in the next world for not having any materialistic desires, which is very noble in the world to come being that it is devoid of materialism. Rav Yehoshua then asked his son what he had seen with respect to the honor given to Torah Scholars like themselves in the world to come. Rav Yosef answered that just like we are considered important and are honored in this world, similarly in the world to come, we are considered important and honored in the world to come. The Maharal explains that intelligence is valued both in this world and in the world to come.

Rav Moshe is bothered by how Rav Yehoshua could even think to call the world to come an upside-down world when he obviously knew that the world to come was the world of truth and that this world is typically referred to as a world of falsity. Because of this problem, he presents a unique interpretation of this Gemorah and says that what Rav Yehoshua referred to as people at the top in this world are people who, because of their abilities, have accomplished much good. People at the bottom are people who have not accomplished much good in this world because of their very limited talents and abilities. The people at the top are considered people at the top in both this world and in the world to come since they have accomplished much good. Similarly, the people at the bottom of this world who have accomplished little are considered as people of the bottom in both this world and the next. This is all with regard to how these people are respected. However, despite people at the bottom receiving little respect even in the world to come, Rav Yehoshua saw that in many cases, the people at the bottom received more reward than the people at the top. The reason is that if the person at the bottom did everything possible for the abilities and talents he was given, even though he did not accomplish very much, he receives a full reward. On the other hand, people at the top who, because of their tremendous talent and abilities, accomplished much are held accountable if proportionate to their talent and abilities; they could have accomplished much more. Despite this person being respected for all that he accomplished, in terms of reward, he can receive much less reward than a person who has accomplished little, and therefore, Rav Yehoshua termed the world to come an upside-down world.

The Ben Yehoyoda presents another case where someone who has accomplished less than someone else can still reap a much greater reward. He builds a case of someone who has very righteous parents and is brought up in an environment in which he only experiences righteousness and fear of Hashem. He contrasts this to someone who did not have either this type of parents nor the righteous environment and yet, due to spending much time and effort working on himself, reach the same level of righteousness as the first person. Similar to Rav Moshe, he says that the second person gets much more reward in the world to come since reward in the world to come is proportionate to effort and not to accomplishments.

The Yepheh Kol on the Midrash Shir HaShirim Raba (4:5) says that indeed Moshe and Aharon were equal even when the Torah describes Moshe as a prophet that there was no one else like him in Yisroel. The Mishna in Pirkei Avos (1:12) quotes Hillel, who says, "be among the students of

Vaera

Aharon, loving peace and pursuing peace, loving people and bringing them closer to the Torah. The Yepheh Kol says that in this attribute, Aharon was greater than Moshe, and therefore, in sum total Aharon and Moshe were equal. The Yepheh Kol compares Aharon and Moshe to two different gems of equal value, each of which has its own unique attributes.

2) Rabeinu Bechay, the Chizkuni, the Eben Ezra, the Toldos Yitzchak, and Maharil Diskin answer our question similarly. They say that our Posuk is speaking about the genealogy of Aharon and Moshe. Since Aharon was older than Moshe, he is listed first in our Posuk. In the Posuk after ours, it says, "They are the ones who spoke to Pharaoh, the King of Egypt, to let the Bnei Yisroel out of Egypt; they are Moshe and Aharon." Rabeinu Bechay, the Chizkuni, the Eben Ezra, and the Toldos Yitzchak explain that since this Posuk is speaking about the mission of taking the Bnei Yisroel out of Egypt, Moshe is mention before Aharon since he led this mission and his contribution was greater than Aharon's was. Rabeinu Bechay explains in a similar way why Yehoshua is typically mentioned before Calev since he was greater than Calev in prophecy. We have mentioned previously that in Bamidbar (14:30), Calev is mentioned before Yehoshua when the Torah says, "You shall not come into the Land concerning which I raised My hand that you would settle in it, except Calev the son of Yephuneh and Yehoshua the son of Nun." The reason Calev is mentioned before Yehoshua in this Posuk is that Calev was greater than Yehoshua in terms of more honorable family genealogy. He also explains that the reason sometimes Heaven is mentioned before the earth is because the spiritual beings found in the heavens are greater than the physical beings found on earth, being that the spiritual beings are eternal. However, on many occasions, the earth is mentioned before Heaven since the earth has the advantage of being the main resting place of Hashem's Shechinah, especially when the Beis Hamikdosh existed.

3) The Eben Ezra, Akeidah, and Maharil Diskin answer our question similarly. They all say that the reason Aharon is mentioned first is that he had already previously been the prophet for the Bnei Yisroel in Egypt. The Shemos Raba (3:16) and Midrash Tanchuma on Shemos (27) say that when Moshe said in Shemos (4:13), "I beseech You, Hashem, send now Your message with whom You would send," Moshe was referring to Aharon. The Shemos Raba says that Aharon had prophesized for the past 80 years in Egypt. In Sefer Shmuel I (2:27-28), the prophet (Rashi says that this prophet was Elkanah) tells Ayli the Kohen Godol, "So said Hashem: 'It is well known that I appeared to the house of your father, when they were in Egypt, enslaved to the house of Pharaoh.' And I chose him from all the tribes of Yisroel to be My Kohen, to offer up sacrifices on My altar, to burn incense, to wear an ephod before Me. And I gave to the house of your father all the fire-offerings of the Bnei Yisroel." Based on this Posuk, the Shemos Raba says that it was Aharon who delivered the prophecy quoted in Sefer Yechezkel (20:7) "And I (Hashem) said to them: Every man cast away the despicable idols from before his eyes, and pollute not yourselves with the idols of Egypt; I am Hashem your G-d." We have mentioned that the Shemos Raba and Midrash Tanchuma say that Aharon prophesized for 80 years in Egypt. The Maharif on this Shemos Raba says that Miriam prophesized until Moshe was born and that Aharon became the prophet for the Bnei Yisroel right after that. Since Aharon was three years older than Moshe, this implies that Aharon became the prophet for the Bnei Yisroel when he was only three years old.

Vaera

4) The Alshich HaKodosh presents an answer to our question. When Hashem first appeared to Moshe and asked Moshe to redeem the Bnei Yisroel from Egypt, Moshe gave many excuses why he was not fit for the job and why others, like Aharon in the previous answer, were more appropriate than he was. He rejects the notion that Aharon was ever greater than or even equal in his prophecy to Moshe, an opinion shared by some commentators, as we have mentioned in our first answer to our question. He says that Moshe, and not Aharon, was the only one capable of redeeming the Bnei Yisroel from Egypt. This is consistent with the analysis of the Vayikra Raba (1:5) of Shemos (3:10) which says וְעַתָּה לְכָה וְאֶשְׁלָחֲךָ אֶל פַּרְעֹה וְהוֹצֵא אֶת עַמִּי בְנֵי יִשְׂרָאֵל מִמִּצְרָיִם (So now go, and I (Hashem) will send you (Moshe) to Pharaoh, and take My people, the Bnei Yisroel, out of Egypt). It says that the reason there is a Heh at the end of the word לְכָה is to tell Moshe that if he doesn't redeem the Bnei Yisroel from Egypt, no one else will redeem them. The Matnos Kehunah explains that instead of using the strange word לְכָה to mean "go" the Posuk should have used the same and typical word (לֵךְ) as is used in Shemos (3:16) לֵךְ וְאָסַפְתָּ אֶת זִקְנֵי יִשְׂרָאֵל (Go and assemble the elders of Israel). The reason the Torah added on a Heh at the end of the word לֵךְ is so that the reading of the word would be the same as the word לְךָ (to you). If we used the Hebrew word לֵךְ instead of לְכָה, that Posuk would be translated as "only to you (Moshe) is the mission of going to Pharaoh and taking the Bnei Yisroel out of Egypt.

The Alshich says that as a result of Moshe's many excuses for not immediately accepting the mission of redeeming the Bnei Yisroel from Egypt, Hashem decided to install Aharon as Moshe's "middle man" and spokesman to Pharaoh and to the Bnei Yisroel. Therefore, Shemos (4:30-31) says, "And Aharon spoke all the words that Hashem had spoken to Moshe, and he performed the signs before the eyes of the people. And the people believed, and they heard that Hashem had remembered the Bnei Yisroel and that He saw their affliction, and they kneeled and prostrated themselves." At this point in time, Aharon was taking the lead in the redemption, and that is why our Posuk mentions Aharon before Moshe. Immediately after seeing the belief shown by the people, Moshe joined Aharon in together speaking to Pharaoh as Shemos (5:1) says, "And afterwards, Moshe and Aharon came and said to Pharaoh, 'So said Hashem, G-d of Yisroel, Send out My people, and let them sacrifice to Me in the desert." Since, as we have mentioned previously, only Moshe could complete the mission of redeeming the Bnei Yisroel from Egypt, Hashem welcomed the fact that Moshe over time took the lead in the redemption from Egypt and, therefore, subsequently, Moshe is mentioned before Aharon.

Even after Moshe did agree to the mission when Pharaoh did not immediately listen to Moshe, Moshe again made an excuse for not being fit for the mission when he said in Shemos (6:12), "Behold, the Bnei Yisroel did not hearken to me. How then will Pharaoh hearken to me, seeing that I am of closed lips?" Because of this, says the Alshich, Hashem decided to speak to both Moshe and Aharon

5) The Kli Yakor, Terumas HaDeshen, as quoted by the Tzedah LeDerech, Ponim Yofos, and the Oznayim LeTorah, answer our question similarly. They say that there were two parts to the mission. The first part is being the prophet who is given the commandment to take the Bnei Yisroel out of Egypt. This part is described in our Posuk, which says, "That is Aharon and Moshe, to whom

Vaera

Hashem said, "Take the Bnei Yisroel out of the land of Egypt with their legions." One would think that since Hashem initially gave this commandment to Moshe that Moshe was more important in this part. Therefore, our Posuk mentions Aharon before Moshe to inform us that they were equal. The second part of the mission was to speak to Pharaoh and tell him to let the Bnei Yisroel leave Egypt. This second part is described in the Posuk after ours, which says, "They are the ones who spoke to Pharaoh, the King of Egypt, to let the Bnei Yisroel out of Egypt; they are Moshe and Aharon." Since Aharon was the one who directly spoke to Pharaoh, we might think that Aharon was more important than Moshe with regard to the second part of the mission. Therefore, the Posuk, after ours, mentions Moshe before Aharon to inform us that they are both equal.

The Tzedah LeDerech says that this explanation is similar to what the Gemorah says in Kidushin 30b-31a in explaining why the Torah mentions one's father before one's mother in Shemos (20:12) "Honor your father and your mother," while in Vayikra (19:3) the order is reversed when the Torah says "Every man shall fear his mother and his father." The Gemorah says that it is "revealed and known to the one who spoke and the world came into being" that a son honors his mother more than his father because his mother wins him over with pleasant words. Therefore, when the Torah is speaking about honor, the Torah mentions the father before the mother to inform us that both parents are equal with respect to honor. The Gemorah continues that it is also "revealed and known to the one who spoke and the world came into being" that a son has more fear for his father than for his mother because his father teaches him Torah. Therefore, with respect to fear, the Torah mentions one's mother before one's father to teach us that both parents are also equal with respect to the fear one is to have of them.

6) The Kli Yakor presets another answer to our question. He says that our Posuk is talking about being the prophet to the Bnei Yisroel to take them out of Egypt. As we have mentioned previously, Aharon was the original prophet who began prophesizing to the Bnei Yisroel on enabling the Bnei Yisroel to be redeemed from Egypt as quoted in Sefer Yechezkel (20:7) "And I (Hashem) said to them: Every man cast away the despicable idols from before his eyes, and pollute not yourselves with the idols of Egypt; I am Hashem your G-d." Since Aharon began the process, he is mentioned before Moshe in our Posuk. The Posuk after ours describes the part of the mission to speak to Pharaoh. Originally, Moshe was told to do this as Shemos (3:18) says, "and you (Moshe) shall come, you and the elders of Yisroel, to the King of Egypt, and you shall say to him, 'Hashem G-d of the Hebrews has happened upon us, and now, let us go for a three days' journey in the desert and offer up sacrifices to Hashem, our G-d.'" Since Moshe was first commanded to do this part of the mission, Moshe's name is mentioned before Aharon in the Posuk after ours.

7) The Chasam Sofer and Nitziv answer our question similarly. They say that when the Torah mentions Aharon before Moshe in our Posuk, the Torah is speaking from the perspective of the Bnei Yisroel as our Posuk says, "Take the Bnei Yisroel out of the land of Egypt with their legions." From the perspective of the Bnei Yisroel, at least at this time, they felt Aharon was greater than Moshe. The Nitziv says that since they knew Aharon as a holy person who had been their prophet and had hardly seen Moshe, who was raised in the Pharaoh's palace and then had to escape to

Vaera

Midyan, they felt that Aharon was greater than Moshe. Therefore, in our Posuk, Aharon is mentioned before Moshe.

According to the Chasam Sofer and Nitziv, the Posuk after ours, "They are the ones who spoke to Pharaoh, the King of Egypt, to let the Bnei Yisroel out of Egypt," is talking from Pharaoh's perspective of Moshe and Aharon. Pharaoh knew Moshe from the time that he grew up in Pharaoh's palace, and he knew that Moshe had a very high intellect. Since Pharaoh had never met Aharon before, from Pharaoh's perspective, Moshe was greater than Aharon, and therefore Moshe is mentioned first in the Posuk after ours.

8) The Berditchever Rebbe, in his Sefer Kedushas Levi, also ponders our question. Similar to the Chasam Sofer and Nitziv in the previous answer, he also says that our Posuk is talking from the perspective of the Bnei Yisroel while the Posuk after ours is talking from Pharaoh's perspective. However, he says that our Pesukim are not speaking of just the time when Moshe and Aharon first speak to Pharaoh but are referring to the entire span of the leadership of Moshe and Aharon. With respect to the Bnei Yisroel, the Berditchever Rebbe says that one might think Moshe was greater than Aharon since Hashem spoke only to Moshe, and Moshe told the entire Torah to the Bnei Yisroel. By mentioning Aharon before Moshe in our Posuk, the Torah is telling us that, nonetheless, Aharon was equal to Moshe. In the first answer, we have discussed how this could be true even though the Torah tells us that there was no one greater in prophecy than Moshe.

With respect to dealing with Pharaoh, the Berditchever Rebbe says that only Aharon spoke to Pharaoh as Hashem says to Moshe in Shemos (7:1) "See! I have made you a lord over Pharaoh, and Aaron, your brother, will be your speaker." One might think that since Aharon spoke to Pharaoh, at least from Pharoah's perspective, Aharon was greater than Moshe. Therefore, the Posuk after ours mentions Moshe before Aharon to tell us that in reality, Moshe was equal to Aharon even with respect to dealing with Pharaoh.

9) The Ksav Sofer presents an answer to our question. As we have mentioned previously from him, until they spoke to Pharaoh, Aharon was equal or perhaps even greater than Moshe in prophecy. Only after Moshe began speaking to Pharaoh, one of the greatest Kings in the world at that time, and despite this, was still the most humble person in Yisroel, did Moshe's level of prophecy continue to rise. Our Posuk is speaking about before Moshe and Aharon came to Pharaoh as our Posuk says, "That is Aharon and Moshe, to whom Hashem said, "Take the Bnei Yisroel out of the land of Egypt with their legions." Therefore, since Aharon was equal or perhaps greater than Moshe, Aharon is mention first in our Posuk. We can contrast our Posuk with the previous Posuk in Shemos (6:27), which says, "They are the ones who spoke to Pharaoh, the King of Egypt, to let the Bnei Yisroel out of Egypt; they are Moshe and Aharon." When they were scheduled to speak to Pharaoh, Moshe, with his humbleness, became bigger than Aharon in prophecy and therefore is mentioned before Aharon.

10) The Maor VaShemesh, Malbim, and Ritzvah, as quoted by the Taam V'Daas, answer our question similarly. They say that there were two distinct missions that Moshe and Aharon were

Vaera

given. The first mission was for them to separate the Bnei Yisroel from all the Tumah in Egypt and bring them closer to Hashem. In this mission, Aharon was the main person. As we have mentioned previously, the Shemos Raba (3:16) says that Aharon prophesized for 80 years to try and get the Bnei Yisroel to refrain from worshipping idols. During much of this time, Moshe was not even in Egypt, and even when he was, it was Aharon and not Moshe who Hashem chose to prophecize for the Bnei Yisroel. In addition, since Moshe grew up in Pharaoh's palace, the Bnei Yisroel had little if any contact with him, and the vast majority of the Bnei Yisroel had never even met him. Our Posuk, which describes this mission of taking the Bnei Yisroel out of the Land of Egypt, is talking about this mission. Since Aharon was the exclusive prophet of the Bnei Yisroel, he is mentioned first in our Posuk. The Malbim also points out that the Bnei Yisroel were more drawn to Aharon since, as we have mentioned previously, the Mishna in Pirkei Avos (1:12) quotes Hillel who says, "be among the students of Aharon, loving peace and pursuing peace, loving people and bringing them closer to the Torah.

The second mission was to go to Pharaoh and attempt to convince him to let the Bnei Yisroel leave Egypt. Until this time, Pharaoh had never met Aharon but knew Moshe well since Moshe grew up in Pharaoh's house. In this mission, Moshe was the main person. The Maor VaShemesh points out that the first thing that Hashem tells Moshe when Hashem describes the mission in Shemos (4:10) is, "So now come, and I will send you to Pharaoh." The Posuk after ours, which says, "They are the ones who spoke to Pharaoh, the King of Egypt, to let the Bnei Yisroel out of Egypt," is speaking about this mission. Therefore, the Posuk after ours mentions Moshe before Aharon since Moshe was the main person in this mission.

11) The Maor VaShemesh presents another answer to our question. The Posuk before our Posuk says, "Elazar, the son of Aharon, took for himself one of the daughters of Putiel as a wife, and she bore him Pinchos; these are the heads of the fathers' houses of the Leviyim according to their families." At first glance, it seems to be a strange juxtaposition to put this Posuk speaking about Pinchos next to our Posuk speaking about Moshe and Aharon. To explain this juxtaposition, he quotes a statement from the Arizal, which is essentially found in the Zohar, Shemos 26b. The Zohar ponders how the Posuk before ours says "these are the heads of the fathers' houses of the Leviyim according to their families," after mentioning the birth of one person, Pinchos, instead of saying "this is the head of the fathers' houses of the Leviyim." It answers that when Nadav and Avihu died while bringing a strange fire on the Mizbeach, their image dwelt in Pinchos, and Pinchos inherited their title of being a Kohen and got their spirit in him. The Arizal says that the Neshomos of Nadav and Avihu went to Pinchos and combined with the Neshama Pinchos already had. The Zohar concludes by saying that the Posuk before ours is telling us about what would happen in the future with regard to Nadav, Avihu, and Pinchos. Finally, it says that the reason the Posuk before ours uses the plural in saying "these are the heads of the fathers' houses of the Leviyim according to their families" is because Pinchos was going to have the Neshomos of three people (Nadav, Avihu, and his own). The Maor VaShemesh says that this Posuk is juxtaposed to our Posuk to tell us that there will be a day when Aharon will be greater than Moshe. That day will be when Nadav and Avihu are Niftar, and their Neshomos go to Pinchos. On that day, Aharon paskined that the sin offering should be burnt because his two sons had been Niftar that day, while Moshe got angry with Aharon's

Vaera

decision to burn the sin offering instead of eating from it. After Moshe and Aharon explained their reasoning for their decision to each other, Moshe conceded that Aharon was indeed correct as Vayikra (10:20) says, "Moshe heard (Aharon's reasoning), and it pleased him." Aharon reached this lofty level on that day since, despite his two sons being killed for bringing a strange fire on the Mizbeach, Aharon was silent and did not question Hashem's decree against his two sons. Therefore, our Posuk mentions Aharon before Moshe because, on that day, Aharon was indeed greater than Moshe.

The Maor VaShemesh says that we can alternatively come to the same answer if we say that the day Aharon became greater than Moshe was on the day that Pinchos killed Zimri, prince of the tribe of Shimon, in the last few Pesukim of Parshas Balak. Pinchos was rewarded for his actions by Hashem in Bamidbar (25:13), which says, "It shall be for him and for his descendants after him as an eternal covenant of Kehunah, because he was zealous for his G-d and atoned for the Bnei Yisroel." We have quoted the Zohar, which says that Pinchos inherited their title of being a Kohen and got their spirit in him. It would seem that the Neshomos of Nadav and Avihu entered Pinchos when he inherited the title of being a Kohen which happened when he killed Zimri. The Gemorah in Sanhedrin 82a tells us that Zimri brought the Midyanite woman Kosbi before Moshe and asked Moshe if she was permitted to him. At that moment, Moshe did not remember the Halacha that a zealot may kill one who cohabits with an idolatress, which Zimri was preparing to do. Pinchos saw what was happening and remembered the Halacha. Pinchos went to Moshe and said, "brother of my grandfather (Aharon) didn't you teach me when you came down from Mount Sinai that zealots may kill one who cohabits with an idolatress?" Moshe told Pinchos, "may the one who reads the letter be the person to carry out its instructions." On that day, we see that Aharon's grandson Pinchos was greater than Moshe.

Why Don't We Have Sorcerers in Our Times?

וַיַּשְׁלֵךְ אַהֲרֹן אֶת מַטֵּהוּ לִפְנֵי פַרְעֹה וְלִפְנֵי עֲבָדָיו וַיְהִי לְתַנִּין. וַיִּקְרָא גַּם פַּרְעֹה לַחֲכָמִים וְלַמְכַשְּׁפִים וַיַּעֲשׂוּ גַם הֵם חַרְטֻמֵּי מִצְרַיִם בְּלַהֲטֵיהֶם כֵּן (ז:י-יא) Shemos (7:10-11) Aharon cast his staff before Pharaoh and before his servants, and it became a serpent. Pharaoh too summoned the wise men and the magicians, and the sorcerers of Egypt also did likewise with their magic.

Rav Yaakov Kaminetsky ponders the question of why we do not have sorcerers in our times.

Our question is based on the fact that the sorcerers mentioned in the Torah performed real sorcery as opposed to sleight of hand. In our Posuk, the sorcerers emulate what Aharon did by turning their staffs into serpents. Not all Meforshim are of the opinion that the Egyptian sorcerers performed real sorcery. For example, the Malbim explains that the sorcerers emulated what Aharon did by sleight of hand. As part of his proof that the sorcerers emulated by sleight of hand, he quotes our Posuk which says וַיַּעֲשׂוּ גַם הֵם חַרְטֻמֵּי מִצְרַיִם בְּלַהֲטֵיהֶם כֵּן (which literally means "and they (the sorcerers) also did with their magic likewise"). He says that had the Torah wanted to tell us that they did what Aharon did the Torah would have said וַיַּעֲשׂוּ כֵן גַם הֵם חַרְטֻמֵּי מִצְרַיִם בְּלַהֲטֵיהֶם (which literally means "and they (the sorcerers) likewise also did with their magic"). Rather, only with their magic did the

Vaera

sorcerers make it appear as if they copied Aharon and made their staffs turn into serpents. He explains exactly how they performed their sleight of hand. They started by holding a staff. They then took the skins of serpents and covered both themselves and their staff with it so that it became their costume. They then crawled on the floor, emulating the movement that a serpent does, which was not too difficult, being that they were under the serpent's skin. In the end, Aharon's serpent turn back into a snake and swallowed up the Egyptian serpents, which in effect swallowed up the sorcerers along with their staffs who were under their serpent costumes. He quotes the Shemos Raba (9:7) as a source of his explanation. It says that if Hashem caused Aharon's staff, while it was still a serpent, to swallow the sorcerer's emulation of serpents, it would not be so impressive since it would look like a natural act that a live thing (serpent) swallowed another live thing. Rather Hashem turned Aharon's serpent back into a staff, and it was this inanimate object which did the swallowing, a much more miraculous occurrence. When Pharaoh saw what happened, he became agitated and thought to himself about what would happen if Hashem had also directed Aharon's staff to swallow Pharaoh and his throne. The Malbim explains why Pharaoh was agitated and why he was afraid that Aharon's staff might swallow him. In the next Posuk after ours, it says, "Each one of them (sorcerers) cast down his staff, and they became serpents; but Aharon's staff swallowed their staffs." He ponders why this Posuk says, "Aharon's staff swallowed their staffs," when the Torah nowhere tells us that the Egyptian sorcerers had turned their serpents back to a staff. Rather, since they only did sleight of hand, the sorcerers had their staff along with themselves under their serpent costumes. The Posuk hints to us that Aharon's staff swallowed up the whole serpent costume, which included the sorcerers and their staffs. Pharaoh knew that the sorcerers had used sleight of hand to emulate Aharon and were really inside the Egyptian serpent costumes. Watching Aharon's staff swallow up the sorcerers made Pharaoh worry that Hashem could also cause Aharon's staff to swallow him up. There is a much earlier source than the Malbim that the Egyptian sorcerers did sleight of hand, and this source is of the opinion that all acts of sorcerers are only performing sleight of hand and that there is no such thing as real sorcery.

The Rambam, in his explanation of the Mishnayos of Avodah Zora (4:6), says that all forms of sorcery mentioned in the Torah and forbidden for us to follow, came about from people believing that the sleight of hand performed by sorcerers was real. Though it was sleight of hand, it became accepted by many as real, and therefore the Torah forbid any of these activities. In Hilchos Avodas Kochavim (11:11), he says that if a scorpion bites someone, the person is permitted to use the words (or spells) of sorcerers in an attempt to save himself from the effect of the scorpion's venom. This is permitted, even though using the words (or spells) of sorcerers does absolutely nothing; being that the person is in mortal danger, we are afraid that the psychological effects of not being permitted to use the words (or spells) may increase the mortal danger he is in. In other words, he is allowed to pretend the words (or spells) may help him, to ease his state of mind. In Shulchan Aruch, Yoreh Deah (179:6), the Shulchan Aruch quotes and paskins like the Rambam and says that if a scorpion bites someone, the person is permitted to use the words (or spells) of sorcerers in an attempt to save himself from the effect of the scorpion's venom. Quoting the Rambam, the Shulchan Aruch continues that this is permitted, even though using the words (or spells) of sorcerers does absolutely nothing, since the person is in mortal danger, we are afraid that the psychological effects of not being permitted to use the words (or spells) may increase the mortal danger he is in. The Vilna

Vaera

Gaon on the Shulchan Aruch says the Shulchan Aruch is following the opinion of the Rambam that we have mentioned, who is of the opinion that sorcery is just sleight of hand.

The Vilna Gaon says that many disagree with the Rambam and Shulchan Aruch's opinion and instead say that sorcery can be real and not just sleight of hand. The best proof, he says, is the many times real sorcery or other supernatural means is found in various Gemorohs. The Gemorah in Sanhedrin 95a is such an example. The Gemorah explains the details of what Sefer Shmuel II (21:15-17) tell us. The Pesukim say, "And the Philistines waged war again with Yisroel; and Dovid went down with his servants and they fought against the Philistines, but Dovid became faint. And Yishbi, who was one of the sons of Raphah was in Nov; and the weight of his spear was three hundred shekels of brass in weight; and he was girded with new armor, and he thought to smite Dovid. But Avishay, the son of Tzruiah, aided him, and he struck the Philistine, and killed him. Then the men of Dovid swore to him saying, 'You shall no longer go out with us to battle, so that you extinguish not the lamp of Yisroel.'" The Gemorah explains that when the Posuk tells us about Yishbi, who was in the city of Nov, it is alluding to Dovid being punished for what happened years earlier in the city of Nov. The story of the massacre in Nov is related in Sefer Shmuel I, chapters 21-22. In brief, Dovid was fleeing from being attacked by King Shaul, who wanted to kill him. Dovid came to the city of Nov, which contained a settlement of Kohanim. Dovid told the head Kohen that he was an emissary of King Shaul on a mission from the King. The head Kohen gave Dovid food, provisions, and arms to assist him in his mission. One of Shaul's servants, Doeg, witnessed what occurred and subsequently told Shaul that the Kohanim of Nov had betrayed him by giving Dovid food, provisions, and arms even though they knew Dovid was Shaul's enemy. Shaul ordered Doeg to kill all the Kohanim in Nov, and Doeg fulfilled his request. There were three people culpable for the massacre in Nov. Doeg who lied to Shaul and told Shaul that the Kohanim of Nov knew that Dovid was Shaul's enemy and thereby lost his share in the world to come. Shaul, who accepted Doeg's words, was killed along with his three sons in a war with the Philistines. Dovid, even though he did not intend to cause the Kohanim of Nov any harm, is held by the Gemorah as indirectly responsible for their deaths, for Shaul being killed, and for Doeg losing his portion in the world to come, since he did not tell the Kohanim of Nov that he was running away from Shaul. As punishment, Hashem now, many years after the event, gave Dovid the choice of either his descendants being destroyed or of Dovid being given over into his enemy's hand. The Maharsha explains that the punishment of Dovid's descendants being destroyed would atone for the fact that all future descendants of the Kohanim of Nov were destroyed when they were murdered. The punishment of Dovid being given over into his enemy's hand would atone for Dovid choosing to not give himself over into his enemy's (Shaul's) hand and thereby causing all the Kohanim of Nov to be murdered.

The Gemorah continues and tells us that one day Dovid went hunting. The Satan appeared disguised as a deer. Each time Dovid shot an arrow at the deer, it fell short, causing Dovid to run and try to get closer to the deer, with the chase eventually leading Dovid to the land of the Philistines. Yishbi sees Dovid and recognizes him as the one who killed his brother Golyus, the giant. Parenthetically we see that when the Posuk says that Yishbi was the son of Raphah, the Gemorah is of the opinion that Raphah is the same person as Orpah, the mother of Golyus. We

Vaera

know Orpah from Megilas Rus as the daughter-in-law of Naomi, who left her and returned to her father's house when Naomi returned to Eretz Yisroel.

Yishbi captures Dovid and ties him up. He then threw Dovid under an olive press and sat on top of the press so as to crush Dovid to death. However, a miracle was performed for Dovid, and the ground under him softened, preventing Dovid from being crushed to death. Though this miracle saved Dovid from the immediate threat, he was still a prisoner of Yishbi and, therefore, still in great danger. The Gemorah now tells us how he was eventually saved. The day Dovid was captured was Erev Shabbos. Avishay, the son of Tzruiah, one of Dovid's head army officers, was preparing for Shabbos and was sent a sign from heaven that something was amiss with Dovid. One opinion is that he saw some drops of blood in the water he used to wash his hair, and another opinion is that a dove came and beat itself with its wings until some of its feathers came out. Avishai went to Dovid's house, and he was not there. Sensing that time was of the essence, Avishay asked for a Halachic ruling on whether he could ride on Dovid's mule, which was extraordinarily fast. The ruling was needed since, in ordinary circumstances, one is not allowed to take benefit from the King's designated possessions, like his horse, throne, and scepter. Because of the danger, he was given a ruling that permitted him to use Dovid's mule, which took him to the land of the Philistines in a very short time. When he got to the land of the Philistines, he saw Orpah, Yishbi's mother. She was spinning thread on a spindle. When she noticed Avishay, she broke off the spindle, which had a sharp end, and threw it at Avishay as a dart to kill him. She missed, and Avishay realizing what she was attempting to do, picked up the spindle, threw it back at her, and killed her.

Riding on, Avishay came to Yishbi. When Yishbi saw him, he calculated to himself that if Avishay joined Dovid, it would be two against one, and they could overpower and kill him. Being extremely strong like his brother Golyus, he decided to again try to kill Dovid before Avishay got there. Yishbi threw Dovid high up in the air and stuck his spear into the ground so that Dovid would fall with great force on the spear and be killed. Seeing Dovid in the air, Avishay said Hashem's name, and Dovid was suspended in midair. After bringing down Dovid from midair, the two of them run away with Yishbi in pursuit. Realizing that even the both of them could not overpower Yishbi, they tell Yishbi that they had killed his mother, and in his sorrow, they are able to overpower him and kill him. Though some, like the Maharal, are of the opinion that the whole story is allegorical, the Vilna Gaon and others are of the opinion that the story in the Gemorah actually happened in all its details.

The Gemorah in Bechoros tells another story whereby saying the name of Hashem, Rav Yehoshua, elevates himself in midair. Parenthetically, Rav Yehoshua was a student of Rav Yochanon ben Zakai upon whom he says in Pirkei Avos (2:8), "Praised is the mother who bore him." In short, the Gemorah in Bechoros tells how Rav Yehoshua debated and bested the sages of Athens. One of the things the sages of Athens tested Rav Yehoshua's abilities was by asking him to build a house in the air. Rav Yehoshua said the name of Hashem by which he suspended himself between the sky and earth. He then asked the sages of Athens to hand up bricks and mortar to him so he could build the house. Since the sages of Athens could not raise anything up to the height of where Rav Yehoshua stood, he told them that if you do not have the power to do this, then how can you ask me to build a house in the air? In other words, Rav Yehoshua showed them that he had much more supernatural

Vaera

power than they did. Again, the Vilna Gaon takes what is said in this Gemorah literally. Taken literally, both these Gemorohs say that one can use the power of Hashem's name to float up high in the air and remain suspended there in contradiction to the law of gravity.

The Gemorah in Chulin 105b and Shabbos 81b tell a similar story. Rav Chisda and Rabba bar Rav Huna were traveling on a boat. A noblewoman asked them to seat her together with them on the boat. When they did not seat her on the boat, she became angry and recited a spell that stopped the boat from moving. Rav Chisda and Rabba recited a spell to counter this witchcraft and the boat was able to move again. The noblewoman said in frustration that her sorcery is powerless against them since they did not follow any of the practices of doing things that would make them susceptible to her sorcerous powers. Rashi on the Gemorah in Chulin says that the reason Rav Chisda and Rabba were permitted to use a spell was either that it is permitted to use a spell to counteract a sorcerer's spell or because their spell used the name of Hashem. From these Gemorahs, again, we see that supernatural occurrences by people, both the noblewoman and the two Rabbonim, can happen and that they are not just sleight of hand.

The Gemorah in Sanhedrin 65b tells us that Rava created a person. Rashi explains that he put together various letters of Hashem's name and through it created this person (or Golem). Rava sent the person to Rav Zeira. Rav Zeira spoke to it, but it would not answer. The Maharsha explains that speech requires the presence of a Neshama, which only Hashem can create. This creature was like an animal with the power of life but no Neshama. Seeing that it could not talk, Rav Zeira concluded that it was just a creation of one of his fellow Talmedei Chachomim, and he told it to return to being dust. The Gemorah continues and tells us about Rav Chanina and Rav Oshaya who would sit together every Erev Shabbos and create a calf which was at one-third of its full growth, and they would then eat it on Shabbos. Rashi explains that a calf at one-third of its full growth is the tastiest. Rashi on Sanhedrin 67b says that they also created this calf by putting together various letters of Hashem's name. Again, says the Vilna Gaon, we see supernatural acts occurring and not sleight of hand.

We should mention that all the above cases deal with the Rabbonim using the power of Hashem's name to change something in nature. The Gemorah in Sanhedrin 67b says that putting together the letters of Hashem's name is the one thing with which it is permitted to change something in nature with. Since we are talking about righteous Jews in the above, this is what they were permitted to do to aid in the situation at hand for them. Using sorcery, on the other hand, is forbidden. The Gemorah in Sanhedrin 67b tells us a story of Zeiri, who came to the city of Alexandria in Egypt and purchased a donkey that had been made through sorcery. When he came to a stream of water to give it a drink, the sorcery dissolved and became a piece of wood. The Gemorah in Sanhedrin 67b says that water from a spring takes away the power of sorcery. The Anaf Yosef explains that spring water is the source of purity, and that is why the ashes of the Porah Adumah (Red Heifer) require spring water to be mixed with the ashes to make a Tameh person pure. On the other hand, the source of sorcery is Tumah, and that is why spring water takes away the power of sorcery.

Vaera

There is a very interesting Rashi found in Sanhedrin 44b about Baya, the tax collector. Rashi tells us that he was a corrupt Jewish tax collector. On the same day and in the same city that Baya was Niftar, a righteous Talmid Chochom was also Niftar. The entire city came to the Levaya of the righteous Talmid Chochom while only a few relatives of Baya, the tax collector, came to his Levaya. Many people accompanied the righteous Talmid Chochom to the cemetery, and in the back of the big processional, Baya's relatives carried him to the cemetery. Seeing all these people, bandits decided to attack them, and everyone put down the two coffins and ran for their lives. Only one disciple of the righteous Talmid Chochom was brave enough to hide near the coffin of his Rebbe and protect it as best he could. When the people of the town returned later to bury the coffins, they confused the two coffins. Despite the disciple complaining and protesting bitterly about their mistake, the people of the town did not listen to him. Baya, the corrupt Jewish tax collector, was buried with the highest of honors, while the righteous Talmid Chochom received a quick and non-honorable burial by Baya's relatives.

The disciple of the righteous Talmid Chochom was very upset about the dishonor that was given to the righteous Talmid Chochom at his burial, not to mention the honor given to Baya. That night his Rebbe appeared to him in a dream. His Rebbe told his disciple not to be upset since he was now receiving great honor in Gan Eden, while Baya, the corrupt tax collector, was suffering much pain in Gehenom. The Rebbe showed the disciple that the full weight of the hinge of the door to Gehenom was rotating on Baya's ear. The Rebbe also explained to the disciple that the reason he had received dishonor at his burial was that one time the shaming of a Torah Scholar came to his attention, and the Rebbe did not protest against this. With regard to Baya, the reason he received so much honor at his burial was that one time he prepared a banquet for the head of the city, but the head of the city did not show up. Instead, Baya distributed the food to the poor, and the honor at his burial was his reward. Upon seeing the anguish that Baya was undergoing, the disciple asked his Rebbe how long Baya would be receiving this punishment. His Rebbe answered that he would be receiving it till Rav Shimon ben Shetach was Niftar, and Rav Shimon ben Shetach would take his place under the door to Gehenom. For reference, Rav Shimon ben Shetach is listed in Pirkei Avos (1:8) as one of the pairs of religious leaders during the time of the second Beis Hamikdosh.

The disciple was astounded by the news that the great sage, Rav Shimon ben Shetach, had such a horrible punishment in store for him, and he asked his Rebbe for an explanation. His Rebbe explained that Rav Shimon ben Shetach was being punished for allowing Jewish women sorcerers to live in the city of Ashkelon without bringing them to trial. The next morning the disciple hurried over to Rav Shimon ben Shetach and related his dream to him.

Rav Shimon ben Shetach came up with a plan to be able to deal with the women sorcerers. He gathered 80 handsome young men. It turned out that it was raining heavily that day. Rav Shimon ben Shetach gave each of the men a large covered pot with a clean, dry robe folded inside. He instructed the men that there were exactly 80 women sorcerers and when he signaled, each of them should lift one of the women up from the ground. Rav Shimon ben Shetach explained that when a sorcerer is not in contact with the ground, they can not do their sorcery. As long as they could take the sorcerers by surprise and simultaneously lift them off the ground, they would be successful. Rav

Vaera

Shimon ben Shetach then went to their palace in Ashkelon, instructing the men to remain outside until he called them. Upon knocking on the door of the palace, the sorcerers asked him who he was and why he had come. Rav Shimon ben Shetach told them that he was also a sorcerer and that he had come to test their powers of witchcraft. The women sorcerers challenged him to show them an example of his witchcraft. Rav Shimon ben Shetach told them that he could bring the women sorcerers 80 young men all wearing dry clothes despite the heavy rains. They challenged him to do as he had said, and he motioned to the men to take the robes out of the pots, put them on, and all come in at once to lift each of them off the ground. They carried the women sorcerers to ensure that they made no contact with the ground and the women sorcerers could not harm them. Rav Shimon ben Shetach judged them all with the penalty of murder, and all 80 were hung on the same day.

Subsequently, the relatives of these sorcerers came up with a plot to avenge the deaths of their relatives, the sorcerers. Two of them came before a Beis Din and testified that they saw the son of Rav Shimon ben Shetach commit a sin for which he deserved to be killed by Beis Din. As is the case in any capital crime, the court rigorously grilled the witnesses, but the witnesses were able to pass all of Beis Din's investigations, and their testimony was accepted. After the death sentence was announced, Rav Shimon ben Shetach's son was taken out to be executed. As is the case in all executions, the son was asked to confess his sins before being executed. The son said that "If I have committed this sin, let my death not atone for any of my sins, but if I have not committed this sin, then my death should atone for all my sins and let the witnesses who conspired against me never find forgiveness for what they have done." Upon hearing this statement, the witnesses were shaken and admitted to the Beis Din that they had testified falsely to avenge the death of their relatives, the sorcerers. Despite this admission of the witnesses, the Beis Din was not able to overturn their verdict since once witnesses have given over their testimony to Beis Din, the testimony cannot be changed, and Rav Shimon ben Shetach's son was executed by Beis Din. This story is also told in the Yerushalmi Chagigah (2:2) with a few minor differences from the story that Rashi tells us in Sanhedrin 44b. Among the minor differences is that according to the Yerushalmi in Chagigah (2:2), Rav Shimon ben Shetach had promised before he became prince of the Bnei Yisroel that he would eradicate the sorcerers if he became the prince. Therefore, when he didn't initially keep this promise, he was set to be punished in Gehenom. Another difference is that the Yerushalmi says that Rav Shimon ben Shetach prearranged with the 80 young men that when he made certain sounds, they were to come in dressed in their dry clothes, and that is how they knew when to come in. Again from this story, we see that even though Rav Shimon ben Shetach used sleight of hand, had the sorcerers been able to contact the ground, they could have done real sorcery and harmed Rav Shimon ben Shetach and those that accompanied him.

The Gemorah in Sanhedrin 67b and Chulin 7b ponders why the power of sorcery is called in Hebrew כְּשָׁפִים. The Gemorah says that sorcery contradicts the heavenly council. Rashi explains that כְּשָׁפִים is a contraction of this phrase in Hebrew. The Chinuch in Mitzvah 62 explains that Hashem has put into nature how things should act, and the sorcerers go against this by causing them to act in a way they were not created to act in. The Vilna Gaon offers this as proof that sorcery is not just sleight of hand but rather has the power to actually change the laws of nature.

Vaera

Rav Yaakov Kaminetsky follows the view of the Vilna Gaon, which most Poskim and Meforshim follow and therefore ponders why it is that nowadays we no longer see real sorcery. In general, one also does not see Dibukim (spirits that invade and take over a person's body), which one did find in previous generations. We do note that less than twenty years ago, there was a story about a Dibuk in a man in Brazil, which did generate worldwide Jewish attention but was later found out to be a hoax.

Rav Yaakov explains that Hashem has created the world so that the forces of holiness have corresponding forces of Tumah such that a logical person was always left with the freedom of choice and was not forced to conclude that only the power of holiness was correct. For example, the Ramban on Shemos (14:21) ponders why Hashem made a strong east wind blow right before the Red Sea was split as the Torah says, "And Moshe stretched out his hand over the sea, and Hashem led the sea with the strong east wind all night, and He made the sea into dry land and the waters split." In this way, says the Ramban, Pharaoh was left with the freedom of choice to decide if the sea was split because of the natural force of the east wind or if it was a miracle of Hashem. Pharaoh decided that it was because of the east wind, and therefore Pharaoh ordered his army to go into the split Red Sea, and his army was drowned. In a similar way, when there were prophets of Hashem who at times could do miracles, there also had to be sorcerers who could also do supernatural acts, so that a person still had free choice to decide to follow Hashem or, Chas VeShalom, the powers of Tumah. In this same vein, Devorim (34:10) says, "And there was no other prophet who arose in Yisroel like Moshe, whom Hashem knew face to face." The Sifrei on that Posuk says that though there were no other in Yisroel, there was a prophet like Moshe in the Gentiles whose name was Bilam. Rav Yaakov says that Hashem had to put Bilam in the world at the same time as Moshe so that people would have free choice to believe in Hashem and Moshe or believe, Chas VeShalom, in Bilam.

Rav Yaakov concludes that he remembers when he was in Kelm that he saw a written note from Rav Elchonon Wasserman in the name of the Chofetz Chaim who said that in all probability, the Dibuk that was publicized in their time was probably the last one that would occur. The reason for this, writes Rav Elchonon, is that parallel to the diminishing of the power of Torah and spirituality, the power of Tumah, which brought about the Dibuk, would also be diminished.

What Was the Reason for the Particular Order and Kinds of Plagues for the Ten Plagues?

Shemos (7:17) כֹּה אָמַר ה' בְּזֹאת תֵּדַע כִּי אֲנִי ה' הִנֵּה אָנֹכִי מַכֶּה בַּמַּטֶּה אֲשֶׁר בְּיָדִי עַל הַמַּיִם אֲשֶׁר בַּיְאֹר וְנֶהֶפְכוּ לְדָם (ז:יז) So said Hashem, "With this you will know that I am Hashem." Behold, I will smite with the staff that is in my hand upon the water that is in the Nile, and it will turn to blood.

What was the reason for the particular order and kinds of plagues that took place in the ten plagues?

1) The Daas Zekanim on Shemos (11:4) says that the ten plagues parallel what a human King would do when one of his countries or states rebelled against him. The first thing the King would do to stop the rebellion is to block off the rebel's water supply. Hashem did that by turning the Egyptian's

Vaera

water into blood so that they would not have water to drink. The next step is to make a lot of noise by blowing trumpets, and therefore Hashem sent the plague of frogs to make noise even inside the Egyptian's bodies. Next, the King would start shooting arrows to pierce the enemy's bodies, which was why Hashem sent lice to bite and pierce the bodies of the Egyptians. After shooting arrows from a distance, the King next sends in wild animals to cause havoc among the rebels in the hope of squashing the rebellion. Next, the King sends in people to raid and take away their animals, which was done with the plague of pestilence, and the animals were killed. The King next sends in foul-smelling odors to further disgust and demoralize the rebels, which was the purpose of boils that made the Egyptian's bodies foul-smelling and disgusting. Next, the King attacks with a barrage of stones, which was the hail that rained down on the Egyptians. The King next destroys the food supply, which was the purpose of the locusts that ate up all the Egyptian crops. The King then captures the leaders of the rebelling state and puts them into a prison which was the purpose of darkness that imprisoned the Egyptians in their own homes. If that still does not squash the rebellion, the King begins killing the leaders and important people, which was the purpose of killing the firstborns.

2) The Kli Yakor notes that we say in the Hagadah on Pesach: "רַבִּי יְהוּדָה הָיָה נוֹתֵן בָּהֶם סִמָּנִים דְּצַ"ךְ עֲדַ"שׁ בְּאַחַ"ב (Rabi Yehuda referred to them by acronyms: DeTzaCh (blood, frogs, lice); ADaSh (wild animals, pestilence, boils); BeAChaV (hail, locust, darkness, killing of firstborn)). The Abarbanel, Kli Yakor, and Malbim explain that Rabi Yehuda did not just superficially give us three acronyms to remember the plagues by but rather also said that the plagues could be grouped into three groups. In our Posuk, which prefaces the first group, Hashem told Pharaoh that with the first group of plagues, he would come to the proof that "I am Hashem." Similarly, before the second group of plagues which begin with the plague of wild animals, Hashem says in Shemos (8:18) וְהִפְלֵיתִי בַיּוֹם הַהוּא אֶת אֶרֶץ גֹּשֶׁן אֲשֶׁר עַמִּי עֹמֵד עָלֶיהָ לְבִלְתִּי הֱיוֹת שָׁם עָרֹב לְמַעַן תֵּדַע כִּי אֲנִי ה' בְּקֶרֶב הָאָרֶץ (And I will separate on that day the land of Goshen, upon which My people stand, that there will be no mixture of noxious creatures there, in order that you know that I am Hashem in the midst of the earth). Finally, before the third group of plagues which begins with the plague of hail, Hashem says in Shemos (9:14), כִּי בַּפַּעַם הַזֹּאת אֲנִי שֹׁלֵחַ אֶת כָּל מַגֵּפֹתַי אֶל לִבְּךָ וּבַעֲבָדֶיךָ וּבְעַמֶּךָ בַּעֲבוּר תֵּדַע כִּי אֵין כָּמֹנִי בְּכָל הָאָרֶץ (Because this time, I am sending all My plagues into your heart and into your servants and into your people, in order that you know that there is none like Me in the entire earth).

When Moshe first comes to Pharaoh, he says to him in Shemos (5:1) "So said Hashem G-d of Yisroel, 'Send out My people, and let them sacrifice to Me in the desert.'" Pharaoh answers in Shemos (5:2), "Who is Hashem that I should heed His voice to let Yisroel out? I do not know Hashem, neither will I let Yisroel out." The Shemos Raba (5:14) says that when Moshe asked in the name of Hashem, Pharaoh said to wait for a bit while he looked up Hashem's name in his book, which contained a listing of the idols of all the nations. Pharaoh comes back and says that he looked in the entire book, and he does not see Hashem's name anywhere. The Shemos Raba offers a Moshul to the situation in this case. A Kohen once had a foolish servant. The Kohen went traveling, and the servant decided to try and find him. The servant went to a cemetery and started asking people there if they had seen his master. One of the people he asked recognized him and said, "isn't your master a Kohen?" "Yes," answered the servant. "You fool, have you ever seen a

Vaera

Kohen in a cemetery?" exclaimed the person. Similarly, Moshe and Aharon told Pharaoh, "You fool does it make sense to look for a live being in a book about dead beings. Our Hashem is live and the King over the universe, while the idols in your book are dead." In describing the Bnei Yisroel serving idols as a result of Bilam's plan, the Gemorah in Avodah Zora 29b quotes Tehillim (106:28), which says, "They became attached to Baal Peor and ate sacrifices of the dead." The Metzudos Dovid on the Posuk explains that idols are inanimate, powerless, and not alive, like a dead person.

The Kli Yakor says that the bottom line is that Pharaoh did not believe that Hashem was a G-d since Hashem was not listed in Pharaoh's book of G-ds, and therefore the first three plagues proved to him and the Egyptians that Hashem is a G-d. The Shemos Raba (9:9) says that the first plague was against the Nile River because the Egyptians served it as their main idol. It rains very little in Egypt, and the only way they have enough water to exist in Egypt is from the Nile River overflowing its banks and providing water for both humans and their crops to exist on. To stay in its good graces, the Egyptians served the Nile River as their idol. When Hashem turned the water of the Nile River to blood, it showed that Hashem was more powerful than the Egyptian's idol, and therefore Hashem was a G-d. The Gemorah in Pesachim 53b tells us how Chananyah, Mishael, and Azariah convinced themselves that they should allow themselves to be thrown into a fiery furnace in order to sanctify Hashem's name. The Gemorah says that they made a Kal VeChomer of what they should do from what the frogs did in the second plague. They reasoned that if frogs that are not commanded to sanctify Hashem's name nonetheless went into the ovens and kneading bowls of the Egyptians, they, as Jews, commanded to sanctify Hashem's name, should certainly allow themselves to be thrown into the furnace. Concerning the frogs, Shemos (7:28) says, "And the Nile will swarm with frogs, and they will go up and come into your house and into your bedroom and upon your bed and into the house of your servants and into your people, and into your ovens and into your kneading troughs." By going into the ovens and into the kneading troughs, which were subsequently placed in the oven, the frogs allowed themselves to be thrown into a furnace to sanctify Hashem's name. The Egyptians also observed the frogs allowing themselves to be thrown into the ovens and had to conclude that they were only doing this for the purpose of sanctifying Hashem. Finally, in the third plague, that of lice, even the sorcerers, for the first time admitted in Shemos (8:15) that the plague was "the finger of G-d." Based on these three plagues, Pharaoh had to conclude that Hashem was a G-d and at the very least belonged in Pharaoh's book of G-ds.

Now that Hashem proved to Pharaoh and the Egyptians that he indeed was a G-d, the next three plagues, wild animals, pestilence, and hail proved, as the Torah says in introducing these three plagues, "I am Hashem in the midst of the earth." Otherwise, Pharaoh could say that he admits that Hashem is a G-d, but what proof does he have that Hashem takes an interest in what happens on earth and even more so directs what happens here on an individual basis. These three plagues proved that Hashem, on a widespread basis, would direct the plague to only affect those that deserved it. The first plagues of this set, wild animals, are very mobile and naturally move around over large distances. Yet Hashem says in Shemos (8:18), "And I will separate on that day the land of Goshen, upon which My people stand, that there will be no mixture of noxious creatures there." Similarly, by the next plague, pestilence, it says in Shemos (9:4), "And Hashem will make a separation between the livestock of Israel and the livestock of Egypt, and nothing of the Bnei Yisroel will die." Likewise, by boils, despite the fact that Shemos (9:8) says that Moshe performed the plagues by throwing soot up into the skies which ostensibly could fly on anyone, Shemos (9:11) says, "the boils were upon the sorcerers and upon all Egypt." Even more so, says the Kli Yakor, by saying that the boils were "upon the sorcerers and upon all Egypt," implies that the boils first came on the sorcerers before the rest of the Egyptians. The boils first came on the sorcerers because, until this plague, they had helped Pharaoh harden his heart by showing that they also could copy the plagues. Therefore, in all the three plagues of this set, Hashem showed that he directed the plague precisely to only those who deserved to be affected by the plagues. After these three plagues, Pharaoh was forced to conclude that not only was Hashem a G-d, but Hashem was a G-d who directs what happens on the earth on an individual basis.

Finally, in the last set of plagues, Hashem proved to Pharaoh and the Egyptians "that there is none like Hashem in the entire earth." That is, not only is Hashem a G-d, and not only is Hashem a G-d who directs what happens on the earth on an individual basis, but in addition, there is no other idol that has any power. When the Egyptians worshipped idols, like the sheep, it didn't mean that they were so naïve to believe that an animal had any power but rather that the power in heaven who controlled the sheep on this world was the idol. They reasoned that by making the sheep holy, they would be in good graces of the power in heaven who controlled the sheep since they were making his sheep holy. Therefore, says the Kli Yakor, in all of the plagues of this third and final set, the sky was completely covered, and all heavenly forces which the Egyptians served were powerless in uncovering the sky and could not counteract the plague that was happening because of the covered sky. In the plague of hail, though the Torah does not say it explicitly, it stands to reason that the sky was all covered in clouds to facilitate the hail, and therefore neither the sun nor any of the constellations could be seen. In the plague of locusts, there were so many of them that one could not see neither other parts of the earth or the sky as Shemos (10:5) says, "And they (the locusts) will obscure the view of the earth, and no one will be able to see the earth." The plague of darkness obviously blocked out any light from the sun or the constellations; otherwise, it would not have been so dark. Though in Rabi Yehuda's acronyms, the last set includes the plague of the killing of the firstborns, the Malbim says that different than the first nine plagues, the plague of the killing of the firstborns was not meant to punish the Egyptians but rather to force the Egyptians to let the Bnei Yisroel go free.

The Abarbanel, in his Sefer on the Hagadah Shel Pesach called Zevach Pesach, the Malbim, and Rav Hirsch say that the grouping of Rabi Yehuda into acronyms DeTzaCh (blood, frogs, lice); ADaSh (wild animals, pestilence, boils); BeAChaV (hail, locust, darkness, killing of firstborn)) also emphasizes that in each of these sets, the third plague (lice, boils, and darkness) came without any previous warning that the plague was about to occur. The Malbim explains that since each of the three groups came to prove a point about Hashem, it is enough to bring two proofs, just like one brings two witnesses to prove some fact. Lice, boils, and darkness came to punish the Egyptians, and since none of these plagues are life-threatening, there was no need for a warning. Rav Hirsch explains that the third plague of each set (lice, boils, and darkness) just came as punishment for Pharaoh and the Egyptians for not listening to the first two plagues in the set. The Malbim also

Vaera

points out that Moshe came to warn Pharaoh early in the morning when he went out to bathe in the Nile River for the first plague of each of the three sets. For the second plague in each set (frogs, pestilence, and locusts), Moshe went to Pharaoh's palace to warn him, in front of all his servants who were in the palace. In this way, it would be known to all Pharaoh's servants and thereby the entire country that Moshe had given a warning about the upcoming plague.

3) In the Bris Bain HaBesorim, Hashem tells Avrohom in Shemos (15:13) יָדֹעַ תֵּדַע כִּי גֵר יִהְיֶה זַרְעֲךָ בְּאֶרֶץ לֹא לָהֶם וַעֲבָדוּם וְעִנּוּ אֹתָם אַרְבַּע מֵאוֹת שָׁנָה (You shall surely know that your seed will be strangers in a land that is not theirs, and they will enslave them and oppress them, for four hundred years). From this Posuk, we see that there will be three stages of slavery (being strangers in a strange land, being enslaved, and being oppressed). Rav Hirsch says that the reason Rabi Yehuda referred to them by acronyms: DeTzaCh (blood, frogs, lice); ADaSh (wild animals, pestilence, boils); BeAChaV (hail, locust, darkness, killing of firstborn)), is because each of these sets corresponds to these three stages of slavery. Each of these sets proves the falseness of the premise of the Egyptians that they had a right to use these three stages of slavery against us, and brought home to the Egyptians the misery they gave to the Bnei Yisroel in each of these three stages.

The first plague in each set (blood, wild animals, and hail) showed the Egyptians how they themselves were no better than strangers in the land of Egypt and how little justification they could find for treating the Bnei Yisroel as strangers. A stranger is someone whose stay in a country is dependent on the goodwill and tolerance of others. The Egyptians, because of the annual overflowing of the Nile River, felt more secure and prouder than any other nation. They did not even have to worry about rain and therefore felt themselves independent of heaven. With the plague of blood, Hashem showed the Egyptians that if he wanted, he could change the Nile River from giving blessings to bringing foulness and disease and driving them out of the land since the disease made the land unlivable. The plague of blood showed that it was only the goodwill and tolerance of Hashem which allowed the Egyptians to stay in Egypt. Wild animals stay away from where people are living only because of the decree of Hashem in Beraishis (9:2) "And your fear and your dread shall be upon all the beasts of the earth." Hashem has only to give the word, and the barrier falls, and in his own house, Man is no longer secure. Moreover, in the plague of wild animals, the only land that the wild animals respected and kept away from was the land of Goshen, whose inhabitants, the Bnei Yisroel, are treated by the Egyptians as strangers without any rights to the land. In the plague of hail, Hashem showed the Egyptians that he could change the entire climatic conditions of the land. Egypt, which has very little moisture from the atmosphere and rather gets its moisture from the Nile River, for the first time gets a gigantic storm of hail, and suddenly its whole atmospheric nature has changed. With its first storm of hail, Egypt has the threatened possibility of becoming changed into an entirely different country, and only with the consent of Hashem could the Egyptians continue living there in the way they were accustomed to.

The second plague in each set (frogs, pestilence, and locusts) showed the Egyptians how they had no right to enslave the Bnei Yisroel. Two false ideas fill the mind of the slave owner with a conceit that his superiority over a slave is justified. First is that he belongs to an altogether higher order of beings, and second is the idea of haughty superiority due to power and riches. The frog, one of the

Vaera

most timorous and remote of animals, now leaves its secluded retreat and boldly enters the domain of the humans, hops up even on the sacred person of his Majesty, Pharaoh, himself and so teaches the Egyptians how even one of the lowest and smallest animals has lost all respect for them. The frogs show the Egyptians that they have no reason for their arrogance. The plague of pestilence kills the Egyptian horses, the pride and renown of Egypt, and also kills their donkeys and camels, which are their beasts of burden, along with killing their cattle and flocks, which are their riches and meat food supply. Finally, the locusts came and finished off all the fruit and produce of Egypt. Without food or possessions, the Egyptians could not justifiably enslave the Bnei Yisroel due to the Egyptians power and riches.

The third plague in each set (lice, boils, and darkness) came to inflict the Egyptians with excruciating pain and show them how the Bnei Yisroel felt when they were made to lead a harassed, painful, and starving life. Both lice and boils cause much pain and affliction. Darkness imprisoned the Egyptians in their own houses along with causing them to go without food since they were incapable of moving from their positions. During the plague of darkness, they sat there chained to the spot and went hungry until Hashem gave them light again.

Where Did the Egyptian Sorcerers Get Water From to Turn Into Blood If There Was Blood Throughout Egypt?

וְהַדָּגָה אֲשֶׁר בַּיְאֹר מֵתָה וַיִּבְאַשׁ הַיְאֹר וְלֹא יָכְלוּ מִצְרַיִם לִשְׁתּוֹת מַיִם מִן הַיְאֹר וַיְהִי הַדָּם בְּכָל אֶרֶץ מִצְרָיִם. וַיַּעֲשׂוּ כֵן חַרְטֻמֵּי מִצְרַיִם בְּלָטֵיהֶם וַיֶּחֱזַק לֵב פַּרְעֹה וְלֹא שָׁמַע אֲלֵהֶם כַּאֲשֶׁר דִּבֶּר ה' (ז':כא-כב) Shemos (7:21-22) And the fish that were in the Nile died, and the Nile became putrid; the Egyptians could not drink water from the Nile, and there was blood throughout the entire land of Egypt. And the sorcerers of Egypt did likewise with their secret rites, and Pharaoh's heart was steadfast, and he did not heed them, as Hashem had spoken.

Where did the Egyptian sorcerers get water from to turn into blood if there was blood throughout the entire land of Egypt?

Introduction
The Zohar in Shemos 29a says that when it is decreed that blood should be brought on a nation, it comes through another nation attacking them and killing some of them. However, since the Bnei Yisroel were living among the Egyptians, Hashem did not want to bring another nation to attack the Egyptians. Instead, Hashem brought the plague of blood so that the Bnei Yisroel would not be affected by the decree of blood against the Egyptians.

Assuming that the purpose of the plague was so that the Egyptians would not have any water to drink, the Hegyona Shel Torah ponders why Hashem didn't just make the water very bitter tasting to accomplish the same goal in a less miraculous way. The Ramban in Parshas Noach writes that it was a miracle that Noach's Ark held Noach, his family, and all the animals since, in reality, even an ark ten times as big as the one Noach made could not have held all the animals. If saving everyone was a miracle anyway, why did Hashem make Noach spend 120 years making a big ark instead of

Vaera

just having Noach make a small ark and not spend so much time and energy making a gigantic ark? He answers that Hashem always does a miracle in the most natural way possible so that the miracle would be as minimum as possible. As a result, Hashem has the people do the most that they can do, and for the rest, Hashem makes a miracle. In a similar way, Hashem could have minimized taking away all drinking water from the Egyptians by making the water very bitter and undrinkable instead of the much bigger miracle of turning all the water into blood. The Hegyona Shel Torah answers that there is another principle which is that Hashem punishes measure for measure. The Egyptians, in their cruelty, shed much blood of the Bnei Yisroel. Shemos (2:23) says, "Now it came to pass in those many days that the King of Egypt died, and the Bnei Yisroel sighed from the labor, and they cried out, and their cry ascended to G-d from the labor." The Targum Yonason ben Uziel on this Posuk and the Shemos Raba (1:34) tells us that Pharaoh did not die but rather got leprosy. The Shemos Raba says that Pharoah's sorcerers told him that the only way to be cured was for him to slaughter 150 Jewish children in the morning and another 150 Jewish children in the evening and bathe in their blood. As a measure for measure punishment for all the Jewish blood, the Midrash Lekach Tov and the Hegyona Shel Torah say Hashem turned all the Egyptian water to blood. Similarly, the Abarbanel says that the reason Hashem brought the plague of blood was that the Egyptians had killed the Bnei Yisroel's baby boys by throwing them into the Nile River so that they were killed, and figuratively, their blood was spilled in the Nile River.

The Midrash Lekach Tov and the Toldos Yitzchak observe that different from what happened in Noach's flood, the fish were killed in this plague. The Toldos Yitzchak says that the fish as property of the Egyptians were killed since the Egyptians sinned by throwing the Bnei Yisroel's baby boys into the Nile River, where the fish ate the bodies of the babies. With regard to the flood, Beraishis Raba (28:8) writes that everyone corrupted their way in the generation of the flood. The dog mated with the wolf, and the chicken mated with the turkey. That is why Beraishis (6:12) says that "all flesh," i.e., everyone was corrupt and not just all humans were corrupt. That is also why not only all the humans but also all the animals were destroyed by the flood. Since the fish did not mate with other species, that is why only the animals and not the fish were killed during the flood.

The Shemos Raba (9:11) presents three different opinions with regard to the extent of the plague of blood. Rav Yehuda says that the water that was in the Nile River turned to blood. In Shemos (7:19), Hashem tells Moshe to tell Aharon, "Take your staff and stretch forth your hand over the waters of Egypt, over their rivers, over their canals, over their ponds, and over all their bodies of water, and they will become blood, and there will be blood throughout the entire land of Egypt, even in wood and in stone." Therefore, says the Maharzav, Rav Yehuda does not mean to say that there was only blood in the Nile River but rather that water below ground did not turn to blood. Rav Nechemia says that both water above ground and below ground was turned to blood. Rav Yehuda questions Rav Nechemia's opinion from Shemos (7:24), which says, "All the Egyptians dug around the Nile for water to drink because they could not drink from the water of the Nile." This Posuk implies that there indeed was water to drink below ground. Rav Nechemia replied that the Egyptians thought that they could find water below ground since a sorcerer can only perform their sorcery on objects that they can see. Thinking that Moshe and Aharon had, Chas VeShalom, also performed sorcery, the desperate Egyptians tried to find water by digging below ground. To their

Vaera

disappointment, no matter how deep they dug, the Egyptians only found blood underground. The third opinion is Rav Yossi, who says that all flowing bodies of water turned to blood. Rav Yossi says that this excluded water found in pits, ditches, and caves.

We have previously quoted the Posuk, which says, "there will be blood throughout the entire land of Egypt, even in wood and in stone." The Shemos Raba presents two opinions as to what blood in wood and in stone means. The first opinion, which is consistent with the opinion of Rav Nechemia that all water turned to blood, is that it refers to water found in wooden and stone bowls. The Shemos Raba and Tanah D'Bay Eliyahu (7) say that when an Egyptian tried to drink any water, it turned to blood. For example, if an Egyptian and a Jew resided in the same house, and there was water gathered on the roof, if the Egyptian filled up his pitcher, it immediately turned to blood. When the Jew gathered some of this water into his pitcher and drank it, it was water. Seeing this, the Egyptian asked the Jew for some water from his pitcher. When he got the water and tried to drink it, the water was blood. The Egyptian then asked the Jew to pour some water into a special vessel which had two places, one on each end, where two people could suck up the water similar to a modern straw. The Egyptian asked that they both drink simultaneously from this vessel. To his disappointment, the Jew sucked up water, and the Egyptian sucked up blood from this vessel. The only way the Egyptians were able to drink water was if they bought the water from the Jews. By selling the Egyptians water, says the Shemos Raba, the Jews became wealthy during the plague of blood. Even seats made of wood and stone like those found in a bathroom or a bathhouse were all covered in blood so that when an Egyptian sat on them, all the clothes became ruined with the blood. The other opinion, which is consistent with the opinion of Rav Yossi and Rav Yehuda, is that wood and stone is referring to the Egyptian idols, which were made of wood and stone. The Maharzav says that even though the idols were not a place that normally had water, they had blood on them. The Yepheh Toar explains to show that Hashem not only smote the Nile River with blood which was one of the Egyptian idols but also all the rest of the Egyptian idols.

The Ksav VeHakabola points out that making even the wooden and stone bowls turn to blood was also a calamity for another reason. He quotes the scientific community in Egypt who discovered that even when the water of the Nile River is polluted, if that water is placed in wooden or stone bowls for several days, the contamination completely separates itself from the water, making the water drinkable. By making the plague of blood affect even the wooden and stone bowls, Hashem took away this method of purifying their water so that the Egyptians would not have what to drink.

The Shemos Raba (9:9) says that the first plague was against the Nile River because the Egyptians served it as their main idol. It rains very little in Egypt, and the only way they have enough water to exist in Egypt is from the Nile River overflowing its banks and providing water for both humans and their crops to exist on. Hashem first wanted to send a plague against the Egyptian idol, so the Egyptians would realize that their idols could not protect them from the plagues of Hashem. Not only couldn't their idol, the Nile River, protect them but, says the Malbim, in the plague of blood, it was the one that sent destruction by flowing blood over all the land of Egypt along with killing their main source of food, fish.

Vaera

The Daas Zekanim ponders why it was necessary for the Torah to tell us, "And the fish that were in the Nile died, and the Nile became putrid; the Egyptians could not drink water from the Nile." The Daas Zekanim and the Ksav VeHakabola say that since Gentiles drank blood, they would have something to drink even when all the water turned to blood. However, since the fish also died, the water which had turned to blood became putrid and undrinkable even for people who would otherwise drink blood. Being that the real plague was that the water was undrinkable because of the dead fish, the Daas Zekanim ponders why we do not refer to this plague as the plague of the dead fish. He answers that since the most obvious visible thing that happened was that the water turned to blood, the plague is referred to as the plague of blood.

In Shemos (7:15), Hashem tells Moshe, "Go to Pharaoh in the morning; behold, he is going forth to the water, and you shall stand opposite him on the bank of the Nile." The Shemos Raba (9:8) and the Midrash Tanchuma in Vaera (14) tell us that Pharaoh went every morning to the Nile River to bathe. In addition, Pharaoh pretended that he was a G-d and told everyone that he did not have to take care of his bodily needs. Instead, Pharaoh would use the time that he was bathing in the Nile River to secretly relieve himself and take care of his bodily needs. The Yalkut Shimoni (182) and the Maharzav say that Hashem told Moshe to show Pharaoh that he was pretending to everyone about not needing to take care of his bodily needs. Moshe grabbed hold of Pharaoh to prevent him from going into the Nile River. Pharaoh asked Moshe to let go of him so that he could take care of his bodily needs. Moshe told Pharaoh, "is it possible that a God, like you are pretending to be, has bodily needs?" The Targum Yonason ben Uziel on Shemos (7:23) says that Pharaoh could not control himself and took care of his physical needs in public after being stopped by Moshe. The Yalkut Yehuda quoting a Sefas Emes tells us another version of how Pharaoh embarrassed himself. After the Nile was turned to blood, there was obviously no sensible possibility or point of Pharaoh bathing in the Nile River since it was now blood. That being the case, by then being desperate, Pharoah took care of his bodily needs in front of everyone who was there and then headed back to the Palace. Interestingly enough, Pharaoh still did not stop pretending even after this happened in front of everyone.

The Gemorah in Sotah 11a says that the plague of frogs first affected Pharaoh because he was the first to offer the suggestion to begin enslaving the Jews in the beginning of Parshas Shemos. The Gemorah also says that according to one opinion, the Pharaoh that offered the suggestion was the same Pharaoh who appointed Yosef as viceroy over Egypt. The Ponim Yofos puts these two facts together to say that the present Pharaoh was the same Pharaoh who had been given a Brocha from Yaakov that the Nile should rise up when Pharaoh walked up to it. Pharaoh was very happy with this Brocha of Yaakov since it caused the famine to end, especially since it allowed him to get the Nile to flow towards him and thereby water all of Egypt. However, it caused a big problem when the Nile River turned to blood since now the blood rushed up from the Nile River to Pharaoh. That is why instead of spending time at the Nile River as he usually did, Pharaoh quickly went back to his Palace as Shemos (7:23) says, "Pharaoh turned and went home, and he paid no heed even to this." We note that the Chizkuni also says that Pharaoh went to the Nile River every morning because it rose up when he came to it.

Vaera

The Pirkei D'Rabi Eliezer (9) and the Yalkut Shimoni in Sefer Yona (450) both say that the plague of blood, as well as the day the Bnei Yisroel went out of Egypt, were both on a Thursday. The Malbim, in his Sefer Eretz Chemdah, calculates how we can figure this out and how both events are intertwined to be able to calculate this. Since the Bnei Yisroel went out on the first day of Pesach, which is on the 15th day of the month of Nisan, and it was a Thursday, it implies that the first day of Nisan (Rosh Chodesh) was also on a Thursday. Since Rosh Chodesh Iyar is always two days, Rosh Chodesh Iyar was on a Friday and Shabbos in the year the Bnei Yisroel went out of Egypt and that the first day of Iyar was on a Shabbos. The Malbim quotes a Raavad that the ten plagues began in Iyar since, just like wicked people are judged for a period of twelve months after their death, so the Egyptians were punished in Egypt. Assuming a normal Hebrew calendar year where alternate months are 29 and 30 days implies that the Hebrew year contained six times 29 plus six times 30 days for a sum total of 354 days. A 354-day year is composed of 50 weeks and four days. This implies that if the first day of Iyar was on a Shabbos in the year, the Bnei Yisroel went out of Egypt that it fell four days before or on a Tuesday in the previous year when the plagues began. Shemos (7:25) tells us that the plague of blood lasted for seven days and the Shemos Raba (9:12) on this Posuk says that Moshe warned Pharaoh for 24 days before the plague came. We have calculated that the first day of Iyar was on a Tuesday, which implies that the 22nd day was also on a Tuesday, which makes the 24th day when the plague of blood started on a Thursday. That, says the Malbim, is how we know that the plague of blood started on a Thursday.

The Oznayim LeTorah ponders why the Egyptians didn't use the Jewish slaves to dig for water around the Nile and rather did the digging themselves. He says that it would seem from this question that with the plague of blood, the Jews were no longer forced to work. He also says that even if the Jews were still working for the Egyptians, we could still understand why the Jews were not used to dig for water. We have mentioned before in the introduction that the Egyptians found out that any water given to them by a Jew would turn to blood. Therefore, there would be no point in having the Jews digging for the water since it would turn to blood when they handed it over to the Egyptians.

1) We have mentioned in the introduction that both according to the opinion of Rav Yehuda and according to the opinion of Rav Yossi, not all water in Egypt was turned to blood. According to Rav Yehuda, only water above ground was turned into blood, and according to Rav Yossi, even non-flowing water like that found in pits, ditches, and caves did not turn into blood. Though this only provided limited water for the Egyptians, the Eben Ezra, Rabeinu Bechay, Ralbag, Toldos Yitzchak, Ohr HaChaim, and Malbim all say that our question does not begin according to Rav Yehuda or Rav Yossi since the sorcerers could have turned this water into blood. Much effort had to be expended, especially for the underground water, which is consistent with Shemos (7:18), which says, "the Egyptians will get weary in their efforts to drink water from the Nile." Rav Hirsch also says that only that water that was physically connected to the Nile River became blood. He says that water in wells did not become blood since they are not connected to the Nile River. Therefore, the sorcerers could have used water from wells. It would seem that the Egyptians did not have an abundance of wells and that they more typically used the water of the Nile River for their drinking water. Otherwise, the plague would not have had much effect on the Egyptians.

Vaera

The Daas Zekanim says that if we use Rav Yehuda's opinion to say that the sorcerers used water that was obtained by digging underground around the Nile River, there is a chronological problem in how the Torah presents what happened. The Torah tells us first in Shemos (7:22) that the sorcerers also turned water into blood. Only two Pesukim later (7:24) does the Torah tell us, "All the Egyptians dug around the Nile for water to drink because they could not drink from the water of the Nile."

2) The Targum Yonason ben Uziel provides an answer to our question. He says that the sorcerers used water from Goshen and turned it into blood. It is not clear to me if he is of the same opinion as the Shemos Raba and Tanah D'Bay Eliyahu we presented in the introduction that when an Egyptian took water and tried to drink it, the water turned to blood. If he is of this opinion, then the sorcerers had to not try to drink the water since everyone knew that it turned to blood for every Egyptian if they tried to drink it. Alternatively, we will see later that many Meforshim say that the sorcerers used sleight of hand to change the water into blood. All they had to do was secretly try to drink it for the water to turn into blood.

3) Rabeinu Bechay, the Malbim, and the Ksav VeHakabola tell us about a general rule that Rabeinu Saadia Gaon speaks about. From the perspective of man, there are two types of water. One is drinkable water, and the other is non-drinkable water like saltwater which is found in an ocean. Rabeinu Saadia Gaon ponders the question of how the Egyptians survived for seven days without drinking water. He answers that the Egyptians drank non-drinkable water like saltwater during that time.

In Shemos (7:19) Aharon was commanded to קַח מַטְּךָ וּנְטֵה יָדְךָ עַל מֵימֵי מִצְרַיִם עַל נַהֲרֹתָם עַל יְאֹרֵיהֶם וְעַל אַגְמֵיהֶם וְעַל כָּל מִקְוֵה מֵימֵיהֶם וְיִהְיוּ דָם וְהָיָה דָם בְּכָל אֶרֶץ מִצְרַיִם וּבָעֵצִים וּבָאֲבָנִים (Take your staff and stretch forth your hand over the waters of Egypt, over their rivers, over their canals, over their ponds, and over all their bodies of water, and they will become blood, and there will be blood throughout the entire land of Egypt, even in wood and in stone). Rabeinu Saadia Gaon says that when referring to water, there is a big difference when a Posuk says מֵי or מֵימֵי. מֵי refers to all water which includes drinkable and non-drinkable water while מֵימֵי (a word with two Mems) only refers to water suitable for drinking. For example, when the Torah refers to the drinking water from the well of Miriam in the desert, Bamidbar (20:8) says, וְנָתַן מֵימָיו. When Hashem says that if we follow in his ways, Hashem will bless our food and (drinking) water, Shemos (23:25) says וּבֵרַךְ אֶת לַחְמְךָ וְאֶת מֵימֶיךָ. In Megilas Eichah (5:4), when the Megilah describes that drinking water was so scarce that they had to purchase it, it says מֵימֵינוּ בְּכֶסֶף שָׁתִינוּ. On the other hand, with regard to the waters of Noach's flood, which was not necessarily drinking water, Braishis (7:7) says that Noach was forced to enter the Ark because of the floodwater. In that case, the Torah says מִפְּנֵי מֵי הַמַּבּוּל. Similarly, when the Torah describes the water of the Red Sea drowning the Egyptians, Shemos (15:19) says וַיָּשֶׁב ה' עֲלֵהֶם אֶת מֵי הַיָּם. Rav Saadia Gaon does point out that sometimes the Jordan River is referred to as מֵי and other times as מֵימֵי. He says that the reason for using both words is because parts of the Jordan River contain drinkable water while other parts are not drinkable. When our Posuk says that Aharon stretched his hand and changed the water of Egypt into blood, it uses the term for drinkable water

Vaera

(מֵימֵיהֶם). From here, we derive that the plague of blood was not on non-drinkable water, and it was this water that the sorcerers changed to blood.

4) The Daas Zekanim, Ponim Yofos, and Oznayim LeTorah answer our question similarly. They say that they brought it from a different place or land. The Oznayim LeTorah explains how this could be. The Nile River is one of the few rivers that flow north. The reason it flows north is that its source of water is from high elevation lakes in Africa, and since Egypt is at a much lower elevation, the Nile River flows from central Africa till it empties into the Mediterranean Sea. Among the countries it flows through are Ethiopia, Congo, Sudan, and Kenya. Obviously, the Nile River only turned to blood when it entered Egypt. In present-day countries, the Nile River enters Egypt through the country of Sudan. The Oznayim LeTorah says that sorcerers went to the border when the Nile came into Egypt, and at the border, they performed their sorcery of turning the water into blood. We will later see that many commentators are of the opinion that the sorcerers used sleight of hand to turn the water into blood. Being that they were right next to the border where Hashem turned the water to blood, it is not hard to imagine that they could have used sleight of hand to pretend that it was they who were turning the water to blood when it was really happening through Hashem.

5) The Chizkuni, Bechor Shor, and Moshav Zekanim, as quoted by the Taam V'Daas, answer our question similarly. They say that at the beginning of the plague, all the water of Egypt turned into blood. Because of this, the fish in the Nile all died, and the water became polluted and undrinkable. Soon after this, Hashem turned the water in the Nile River back into water, though it was still undrinkable because of the dead fish. Being that it hardly rains in Egypt, it is the Nile River's water that fed the rivers, ponds, and canals. The Nile River's water, polluted from the dead fish, fed into these other water sources, both slowly changing the blood back to water and spreading the polluted water into these other water sources. The Chizkuni and Bechor Shor say that this is what Shemos (7:21) means when it says, "And the fish that were in the Nile died, and the Nile became putrid; the Egyptians could not drink water from the Nile, and there was blood throughout the entire land of Egypt." That is the reason the Egyptians could not drink the water from the Nile because it was polluted, and in addition, there was blood in the other sources of water. That is also why the next Posuk is understandable when it says, "And the sorcerers of Egypt did likewise with their secret rites, and Pharaoh's heart was steadfast, and he did not heed them, as Hashem had spoken." The Chizkuni and Bechor Shor say that the sorcerers used the polluted water of the Nile River to change it back into blood, and the fact that the sorcerers had water is proof that the Nile River turned back to water. The Tur also says that it took seven days for the putrid water to become drinkable again.

6) The Ohr HaChaim, Alshich, Ponim Yofos, and Eitz Yosef, on the Midrash Tanchuma, answer our question similarly. They say that the sorcerers bought water from the Jews and used that water to turn into blood.

7) The Midrash Lekach Tov, Rabeinu Bechay, Eben Ezra, and Ohr HaChaim all say that the sorcerers used sleight of hand to turn the water into blood. Rabeinu Bechay explains what they did. In Shemos (7:17), Moshe is told to tell Pharaoh, "Behold, I will smite with the staff that is in my

Vaera

hand upon the water that is in the Nile, and it will turn to blood." In addition, Hashem tells Moshe to tell Aharon in Shemos (7:19) "'Take your staff and stretch forth your hand over the waters of Egypt, over their rivers, over their canals, over their ponds, and over all their bodies of water, and they will become blood, and there will be blood throughout the entire land of Egypt, even in wood and in stone." Therefore, says Rabeinu Bechay, there were two parts to the plague. First, Aharon used Moshe's staff to smite the water in the Nile River. Subsequently, Aharon waved his staff in all four directions to cause all the rest of the water in Egypt to turn into blood. Since the sorcerers were told that there would be two parts to the plague, they quickly went to one of the other bodies of water, as opposed to the Nile River, and when Aharon waved the staff in their direction, they pretended that it was them and not Aharon who was changing the water to blood. Parenthetically the Ohr HaChaim points out that since the fish died, it was obvious that Aharon was not, Chas VeShalom, using any sleight of hand in this plague and that the water becoming blood through Aharon was not an illusion.

8) Rav Sternbuch, in his Sefer Taam V'Daas, also presents an answer to our question. He says that only the water of the Nile River was totally changed to blood. The rivers, ponds, and canals got blood by being fed from the blood of the Nile River. Therefore, their water was a mixture of blood and water. It was this water blood mixture, which the sorcerers used to turn into blood. It would also not be hard to imagine that all the sorcerers had to do was take out some of the water so that the blood water mixture became blood.

The Gevuras Yitzchak explains that there were two aspects to the plague of blood. One aspect was to show the power of Hashem that he could change water into blood. The Nile River was used to show this power. The second aspect was to punish the Egyptians such that they would have no drinkable water. The rivers, ponds, and canals were used for this purpose, and for this purpose, it was enough that they got blood in their water from the Nile River without having the supernatural miracle of water being turned to blood.

Why Did Moshe Need to Daven by Crying Out in the Plague of Frogs?

Shemos (8:8) וַיֵּצֵא מֹשֶׁה וְאַהֲרֹן מֵעִם פַּרְעֹה וַיִּצְעַק מֹשֶׁה אֶל ה' עַל דְּבַר הַצְפַרְדְּעִים אֲשֶׁר שָׂם לְפַרְעֹה (ח:ח) And Moshe and Aharon went away from Pharaoh, and Moshe cried out to Hashem concerning the frogs that He had brought upon Pharaoh.

Why did Moshe need to daven by crying out in the plague of frogs?

Introduction
The Toldos Yitzchak and Maharil Diskin point out that in all the other plagues when Moshe davened that the plague should end, the Torah does not describe the davening as "crying out." For example, in Shemos (8:26) and Shemos (10:18), after the plague of the wild animals and locusts respectably it says, וַיֵּצֵא מֹשֶׁה מֵעִם פַּרְעֹה וַיֶּעְתַּר אֶל ה' (So Moshe went away from Pharaoh and davened to Hashem). After the plague of hail, Shemos (9:33) describes Moshe's davening as וַיִּפְרֹשׂ כַּפָּיו אֶל ה' (and he spread out his hands to Hashem).

Vaera

In Shemos (8:5) Moshe makes an offer to Pharaoh הִתְפָּאֵר עָלַי לְמָתַי אַעְתִּיר לְךָ וְלַעֲבָדֶיךָ וּלְעַמְּךָ לְהַכְרִית הַצְפַרְדְּעִים מִמְּךָ וּמִבָּתֶּיךָ רַק בַּיְאֹר תִּשָּׁאַרְנָה ("Glorify yourself over me. For when shall I entreat for you, for your servants, and for your people, to destroy the frogs from you and from your houses, that they should remain only in the Nile River?") Pharaoh responds in the next Posuk "tomorrow," And he (Moshe) said, "As you say, in order that you should know that there is none like Hashem, our G-d." There is a difference of opinion as to whether Moshe immediately davened after Pharaoh requested that the plague of frogs should stop tomorrow or whether Moshe waited until the next day to daven to Hashem to remove the plague of frogs. Rashi, the Ralbag, and the Ohr HaChaim are of the opinion that Moshe davened immediately. Rashi proves his opinion by the fact that the Torah uses the terminology לְמָתַי אַעְתִּיר לְךָ (for when shall I daven for you) instead of מָתַי אַעְתִּיר לְךָ (when shall I daven for you). The Ohr HaChaim says that davening today that the plague should be removed tomorrow is an unheard-of request to a deity. Moshe wanted to show that Hashem would accept even such a request. That is why Moshe tells Pharaoh in Shemos (8: 6), "As you say, in order that you should know that there is none like Hashem, our G-d.'" that by having such a request come true, Hashem will show that he is greater than any deity Pharaoh has worshipped.

The Ramban is of the opinion Moshe waited and davened the next day that the plague should be removed immediately. The Ramban proves his opinion by referencing Shemos (8:9) after Moshe davened, saying, "And Hashem did according to Moshe's word, and the frogs died from the houses, from the courtyards, and from the fields." Had Moshe done as Rashi says, i.e., davened immediately that the frogs should be removed the next day, the Ramban says that the Torah would have instead said, "and the frogs died the next day from the houses, from the courtyards, and from the fields." As to Rashi's proof from the Torah using the terminology לְמָתַי אַעְתִּיר לְךָ (for when shall I daven for you), the Ramban cites several examples where using the Hebrew letter ל in front of the word does not mean "for." For example, a few Pesukim after our Posuk, Shemos (8:19) says, לְמָחָר יִהְיֶה הָאֹת הַזֶּה (tomorrow this sign will come about). The ל in front of this phrase does not mean that anything was done now for the sign to occur tomorrow, says the Ramban.

It seems crazy that Pharaoh would want to suffer an extra day with the plague of frogs, so it is perplexing why he asked that they only be removed the next day. The Eben Ezra quotes Rav Shmuel ben Chofni, who lived during the time of the Gaonim, who says that Pharaoh thought the reason Moshe made this offer was that Moshe knew that the plague was going to end by itself immediately. Since Pharaoh also assumed Moshe was certain that Pharaoh would choose to have the plague over immediately, Pharaoh chose the next day in hopes of proving Moshe wrong. Proving Moshe wrong was far more important to Pharaoh than putting up with the plague for another day. The Yismach Moshe presents another reason why Pharaoh wanted to wait until the next day. Shemos (8:4) tells us how Pharaoh called Moshe and Aharon to daven and stop the plague because he could not withstand its pain. A good number of people saw Moshe and Aharon being summoned to Pharaoh, and if the plague immediately stopped when they went out of the palace, the people would assume that the plague ceased through Moshe and Aharon's davening. This would thereby cause a big sanctification of Hashem's name since they knew that their idols could not do such a thing. The last thing that Pharaoh wanted was that he should cause a sanctification of

Vaera

Hashem's name. Since Pharaoh was given a choice as to when the plague should stop, he told Moshe and Aharon that it should stop the next day. In this way, the people would not associate Moshe and Aharon's coming and praying with the end of the plague and would not cause a sanctification of Hashem's name.

The Abarbanel and Ohr HaChaim point out that the plague of frogs was the first plague that affected Pharaoh personally. In the plague of blood, Pharaoh could get water either by having his servants dig into the earth for water or buying it from the Bnei Yisroel, neither method being a problem for the King nor personally affecting him. However, as the Shemos Raba (10:3) points out, the Torah makes it quite clear that the plague of frogs was sent to attack Pharaoh first. Shemos (7:28-29) say, "And the Nile will swarm with frogs, and they will go up and come into your house and into your bedroom and upon your bed and into the house of your servants and into your people, and into your ovens and into your kneading troughs. Into you and into your people and into all your servants, the frogs will ascend." These Pesukim make it quite clear that the frogs will first go to Pharoah's palace and, in fact, also go into his bed before they subsequently attack Pharoah's servants and, lastly, the rest of the Egyptians. The Shemos Raba (10:6) says that the frogs went into the Egyptian's bodies either together with their drinks or food and, once there, made noises in their bodies which were extremely painful for the Egyptians. The Zohar in Shemos 29b explains that the frogs went into the ovens and then made their way into the bread that was baking. These frogs remained alive, and when the Egyptians ate the bread, they went into the stomachs of the Egyptians and made terrible noises.

The Malbim ponders what הִתְפָּאֵר עָלַי (Glorify yourself over me) means in our context. The Malbim points out that in Sefer Shoftim (7:2) Hashem tells Gidon, רַב הָעָם אֲשֶׁר אִתָּךְ מִתִּתִּי אֶת מִדְיָן בְּיָדָם פֶּן יִתְפָּאֵר עָלַי יִשְׂרָאֵל לֵאמֹר יָדִי הוֹשִׁיעָה לִּי (The people that are with you are too numerous for Me to give the Midyanites into their hand, lest Yisroel glorify themselves against Me, saying, 'My own hand has saved me). In the end, Hashem tells Gidon to take 300 people into battle so that the Bnei Yisroel will realize that it was Hashem who caused the victory over the Midyanites. In the same way that if many people went into battle against the Midyanites, the Bnei Yisroel would question the ability of Hashem to perform a miracle, Pharaoh also questioned Hashem's ability to perform a miracle. To prove the plague of frogs was a miracle, Moshe told Pharaoh that (1) he should choose the time the plague would stop, (2) just like the plague started from Pharaoh and then spread to his servants and all of Egypt; similarly, when it stopped, it would first stop from Pharaoh and then from his servants, (3) that the frogs should not disappear entirely from Egypt but should rather continue living in the Nile River and provide a reminder about the plague of frogs. The Abarbanel and Malbim say that the frogs were not normal frogs, but rather crocodiles that had not before lived in the Nile River. As a reminder of the plague and as a warning to Pharaoh that Hashem could have them come back to Pharaoh, the crocodiles remained in the Nile River from that point on in history.

The Midrash Tanchuma in Vaera (14), Tanah D'Bay Eliyahu (Raba 7), and Yalkut Shimoni 182 explain why Hashem brought each of the ten plagues on the Egyptians. With respect to frogs, they say that the Egyptians made the Bnei Yisroel gather all sorts of disgusting creeping animals from the fields for the Egyptians to play games with.

Vaera

1) The Sforno presents an answer to our question. He says that in Shemos (8:5), Moshe not only offered Pharaoh that he could dictate when the plague of frogs would come to an end but also made a second offer לְהַכְרִית הַצְפַרְדְּעִים מִמְּךָ וּמִבָּתֶּיךָ רַק בַּיְאֹר תִּשָּׁאַרְנָה (destroy the frogs from you and from your houses, that they should remain only in the Nile). That means that not only would Hashem get rid of the frogs that were presently in the Egyptians' bodies and in their houses, but Hashem would also make sure that the frogs that were currently in the Nile River would not come back to the Egyptians and their houses. Though the frogs would be removed from the Egyptians' bodies and houses, those in the streets would not be removed but would rather die in the streets. Therefore, Moshe promised three conditions for the end of the plague (1) the frogs in the Egyptians' bodies and houses would be removed, (2) the frogs in the street would die, and (3) the frogs in the Nile River would remain there.

The Sforno quotes a Gemorah in Sanhedrin 64a and Yuma 69b to prove that having all these conditions makes it more unlikely Moshe's davening would be accepted. Nechemia (9:4) says that when the Bnei Yisroel returned to Eretz Yisroel with Ezra and Nechemia to rebuild the Beis Hamikdosh, "they cried out in a huge voice to Hashem." The Gemorah in Yuma 69b and Sanhedrin 64a explains that they cried out, "Woe, woe, it is he who has destroyed the Beis Hamikdosh, burnt the sanctuary, killed all the righteous people, driven all Bnei Yisroel into exile, and is still dancing around among us! Hashem has surely given him to us so that we may receive reward through him. We want neither him nor any reward through him! Rashi explains that they were talking about the Yetzer Horah that entices one to worship idolatry. A tablet fell down from Heaven for them, upon which the word Emes (truth) was written. Rashi explains that this was a sign from Heaven that Hashem agrees with their request. They fasted for three days and three nights, and Heaven gave him (the Yetzer Horah of idolatry) to them. He came out from the Holy of Holies like a fiery young lion. The Toras Chaim ponders what the Yetzer Horah is doing in the Holy of Holies. He answers that each person encompasses a small world similar to the physical world that we live in. Just like the Yetzer Horah is found inside the essence of every person, he is also found inside the essence of the world, which is where Hashem's Shechinah rests in the Holy of Holies.

The Prophet (Zechariah) said to them, "This is the Yetzer Horah of idolatry. As they captured the Yetzer Horah of idolatry, a hair of his beard fell out, and he raised his voice, and it was heard to a distance of 400 parsas. Parenthetically for calibration of how big a parsa is, Tosfos in Baba Metzia 28a says that Eretz Yisroel is 400 parsas by 400 parsas. After hearing this tremendous noise, they said: "How should we act? Perhaps, Chas VeShalom, they might have mercy on him in Heaven!" The prophet said to them: "Put him into a leaden pot, close its opening with lead, because lead absorbs sound well." They said: "Since this is a time of mercy, let us pray for mercy for the Yetzer Horah of sin (immorality)." They davened for mercy, and he was handed over to them. He said to them, "you should realize that if you kill him (me), the world will no longer continue to exist." They put him in prison for three days, then looked in the whole land of Eretz Yisroel for a fresh egg and could not find one. Rashi says that even those eggs which had already started to form stopped continuing to form since the warm environment in the reproductive organs of the chickens cooled off. They said: "What should we do now? Should we kill him? The world would then no longer

Vaera

exist. We can't beg for half mercy since in Heaven they do not grant halves." Rashi on these Gemoros says that by "half mercy," they meant that the Yetzer Horah of immorality would not arouse a person to sin but would allow a person to reproduce. They put out his (the Yetzer Horah of immorality) eyes and let him go. Putting out his eyes helped so that he at least no longer entices men to commit incest. However, Rashi explains that the Yetzer Horah still entices a person to sin with a married woman. Obviously, all the details in the above are not to be taken completely literally.

The Ain Eliyahu on this Gemorah explains that getting rid of the Yetzer Horah to commit idolatry also had a negative effect. As opposed to the first Beis Hamikdosh, in the second Beis Hamikdosh, which was after they had gotten rid of the Yetzer Horah of idolatry, Hashem's Shechinah did not rest in it. The Mishna in Pirkei Avos (5:26) says one is rewarded commensurate with one's pain or trouble in doing a Mitzvah. Since the people of the first Beis Hamikdosh had the trouble of conquering the Yetzer Horah of idolatry, the presence of Hashem rested in the Beis Hamikdosh, at least during times when they conquered the Yetzer Horah of idolatry. When they did not have this trouble, the Shechinah no longer rested in the Beis Hamikdosh. The Ain Eliyahu explains that this is what is meant that the voice of the Yetzer Horah was heard to a distance of four hundred parsas. As we have mentioned previously, four hundred parsas match the dimensions of Eretz Yisroel, implying that all of Eretz Yisroel was affected, being that Hashem's Shechinah no longer rested there.

The Ain Eliyahu also tells of another negative effect of getting rid of the Yetzer Horah of idolatry. The first exile only lasted seventy years since, during the exile, the Bnei Yisroel proved worthy of being redeemed by subduing the Yetzer Horah of idolatry. For example, we know that in Daniyel, chapter 3, we are told about Chananyah, Mishael, and Azariah who were thrown into the fiery furnace by Nevuchadnetzar for not worshipping his idol. After they were miraculously saved, Nevuchadnetzar (3:28) says, "Blessed be the G-d who has sent his angel and delivered His servants who trusted in him, not listening to the King's word and giving their bodies, so that they would not serve any idol besides for Hashem." Therefore, Nevuchadnetzar made a decree that any person, nation, or tongue that speaks anything amiss against Hashem shall be cut into pieces and their house shall be made a dunghill because there is no other G-d that can deliver after this sort." The greatness of this act was magnified since Chananyah, Mishael, and Azariah had a Yetzer Horah of idolatry in them. Because they and others conquered this Yetzer Horah, the first exile only lasted for seventy years. However, our present exile, unfortunately, has already lasted almost two thousand years.

Getting back to the above Gemoros, the Gemorah says, "We can't beg for half mercy since in heaven they do not grant halves." Having three categories of frogs with different scenarios is at least similar to asking for "half mercy." Therefore, ending the plague with the three different scenarios of frogs required a more potent davening than by the other plagues. Therefore, says the Sforno, Moshe had to cry out in prayer for his davening to be accepted.

2) The Akeidah also ponders our question. He says that after Moshe finished his conversation with Pharaoh that culminated in the frogs not being removed until the next day, the plague got even stronger. Moshe was afraid that Hashem was not going to agree to end the plague the next day since

Vaera

if that was the case, he thought the plague should begin to weaken and completely stop the next day. Therefore, Moshe davened very hard that Hashem should listen to his davening and stop the plagues the next day.

3) The Eben Ezra and many years later Rav Hirsch answer our question similarly. After Pharaoh answered tomorrow to Moshe's offer of when to end the plague, Moshe says in Shemos (8:6) כִּדְבָרְךָ (as you say). The Eben Ezra and Rav Hirsch say that Moshe said this on his own without consulting Hashem. This was the first time that Moshe had done such a thing, and therefore Moshe cried out in davening that Hashem should accept and fulfill what Moshe had promised. As proof that Moshe said this on his own, Shemos (8:9) says וַיַּעַשׂ ה' כִּדְבַר מֹשֶׁה (And Hashem did according to Moshe's word) implying that Hashem fulfilled Moshe's words which he said on his own. The Abarbanel also says that the offer which Moshe made to Pharaoh of dictating when the plague would end was Moshe's own offer since Hashem did not tell him to make such an offer. Therefore, Moshe had to daven very hard and cry out in davening so that Hashem would accept to do what Moshe had offered

The Maharil Diskin explains that Moshe wasn't positive that his words were being spoken with Ruach HaKodesh (Holy Spirit), which would have reflected what Hashem wanted. In truth, Moshe was already speaking with Ruach HaKodesh as Hashem promised Moshe in Shemos (4:12) "I will be with your mouth, and I will instruct you what you shall speak." The Shemos Raba (3:15) says that Hashem told Moshe He would shoot words into his mouth like one shoots an arrow. The Maharzav, on this Shemos Raba, explains Hashem purposely did not heal Moshe's closed lips so that it would be obvious when he was speaking on his own since he would speak with an impairment. It would also be obvious when Hashem was shooting words into his mouth, and he was speaking with Ruach HaKodesh since then, his words would come out of his mouth perfectly without any impairment. The Maharil Diskin says from this point forward, after Hashem accepted to fulfill the offer to Pharaoh, Moshe knew that he was speaking with Ruach HaKodesh. The Devorim Raba (1:1) also says that when Moshe was speaking words of Torah, his speech impairment was lifted.

4) The Tur also presents an answer to our question. He says that when Moshe made Pharaoh an offer to choose when the plague of frogs should end, Moshe said in Shemos (8:5), "Glorify yourself over me." Moshe made it sound to Pharaoh that it was his davening which would affect when the plague would be over. Because of this tinge of arrogance, Moshe had to daven much harder and cry out in davening to get his request fulfilled by Hashem.

5) The Toldos Yitzchak also offers an answer to our question. He says the plague of frogs was the only time that Moshe put his honor "on the line" by offering to have Pharoah's request dictate when the plague would stop. Since Moshe's honor and, by extension, Hashem's honor was at stake in whether Moshe's prayer would be accepted, Moshe davened much harder that his prayer would be accepted in the plague of frogs as compared to all the other plagues.

6) The Abarbanel and Alshich answer our question similarly. We have mentioned in the introduction that the plague of frogs was the first plague that personally affected Pharaoh, and in

Vaera

fact, Pharaoh was the first victim and target of the frogs. They say that Pharaoh, therefore, was very interested in getting the plague to be finished. They say that Pharaoh begged Moshe to kill the frogs that were in his palace and ensure that the frogs no longer came to his palace. In addition, Pharaoh begged Moshe to get rid of the frogs that had gotten into his body. The Alshich says that Pharaoh was petrified that the frogs would die in his body and cause him to become very sick. Though Pharaoh only asked about the frogs that had entered his palace and had gotten into the bodies of the Egyptians, the Alshich says that Hashem did more miracles when the plague was removed. He says that Hashem also kept the frogs that had gone into the Egyptians' ovens alive since they were willing to give up their lives for Hashem. Therefore, they were kept alive and returned to the Nile River. Also, because of the honor of the King, all frogs which had gotten into the palace were also returned to the Nile River and did not die in the palace so that the palace would not smell. Since Moshe asked for the frogs to be removed alive from Pharaoh and from the Egyptians, which was quite a miracle, this required Moshe to daven very hard for it to happen.

7) The Chasam Sofer also ponders our question. In Beraishis (25:21), the Torah uses the term וַיֶּעְתַּר יִצְחָק to describe Yitzchak davening to Hashem for children. We have mentioned in the introduction that after the plagues of wild animals and of locusts, Moshe's prayer to Hashem is also described with the Hebrew word וַיֶּעְתַּר. The Beraishis Raba (60:13) says that the reason Rivka was barren was that Lavan and Rivka's mother had blessed Rivka in Beraishis (24:60) with, אַתְּ הֲיִי לְאַלְפֵי רְבָבָה (may you become thousands of myriads), and therefore Hashem did not want idol worshippers to boast that their prayers had been fulfilled. The Gemorah in Sukkah 14a and Yevomos 64a says that the Hebrew word וַיֶּעְתַּר comes from the word to describe a shovel or pitchfork which is used to turn over the grain on a threshing floor. A righteous person is able to turn over a decree of judgment to become a decree of mercy. The Maharsha in Yevomos explains that just like a pitchfork turns over the grain so that the grain is separated from the chaff so also the davening of a righteous person separates the attribute of Hashem's mercy from Hashem's judgement. The Ain Eliyahu explains that typically the attribute of judgement surrounds the attribute of mercy so that the attribute of mercy is not visible. The pitchfork or the davening of a righteous person separates the attribute of mercy from that of judgement so that the attribute of mercy is visible. In the case of Yitzchak, the attribute of judgment had surrounded that of mercy so that idol worshippers would not boast that their prayer had been fulfilled. Yitzchak's prayers help to separate the two attributes such that the attribute of mercy would be visible and allow Rivka to have children.

The Chasam Sofer says that for the plague of frogs, it was not appropriate to use the term וַיֶּעְתַּר since the frogs died and caused the entire land to stink, which meant that the plague was not completely removed and everything was not returned to good. This is to be contrasted with the plague of wild animals and the plague of locusts, where all the wild animals and all the locusts were removed. Since it was not appropriate to use the term וַיֶּעְתַּר the Torah instead described Moshe's davening as crying out.

8) The Oznayim LeTorah also presents an answer to our question. In Shulchan Aruch, Orach Chaim (100:2), we paskin that even when davening the silent Shemoneh Esreh, one should pronounce the words with his lips so that his ears can hear his silent words. During the plague of frogs in Egypt,

Vaera

the sound of the frogs was so loud that one could only concentrate and hear what one was saying if one davened very loud. Therefore, Moshe had to cry out and daven very loudly.

Why Couldn't the Sorcerers Make Lice?

וַיַּעֲשׂוּ כֵן הַחַרְטֻמִּים בְּלָטֵיהֶם לְהוֹצִיא אֶת הַכִּנִּים וְלֹא יָכֹלוּ וַתְּהִי הַכִּנָּם בָּאָדָם וּבַבְּהֵמָה. וַיֹּאמְרוּ הַחַרְטֻמִּם אֶל פַּרְעֹה אֶצְבַּע אֱלֹקִים הִוא וַיֶּחֱזַק לֵב פַּרְעֹה וְלֹא שָׁמַע אֲלֵהֶם כַּאֲשֶׁר דִּבֶּר ה' (ח:יד-טו) Shemos (8:14-15) And the sorcerers did likewise with their secret rites to bring out the lice, but they could not, and the lice were upon man and beast. So the sorcerers said to Pharaoh, 'It is the finger of G-d,' but Pharaoh's heart remained steadfast, and he did not hearken to them, as Hashem had spoken

Why couldn't the sorcerers make lice?

Introduction
The Midrash Tanchuma on Vaera (14), Tanah D'Bay Eliyahu (Raba 7), and Yalkut Shimoni 182 explain why Hashem brought each of the ten plagues on the Egyptians. With respect to lice, they say that the Egyptians appointed the Bnei Yisroel as sweepers of the roads, houses, and fields. Shemos (8:13) says, "Aharon stretched forth his hand with his staff and struck the dust of the earth, and the lice were upon man and beast; all the dust of the earth became lice throughout the entire land of Egypt." Since all the dust of the earth became lice, the Egyptians were punished by not being able to have any dust for the Bnei Yisroel to sweep up since it had all turned to lice. The Tanah D'Bay Eliyahu and Yalkut Shimoni also say that in this plague, Hashem sent fourteen different types of lice on the Egyptians, and it details their names. The Yalkut Shimoni says that the smallest lice were the size of a chicken egg while the biggest were the size of a goose's egg.

The Yalkut Shimoni explains in a different way why Hashem brought each of the plagues on the Egyptians. With respect to lice, it says that the Egyptians were punished by having their dust turned to lice since they oppressed the Bnei Yisroel who are compared to the dust of the earth, as for example, the Torah says in Beraishis (27:14), "And your seed shall be as the dust of the earth." The Midrash Lekach Tov says that the Egyptians were punished with lice since they did not allow the Bnei Yisroel to take baths which caused the Bnei Yisroel to have lice. As a measure for measure punishment, the Egyptians were punished with lice.

The Malbim points out that this plague of lice remained on the Egyptians as long as they lived. He derives this from Sefer Tehillim (105:31), which says, "He (Hashem) commanded and a mixture of noxious beasts came, lice throughout all their boundary." This Posuk implies that even after the next plague after lice (wild animals), came the lice remained in Egypt.

The Ramban ponders why the sorcerers call the plague a finger of Hashem instead of a hand of Hashem. Typically, the Torah uses the phrase "hand of Hashem" like in Shemos (14:31), "And Yisroel saw the great hand, which Hashem had used upon the Egyptians." Similarly, Sefer Shmuel I (12:15) says, "But, if you will not hearken to the voice of Hashem, and you will rebel against the commandments of Hashem, Hashem's hand will be against you and against your fathers." Also,

Vaera

similarly, Sefer Shmuel I (5:11) says, "And they sent and gathered all the lords of the Philistines, and they said, 'Send away the Ark of the G-d of Yisroel, and let it return to its place, so that it will not kill me and my people,' for there was a panic of death in the entire city; the hand of G-d was very heavy there." The Ramban answers that the sorcerers wanted to encourage Pharaoh by saying that the plague is a small plague, only a finger, and we can withstand it.

The Ramban notes that for the plagues of lice, boils, and darkness, Hashem does not warn Pharaoh that these plagues are going to happen. Since these plagues did not threaten the lives of the Egyptians and just made them very uncomfortable, Hashem did not give Pharaoh any warning. The plague of pestilence, even though it is mainly a plague on animals, can also infect humans, and that is why Moshe tells Pharaoh with regard to the plague of pestilence in Shemos (9:16) that despite this possibility, Pharaoh does not have to fear for his life since, "But, for this reason, I have allowed you to stand, in order to show you My strength and in order to declare My name all over the earth." With regard to the plague of locusts, the locusts threatened the Egyptian's food supply and thereby death through starvation. The only other plague that, at first glance, did not seem life-threatening is the plague of frogs. However, the Ramban shows that this is not the case by quoting Sefer Tehillim (78:45), which says, "He (Hashem) incited against them a mixture of wild beasts, which devoured them, and frogs, which mutilated them." Along with "mutilation" implying the possibility of death, he quotes the Shemos Raba (10:3), which says that the frogs went into the Egyptian's bodies and mutilated their reproductive organs.

The Pirkei D'Rabi Eliezer 48 says that the sorcerers of Egypt tried to do every plague all the way through the plagues of boils. For the plague of boils, Shemos (9:11) says, "And the sorcerers could not stand before Moshe because of the boils, for the boils were upon the sorcerers and upon all Egypt." The Radal explains that even though they were unsuccessful, the plague of lice is included in the list of plagues that the sorcerers tried since they at least tried to do the plague. However, the Shemos Raba disagrees and says that the last plague the sorcerers tried to copy was the plague of lice. The Ramban and Rabeinu Bechay explain that once they realized that they couldn't do it, and admitted that the plague was a "finger of G-d" the sorcerers were no longer called by Pharaoh to try and copy the plagues that Hashem brought. Until the plague of boils, the sorcerers at least gave encouragement to Pharaoh for continuing to oppose Moshe's demand to let the Bnei Yisroel go. During the plague of boils, the sorcerers were so embarrassed by their boils that they didn't even go to give encouragement to Pharaoh. The Ponim Yofos says that the plague of boils remained on the sorcerers even after the plague finished, and therefore they were too embarrassed to come anymore from the plague of boils and onward to Pharaoh.

Rabeinu Bechay says that when the sorcerers in the Posuk after ours admit that they could not copy Hashem and do the plagues of lice, the Torah from then and onwards spells the Hebrew word for their name הַחַרְטֻמָּם without a yud. In our Posuk and before, their Hebrew name is spelled with a yud, הַחַרְטֻמִּים. They lost their Yud since, after their admission, their stature decreased considerably in the eyes of Pharaoh.

Vaera

The Chizkuni and Bechor Shor ponder why Pharaoh just hardened his heart, and he did not ask Moshe to remove the plague of lice. The Chizkuni and Bechor Shor answer that since Pharaoh lived in a marble palace, he wasn't concerned about all the dirt turning into lice. All Pharaoh had to do was make sure that his palace was well swept at all times. Pharaoh was not so concerned about everyone else since, at that time, having lice around was not unheard of for the common people.

The Eben Ezra and Ralbag explain in a unique fashion how the sorcerers explained to Pharaoh why they could not create lice. According to them, the sorcerers did not at all admit that the plague of lice was a sign that the plagues were from Hashem. Rather the sorcerers said that the constellations at that point were in such a configuration just at that point in time that the constellations caused there to be lice in Egypt. The sorcerers argued that the plague of lice had nothing to do with Hashem bringing a plague on the Egyptians on behalf of the Bnei Yisroel. As proof that natural phenomena caused it, the sorcerers pointed out to Pharaoh that unlike the plagues of blood and frogs, Moshe did not warn Pharaoh that the plague of lice was coming. The sorcerers took this as proof that Moshe had no idea, Chas VeShalom, that the plague was coming since natural events caused it. In addition, the sorcerers explained that the reason they couldn't imitate the plague was that the constellations were no longer in a configuration to produce the lice. Furthermore, the Eben Ezra says that the reason the sorcerers said that it was אֶצְבַּע אֱלֹקִים הוּא (a finger of G-d) and not אֶצְבַּע ה' הוּא (a finger of Hashem) was that they ascribed Hashem to the G-d of the Bnei Yisroel while the term אֱלֹקִים (G-d) they ascribed to any nation's G-d. The Nodeh BeYehudah in his Sefer Tzlach on Chagigah 12a says that the term אֱלֹקִים (G-d) has the same Gematria (numerical value) as הטבע (nature). Using the term אֱלֹקִים (G-d) implies how Hashem deals with this world through the laws of nature. Therefore, the sorcerers said that the plague of lice was caused by a natural phenomenon.

The Rambam, Rabeinu Yona, and the Meiri on the Mishna in Pirkei Avos (5:4) say that the plague of lice was unique in that it was not only where the Egyptians were but was also where the Bnei Yisroel were. The Rambam offers as proof that in all the other nine plagues, the Torah in some way tells us that the plague was only on the Egyptians. With regard to the plague of blood, Shemos (7:21) says, "the Egyptians could not drink water from the Nile, and there was blood throughout the entire land of Egypt." With regard to frogs, Shemos (7:28) says, "And the Nile will swarm with frogs, and they will go up and come into your (Egyptian) house and into your bedroom and upon your bed and into the house of your servants and into your people, and into your ovens and into your kneading troughs." With regard to wild animals, Shemos (8:18) says, "And I will separate on that day the land of Goshen, upon which My people stand, that there will be no mixture of noxious creatures there." With regard to the plague of pestilence, Shemos (9:7) says. "And Pharaoh sent, and behold, not even one of the livestock of Yisroel died." With regard to boils, Shemos (9:11) says, "for the boils were upon the sorcerers and upon all Egypt." For the plague of hail, Shemos (9:26) says, "Only in the land of Goshen, where the Bnei Yisroel were, there was no hail." With regard to locusts, Shemos (10:14) says, "The locusts ascended over the entire land of Egypt." The Rashash has a problem with the Rambam quoting this Posuk as proof the locust were only on the Egyptians as opposed to lice since Shemos (8:13) says, "all the dust of the earth became lice throughout the entire land of Egypt." Therefore, it would seem that both lice and locusts affected the entire land of Egypt. Rather the Rashash says that a better Posuk to quote about locusts only

Vaera

being on the Egyptians would be Shemos (10:13), "And your houses and the houses of all your servants and the houses of all the Egyptians will be filled." As opposed to the Posuk the Rambam quotes, this Posuk explicitly says that the locusts only went into the house of the Egyptians. We now continue with the Rambam's proof from Pesukim that only the plague of lice was also where the Bnei Yisroel lived. With regard to the plague of darkness, Shemos (10:23) says, "but for all the Bnei Yisroel there was light in their dwellings." Finally, though the Rambam doesn't mention it since it is quite obvious, for the plague of the death of the firstborn Hashem passed over the house of the Bnei Yisroel as it says in Shemos (12:23), "Hashem will pass to smite the Egyptians, and He will see the blood on the lintel and on the two doorposts, and Hashem will pass over the entrance, and He will not permit the destroyer to enter your houses to smite you."

The Rambam and Rabeinu Yona say that even though lice were everywhere, including where the Bnei Yisroel were, it was handed down by tradition to our Chachomim, who tell us that the lice did not affect the Bnei Yisroel. The Meiri goes a step further and says that this was not only passed down by tradition, but it is found in the explanation of the Gemorah. The only problem is that the commentators point out that they are not aware of such an explanation being brought anywhere in the Gemorah or in the Midrashim.

Both the Oznayim LeTorah and Rav Schwab, in his Sefer Mayan Beis HaShoaivah, offer a similar proof as to where at least in the Midrashim, we see that the plague of lice was also where the Bnei Yisroel lived. Amongst the reasons the Beraishis Raba (96:6) presents as to why Yaakov did not want to be buried in Egypt was because the dirt of Egypt would be turned into lice, and Yaakov did not want the lice to be crawling through his body. If the plague of lice was not found where the Bnei Yisroel lived in Goshen, then this reason which the Beraishis Raba presents would not be valid since Yaakov could have been buried in Goshen without having to worry that lice would crawl through his body. The Oznayim LeTorah ponders why the plague of lice was different than all the other plagues in that t it was also found where the Bnei Yisroel lived. The Oznayim LeTorah answers that since even the sorcerers admitted that this plague was a "finger of G-d," it may not have been possible for Pharaoh to harden his heart and not send out the Bnei Yisroel when it was clear, at least to the sorcerers, that Hashem was sending the plagues. Therefore, Hashem had to balance this out by allowing the lice to go where the Bnei Yisroel lived so that Pharaoh could rationalize to himself that Hashem was punishing both Egyptians and Jews, and therefore there was no need to send out the Bnei Yisroel. He also presents a second reason why it was necessary for the lice to also be in Goshen, where the Bnei Yisroel lived. Mishnas Rabi Eliezer (Chapter 19) says that the Bnei Yisroel were no longer required to work for the Egyptians beginning from when the plague of lice occurred. The reason is that the Bnei Yisroel could no longer make bricks since they could no longer find clean sand to make it from. Had the plague of lice not occurred in Goshen, the Egyptians would have required the Bnei Yisroel to continue making bricks from the sand in Goshen.

The previous to our Posuk says, "and the lice were upon man and beast; all the dust of the earth became lice throughout the entire land of Egypt." That being the case, the Shach quotes Rav Saadia Gaon as to why our Posuk repeats and says, "and the lice were upon man and beast." He says that until the sorcerers told all the Egyptians that this plague was "the finger of G-d," the Egyptians

Vaera

thought that the lice were only a sleight of hand and was not real lice meaning they had a lot less to worry about. After the sorcerers confirmed that the plague of lice was indeed a 'finger of G-d," the Egyptians knew that the lice were real, and they started scratching themselves, knowing that they were real.

1) The Gemorah in Sanhedrin 67b, Shemos Raba (10:7), and the Midrash Tanchuma on Vaera (14) are the sources for the answer that Rashi presents to our question. In our Posuk it says that the sorcerers tried to make the plague of lice, בְּלָטֵיהֶם. When Aharon made the sign in front of Pharaoh of his staff turning into a scorpion, and the sorcerers wanted to copy him, Shemos (7:11) says that the sorcerers made the sign בְּלַהֲטֵיהֶם. The Gemorah in Sanhedrin 67b and the Midrash Tanchuma on Vaera (14) says that when the Torah uses the term בְּלָטֵיהֶם (as in our Posuk), it means that the sorcerers used demons to do their sorcery. When the Torah uses the term בְּלַהֲטֵיהֶם, it means that the sorcerers used witchcraft to do their sorcery. Rashi uses as his sources the Gemorah, Shemos Raba, and Midrash Tanchuma to say that a demon has no power over something smaller than a grain of barley. Since the sorcerers needed to use demons to make the lice, they could not make the lice that are ostensibly smaller than a grain of barley. Seeing this, the sorcerers admitted that this plague was not made by demons but was rather, as the Torah quotes the sorcerers in the Posuk after ours, a "finger of Hashem." We note that the Tanah D'Bay Eliyahu says that the reason the sorcerers could not make the lice was because it was less than the size of a lentil. We do also note that the Shai LeMorah, in his comments on the Tanah D'Bay Eliyahu, says that the Yeshuos Yaakov had the text of a grain of barley consistent with the Gemorah and Midrashim. However, the Maharzav disagrees and says the text should be a lentil. In his written manuscript, which Rav Shavel used, the Ramban does, however, say that the lice were less than the size of a lentil, and Rabeinu Bechay, when he quotes the Ramban, also says the size of a lentil and not the size of a grain of barley.

The Maharal in Gur Aryeh, the Toras Chaim in Sanhedrin 67b, the Maskil LeDovid, and the Eitz Yosef, quoting the Baer Hetev, explain similarly why a demon does not have any power over an object smaller than a grain of barley. Like a Niftar, a human bone is Tameh and renders someone who comes in contact with it Tameh. However, a piece of human bone that is less than the size of a grain of barley is not Tameh and does not render Tameh someone who comes in contact with it. A demon works with the powers of Tumah to accomplish what it accomplishes. Since something smaller than a grain of barley cannot become Tameh, the demon has no power over it. Similarly, the Gemorah in Sanhedrin 67b says that water from a spring takes away the power of sorcery. The Anaf Yosef explains that spring water is the source of purity, and that is why the ashes of the Porah Adumah (Red Heifer) require spring water to be mixed with the ashes to make a Tameh person pure. On the other hand, the source of sorcery is Tumah, and that is why spring water takes away the power of sorcery. The Maharal, both in his commentary on the Gemorah in Sanhedrin 67b and in his Sefer Gur Aryeh, presents another explanation of why a demon does not have any power over an object smaller than a grain of barley. An object at least the size of a grain of barley has importance as an object in its own right. An object less than that size is just part of the general makeup of the earth. A demon does not have power over the world itself, so, for example, it cannot control the wind and dust of the earth. The Maharal explains that this is the reason that a human bone less than the size of a grain of barley cannot become Tameh. This bone is so small that it is not an object in

Vaera

its own right and is just part of the general makeup of the earth. The earth itself cannot become Tameh.

We have quoted the Yalkut Shimoni in the introduction that the size of the lice during the plague was much bigger than the size of a grain of barley or lentil and, in fact, was between the size of a chicken and a goose egg. Therefore, the Yepheh Toar, the Eyun Yaakov on the Gemorah in Sanhedrin 67b, and the Maskil LeDovid ponder the question of why the demons could not make lice of this size. They answer that a demon can only make something in its natural size. Since the natural size of a lice is less than the size of a grain of barley, the demon cannot make it. The Ben Yehoyoda says that the sorcerers specifically wanted to make the lice in their natural size so that they could differentiate their lice from those that Hashem made and show off the lice they made to everyone. However, since its natural size was less than the size of a grain of barley, the demons could not make it. According to this answer of the Ben Yehoyoda, it is not clear to me why the sorcerers did not have the demons make lice of a size bigger than a grain of barley. Ostensibly, according to this answer, they could do this if we don't use the opinion that demons can only make something in its natural size.

2) The Gemorah in Sanhedrin 67b, the Shemos Raba (10:7), and the Midrash Tanchuma on Vaera (14) all present an opinion which argues with the previous answer. This opinion says that demons cannot even make something as big as a camel. All demons can do is gather such creatures from somewhere else and transport them to where they are told to bring them. The Maharal in Sanhedrin 67b explains that according to Pirkei Avos (5:8), some opinions say that demons called Mazikim were created right before the first Shabbos of creation. Since they themselves were created during creation, they have no power to create anything else and can only gather creatures from elsewhere and transport them.

Rashi on the Gemorah in Sanhedrin explains that since lice are so small, they cannot survive being brought from such a great distance, and that is why the sorcerers could not "make" lice. The Chizkuni and Maharsha ponder why the sorcerers could not have used the demons in the next plague of wild animals to create the wild animals. The Maharsha says that since the sorcerers realized that the plague of lice was made by Hashem and not by demons, they recognized that even the big wild animals were made by Hashem, and therefore there was no point in asking the demons to copy it. The Chizkuni, because of this question, rejects this answer.

The Ben Yehoyoda ponders why the sorcerers didn't have the demons bring the lice from nearby so that they could survive being transported. Moreover, he ponders why the lice couldn't survive being brought over a large distance since it was the demon that transported them. He answers that since the lice were less than the size of a grain of barley, the demons do not have the ability to transport them since demons can only deal with Tameh objects greater than the size of a grain of barley.

The Maskil LeDovid explains the perhaps obvious answer of why the demons could not have transported the bigger lice that were at least the size of chicken eggs that Hashem made in this

Vaera

plague. He says that there was nowhere to transport them from since they didn't exist anywhere else in the world.

3) The Ramban also presents an answer to our question. He says that the sorcerers did as they would normally do to bring forth lice, and they were unsuccessful, even though they were fully confident that they could bring forth the lice. The Tur explains that they used the exact same recipe they had previously used, which did bring forth lice, but that this time they were unsuccessful. Rav Shavel quotes a Droshos Ramban, which says that Hashem did not allow them to succeed since Hashem wanted to nullify their ability to do such things, starting from this plague. The Chizkuni explains that since this was the third plague and the sorcerers had imitated the first two plagues, Hashem did not want them to be successful this third time, since in Halacha, successfully doing something three times without failure creates a presumption (Chazakah) that the person will continue to be successful in doing it.

Our Posuk says וַיַּעֲשׂוּ כֵן הַחַרְטֻמִּים בְּלָטֵיהֶם לְהוֹצִיא אֶת הַכִּנִּים וְלֹא יָכֹלוּ (And the sorcerers did likewise with their secret rites to bring out the lice, but they could not). The Ksav VeHakabola ponders why our Posuk puts in the Hebrew word כֵן (likewise). It would seem, at first glance, that our Posuk would have been more precise if it said וַיַּעֲשׂוּ הַחַרְטֻמִּים בְּלָטֵיהֶם לְהוֹצִיא אֶת הַכִּנִּים וְלֹא יָכֹלוּ (And the sorcerers tried with their secret rites to bring out the lice, but they could not). Based on our Posuk using the Hebrew word כֵן (likewise), he says that in their houses, when they were practicing, the sorcerers had no issues bring forth lice. It was only when they tried to do it in front of Moshe that it did not work. Therefore, our Posuk should be translated, "And the sorcerers did likewise (in their houses) with their secret rites to bring out the lice, but they could not (do it in front of Moshe)."

4) The Ramban presents another answer to our question. He says that sorcerers could not do this plague since the plague involved creating lice from dirt. The sorcerers could not create anything; they could just use things there were already created. For example, the sorcerers could use something already created, and bring them to where they wanted them. In a similar way, by the plague of blood, the sorcerers could bring blood and mix it with water to create bloody water. I do not fully understand why the sorcerers, for the plague of lice, could not just remove the dirt and replace it with lice instead of creating lice from dirt.

5) The Ralbag is of the opinion that the sorcerers in Egypt did not perform any real witchcraft, but rather, they just used sleight of hand. Since lice are so small, they were not able to use sleight of hand to pretend that they were creating lice.

6) The Chizkuni, Bechor Shor, Rosh, as quoted by the Ksav VeHakabola, and Malbim answer our question similarly. They all say that the sorcerers did not want to create more lice, but rather they wanted to get rid of at least some of the lice. As the Chizkuni explains, no one would be able to notice if the sorcerers created more lice since all the dirt of the land was already lice. The only thing they could do to show off that they also had power was to get rid of the lice. The Bechor Shor says that the sorcerers wanted to test if Moshe was also, Chas VeShalom, using sorcery to create the plagues or not. The sorcerers could prove that Moshe was using sorcery if they could get rid of the

237

Vaera

lice since sorcery could be undone by other sorcery. However, if they were unable to undo Moshe's plague, then they would know that it was an act of Hashem. When the sorcerers were unable to get rid of the plague, they knew that it was an act of Hashem, as they confessed.

The Malbim explains that the sorcerers already realized by the plague of frogs that Pharaoh was not impressed by the fact that they created more frogs since all he wanted from Moshe was to get rid of the frogs. Therefore, the sorcerers knew that Pharaoh would only be impressed by them if they got rid of the lice. He also explains that despite the fact that the sorcerers knew remedies to get rid of the lice, at least from people's bodies, since lice were not uncommon in Egypt, even these remedies did not work now since the lice were a miracle of Hashem.

The Maharal, in Gur Aryeh, and the Oznayim LeTorah are not happy with this answer since we never find by any of the plagues that the sorcerers tried to remove the plague. The Oznayim LeTorah says that the sorcerers only had the power to do bad and not do good as needed to remove the plague.

7) The Abarbanel also presents an answer to our question. He has a unique interpretation of our Posuk. When our Posuk says וַיַּעֲשׂוּ כֵן הַחַרְטֻמִּים בְּלָטֵיהֶם (And the sorcerers did likewise with their secret rites) he says that it means that the sorcerers imitated Moshe and Aharon and successfully created lice, just like they imitated them for the plagues of blood and frogs. However, when Pharaoh saw what they did, Pharaoh castigated them for creating more lice and more of a problem, and instead, Pharaoh asked the sorcerers to remove the lice. However, the sorcerers were not successful at removing the lice. This is what our Posuk means when it says וְלֹא יָכֹלוּ (and they were not able). When Pharaoh asked the sorcerers why they could not remove the lice, the sorcerers were forced to admit that the lice which Hashem had created were "the finger of G-d."

8) The Chizkuni, Daas Zekanim, and Toldos Yitzchak answer our question similarly. We can understand this answer better if we first examine a very interesting Rashi found in Sanhedrin 44b about Baya, the tax collector. Rashi tells us that he was a corrupt Jewish tax collector. On the same day and in the same city that Baya was Niftar, a righteous Talmid Chochom was also Niftar. The entire city came to the Levaya of the righteous Talmid Chochom while only a few relatives of Baya, the tax collector, came to his Levaya. Many people accompanied the righteous Talmid Chochom to the cemetery, and in the rear of the big processional, Baya's relatives carried him to the cemetery. Seeing all these people, bandits decided to attack them, and everyone put down the two coffins and ran for their lives. Only one disciple of the righteous Talmid Chochom was brave enough to hide near the coffin of his Rebbe and protect it as best he could. When the people of the town returned later to bury the coffins, they confused the two coffins. Despite the disciple complaining and protesting bitterly about their mistake, the people of the town did not listen to him. Baya, the corrupt Jewish tax collector, was buried with the highest of honors, while the righteous Talmid Chochom received a quick and non-honorable burial by Baya's relatives.

The disciple of the righteous Talmid Chochom was very upset about the dishonor that was given to the righteous Talmid Chochom at his burial, not to mention the honor given to Baya. That night his

Vaera

Rebbe appeared to him in a dream. His Rebbe told his disciple not to be upset since he was now receiving great honor in Gan Eden, while Baya, the corrupt tax collector, was suffering much pain in Gehenom. The Rebbe showed the disciple that the full weight of the hinge of the door to Gehenom was rotating on Baya's ear. The Rebbe also explained to the disciple that the reason he had received dishonor at his burial was that one time, the shaming of a Torah Scholar came to his attention, and the Rebbe did not protest against this. With regard to Baya, the reason he received so much honor at his burial was that one time he prepared a banquet for the head of the city, but the head of the city did not show up. Instead, Baya distributed the food to the poor, and the honor at his burial was his reward. Upon seeing the anguish that Baya was undergoing, the disciple asked his Rebbe how long Baya would be receiving this punishment. His Rebbe answered that he would be receiving it till Rav Shimon ben Shetach was Niftar, and Rav Shimon ben Shetach would take his place under the door to Gehenom. For reference, Rav Shimon ben Shetach is listed in Pirkei Avos (1:8) as one of the pairs of religious leaders during the time of the second Beis Hamikdosh.

The disciple was astounded by the news that the great sage, Rav Shimon ben Shetach, had such a horrible punishment in store for him, and he asked his Rebbe for an explanation. His Rebbe explained that Rav Shimon ben Shetach was being punished for allowing Jewish women sorcerers to live in the city of Ashkelon without bringing them to trial. The next morning the disciple hurried over to Rav Shimon ben Shetach and related his dream to him.

Rav Shimon ben Shetach came up with a plan to be able to deal with the women sorcerers. He gathered 80 handsome young men. It turned out that it was raining heavily that day. Rav Shimon ben Shetach gave each of the men a large covered pot with a clean, dry robe folded inside. He instructed the men that there were exactly 80 women sorcerers and when he signaled, each of them should lift one of the women up from the ground. Rav Shimon ben Shetach explained that when a sorcerer is not in contact with the ground, they can not do their sorcery. As long as they could take the sorcerers by surprise and simultaneously lift them off the ground, they would be successful. Rav Shimon ben Shetach then went to their palace in Ashkelon, instructing the men to remain outside until he called them. Upon knocking on the door of the palace, the sorcerers asked him who he was and why he had come. Rav Shimon ben Shetach told them that he was also a sorcerer and that he had come to test their powers of witchcraft. The women sorcerers challenged him to show them an example of his witchcraft. Rav Shimon ben Shetach told them that he could bring the women sorcerers 80 young men all wearing dry clothes despite the heavy rains. They challenged him to do as he had said, and he motioned to the men to take the robes out of the pots, put them on, and all come in at once to lift each of them off the ground. They carried the women sorcerers to ensure that they made no contact with the ground and the women sorcerers could not harm them. Rav Shimon ben Shetach judged them all with the penalty of murder, and all 80 were hung on the same day.

Subsequently, the relatives of these sorcerers came up with a plot to avenge the deaths of their relatives, the sorcerers. Two of them came before a Beis Din and testified that they saw the son of Rav Shimon ben Shetach commit a sin for which he deserved to be killed by Beis Din. As is the case in any capital crime, the court rigorously grilled the witnesses, but the witnesses were able to pass all of Beis Din's investigations, and their testimony was accepted. After the death sentence was announced, Rav Shimon ben Shetach's son was taken out to be executed. As is the case in all executions, the son was asked to confess his sins before being executed. The son said that "If I have committed this sin, let my death not atone for any of my sins, but if I have not committed this sin, then my death should atone for all my sins and let the witnesses who conspired against me never find forgiveness for what they have done." Upon hearing this statement, the witnesses were shaken and admitted to the Beis Din that they had testified falsely to avenge the death of their relatives, the sorcerers. Despite this admission of the witnesses, the Beis Din was not able to overturn their verdict since once witnesses have given over their testimony to Beis Din, the testimony cannot be changed, and Rav Shimon ben Shetach's son was executed by Beis Din. This story is also told in the Yerushalmi Chagigah (2:2), with a few minor differences from the story that Rashi tells us in Sanhedrin 44b. Among the minor differences is that according to the Yerushalmi in Chagigah (2:2), Rav Shimon ben Shetach had promised before he became prince of the Bnei Yisroel that he would eradicate the sorcerers if he became the prince. Therefore, when he didn't initially keep this promise, he was set to be punished in Gehenom. Another difference is that the Yerushalmi says that Rav Shimon ben Shetach prearranged with the 80 young men that when he made certain sounds, they were to come in dressed in their dry clothes, and that is how they knew when to come in.

The Chizkuni, Daas Zekanim, and Toldos Yitzchak say that since all the dirt of Egypt was changed into lice, the feet of the sorcerers no longer were touching the ground but rather were touching the lice. Since their feet were not touching the ground, their sorcery could no longer work, and therefore they were unable to imitate the plague of lice.

9) The Chizkuni presents another answer to our question. He says the sorcerers were embarrassed to be seen in public because of the lice that were all over them. Therefore, they would not imitate the plague. The Tzedah LeDerech does not like this answer of the Chizkuni. He says that our Posuk contradicts this answer when it says, "And the sorcerers did likewise with their secret rites to bring out the lice, but they could not." This implies that they did come out in public and did indeed try to imitate this plague.

Why Did Pharoah's Heart Become Hardened After Seeing That Not Even Till One of the Livestock of the Bnei Yisroel Died During the Plague of Pestilence?

Shemos (9:7) וַיִּשְׁלַח פַּרְעֹה וְהִנֵּה לֹא מֵת מִמִּקְנֵה יִשְׂרָאֵל עַד אֶחָד וַיִּכְבַּד לֵב פַּרְעֹה וְלֹא שִׁלַּח אֶת הָעָם (ט:ז) And Pharaoh sent, and behold, not even till one of the livestock of Yisroel died, and Pharaoh's heart became hardened, and he did not let the people out.

In Shemos (9:4), Hashem tells Moshe to inform Pharaoh, "And Hashem will make a separation between the livestock of Yisroel and the livestock of Egypt, and nothing of the Bnei Yisroel will die." Why did Pharoah's heart become hardened after seeing that not even till one of the livestock of the Bnei Yisroel died during the plague of pestilence? Ostensibly, after seeing Hashem fulfill his

Vaera

word, Pharaoh should have at best heeded Hashem's request to let the Bnei Yisroel leave Egypt, but at worst, it should not have caused Pharaoh to harden his heart.

Introduction
The Shemos Raba (11:4), Midrash Tanchuma on Vaera (14), Midrash Lekach Tov, and the Tanah D'Bay Eliyahu (7) say that the reason Hashem brought the plague of pestilence on the Egyptians was that the Egyptians made the Bnei Yisroel be shepherds of the Egyptian's horses, cattle, sheep, and donkeys in the mountains, valleys, and deserts far from where the Bnei Yisroel lived. They did this to prevent the husbands from coming home to their wives and thereby attempted to cause the Jewish population to increase much slower. With the plague of pestilence, Hashem figuratively said that he would send a new shepherd to take care of the Egyptian's animals. After this new shepherd came and killed the cattle, they would no longer need a shepherd to watch them.

The Midrash Tanchuma on Vaera (3) and the Shemos Raba (13:3) are the sources for Rashi's statement on Shemos (7:3) that for the first five plagues, Pharaoh hardened his own heart while for the last five plagues Hashem hardened Pharaoh's heart. The Midrash Tanchuma says that we can see this because, in the first five plagues (the plague of pestilence being the fifth plague), the Torah says that Pharaoh hardened his heart. In the last five plagues, the Torah says, "And Hashem hardened Pharaoh's heart." After Pharaoh hardened his heart for the first five plagues, Hashem figuratively said that from this point and onwards, even if Pharaoh would want to send the Bnei Yisroel, Hashem will not listen to his desires causing Pharaoh to refuse to send out the Bnei Yisroel, no matter what.

The Ramban on Shemos (7:3) ponders the question, which he describes as a question asked by all, of why Pharaoh should be punished if Hashem hardened his heart. He says that there are two answers to this question and that they are both truthful answers. The first answer is that Pharaoh, in his wickedness, did many horrible things to the Bnei Yisroel, which were completely unjustifiable. As the Rambam says, in the eighth Perek of Shemoneh Perakim, had the punishment to Pharaoh and the Egyptians only been for not sending the Bnei Yisroel out of Egypt, Hashem would not have punished them since Hashem hardened Pharoah's heart to not send the Bnei Yisroel out. Rather, the punishment was because Pharaoh and his helpers used their freedom of choice to persecute a nation of people who had come to live amongst them. Therefore, Hashem took away Pharoah's free will to send the Bnei Yisroel out of Egypt so that Pharaoh could get punished for all the horrible things the Egyptians did to the Jews during the exile in Egypt. Though Hashem could have chosen to punish Pharaoh in the world to come for his wickedness, Hashem chose to punish Pharaoh in this world since Hashem had promised Avrohom in Beraishis (15:14). "And also the nation that they will serve will I judge." He also offers a second reason as to why Pharaoh should be punished in light of the fact that Hashem had hardened his heart, and Pharaoh had no choice but to refuse to allow the Bnei Yisroel to leave. During the first five plagues, the Torah says either וַיֶּחֱזַק לֵב פַּרְעֹה וְלֹא שָׁמַע אֲלֵהֶם (But Pharaoh's heart remained steadfast, and he did not hearken to them) or וַיַּכְבֵּד פַּרְעֹה אֶת לִבּוֹ (But Pharaoh hardened his heart). That is, Pharaoh did not really want to send the Bnei Yisroel out of Egypt to serve and honor Hashem. However, once the plagues became so intense, Pharaoh did not have the desire to endure the plagues, and therefore Pharaoh would have sent the Bnei Yisroel out in

Vaera

order to not have to put up with the plagues. Nonetheless, in the absence of the threat of future plagues, Pharaoh would never have sent the Bnei Yisroel out to serve and honor Hashem. Not just in our case of Pharaoh but also in general, Hashem controls the heart and actions of a King as Mishlay (21:1) says, "A king's heart is like rivulets of water in Hashem's hand; wherever He wishes, He turns it."

The Rambam in Hilchos Teshuva (6:3) presents other examples where Hashem hardened leader's hearts. For example, Devorim (2:30) says, "But Sichon, king of Cheshbon, did not wish to let us (Bnei Yisroel) pass by him, for Hashem your G-d caused his spirit to be hardened and his heart to be obstinate, in order that He would give him into your hand, as this day." Another example is in Sefer Yehoshua (11:19-20), which says, "There was not a city that made peace with the Bnei Yisroel, save the Chivites, the inhabitants of Givon; they took all in battle. For it was from Hashem to harden their hearts, (that they should come) against Yisroel in battle, that they might destroy them completely, and that they might have no favor, that they might destroy them as Hashem had commanded Moshe."

In his Sefer Shaarei Orah (2), Rav Meir Bergman uses this concept to explain a well-known Gemorah in Brochos 10a. The Gemorah tells us that there were some people who lived in Rav Meir's neighborhood and who were careless of the Torah's laws and caused Rav Meir much distress. The Gemorah says that Rav Meir asked for mercy on these people that they should die. His wife Beruriah pondered why Rav Meir had prayed for their deaths. Sefer Tehillim (104:35) says, יִתַּמּוּ חַטָּאִים מִן הָאָרֶץ וּרְשָׁעִים עוֹד אֵינָם בָּרְכִי נַפְשִׁי אֶת ה' הַלְלוּקָהּ (Sinners will be destroyed from the earth and the wicked will be no more; my soul, bless Hashem. Hallelukah). At first glance, Beruriah thought that Rav Meir was following what Dovid HaMelech said and was davening to destroy sinners from the earth. However, Beruriah disagreed that this was what Dovid HaMelech meant in this Posuk, and rather she said that Dovid meant that the entity which causes sinners (the Yetzer Horah) should be destroyed. She proved that her interpretation was correct from the next phrase in the Posuk, which says, "the wicked shall be no more." If one set of sinners were destroyed, then how could Dovid say that this would cause that "the wicked shall be no more." However, if the Posuk meant that the entity which causes sinners should be destroyed, then it is understandable that this would cause "the wicked shall be no more." Rather Beruriah told Rav Meir that he should daven that these people who were careless of the Torah's laws should do Teshuva. Rav Meir listened to her advice, and after davening for them to do Teshuva, they indeed repented of their wickedness.

The Gemorah In Brochos 33b says הכל בידי שמים – חוץ מיראת שמים (Everything is in the hands of Heaven (Hashem) except for fear of Heaven (Hashem)). The Maharsha on this Gemorah ponders the question of how Rav Meir could have davened that his neighbors should fear Hashem and do Teshuva if fearing Hashem is not in the hands of Hashem. He answers that it is understandable how a person can daven for himself to fear Hashem since the Gemorah in Makos 10b says that "Heaven leads a person in the way that the person wants to go." There is also a corollary principle in Yuma 38b that "a person who comes to purify himself is helped by Heaven to attain purity." Since the person is davening because he wants to fear Hashem, therefore Heaven will lead that person to fear

Vaera

Hashem. The Maharsha says that it is also understandable how we can daven in Shemoneh Esreh and ask Hashem וְהַחֲזִירֵנוּ בִּתְשׁוּבָה שְׁלֵמָה לְפָנֶיךָ (and return us in complete Teshuva before you) since the person is including himself in this request, and we have just established that a person can daven for himself to fear Hashem and do Teshuva. However, it is difficult to understand how Rav Meir could daven for others to fear Hashem. The Maharsha concludes that it is possible to explain this difficulty though he does not elaborate as to how. Parenthetically, the Ben Yehoyoda says that it is also possible to daven for another person who at this point is righteous that they stay righteous and continue fearing Hashem. As proof, he offers the case of Moshe davening that Yehoshua remains fearing of Hashem and not be influenced by his fellow spies of Eretz Yisroel.

The Anaf Yosef answers the question that the Maharsha ponders by saying that there are many cases where a person sins and does not fear Heaven because of circumstances around him. For example, the Gemorah in Eruvin 41b says that there are three things that cause a person to violate his own will and the will of his creator. The three things are idolaters who pressure him to violate the Torah, evil spirits which cause the person to have problems mentally, and the problems induced by poverty. Though a person cannot daven to Hashem to give another person fear of Heaven not to sin, a person can daven to Hashem to remove the circumstances around the other person, so that the person will have a better chance of coming to fear of Hashem on his own. This is what Rav Meir davened about for his neighbors, and they were successful in bringing themselves to fear Hashem. The Nisivos, in his Sefer Emes LeYaakov on Shas, similarly says that people can be born with characteristics that make it more difficult for them to fear Hashem, and such was the case with Rav Meir's neighbors. In this case, also someone davening to Hashem to modify these character traits of the other person can successfully bring the other person to fear Hashem, as was the case with Rav Meir's davening for his neighbors.

Rav Meir Bergman answers the Maharsha's question of how Rav Meir could have davened that his neighbors should fear Hashem and do Teshuva if fearing Hashem is not in the hands of Hashem. He says that Rav Meir had tried mightily to get his neighbors to do Teshuva. However, Rav Meir eventually came to the conclusion that he was not being successful since Hashem had taken away their ability to do Teshuva, similar to what Hashem did to Pharaoh. That being the case, he decided that the best thing for these neighbors would be for them to die; since then, they would stop doing more sins which they could not Teshuva for. Rav Meir's wife Beruriah argued that a better way was possible, and that was to daven to Hashem that He should allow them to have the ability to do Teshuva. Rav Meir accepted Beruriah's argument, and his davening was successful in Hashem, allowing the neighbors to have the ability to do Teshuva. Now that they had this ability, Rav Meir was able to convince them to do Teshuva.

At the time of Kriyas Yam Soof, Shemos (14:28) says, וַיָּשֻׁבוּ הַמַּיִם וַיְכַסּוּ אֶת הָרֶכֶב וְאֶת הַפָּרָשִׁים לְכֹל חֵיל פַּרְעֹה הַבָּאִים אַחֲרֵיהֶם בַּיָּם לֹא נִשְׁאַר בָּהֶם עַד אֶחָד (And the waters returned and covered the chariots and the horsemen, the entire force of Pharaoh coming after them into the sea; not even till one of them survived). The Mechilta on the Posuk ponders whether Pharaoh was killed at Kriyas Yam Soof. Rav Yehuda's opinion is that Pharaoh did not survive, as Shemos (15:4) in Oz Yashir seems to imply when it says, "Pharaoh's chariots and his army He (Hashem) cast into the sea, and the elite of

Vaera

his officers sank in the Red Sea." Rav Nechemia's opinion is that Pharaoh did indeed survive as Shemos (9:16) says, "But, for this reason I have allowed you to survive, in order to show you My strength and in order to declare My name all over the earth." The Pirkei D'Rabi Eliezer (43) and the Yalkut Shimoni (176) say that not only did Pharaoh survive, but he eventually became King in Ninveh and was the King who caused the entire city of Ninveh to repent when Yona comes and proclaims that in forty days Ninveh will be destroyed. In this way, Pharaoh does Teshuva for not listening to Hashem in Egypt and letting the Bnei Yisroel leave Egypt. Both the Posuk at Kriyas Yam Soof and our Posuk use the similar words of עַד אֶחָד (until one). Based on the Posuk in Kriyas Yam Soof, we know that it is debatable if "until one" means everyone or that one was left. Similarly, in our Posuk we will see that some commentators say that לֹא מֵת מִמִּקְנֵה יִשְׂרָאֵל עַד אֶחָד means that not even one of the cattle of the Bnei Yisroel died and others take our Posuk to mean that only one of the cattle of the Bnei Yisroel died. The Malbim brings Sefer Shoftim (4:16) which says וּבָרָק רָדַף אַחֲרֵי הָרֶכֶב וְאַחֲרֵי הַמַּחֲנֶה עַד חֲרֹשֶׁת הַגּוֹיִם וַיִּפֹּל כָּל מַחֲנֵה סִיסְרָא לְפִי חֶרֶב לֹא נִשְׁאַר עַד אֶחָד (And Barak pursued the chariots and the camp, to Haroshes-goiim; and all of Sisra's camp fell by the edge of the sword, not even till one was left). The next Posuk says, "And Sisra fled on foot to the tent of Yael, the wife of Chever the Kenite; for there was peace between Yavin the king of Chatzor and the house of Chever the Kenite." Since Sisra did indeed survive, it would seem that when the Posuk says "till one," it means that one was left. Others like the Metzudos Dovid on the Posuk are of the opinion that "till one" is speaking about the camp of Sisra as opposed to Sisra himself. In that case, every one of Sisra's camp was killed out.

In Shemos (9:4), we are told, "And Hashem will make a separation between the livestock of Yisroel and the livestock of Egypt, and nothing of the Bnei Yisroel will die. Rav Schwab, in his Sefer Mayan Beis HaShoaivah, says that by the Torah saying that "nothing of the Bnei Yisroel will die," the Torah means that even if the cattle of the Bnei Yisroel were in central Egypt as opposed to being in Goshen, the Bnei Yisroel's cattle would not die. This is despite the fact that it could be right next to the cattle of the Egyptians, which will die; the typically contagious pestilence will not affect the cattle of the Bnei Yisroel.

The Shach points out that just by natural statistics, a few of the cattle of the Bnei Yisroel should have died during the period of seven days that the plague of pestilence occurred over. However, Hashem made a miracle, and not even one of the Bnei Yisroel's cattle died even though it would have died under normal circumstances.

We should mention that both the Chizkuni and Bechor Shor are of the opinion that not all of the cattle of the Egyptians died during the plague of pestilence. Rather they say that of the cattle that died, all the deaths were from the cattle of the Egyptians. They explain that that is why we see in the later plague of hail where Shemos (9:20) mentions the Egyptians still having animals when it says, "He who feared the word of Hashem of Pharaoh's servants drove his servants and his cattle into the houses."

1) We will first examine the opinions of those who say that when our Posuk relates לֹא מֵת מִמִּקְנֵה יִשְׂרָאֵל עַד אֶחָד it means that not even one of the cattle of the Bnei Yisroel died. The Shemos Raba

Vaera

(11:4) and the Midrash Tanchuma on Vaera (14) say that even cattle which was jointly owned by an Egyptian and a Jew did not die. Not only that, but the Shemos Raba says that even cattle which was in possession of an Egyptian but about which a Jew had claims on, even just a partial ownership of the animal, also did not die. The Rashash says that the Shemos Raba derives this last category of animals from our Posuk saying לֹא מֵת מִמִּקְנֵה יִשְׂרָאֵל which literally means "it did not die from the cattle of the Bnei Yisroel." The word "from" (and not necessarily all) means even if only a portion of it was owned by a Jew. The Yepheh Toar says that the Hebrew word עַד can sometimes mean even. For example, he quotes Sefer Shoftim (15:5) which says about Shimshon, וַיַּבְעֶר אֵשׁ בַּלַּפִּידִים וַיְשַׁלַּח בְּקָמוֹת פְּלִשְׁתִּים וַיַּבְעֵר מִגָּדִישׁ וְעַד קָמָה וְעַד כֶּרֶם זָיִת (And he kindled fire on the torches and set them loose in the standing grain of the Philistines, and burnt up from the stacks and even the standing grain and even the vineyards and olive trees). If we translate עַד in our Posuk as even, it would mean that our Posuk is saying that not even cattle that belonged partially to an Egyptian died. From Pharoah's perspective, Pharaoh was looking for an excuse to say that not all of the cattle of the Egyptians died. With this excuse, he could convince himself that the cattle of the Bnei Yisroel were essentially the same as the cattle of the Egyptians since at least some of the cattle of the Egyptians remained alive. He could delude himself that the prophecy of "And Hashem will make a separation between the livestock of Yisroel and the livestock of Egypt, and nothing of the Bnei Yisroel will die," had, Chas VeShalom, not happened since even some cattle in the Egyptians possession had not died. He was not interested that the cattle were either cattle that a Jew had some claim to or that a Jew had partial ownership of.

2) The Toldos Yitzchak, Oznayim LeTorah, and Rav Schwab, in his Sefer Mayan Beis HaShoaivah, answer our question similarly. They say that even when Pharaoh saw all the cattle of the Bnei Yisroel had survived, he concluded that the plague of pestilence was not that bad from his perspective. Pharaoh decided that he had an easy way to replenish the stock of Egyptian cattle, and that was by stealing the cattle of the Jews. Since Pharaoh had already "stolen" the bodies of the Bnei Yisroel by enslaving them, Pharaoh had no qualms about stealing their cattle. Therefore, Pharoah's heart was hardened even though all the cattle of the Egyptians died and all the cattle of the Bnei Yisroel survived.

In Shemos (12:37-38), when the Bnei Yisroel are leaving Egypt, the Torah tells us, "The Bnei Yisroel journeyed from Ramses to Succos, about six hundred thousand on foot, the men, besides the young children. And also, a great mixed multitude went up with them, and flocks and cattle, very much livestock." Since the Bnei Yisroel only borrowed vessels of gold, vessels of silver, and fine clothes from the Egyptians, the Ksav Sofer draws the obvious conclusion that the livestock had always belonged to the Bnei Yisroel in the Egyptian exile. Being that the Egyptians had stolen even the bodies of the Bnei Yisroel, he ponders why they didn't also steal their cattle. He answers that the Egyptians did this out of their wickedness so that they could inflict psychological pain on the Bnei Yisroel. A rich person who is forced to work under tremendous hardship is much more psychologically pained than a poor person who is used to working very hard and doing even menial jobs to earn money to feed himself. By allowing the Bnei Yisroel to keep their many flocks of cattle, the Egyptians made the Bnei Yisroel feel like they were rich.

Vaera

The Nitziv says that the Bnei Yisroel got essentially all their cattle in this plague of pestilence. With regard to the plague of pestilence, Shemos (9:5) says, "Hashem set an appointed time, saying, 'Tomorrow, G-d will do this thing in the land.'" The reason Hashem had Moshe announce to the Egyptians that the plague of pestilence would start on the next day was so that many of the Egyptians would take advantage and sell their cattle to the Bnei Yisroel at a very low price. These Egyptians would calculate that it would be better to at least get something for their cattle before they would die and be worthless once the plague of pestilence started.

3) The Taam V'Daas, quoting the Mashgiach Rav Leib Chasman, one of the great masters of Mussar, presents another answer to our question. Rav Chasman says that one of the hard-to-understand character traits of a person is that a person has a hard time saying that he is wrong. A person almost always sees himself as correct and gives himself many excuses for doing wrong actions, even in a case when "the whole world" says that what he is doing is wrong. In fact, in such a case, many people become even more stubborn when "the whole world" says that what they are doing is wrong since he can only see himself as correct. This was exactly the psychology of Pharaoh. When it was obvious to the whole world that it was no happenstance that every single cattle of the Bnei Yisroel lived during the plague of pestilence, Pharaoh had to harden his heart and become even more stubborn since it was obvious to "the whole world" that Pharaoh was wrong and that he should let the Bnei Yisroel leave Egypt.

With regard to how it was possible for Pharaoh to delude himself, the Akeidah offers a possible explanation. Until this plague, Pharaoh had deluded himself into believing that the constellation, which was the power over Goshen, saved the inhabitants of Goshen while the constellation over the rest of Egypt did not. In this plague of pestilence, where Jewish-owned cattle remained alive even though they were amongst the Egyptians in Egypt, Pharaoh started blaming the constellation over the Egyptians for not saving their cattle, whereas the constellation over the Jews did save their cattle, even when it was amongst the Egyptians.

4) We will now examine the opinions of those who say that when our Posuk relates לֹא מֵת מִמִּקְנֵה יִשְׂרָאֵל עַד אֶחָד it means that one or one categories of the cattle of the Bnei Yisroel indeed did die. The Malbim and the Vilna Gaon, as quoted by the Mayanah Shel Torah, say that the one cattle which did die was the cattle that belonged to the son of Shlomis bas Divri. The Shemos Raba (1:28) says that Shlomis bas Divri's husband was Dasan, the same Dasan along with Avirom that rebelled against Moshe in the rebellion of Korach. The Egyptian taskmaster, who Moshe later killed, became attracted to Shlomis bas Divri and to satisfy his desires, he awoke Dasan in the middle of the night and forced him to leave his house. The Egyptian then came in and replaced Dasan in bed with her to satisfy his desires. Since it was in the middle of the night, Shlomis bas Divri had no idea that it was an Egyptian and not her husband. Dasan later returned and figured out what had happened. When the Egyptian realized that he had figured out what had happened, the Egyptian began hitting Dasan without remorse. When Moshe saw this, he killed the Egyptian. The Ramban on Vayikra (25:10) quotes the opinion of the French Rabonim that, before the Torah was given, in such a situation as what happened to Shlomis bas Divri, the child follows the pedigree of the father and is an Egyptian. That being the case, his cattle died during the plague of pestilence, just like the cattle of all the rest

Vaera

of the Egyptians. Pharaoh, however, had no idea that the son of Shlomis bas Divri had an Egyptian father, and Pharaoh thought that this son was Jewish. Since Pharaoh thought he had, Chas VeShalom, found an animal which contradicted what Moshe had told him that all of the cattle of the Jews would not die, Pharaoh had his excuse to not believe Moshe, and therefore he hardened his heart.

5) The Nitziv also answers our question by presenting a case where one category of the cattle of the Bnei Yisroel indeed did die. He says that there were some cattle which the Jews rented from the Egyptians in order to benefit from their milk and wool. Even though the Egyptians still owned these cattle, the cattle did not die since they were in possession of a Jew. However, he says that the Egyptian cattle rented out to the Bnei Yisroel did die if the Jewish renter was wicked and was destined to die in the three days of darkness. Cattle owned by even a wicked Jew who was destined to die in the three days of darkness remained alive in the plague of pestilence so that the righteous Jews who did not die in the three days of darkness could inherit the possessions of the wicked Jews who died. Therefore, there were three classes of people with respect to the plague of pestilence. All the cattle of the Egyptians died. All the cattle of the righteous Jews remained alive, including those they had rented from the Egyptians. All the cattle of the wicked Jews remained alive except for those that they had rented from the Egyptians.

With this approach, the Nitziv explains the seeming repetitiveness of our Posuk and the previous Posuk, which says, "G-d did this thing on the morrow, and all the livestock of the Egyptians died, but of the livestock of the Bnei Yisroel, not one died (according to the Nitziv these are the righteous Jews where even the rented Egyptian cattle remained alive). And Pharaoh sent, and behold, not until one of the livestock of Yisroel died (these are the wicked Jews where one category of cattle, those that they had rented from the Egyptians died), but Pharaoh's heart became hardened, and he did not let the people out." From the perspective of Pharaoh, who had no idea of the difference between righteous and wicked Jews, the inconsistency of which cattle died allowed Pharaoh to justify to himself that Hashem's words had, Chas VeShalom, not been fulfilled.

Since Hashem Hardened Pharoah's Heart, How Could Hashem Punish Him for Not Listening to Moshe?

וְלֹא יָכְלוּ הַחַרְטֻמִּים לַעֲמֹד לִפְנֵי מֹשֶׁה מִפְּנֵי הַשְּׁחִין כִּי הָיָה הַשְּׁחִין בַּחַרְטֻמִּם וּבְכָל מִצְרָיִם. וַיְחַזֵּק ה' אֶת לֵב פַּרְעֹה וְלֹא שָׁמַע אֲלֵהֶם כַּאֲשֶׁר דִּבֶּר ה' אֶל מֹשֶׁה (ט:יא-יב) Shemos (9:11-12) And the sorcerers could not stand before Moshe because of the boils, for the boils were upon the sorcerers and upon all Egypt. But Hashem strengthened Pharaoh's heart, and he did not hearken to them, as Hashem spoke to Moshe.

Since Hashem strengthened Pharoah's heart, how could He punish him for not listening to Moshe?

Introduction
The Ramban on Shemos (7:3) describes our question as a question asked by all.

Vaera

The Midrash Tanchuma in Vaera (3) and the Shemos Raba (13:3) are the sources for Rashi's statement on Shemos (7:3) that for the first five plagues, Pharaoh hardened his own heart while for the last five plagues Hashem hardened Pharaoh's heart. The Midrash Tanchuma says that we can see this because, in the first five plagues (the plague of pestilence being the fifth plague), the Torah says that Pharaoh hardened his heart. In the last five plagues, the Torah says, "And Hashem hardened Pharaoh's heart." They say that after Pharaoh hardened his heart for the first five plagues, Hashem figuratively said that from this point and onwards, even if Pharaoh would want to send the Bnei Yisroel, Hashem will not listen to his desires. This statement caused Pharaoh to refuse to send out the Bnei Yisroel, no matter what.

Not only was Pharoah's heart hardened, but also his servants' hearts were hardened as Hashem tells Moshe in Shemos (10:1), "Come to Pharaoh, for I have hardened his heart and the heart of his servants, in order that I may place these signs of Mine in his midst."

1) The Rambam, in Hilchos Teshuva (6:3), the Ramban on Shemos (7:3), and Rabeinu Bechay answer our question similarly. They say that Pharaoh, in his wickedness, did many horrible things to the Bnei Yisroel, which were completely unjustifiable. As the Rambam says in the eighth Perek of Shemoneh Perakim, had the punishment to Pharaoh and the Egyptians only been for not sending the Bnei Yisroel out of Egypt, Hashem would not have punished them since Hashem hardened Pharoah's heart to not send the Bnei Yisroel out. Rather, the punishment was because Pharaoh and his helpers used their freedom of choice to persecute a nation of people who had come to live amongst them. Therefore, Hashem took away Pharoah's free will to send the Bnei Yisroel out of Egypt so that Pharaoh could get punished for all the horrible things the Egyptians did to the Jews during the exile in Egypt. The Rambam in Shemoneh Perakim says that though Hashem could have chosen to punish Pharaoh in the world to come for his wickedness, Hashem chose to punish Pharaoh in this world. The reason is that Hashem had promised Avrohom in Beraishis (15:14) "And also the nation that they will serve will I judge."

The Mishna says in Pirkei Avos (5:18) וְכָל הַמַּחֲטִיא אֶת הָרַבִּים אֵין מַסְפִּיקִין בְּיָדוֹ לַעֲשׂוֹת תְּשׁוּבָה (anyone who causes the public to sin, is not given the wherewithal to do Teshuva). The Rambam says that Pharaoh would be an example of this principle. The Bnei Yisroel came down to Egypt as G-d fearing people and were corrupted by the Egyptians. For example, the Yalkut Shimoni (268) at the end of Parshas Beshalach tells us that the Bnei Yisroel had one main Mitzvah, that of doing a Bris Milah, which they kept in Egypt being that it had been given to and handed down from Avrohom. The Egyptians, seeing that it was their main Mitzvah, went to the Bnei Yisroel and told them to give up the Mitzvah of Bris Milah, thereby becoming similar to the Egyptians, and as a reward, the Egyptians promised to lighten the slavery work. Therefore, we see that the Egyptians, under the guidance of their leader Pharaoh, caused the public to sin. Because of this, says the Rambam, Pharaoh and the Egyptians are not given the opportunity to do Teshuva. We note that many other commentators disagree with the Rambam and say that the Mishna is telling us that a person who causes the public to sin is not given any help from Heaven to do Teshuva, but not that he is not given the opportunity at all to do Teshuva.

Vaera

The Shemos Raba (11:6) says that when Hashem saw that Pharaoh did not do Teshuva in the first five plagues, Hashem said that after this had occurred, even if Pharaoh will want to do Teshuva in the last five plagues, Hashem will harden his heart so as not to Teshuva. The reason is so that Pharaoh will get the full punishment that he deserves. The Abarbanel says that this Shemos Raba seems to be completely consistent with the opinion of the Rambam, Ramban, and Rabeinu Bechay that Pharoah's ability to do Teshuva was taken away after the fifth plague.

In his Sefer Shaarei Orah (2), Rav Meir Bergman uses this concept to explain a well-known Gemorah in Brochos 10a. The Gemorah tells us that there were some people who lived in Rav Meir's neighborhood and who were careless of the Torah's laws and caused Rav Meir much distress. The Gemorah says that Rav Meir asked for mercy on these people that they should die. His wife Beruriah pondered why Rav Meir had prayed for their deaths. Sefer Tehillim (104:35) says, יִתַּמּוּ חַטָּאִים מִן הָאָרֶץ וּרְשָׁעִים עוֹד אֵינָם בָּרְכִי נַפְשִׁי אֶת ה' הַלְלוּקָה (Sinners will be destroyed from the earth and the wicked will be no more; my soul, bless Hashem. Hallelukah). At first glance, Beruriah thought that Rav Meir was following what Dovid HaMelech said and was davening to destroy sinners from the earth. However, Beruriah disagreed that this was what Dovid HaMelech meant in this Posuk, and rather she said that Dovid meant that the entity which causes sinners (the Yetzer Horah) should be destroyed. She proved that her interpretation was correct from the next phrase in the Posuk, which says, "the wicked shall be no more." If one set of sinners were destroyed, then how could Dovid say that this would cause that "the wicked shall be no more." However, if the Posuk meant that the entity which causes sinners should be destroyed, then it is understandable that this would cause "the wicked shall be no more." Rather Beruriah told Rav Meir that he should daven that these people who were careless of the Torah's laws should do Teshuva. Rav Meir listened to her advice, and after davening for them to do Teshuva, they indeed repented of their wickedness.

The Gemorah In Brochos 33b says הכל בידי שמים – חוץ מיראת שמים (Everything is in the hands of Heaven (Hashem) except for fear of Heaven (Hashem)). The Maharsha on this Gemorah ponders the question of how Rav Meir could have davened that his neighbors should fear Hashem and do Teshuva if fearing Hashem is not in the hands of Hashem. He answers that it is understandable how a person can daven for himself to fear Hashem since the Gemorah in Makos 10b says that "Heaven leads a person in the way that the person wants to go." There is also a corollary principle in Yuma 38b that "a person who comes to purify himself is helped by Heaven to attain purity." Since the person is davening because he wants to fear Hashem, therefore Heaven will lead that person to fear Hashem. The Maharsha says that it is also understandable how we can daven in Shemoneh Esreh and ask Hashem וְהַחֲזִירֵנוּ בִּתְשׁוּבָה שְׁלֵמָה לְפָנֶיךָ (and return us in complete Teshuva before you) since the person is including himself in this request, and we have just established that a person can daven for himself to fear Hashem and do Teshuva. However, it is difficult to understand how Rav Meir could daven for others to fear Hashem. The Maharsha concludes that it is possible to explain this difficulty though he does not elaborate as to how. Parenthetically, the Ben Yehoyoda says that it is also possible to daven for another person who at this point is righteous that they stay righteous and continue fearing Hashem. As proof, he offers the case of Moshe davening that Yehoshua remains fearing of Hashem and not be influenced by his fellow spies of Eretz Yisroel.

Vaera

The Anaf Yosef answers the question that the Maharsha ponders by saying that there are many cases where a person sins and does not fear Heaven because of circumstances around him. For example, the Gemorah in Eruvin 41b says that there are three things that cause a person to violate his own will and the will of his creator. The three things are idolaters who pressure him to violate the Torah, evil spirits which cause the person to have problems mentally, and the problems induced by poverty. Though a person cannot daven to Hashem to give another person fear of Heaven not to sin, a person can daven to Hashem to remove the circumstances around the other person, so that the person will have a better chance of coming to fear of Hashem on his own. This is what Rav Meir davened about for his neighbors, and they were successful in bringing themselves to fear Hashem. The Nisivos, in his Sefer Emes LeYaakov on Shas, similarly says that people can be born with characteristics that make it more difficult for them to fear Hashem, and such was the case with Rav Meir's neighbors. In this case, also someone davening to Hashem to modify these character traits of the other person can successfully bring the other person to fear Hashem, as was the case with Rav Meir's davening for his neighbors.

Rav Meir Bergman answers the Maharsha's question of how Rav Meir could have davened that his neighbors should fear Hashem and do Teshuva if fearing Hashem is not in the hands of Hashem. He says that Rav Meir had tried mightily to get his neighbors to do Teshuva. However, Rav Meir eventually came to the conclusion that he was not being successful since Hashem had taken away their ability to do Teshuva, similar to what Hashem did to Pharaoh. That being the case, he decided that the best thing for these neighbors would be for them to die; since then, they would stop doing more sins which they could not Teshuva for. Rav Meir's wife Beruriah argued that a better way was possible, and that was to daven to Hashem that He should allow them to have the ability to do Teshuva. Rav Meir accepted Beruriah's argument, and his davening was successful in Hashem, allowing the neighbors to have the ability to do Teshuva. Now that they had this ability, Rav Meir was able to convince them to do Teshuva.

2) The Ramban, Rabeinu Bechay, and Sforno all on Shemos (7:3) offer a second answer to our question. During the first five plagues, the Torah says either וַיֶּחֱזַק לֵב פַּרְעֹה וְלֹא שָׁמַע אֲלֵהֶם (But Pharaoh's heart remained steadfast, and he did not hearken to them) or וַיַּכְבֵּד פַּרְעֹה אֶת לִבּוֹ (But Pharaoh hardened his heart). That is, says the Ramban, Pharaoh, did not really want to send the Bnei Yisroel out of Egypt to serve and honor Hashem. However, once the plagues became so intense, Pharaoh did not have the desire to endure the plagues, and therefore Pharaoh would have sent the Bnei Yisroel out in order to not have to put up with the plagues. Nonetheless, in the absence of the threat of future plagues, Pharaoh would never have sent the Bnei Yisroel out to serve and honor Hashem. The Ramban says that not just in our case of Pharaoh but also in general, Hashem controls the heart and actions of a King as Mishlay (21:1) says, "A king's heart is like rivulets of water in Hashem's hand; wherever He wishes, He turns it." However, says the Sforno, if Pharaoh would have changed his mind and decided to send the Bnei Yisroel out of Egypt to serve and honor Hashem, Hashem would have in no way prevented this and Pharaoh could have done Teshuva.

Vaera

The Rambam in Hilchos Teshuva (6:3) presents other examples where Hashem hardened leader's hearts. For example, Devorim (2:30) says, "But Sichon, king of Cheshbon, did not wish to let us (Bnei Yisroel) pass by him, for Hashem your G-d caused his spirit to be hardened and his heart to be obstinate, in order that He would give him into your hand, as this day." Another example is in Sefer Yehoshua (11:19-20), which says, "There was not a city that made peace with the Bnei Yisroel, save the Chivites, the inhabitants of Givon; they took all in battle. For it was from Hashem to harden their hearts, (that they should come) against Yisroel in battle, that they might destroy them completely, and that they might have no favor, that they might destroy them as Hashem had commanded Moshe."

3) The Sforno on Shemos (7:3) presents another answer to our question. He says that Hashem always wants everyone to do Teshuva. As Sefer Yechezkel (33:11) says, "Say to them: As I live, says Hashem G-d, I do not wish for the death of the wicked, but for the wicked to repent of his way so that he may live." The purpose of the ten plagues was for Pharaoh and all the Egyptians to do full Teshuva and come to serve and honor Hashem. Since they started off not believing in Hashem at all, the only way to do this was to show the Egyptians many wondrous signs through the plagues. Since some of the wondrous signs involved hardships, Pharoah's heart had to be hardened so that he would be able to withstand the plagues, each one showing the greatness of Hashem. The goal was for Pharaoh to come to a state where he would send out the Bnei Yisroel for the honor of Hashem and thereby do full Teshuva. Not only was Pharaoh able to do full Teshuva, but Hashem also aided him to do full Teshuva. Similar to the Sforno, Rabeinu Yona also says that hardening Pharoah's heart was just so that he would be able to withstand the plagues and not die because of the fright or pain of the plagues. In no way did this hardening of Pharoah's heart prevent him from doing Teshuva.

4) The Akeidah also ponders our question. He says that Pharoah's ability to do Teshuva was in no way taken away from him. Rather there were three fundamental principles at play here. Firstly, a person can become responsible for many different punishments and afflictions for what the person has done. It works this way in Halacha also. For example, he quotes the Gemorah in Makos 16b, which says that there are many negative Mitzvos, one can come in violation of by eating creeping creatures. Some of these violations are for, in general, eating creeping creatures while others are specific to creeping creatures in the water, others to creeping creatures on land, and others for creeping creatures that fly. Violating each negative Mitzvah comes with the penalty of lashes, and therefore one can get many sets of lashes for eating a creeping creature. For example, the Gemorah says that one who ate a certain small nonkosher water creature has violated four different negative Mitzvos and is due four sets of lashes. Even worse, eating a creeping creature that flies violates six different negative Mitzvos since it includes both the land and the flying negative Mitzvos of creeping creatures. The Akeidah says that in his time, the Gentile courts had laws such that a person would first be punished by taking away all his money, then by lashes, then by chopping off his feet first, then his hands next, and subsequently other parts of his body until the person died.

Secondly, a person who has received a verdict for punishment by a human court cannot have the punishment annulled by doing Teshuva. Otherwise, there would never be the possibility of capital

Vaera

punishment since no one facing the death penalty would ever allow himself to be killed and would choose to do Teshuva and be saved from the death penalty. Many times, the Torah says similar to what it says in Devorim (13:12) "And all Yisroel shall listen and fear, and they shall no longer do any evil such as this in your midst." "Had a person been allowed to do Teshuva and have the punishment erased," says the Akeidah, "he would never fear of doing any Aveirah since he will say that he will just do Teshuva, after committing the Aveirah." It is not just in punishments meted out by human courts where Teshuva does not work to erase the punishment but also in punishment meted out by the heavenly court. For example, the Gemorah in Yuma 86a says that if someone has done the sin of Chilul Hashem, it is such a grave sin that neither Teshuva, Yom Kippur, nor suffering punishment alone is powerful enough to even just protect the person from a full punishment. Rather only the combination of Teshuva, Yom Kippur, and suffering punishment is able to protect the person from a full punishment, and the person is only fully forgiven when he is Niftar. The Gemorah proves this from Sefer Yeshayahu (22:14), which says, "And it was revealed in My ears, Hashem of Hosts; that this sin shall not be atoned for you until you die." Rashi on the Gemorah explains that this Posuk shows that there is a sin that is only atoned for on death. Since Chilul Hashem is the gravest sin, the Gemorah concludes that this Posuk must be talking about the punishment for Chilul Hashem. An example of Chilul Hashem was the sin of hitting the rock instead of speaking to it where Moshe and Aaron were punished in Bamidbar (20:12) "Since you did not have faith in Me to sanctify Me in the eyes of the Bnei Yisroel, therefore you shall not bring this assembly to the Land which I have given them." No amount of Teshuva or davening was able to unlock the gate of Teshuva and allow Moshe and Aharon to go to Eretz Yisroel.

Thirdly, when a person becomes responsible for many types of punishment, it is much more likely that the person will be able to receive these punishments if they are spaced out in time. Otherwise, it is likely that the person will soon die if the punishments come one right after the other without any time to recover between them. Also, it will help if the person is given ample food and medical attention to recover from the first punishment so that the person will be able to withstand subsequent punishment. Since the purpose of all the punishments is to act as a deterrent for others to not follow in this person's footsteps, it is in the court's best interests to do everything they can to facilitate the person withstanding all the punishments.

The Akeidah says that the three principals were all in play with respect to Pharaoh. Pharaoh had done much evil by ignoring all the good that Yosef had done in saving Egypt and had mercilessly persecuted the Jews themselves and even their babies. In addition, he had violated Chilul Hashem, for example, by saying in Shemos (5:2), "Who is Hashem that I should heed His voice to let Yisroel out? I do not know Hashem, neither will I let Yisroel out." Therefore, Pharaoh was punished with multiple punishments, and consequently, Teshuva would not help to take away the punishments as we have seen in the principals. All that was left to do was to punish Pharaoh in such a way that he would be able to withstand all the punishments, as the Akeidah detailed in the third principle. As a result, Pharaoh was afforded 24 days to recover from each punishment and was given the right temperament, including a hardened heart to be able to get all the punishments that he deserved. This fits in very well with what Hashem tells Moshe to tell Pharaoh in Shemos (9:16), "But, for this

Vaera

reason I have allowed you to stand, in order to show you My strength and in order to declare My name all over the earth."

5) The Akeidah presents another answer to our question. The Gemorah says in Makos 10b that "they lead a person in the way that the person wants to go." The Maharsha explains that "they" refers to the deeds that a person does. Every good or bad deed that a person does creates either a good or bad angel for that deed. These good or bad deeds influence a person so that the person goes in the way that he originally wanted to go. For example, says the Gemorah, Bilam, wanted to go with the princes of Midyan to curse the Bnei Yisroel. Hashem made it clear to Bilam that he should not go with the princes of Midyan as Hashem tells Bilam in Bamidbar (22:12), "You shall not go with them (princes of Midyan)! You shall not curse the people because they are blessed." Yet when Bilam still very much wants to go with the princes of Midyan, Hashem tells him in Bamidbar (22:20), "If these men have come to call for you, arise and go with them, but the word I speak to you that you shall do." This concept is also similar to the concept in Yuma 38b that if one comes to defile himself, an opening is made for him to allow him to defile himself. As Rashi on the Gemorah explains, the person is not prevented by Heaven from defiling himself. Similarly, if one comes to purify himself, he is given assistance from Heaven to purify himself. The Eyun Yaakov explains that one's Yetzer Horah is so strong that unless Heaven helps a person, he cannot, in general, overcome it. Therefore, when the person comes to defile himself, Heaven does not help him, and this leads to the person tending to defile himself further. In the case of the person coming to purify himself, Heaven actively helps that person against his Yetzer Horah so that the person is given assistance by Heaven to further purify himself. The Akeidah says that we see an example of this with Pharaoh himself. Pharaoh never really wanted to send the Bnei Yisroel out of Egypt. Therefore, when Hashem told Moshe to tell the Bnei Yisroel in Shemos (14:2), "Speak to the Bnei Yisroel, and let them turn back and encamp in front of Pi Hachiros, between Migdol and the sea; in front of Baal Tzphon, you shall encamp opposite it, by the sea," Pharaoh thought that the Bnei Yisroel were lost in the desert and it was an opportunity for Pharaoh to capture back the Bnei Yisroel. This is what the next Pesukim (14:3-4) tell us when they say, "And Pharaoh will say about the Bnei Yisroel, they are trapped in the land. The desert has closed in upon them. And I will harden Pharaoh's heart, and he will pursue them, and I will be glorified through Pharaoh and through his entire force, and the Egyptians will know that I am Hashem and they did so." The Akeidah explains that when this Posuk says that Hashem will harden Pharoah's heart, all it means is that Hashem will provide Pharaoh the opportunity to go in the way he wanted to go. This will occur by setting up the conditions so that he will think the Bnei Yisroel are trapped in the desert and thereby go and chase the Bnei Yisroel. Since by hardening Pharoah's heart, Hashem was just leading Pharaoh in the way he wanted to go, he could have done Teshuva at any time, and therefore our question is answered. The Abarbanel also is of a similar opinion as to the Akeidah.

6) The Abarbanel also ponders our question. He says that with regard to sins between man and Hashem, Teshuva always helps. He says that even a great sinner like King Menashe about whom Divrei HaYomim II (33:9) says, "And Menashe led the kingdom of Yehuda and the inhabitants of Yerushalayim astray to do what was evil, more than the nations whom Hashem had destroyed from before the Bnei Yisroel," was able to do Teshuva. Divrei HaYomim II (33:11-13) says, "And

Vaera

Hashem brought upon them the generals of the king of Assyria, and they seized Menashe with hooks and bound him with copper chains and brought him to Babylon. And when he was distressed, he entreated Hashem his G-d, and he humbled himself greatly before the G-d of his fathers. And he prayed to Him, and He accepted his prayer, and He heard his supplication and He restored him to Yerushalayim to his kingdom, and Menashe knew that Hashem was G-d." The Yismach Yisroel says that for a person who "humbles himself greatly," as Menashe did, Hashem opens up a path of Teshuva, so that he can do Teshuva even when there is a decree, because of his sin, that he cannot do Teshuva.

The only time when Hashem does not accept Teshuva is for sins that are done between man and his fellow man. Pharaoh not only sinned to Hashem with his belief in idols, but he also sinned terribly to his fellow man, the Bnei Yisroel, by horribly persecuting them, not to mention murdering their children. For these sins, even if Pharaoh did complete Teshuva, it would not be accepted so that he could be punished for all these sins. When Sefer Yechezkel (33:11) says "Say to them: As I live, says Hashem G-d, I do not wish for the death of the wicked, but for the wicked to repent of his way so that he may live," the Abarbanel says that this Posuk is only talking with regard to sins between man and Hashem.

7) The Abarbanel presents another answer to our question. He says that Teshuva is a gift and that this gift was only given to the Bnei Yisroel. However, a Gentile who does Teshuva and still believes in his idols has not done full Teshuva. Pharaoh never gave up serving his idols, and therefore he was not given the gift of Teshuva. Only if a Gentile gives up his idols and commits to serving Hashem will the Gentile also be given the gift of Teshuva. With this principle, the Abarbanel explains how Hashem accepted the Teshuva of Ninveh in the time of the prophet Yona since they all gave up their idols and accepted Hashem, and therefore Ninveh was spared at that time.

8) The Maharal, in his Sefer Gevuras Hashem (31), also ponders our question. He says that Pharaoh caused a great Chilul Hashem at the time Moshe and Aharon first came to him when he said in Shemos (5:2), "Who is Hashem that I should heed His voice to let Yisroel out? I do not know Hashem, neither will I let Yisroel out." The wicked Pharaoh and his nation caused that Hashem should not be known, and therefore Pharaoh and his nation had to atone for this by allowing everyone to know the name of Hashem. By hardening Pharoah's heart, Hashem caused everyone to know the name of Hashem. Had his heart not been hardened, he would not have been able to withstand the plagues, and he would have sent the Bnei Yisroel out before all the miraculous miracles came on the Egyptians and showed everyone the greatness of Hashem. Therefore, hardening Pharoah's heart was just a necessary part of Pharoah's atonement for his Chilul Hashem.

9) The Maharal, in his Sefer Gevruas Hashem (31), the Beis HaLevi towards the end of Parshas Shemos, and the Oznayim LeTorah answer our question similarly. The reason Hashem hardened Pharoah's heart was so that Pharoah should have free will in whether he wanted to send the Bnei Yisroel out of Egypt. The plagues, especially the last five ones, would have taken away Pharoah's free will since their severity would have forced Pharaoh to send the Bnei Yisroel out of Egypt. By

Vaera

hardening his heart, Hashem counterbalanced the desire to send the Bnei Yisroel out because of the severity of the plagues, which left Pharaoh with free will to decide whether he really wanted to send the Bnei Yisroel out. As the Beis HaLevi puts it, Hashem evened things up when before each plague, Pharaoh had a choice whether to send the Bnei Yisroel out. The pressure to not allow the Bnei Yisroel to leave because of how much Pharoah's heart was hardened equaled the pressure of how much each plague caused Pharoah to want to let the Bnei Yisroel leave so that Pharoah would not have to endure that particular plague. If Pharaoh would under these circumstances have allowed the Bnei Yisroel to leave, then it meant that if both the threat of the plague and the hardening of Pharoah's heart were removed, Pharaoh would have still wanted to send the Bnei Yisroel out of Egypt. This would have been true Teshuva.

The Beis HaLevi cites a Gemorah in Menochos 53b. The Gemorah describes how at the time the first Beis Hamikdosh was being destroyed, Avrohom Aveinu came to the place of the Beis Hamikdosh on behalf of the Bnei Yisroel. After being told that the Bnei Yisroel had sinned and were sent into exile, Avrohom reacted by putting his hands on his head, crying and weeping while wondering if, Chas VeShalom, the Bnei Yisroel, had no hope of doing Teshuva and returning from exile. A heavenly voice called out and said the Bnei Yisroel are similar to a leafy olive tree which will have beautiful fruit. In the same way that an olive tree's destiny is fulfilled at its end, so too will the Bnei Yisroel's destiny be fulfilled at their end. The Beis HaLevi says that Avrohom was concerned that even if the Bnei Yisroel did Teshuva, it would not be accepted since it will only have come through being afflicted in exile. The Heavenly voice came out and said that the Bnei Yisroel are comparable to an olive tree. An olive only emits its most oil by being crushed. In a similar way, the Bnei Yisroel only do their best Teshuva when they are being crushed by their enemies. The fact the crushing process emits much more oil than just the squeezing process proves that inherently the olive has oil in it. In a similar way, being crushed by their enemies brings out the best Teshuva of the Bnei Yisroel, which shows that inherently they are capable of doing Teshuva and following Hashem's ways. The Oznayim LeTorah quotes a famous Rambam in Hilchos Gerushin (2:20). A Get (divorce) can only be given willingly by the husband. The Rambam describes what happens in a case where the Halacha says that we force the husband to divorce his wife, and the husband does not want to grant a divorce. In such a case, the Jewish court is given the authority to hit and punish the husband until the point the husband says that he is willing to give the divorce. He ponders why such a divorce is valid since the husband was forced to do so against his will. He answers that Halachically, something is only called forced if it does not force a person to do something that the Torah does not obligate him to do. For example, if someone is forced to gift or sell an object. A Jew at his base wants to do the positive Mitzvos and not violate the negative Mitzvos. It is just one's Yetzer Horah that forces the person to not do what his base will wants him to do. By adding in the force of Beis Din hitting and punishing the husband, we are just negating the force of the Yetzer Horah and the true will of the husband to follow the Torah and grant his wife a divorce. Therefore, the divorce is valid since it was given by the husband's true will. In a similar way, being crushed by our enemies in exile allows the true character of the Jews to shine forth when they do Teshuva and follow in the path of Hashem. On the flip side, hardening Pharoah's heart allowed the true character of Pharoh to shine forth when he refused to listen to Hashem and send the Bnei Yisroel out of Egypt.

Vaera

10) The Sifsei Chachomim on Rashi also presents an answer to our question, and he is of the opinion that this is also Rashi's opinion. He says that Hashem knew that Pharaoh will not do a complete Teshuva and that without hardening Pharoah's heart, he would have sent out the Bnei Yisroel because of his desire not to have to endure the pain of further plagues. That being the case, Pharaoh would still need to be punished since he would not have done a complete Teshuva. However, not knowing Pharoah's intention, the people of the world would think that Pharaoh did complete Teshuva by sending out the Bnei Yisroel, and it would be a Chilul Hashem to punish him after he sent out the Bnei Yisroel from Egypt. Therefore, Hashem hardened Pharoah's heart so that both the correct punishment would be meted out to him, and it would be without a Chilul Hashem being caused later if Pharaoh would be properly punished after sending the Bnei Yisroel out of Egypt.

11) The Chofetz Chaim also presents an answer to our question. He says that there are sinners whom Hashem helps to do Teshuva. We see this concept in our everyday Shemoneh Esreh when we daven to Hashem and say וְהַחֲזִירֵנוּ בִּתְשׁוּבָה שְׁלֵמָה לְפָנֶיךָ (and bring us back in complete Teshuva before you). However, Pharaoh was punished that Hashem would not help him to do Teshuva, and rather would need to decide purely on his own to do Teshuva. If Pharaoh on his own decided to do Teshuva then, it would have been accepted. The Gemorah in Chagigah 15a tells us about Acher, a great scholar who abandoned being religious. The Gemorah says that once, Acher was riding on a horse on Shabbos, and Rav Meir was walking behind him in order to learn some Torah from him. When they came to a certain point along the way, Acher told Rav Meir to turn around and go back since Acher had calculated using the footsteps of his horse that they had reached the furthest distance outside of a city that one is permitted to travel on Shabbos. Rav Meir replied to Acher, "you should also turn around and go back to your Torah observance." Acher replied, "didn't I already tell you that I have heard from the other side of the Heavenly partition a heavenly voice saying, "Do Teshuva wayward sons except for Acher." "Therefore," said Acher, "there is no point of my doing Teshuva since it will not be accepted." The Chofetz Chaim explains that all the heavenly voice was saying is that Acher would not be helped by Hashem in doing Teshuva but would need to decide to do so on his own accord. If Acher, on his own, did a complete Teshuva, it would be accepted.

Bo

Why Would Hashem Hardening Pharaoh's Heart Be a Reason to Go to Pharaoh?

Shemos וַיֹּאמֶר ה' אֶל מֹשֶׁה בֹּא אֶל פַּרְעֹה כִּי אֲנִי הִכְבַּדְתִּי אֶת לִבּוֹ וְאֶת לֵב עֲבָדָיו לְמַעַן שִׁתִי אֹתֹתַי אֵלֶּה בְּקִרְבּוֹ (י:א) (10:1) Hashem said to Moshe: 'Come to Pharaoh, for I have hardened his heart and the heart of his servants, in order that I may place these signs of Mine in his midst.'

Why would Hashem hardening Pharaoh's heart be a reason to go to Pharaoh? It would seem that once Pharaoh's heart is hardened, there would be no point in going to Pharaoh.

Introduction.
The upcoming plague Moshe was coming to warn Pharaoh about was the plague of locusts.

1) The Bechor Shor presents an answer to our question. He points out that Hashem in our Posuk does not tell Moshe to "go to Pharaoh" but rather to "come to Pharaoh," which is a strange phraseology. He says that "come to Pharaoh" implies that Hashem would go along with Moshe to Pharaoh, and therefore despite the fact that Hashem hardened Pharaoh's heart, there was a purpose in going to Pharaoh.

2) The Mizrachi, Abarbanel, and Maharil Diskin present an answer to our question. After the previous plague of hail, Pharaoh says in Shemos (9:28), "Daven to Hashem, and let it be enough of G-d's thunder and hail, and I will let you (Bnei Yisroel) go, and you shall not continue to stand." The Maharil Diskin points out that Shemos (9:14) introducing the plague of hail says, "Because this time, I am sending all My plagues into your heart and into your servants and into your people, in order that you know that there is none like Me in the entire earth." Coupling together the fact that Pharaoh promised to let the Bnei Yisroel go after the plague of hail, the Mizrachi, Abarbanel, and Maharil Diskin say that Moshe thought Pharaoh would soon contact him in arranging for the Bnei Yisroel to leave Egypt. In fact, the Maharil Diskin says, no matter what Pharaoh did, Moshe felt that there was no need now to go to Pharaoh. Either Pharaoh would keep his word, and therefore it was up to Pharaoh to contact Moshe, or Pharaoh would renege on his promise, and therefore Hashem should just punish Pharaoh for reneging without any warnings. Hashem informed Moshe that Pharaoh was not going to keep his promise and because it was Hashem who hardened Pharaoh's heart, it was not fair to punish Pharaoh just for reneging on his promise. That being the case, there was still a need to go to Pharaoh and warn him about the upcoming plague of locusts.

257

Bo

3) The Nachalas Yaakov disagrees with the Mizrachi, Abarbanel, and Maharil Diskin and says that Moshe was aware that Pharaoh was going to renege on his promise, as the last Posuk in Parshas Vaera says, "And Pharaoh's heart was hardened, and he did not let the Bnei Yisroel go out, as Hashem had spoken through the hand of Moshe." Moreover, after Pharaoh made his promise, Shemos (9:30) says that Moshe tells Pharaoh, "But you and your servants I know that you still do not fear Hashem G-d." Rather, the reason Hashem wanted Moshe to now go to Pharaoh was that for the first time, Hashem had also hardened the hearts of Pharaoh's servants. The reason Hashem had to now harden the hearts of Pharaoh's servants was that in the last plague, hail, Shemos (9:20) says, "He who feared the word of Hashem of Pharaoh's servants drove his servants and his livestock into the houses." Therefore, these servant's hearts also had to be hardened less they force Pharaoh to send out the Bnei Yisroel before the Egyptians had been punished sufficiently with all the plagues. This plague of locusts would be a test of Pharaoh's servants to see if after their hearts had been hardened, they would still choose to demand the Bnei Yisroel be sent out. The Nachalas Yaakov is of the opinion that Hashem hardening Pharaoh and his servants' hearts did not prevent them from repenting if they only chose to.

4) The Maharil Diskin presents another answer to our question. Pharaoh was stubborn and held onto even the slightest strand of evidence to try and prove that Moshe was doing the plagues with some sort of sorcery and was not being truthful when he said that he was an emissary of Hashem. For this plague of locusts, Hashem wanted to put the stubborn Pharaoh in a position that whatever he did would go against Pharaoh's beliefs. Moshe was sent to Pharaoh to tell him that it was Hashem who hardened Pharaoh's heart so that he wouldn't send out the Bnei Yisroel resulting in Pharaoh being punished more. On one side, Pharaoh was inclined to prove Moshe wrong and send out the Bnei Yisroel. However, to do this, Pharaoh would have to send out the Bnei Yisroel from being his slaves, something that Pharaoh, especially without being forced to, had no intention of doing. Therefore, Pharaoh found himself "between a rock and a hard place" with respect to how to proceed. This mockery of Pharaoh is what the Posuk after ours means when it says, "and in order that you tell into the ears of your son and your son's son how I made a mockery of the Egyptians."

5) The Chasam Sofer presents an answer to our question. He says Pharaoh could have thought to himself that there was something that didn't make any sense going on. If Hashem really wanted the Bnei Yisroel to go out to freedom, why hadn't Hashem already caused this to happen? Couldn't Hashem either force Pharaoh to send out the Bnei Yisroel by the sheer force of a plague, or couldn't Hashem change Pharaoh's heart such that he would want to send out the Bnei Yisroel? Parenthetically we cannot answer Pharaoh's question of "why Hashem couldn't change Pharaoh's heart such that he would want to send out the Bnei Yisroel" by saying that Hashem made the world based on giving people freedom of choice. Mishlay (21:1) says, פַּלְגֵי מַיִם לֶב מֶלֶךְ בְּיַד ה' עַל כָּל אֲשֶׁר יַחְפֹּץ יַטֶּנּוּ (A king's heart is like small streams of water in Hashem's hand; wherever He wishes, He turns it). A King, like Pharaoh, as opposed to everyone else, does not have free choice. Therefore, in our Posuk, Hashem tells Moshe to go to Pharaoh and tell him that Hashem has purposely hardened Pharaoh's heart so that he does not send the Bnei Yisroel out of Egypt. The reason for this is said in Shemos (10:2), "in order that you tell into the ears of your son and your son's son how I made a

Bo

mockery of the Egyptians, and that you tell of My signs that I placed in them, and you will know that I am Hashem."

6) The Chasam Sofer also presents another answer to our question. The Gemorah in Gittin 88a says that Eretz Yisroel was only destroyed after seven courts performed idolatry in Eretz Yisroel. Rashi on the Gemorah explains that seven courts mean seven royal families. The Gemorah says that having the destruction not occur until the sin was repeated seven times is based on Sefer Yirmiyahu (15:9) which says, אֻמְלְלָה יֹלֶדֶת הַשִּׁבְעָה נָפְחָה נַפְשָׁהּ בָּא שִׁמְשָׁהּ בְּעֹד יוֹמָם בּוֹשָׁה וְחָפֵרָה וּשְׁאֵרִיתָם לַחֶרֶב אֶתֵּן לִפְנֵי אֹיְבֵיהֶם נְאֻם ה' (She who bore seven has been cut off, her soul grieves, her sun sets when it is still day. She is ashamed and confounded. And her remnant I shall deliver to the sword before their enemies says Hashem). Being that the present plague (locusts) is the eighth plague, Moshe calculated that since Pharaoh had sinned by the previous seven plagues, there was no reason for an eighth plague, and Egypt would just be destroyed, and certainly, there was no more reason to warn Pharaoh. Hashem, however, explained that Moshe's calculation had a couple of errors in it. Firstly, when Moshe and Aharon had come and done the sign of Aharon's staff swallowing up all the staffs of the Egyptians, this is counted as the first sin of Pharaoh. After the fifth plague of pestilence, Hashem hardened Pharaoh's heart so that he could be punished more. Five plagues plus the preceding sign of Aharon's staff meant that Pharaoh had only, by himself, sinned six times. This is what Hashem means when he tells Moshe that he must still go to Pharaoh, despite Moshe's calculation, because "I have hardened his (Pharaoh's) heart and the heart of his servants, in order that I may place these signs of Mine in his midst."

7) The Chasam Sofer presents a third answer to our question. To better appreciate his answer, we reference a Gemorah in Sanhedrin 81b. The Mishnah speaks about a person who was sentenced to Makos (flogging) twice and then repeated a third time the sin for which the person was sentenced to Makos twice before. Since this person is a habitual sinner, the Mishna says that he is put in a jail cell and fed barley until his stomach bursts and he dies. That is, the Beis Din cannot directly sentence the person to death but can indirectly cause the person's death. The Gemorah explains that the sin which the person committed is a sin for which the person gets the punishment of Kores (a heavenly punishment that causes the premature death of the person who did such a sin). The Gemorah also explains that the person transgressed the same sin three times, which shows that the person never did Teshuva from committing the sin. Since the person knows that he will get Kores which will cause his premature death, this indicates that the person has relinquished his life such that Beis Din causing his death is justified. The Gemorah also explains that we would paskin that it would take three times getting Makos for Beis Din to indirectly cause his death on the fourth time that he repeated doing this same sin.

The Chasam Sofer says that Pharaoh had also previously to this plague committed the same offense three times. First, Pharaoh had seen the staff of Aharon turn into a serpent when Moshe and Aharon came to Pharaoh's palace. Then Moshe went to the Nile River to warn Pharaoh about the plague of blood, and again Pharaoh sinned and took no heed of what Moshe requested. These two different plagues cannot be counted as the same sin since they differed by where Moshe came to warn Pharaoh. The second set of times that Pharaoh sinned was when Moshe came to the palace to warn

Bo

Pharaoh about the upcoming plague of frogs coupled together with coming to the Nile to warn Pharaoh of wild animals. We note that no explicit warning was given to Pharaoh about lice, so this plague cannot be counted as a sin of Pharaoh. The third set of times that Pharaoh sinned was for the sin of pestilence when Moshe went to Pharaoh's palace and for the plague of hail where Moshe went to the Nile to warn Pharaoh. Again, the plague of boils does not count since there was no explicit warning to Pharaoh. Since Pharaoh had now three times transgressed the same sin and never done Teshuva from transgressing the same sin, the Chasam Sofer says that Pharaoh was now classified as a wicked person. The Gemorah in Megilah 28a quotes Rav Yochanon, who says that it is forbidden to gaze at the face of a wicked person. As Sefer Melachim II (3:14) says when Elisha is summoned by the wicked King of the Ten Tribes, Yehoram, "And Elisha said, "As Hashem of Hosts, before Whom I have stood, lives, for were it not that I respect Yehoshophot (who also went to war with Yehoram) King of Yehuda, I would neither look at you nor would I see you." The Gemorah continues and says that if one does gaze at a wicked person, the eyesight of the one who gazes dims. That is why Yitzchak's eyesight dimmed since he gazed at his wicked son Esav. Being that Pharaoh had now earned the title of being a wicked person, Moshe no longer wanted to go to him. Hashem, however, tells Moshe that since Hashem hardened Pharaoh's heart, it is like Hashem is together with Pharaoh keeping Pharaoh's heart hardened. Therefore, it is no longer a problem to go to Pharaoh or even gaze at him since he will also be gazing at Hashem.

8) The Nitziv, also citing the above Gemorah in Sanhedrin 81a, presents another answer to our question. He says Moshe calculated that Pharaoh had sinned at least three times. Since he does not explicitly say how we count the three times, we can use the calculation of the Chasam Sofer in the previous answer. Hashem tells Moshe that one cannot calculate that Pharaoh had sinned three full times since Hashem has hardened Pharaoh's heart during some of the plagues. Rather Hashem tells Moshe that He is slowly causing opportunities for Pharaoh to increase his sin so that Pharaoh would merit great punishments. There are times when Hashem presents opportunities for someone to either prove himself as not fit for the punishment or to prove himself to be fit for the punishment. An example of this is in Beraishis (19:1), when Hashem sends two angels to Sodom immediately before punishing Sodom. Through the angels, Lot proves himself worthy of being saved by giving the angels lodging, while the people of Sodom prove themselves worthy of being destroyed through their behavior with the angels. Therefore, Moshe is to continue to go and warn Pharaoh about the upcoming plague so that Pharaoh, like the people of Sodom, will merit his fitting punishment.

9) The Yismach Moshe also ponders our question and says that not only did Moshe think he no longer had to warn Pharaoh, as we have presented in the previous two answers, but that Moshe thought he was not even allowed to warn Pharaoh any more. The Gemorah in Yevomos 65b says that just as there is a Mitzvah for a person to say words of rebuke which will be accepted, so too there is a Mitzvah for a person not to say words of rebuke that will not be accepted. The Gemorah adds that it is not only a Mitzvah to hold back from speaking words of rebuke which will be ignored, but it is an obligation not to say those words as Mishlay (9:8) says, "Rebuke not a scorner lest he hate you; rebuke a wise man and he will love you." If one offers rebuke, which will not be listened to, the rebuker is doing a sin by causing the one rebuked to do the sin intentionally since the rebuker has informed him that it is a sin. Bringing a person to sin is putting a stumbling block in front of the

Bo

person. The Gemorah in Pesachim 22b says that handing wine to a Nazir or a limb that was taken from a live animal to a Gentile is prohibited based on Vayikra (19:14), which says, "You shall not place a stumbling block before a blind person." Putting these two Gemoros together implies that it is even prohibited to rebuke a Gentile if the rebuke will not be accepted. More concretely, the Gemorah in Shabbos 55a says that not rebuking when the rebuke will not be accepted only applies when one is certain that the rebuke will not be accepted.

Till this point, Moshe had no problem warning and rebuking Pharaoh since Moshe was not certain that Pharaoh would not listen. As we have mentioned above, in the plague of hail, Pharaoh first promised to send out the Bnei Yisroel, and only later, when his heart was hardened, did Pharaoh completely renege on what he had said. Such an about-face convinced Moshe that Pharaoh would never accept Moshe's warnings and rebuke, and therefore Moshe felt it was now prohibited to go to Pharaoh. Hashem, however, informed Moshe that since it was Hashem who hardened Pharaoh's heart, it is permitted to keep on warning and rebuking Pharaoh since Pharaoh on his own might have listened to the rebuke.

10) The Maor VaShemesh also ponders our question. He first ponders the question of why Hashem tested Avrohom at the Akeidah since Hashem already knew even before the test that Avrohom would pass the test and follow Hashem's commandment completely. That being the case, why was this test needed? He answers that the reason Hashem tests a righteous person is to show everyone else how righteous this Tzadik is, which also causes a sanctification of Hashem. The opposite is also true in showing how wicked a wicked person is. Even though Hashem knows how wicked the person is, all the other people of the world might think that the wicked person did Teshuva, even though in reality, he did not. He points out that in the last plague of hail Pharaoh tells Moshe in Shemos (9:27), חָטָאתִי הַפָּעַם ה' הַצַּדִּיק וַאֲנִי וְעַמִּי הָרְשָׁעִים (I have sinned this time. Hashem is the righteous One, and I and my people are the guilty ones.). Anyone hearing this statement could have concluded that Pharaoh did Teshuva. However, Hashem knew that Pharaoh did not really mean what he said. Publicizing this to the people of the world was the reason Moshe was to come now to Pharaoh. In our Posuk, Hashem tells Moshe to go to Pharaoh כִּי אֲנִי הִכְבַּדְתִּי אֶת לִבּוֹ (for I have hardened his heart). As a hint, the Maor VaShemesh says the Gematria (numerical value) of the word הִכְבַּדְתִּי is אֱמֶת (truth).

The Shach explains that when Pharaoh made the statement "I have sinned this time. Hashem is the righteous One, and I and my people are the guilty ones," he really said and thought, "I have sinned this time. Hashem is the righteous One and I. And my people are the guilty ones." Pharaoh, in his arrogance, still held that he was righteous and that only his people were the guilty ones. Coming now to Pharaoh would get people to understand what Pharaoh really said and that Pharaoh had never done Teshuva.

11) The Maor VaShemesh presents a second answer to our question. He references a Beraishis Raba (90:2). After appointing Yosef as viceroy, Pharaoh says in Beraishis (41:44): וַיֹּאמֶר פַּרְעֹה אֶל יוֹסֵף אֲנִי פַרְעֹה וּבִלְעָדֶיךָ לֹא יָרִים אִישׁ אֶת יָדוֹ וְאֶת רַגְלוֹ בְּכָל אֶרֶץ מִצְרָיִם (And Pharaoh said to Yosef, "I am Pharaoh, and besides you, no one may lift his hand or his foot in the entire land of Egypt.") The

Bo

Shemos Raba says that from the meaning of when Pharaoh said אֲנִי פַרְעֹה (I am Pharaoh) we derive what it means when Hashem says אֲנִי. The Maor VaShemesh explains that through Yosef's interpretation of Pharaoh's dream, not only was Pharaoh's mind assuaged from the dream but also Egypt, and by extension Pharaoh, became the most powerful and wealthiest nation of the world at that time. That being the case, one would expect Pharaoh would act subservient to Yosef. Instead, Pharaoh showed his haughtiness by saying אֲנִי פַרְעֹה (I am Pharaoh). Due to Pharaoh's arrogance many years earlier, Hashem now sent ten plagues against Pharaoh, until Pharaoh was forced to admit that he really was nothing and only Hashem is the complete ruler of everything that goes on in the world. Based on what happened to Pharaoh for saying אֲנִי פַרְעֹה we learn that no one else except for Hashem should say "I am." Consistent with this answer, the Baalei Mussar typically paraphrase Devorim (5:5) immediately preceding the second writing of the Ten Commandments, which says, "I am standing between Hashem and you." That is, the Baalei Mussar say, the capital I is typically the one thing that prevents one from getting close to Hashem.

The Maor VaShemesh says that Moshe was hesitant to go again to Pharaoh and warn him. Hashem explained in our Posuk: כִּי אֲנִי הִכְבַּדְתִּי אֶת לִבּוֹ (Because I have hardened his heart). Hashem was telling Moshe that Pharaoh's use of the word אֲנִי when addressing Yosef, caused that Hashem should harden Pharaoh's heart to withstand the plagues so that Hashem could show that Pharaoh had no business saying "I am."

12) Rav Moshe Feinstein, in his Sefer Dorash Moshe, also ponders our question. He says that since both Pharaoh and his servants' hearts had been hardened, there was no longer a need to go to Pharaoh and warn Pharaoh about any plagues. As we have mentioned previously, the last plague of hail had already caused Pharaoh to agree to send out the Bnei Yisroel and had caused many of his servants to show belief in what Moshe said by protecting themselves and their cattle from the plague of hail. If Hashem chose to stop hardening Pharaoh and his servant's hearts, they would send out the Bnei Yisroel. The only reason which remained for the plagues was for the Bnei Yisroel to witness enough plagues and wonders so that they would believe in Hashem forever. That is what the Posuk after ours means when it says, "and in order that you tell into the ears of your son and your son's son how I made a mockery of the Egyptians, and that you tell of My signs that I placed in them, and you will know that I am Hashem." The Chidushay HaRim also is of the opinion that hardening Pharaoh's heart was for the purpose of strengthening the Bnei Yisroel's belief in Hashem

13) Rav Moshe Feinstein also presents a second answer. Moshe only knew that Pharaoh's heart was hardened because Hashem had told him. By sending Moshe to warn Pharaoh, Hashem taught Moshe that a human court must always warn a person even if they suspect that the warning will not stop the person from committing the crime. A human court can never completely know what is in the heart of a person, and therefore they must always suspect that their warning will stop a person from committing a crime. In light of what we have quoted above from the Chasam Sofer and Nitziv that Moshe thought Pharaoh had already been warned a sufficient number of times, we must say, according to Rav Moshe, that Hashem also told Moshe why the previous warnings to Pharaoh were not sufficient.

Bo

Why Did Moshe Turn Before He Went Out From Before Pharaoh in the Plague of Locusts?

וּמָלְאוּ בָתֶּיךָ וּבָתֵּי כָל עֲבָדֶיךָ וּבָתֵּי כָל מִצְרַיִם אֲשֶׁר לֹא רָאוּ אֲבֹתֶיךָ וַאֲבוֹת אֲבֹתֶיךָ מִיּוֹם הֱיוֹתָם עַל הָאֲדָמָה עַד הַיּוֹם הַזֶּה וַיִּפֶן וַיֵּצֵא מֵעִם פַּרְעֹה (י:ו) Shemos (10:6) And your houses and the houses of all your servants and the houses of all the Egyptians will be filled, which your fathers and your fathers' fathers did not see since the day they were on the earth until this day. He turned and went out from before Pharaoh.

Why did Moshe turn before he went out from before Pharaoh in the plague of locusts?

Introduction
The Maharzav, Toldos Noach, Maharif on the Shemos Raba (13:4), and Alshich all say that this is the only time in Moshe's interaction with Pharaoh that the Torah says Moshe first turned. For example, Shemos (8:26) says וַיֵּצֵא מֹשֶׁה מֵעִם פַּרְעֹה. Shemos (9:33) says וַיֵּצֵא מֵעִם פַּרְעֹה. Shemos (10:18) says וַיֵּצֵא מֵעִם פַּרְעֹה. Shemos (11:8) says וַיֵּצֵא מֵעִם פַּרְעֹה בָּחֳרִי אָף.

1) The Shemos Raba (13:4) ponders our question. This answer is also found in the Ramban and Abarbanel. Moshe saw the Egyptian advisors turning towards each other and saw that they believed what Moshe was saying was going to happen. Therefore, Moshe left so that they could advise each other to do Teshuva. The Toldos Noach and Maharif explain that when Moshe saw the advisors turning towards each other, Moshe turned to hear what they were saying and overheard that they believed what Moshe was saying was going to happen. Therefore, Moshe left so that they could continue the discussion without Moshe being present and be more apt to do Teshuva. The Yepheh Toar ponders the question of how they would be able to do Teshuva when Hashem hardened their hearts. The Yepheh Toar concludes that this Shemos Raba is of the opinion the Egyptians could still do Teshuva if they decided to do it.

The Rashash ponders why the Shemos Raba did not simply say that when the Torah says that Moshe turned, it means that Moshe turned around to leave Pharaoh so that his back was to Pharaoh as he was leaving. The Mishna in Yuma 52b says that the Kohen Godol on Yom Kippur walked out of the holy of holies in the same way that he came in, i.e., backward. The Gemorah in Yuma 53a analyzes where this Halacha is derived from. It ponders the meaning of Divrei HaYomim II (1:13) which says, וַיָּבֹא שְׁלֹמֹה לַבָּמָה אֲשֶׁר בְּגִבְעוֹן יְרוּשָׁלִַם מִלִּפְנֵי אֹהֶל מוֹעֵד וַיִּמְלֹךְ עַל יִשְׂרָאֵל (And Shlomo, came to the Bamah (Place for bringing Korbanos when there is no Beis Hamikdosh), which was in Givon, Yerushalayim, from before the Tent of Meeting, and he reigned over Yisroel.). The Nach is speaking about the time in history when the Beis Hamikdosh had yet to be built in Yerushalayim. The Gemorah is bothered by the phrase "Givon, Yerushalayim," given that they are both cities geographically far apart from each other, and the Nach refers to them as if they were one place. It answers that the Nach is comparing Shlomo's going from Givon back to Yerushalayim after offering his Korbanos in Givon to Shlomo's initial coming from Yerushalayim to Givon to bring his sacrifices. The Gemorah says that just like when Shlomo was going to Givon from Yerushalayim, his face was towards the Bamah in Givon, similarly on his way back, he also faced the same way. Similarly, says the Gemorah, Kohanim when they are doing their sacrificial services, Leviyim when they provide musical accompaniment to the service, and Yisraelim when they attended the service,

Bo

would also not turn their faces away and go when they departed their services. Rather they would turn their faces sideways and go. Besides, says the Gemorah, a student when he is taking leave of his Rebbe should not turn his face away from the Rebbe and go but rather should turn his face sideways and go. The Gemorah cites how Rava took leave of his Rebbe, Rav Yosef. Rava walked backward, not looking where he was going until his legs became bruised. The Gemorah says that the threshold of Rav Yosef's house was stained with Rava's blood because of the bruises. The Ben Yehoyoda explains that Rava conducted himself beyond the letter of the law when he took leave of Rav Yosef. It is extra beneficial spiritually to keep one's gaze on one's Rebbe at all times possible. Since Rava's gaze was fixated on Rav Yosef and not on looking down, he could not also see where he was going, and that is why he injured himself walking backward.

The Rashash answers that the Shemos Raba (7:3) says, at the beginning of the mission to Pharaoh, Moshe was specifically commanded to give respect to Pharaoh and treat him like the King he was, despite the fact that Pharaoh was going to be punished. It highlights an example of how Moshe and Aharon did this. When describing what would happen on the night of Pesach when all the Egyptian firstborn were killed, Shemos (11:8) says, "And all these servants of yours (Pharoah's) will come down to me and prostrate themselves to me, saying, 'Go out, you and all the people who are at your feet,' and afterwards I will go out." In actuality, Pharaoh himself, and not his servants went to find Moshe and Aharon as Shemos (12:30-31) says, "And Pharaoh arose at night, he and all his servants and all the Egyptians, and there was a great outcry in Egypt, for there was no house in which no one was dead. So he called for Moshe and Aharon at night, and he said, 'Get up and get out from among my people, both you, as well as the Bnei Yisroel, and go, worship Hashem as you have spoken.'" However, because of respect to Pharaoh, Moshe and Aharon did not tell him that he would break the laws of decorum for a King and go himself looking for Moshe and Aharon. In a similar way in our Posuk, Moshe walked backward from Pharaoh when he took leave of him, and therefore it is not possible to say that וַיִּפֶן in our Posuk means that Moshe turned his back to Pharaoh as he left.

Parenthetically, in a similar vein, the Mishnah Berurah in Simon 128, Sif Koton 61 says that Kohanim, when they depart after Duchaning, should not turn around with their back to the Aron, but rather should turn to the side, like the example in the Gemorah above of a student takin leave of their Rebbe. Similarly, when leaving a Shul, instead of turning around and leaving the Shul, many walk backward out the door of the Shul as a sign of respect to the Shechinah, which is present when a minyan davens together. With this concept, we can understand Beraishis (18:2), which says, "He (Avrohom) saw so he ran toward them (the three angel guests)," which seems at first glance to be in opposition to the events the Gemorah in Baba Metzia (86b) relates. According to the Gemorah, Avrohom noticed the three visitors had begun to leave Avrohom's tent, and therefore it would seem that the Torah should have said that "Avrohom ran after the visitors." The Vilna Gaon, in Kol Eliyahu, and the Taam V'Daas, quoting Rav Shamshon Ostropola, both note that we must remember when the visitors decided to change course and go away from Avrohom's tent, both Hashem and Avrohom were at the doorway of Avrohom's tent. That being the case, the angel visitors walked backward from Avrohom's tent, and therefore Avrohom ran towards them (their faces).

Bo

The Eben Ezra and Tzedah LeDerech quote an opinion that וַיִּפֶן does not mean he turned but rather means he faced. According to this opinion, וַיִּפֶן comes to inform us that Moshe faced Pharaoh when he took leave of Pharaoh. The Alshich on Sefer Yirmiyahu (32:33) also is of this opinion. Both the Eben Ezra and the Tzedah LeDerech reject this opinion and bring proofs of Pesukim when it would be difficult to translate וַיִּפֶן as he faced. For example, the Eben Ezra quotes Shemos (2:12) which says, וַיִּפֶן כֹּה וָכֹה וַיַּרְא כִּי אֵין אִישׁ ("He (Moshe) turned this way and that way, and he saw that there was no man"). The Tzedah LeDerech quotes Shemos (7:23) which says, וַיִּפֶן פַּרְעֹה וַיָּבֹא אֶל בֵּיתוֹ וְלֹא שָׁת לִבּוֹ גַּם לָזֹאת ("Pharaoh turned and went home, and he paid no heed even to this"). In the case of either of these Pesukim, וַיִּפֶן means he turned and not he faced.

2) The Eben Ezra also presents an answer to our question. He says that וַיִּפֶן does not mean Moshe physically turned but rather that Moshe left Pharaoh without permission, and did not do what was proper when leaving from a King or other important official. This incensed Pharaoh, and after calling Moshe and Aharon back in and speaking to them for a bit, Shemos (10:11) says, "And he chased them (Moshe and Aharon) out from before Pharaoh." We may take this explanation a step further if we examine how the Ohr HaChaim explains what happened when Pharaoh, a week later, needed to call back Moshe and Aharon to stop the plague of locusts. To get on their good side for having chased them out previously, Pharaoh says in Shemos (10:16), "Pharaoh hastened to summon Moshe and Aharon, and he said, "I have sinned against Hashem your G-d and against you." The Ohr HaChaim says that the admission of sin against them was the fact that he had, in their last meeting, chased them out of his palace.

3) The Ramban and Rabeinu Bechay also ponder our question. They say that Moshe's intuition told him the Egyptians would be very afraid of dying from hunger when he told them that the plague of locusts was coming. For the first time, in order to get the plague of hail to stop, Pharaoh in Shemos (9:27) admits, "I have sinned this time. Hashem is the righteous One, and I and my people are the guilty ones." With regard to the locusts, Moshe says in Shemos (10:5), "they will eat the surviving remnant, which remains for you from the hail, and they will eat all your trees that grow out of the field." Therefore, the plague of locusts would worsen what the hail started doing, and with all the crops and trees eaten by the locusts, there was a good chance that they would die from hunger. So that the full ramification of what Moshe said could be realized, Moshe and Aharon abruptly left Pharaoh and his servants so that they could discuss the upcoming plague and maybe come to their senses before it occurred. וַיִּפֶן signified that they left abruptly and without waiting for permission to leave. Moshe's intuition was completely correct, and Pharaoh's servants immediately began pressuring Pharaoh to give in and let the Bnei Yisroel leave when they say in Shemos (10:7), "How long will this one be a stumbling block to us? Let the people go, and they will worship their G-d. Don't you yet know that Egypt is lost?" The way Rabeinu Bechay describes it, Moshe did this with great smarts and shrewdness.

4) The Ramban presents another answer to our question. He says that even though this is the only time the word וַיִּפֶן is mentioned, Moshe did this for all the plagues. Presumably, what he means is that Moshe gave the warning and left Pharaoh without waiting for permission to leave. We say in the Hagadah on Pesach: רַבִּי יְהוּדָה הָיָה נוֹתֵן בָּהֶם סִימָנִים, דְּצַ"ךְ עֲדַ"שׁ בְּאַחַ"ב (Rabi Yehuda referred to them by

Bo

acronyms: DeTzaCh (blood, frogs, lice); ADaSh (wild animals, pestilence, boils); BeAChaV (hail, locust, darkness, killing of firstborn)). The Abarbanel, Kli Yakor, and Malbim explain that Rabi Yehuda did not just superficially give us three acronyms to remember the plagues by but rather also said that the plagues could be grouped into three groups. The Malbim points out that for the first plague of each of the three sets (blood, wild animals, and hail), Moshe came to warn Pharaoh early in the morning when he went out to bathe in the Nile River. For the second plague in each set (frogs, pestilence, and locusts), Moshe went to Pharaoh's palace to warn him, in front of all his servants who were in the palace, so that it should be known to all Pharaoh's servants and thereby the entire country that Moshe had given a warning about the upcoming plague. Finally, no warning was given for the third plague in each set (lice, boils and darkness).

The Oznayim LeTorah explains this Ramban by observing that Moshe came to Pharoah's palace only for three plagues (frogs, pestilence, and locusts). In the case of the plagues of both frogs and pestilence, the Torah only records Hashem's instructions to Moshe of what to warn Pharaoh and not Moshe's actual warning to Pharaoh. Therefore, there is no description of Moshe coming into or leaving Pharaoh's palace. Our plague of locusts is described differently, with the Torah describing how Moshe came to Pharaoh and how he warned him about the plague of locusts. Therefore, only in the plague of locusts does it make sense to describe how Moshe left Pharoah's palace. We note that all the Pesukim we quoted in the introduction which describes Moshe leaving Pharaoh and not using the word וַיִּפֶן, are describing what happened after Pharaoh summoned Moshe to come to him to stop a plague from continuing. Only our Posuk talks about Moshe leaving Pharaoh after warning him. Therefore, says the Ramban, we derive from our Posuk that Moshe behaved the same way in all the plagues after warning Pharaoh.

5) The Tur also presents an answer to our question. He says that וַיִּפֶן does not refer to Moshe but rather refers to Pharaoh. Pharaoh turned and looked at Moshe, fully expecting him to still be there since he had not asked for permission to leave. It may be that it was disrespectful to stand directly in front of the King or that Pharaoh had turned away in disdain from Moshe when Moshe started warning him what would happen when the plague of locusts came. For whatever reason, Pharaoh now turned; Pharaoh saw that Moshe was un-expectantly to Pharaoh, no longer there.

6) The Ohr HaChaim, as explained by the Ohr Yakor, the Malbim, and the Nitziv, answer our question similarly. They say that in the plague of locusts, Moshe showed disrespect to Pharaoh and turned his back on Pharaoh, similar to what one does when one leaves an ordinary person. The Ohr HaChaim and Nitziv explain that to stop the previous plague of locusts, Pharaoh, for the first time, admitted in Shemos (9:27), "I have sinned this time. Hashem is the righteous One, and I and my people are the guilty ones." Moshe was flabbergasted that after this admission, Pharaoh had returned to his stubborn ways, refusing to recognize Hashem. To show his displeasure, Moshe ignored protocol and turned his back on Pharaoh when leaving. We have previously mentioned that Pharaoh got incensed with Moshe in this plague, and after calling Moshe and Aharon back in and speaking to them for a bit, Shemos (10:11) says, "And he chased them (Moshe and Aharon) out from before Pharaoh." The Ohr HaChaim explains that Pharaoh was forced to hastily retreat from his behavior a week later when he needed to call back Moshe and Aharon to stop the plague of

Bo

locusts. To get on their good side for having chased them out previously, Pharaoh says in Shemos (10:16), "I have sinned against Hashem your G-d and against you." The admission of sin against them was the fact that he had, in their last meeting, chased them out of his palace.

The Nitziv points out that we find in another situation where the word וַיִּפֶן means Moshe turned around. Shemos (32:15) says, וַיִּפֶן וַיֵּרֶד מֹשֶׁה מִן הָהָר וּשְׁנֵי לֻחֹת הָעֵדֻת בְּיָדוֹ לֻחֹת כְּתֻבִים מִשְּׁנֵי עֶבְרֵיהֶם מִזֶּה וּמִזֶּה הֵם כְּתֻבִים (Now Moshe turned and went down from the mountain bearing the two tablets of the testimony in his hand, tablets inscribed from both their sides; on one side and on the other side they were inscribed.). He contrasts this Posuk to Shemos (19:14) which says וַיֵּרֶד מֹשֶׁה מִן הָהָר אֶל הָעָם וַיְקַדֵּשׁ אֶת הָעָם וַיְכַבְּסוּ שִׂמְלֹתָם (So Moshe descended from the mountain to the people, and he prepared the people, and they washed their garments.). He explains that in Shemos (19:14), Moshe went backward down from the mountain since Hashem's Shechinah rested on the mountain, which, as we have explained previously from the Gemorah in Yuma 53a, is the proper behavior. In fact, Moshe was stringent and went down completely backward even though this left open the possibility of hurting himself as what happened to Rava. However, in Shemos (32:15), Moshe had a logistical problem. If he walked down backward from the mountain holding onto the two tablets, there was a possibility that he would trip and fall, causing the tablets to fall from his hands. Therefore, וַיִּפֶן signified that Moshe at least partially turned to his side so that he could ensure that he could see what was in his path and not, Chas VeShalom, trip. This Posuk is consistent with our Posuk, which also describes Moshe's actions with the word וַיִּפֶן, signifying that Moshe turned, and therefore his back was to Pharaoh.

7) The Kli Yakor also ponders the question of what וַיִּפֶן means in our Posuk and says that Moshe only turned away from Pharaoh and was still standing in the middle of Pharaoh's servants. Presumably, we can envision that Pharaoh was encircled by his many advisors and other government officials. Previously Moshe had been standing right in front of Pharaoh, and now he moved backward and was now found standing next to Pharaoh's advisors. He offers proof to his explanation by examining the Posuk after ours, which says, Pharaoh's servants said to him, "How long will this one be a stumbling block to us?" Using this way of speaking implies that they pointed to Moshe when they said "this one," proving that he was still there. We can appreciate this answer more if we also consider something the Alshich says. He says the advisors were so afraid of what Moshe had just said that they couldn't hold themselves back from expressing their feelings, fears, and advice to Pharaoh even though Moshe had not completely left the room. Otherwise, sit would have been very undignified for them to say to Pharaoh in the Posuk after ours, "Don't you yet know that Egypt is lost?"

Why Would "a Festival of Hashem to Us" Cause the Bnei Yisroel a Need to Bring Their Young Children and Cattle?

Shemos (10:9) וַיֹּאמֶר מֹשֶׁה בִּנְעָרֵינוּ וּבִזְקֵנֵינוּ נֵלֵךְ בְּבָנֵינוּ וּבִבְנוֹתֵנוּ בְּצֹאנֵנוּ וּבִבְקָרֵנוּ נֵלֵךְ כִּי חַג ה' לָנוּ (י:ט) Moshe said, "With our youth and with our elders we will go, with our sons and with our daughters, with our flocks and with our cattle we will go, for it is a festival of Hashem to us."

Bo

Why would "a festival of Hashem to us" cause the Bnei Yisroel a need to bring their young children and cattle?

Introduction
Rabeinu Bechay says that the Festival Moshe is truthfully referring to is Shavuos, the day of the giving of the Torah. This is the meaning of what Hashem told Moshe months before at the burning bush when Hashem says in Shemos (3:12), "And He (Hashem) said, "For I will be with you, and this is the sign for you that it was I who sent you. When you take the people out of Egypt, you will worship G-d on this mountain." Rabeinu Bechay reasons that Moshe could not have been referring to Pesach since they were still in Egypt when they celebrated Pesach.

The Yismach Moshe, as quoted by the Meorah Shel Torah, explains what Moshe was truthfully referring to when he says, "it is a festival of Hashem to us." Whenever the young people and older people go together for an activity, it is a great festival for any nation, including the Bnei Yisroel.

The Beis HaLevi points out that Pharaoh, despite all the plagues, really did not want to send any of the Bnei Yisroel out of Egypt. However, since Pharoah's servants said to him two Pesukim before our Posuk in Shemos (10:7), "How long will this one (Moshe) be a stumbling block to us? Let the people go, and they will worship their G-d. Don't you yet know that Egypt is lost?" Pharaoh had no choice but to follow his servants' advice and at least offer to send the grown men. Fortunately for Pharaoh, when Moshe and Aharon say in our Posuk that even the young men and cattle must also go, Pharaoh could say that he did everything his servants asked, but Moshe and Aharon wanted more. Therefore, Pharaoh could say that he was not sending any of the Bnei Yisroel out while still being able to say that he listened to his servants' request. Shemos (10:11) says, "Not so; let the men go now and worship Hashem, for that is what you request." And he (Pharaoh) chased them (Moshe and Aharon) out from before Pharaoh." Pharaoh chased out Moshe and Aharon because he was afraid that they would accept his offer of only the men going to serve Hashem. If they accepted, Pharaoh would have to bend to the pressure of his servants and allow the men to go out of Egypt, a scenario Pharaoh did not want.

Pharaoh answers Moshe's request by saying in Shemos (10:10), "See that evil is before your faces." Rashi, quoting the Yalkut Shimoni 392 in Parshas Ki Sisa, explains what Pharaoh meant by, "See that evil is before your faces." By "evil," Pharaoh referred to a cloud that his astrological signs told him meant that blood would be spilled. That is why, when the Bnei Yisroel sinned by making the Golden Calf, Moshe defended the Bnei Yisroel by saying in Shemos (32:12), "Why should the Egyptians say, 'He (Hashem) brought them out with evil to kill them in the mountains and to annihilate them from upon the face of the earth'? Retreat from the heat of Your anger and reconsider the evil intended for Your people." Hashem accepted Moshe's defense of the Bnei Yisroel and changed the blood to that of the blood of Bris Milah. This occurred when Yehoshua gave a Bris Milah to all the people born in the desert as Sefer Yehoshua (5:6-7) says, "For the Bnei Yisroel walked forty years in the wilderness, until all the people, the men of war, that came out of Egypt were consumed, those who did not listen to the voice of Hashem, to whom Hashem had sworn that He would not show them the land, which Hashem had sworn to their forefathers that He would give

Bo

us, a land that flows with milk and honey. And their children, whom he raised up in their stead, them Yehoshua circumcised, for they had not circumcised them by the way." After Yehoshua gives them a Bris Milah, Hashem says to Yehoshua in Shemos (5:9), "This day have I rolled away the reproach of Egypt from off you." The reproach that is being referred to is this that Pharaoh says in our Pesukim, "See that evil is before your faces."

The Alshich says that by saying, "See that evil is before your faces," Pharaoh was pretending to care about the young children and say that it is a bad idea to take them. Pharaoh argued that the "evil' or "blood" that was coming towards them signaled that there was going to be a battle in the desert. During a battle, argued Pharaoh, you will be much relieved if the children won't be with you since without children to protect you will fight the battle differently. Instead of having to be defensive to protect the children, you can take a more offensive approach and, if need be, run away if the battle becomes too intense without having to worry about leaving the children behind. The Oznayim LeTorah points out how ironic it is that Pharaoh, who had murdered so many Jewish children, suddenly now becomes their protector. He says that it was probably a self-centered request since Pharaoh wanted to make sure that he could be able to murder even more children and use their blood for bathing in to attempt to cure himself completely of the remnant of the plague of boils. The Mayanah Shel Torah says that it was a very calculated decision by Pharaoh. If Pharaoh keeps the children and trains them to keep from serving Hashem, he can ensure that there will be no continuity in the next generation of having the desire to serve Hashem.

The Shemos Raba (13:5) says Pharaoh had a different intention when he said to Moshe in Shemos (10:10), "See that evil is before your faces." Pharaoh accused Moshe of attempting to escape forever by the fact that Moshe wanted all the Bnei Yisroel and all their possessions to leave Egypt. The "evil" that Pharaoh is referring to is the evil plan Moshe had of escaping forever from Egypt under the excuse of going for three days to serve Hashem in the desert. After coming to this conclusion, Pharaoh was so incensed that Shemos (10:11) says, "And he chased them (Moshe and Aharon) out from before Pharaoh" and told them that now after they lied about their plans, Pharaoh would not agree to anyone leaving Egypt.

The Ponim Yofos explains why Pharaoh was so against the children leaving and going along with their parents into the desert. Pharaoh was aware that Hashem promised Avrohom in the Bris Bain HaBesorim in Beraishis (15:16), "And the fourth generation will return here (Eretz Yisroel), for the iniquity of the Amorites will not be complete until then." Moshe's grandfather Kehas was one of the 70 people who came down to Egypt, making Moshe the third generation from the point of coming to Egypt. Pharaoh knew that the children, the fourth generation, were destined to go into Eretz Yisroel. Therefore, Pharaoh did everything he could to keep the children (fourth generation) under his control in Egypt.

We note that the Noam Elimelech understands our entire Posuk in a completely Kabbalistic or Chasidic way. He bases his way of learning on a Gemorah in Sukkah 53a, which describes what people would sing at the Simchas Beis HaShoaivah in the Beis Hamikdosh on Chol Hamoed Succos. One thing they would sing is: "Happy is our youth which did not shame our old age."

Bo

Rashi on the Gemorah explains they meant that they didn't do any sin in their youth which would come back to embarrass them in their old age. The Noam Elimelech says this is what Mishlay (22:6) means when it says, "Train a child according to his way; even when he grows old, he will not turn away from it." If the child was trained to do good in his youth, he will not turn away from the path he gained in his youth even when he gets old. With this concept, the Noam Elimelech explains our Posuk. "With our youth and with our elders we will go" means that we will go on the same path in both our youth and in our old age. "With our sons and with our daughters" means that not only will we keep on the same path in our youth and in our old age, but we will also train our sons and daughters to go on this path. "With our flocks and with our cattle we will go" means that even in physical matters like eating, drinking, working to make a living, etc., we will also do these with the intention to serve Hashem. "For it is a festival of Hashem to us" means that the reason we are doing everything we can to serve Hashem is that we have a burning desire to serve Hashem, and doing his service is a "festival of Hashem."

1) The Midrash Lekach Tov presents an answer to our question. Included in making a festival to Hashem is to temporarily change (at this point, since they were only asking for three days) from serving Pharaoh and the Egyptians to serving Hashem. Since Pharaoh and the Egyptians took control over even our children, then we must change their master from Pharaoh to Hashem. "That is why," said Moshe, "we must also bring our children." It would seem that Moshe did not have to explain why the Bnei Yisroel needed to take their cattle and sheep since they would be needed in case the Bnei Yisroel are required to bring many Korbanos to Hashem.

2) The Chizkuni, Ralbag, Tur, Alshich, Kli Yakor, Nitziv, and Ksav VeHakabola answer our question similarly. They point out that Moshe called it "a festival of Hashem to us." Ostensibly, the phrase "to us" is unnecessary. They explain that "to us" means that the Festival also had a component to being a "festival to us" and not just a "festival of Hashem." For something to be a "festival to us" and a joyous occasion, a person can only be completely joyous if his wife, children, and possessions are visible to the person. In addition, the person would worry about the welfare of his wife, children, and cattle if they weren't with him. Therefore, Moshe insisted the Bnei Yisroel bring along their wives, children, and cattle (possessions).

The Alshich ponders why Moshe said, "With our youth and with our elders we will go, with our sons and with our daughters, with our flocks and with our cattle we will go" instead of combining into one phrase and saying, "With our youth and with our elders, with our sons, and with our daughters, with our flocks and with our cattle we will go." He answers that had Moshe and Aharon said, "With our youth and with our elders, with our sons, and with our daughters, with our flocks and with our cattle we will go," one could have mistakenly said, "With our youth and with our elders" implies that this statement is said from the perspective of the middle-aged people. That being the case, Pharaoh could have interpreted "our sons, and with our daughters our flocks and with our cattle" is only referring to the children, flocks, and cattle of the middle-aged people, and would not include the children, flocks, and cattle of the elders or the youth. Therefore, Moshe put in the phrase "we will go" after the phrase "with our youth and with our elders" to emphasize that the

Bo

phrase "with our sons and with our daughters, with our flocks and with our cattle" was referring to that of all the Bnei Yisroel.

The Kli Yakor presents a different reason why Moshe repeats "we will go" twice in out Posuk. Before presenting his reason for the repetition, he points out several other difficulties in our Posuk and in the preceding Posuk. Pharaoh asks Moshe who is going by inquiring מִי וָמִי הַהֹלְכִים (who and who are the ones that go). This is strange that Pharaoh says "who and who" instead of who. It is also strange that Pharaoh uses the present tense when he says "are the ones that go" instead of using future tense and saying "will go." Pharaoh was making a generic statement and said that if one searched around the world to see "who and who" typically goes to offer sacrifices to their deity, one would find that only those who are of the age to make the actual offering are the ones that go. This approach answers why Pharaoh used the strange terminology of "who and who" and uses the present tense when he says "who and who are the ones that go." Moshe answers Pharaoh by saying that not only will we go like the rest of the world "with our youth and with our elders," but in addition, we will also go "with our sons and with our daughters, with (all) our flocks and with (all) our cattle." The reason that our going is different than all the nations of the world is that we are going (1) to serve Hashem by bringing sacrifices and (2) to make a "festival to us" and a joyous occasion, in which a person can only be completely joyous if his wife, children, and possessions are visible to the person.

Pharaoh, in addition to saying "See that evil is before your faces," that we have talked about in the introduction, also says in Shemos (10:11), "Not so; let the men go now and worship Hashem, for that is what you request." The Kli Yakor points out that Pharaoh cast doubt on Moshe's reason as to why they needed to take everyone by pointing out Moshe's original request from Pharaoh in Shemos (5:1) is, שַׁלַּח אֶת עַמִּי וְיָחֹגּוּ לִי בַּמִּדְבָּר (Send out My people and let them sacrifice to Me in the desert.). Nowhere in that request, says Pharaoh, is there any mention of a חַג ה' לָנוּ (it is a festival of Hashem to us)." Therefore, argues Pharaoh in his reply, "Not so; let the men go now and worship Hashem" for that was your original request. In fact, Pharaoh said that it just couldn't be that Hashem has, Chas VeShalom, changed his mind, so it must be that this new request of a "festival to us" is something that Moshe made up on his own.

Parenthetically, the Baal HaTurim, Abarbanel, and Shach quote a Midrash that when Pharaoh said "who and who are the ones that go," he was referring to something he saw through astrology. Pharaoh saw that only two of all the Bnei Yisroel that left Egypt, Yehoshua and Calev, would go into Eretz Yisroel. All the rest would die out in the desert. With such danger, Pharaoh was trying to convince Moshe and Aharon it did not make sense to go out of Egypt and into the desert. The Baal HaTurim and Shach say that Moshe answered Pharaoh's astrology when he said in our Posuk, "with our youth and with our elders we will go." Neither the youth (below age 20) nor the elders (about age 60) are part of the decree of dying out in the desert.

3) The Eben Ezra, Ramban, and many years later the Oznayim LeTorah answer our question similarly. They say Moshe told Pharaoh with the words it is a "festival to us" that everyone is commanded to celebrate this Festival. In his Sefer Pirkei Torah, Rav Mordechai Gifter is perplexed

Bo

at how it is possible that children would have a commandment to do a Mitzvah since children are not obligated to do Mitzvos. He answers that the Mitzvah is not on the children but rather on the adults that all their household should participate in this Mitzvah of a festival to Hashem. Presumably, this is similar to the Mitzvah of Hakhel where Devorim (31:11-12) says, every seven years during Succos of the year after Shemitah: "When all Yisroel comes to appear before Hashem, your G-d, in the place He will choose, you shall read this Torah before all Yisroel, in their ears. Assemble the people: the men, the women, and the children, and your stranger in your cities, in order that they hear, and in order that they learn and fear Hashem, your G-d, and they will observe to do all the words of this Torah." The Gemorah in Chagigah 3a says that the men are command to come to learn, the women are commanded to come to listen, and the children are command to come in order to bring reward to those that brought them. Moreover, as we have pointed out in the introduction, Moshe was really referring to the Festival of Shavuos and receiving the Torah. In this Festival, it was imperative that everyone be at Mount Sinai to accept the Torah.

4) The Abarbanel and Maharil Diskin answer our question similarly. They say Moshe told Pharaoh we need to bring all our sheep and cattle for the Festival since we will need to slaughter them for the Festival. In addition, we need to bring our wives and children because part of being a festival is making sure that our wives and children are also joyous. The Maharil Diskin is also sensitive as to why our Posuk repeats the phrase "we will go" twice in our Posuk, one with the phrase "With our youth and with our elders" and then again with the phrase "with our sons and with our daughters, with our flocks and with our cattle." He explains that the youth and elders will walk on their own accord while the small sons and daughters will need animals to carry them. This was why the Bnei Yisroel would need to bring all their cattle so that the children will have what to ride on, even on the way back to Egypt. It is not obvious to me that cattle in our Posuk include the typical animals one rides on, which are horses and donkeys. The Gemorah in Bechoros 5b and the Mechilta in Parshas Beshalach on Shemos (17:8) tells us there was not one Yisroel who did not take 90 donkeys laden with the gold and silver of Egypt. Therefore, it seems that the Bnei Yisroel also had a large number of donkeys. Though Moshe did not mention donkeys explicitly, it would seem to me that Moshe would also want the Bnei Yisroel to bring all the donkeys with them. It seems to me that Moshe included the donkeys in the phrase "with our sons and daughters" since they would need the donkeys to ride on.

5) The Malbim also presents an answer to our question. He explains that at that time, Pharaoh and, in fact, all idol worshippers of the world thought that there were, Chas VeShalom, two distinct deities, one for bringing all good to the world and the other for all afflictions and punishments. They would serve the idol of bad so that the idol would not bring bad to the world. The method of serving each of these idols was entirely different. They would not bring any sacrifices to the idol of good since they thought the idol of good did not want the blood spilled by the slaughtering of sacrifices. Instead, the idol of good was served by bringing their women and children together to rejoice, together with music and food for everyone. They used to serve the idol of bad by slaughtering sacrifices so that this idol could be satiated in seeing all the blood spilled in sacrificing the animals. They would keep the women and children away from serving the idol of bad so that the women and children could not be harmed if the idol of bad wanted to do bad and also so that the idol

Bo

of bad would not demand that they be brought as sacrifices to him. That is why Pharaoh asks in the previous Posuk to ours, "who and who are the ones that go." Pharaoh wanted to know if they were going to serve the idol of good, in which case they would need to take along their wives and children but not their animals or if they were going to serve the idol of bad such that they would need their animals and not their wives and children. In our Posuk, Moshe answers Pharaoh's question by telling Pharaoh that Hashem is the G-d over both good and bad. Therefore, the Bnei Yisroel will need to bring both their wives and children to rejoice along with their cattle and sheep to slaughter before Hashem. The Malbim, in his Ayeles HaShachar (rule 545), says that since the name festival includes rejoicing by bringing Korbanos of joy, Rosh Hashana and Yom Kippur are not referred to in the Torah as a Chag (Festival) since there is no obligation to offer Korbanos of joy on those days.

The Ralbag many years earlier writes that he saw in a Sefer that Pharaoh was of the opinion each idol was either an idol for good or an idol for bad. Pharaoh sized up that Hashem was, Chas VeShalom, only for bad, especially after experiencing many plagues, and that is why he says in Shemos (10:10), "See that evil is before your faces."

6) The Malbim, in his Sefer Eretz Chemdah, presents another answer to our question. Pharaoh knew that there were two possible reasons for going into the desert to serve Hashem. It could be that the place they were going to in the desert was a holy place where they would receive a flow of blessings and holiness. If this was the case, there was no need to bring any animals for sacrifices. The second reason the Bnei Yisroel could be going to the desert would be to bring presents for Hashem in the form of sacrifices. If this was the case, there was no need to bring along the children since children do not bring sacrifices. Moshe informed Pharaoh that with regard to serving Hashem, one served Hashem in both ways. This is what Moshe meant when he said that they were going to the desert for "a festival of Hashem to us." For example, three times a year, on the three festivals, the Bnei Yisroel were commanded to come up to Yerushalayim. There were two purposes for this. Firstly, to come up to a holy place where they would receive a flow of blessings and holiness. In addition, Devorim (16:16) says that when one came up to Yerushalayim, "and he shall not appear before Hashem empty-handed (without sacrifices)." Therefore, said Moshe, we need both our children and our animals.

7) Rav Hirsch also ponders our question. He says that Moshe explained to Pharaoh that Judaism is unlike any religion Pharaoh is used to. In Judaism, there are no intermediaries, nor any representatives before our G-d. Though there are spiritual leaders, their function is to teach the people how each individual should serve Hashem. That being the case, if we are to go serve Hashem, we must all go, even the tiniest baby in the cradle and the last sheep of our possessions. Sefer Yeshayahu (40:22) says הַיֹּשֵׁב עַל חוּג הָאָרֶץ (He (Hashem) that sits above the circle of the earth). Based on this Posuk, He takes the word חַג in our Posuk to be a circle that all are to form around Hashem. For this circle, we need every member of all the families along with all our possessions.

8) The Yismach Moshe also presents an answer to our question. He says the phrase "a festival of Hashem to us" is only referring to why the Bnei Yisroel have to bring their children. With regard to why they had to bring their cattle and sheep, Moshe and Aharon had already addressed this issue the

Bo

first time they met Pharaoh when they said in Shemos (5:3): "Now let us go on a three day journey in the desert and sacrifice to Hashem our G-d." Obviously, "sacrificing to Hashem" requires cattle and sheep.

The Yismach Moshe references the Poroshas Derochim, Chapter 24. The Eicha Raba (1:32) explains Eichah (1:5) which says, הָיוּ צָרֶיהָ לְרֹאשׁ אֹיְבֶיהָ שָׁלוּ כִּי ה' הוֹגָהּ עַל רֹב פְּשָׁעֶיהָ עוֹלָלֶיהָ הָלְכוּ שְׁבִי לִפְנֵי צָר (Her (Bnei Yisroel's) adversaries have become the head, her enemies are at ease; for Hashem has afflicted her for the multitude of her transgressions; her young children are gone into captivity before the enemy.). The following Posuk says, וַיֵּצֵא מִבַּת צִיּוֹן כָּל הֲדָרָהּ (And gone is from the daughter of Tzion all her splendor). These Pesukim tells us how beloved young children are to Hashem. Even though the Sanhedrim went into exile, the Shechinah remained. Even when the Kohanim and Leviyim who served in the Beis Hamikdosh were exiled, the Shechinah remained. Only when the young children went into exile was all the splendor (The Shechinah) gone from Yerushalayim. The Poroshas Derochim quotes the Pesichta to the Eichah Raba (24) to show the ramifications of Hashem's Shechinah leaving. At the time Hashem decided to destroy the Beis Hamikdosh; Hashem said that as long as the Shechinah is in the Beis Hamikdosh, no Gentile will be able to destroy it. Therefore, the Shechinah left, and the Gentiles were able to destroy the Beis Hamikdosh. This is what Sefer Hoshea (5:15) means when it says, אֵלֵךְ אָשׁוּבָה אֶל מְקוֹמִי עַד אֲשֶׁר יֶאְשְׁמוּ וּבִקְשׁוּ פָנָי בַּצַּר לָהֶם יְשַׁחֲרֻנְנִי (I will go (from the Beis Hamikdosh) and return to My place, till they acknowledge their guilt, and seek My face; in their trouble, they will seek Me earnestly).

The Gemorah in Shabbos 119b discusses the possible reasons as to why the Beis Hamikdosh was destroyed. Among the reasons is that the generation's leaders did not maintain having the children focus entirely on their Torah Studies. The Gemorah derives this reason from Sefer Yirmiyahu (6:11), which says, "Therefore, I am full of the fury of Hashem, I am weary of containing it, to pour it out upon the babes in the street and upon the assembly of young men together, for a man with a woman shall be seized, an old man with one full of days." The Gemorah explains that the reason why the fury of Hashem is poured out on the babies (little children) in the street is that the little children are in the streets instead of being inside the classroom learning Torah. The Maharsha says the reason the Posuk also talks about "for a man with a woman shall be seized, an old man with one full of days" is because the parents will be punished for the sins of their children being that they did not make sure the children went and stayed inside learning Torah. The Gemorah, a bit further down on Shabbos 119b, says that the world only exists because of the merit from school children's breath. When Rav Pappa questioned Abaye why their breaths taken in Torah learning were not as important, Abaye told him that breath which contains the taint of sin cannot be compared to breath which does not contain the taint of sin. The reason being that children below Bar Mitzvah are not held accountable for their sins. The Gemorah continues and says the learning of schoolchildren is so important that we do not stop children from learning even for the sake of building the Beis Hamikdosh. Shulchan Aruch, Yoreh Deah (245:7) says that we make sure there are teachers for schoolchildren in every city. Any city which does not have a teacher for schoolchildren is put into Cherem until they obtain such teacher(s). Subsequent to being put into Cherem, if the city still does not obtain these teachers, we destroy the city since the world only exists because of the merit of the breath that comes from school children while learning Torah.

Bo

Vayikra (26:25), in the middle of the Tochaycha (rebuke), says, "I will incite the plague in your midst, and you will be delivered into the enemy's hands." Rashi quoting the Sifrah (Toras Kohanim) on this Posuk, explains what the connection of sending a plague has to with being delivered into the enemy's hand. It says the plague will cause people in Yerushalayim to die. The Gemorah in Baba Kama 82b relates that ten decrees were made by the Rabonon to increase the holiness of Yerushalayim. Among the decrees is that one cannot allow a dead body to remain in Yerushalayim overnight. In addition, there are no cemeteries allowed in Yerushalayim. Because of these two decrees, one had to take out the dead bodies by day even though Yerushalayim was being besieged by the enemies, causing those that bring out the dead bodies to be captured by the enemy. The Oznayim LeTorah and Rav Sternbuch, in his Sefer Taam V'Daas, ponder why the Bnei Yisroel had to risk their lives to take out the dead bodies from Yerushalayim. As Rav Sternbuch puts it, the prohibitions of burying a dead body in Yerushalayim are Rabbinic, and they do not require one to risk one's life to fulfill them. Rather, they should have temporarily buried the dead inside Yerushalayim until the end of the siege and then buried them outside of Yerushalayim. In addition, at the point this Posuk appears in the Tochaycha, the people were no longer keeping many of the Mitzvos of the Torah, and it seems peculiar that they would keep this Rabbinic prohibition even in a life-threatening situation.

The Oznayim LeTorah answers that the people of Yerushalayim were so petrified of the Shechinah leaving the Beis Hamikdosh and Yerushalayim they did everything possible to preserve the sanctity of Yerushalayim by, for example, not burying dead bodies there. As we have previously quoted, they knew that as long as the Shechinah was in Yerushalayim, Yerushalayim would be protected from its enemies. This is the meaning of the rebuke Yirmiyahu tells them in Sefer Yirmiyahu (7:4-6): "Do not rely on false words, saying: The Temple of Hashem, the Temple of Hashem, the Temple of Hashem, are they. For if you improve your ways and your deeds, if you perform judgment between one man and his fellowman. If you do not oppress a stranger, an orphan, or a widow, and you do not shed innocent blood in this place, and you do not follow other gods for your detriment." The false words is the premise that because it is the Beis Hamikdosh of Hashem, Hashem will protect it and it doesn't matter how the Bnei Yisroel themselves behave. Rather "the temple of Hashem are they" and their behavior especially in fulfilling the Mitzvos outlined in the Pesukim affects whether Hashem's Shechinah remains in the Beis Hamikdosh.

The Oznayim LeTorah quotes a story along these same lines, recorded by the Gemorah in Yuma 23a. Before discussing the Gemorah, we should quote the Mishna on Yuma 22a. The first service in the Beis Hamikdosh is called Terumas HaDeshen and involves separating a shovelful of ash from the ashes of the Korbanos, which burned all night on the Mizbeach (Altar). The Kohen took the shovelful and deposited it on the floor of the courtyard (Azarah) east of the ramp of the Mizbeach. The Mishna says that originally whoever wanted to do this service could do it. If there were many Kohanim who sought this privilege, they would all run up the ramp of the Mizbeach, and the first that got within four cubits of the top of the ramp got to do the service. One time it happened that two Kohanim were even as they went up the ramp, and one of the Kohanim pushed the other Kohen, who fell and broke his leg. When Beis Din saw that this system could be dangerous, they decreed

Bo

that the Kohen to perform Terumas HaDeshen would be selected by drawing lots. The Gemorah in Yuma 23a tells us about another incident that occurred. Two Kohanim were even as they went up the ramp, and one Kohen took out a knife and stabbed the other Kohen in the heart, mortally wounding him. Rav Tzadok, seeing what had happened, got up and said a few words that got all the people around crying about the calamity which had just occurred. At that point, the father of the slain Kohen, who had come to try to help his son, called out that his son was still writhing on the floor and had not yet died. Therefore, he called out that the knife should be quickly removed from his son so that it did not become Tameh because of contact with a dead person. The Gemorah says we see from this story that keeping a vessel of the Beis Hamikdosh from becoming Tameh was more serious to them than murder. Parenthetically the Gemorah analyzes which story, the one in the Mishna of a Kohen breaking his leg or the one in the Gemorah of a Kohen being murdered, happened first in time. The Gemorah concludes that the murder happened first. The Sefas Emes explains that murder was committed by a very wicked person, and the Rabonon felt it was highly unusual that a Kohen would be so wicked. It was only subsequent to the incident with the broken leg occurring that the Rabonon decide that such an incident, breaking a leg, could happen even with Kohanim, and therefore the Rabonon instituted the system of lots.

The Ain Eliyahu quotes a Gemorah in Nedorim 22a to give us an even deeper insight into the Gemorah in Yuma. The Gemorah tells us what happened when Ulla was coming up from Babylonia to Eretz Yisroel. He was accompanied by two people from the city of Chuzai. Along the way, one of them got angry at the other and slit the throat of the other person. He then asked Ulla, "Did I do the right thing?" Ulla replied, "Yes, you did, and in addition, you should continue and open up the place where you slit his throat." The Ran and Rosh explain that by doing so, he will die quicker. The Rosh explains that Ulla was afraid if he answered no, he would also be killed. When Ulla reached Eretz Yisroel, he went to Rav Yochanon and confided that he was worried if he had, Chas VeShalom, given support to a sinner. Rav Yochanon replied, "on the contrary, you saved your own life by doing so; otherwise, he would have also killed you. Rav Yochanon told Ulla that he was puzzled about a Posuk in the Tochaycha (rebuke) in Devorim (28:65), which says, "And among those nations, you will not be calm, nor will your foot find rest. There, Hashem will give you an angry heart, dashed hopes, and a depressed soul." Rav Yochanon explained that this Posuk is talking about the Jews in exile in Babylonia having "an angry heart," not the Jews in Eretz Yisroel where this incident occurred. Ulla informed Rav Yochanon that at the point the murder took place, they had not passed over the Jordan River and were not yet in Eretz Yisroel.

The Ain Eliyahu explains that the more holiness a place has, the less likely it is that murder will occur there. Therefore, Rav Yochanon was puzzled about how the murder could occur in Eretz Yisroel and not in Babylonia since Eretz Yisroel has more holiness than Babylonia. In a similar way, it was extremely puzzling that there would be a murder in the Beis Hamikdosh and that its holiness would not prevent the murder from taking place. At this point, the father said that he could solve their puzzlement by announcing that his son had not yet died, and therefore the holiness of the Beis Hamikdosh had indeed at least delayed the death. The Gemorah concludes that the father's priorities were not correct since he was more worried about answering their worry concerning the holiness of the Beis Hamikdosh as opposed to his own son being murdered. The Oznayim LeTorah

Bo

concludes it was a widespread belief that as long as the Bnei Yisroel ensured the Shechinah would remain in the Beis Hamikdosh, they could do even the most heinous sins, and the Beis Hamikdosh would not be destroyed.

The Yismach Moshe says Pharaoh put together the fact that the Shechinah stays and remains with the schoolchildren with the concept that whatever place the Shechinah is cannot be destroyed. Pharaoh understood that when Moshe said in our Posuk that we want to leave Egypt for "a festival of Hashem to us," Hashem would be there and protect the Bnei Yisroel if the children were allowed to come along with them to serve Hashem in the desert. Pharaoh knew if the Bnei Yisroel went with the schoolchildren, he would not be able to militarily force the Bnei Yisroel to return to Egypt since the schoolchildren would ensure Pharaoh would not be victorious in a war with the Bnei Yisroel. Therefore, Pharaoh refused to even consider sending the schoolchildren with them. In summary, in order for it to be "a festival of Hashem to us," it was imperative the schoolchildren be brought along.

9) The Yismach Moshe presents another reason why it was imperative the schoolchildren be brought along, which in turn caused Pharaoh to refuse to send the schoolchildren with the Bnei Yisroel. The Gemorah in Sanhedrin 97b has a discussion about when Moshiach will come. The Gemorah quotes Rav, who says that all the ends have passed and Moshiach's coming depends only on Teshuva and good deeds. The Maharal on this Gemorah explains that all the various times predicted as suitable for Moshiach's arrival have passed. Waiting for a time suitable for Moshiach to come could delay his arrival until that suitable time occurred. At this point, since all the suitable times have passed, there is nothing delaying his arrival except for the Bnei Yisroel doing Teshuva and good deeds. The Maharal explains that Rav is of the opinion Moshiach must eventually come, except if necessary, Hashem will help us do Teshuva by making us more sensitive to the need to do Teshuva. Alternatively, Hashem will put a King or leader in power over us, whose decrees are as harsh as Haman's decrees which will cause the Bnei Yisroel to do Teshuva and perform good deeds. The Gemorah quotes Shmuel, who is of the opinion that it is enough for a mourner (Hashem) to endure his period of mourning. Even if the Bnei Yisroel do not do Teshuva or perform good deeds, the redemption will occur at its preordained time.

Micha (7:15) describes the redemption of Moshiach "As in the days of your exodus from the land of Egypt, I will show wonders." Based on this Posuk, the Yismach Moshe says the redemption from Egypt presumably had similar criteria as the redemption of Moshiach. Though the Yismach Moshe doesn't exactly say this, it would seem Pharaoh was of the opinion that the Bnei Yisroel were not on the level of doing Teshuva and good deeds to merit the redemption from Egypt. Pharaoh was afraid of Shmuel's opinion that Teshuva and redemption will occur at the preordained time since "it is enough for a mourner (Hashem) to endure his period of mourning." Therefore, Pharaoh felt that he had nothing to worry about as long as the Shechinah was not together with the Bnei Yisroel when they went to serve Hashem in the desert. However, when Pharaoh heard Moshe demand the schoolchildren also be taken, which implied the Shechinah was going to go with them being that it was a "festival of Hashem to us," he now had to worry about the redemption coming even without Teshuva and good deeds. Therefore, Pharaoh completely refused to send the schoolchildren.

Bo

10) Rav Sternbuch, is his Sefer Taam V'Daas, presents an answer to our question. He references how the Rambam in the last Halacha of Hilchos Lulav (8:15) describes the joy of a Chag. "The happiness with which a person should rejoice in the fulfillment of the Mitzvos and the love of Hashem who commanded them is a great service. Whoever holds himself back from this rejoicing is worthy of retribution, as Devorim (28:47) says, 'because you did not serve Hashem, your G-d, with happiness and a glad heart.' Whoever holds himself proud, giving himself honor, and acts haughtily in such situations is a sinner and a fool. Concerning this, Shlomo warned in Mishlay (28:10): "Do not seek glory before the King." In contrast, anyone who lowers himself and thinks lightly of his person in these situations is a great person, worthy of honor, who serves Hashem out of love. Thus, Dovid, King of Yisroel, says in Sefer Shmuel II (6:22): 'I will hold myself even more lightly esteemed than this and be humble in my eyes,' because there is no greatness or honor other than celebrating before Hashem, as Sefer Shmuel II (6:16) says, 'King Dovid was dancing wildly and whistling before Hashem.'" The Rambam is referring to Dovid's reaction to Michal, who criticized Dovid's behavior as not fitting for a King at the time the Aron was being moved to Yerushalayim from its temporary quarters.

Rav Sternbuch says we see from this Rambam that when we have a festival and are commanded to be happy, the being happy is part of our services of Hashem and not happiness for its own sake. In fact, our happiness is a service to Hashem, and this service can and needs to be performed by everyone. Pharaoh could only understand bringing sacrifices to serve a deity and therefore could not comprehend how Moshe could think that everyone needed to participate. Therefore, Pharaoh could understand why the cattle and sheep had to be brought along for sacrifices, but not why the women and children had to also come.

11) Rav Mordechai Gifter, in his Sefer Pirkei Torah, also ponders our question. He says Pharaoh argued there was no reason to bring children to the desert since all the sacrifices being offered were completely burnt offerings, and there was no meat to eat from these sacrifices. The Gemorah in Zevochim 116a has a difference of opinion in whether Gentiles can only bring completely burnt offerings or if they can also offer Shelomim (peace offerings) where a portion of the sacrifice is eaten by the one who brought the sacrifice along with his family. Pharaoh was of the opinion that Gentiles could only bring burnt offerings. Moshe answered Pharaoh that they were going to the desert for "a festival of Hashem to us." In a festival, one offers Shelomim an offering that would provide meat for the entire family, including the children, to eat. Therefore, said Moshe, we also need to bring our children.

What Did Pharaoh Mean When He Said "Evil" Is Before Your Faces?

Shemos (10:10) וַיֹּאמֶר אֲלֵהֶם יְהִי כֵן ה' עִמָּכֶם כַּאֲשֶׁר אֲשַׁלַּח אֶתְכֶם וְאֶת טַפְּכֶם רְאוּ כִּי רָעָה נֶגֶד פְּנֵיכֶם (י:י) So he (Pharaoh) said to them, "So may Hashem be with you, just as I will let you and your young children out. See that evil is before your faces."

What did Pharaoh mean when he said "evil" is before your faces?

Bo

Introduction

The Eben Ezra explains that by using the phrase "before your faces," Pharaoh was telling Moshe that the "evil" is very close to happening, and it is as if it is "right in front of your faces."

The Ponim Yofos explains why Pharaoh was so against the children leaving and going along with their parents into the desert. Pharaoh was aware that Hashem promised Avrohom in the Bris Bain HaBesorim in Beraishis (15:16). "And the fourth generation will return here (Eretz Yisroel), for the iniquity of the Amorites will not be complete until then." Moshe's grandfather Kehas was one of the 70 people who came down to Egypt, making Moshe the third generation from the point of coming to Egypt. Pharaoh knew that the children, the fourth generation, were destined to go into Eretz Yisroel. Therefore, Pharaoh did everything he could to keep the children (fourth generation) under his control in Egypt.

1) Rashi and Rabeinu Bechay, quoting the Yalkut Shimoni 392 in Parshas Ki Sisa, present an answer to our question. They say Pharaoh was referring to a cloud which his astrological signs told him meant that blood would be spilled. That is why, when the Bnei Yisroel sinned by making the Golden Calf, Moshe defended the Bnei Yisroel by saying in Shemos (32:12), "Why should the Egyptians say: 'He (Hashem) brought them out with evil to kill them in the mountains and to annihilate them from upon the face of the earth'? Retreat from the heat of Your anger and reconsider the evil intended for Your people." Hashem accepted Moshe's defense of the Bnei Yisroel and changed the blood to that of the blood of Bris Milah when Yehoshua gave a Bris Milah to all the people born in the desert as Sefer Yehoshua (5:6-7) says, "For the Bnei Yisroel walked forty years in the wilderness, until all the people, the men of war, that came out of Egypt were consumed, those who did not listen to the voice of Hashem, to whom Hashem had sworn that He would not show them the land, which Hashem had sworn to their forefathers that He would give us, a land that flows with milk and honey. And their children, whom he raised up in their stead, them Yehoshua circumcised, for they had not circumcised them by the way." After Yehoshua gives them a Bris Milah, Hashem says to Yehoshua in Shemos (5:9), "This day have I rolled away the reproach of Egypt from off you." The reproach that is being referred to is this that Pharaoh says in our Pesukim, "See that evil is before your faces."

The Maskil LeDovid ponders the question that Pharaoh implied this cloud was in the desert, since that is where Moshe asked to go with the Bnei Yisroel, yet Yehoshua did not give this Bris Milah till they were out of the desert and in Eretz Yisroel. He says that both the Pirkei D'Rabi Eliezer (29) and the Tosfos in Yevomos 71b say that the Bnei Yisroel did the Mitzvah of Bris Milah even in the desert. This is the blood that Pharaoh saw. However, a Bris Milah is composed of two parts, Milah (cutting off the foreskin) and Priah (cutting or peeling back the thin membrane). They only did the first part (Milah) in the desert since they felt that doing Priah was dangerous health-wise to someone traveling. According to the Pirkei D'Rabi Eliezer and Tosfos, Yehoshua performed Priah on them when they got to Eretz Yisroel. Therefore, the Milah all of the Bnei Yisroel did in the desert was the cloud of blood that Pharaoh's astrologers saw.

Bo

The Alshich says that by saying, "See that evil is before your faces," Pharaoh was pretending to care about the young children and say that it is a bad idea to take them. Pharaoh argued that the "evil' or "blood" that was coming towards them signaled that there was going to be a battle in the desert. During a battle, argued Pharaoh, you will be much relieved if the children won't be with you since, without children to protect, you will fight the battle differently. Instead of having to be defensive to protect the children, you can take a more offensive approach and, if need be, run away if the battle becomes too intense without having to worry about leaving the children behind. The Oznayim LeTorah points out how ironic it is that Pharaoh, who had murdered so many Jewish children, suddenly now becomes their protector. He says that it was probably a self-centered request since Pharaoh wanted to make sure he could murder even more children and use their blood for bathing to attempt to cure himself completely of the remnant of the plague of boils. The Mayanah Shel Torah says that it was a very calculated decision by Pharaoh. If Pharaoh keeps the children and trains them to keep from serving Hashem, he can ensure that there will be no continuity in the next generation of having the desire to serve Hashem.

The Baal HaTurim, Abarbanel, and Shach quote a Midrash that Pharaoh saw through astrology only two of all the Bnei Yisroel that left Egypt, Yehoshua, and Calev would go into Eretz Yisroel. All the rest would die out in the desert. This could be an even more specific astrological interpretation of what the evil cloud coming toward the Bnei Yisroel meant.

2) The Shemos Raba (13:5), Targum Onkelos, according to the Ramban, Rabeinu Bechay, Chizkuni, Bechor Shor, Abarbanel, Maskil LeDovid, and Chasam Sofer answer our question similarly. They say that Pharaoh accused Moshe of wanting to escape forever by the fact that Moshe wanted all the Bnei Yisroel and all their possessions to leave Egypt. The "evil" that Pharaoh is referring to is the evil plan Moshe had of escaping forever from Egypt under the excuse of going for three days to serve Hashem in the desert. After coming to this conclusion, Pharaoh was so incensed that Shemos (10:11) says, "And he chased them (Moshe and Aharon) out from before Pharaoh" and told them that now after they lied about their plans, Pharaoh would not agree to anyone leaving Egypt. The only problem with this explanation is how the phrase in our Posuk, "evil is before your faces," fits in with this explanation. The Shemos Raba says that "before your faces" means that Pharaoh said he would no longer give you permission to leave. To borrow an idiom from the English language, Pharaoh was saying that Moshe's plan had "blown up in his face." The Bechor Shor says that "before your faces" means Pharaoh said that he could see or read it in their faces that this is their real intention. He compares this to what Yaakov said about Lavan in Beraishis (31:5) רֹאֶה אָנֹכִי אֶת פְּנֵי אֲבִיכֶן כִּי אֵינֶנּוּ אֵלַי כִּתְמֹל שִׁלְשֹׁם (I see your father's face, that he is not disposed toward me as he was yesterday and the day before). Finally, the Abarbanel says that Pharaoh was talking to his advisors when he said, "evil is before your faces." Pharaoh was referring to Moshe and Aharon as evil since they were planning to escape, and this is how Pharaoh answered back his servants who were trying to convince Pharaoh to send out the Bnei Yisroel when they said in Shemos (10:7), "How long will this one be a stumbling block to us? Let the people go, and they will worship their G-d. Don't you yet know that Egypt is lost?"

Bo

The Alshich takes the "evil" plan Pharaoh accused Moshe and Aharon of a step further. Pharaoh pointed out to Moshe that when he first came to him, Moshe said in Shemos (5:3): "And they (Moshe and Aharon) said, "The G-d of the Hebrews has happened upon us. Now let us go on a three-day journey in the desert and sacrifice to Hashem our G-d, lest He strike us with a plague or with the sword." Even Hashem only wants you to go out for three days instead of forever, argued Pharaoh and therefore Pharaoh argues this was even an "evil" plan against Hashem.

3) The Midrash Lekach Tov also presents an answer to our question. When the Bnei Yisroel are traveling away from Egypt and coming close to the Red Sea, Shemos (14:2) says, "Speak to the Bnei Yisroel, and let them turn back and encamp in front of Pi Hachiros, between Migdol and the sea; in front of Baal Tzephon, you shall encamp opposite it, by the sea." Rashi, on this Posuk, quoting the Mechilta, says that only this idol was left from all the Egyptian deities in order to mislead the Egyptians, so they would say that their deity is powerful. Concerning this tactic, Iyov (12:23) says, "He (Hashem) misleads nations and destroys them." Pharaoh was so sure that his Baal Tzephon idol was going to stop the Bnei Yisroel that he chased after the Bnei Yisroel, eventually leading to the Egyptians drowning in the Red Sea. The Midrash Lekach Tov says that the "evil" Pharaoh saw was this idol of Baal Tzephon, which would stop and destroy the Bnei Yisroel according to Pharaoh's interpretation when they were leaving Egypt.

4) The Ramban and Abarbanel present another answer to our question. The Ramban labels this answer "the simple explanation." They say that the "evil" Pharaoh was referring to was the bad things he was going to punish the Bnei Yisroel with for planning to escape.

5) The Ralbag, Toldos Yitzchak, and Malbim answer our question similarly. They explain that at that time, Pharaoh and, in fact, all idol worshippers of the world thought that there were, Chas VeShalom, two distinct deities, one for bringing all good to the world and the other for all afflictions and punishments. They would serve the idol of bad so that the idol would not bring bad to the world. The Ralbag writes that he saw in a Sefer that Pharaoh was of the opinion each idol was either an idol for good or an idol for bad. Pharaoh sized up that Hashem was, Chas VeShalom, only for bad, especially after experiencing many plagues, and that is why he says in our Posuk, "See that (a G-d of) evil is before your faces." Due to this assessment, Pharaoh is both advising Moshe and Aharon to be cautious and explaining why Moshe's request to take the children along is wrong. An idol of bad is served by slaughtering sacrifices so that this idol could be satiated in seeing all the blood spilled in sacrificing the animals. They would keep the women and children away from serving the idol of bad so that the women and children could not be harmed if the idol of bad wanted to do bad and also so that the idol of bad would not demand that they be brought as sacrifices to him.

6) The Beis HaLevi also ponders our question. He says Pharaoh was predicting that Hashem would, Chas VeShalom, bring "evil" against the Bnei Yisroel just like Hashem brought the ten plagues against the Egyptians. Pharaoh argued that he had first-hand experience that when one did not listen to Hashem, one got punished. Since Koheles (7:20) says, "For there is no righteous man on earth who does good and sins not," it is not possible that over time you will not sin, and when you do,

Bo

warned Pharaoh, "evil will be before your faces." This is similar to what Yehoshua says to the Bnei Yisroel in Sefer Yehoshua (24:19-20): "You will not be able to serve Hashem, for He is a holy G-d: He is a jealous G-d: He will not forgive your transgressions or your sins. When you forsake Hashem and serve strange gods, then He will turn and do you evil, and destroy you, after He has done you good." Though Yehoshua was talking about the grave sin of serving idols, Pharaoh generalized this concept to any sin.

7) The Nitziv also offers an answer to our question. He says that the "evil before your faces" refers to the whole plan of taking the children with them. Pharaoh pointed out that a desert is not a suitable place to take children to since children constantly need food and supplies, and there is no place to get or make them in a desert.

What Does "for All the Bnei Yisroel There Was Light in Their Dwellings" Come to Include?

Shemos (10:23) לֹא רָאוּ אִישׁ אֶת אָחִיו וְלֹא קָמוּ אִישׁ מִתַּחְתָּיו שְׁלֹשֶׁת יָמִים וּלְכָל בְּנֵי יִשְׂרָאֵל הָיָה אוֹר בְּמוֹשְׁבֹתָם (י:כג) They did not see each other, and no one rose from his place for three days, but for all the Bnei Yisroel there was light in their dwellings.

What does "for all the Bnei Yisroel there was light in their dwellings" come to include?

Introduction
Rabeinu Bechay says that the darkness was not something that also happened in the rest of the world, by, for example, the sun not shining in the world. Rather the sun was shining as normal in the world, but there was a thick air that prevented the sun and its light from illuminating where each Egyptian was. This is what the Shemos Raba (14:1) and Midrash Tanchuma on Bo (2) mean when they say that the darkness was the thickness of a coin. However, where the Bnei Yisroel were, the air was not thick, and the sun was able to illuminate that place. The Rashash on the Shemos Raba explains that there was a blanket of thick air between the sun and the Egyptians, which prevented the sun's rays from penetrating.

Rabeinu Bechay says that the plague of darkness began after the sun had already risen so that the Egyptians should not think the sun never rose for the days of the plague. He says that it was a greater miracle to make it dark even when the sun shone than making it dark without the sun shining. He points out that Targum Onkelos also says that it got dark after it had been light. The Shach extends this concept to the light which the Bnei Yisroel received. He says that it only became light after it was first dark so that the Bnei Yisroel would not think that the daylight just extended itself.

Shemos (7:25) tells us that the plague of blood lasted for seven days. The Posuk before ours says, "So Moshe stretched forth his hand toward the heavens, and there was thick darkness over the entire land of Egypt for three days." Our Posuk begins with, "They did not see each other, and no one rose from his place for three days." The Shemos Raba (14:3) and Tanah D'Bay Eliyahu (7) ponder why

Bo

Hashem brought the plague of darkness. They say that some of the Bnei Yisroel were officers under the Egyptians, and because of their positions, they had honor and some wealth. Due to this, these people did not want to leave Egypt. Hashem could not publicly cause these Bnei Yisroel to die since the Egyptians would see this and say that the Bnei Yisroel are getting punished just like they were. Therefore, Hashem brought three days of darkness, dark enough so that one Egyptian could not see another Egyptian so that during this time Hashem killed these Bnei Yisroel and the Egyptians were not able to see what happened. The Shemos Raba says that there was a second period of three days, described by our Posuk, in which it was even darker so that no one who was sitting could rise up from his place and no one who was standing was able to sit. The Shemos Raba and the Midrash Tanchuma on Bo (3) say that during these three days, Hashem put the favor of the Bnei Yisroel into the eyes of the Egyptians so that they lent them gold and silver. During these days, the Bnei Yisroel went into the houses of the Egyptians, and wherever they went, the light that was with them showed them where all the Egyptian valuables were hidden. When the Bnei Yisroel asked the Egyptians to borrow their valuables, if the Egyptian said that he didn't have any, the Bnei Yisroel told them exactly what and where their valuables were. The Egyptians then willfully lent these valuables since they reasoned that the Bnei Yisroel were very trustworthy, being that otherwise, they could have just taken the valuables by themselves, and the Egyptians would have been completely unable to stop them since the Egyptians could not even move during these three days. The Alshich and Oznayim LeTorah point out that this darkness had to be much darker than the first darkness so that the Egyptians could not stop the Bnei Yisroel from entering into their houses. Finally, this Shemos Raba and the Midrash Tanchuma on Bo (3) say that the plague of darkness also lasted for another day, such that in total, there were seven days of darkness, just like the previous plagues. The last day of darkness happened when the Egyptians were chasing the Bnei Yisroel to the Red Sea, and on the night before the sea split, Hashem again put the Egyptians into darkness while making it light for the Bnei Yisroel. This is what Shemos (14:20) means when it says, "there were the cloud and the darkness, and it illuminated the night, and one did not draw near the other all night long." The "cloud and darkness" was for the Egyptians, and the "it illuminated the night" was for the Bnei Yisroel. Parenthetically the Oznayim LeTorah says that this is the only plague where the severity of the plague changed and markedly did so, in the middle of the plague.

When describing the plague of darkness, Shemos (10:21) says, וִיהִי חֹשֶׁךְ עַל אֶרֶץ מִצְרָיִם וְיָמֵשׁ חֹשֶׁךְ (that there may be darkness over the land of Egypt, even darkness which may be felt). We have translated the Posuk as Rashi, quoting the Shemos Raba (14:1) and Midrash Tanchuma on Bo (2), translates it. They take the Hebrew word וְיָמֵשׁ to mean to feel or grope as Devorim (28:29) says, וְהָיִיתָ מְמַשֵּׁשׁ בַּצָּהֳרַיִם (And you shalt grope at noonday). The Ralbag ponders the question that such a thick air would make breathing it a health risk. He says that Hashem had to stuff up the mouth and nostrils of the Egyptians so this thick air would not kill them. The Ralbag says that this was very painful for the Egyptians.

The Shemos Raba (14:2) and Midrash Tanchuma on Bo (2) ponder the question of where the darkness used in the plague of darkness came from. The Eitz Yosef and Nisivos Shalom explain that since the darkness was not just a lack of light but was something one could feel, they wanted to know where this new type of darkness came from. Being that after the first seven days of creation,

Bo

Hashem does not create something new, the darkness had to already be in existence somewhere. They answer that it is a difference of opinion between Rav Yehuda and Rav Nechemia. Rav Yehuda is of the opinion that the darkness came from darkness in the heavens. To prove there is darkness in Heaven, he quotes Tehillim (18:10), "And He (Hashem) bent the heavens, and He came down, and thick darkness was under His feet." Rav Nechemia is of the opinion that the darkness came from Gehenom. Though it is perhaps understandable that there is darkness in Gehenom, nonetheless, he quotes Iyov (10:21), which says, "before I go and do not return, to a land of darkness and the shadow of death."

The Shach says it is not possible that there is darkness in the heavens. Rather as Sefer Daniyel (2:22) says, וּנְהוֹרָא עִמֵּהּ שְׁרֵא (and light dwells with Him). The Shach says that even with physical light when one has too much light, one sees darkness. For example, says Rav Schwab in his Sefer Mayan Beis HaShoaivah, if one looks at the sun and then looks away, one will see darkness as one's eyes become adjusted to normal light. Similarly, with spiritual light, one who is not on the spiritual level to handle the spiritual light will see (spiritual) darkness instead.

Shemos (10:21-22) say, "Hashem said to Moshe, 'Stretch forth your hand on the heavens, and there will be darkness over the land of Egypt, and the darkness will become darker.' So Moshe stretched forth his hand on the heavens, and there was thick darkness over the entire land of Egypt for three days." The Zohar in Parshas Pekuday (260b) ponders the question of how a human being would be able to lift his hand on top of the heavens. It explains that Moshe was not commanded to put his hand on Heaven but rather to use his hand to draw down a heavenly flow from the heavens to the earth. The Nisivos Shalom explains that this heavenly flow was the light from Heaven, which turned into darkness for the wicked Egyptians.

The Tzedah LeDerech quotes a question pondered by the Terumas HaDeshen. After the flood, Hashem promises in Beraishis (8:22), "and day and night shall not cease." That being the case, "How was it possible that night lasted for six days straight in Egypt?" He answers that since it was light for the Bnei Yisroel, even when they went into the home of an Egyptian, there was light for Jews everywhere. The promise of "and day and night shall not cease" is not violated when some people (like the Jews in this case) do indeed have day and night in that land. The Tzedah LeDerech answers the question by saying that the promise is only violated when the whole world does not have night and day. As we have previously quoted from the Rabeinu Bechay, this was not the case in the plague of darkness when outside of Egypt; it was day and night as usual. The Meam Loez answers that it was as dark as night during the day but that at night it was even darker than is typical at night. Therefore, there is no violation of the promise "and day and night shall not cease" since relative to each other, there was day and night even in Egypt.

The Chasam Sofer ponders the question of why Hashem could not have just made a smaller miracle and smitten the Egyptians with blindness and disorientation. In Beraishis (19:11), when the people of Sodom surrounded Lot's house to force him to give them the two visitors/angels who had come to his house, the Torah says, "And the men who were at the entrance of the house they struck with blindness, both small and great, and they toiled in vain to find the entrance." As the Malbim on that

Bo

Posuk explains, the people of Sodom were not just smitten with blindness, but they were also smitten with disorientation. Otherwise, even a blind person would have eventually felt their way and found the door. It would seem that doing the same thing to the Egyptians would have been a smaller miracle than changing the entire climate where an Egyptian went. The Chasam Sofer answers that a blind person, especially over time, becomes much more sensitive with his other senses to make up for the fact that he cannot see. However, someone whose eyesight is just fine and makes every effort to see will not have his other senses become more sensitive. Making the plague in the way it was made ensured that the Egyptians would be completely helpless and not have any of their other senses compensate for not seeing, especially in the second part of the plague of darkness.

Tehillim (105:28), when describing the plague of darkness, says, "He (Hashem) sent darkness and it darkened, and they did not disobey His word." The Chasam Sofer says that the phrase "They did not disobey his word" is referring to the Bnei Yisroel. During the plague of darkness, the Egyptians were so immobilized that the Bnei Yisroel could have killed them, robbed them of all their money, or perhaps most appropriately taken the opportunity to leave Egypt taking whatever they wanted with them. Beraishis (50:25) says, "And Yosef made the Bnei Yisroel take an oath, saying, 'G-d will surely remember you, and you shall take up my bones out of here.'" The Targum Yonason ben Uziel explains that part of this oath was not to leave Egypt on their own until they were redeemed. Even though they could have easily done so, the Bnei Yisroel were bound by this oath, and "they did not disobey his word."

1) The Shemos Raba (14:3) and Midrash Tanchuma on Bo (3) are the sources to the answer that the Rabeinu Bechay, Chizkuni, Bechor Shor, and Ohr HaChaim present to our question. They say that our Posuk is telling us that even if a Jew walked into the home of an Egyptian, he would have light so that he could see, and as we have quoted from the Shemos Raba, the Jew was able to see all the Egyptian valuables, even those hidden, during this plague. Unlike many of the preceding plagues, the Torah does not say that there was darkness in Egypt while there was light in Goshen. For example, in the plague of hail, Shemos (9:25) says, "The hail struck throughout the entire land of Egypt," and Shemos (9:26) says, "Only in the land of Goshen, where the Bnei Yisroel were, there was no hail." The Chizkuni, Rabeinu Bechay, and Maharzav explain that the Shemos Raba derives that a Jew had light in the house of an Egyptian by the fact that our Posuk uses the seemingly superfluous phrase "in their dwelling" when it says "for all the Bnei Yisroel there was light in their dwellings." They say that "their dwellings" means the dwellings of the Egyptians. The Bechor Shor says that the Shemos Raba took "in their dwellings" to be the dwellings of the Bnei Yisroel and that our Posuk attributes anywhere a Jew went to be (even in the house of an Egyptian) to be the Jew's (at least temporary) dwelling so that there was light for the Jew there.

The Ksav VeHakabola says that because there was light for the Bnei Yisroel, even when they were in the Egyptian houses, there was no need to differentiate Goshen from the rest of Egypt. He says that there were many Egyptians who lived in Goshen. In some of the previous plagues which did not occur in Goshen, these Egyptians were spared so that the Bnei Yisroel who lived in Goshen would not be subjected to the plague. Parenthetically, Rabeinu Bechay, the Toldos Yitzchak, the Tur, and the Tzedah LeDerech say that it was Pharaoh who built houses for the Egyptians in

Bo

Goshen. When Pharaoh failed to get the Midwives to murder the Jewish boys, Pharaoh still wanted to make sure that all the Jewish baby boys were found, and therefore he built houses between every Jewish house and settled Egyptian people in those houses so that the Bnei Yisroel could not hide their Jewish sons from being heard by the Egyptians.

2) The Bechor Shor presents another answer to our question. He says that the plague of darkness was similar to the previous plagues where the plague was only found in all of Egypt besides for the land of Goshen, where there was no plague. He says that the phrase in our Posuk, "for all the Bnei Yisroel there was light in their dwellings," means in the land of Goshen. Everywhere else in Egypt, there was darkness.

3) The Kli Yakor and Kli Chemdah answer our question similarly. They say that the Bnei Yisroel had an extra amount of light during the plague of darkness. During the day, just like it was as dark as night for the Egyptians, it was as light as daytime for the Bnei Yisroel during the night. Otherwise, they reason, there was no reason for the Torah to tell us "for all the Bnei Yisroel there was light in their dwellings." The Maor VaShemesh says that it was similar to what took place during the creation of the world where before Beraishis (1:4) which says, "G-d separated between the light and between the darkness" both light and dark existed at the same time.

4) The Akeidah also ponders our question. He says that the phrase "for all the Bnei Yisroel there was light in their dwellings" means that Hashem gave each member of the Bnei Yisroel the intellectual understanding to figure out where and how the Egyptians hid their treasures and valuables. He also takes the portion of the phrase "in their dwellings" to mean in the dwellings of the Egyptians.

5) The Yalkut Reuveni also presents an answer to our question. We have mentioned previously that many of the Bnei Yisroel died during the plague of darkness. I'm not sure what the source for this is, but he says that they all died doing Teshuva. Because of this, even the people who did not merit to leave Egypt had "light in their dwellings." "Their dwellings" is referring to Gan Eden, and they had spiritual light there since they did Teshuva before they were Niftar.

6) The Shach also presents an answer to our question. He says that when our Posuk relates, "for all the Bnei Yisroel there was light in their dwellings," the Torah is not referring to physical light but rather spiritual light. The spiritual light was that of the Ohr HaGanuz, the light created on the first day of creation, which Hashem hid for the Righteous ones after Moshiach comes. The Nitziv explains why Hashem had to create the spiritual Ohr HaGanuz, even though he was soon to hide it because there are no new creations allowed, even after Moshiach comes. The Shach says that after Hashem had killed all the wicked people of the Bnei Yisroel, the remainder of the Bnei Yisroel were righteous, and they were able to use this Ohr HaGanuz. It is understandable that with this light, the Bnei Yisroel were able to see inside all the Egyptian containers and hiding places since the Ohr HaGanuz is not stopped by the physical walls of vessels. Since the Ohr HaGanuz has nothing to do with the physical light of the sun, it was light for the Bnei Yisroel during all the days of the plague of darkness. Similarly, the wicked Egyptians were blinded by the light of the Ohr HaGanuz so that

Bo

it was dark for them during the entire time of the plague of darkness. The Shach and the Kedushas Levi quote the Gemorah in Nedorim 8b, which says that in the time of Moshiach, Hashem will take out the sun from its sheath, and it will cure the righteous people while simultaneously burning the wicked people. Taking the sun out of its sheath is referring to the light of the Ohr HaGanuz, which has the power to cure righteous people and burn wicked people. This is similar to the way the Chasam Sofer in his Divrei Torah on Succos explains the Gemorah in Avodah Zora 3a. The Gemorah says that at the time of Moshiach, the Gentiles will ask for a Mitzvah to do to show that they are also ready to do Mitzvos, and Hashem will tell them to do the Mitzvah of Sukkah. The Gemorah relates how Hashem makes it an extremely hot day. Because of the extreme heat, the Gentiles leave their Sukkos, kicking them on the way out. The Chasam Sofer ponders whether the Jews also left their Sukkos and what the problem with the Gentiles leaving their Sukkah was since one who is in pain from a great heat is not obligated to sit in a Sukkah. The Chasam Sofer says that the heat was not a physical heat but rather a spiritual heat of the Ohr HaGanuz, which Hashem released at that point, as we have seen from the Gemorah in Nedorim 8b, that Hashem will do at the time of Moshiach. The Bnei Yisroel, who were on a much higher spiritual level than the Gentiles, were not bothered by this heat and light and therefore had no reason to leave their Sukkos. The Gentiles are not able to spiritually handle this light, and therefore they are in pain because of it. By showing the Gentiles that the Bnei Yisroel are not at all in pain and are rather being cured by this heat/light, Hashem shows the Gentiles why they are not able or fit to handle doing Mitzvos.

7) The Malbim takes the Shach's answer a step further. He says that not only was the light a spiritual light of the Ohr HaGanuz but, consistent with Rav Yehuda's opinion; the darkness was also a spiritual darkness. According to this opinion, the darkness could have just been in the eyes of each Egyptian.

8) The Kotzker Rebbe, as quoted by the Mayanah Shel Torah, also presents an answer to our question. We have mentioned previously, quoting the Shemos Raba and Tanah D'Bay Eliyahu, that all the wicked people of the Bnei Yisroel died during the plague of darkness. We also know all the Egyptians were in darkness during the plague of darkness. Rashi on Beraishis (1:4) says Hashem saw that it was not proper for the wicked people to use the Ohr HaGanuz, and therefore Hashem hid the Ohr HaGanuz for righteous people at the time of Moshiach. Now that both the wicked of the Bnei Yisroel were dead and the Egyptians not getting any light to use, Hashem could bring out the Ohr HaGanuz for the remaining Bnei Yisroel. That is what the Torah is telling us when it says, "for all the Bnei Yisroel there was light in their dwellings."

Why Was Hashem Concerned About What Avrohom Would Say About Fulfilling the Promise of Leaving Egypt With Riches?

Shemos (11:2) דַּבֶּר נָא בְּאָזְנֵי הָעָם וְיִשְׁאֲלוּ אִישׁ מֵאֵת רֵעֵהוּ וְאִשָּׁה מֵאֵת רְעוּתָהּ כְּלֵי כֶסֶף וּכְלֵי זָהָב (יא:ב) Please, speak into the ears of the people, and let them borrow, each man from his friend and each woman from her friend, silver vessels and golden vessels.

Bo

The Gemorah in Brochos 9a ponders why Hashem requests from Moshe "Please Speak." Rashi quotes the Gemorah's answer that the reason is "so that the righteous man, Avrohom, will not say Hashem fulfilled with them His promise in Beraishis (15:13) "and they will enslave them and oppress them," but Hashem did not fulfill with them His promise in the next Posuk (Beraishis (15:14)): "afterward they will go forth with great possessions." The Gemorah presents a Moshul to explain this. A prisoner once was promised great possessions tomorrow when he would be freed from prison. The prisoner replies that he is so sick of prison that he would prefer to get out of jail today, and he will forego the great possessions which he will receive the next day. In addition, Hashem had to fulfill the promise that Hashem made independent of what Avrohom or anyone else would say. That being the case, why would Hashem only be concerned with what Avrohom would say?

Why was Hashem concerned about what Avrohom would say about fulfilling the promise of leaving Egypt with riches?

Introduction
The Gemorah in Sanhedrin 91a describes what happened when the Egyptians brought a court case to the court of Alexander the Great demanding that the Bnei Yisroel return all the money they borrowed from Egypt. As proof to their claim, the Egyptians quoted Shemos (12:36), which says, "Hashem gave the people favor in the eyes of the Egyptians, and they lent them, and they emptied out Egypt." The Gemorah relates that there was a person called Geviha ben Pesisa who asked permission from the Jewish elders to answer the claim of the Egyptians. Geviha ben Pesisa argued that if the Egyptians win against me in the court case, you can say that the Egyptians won against a simple Jew, and if I win against them, you can say that the Torah taught to us by Moshe has defeated them. The Jewish elders gave him permission to answer the claim of the Egyptians. He began his rebuttal by noting to the Egyptians that their entire claim is based on the Torah. Therefore, he said that he would refute their claim from the same Torah, which says only a few Pesukim later in Shemos (12:40) "And the habitation of the Bnei Yisroel, that they dwelled in Egypt, was four hundred and thirty years." He asked the Egyptians to first pay us wages for 600,000 men working for 430 years which far exceeds the amount of money we borrowed from Egypt, and then we will pay you for what we borrowed from Egypt. Alexander the Great then asked the Egyptians to counter Geviha ben Pesisa's claim. The Egyptians pleaded to be given three days to prepare an answer, to which Alexander the Great agreed. When the Egyptians realized they did not have an answer, they abandoned all their fields and vineyards with their crops and ran away. The Gemorah tells us that it was the Shemitah year where we are forbidden to plant, and because of that, we had a big windfall of food in a year where food is typically difficult to get.

The Malbim on Shemos (3:22) presents another justification for taking the Egyptians gold and silver vessels. The Torah says, "Each woman shall borrow from her neighbor and from the dweller in her house silver and gold objects and garments, and you shall put them on your sons and on your daughters, and you shall empty out Egypt." The Malbim explains that the focus on borrowing the gold and silver objects from their neighbors was because when the Bnei Yisroel left Egypt, these

Bo

neighbors took over the houses and anything the Bnei Yisroel left in the houses. Therefore, the gold and silver vessels were payment for the Bnei Yisroel's houses and their contents.

The Nisivos, in his Sefer Nachalas Yaakov, presents another justification for taking the Egyptian gold and silver vessels. Moshe only asked Pharaoh for the Bnei Yisroel to be allowed to travel three days in the desert and bring sacrifices to Hashem as Moshe says in Shemos (5:3), "Now let us go on a three-day journey in the desert and sacrifice to Hashem our G-d, lest He strike us with a plague or with the sword." Hashem tells Moshe in Shemos (6:1): כִּי בְיָד חֲזָקָה יְשַׁלְּחֵם וּבְיָד חֲזָקָה יְגָרְשֵׁם מֵאַרְצוֹ (for with a mighty hand he (Pharaoh) will send them out, and with a mighty hand he will drive them out of his land). At first glance, this Posuk seems repetitious. The Nisivos explains that the first phrase means that Pharaoh will allow the Bnei Yisroel to go out of Egypt and return (in three days). The second phrase tells us that Pharaoh will drive out the Bnei Yisroel under threat that they should never return. Shemos (12:39) says, "for they (Bnei Yisroel) were driven out of Egypt, and they could not tarry, and also, they had not made provisions for themselves," proving that the Bnei Yisroel were driven out and informed not to return. Telling the Bnei Yisroel not to return amounted to disowning the articles which they had lent the Bnei Yisroel since they never wanted to see the Bnei Yisroel again. More poignantly, the Posuk immediately before ours says, "When he (Pharaoh) lets you out, he will completely drive you out of here." Therefore, the Bnei Yisroel already knew when they were told to borrow gold and silver vessels in our Posuk that the Egyptians would completely drive them out so that they would relinquish ownership from the gold and silver vessels.

We must also understand how Hashem would have fulfilled his promise even if the people did not ask to borrow silver and golden vessels. The Nisivos, in his Sefer Nachalas Yaakov, and the Anaf Yosef on Brochos 9a say that Hashem's promise of getting great riches would have been fulfilled from all the booty the Bnei Yisroel gathered when the Egyptians drowned in the Red Sea. The old Midrash Tanchuma (typically published at the end of the Midrash Tanchuma) on Shemos (15:22) says that Pharaoh dressed all the horses that he used to chase after the Bnei Yisroel with precious stones and pearls. When the Egyptians, along with their horses, were drowned in the Red Sea, the precious stones and pearls floated on the water toward the shore where the Bnei Yisroel were. Each day they spent at the shores of the Red Sea, the Bnei Yisroel gathered all these riches. The Bnei Yisroel were so enthralled by these riches that they wished to remain at the shores of the Red Sea. Moshe had to force them to travel as Shemos (15:22) says, "Moshe led Yisroel away from the Red Sea, and they went out into the desert of Shur." The Mechilta on Shemos (12:36) says that the booty gathered at the Red Sea was more than all the riches the Bnei Yisroel took with them when they left Egypt. The Ben Yehoyoda points out that Beraishis (15:14) says, "And also the nation that they will serve will I judge, and afterward they will go forth with great possessions." The end of the judgment of the Egyptians did not occur until they drowned in the Red Sea. As Rav Yossi HaGlili proves in the Hagadah, the Egyptians were stricken by ten plagues in Egypt and then were struck by fifty plagues at the Red Sea. As prophesized, the receiving of great possessions by the Bnei Yisroel occurred right away after the end of the Egyptian's judgment. The Vilna Gaon, in his Sefer Kol Eliyahu, and the Nodeh BeYehudah, in his Sefer Tzlach on Brochos 9a, are also of the opinion that great riches and, in fact, the real redemption from Egypt only happened with the drowning of the Egyptians at the Red Sea. Using this idea, they explain what the Gemorah in Brochos 9a means

Bo

when it presents a Moshul of a prisoner who once was promised great possessions tomorrow when he would be freed from prison. The prisoner replies that he would prefer to get out of jail today, and he will forego the great possessions which he will receive the next day. Shemos (12:33) says, "So the Egyptians took hold of the people (Bnei Yisroel) to hasten to send them out of the land, for they said, 'We are all dead.'" As the Nodeh BeYehudah and Vilna Gaon explain, had the Bnei Yisroel asked for a present of golden and silver vessels instead of borrowing them, the Egyptians were so petrified of dying that they would have gladly given them. The Bnei Yisroel were ready to forego all the riches at the Red Sea seven days after they left Egypt in exchange for being redeemed immediately and not causing the Egyptians to pursue them by borrowing golden and silver vessels from them and thereby drown with their riches.

The Ain Eliyahu says that Hashem was not obligated to fulfill his promise since the promise was only made for after the Bnei Yisroel served 400 years of slavery. Since the Bnei Yisroel were only in slavery for 210 years, Hashem did not have to fulfill his promise. The Chidushay HaRim says that the riches being referred to were not physical riches, which of course, Avrohom would not be impressed with, but rather was the spiritual riches of receiving the Torah on Mount Sinai. Therefore, if not for worrying about what Avrohom would say, there was no obligation for Hashem to fulfill the promise at that time of "afterward they will go forth with great possessions."

Along with the Moshul presented by the Gemorah in Brochos 9a to why the Bnei Yisroel had to be convinced to take riches from the Egyptians, the Nachalas Yaakov on Rashi presents another reason. He explains that the Bnei Yisroel were concerned that if they borrowed the gold and silver vessels, the Egyptians would chase after them once they realized the Bnei Yisroel were not returning to Egypt. In fact, Rashi on Shemos (14:5) says that the incentive to chase after the Bnei Yisroel, after realizing they weren't returning, was to take back the gold and silver vessels they lent the Bnei Yisroel. Therefore, the Bnei Yisroel calculated it was better not to borrow the riches so as not to take the risk of being chased by the Egyptians.

Though our Posuk only speaks of the Bnei Yisroel being told to borrow gold and silver vessels from the Egyptians, Shemos (12:38) says, "And the Bnei Yisroel did according to Moshe's order, and they borrowed from the Egyptians silver vessels, golden vessels, and garments." We must ponder the question of how the Bnei Yisroel decided to also borrow garments, which we are told by the Mechilta, had jewels that made them even more precious than the gold and silver vessels.

The Toldos Yitzchak has a unique approach as to how the Bnei Yisroel received the precious clothes even though Moshe did not tell the Bnei Yisroel to ask for clothes. On the night of the killing of the firstborn, along with the commandment to eat the Korban Pesach, the Bnei Yisroel were also commanded in Shemos (12:22) וְאַתֶּם לֹא תֵצְאוּ אִישׁ מִפֶּתַח בֵּיתוֹ עַד בֹּקֶר (and you shall not go out, any man from the entrance of his house until morning). At midnight, the Egyptian firstborns were killed, and soon after we are told in Shemos (12:33), "So the Egyptians took hold of the people to hasten to send them out of the land, for they said, 'We are all dead.'" The Bnei Yisroel remembered that they were commanded to ask the Egyptians for their gold and silver before leaving, and therefore they asked the Egyptians for it. Rashi quoting the Mechilta on Shemos (12:35), says that the Egyptians

Bo

were so eager to get the Bnei Yisroel to hurry up and leave that instead of bringing them the specific article of gold and silver that the Bnei Yisroel asked for, they brought two of the same articles. All of this was an attempt to get the Bnei Yisroel to leave quickly since the Egyptians feared that soon all the Egyptians would die. The haste of the Egyptians left the Bnei Yisroel is a quandary since they still had a number of hours to go till morning, and they were commanded not to leave their house until morning. The Bnei Yisroel came up with an ingenious idea to stall for time. The Bnei Yisroel asked the Egyptians for their precious clothes. By asking for clothes, the Bnei Yisroel could stall the Egyptians because even if they did bring them clothes, the Bnei Yisroel could complain that the clothes needed to be adjusted to fit or needed a different color. This caused the Egyptians to frantically run around for hours trying to fulfill the specifications of the Bnei Yisroel for clothes. Because of their request for clothes, the Bnei Yisroel managed to stall the Egyptians until morning, when they were allowed to leave their houses to go out of Egypt. Hashem predicted this ingenuity to Moshe when he told him at the beginning of his mission that the Bnei Yisroel would ask for expensive clothes from the Egyptians.

1) The Ponim Yofos presents an answer to our question and says that the statement "afterward they will go forth with great possessions" is subjective and therefore problematic. In general, a person is never satisfied with how much wealth he has. Koheles (5:9) says that "A lover of money will never be satisfied with money." The Koheles Raba (1:13) explains that such a person will leave this world with only half of his desires fulfilled since he will want double the amount of whatever amount he has. For example, if he has one million dollars, he will want two million; if he has two million, he will want four million. Therefore, great possessions to a rich man can be very different than great possessions to a poor man. The Mishna in Pirkei Avos (4:1) says, אֵיזֶהוּ עָשִׁיר הַשָּׂמֵחַ בְּחֶלְקוֹ (Who is the rich one? He who is happy with his lot). Only to such a person can we be guaranteed that getting something extra is a great possession.

The Ponim Yofos explains Hashem changed the nature of the Bnei Yisroel such that when they went out of Egypt, they were completely happy with their lot. Because they were happy with their lot, they considered even getting gold and silver vessels from the Egyptians to be an unnecessary burden for them to carry with them out of Egypt. Therefore, Hashem had to beg them to ask for the vessels. Only in this fashion could Avrohom be assured that everyone, no matter how rich or how poor they were, who came out of Egypt considered golden and silver
vessels to be a "great possession."

2) The Dubna Magid also presents an answer to our question. We have mentioned in the introduction that the riches gained at the Red Sea dwarfed the riches the Bnei Yisroel came out of Egypt with. As is typical with him, he gives a Moshul to explain his answer. In his Moshul, there were once two Kings who fought a long-running war, causing numerous casualties and damage to their Kingdoms. One day they decided to resolve the war by choosing two warriors, one from each side, and depending on which one bested the other, it would decide which King got to take over the other's kingdom. They also decided to dig a very deep pit and have the winner of the two warriors be the one who threw the other into the pit. With so much at stake, the two Kings stood by to watch what would happen. Right at the start, one of the warriors went over, grabbed the second warrior,

Bo

put him on his shoulder, and headed to the pit to drop him in it. When they got close to the edge of the pit, the second warrior easily overpowered the first warrior and threw the first warrior down into the pit. The King of the second warrior went over to the second warrior and, after thanking him for winning, told him that he had a complaint. "When you were close to the edge of the pit, I was so afraid that I was going to lose my Kingdom that I almost had a heart attack," said the second King. "Since you had the strength to overpower the first warrior, why didn't you do it a lot sooner and prevent me from having so much pain?" With this Moshul, the Dubna Magid explains that Avrohom would have felt the same way as the second King, had Hashem waited until the Bnei Yisroel got to the Red Sea. Hashem wanted to prevent this pain and therefore beseeched the Bnei Yisroel to get some riches from the Egyptians before leaving Egypt.

3) The Dubna Magid presents a second answer to our question. Avrohom had been promised that the Bnei Yisroel would be slaves for 400 years. However, Chazal tell us that the Bnei Yisroel were on the 49th and last level of Tumah in Egypt, and if they had stayed in Egypt any longer, they would have fallen to the 50th level of Tumah for which there would be no hope of redemption. Therefore, Hashem had to redeem the Bnei Yisroel early and made the remaining years of exile occur later in the history of the Bnei Yisroel. That being the case, there was no need for the Bnei Yisroel to be rewarded with richness until they had fulfilled the entire 400 years of their exile. He presents a Moshul to explain what would have been wrong with rewarding the Bnei Yisroel when they had completed their 400 years of exile. The Moshul involves a person from a small town who suddenly decided that he was going to go into the catering business. However, the person had never been at a lavish meal, so he consulted with those who had been at lavish meals to explain what happens at such a meal. They explained that first one brings out fish, and after that course, broiled meat is brought out with condiments. There were many guests who attended the first meal the new caterer catered, such that he needed to make two rows of tables. First, he brought out two large platters of fish, which he skillfully balanced in each hand, and placed one at each table. Then he brought out two more platters, one which contained the broiled meat and one which contained a special sauce or condiments for the meat. Seeing that his first course had been well received, he decided to repeat what he had done previously and put the meat on one table and the sauce/condiments on the other table. The people started laughing at the caterer, asking why he had given the sauce/condiments to a table that had no meat to eat it with. In a similar way, if Hashem waited with the riches until the future generation finished the exile, Avrohom would complain that they would be getting a reward for enduring an exile they had not endured, while those that did endure the exile got nothing for all their pain and suffering.

4) The Ksav Sofer presents an answer to our question. He says that the Bnei Yisroel did not have to ask the Egyptians to lend them gold and silver vessels but rather could have asked them to give the Bnei Yisroel their gold and silver as a present. After all, Shemos (12:33) says, "So the Egyptians took hold of the people to hasten to send them out of the land, for they said, 'We are all dead.'" A person would give up all his money to keep himself alive. However, Hashem did not want the Bnei Yisroel to ask for a present since they would then have to have gratitude to the Egyptians for making them rich. Avrohom, when the King of Sodom offered to give him a present of all the booty which he won in the war with the four Kings, says to the King of Sodom in Beraishis (14:22-23), "I raise

Bo

my hand to Hashem, the Most High G-d, Who possesses heaven and earth. Neither from a thread to a shoe strap nor will I take from whatever is yours, that you should not say, 'I have made Avrom wealthy.'" In Avrohom's eyes, taking a present from a person was not the proper way to get rich since Avrohom would rather get rich directly from Hashem and not have to be beholden to a person. Avrohom was of the opinion that when Hashem promised to make him rich, it should not come through presents from a person. Though the Bnei Yisroel would have preferred being given presents from the Egyptians, which they immediately would know was theirs, as opposed to borrowing the articles, because of sensitivity to Avrohom, Hashem commanded them to borrow the gold and silver vessels. In this way, when the Bnei Yisroel acquired the gold and silver vessels when the Egyptians drowned, they only had to have gratitude to Hashem for giving them these riches. Therefore, Hashem commanded the Bnei Yisroel to please borrow and not ask for the gold and silver as presents. With this answer, we can understand what the Gemorah in Brochos 9a means when it says that Hashem's concern for Avrohom, who would not label getting presents from people as becoming rich, is what caused Hashem to ask the Bnei Yisroel to borrow golden and silver vessels. We can also understand why the Gemorah labels Avrohom as "the righteous one" since only a righteous person could give up all the riches a person (the King of Sodom) was volunteering to give him.

The Ksav Sofer takes this concept a step further. In Sefer Shmuel II, chapter 24, Dovid realizes that he has sinned by taking a census of the Bnei Yisroel. Sefer Shmuel II (24:10) says, "And Dovid's heart smote him after he had counted the people. And Dovid said to Hashem: 'I have sinned greatly in what I have done; and now, 'O Lord, put aside please, the iniquity of your servant, for I was very foolish!'" Dovid is offered to choose among three different punishments to which Dovid answers in Sefer Shmuel II (24:14): "I am greatly oppressed; let us fall now into the hand of Hashem; for His mercies are great, but into the hand of man let me not fall." We have previously quoted the Gemorah in Brochos 9a, which says that Avrohom would say: "Hashem fulfilled with them His promise in Beraishis (15:13) "and they will enslave them and oppress them," but Hashem did not fulfill with them his promise in Beraishis (15:14): "afterward they will go forth with great possessions." Avrohom would complain that since the punishment (enslavement) came in the worst way, through a person, it would not be nice if the reward also came in the worst way, which would be through receiving presents from a person or people.

5) The Ksav Sofer presents another answer to our question. He first quotes a Yalkut Shimoni (258) in Parshas Beshalach about the Mon to motivate the answer. Shemos (16:15) says, "When the Yisroel saw it, they said to one another, It is Mon, because they did not know what it was, and Moshe said to them, It is the bread that Hashem has given you to eat." Further on, Shemos (16:31) says, "The house of Yisroel named it Mon, and it was like coriander seed, it was white, and it tasted like a wafer with honey." Bamidbar (11:8) says, "It had a taste like the taste of oil cake." The Yalkut Shimoni explains why the Mon had so many different descriptions by explaining that it depended on who was eating it. When a nursing child ate the Mon, it tasted like milk; when a lad ate the Mon, it tasted like honey on a cracker, when an elder ate the Mon, it tasted like bread, and when a sick person ate the Mon, it tasted like flour mixed with oil and honey as is given to a sick person. The Sifrei in Bamidbar (11:8) says that the Mon could taste like any food, be the food something which grows or be it cooked, baked, or ground up. That being the case, the Ksav Sofer

Bo

ponders why when an elder ate the Mon, it tasted like bread. He explains that the base or default taste of Mon was like bread. However, a person who desired a different taste could think of the taste, and the Mon would taste like that. Young lads who wanted to have pleasure from the taste could taste the sweetest taste of honey on a cracker or any other taste they desired. Nevertheless, the elders did not have any thoughts of getting physical pleasures from the Mon and just desired food to give them the energy to serve Hashem. Consequently, the Mon kept its base taste of bread. This is what Mishlay (13:25) means when it says, "A righteous man eats to satiate his appetite, but the stomach of the wicked shall feel want." As Rashi explains, to the wicked people, it does not seem to them that they are ever satisfied.

Devorim (8:12-14) says, "lest you eat and be satiated, and build good houses and dwell therein, and your herds and your flocks multiply, and your silver and gold increase, and all that you have increases, and your heart grows haughty, and you forget Hashem, your G-d, Who has brought you out of the land of Egypt, out of the house of bondage." From these Pesukim, we see that wealth can lead to haughtiness and forgetting Hashem unless one controls one's desire for physical pleasure. The Mon, which could taste like any dish without needing to do any physical work of preparation, was a test to see if one could nonetheless curb one's desires for physical pleasure. The elders understood this, and that is why they only got the base taste of bread from eating the Mon. Devorim (8:2-3) says, "And you shall remember the entire way on which Hashem, your G-d, led you these forty years in the desert, in order to afflict you, to test you, to know what is in your heart, whether you would keep His commandments or not. And He afflicted you and let you go hungry, and then fed you with Mon, which you did not know, nor did your forefathers know." The Mayanah Shel Torah quoting the Kehilas Moshe, explains why the eating of Mon, which could taste like any food, is described as "And He afflicted you and let you go hungry." He says that the test was knowing Mon could taste like any food and yet keeping oneself from these desires and allowing the Mon to taste like bread. By ignoring physical pleasures, one is more likely to improve spiritually by learning Torah and serving Hashem better. The Ksav Sofer concludes that such righteous people would not be led astray if they had riches.

In general, richness and, for that matter, honor and high office can bring a person to becoming haughty and forgetting Hashem. It is especially dangerous for someone who was previously poor and suddenly became rich, like the oppressed Bnei Yisroel did when they were redeemed from Egypt. The Ksav Sofer says that Avrohom was very worried for the Bnei Yisroel when he heard that they would be servants for 400 years and suddenly be redeemed and made rich. However, Hashem prevented this from happening by constantly reminding the Bnei Yisroel of His presence. For example, many miracles were seen both in the redemption and in the desert. They always saw the cloud protecting and guiding them, along with Mon falling every day except Shabbos. If they ever slipped up like in Shemos (17:7), which says, "He (Moshe) named the place Massah (testing) and Meribah (quarreling) because of the quarrel of the Bnei Yisroel and because of their testing Hashem, saying, Is Hashem in our midst or not?" Immediately the next Posuk says, "Amalek came and fought with Yisroel in Refidim." The next generation, which came into Eretz Yisroel, having grown up in wealth, were not so much a threat to forget Hashem, even though they inherited a beautiful land flowing with milk and honey. It was, therefore, necessary for the people coming out

Bo

of Egypt to be rich such that the next generation would be much less likely to forget Hashem when they came to Eretz Yisroel.

With this introduction, the Ksav Sofer answers our question. Once Hashem had informed the Bnei Yisroel to gather all the riches of Egypt by borrowing multitudes of gold and silver vessels, Hashem had technically fulfilled his promise of taking the Bnei Yisroel out of Egypt with much riches. This would be true even if the Bnei Yisroel refused to do so. However, Avrohom would not be happy with such a scenario since Avrohom feared that the generation that went into Eretz Yisroel would forget Hashem when they were given such a precious land. Therefore, Hashem beseeched the Bnei Yisroel to actually borrow the vessels so that Avrohom would not have any complaints.

6) The Ksav Sofer presents a third answer to our question. He says that "afterward they will go forth with great possessions" is relative. For a very poor person, like the Bnei Yisroel were in Egypt, even having a bit of richness is considered by him to be "great possessions." For a rich person, it would take humongous riches for that person to consider it "great possessions." For the impoverished Bnei Yisroel in Egypt, there was no need for them to get golden and silver vessels for them to feel they had "great possessions." However, Avrohom, who was a very wealthy man, would only consider it "great possessions" if the Bnei Yisroel received riches of high value like golden and silver vessels. Therefore, Hashem begged the Bnei Yisroel to ask for golden and silver vessels, even though they would have been delighted with something much less in value.

7) The Ksav Sofer on Shemos (12:38) presents a fourth answer to our question. Shemos (12:38) describes the Bnei Yisroel leaving from Egypt and says, "and flocks and cattle, very much livestock." Since the Bnei Yisroel only borrowed gold and silver vessels along with precious clothing, he ponders how it was that they had "and flocks and cattle, very much livestock." Moreover, being that the Egyptians had stolen even the bodies of the Bnei Yisroel by enslaving them, he ponders why they didn't also steal their cattle. He answers that the Egyptians did this out of their wickedness so that they could inflict psychological pain on the Bnei Yisroel. A rich person who is forced to work under tremendous hardship is much more psychologically pained than a poor person who is used to working very hard and doing even menial jobs to earn money to feed himself. By allowing the Bnei Yisroel to keep their many flocks of cattle, the Egyptians made the Bnei Yisroel feel like they were rich and yet forced them to endure unbearable labor. Since the Bnei Yisroel were rich by virtue of the Egyptians wanting them to remain rich and psychologically tormented, even if they had not taken anything else with them, Hashem's promise of "afterward they will go forth with great possessions" was fulfilled. However, since these riches were used to torment the Bnei Yisroel, also using them to say that Hashem's promise was fulfilled would not impress Avrohom. Therefore, Hashem asked them to in addition borrow golden and silver vessels so that they would have riches besides the riches which were used to afflict them.

Parenthetically we should mention that the Nitziv presents a different answer as to how the Bnei Yisroel leaving Egypt had "and flocks and cattle, very much livestock." He says that the Bnei Yisroel got all their cattle essentially in the plague of pestilence. With regard to the plague of pestilence, Shemos (9:5) says, "Hashem set an appointed time, saying, 'Tomorrow, G-d will do this

Bo

thing in the land.'" The reason Hashem had Moshe announce to the Egyptians that the plague of pestilence would start on the next day was so that many of the Egyptians would take advantage and sell their cattle to the Bnei Yisroel at a very low price. These Egyptians would calculate that it would be better to at least get something for their cattle before the cattle would die and be worthless once the plague of pestilence started.

8) The Yismach Moshe also ponders our question. He points out that ostensibly Avrohom would be the last person to question what Hashem does. Avrohom did not question Hashem when He told him to go to Eretz Yisroel, and almost immediately after Avrohom arrived, there was a famine. Avrohom did not question Hashem when after telling Avrohom that Yitzchak would inherit him spiritually and physically, He then commanded Avrohom to take Yitzchak and bring him as a sacrifice. It would seem incongruous for Avrohom to question Hashem's way in Egypt whether or not they came out with riches.

The Mechilta on Shemos (12:6) quotes Rabi Elazar HaKapor who says that indeed the Bnei Yisroel had four Mitzvos that they kept in Egypt: (1) they did not do immoral acts, (2) they did not speak Loshon Horah, (3) they did not change their Hebrew names, and (4) they did not change their language from Hebrew. Rabi Elazar proves all these four Mitzvos from Pesukim. In particular, with regard to not speaking Loshon Horah, a year before the Bnei Yisroel were scheduled to go out of Egypt, Hashem told Moshe in Shemos (3:22): "Each woman shall borrow from her neighbor and from the dweller in her house silver and gold vessels and garments, and you shall put them on your sons and on your daughters, and you shall empty out Egypt." During this entire year, not one Jew told any of the Egyptian neighbors that they would get these riches from the Egyptians or that the Bnei Yisroel would empty out Egypt from all these articles. Had they done so, the Egyptians would not have been amenable to lend them anything.

The Yismach Moshe says that by telling Avrohom his children would go out with great riches, Hashem was telling Avrohom the major merit of why the Bnei Yisroel would merit to be redeemed from Egypt was that they would not talk Loshon Horah. Since Avrohom would be proud of his children's excellent behavior, Hashem told Avrohom about this good deed. The Yismach Moshe says that if the Bnei Yisroel had left Egypt without riches, Avrohom would be highly disappointed in the Bnei Yisroel. This is because he would ascribe Hashem not fulfilling his promise to the Bnei Yisroel speaking Loshon Horah and causing the Egyptians not to want to lend them anything. Hashem wanted to show Avrohom that indeed the Bnei Yisroel did not talk Loshon Horah and therefore they were worthy of redemption from Egypt, and therefore Hashem made sure they would get the riches.

9) Rav Aryeh Leib Tzuntz of Plotsk, in his Hagada Birchos HaShir, presents another answer to our question. He references the Yalkut Shimoni 241, which says that before the Egyptians were drowned in the Red Sea, Uza (or Uziel) came to Hashem and demanded a court case with the angel Michoel who represented the Bnei Yisroel. Uza began the court case by saying that the Bnei Yisroel had been prophesized to be in slavery for 400 years, and since they had only been in real slavery in Egypt for 86 years, from when Miriam was born, Uza demanded the Bnei Yisroel be returned to the

Bo

slavery of the Egyptians until the 400 years were up. In fact, Uza brazenly said that the 400 years was an oath of Hashem and therefore demanded that it be fulfilled. When Hashem asked Michoel to answer Uza's charges, Michoel could not answer and was silent. Hashem answered Uza that the only reason the Bnei Yisroel were enslaved was because of one mistaken phrase that Avrohom uttered at the Bris Bain HaBesorim when Avrohom said in Beraishis (15:8): "how will I know that I will inherit it (Eretz Yisroel)?" "After Avrohom said this phrase," said Hashem, "I answered him in Beraishis (15:13): 'You shall surely know that your seed will be strangers in a land that is not theirs.'" "As you can see," said Hashem, "I never said that they would be slaves in Egypt." Hashem also pointed out that they were already "strangers in a land that was not theirs" from the time Yitzchak was born, and therefore they had indeed fulfilled the promise of 400 years. The Yalkut Shimoni says that Hashem's saving of the Bnei Yisroel with this argument is what is meant when Shemos (14:30) says, וַיּוֹשַׁע ה' בַּיּוֹם הַהוּא אֶת יִשְׂרָאֵל מִיַּד מִצְרָיִם (and Hashem on that day saved the Bnei Yisroel from the hand of (the angel of) Egypt). The Yalkut Shimoni continues and says that Uza was not finished with his argument. When Hashem was ready to drown the Egyptians in the Red Sea, Uza asked for another court case where he argued that the Egyptians had been punished enough by having all their gold and silver taken from them as payment for the time that they had enslaved the Bnei Yisroel. This time Hashem convened His heavenly court to decide the case. Hashem argued that originally after bringing hunger to the Egyptians, Hashem sent them Yosef to save them, and the Egyptians all became servants to Yosef. Afterward, Hashem's children, the Bnei Yisroel, came down as guests and were enslaved by the Egyptians to such a degree that their cries reached the Heavens. Hashem sent Moshe and Aharon to Pharaoh with a message from Hashem. At that time, Pharaoh was sitting together with all the Kings of the east and west, and in front of them, Pharaoh began belittling Hashem by showing them all his reference books which made no mention of Hashem. When Moshe and Aharon explained to Pharaoh and his entourage that Hashem was the one who created heaven and earth, sends winds, rain, and dew, makes trees and vegetation grow, and who holds the life of everyone in His hands, Pharaoh answered that there is no such G-d with such power. In fact, Pharaoh also claimed, as is recorded in Sefer Yechezkel (29:3): לִי יְאֹרִי וַאֲנִי עֲשִׂיתָנִי (the Nile River is mine, and I made it). Being that Pharaoh had denied the existence of Hashem, Hashem sent ten plagues against Pharaoh. Even till the tenth plague, Pharaoh still had not changed his attitude until Hashem forced his hand with the final plague so that Pharaoh sent the Bnei Yisroel out. Even after sending the Bnei Yisroel out, Pharaoh still did not recognize Hashem since Pharaoh insisted on chasing after the Bnei Yisroel to try to re-enslave them in Egypt. Hashem concluded his argument by saying: "isn't such a person deserving of death?" The heavenly court agreed with Hashem, and the Egyptians were drowned.

Based on the argument of Uza, Rav Aryeh Leib presents a Moshul of a person who tells his servant that if he works doing a specific job for a set amount of time, he will set him free after this time and will pay him for the job that he did. The work was very hard, and after some time, the servant became sick because of all the hard work. In fact, the servant became so sick that he would die if, even after recovering, he kept on working this type of work, especially since this type of work was so hard that it would kill any typical person who did it. Rav Aryeh Leib says that the person who hired this servant obviously has no claims against the servant for why the servant did not finish the job that he was assigned. As the Arizal tells us, the Bnei Yisroel in Egypt had sunk down to the 49th

Bo

level of spiritual Tumah. If they had remained in Egypt even just a bit longer, they would have sunk into the 50th level of Tumah, for which there is no hope of spiritually recovering. Under the influence of the Egyptians, they had fallen down the levels of spiritual Tumah by serving all sorts of idols. Since the Egyptians caused the Bnei Yisroel to be unable to carry on their slavery, according to the above Moshul, they should have no claims against the Bnei Yisroel leaving Egypt and should even pay them for their years of work. However, the Bnei Yisroel had the choice not to listen to the Egyptians and not to serve idols. As proof, the tribe of Levi did not serve idols, despite being in Egypt. If the cause of the Bnei Yisroel not being able to continue working was due to the fault of the Bnei Yisroel, they no longer have a claim to be paid for their work. Indeed, the Bnei Yisroel did contribute to their falling to the lowest level of Tumah and had no complete claim on being paid. However, if they did not get paid, Avrohom would have to conclude that the Bnei Yisroel contributed to their being on such a low level of Tumah that they had to leave Egypt. This would cause much pain to Avrohom, and Hashem did not want to do this. On the other hand, Hashem could not force the Egyptians to pay the Bnei Yisroel for their work since the Beni Yisroel contributed to their not being able to remain in Egypt. Therefore, Hashem begged the Bnei Yisroel to borrow gold and silver, which eventually became theirs when the Egyptians drowned in the Red Sea so that Avrohom would think that the Egyptians caused the Bnei Yisroel to not be able to remain in Egypt and consequently paid them. There was also another reason to have the Bnei Yisroel borrow gold and silver vessels. The Gemorah in Baba Basra 166a says that if it is unclear if someone is obligated to give money, the money remains by default in the hands of the person who currently has it. Before borrowing the money, this would have caused the money to remain in the Egyptian's hands since it was unclear whether they owed wages to the Bnei Yisroel. Now that the money was now in the hands of the Bnei Yisroel, they would get to keep it since they currently had it.

10) The Be'er, as quoted by the Mayanah Shel Torah, presents another answer to our question. As we have mentioned previously from the Ksav Sofer, much riches are not necessarily advantageous in serving Hashem and are frequently disadvantageous. Therefore, the Bnei Yisroel, on their own accord, would have preferred not to have taken any riches so as not to be tested with the test of richness. Hashem could have accepted their request and allowed the Bnei Yisroel to choose not to take riches out of Egypt. However, Avrohom, both when he was poor and also when he was very wealthy, had no issues in serving Hashem. Therefore, from Avrohom's perspective, he could not comprehend that there was any test of faith even when one was very wealthy. That being the case; specifically, Avrohom would complain if Hashem accepted the request of the Bnei Yisroel and allowed them to choose not to take riches. We should mention that the Bnei Yisroel's behavior at gathering even more wealth after the Egyptians drowned at the Red Sea cannot be used as proof that the Bnei Yisroel wanted the test of richness. Since at that time they were already rich from the gold and silver vessels they had taken out of Egypt, they already had the test of richness, and adding on additional riches did not appreciably increase the test of richness.

In the first Posuk of Devorim, Moshe rebukes the Bnei Yisroel for the sins that they committed at different places in the desert. Amongst the places, the sin committed at דִּי זָהָב is mentioned. The Sifrei points out that there is no such place name but rather the Torah is referring to the sin of the

Bo

Golden Calf which was caused by the Bnei Yisroel having דֵּי זָהָב (sufficient gold to use for the Golden Calf). In response to the sin of the Golden Calf, Moshe davens for the Bnei Yisroel to be forgiven. In Shemos (32:32), Moshe concludes וְעַתָּה אִם תִּשָּׂא חַטָּאתָם וְאִם אַיִן מְחֵנִי נָא מִסִּפְרְךָ אֲשֶׁר כָּתָבְתָּ (And now, if You forgive their sin But if not, erase me now from Your book, which You have written.). Consistent with this answer, the Be'er has a cute interpretation of this Posuk. When Moshe said מְחֵנִי נָא מִסִּפְרְךָ אֲשֶׁר כָּתָבְתָּ instead of translating נָא as now or please, the Be'er says that it refers to the word נָא in our Posuk when Hashem asks the Bnei Yisroel to please take all the riches out of Egypt. Had the Bnei Yisroel not been beseeched from Hashem to take the riches, they could have opted not to and then would not have had all the gold to make the Golden Calf.

11) The Oznayim LeTorah also presents an answer to our question. He says that we can best understand this in the time he wrote his commentary within ten years of the end of World War II. At that time, there was a big debate in Eretz Yisroel about whether it was appropriate to accept reparations from the Germans for the atrocities of the Nazis, Yimach Shemom. One side of the debate said it was appropriate to accept reparations for all the property that was taken away. The other side of the debate said that that it was inappropriate to take reparations less the world would consider it that we were repaid for all the atrocities committed against us, and we should therefore forget about what happened. He says that this same debate raged in Egypt at the time of the redemption as to whether taking riches from the Egyptians would cheapen all the atrocities committed by the Egyptians against us, including murdering our children for the King to bathe in their blood. That is why Hashem had to beg the Bnei Yisroel to take the riches; less Avrohom would complain that the prophecy of going out with riches from Egypt was unfulfilled.

It is possible that the reason Avrohom would complain is that he took riches from Pharaoh after he abducted Sorah and did not refuse to take presents to cover up Pharaoh's crime. On the other hand, Avrohom refused to take presents from the King of Sodom. The Oznayim LeTorah on Beraishis (15:23) says that the only reason Avrohom accepted presents from Pharaoh was that he wanted to prevent a Chilul Hashem. As an introduction to his answer, we note that Rashi on Beraishis (13:3) says that when Avrohom returned from Egypt to Eretz Yisroel, he made sure to lodge at the exact same hotels that he had stayed in when he went down to Egypt so that he could pay the bills that he owed them from the first time he was there. Though in our days of credit cards and credit history searches, such an occurrence can easily be understood, the Oznayim LeTorah questions how it was possible in the time of Avrohom for the innkeepers to extend credit to someone who they had no idea of who he was and was just passing through on the way to Egypt.

Ever since Avrohom had come to Eretz Yisroel, he had been broadcasting the existence of Hashem and that only Hashem had created the world and actively managed everything in the world. When the hunger came to Eretz Yisroel, Avrohom, because he had a large group of people and animals, had to pay enormous sums of money just to feed everyone, and gradually Avrohom became poorer. Having exhausted most of his possessions, Avrohom decided to go to Egypt, staying at inns on the way down to Egypt. Avrohom had already become somewhat famous for broadcasting the existence of Hashem, and therefore the innkeepers wondered how it could be that Hashem would not provide sustenance to Avrohom, as a reward for proclaiming the existence of Hashem, especially since

Bo

Avrohom had in fact spent large sums of money inviting all wayfarers in to teach them about Hashem. Therefore, a Chilul Hashem was created since the contradiction led the innkeepers to conclude that Hashem did not manage everything in the world. Only a few months later, Avrohom returned from Egypt with much wealth. Avrohom decided to repay the "bill of Chilul Hashem" by making sure that he stayed at the exact same inn where the innkeeper could now see how Hashem took care of Avrohom and, in fact, made him richer than he was previously. Obviously, this is the bill Chazal were referring to since we cannot be talking about repaying Avrohom's lodging bill due to the fact that, of course, Avrohom was not allowed to stay at an inn unless he paid his bill in full.

Even though Avrohom had a disdain for taking presents, with the above as background, we can understand why Avrohom felt that to counteract Chilul Hashem; he needed to take Pharaoh's presents. When there were no considerations of Chilul Hashem, like with the King of Sodom, Avrohom had no desire to accept presents. We can also say that had the Bnei Yisroel not taken the riches of the Bnei Yisroel; there would be a Chilul Hashem. Only 50 days after leaving Egypt, the Bnei Yisroel stood on Mount Sinai to accept the Torah and were told that they were a special nation to Hashem. It would be a Chilul Hashem for an impoverished nation to be declared and chosen by Hashem, and therefore it was necessary to increase their honor amongst the nations of the world by making them rich. The Bechor Shor says the Bnei Yisroel had to be respectable and able to celebrate the holiday for Hashem that they were going to rejoice in the desert. Having riches, not to mention beautiful clothing, would help them rejoice. Parenthetically with this approach, we could not solve the debate of whether reparations should have been taken from the Yimach Shemom unless taking the reparations would prevent a Chilul Hashem.

12) Rav Meir Bergman in volume 2 of his Sefer Shaarei Orah also ponders our question. He says that the reason for the exile in Egypt was so that the Bnei Yisroel should get closer to Hashem so that they could accept the Torah at Mount Sinai. Afflictions bring a person closer to Hashem since a person realizes that only Hashem has the power to free the person from these afflictions. Because of having to endure all the afflictions, it made sense that the Bnei Yisroel would be rewarded with many riches after this exile. However, instead of becoming closer to Hashem, the Bnei Yisroel in Egypt learned to worship idols from their Egyptian oppressors. That being the case, they were no longer deserving of receiving a reward.

The Gemorah in Baba Metzia 83a tells how Rabba bar bar Chanan had a keg of wine broken by porters. Rashi on the Gemorah explains that they broke it through their own negligence. Since it was through their negligence, Rabba bar bar Chanan took their coats as payment for the wine. The porters went and told Rav what had happened. Rav told him to give them back their coats. He questioned Rav whether this was the Halacha. Rav answered that it was indeed the law. After getting back their coats, the porters said to Rav that they are poor people who are starving and have nothing to eat and have worked the entire day transporting the keg of wine with nothing to show for it. Rav then told Rabba bar bar Chanan to pay them their wages for transporting the keg of wine. He again questioned Rav whether this was the law. Raba told him that this was the law for him since Mishlay (2:20) says, "in order that you go in the way of the good, and you keep the ways of the righteous." As Rashi on the Gemorah explains, since he was a righteous person, Rav instructed

Bo

him to go beyond the letter of the law and do a righteous act by paying the poor porters their wages even though they were negligent.

The Gemorah in Brochos 9a says that the reason Hashem begged the Bnei Yisroel to borrow golden and silver vessels was so that the righteous Avrohom should not complain. Rav Meir Bergman says that since Avrohom was righteous, similar to what Rav told Rabba bar bar Chanan, Avrohom would still pay the poor Bnei Yisroel for their efforts in the exile of Egypt even though they failed to become closer to Hashem due to their own negligence. The way Hashem acts with people is a reflection of how the person behaves; as Tehillim (121:5) says, "Hashem is your shadow." Though according to the letter of the law, the Bnei Yisroel should not have expected any payment, Hashem reflected the righteous, Avrohom's way, so that Avrohom would not have any complaints.

Why Do We Need to Know That No Dog Barked During the Plague of Killing of the Firstborns?

וּלְכֹל בְּנֵי יִשְׂרָאֵל לֹא יֶחֱרַץ כֶּלֶב לְשֹׁנוֹ לְמֵאִישׁ וְעַד בְּהֵמָה לְמַעַן תֵּדְעוּן אֲשֶׁר יַפְלֶה ה' בֵּין מִצְרַיִם וּבֵין יִשְׂרָאֵל (יא:ז)
Shemos (11:7) But to all the Bnei Yisroel, not one dog will whet its tongue against either man or beast, in order that you shall know that Hashem will separate between the Egyptians and between Yisroel.

Why do we need to know that no dog barked during the plague of the killing of the firstborns?

Introduction
The Ohr HaChaim, when he asks this question, says that if the Torah was just trying to tell us that not even one member of the Bnei Yisroel died during the plague, it should have said that explicitly. Since the Torah did not do this, it implies that this was not the reason the Torah told us that the dogs did not bark.

There are two categories of meat from a kosher animal that cannot be eaten. The first category is meat that was not slaughtered properly, including carcasses. About this meat Devorim (14:21) says: "You shall not eat any carcass. You may give it to the stranger who is in your cities, that he may eat it, or you may sell it to a foreigner." That is, the meat may be given or sold to people who are not required to eat slaughtered meat. The second category of meat is an animal whose flesh was torn in the field and therefore could not live for a long time. About this meat, Shemos (22:30) says: "And you shall be holy people to Me, and flesh torn in the field you shall not eat; you shall throw it to the dogs." Rashi, quoting the Mechilta, says that Hashem does not withhold the reward of any creature, as it is said in our Posuk: "But to all the Bnei Yisroel, not one dog will whet its tongue." Said Hashem, "Give it its reward." The Mechilta concludes that if Hashem gives a reward to an animal that does not have freedom of choice, it is even more logical that Hashem would reward each person who does a good deed despite having freedom of choice. The Eben Ezra points out that the Posuk does not say "you shall throw it to **a** dog" but rather "you shall throw it to **the** dog." Using this Eben Ezra, the Malbim explains that this is how the Mechilta knows that the Torah is speaking of a specific dog, i.e., the dog that did not bark in Egypt. He explains that we learn other ethical

Bo

principles from animals, even though animals do not have freedom of choice. For example, Sefer Yirmiyahu (17:11) says: "The cuckoo calls but has not laid, so it is he who gathers riches but not by right; he shall leave them in the midst of his days, and at his end, he stands dishonored." Rashi on that Posuk explains that a cuckoo bird is able to pretend it is the parent of other birds and use its call voice to get young birds to run after it. However, when the birds get older, they will realize that the cuckoo bird is not its parent and will no longer run after it. In a similar way, one who deceitfully gathers riches that do not rightfully belong to him will also lose these riches over time.

1) We can derive an answer to our question from the Gemorah in Baba Kama 60b. The Gemorah says that when dogs are crying, the Angel of Death has come to the city, while when dogs are acting joyously, Eliyahu the Prophet has come to the city. The Meorah Shel Torah on our Posuk explains the simplest meaning of this Gemorah. In Melachim I, chapter 18, Eliyahu HaNavi goes to Mount Carmel along with 450 priests who served the idol, Baal. On Mount Carmel, they make a test to see whose offering will be accepted, the priests offering to their idol Baal or Eliyahu's offering to Hashem. When the priest's offering is ignored, and Hashem accepts Eliyahu's offering by bringing down fire from Heaven, the people who are observing say in Melachim I (18:39), "And all the people saw and fell on their faces, and they said, 'Hashem is G-d, Hashem is G-d.'" The following Posuk says: "Eliyahu said to them, 'Seize the prophets of the Baal; let no one of them escape.' And they seized them. Eliyahu took them down the brook Kishon and slew them there." The Meorah Shel Torah says that since the dogs remember how they ate the bodies of these prophets, the dogs are happy when they see Eliyahu. It could also be that the dogs are happy since they expect to get more meat to eat from Eliyahu's future actions. When the dogs see the Angel of Death, they are reminded of seeing him in Egypt, where their mouths were not allowed or able to bark, a state which was painful to the dogs. Therefore, this remembrance causes the dogs to cry when they see the Angel of Death.

The Toras Chaim on this Gemorah explains that dogs do not have a keener sense of knowing whether the Angel of Death or Eliyahu is present then do humans. In fact, Hashem just put this ability in dogs so that Humans would know if the Angel of Death or Eliyahu was in the city at that time. The Gemorah in Chulin 7a relates how Hashem does not bring pitfalls through the animals of righteous people. As proof, the Gemorah says that Rav Pinchos Ben Yair once arrived at a certain inn where the innkeepers poured barley into a feeding trough for his donkey to eat. However, the donkey refused to eat any of the barley. Thinking that the donkey was a finicky eater, they first tried sifting the barley and then washing it, but still, the donkey refused to eat it. Finally, Rav Pinchos Ben Yair asked them if perhaps the barley was bought from an Am HaAretz, who we suspect did not take off Maaser (a tenth), and Maaser was not subsequently taken after they purchased it. The innkeepers admitted that this was the case. They then took off Maaser, and immediately the donkey ate the barley. The Toras Chaim explains that the donkey did not have a keen sense of knowing whether Maaser was taken off of the barley. Rather Hashem prevented the donkey from eating the barley so that the innkeepers would do the mitzvah of taking off Maaser and would not be punished because of the actions of Rav Pinchos Ben Yair's donkey. Being that Rav Pinchos Ben Yair was so righteous, it would not be correct for Hashem to allow sin to be caused by him or his possessions.

Bo

The Chidushay Geonim on the Gemorah in Baba Kama 60b explains on a deeper level why when dogs are crying, the Angel of Death has come to the city, while when dogs are acting joyously, Eliyahu the Prophet has come to the city. As an introduction to his answer, he quotes the Beraishis Raba (10:6), which says that each blade of grass has a constellation in Heaven that hits it and tells it to grow. "Hitting it" does not mean physically hitting it but rather channeling the flow of energy to it so it can grow. Also, the constellation in Heaven which "hits it" is referring to an angel. Since even every blade of grass has an angel guiding it, it stands to reason that every animal also has an angel guiding it. He further extends this concept to say that every angel who guides each animal has another angel guiding them. This chain of angels continues so that each group of angels has one angel above it, etc. Furthermore, any type of animal which rules over another type of animal has an angel who is a higher angel than the one over the subdued type of animal.

The dog is the most faithful servant to its human master. In fact, the Hebrew name of the dog, כֶּלֶב, comes from the Hebrew word for the heart, meaning that the dog and its master are so tied together that they have the same heart and intentions, at least from the dog's perspective. Therefore, the source of its angels is from a truthful source. In contrast, the fox is a deceitful animal, so the source of its angel is from a deceitful source. The deceitful source is the Satan, who, according to the Gemorah in Baba Basra 16a, is one and the same angel as the Yetzer Horah and the Angel of Death. The Gemorah there says that the Satan goes down and lures people into sin and then goes up to the Heavenly court and incites Hashem's anger by denouncing the sinner and then he takes permission to kill the sinner and when granted he kills the sinner, a process which is about as deceitful as possible. As another example of a faithful animal, the Chidushay Geonim presents the dove. The Gemorah in Eruvin 100b says that if, Chas VeShalom, the Torah had not been given, we would have been able to learn character traits from the animals. An example is that we would learn faithfulness from the dove, which only has relations with its one and only partner. We see another example of the dove being faithful in Gittin 45a. The Gemorah tells us about Rav Elish, who unfortunately was captured and put in jail. One day, he found himself sitting next to someone who understood bird language. It seems from the story that this person was a Gentile. A raven came and said something. Rav Elish turned to the man and asked him what the raven said. The man answered that the raven said, "Elish, escape. Elish, escape." Rav Elish said that a raven is a liar, and one cannot trust what he says. The Maharsha explains that he was referring to the raven that Noach tried to send from the ark. As Rashi explains on Beraishis (8:7), the raven refused to listen to Noach and go on the mission that Noach sent it out for. Soon a dove came by and also said something. He asked the man what the dove said. The man answered that the dove said, "Elish, escape. Elish, escape." Rav Elish said that since the Bnei Yisroel are compared to a dove, it would seem that this is a sign that a miracle will happen to me, and I will be able to escape. The Maharsha explains that the dove did listen to Noach and go on the mission that Noach sent him. However, Rav Elish was also worried that the person could have been lying about what the dove really said. Therefore, he reasoned that since the Bnei Yisroel are compared to a dove, Hashem would not have sent a dove unless the news was true. The Gemorah concludes that a miracle happened to Rav Elish, and he escaped and was transported to the other side of the river so that the guards could not catch him. The person who understood bird language also escaped, but he was caught and executed. From this Gemorah, we see that a dove, as opposed to a raven, is trustworthy.

Bo

The Chidushay Geonim puts together these two ideas and says that each person, animal, or even blade of grass has their own angel who oversees it, and its angel is grouped along with another angel in a hierarchy of angels. Therefore, a righteous person after being Niftar is put together with angels, which epitomized their behavior when they were alive. For example, a person who excelled in doing merciful, good deeds is put together with the angel of mercy, a person who excelled in good deeds of kindness is put together with the angle of kindness, etc. In the case of Eliyahu, his behavior was epitomized by being zealous for defending Hashem. Through his zealousness, we have mentioned how Eliyahu proved to the people at Mount Carmel that Hashem is the one and only G-d and how he also killed all the false prophets of Baal. As another example, when Eliyahu sees that King Achav is sinning against Hashem, he says to Achav in Sefer Melachim I (17:1), "As Hashem, the G-d of Yisroel, whom I serve, lives, if there will be during these years dew or rain except according to my word." When Achav next meets Eliyahu in Sefer Melachim I (18:17-18), the Pesukim say, "And it was when Achav saw Eliyahu, that Achav said to him, 'Is this you, the one who brings trouble upon Yisroel?' And he said, 'I have not brought trouble upon Yisroel, but you and your father's house, since you have forsaken the commandments of Hashem, and you went after the Baal." If we make the assumption that most Meforshim make, that Eliyahu and Pinchos are one and the same person, we have other acts of zealousness for Hashem's honor. Bamidbar (25:11) says, "Pinchos the son of Elazar the son of Aharon the Kohen has turned My anger away from the Bnei Yisroel by his zealously avenging Me among them so that I did not destroy the Bnei Yisroel because of My zeal." With Eliyahu's zealousness, says the Chidushay Geonim, Eliyahu, after he left this world, was put together with the class of angels who are zealous. Putting together the fact that the dog is the most faithful servant to its human master means that the dog and Eliyahu both are in the hierarchy of angels who are zealous and faithful to their master. It should be obvious that when Eliyahu comes back to visit this world, he comes back accompanied by the angel he is grouped with, that of zealousness. He makes the argument that if righteous people, like Yaakov, are accompanied in this world by angels, then it begs to reason that beings, like Eliyahu, coming from the world of angels are accompanied by angels. At the end of Parshas Vayetze in Beraishis (32:2-3), we see that Yaakov was accompanied by angels when the Pesukim say, "And Yaakov went on his way and angels of G-d met him. And Yaakov said when he saw them, "This is the camp of G-d," and he named the place Machanaim."

We can now explain what the Gemorah means when it says that when dogs are crying, the Angel of Death has come to the city, while when dogs are acting joyously, Eliyahu the Prophet has come to the city. When Eliyahu comes to the city accompanied by the top faithful and zealous angel, the dog who also derives its source of energy from this same angel is joyous. When the deceitful Angel of Death, who is in the chain of angels who are deceitful and not faithful, comes to the city, the dogs are crying since these angels are completely opposite the source of energy of the faithful dog.

With the above Chidushay Geonim, we can understand the answer the Ohr HaChaim presents to our question. He says that the dogs not barking signifies the Angel of Death was not at all where the Bnei Yisroel lived in Goshen since otherwise they would be crying and barking. This is similar to the answer that the Alshich and Chasam Sofer present, that the dogs not barking proved that Hashem

Bo

Himself, and not an angel, came to perform the killing of the firstborns. In the Hagadah, we say: "Rabi Akiva says, 'From where can we derive that every plague that the Holy One, blessed be He, brought upon the Egyptians in Egypt was composed of five plagues? As it says in Tehillim (78:49): 'He sent upon them the fierceness of His anger, wrath, and fury, and trouble, a delegation of evil angels.' 'The fierceness of His anger' corresponds to one; 'wrath' two; 'and fury' three; 'and trouble' four; 'a delegation of evil angels' five." The Alshich explains that Hashem came with this delegation of angels when he came to Egypt. However, in the homes of the Bnei Yisroel, Hashem set up a barrier to protect the Bnei Yisroel from this delegation of angels who, because of the barrier, stayed away. The dogs only barked at the home of the Egyptians, where they could see these evil angels. However, at the homes of the Bnei Yisroel, where these angels kept away from, the dogs did not bark. According to the Chasam Sofer, who differs from the Alshich, the dogs did not bark at any house since Hashem did not take along these angels when Hashem killed the firstborn.

The Shach explains why the dog is given meat from an animal that was torn in the field and not meat from the carcass of an animal that died. He explains that since the animal that died of "natural causes" was killed by the Angel of Death, which is the dog's complete antithesis, the dog is not given this meat. The Zohar in Shemos 151b explicitly says that this animal that died of natural causes is killed by the Angel of Death. The dog is only given the meat of an animal that was torn up by another animal and did not die from natural causes.

2) The Rashbam, Bechor Shor, Ralbag, and Ksav VeHakabola answer our question similarly. The Posuk before our Posuk says, "And there will be a great cry throughout the entire land of Egypt, such as there never has been and such as there shall never be again." They say that this great cry took place by the Egyptians, while for the Bnei Yisroel, it was so tranquil, quiet, and peaceful that not even the slight fright that happens when dogs bark would occur. This shows how Hashem protected us even to the tiniest detail such that we would have absolutely no fear while the Egyptians were being utterly destroyed.

The Toldos Yitzchak, Chizkuni, and Tzedah LeDerech sensitize us even further as to how unusual this night was. The Gemorah in Brochos 3a tells us that the twelve-hour night is divided up into three portions or watches each four hours long, where Hashem has built into nature signs to delineate them. The Gemorah says that at the end of the first watch, donkeys bray, in the middle of the second watch, dogs bark, and at the beginning of the third watch, infants wake up to nurse from their mothers. The killing of the firstborn took place exactly at midnight, which corresponds to the time that normally dogs would bark. Shemos (12:11) says, "And this is how you shall eat it: your loins girded, your shoes on your feet, and your staff in your hand; and you shall eat it in haste it is a Korban Pesach to Hashem." A dog normally will also bark when he sees a person holding a stick. Despite this, the dogs, when they awoke at midnight, neither barked nor began barking when they saw the Bnei Yisroel with sticks in their hands.

3) The Ohr HaChaim presents an answer to our question. The Shemos Raba (18:2) says that those Egyptians who were afraid that Moshe's prophesy of the killing of the firstborn would take place brought their firstborn to stay in the house of a Jew and forced the Jews to let the firstborn stay.

Bo

Therefore, a lot of Jewish houses had Egyptians hiding in them during the plague. Our Posuk tells us that dogs did not bark only in houses where everyone was Jewish. In the houses where the Egyptians were hidden, and not everyone was Jewish, the dogs did indeed bark. The difference in the dog's behavior informed the Bnei Yisroel of the greatness of the miracle that had occurred. In Jewish houses where there were Egyptians, Hashem sent in the destroying angel to kill the Egyptian while protecting the Bnei Yisroel such that nothing happened to the Jews. Sending in the destroying angel is very dangerous since the destroying angel does not differentiate between righteous and wicked people as the Mechilta says on Shemos (12:22), and therefore all the Jews in the house were at great risk. The dogs barking when there was an Egyptian hiding in the house informed the Bnei Yisroel that the destroying angel had indeed been in their house, while the fact that no one else besides the Egyptian was harmed informed the Bnei Yisroel that Hashem had completely protected the Bnei Yisroel from the destroying angel.

4) The Abarbanel, Tzedah LeDerech, and Meam Loez answer our question similarly. They say that the dog is referring to the Egyptians. Even though their main idol, the Lamb, was being slaughtered, they did not utter a word nor make any attempt to stop the Bnei Yisroel from totally denigrating their main idol. The Meam Loez points out that Moshe was no longer afraid of the Egyptians, and he could now refer to them as dogs without fearing retribution. After this plague, neither Pharaoh, nor his advisors, nor his people were going to be able to say a word against the Bnei Yisroel.

5) The Meam Loez presents another answer to our question. The Gemorah in Pesachim 118a and in Makos 23a say that anyone who speaks or accepts Loshon Horah about another Jew and anyone who bears false witness about his fellow Jew deserves to be thrown to the dogs. The Gemorah proves this principle from the juxtaposition of the Posuk we have quoted in the introduction, which instructs us to give the flesh of an animal torn in the field to dogs, to the next Posuk which says, "You shall not accept a false report; do not place your hand with a wicked person to be a false witness." The Maharsha in Makos 23a and the Eyun Yaakov in Pesachim 118a explain that a person telling or accepting Loshon Horah about a fellow Jew is figuratively barking against the fellow Jew. If even the dog which has no intellect did not bark at the Bnei Yisroel, despite his innate nature to bark, the person with intellect who does bark against a fellow Jew is worse than a dog. Therefore, he is fit to be thrown to the dogs to learn a lesson from them on controlling his barking. The Ain Eliyahu explains that a dog is its master's best friend and is always looking to do something good for the master. A person talking or accepting Loshon Horah or bearing false witness is exactly the opposite, someone who is looking to do bad to his friend. Therefore, this person should be thrown to the dogs to learn from them how to relate to his fellow man.

The Meam Loez says that there were Jews who spoke Loshon Horah in Egypt at the time the Jews left Egypt. An example of this is Dasan and Avirom, who spoke Loshon Horah about Moshe to Pharaoh after he had killed the Egyptian, the first time Moshe had ventured forth from the palace. Despite these people deserving to be thrown to the dogs, Hashem silenced the dogs and overlooked this sin by keeping the dogs from barking.

Bo

It would seem to me that the Chazal stress the exact opposite of the Meam Loez's answer. The Mechilta on Shemos (12:6) quotes Rabi Elazar HaKapor who says that indeed the Bnei Yisroel had four Mitzvos that they kept in Egypt: (1) they did not do immoral acts, (2) they did not speak Loshon Horah, (3) they did not change their Hebrew names, and (4) they did not change their language from Hebrew. Rabi Elazar proves all these four Mitzvos from Pesukim. In particular, with regard to not speaking Loshon Horah, a year before the Bnei Yisroel were scheduled to go out of Egypt, Hashem told Moshe in Shemos (3:22), "Each woman shall borrow from her neighbor and from the dweller in her house silver and gold objects and garments, and you shall put them on your sons and on your daughters, and you shall empty out Egypt." During this entire year, not one Jew told any of the neighbors that they would get these riches from the Egyptians or that the Bnei Yisroel would empty out Egypt from all these articles. Rather, says Rabi Elazar, each Jew loved the other and had no issues with allowing the other Jews to get rich. In addition, though the Bnei Yisroel knew that they would be redeemed from Egypt completely, no one revealed to Pharaoh nor any other Egyptian that this was the case. Therefore, Moshe could ask Pharaoh to go for just three days into the desert to serve Hashem, without Pharaoh contradicting him from what Moshe told the Bnei Yisroel. Rather says Rav Mordechai Benet as quoted by the Mayanah Shel Torah, the Bnei Yisroel were at this point completely clean from talking Loshon Horah. Though Dasan and Avirom many years earlier had talked Loshon Horah and reported to Pharaoh that Moshe had killed an Egyptian task-master, the Bnei Yisroel had repented and mended their ways. Instead of being a talker of Loshon Horah, who is fit to be thrown to dogs, the dogs held the Bnei Yisroel in the highest esteem by not barking at them and showing that they did not deserve to be thrown to dogs.

6) The Yalkut Reuveni and Meam Loez present another answer to our question. The Egyptians painted different images of animals on the gates of the city. The reason for this was to prevent anyone from escaping out of the city. If a person attempted to escape, by means of sorcery, the image on the gate started screaming, causing all the real animals to also start screaming, giving the guards the time to catch the person escaping. Hashem wanted the Bnei Yisroel to walk out of the gate where the image of a dog was since dogs typically scream more than any other animal. In this way, Hashem would show how totally redeemed the Bnei Yisroel were by having them pass through this gate without the dog of sorcery nor any other dog even screaming once. Therefore, the dogs were instrumental in showing how totally redeemed the Bnei Yisroel were from Egypt.

7) The Shach also ponders our question. The Yalkut Shimoni 208 says that the Egyptians buried their firstborns in caves in their houses to hide their deaths from the Bnei Yisroel. The dogs then came, burrowed into their houses, and took the firstborn corpses out of the caves causing the Egyptians great anguish. The Shach says that since the dogs did not eat the corpses of the Egyptian firstborn, they were rewarded for all time by the Torah with meat from an animal that was torn in the field, as opposed to meat from a carcass that died of natural causes.

8) The Ksav Sofer also presents an answer to our question. He says that the dogs showed how much Hashem loved the Bnei Yisroel. Koheles (3:15) says, וְהָאֱלֹקִים יְבַקֵּשׁ אֶת נִרְדָּף (and G-d seeks the pursued). Rashi on that Posuk explains that Hashem seeks the pursued to punish the pursuer. The Vayikra Raba (27:5) says that in all cases, even if a righteous person is pursuing a wicked person,

Bo

Hashem will still punish the pursuer. That being the case, says the Ksav Sofer, in all the previous nine plagues, there was no indication the Bnei Yisroel were beloved by Hashem nor chosen by Hashem, since even if they were, Chas VeShalom, wicked and the Egyptians righteous, Hashem would still have punished the pursuing Egyptians. However, during the killing of the firstborn, when there was a huge outcry by the Egyptians, as the Posuk before our Posuk says, it is natural that the dogs should have been barking. Nonetheless, Hashem wanted the Bnei Yisroel to be calm and not bothered when they were redeemed from Egypt, so he performed a miracle and kept the dogs completely quiet. Since this miracle had nothing to do with punishing the Egyptians for their pursuing and persecuting of the Bnei Yisroel, it was done to show the Bnei Yisroel and, by extension, the rest of the world that Hashem loves the Bnei Yisroel as his chosen people. In the introduction, we have quoted Shemos (22:30), which says, "And you shall be holy people to Me, and flesh torn in the field you shall not eat; you shall throw it to the dogs." Since it was the dogs who first showed how special the Bnei Yisroel were to Hashem and that the Bnei Yisroel are a holy people to Hashem, it is fitting that the dogs should highlight the fact that as holy people, we do not eat meat from an animal whose flesh is torn in the field. The Ksav Sofer says that this explanation also explains why our Posuk concludes with the phrase "in order that you **shall know** that Hashem will separate between the Egyptians and between Yisroel" instead of "in order that you **did know** that Hashem will separate between the Egyptians and between Yisroel." The use of the future tense implies that the dogs not barking is a lesson for all time about how special we are to Hashem. The Shemos Raba (31:9) also says that, by not barking, the dogs showed that the Bnei Yisroel are a holy people.

9) Rav Hirsch presents an answer to our question. Despite slaughtering the main idol of the Egyptians, the Egyptians treated the Bnei Yisroel with complete respect and did not say nor do anything to them. Even when the Egyptians were in total anguish from the deaths of all their firstborns, the Egyptians did not say or do anything to the Bnei Yisroel. In fact, the Shemos Raba (18:10) says that when the firstborns were killed, the Egyptians, instead of venting their anger on the Bnei Yisroel, tried to kill Pharaoh. Pharaoh was only able to save himself when he commanded his servants to find Moshe and Aharon and have all the Bnei Yisroel leave Egypt immediately. Even the dogs held the Bnei Yisroel in such respect that they would not even bark harmlessly at the Bnei Yisroel. With this, Hashem showed the Bnei Yisroel that not only were they going to go free from Egypt but that they would be sent out in the most respectful of ways as honorable people without any stigma of previously being slaves.

Why Did the Korban Pesach Have to Be Specifically a Lamb?

שֶׂה תָמִים זָכָר בֶּן שָׁנָה יִהְיֶה לָכֶם מִן הַכְּבָשִׂים וּמִן הָעִזִּים תִּקָּחוּ (יב:ה) Shemos (12:5) You shall have a perfect male lamb in its first year; you may take it either from the sheep or from the goats.

Why did the Korban Pesach have to be specifically a lamb (sheep or goat) and not any other animal?

Introduction

Bo

By commanding us to take "a perfect male lamb in its first year," the Chizkuni points out that we could not assuage the Egyptians by claiming that the lamb was not fit to be used as their idol, and therefore they should not be so antagonized. Had we been able to use a blemished, old, or female lamb, it would have been possible to try and make this claim to the Egyptians. "A perfect male lamb in its first year" was the prime lamb that would be used as the Egyptian idol.

The Yalkut Shimoni points out that in Devorim (14:4), we also see that a lamb שֶׂה can refer either to a sheep or a goat. The Torah says, זֹאת הַבְּהֵמָה אֲשֶׁר תֹּאכֵלוּ שׁוֹר שֵׂה כְשָׂבִים וְשֵׂה עִזִּים (These are the animals that you may eat: bull, sheep, and goat).

1) The Zohar in Parshas Pinchos 250b ponders our question. It says that since the Egyptians served the idol of the Heavenly constellation of the lamb, they also served the lamb animal. As proof, it quotes Shemos (8:22), which says, "But Moshe said, 'It is improper to do that, for we will sacrifice the abomination of the Egyptians to Hashem our Lord. Will we sacrifice the deity of the Egyptians before their eyes, and they will not stone us?'" Though in truth, this Posuk is describing Moshe's reaction to Pharaoh's offer of serving Hashem in Egypt instead of in the desert, the Zohar is of the opinion that the Bnei Yisroel would also serve Hashem by slaughtering a lamb when they went to the desert.

The Zohar next discusses Yosef's intelligence. Beraishis (47:2-3) says, "And from among his brothers he (Yosef) took five men, and he presented them before Pharaoh. And Pharaoh said to his brothers, 'What is your occupation?' And they said to Pharaoh, 'Your servants are shepherds of sheep, both we and our forefathers.'" Previously, in Beraishis (46:33-34), Yosef coaches his brothers in what to tell Pharaoh when he later will ask what their occupation is when the Pesukim say, "And if it comes to pass that Pharaoh calls you and asks, 'What is your occupation?' You shall say, 'Your servants have been owners of livestock from our youth until now, both we and our ancestors,' so that you may dwell in the land of Goshen because all shepherds are abhorrent to the Egyptians." The Zohar ponders the question of why Yosef would coach his brothers to say something that will cause the Egyptians to hate and abhor them. It answers that the land of Goshen was the best quality land in all of Egypt. Because of its quality, the Egyptians left the land for their idol to graze there and have the best grazing ground in all of Egypt. Yosef's plan was for Pharaoh to appoint his brothers as shepherds in this land and have the Egyptians consider the brothers as protectors over their idol, the lamb. In that way, not only would the Bnei Yisroel get the best land in Egypt, but they would also be held in esteem by the Egyptians as the caretakers of their idol.

Rav Yossi in the Zohar points out that we know Hashem punishes both people who serve idols and the idols themselves. That being the case, he ponders the question of why Yosef would set up his brothers as caretakers of the Egyptian idol. He answers that the brothers weren't really caretakers over the idols but rather were rulers over the idols and, in fact, hit the lambs with a stick to show they were the rulers. Yosef reasoned that if the brothers were rulers over their idol, then they would also be rulers over the Egyptian people.

Bo

The Beraishis Raba (96:5) says that the reason Yaakov did not want to be buried in Egypt was that he was afraid the Egyptians would make an idol out of his grave. If that happened, Yaakov knew that Hashem exacts punishment both from the people who served the idol and the idol itself. Proof of this concept is brought from an episode in Sefer Daniyel. Sefer Daniyel, chapter two, talks about King Nevuchadnetzar having a dream that he did not remember and when he awoke demanded that his advisors tell him the dream he had along with its interpretation. When the head of the advisors told Nevuchadnetzar that his request was not possible and that no one on earth could do what he requested, in a fit of rage, he made a decree to kill all his advisors. When the decree became known to Daniyel, Daniyel asked for some time during which he, Chananyah, Mishael, and Azariah davened to Hashem to reveal Nevuchadnetzar's dream and its interpretation. Hashem listened to their Tefilos and revealed the dream and its interpretation to Daniyel. Sefer Daniyel (2:27-30) says, "Daniyel answered the King and said, 'The secret that the King asks, no wise men, astrologers, necromancers, or demonologists can tell the King. But there is a G-d in heaven Who reveals secrets, and He lets King Nevuchadnetzar know what will be at the end of days; that is your dream and the visions of your head on your bed. You, O King, your thoughts came while on your bed, what will be after this, and the Revealer of secrets lets you know what will be. And I-not with wisdom that I possess more than all living, did He reveal this secret to me, but in order that they should let the King know the interpretation, and you should know the thoughts of your heart.'" After revealing the dream and its interpretation to Nevuchadnetzar, Posuk (2:46) "Then King Nevuchadnetzar fell on his face and prostrated himself before Daniyel, and he ordered to offer up a meal-offering and libations to bring him satisfaction." The Beraishis Raba says that Daniyel did not allow Nevuchadnetzar to make him into an idol or to make any offerings to him. According to the Maharzav, it derives this from Daniyel (2:46) saying "he ordered to offer up a meal-offering and libations" instead of "he offered up a meal-offering and libations." Daniyel's actions are to be contrasted with that of King Chirom. In prophesizing about Chirom, Sefer Yechezkel (28:2-3) says, "Son of man, say to the prince of Tzor: So said Hashem G-d: Because your heart is proud, and you said, 'I am a god, I have sat in a seat of G-d, in the heart of the seas,' but you are a man and not a god, yet you have made your heart like the heart of G-d. Behold, are you wiser than Daniyel, that no secret is hidden from you?" Because of Chirom's attitude, Yechezkel prophesized that he would be punished as Sefer Yechezkel (28:7-9) say: "Therefore, behold I am bringing foreigners, the strong of the nations, upon you, and they will draw their swords on the beauty of your wisdom and profane your brightness. Into the pit they will lower you, and you will die the deaths of those who are slain, in the heart of the seas. Will you say, 'I am a god' before your slayer? Indeed, you are a man and not a god in the hand of your slayer." Therefore, Yaakov wanted to avoid his grave being made into an idol, less he gets punished as Chirom did.

The Zohar says that the idol of the Egyptians was a lamb. Therefore, Hashem commanded the Bnei Yisroel to hold the Egyptian idol captive in their houses for four days, and on the fifth day, they were commanded to bring the idol to judgment. When the Egyptians heard the sounds of their idol, the sheep, complaining that it was tied up and captive, they began to cry since they were unable to do anything to save it. Psychologically, the Egyptians felt as if they themselves were tied up to be slaughtered, causing the Egyptians to be devastated. On the fifth day, the Bnei Yisroel were commanded to slaughter the lamb in public so the Egyptians would see that their idol was brought to justice. Seeing this judgment was psychologically worse for the Egyptians than any of the previous nine plagues. After the judgment, the Bnei Yisroel were commanded to burn (roast) the lamb. Hashem again commanded that the lamb be roasted instead of cooked so that the lamb roasting would be visible and recognizable to the Egyptians. Cooking the lamb under water would obscure the lamb from being easily recognizable. In addition, roasting ensured that the smell of the roasting would travel far in the air so that the Egyptians would see what was happening to their idol. Furthermore, Hashem commanded the Bnei Yisroel to roast the lamb with its head wrapped around its legs and body so that the Egyptians would see that it was a lamb and not any other animal. Finally, Hashem commanded the Bnei Yisroel to eat it when they were already satiated to further mock the idol and show that it wasn't even slaughtered because the Bnei Yisroel were hungry for food. The Bnei Yisroel were also commanded not to break any bones so that the lamb's bones should be strewn and recognizable everywhere in Egypt.

The Zohar says that the Egyptians, in addition to serving the lamb as their main idol, also made every animal a semi-idol. That is why in the plague of the killing of the firstborn, Hashem also killed all the firstborn animals, so the Egyptians would have further anguish even after their main idol had been so ridiculed as we have described above.

The Akeidah adds on several additional reasons for the Egyptians' anguish by examining Hashem's commandments in how to bring the Korban Pesach. He says that the law in Egypt was that anyone who harmed either a lamb of sheep or of a goat was sentenced to death since they had harmed the idol of the Egyptians. By having the Bnei Yisroel not only harm but slaughter these animals without the Egyptians being able to do anything, this situation also caused intense anguish to the Egyptians. Slaughtering it in the afternoon while it was still light for all the Egyptians to see made this anguish even worse. The Akeidah quotes the Mishna in Keilim (19:2), which says that they tied the lamb to their bed with a string of ten hand-breaths (about 40 inches). Holding the lamb captive with such a short string was a further denigration of the Egyptian idol. Finally, smearing its blood in full view of the Egyptians added to the Egyptian's anguish. The Egyptians could do nothing to prevent the Bnei Yisroel from offering the Korban Pesach despite the Egyptians being right there. The Chizkuni says that this showed the Bnei Yisroel that the Egyptians would surely have no power over the Bnei Yisroel once they left Egypt and were far from the Egyptians.

2) The Ramban, Akeidah, Chizkuni, and Tur answer our question similarly. They point out that the constellation of the lamb falls during the month of Nisan. Slaughtering the lamb on the 15th day of the month when the power of the constellation of the lamb is at its highest showed that, in reality, the constellation of the lamb had no power in stark contrast to the Egyptian's belief that it was all-powerful. Alternatively, from the Egyptian's perspective, Hashem's power was so great that the power of the lamb constellation could do nothing against Hashem's power to prevent the Egyptians from losing all their firstborns and the Bnei Yisroel from leaving Egypt. In addition, having the killing of the firstborn happen at midnight meant that the next powerful idol (the sun) in no way caused the killing of the firstborn, and rather even the Egyptians could see that it was totally the work of Hashem. Furthermore, says the Ramban, by denigrating the lamb, it further showed that the lamb had no power.

Bo

3) The Alshich HaKodosh also presents an answer to our question. Shemos (12:21) says, מִשְׁכוּ וּקְחוּ לָכֶם צֹאן לְמִשְׁפְּחֹתֵיכֶם וְשַׁחֲטוּ הַפָּסַח (Draw forth and acquire for yourselves sheep for your families and slaughter the Korban Pesach). The Mechilta ponders why the seemingly superfluous word מִשְׁכוּ (draw forth) was needed. It says the Bnei Yisroel served idols, and before they could take the Korban Pesach, they needed to draw their hand away from serving idols and only serve Hashem. The Alshich says that since the Bnei Yisroel had been serving the idol of the lamb, the way to show that this was no longer the case was for them to instead bring specifically the lamb as a Korban to Hashem. The Ralbag also says that this was the reason the lamb was chosen for the Korban Pesach. Even more, the Alshich explains why bringing it as a Korban to Hashem would be much greater merit than their previous serving of the idol. Previously, they would each privately serve the lamb. When fulfilling the Mitzvah of bringing the Korban Pesach to Hashem, the entire Bnei Yisroel did this Mitzvah and did it as a united group with families uniting together to bring the Korban as the previous Posuk to ours says, "But if the household is too small for a lamb, then he and his neighbor who is nearest to his house shall take one according to the number of people, each one according to one's ability to eat, shall you be counted for the lamb." In addition, when bringing the lamb as a Korban to Hashem, they would be risking their lives that the Egyptians did not kill them.

The Alshich points out that previous to our going down to Egypt, the lamb represented a great merit for the Bnei Yisroel. At the Akeidah, in lieu of offering Yitzchak as a Korban, Beraishis (22:13) says, "And Avraham lifted up his eyes, and he saw, and lo! There was a ram, and after that it was caught in a tree by its horns. And Avraham went and took the ram and offered it up as a burnt offering instead of his son." A ram is an adult male sheep so that the merit of the Akeidah brought to mind the lamb. We can understand this point of the Alshich a bit deeper when we consider what the Ateres Mordechai, as quoted by the Meorah Shel Torah, says. The Akeidah, for Yitzchak, was the epitome of sacrificing one's life for the sake of Hashem. This character trait was planted into the Bnei Yisroel by the Akeidah and displayed by the Bnei Yisroel that despite risking their lives that the Egyptians did not kill them, they did the Mitzvah of Korban Pesach. It is not a coincidence that Yitzchak was born on Pesach, where his willingness to sacrifice his life would be used many years later by his descendants as a merit to be redeemed from Egypt. This simple belief in Hashem to do his commandments without hesitation, which Yitzchak passed down to his descendants, was the key to the survival of the Jews despite all the persecutions we have endured. The Beis HaLevi, at the end of Parshas Vayerah, explains why we call this event Akeidas Yitzchak (The binding of Yitzchak) and not Nisayon Avrohom (the test of Avrohom). It is the merit of the act and behavior of Yitzchak, which unfortunately has so many times repeated itself through years of exile, which serves as the greatest merit for the Bnei Yisroel. The Alshich points out that following the timeline, we find the lamb was a merit in the time of our forefathers, became a liability when the Bnei Yisroel started serving the lamb as an idol and became a merit again to allow the Bnei Yisroel to be redeemed from Egypt. The Shach points out that the goat lamb also atoned for another sin. When the brothers sold Yosef, Beraishis (37:31-32) says, "And they took Yosef's coat, and they slaughtered a kid goat, and they dipped the coat in the blood. And they sent the fine woolen coat, and they brought it to their father, and they said, 'We have found this; now recognize whether it is your son's coat or not.'" Though the Shach does not say this, it is quite possible that when the Bnei

Bo

Yisroel risked their lives to publicly show the blood of the Korban Pesach, this atoned at least partially for the misuse of the goat's blood which the brothers did when they sold Yosef.

4) The Shach also presents an answer to our question. Bamidbar (25:3-4) says, "This is the fire offering which you shall offer to Hashem, two unblemished lambs in their first year each day as a continual burnt offering. The one lamb you shall offer up in the morning, and the other lamb you shall offer up in the afternoon." The Bamidbar Raba (21:21) explains the reason why this Korban Tamid was brought daily, once in the morning and once in the evening. The Shemos Raba says that the morning Korban Tamid atoned for sins that occurred at night, while the evening Korban Tamid atoned for sins that occurred during the day. The Shach says that by commanding the Bnei Yisroel to bring a lamb as a Korban Pesach, Hashem wanted to show the Bnei Yisroel that he would atone their sins and cleanse their souls from sin, just like the Korban Tamid did. According to the Shach, not only did the Korban Pesach atone for the sin of worshipping the lamb but also for their other sins.

5) The Chasam Sofer also ponders our question. In Bamidbar (28:19), the Korbanos to be brought for the Bnei Yisroel on Pesach are detailed. The Torah tells us that the Korbanos were two bulls, a ram, and seven sheep. Rashi on the Posuk says that the bull was a reminder of Avrohom about whom Beraishis (18:7) says that Avrohom went to the cattle to get food for the angels who had come to visit him after his Bris Milah. The ram was a reminder of Yitzchak, who was exchanged for a ram at the Akeidah. Finally, Rashi says that the sheep were a reminder of Yaakov about whom Beraishis (30:40) says, "And Yaakov separated the sheep, and he turned the faces of the animals toward the ringed ones and every brown one among Lavan's animals, and he made himself flocks by himself, and he did not place them with Lavan's animals." This Posuk tells us that despite Lavan tricking and cheating Yaakov from his wages for watching Lavan's sheep for many years, Yaakov still is very careful about not stealing from Lavan.

When Yaakov came to get the Brochos from Yitzchak, he brought along the meat of two goats. Pirkei D'Rabi Eliezer (32) ponders why Yitzchak needed so much meat. He answers that it was the first night of Pesach and Yitzchak wanted to emulate what the Bnei Yisroel would do on the first night of Pesach. Since the Korban Pesach was only eaten when one was satiated, one also offered a Korban Chagigah so that one would have to meat to eat to be satiated before eating the Korban Pesach. Therefore, Yitzchak wanted two animals, one to be for the Korban Chagigah and the second for the Korban Pesach. Bringing a Korban Pesach from a goat brought the merit of Yitzchak, who many years earlier had emulated eating the Korban Pesach from a goat. Bringing a Korban Pesach from a sheep brought the merit of Yaakov behaving completely honestly despite being cheated by Lavan. The Chasam Sofer says that the merit of Avrohom is not explicitly mentioned since mentioning Avrohom also might bring along a demerit. The Ramban says that the exile to Egypt was foreshadowed by Avrohom traveling to Egypt due to a plague of hunger soon after Hashem had told Avrohom to go to Eretz Yisroel. Avrohom should have remained in Eretz Yisroel and not gone down to Egypt since Hashem had instructed Avrohom to go to Eretz Yisroel and not to Egypt.

Bo

6) The Chasam Sofer presents another answer to our question. As the earth moves in its yearly orbit around the sun, the stars, which are fixed in their positions relative to the sun, appear to be constantly changing relative to the sun. From the perspective of someone on earth, the sun appears to be changing its position relative to the stars. Groups of stars form constellations. Rashi on the Gemorah in Rosh Hashana 11b explains that there are twelve constellations: Sheep, Bull, Twins, Crab, Lion, Maiden, Scales, Scorpion, Bow, Goat, Bucket, and Fish. As the earth rotates on its axis each day, stars rise in the east and eventually slowly disappear in the west. This is a similar phenomenon that we see each day with the sun. It takes approximately two hours for the beginning star of each constellation to begin rising in the east until the time that the entire constellation group is visible. During the course of the twenty-four-hour day, each of these constellations appears on the horizon every two hours so that over the course of the day, all twelve constellations could be visible. However, during the daytime, since the sun is shining, we cannot observe the constellations that appear on the horizon every two hours. Over the course of the year, the constellation which aligns itself with sunrise is called the constellation of the month. For example, during the month of Nisan, the Sheep constellation aligns itself with sunrise. During the next Hebrew calendar month of Iyar, the constellation Bull aligns itself with sunrise, during Sivan the constellation Twins, and so on. Let us focus on the month of Nisan. If the sheep aligns itself with sunrise, at approximately 6 AM, then eighteen hours later at midnight, the constellation of goat rises on the horizon.

The Chasam Sofer says that the Egyptian firstborns did not immediately die at midnight, but rather they were mortally wounded and were killed at the first time of daylight by the destroying angel. In a Teshuva to his father-in-law Rabi Akiva Eiger in Yoreh Deah (346), the Chasam Sofer explains this answer a bit more. He quotes the introduction to Meseches Smochos, which says explicitly that Hashem mortally wounded the Egyptian firstborn at midnight and that they only died in the morning. The Braisah in Meseches Semochos explains the reason for this with a Moshul to someone who gives food to a child and is told to inform the child's mother of this. In a similar way, Hashem wanted to inform the Bnei Yisroel that he had killed the Egyptian firstborn. Therefore, Hashem waited till morning when it was light, not to mention when the Bnei Yisroel were no longer under the prohibition of Shemos (12:22) "and you shall not go out, any man from the entrance of his house until morning," for the firstborns to die and for the Egyptians to begin burying them. Therefore, according to the Chasam Sofer, there were two distinct times the Egyptians were punished, at midnight and at daybreak. These correspond to the constellations of goat and sheep, and therefore the Korban Pesach could be brought from a goat or a sheep to show that neither the constellation of goat nor of sheep had any power to stop the plague against the Egyptians.

7) The Noam Elimelech also ponders our question. He says that a lamb is the most subservient and humble of all animals. Though he uses this concept in explaining the details of the Korban Pesach in an esoteric or Midrashic way, we can take the concept in a simpler way. By having the Korban Pesach be a lamb, Hashem was telling us that the most important characteristic to infuse in the Bnei Yisroel to be proper servants of Hashem is the characteristic of humility. It is not possible to be a true servant of Hashem without realizing that He is infinite and we are mere mortals, and having humility will greatly aid a person in this realization.

Bo

8) The Noam Elimelech presents a second answer to our question. Sefer Yirmiyahu (50:17) says, "A scattered lamb is Yisroel which lions have driven away. First, the King of Assyria devoured him, and this last one broke his bones, Nebuchadrezzar, the King of Babylon." From this Posuk, we see that the Bnei Yisroel are called a lamb. Though he uses this concept in explaining the details of the Korban Pesach in an esoteric or Midrashic way, we can take the concept in a simpler way. When the Bnei Yisroel are first becoming an independent nation using a lamb as a sacrifice is very appropriate to symbolize what the Bnei Yisroel will be termed.

9) The Nodeh BeYehuda in his Sefer Droshos HaTzlach (48) also presents an answer to our question. This answer is also found in the compendium of Nodeh BeYehuda on the Torah. He begins by presenting a question found in the Abarbanel, who ponders why only by the tenth plague of the killing of the firstborn do we stress that Hashem saved the Jewish firstborns from being killed? The Abarbanel compares it to a case of people who come to a King to demand justice for the murdering of their friend(s), and the King kills the murderers and allows the people who demanded justice not to be killed. In such a case, do we say that the King deserves praise for not killing the innocent group of people who demanded justice? In Egypt, the Egyptians enslaved the Jews under the harshest of conditions leading the Bnei Yisroel to eventually daven to Hashem for justice against the Egyptians. When Hashem does justice by killing the Egyptian firstborns, does it make any sense that at the same time, he would also kill the Jewish firstborns? Not to mention, in some plagues like wild animals, pestilence, hail, and darkness, the Torah explicitly tells us that the Jews were not harmed. Chazal even extend this concept to tell us that the Jews were not affected in any of the first nine plagues. That being the case, why do we make many remembrances, like the Korban Pesach itself, to the Jewish firstborns not being killed like the Egyptian firstborns were?

The Nodeh BeYehuda answers that there was a reason the Jewish firstborns should have been killed along with the Egyptian firstborns. The main point of the plague of the killing of the firstborns was to destroy all the Egyptian idols. As such, the Egyptians served the lamb constellation, which is the first constellation, along with giving extra respect to any firstborn, for as firstborns, they were similar to the lamb firstborn constellation. Since the Bnei Yisroel also served the lamb firstborn constellation, their firstborn was also held in esteem because of this and deserved to die along with all the other Egyptian idols, including the Egyptian firstborns. However, in His mercy, Hashem accepted the Jewish firstborns' Teshuva when they agreed to sacrifice lambs for Hashem by making the Korban Pesach. In essence, the Korban Pesach was a sin offering atoning for their sin of serving the lamb idol. As proof the Korban Pesach is a sin offering, the first Mishna in Zevachim says that all Korbanos that were slaughtered not for their own sake, but for that of a different Korban, are valid Korbanos brought on the Altar in the Beis Hamikdosh, except that they do not count towards their owner's fulfillment of the obligation to bring that Korban. For example, if the Korban was an obligatory Korban, like a Korban Asham, the owner must later bring another Korban as an Asham to fulfill his obligation to bring a Korban Asham. However, there are two exceptions to this rule, a Korban Chatos (sin-offering) and a Korban Pesach. In the case of either of these Korbanos being brought for a different type of Korban, the sacrifice itself is invalidated, and the animal may not be brought on the Altar in the Beis Hamikdosh, nor may any other facets of the service of a sacrifice be done on this animal. The Gemorah proves that the Korban Pesach and Chatos have this difference

Bo

from Pesukim in the Torah. A Korban Chatos for the sin of an individual can only be either a sheep or a goat, as the Pesukim say explicitly in Vayikra (4:28) and (4:32). He says that because the Korban Pesach was brought as an atonement for sin, it, therefore, also can only be either a sheep or a goat.

Why Was It Necessary to Take and Inspect the Korban Pesach Four Days Before Using It?

Shemos (12:6) וְהָיָה לָכֶם לְמִשְׁמֶרֶת עַד אַרְבָּעָה עָשָׂר יוֹם לַחֹדֶשׁ הַזֶּה וְשָׁחֲטוּ אֹתוֹ כֹּל קְהַל עֲדַת יִשְׂרָאֵל בֵּין הָעַרְבָּיִם (יב:ו) And you shall keep it for inspection until the fourteenth day of this month, and the entire congregation of the community of Yisroel shall slaughter it in the afternoon.

Shemos (12:3) says, "On the tenth of this month, let each one take a lamb for each parental home, a lamb for each household." Coupled with our Posuk, we are told that they had to take and keep the Korban Pesach for inspection four days before they actually used it. Why was this necessary?

Introduction
The Gemorah in Pesachim 96a explains that only the Korban Pesach brought in Egypt needs to be both designated and inspected for four days before slaughtering it. A Korban Pesach brought in years after the Bnei Yisroel went out of Egypt only had to be examined for four days before being brought. A Korban Pesach brought on Pesach Sheni (the 14th of Iyar) for those unable to bring the Korban Pesach that year, needed neither designating nor examining for four days. It is quite possible to fulfill the requirement of designating without fulfilling the requirement of inspecting and vice versa. One could examine several animals for blemishes without designating any of them. One could also designate an animal four days before slaughtering it, without ever examining it during this time.

1) The Mechilta on our Posuk is the source of the answer presented by the Yalkut Shimoni, Midrash Lekach Tov, and Rashi to our question. It answers that the reason for designating the Korban Pesach in Egypt four days before they slaughtered it is based on what Rabi Masyah ben Chorosh used to say. Sefer Yechezkel (16:8), describing the Bnei Yisroel before they were redeemed says, וָאֶעֱבֹר עָלַיִךְ וָאֶרְאֵךְ וְהִנֵּה עִתֵּךְ עֵת דֹּדִים (And I passed by you and saw you, and behold your time was the time of love). Rabi Masyah explained that the oath which Hashem promised to Avrohom had presented itself (The time of love), but the Bnei Yisroel did not have Mitzvos that they should occupy themselves with as Sefer Yechezkel (16:7) says, וְאַתְּ עֵרֹם וְעֶרְיָה (but you (Bnei Yisroel) were naked and bare). Rabi Masyah explains that the Navi, when it says "naked and bare," is referring to being "naked and bare of all Mitzvos." Therefore, Hashem gave the Bnei Yisroel two Mitzvos, Korban Pesach and Bris Milah, to occupy themselves with. Since one only gets a reward for doing Mitzvos by doing actions, Hashem commanded the Bnei Yisroel to take the Korban Pesach four days before they slaughtered it so that they could be doing a Mitzvah for these four days and get rewarded for it by being redeemed. The Nachalas Yaakov, in his commentary on Rashi, explains that there were four Mitzvos intertwined with the Korban Pesach: (1) walking to take or purchase it, (2) the actual taking or purchasing, (3) examining it, and (4) slaughtering it, all of which the Bnei

Bo

Yisroel got rewarded for. The Shach says that the four days were symbolic of the four Mitzvos the Bnei Yisroel were commanded to do. Presumably, even though the Nachalas Yaakov does not explicitly say this, it would seem that this is the reason he highlighted four Mitzvos of the Korban Pesach. Different than the Nachalas Yaakov, the Shach calculates the four Mitzvos as follows: (1) taking or purchasing the Korban Pesach, (2) slaughtering the Korban Pesach, (3) placing the blood of the Korban Pesach on the doorway, and (4) doing a Bris Milah. Parenthetically we should mention that when Rashi quotes this answer from the Mechilta, he adds that the Mitzvah of Bris Milah was only given to be done on the night the Bnei Yisroel slaughtered the Korban Pesach and not four days before.

The Alshich ponders the question of why the Mechilta refers to Rabi Masyah's explanation as "based on what Rabi Masyah ben Chorosh used to say," instead of saying Rabi Masyah answers the question of why the Korban Pesach needed to be designated four days before it needed to be slaughtered. In addition, Rabi Masyah quotes the Pesukim out of the order they appear in Sefer Yechezkel. Furthermore, why were two Mitzvos (Korban Pesach and Bris Milah) necessary for the Bnei Yisroel to have the merit to be redeemed from Egypt instead of just one Mitzvah? The Alshich answers that the simplest explanation of the Pesukim in Sefer Yechezkel in the order they are presented there is different than Rabi Masyah's explanation. Shemos (12:23) says, "Hashem will pass to smite the Egyptians, and He will see the blood on the lintel and on the two doorposts, and Hashem will pass over the entrance, and He will not permit the destroyer to enter your houses to smite you." Putting aside for a moment the Pesukim in Sefer Yechezkel, the Torah seems to be telling us that the Korban Pesach was needed so that its blood could be sprinkled in the doorway and prevent the Jewish firstborns from dying in the plague of the killing of the firstborn. Shemos (12:48) says, "but no uncircumcised male may partake of it (Korban Pesach)." The Torah also seems to tell us that the only reason a Bris Milah was needed at this time was that only someone who had a Bris Milah could eat from a Korban Pesach, and therefore having a Bris Milah was a prerequisite for making the Korban Pesach. Neither of the above Pesukim implies that either the Korban Pesach or having a Bris Milah in any way was related to being redeemed from Egypt. Rather the redemption from Egypt seemed to be occurring in the merit of our forefathers. At first glance, this approach seems to be consistent with what Sefer Yechezkel (16:6) tells us when it says, "And I passed by you and saw you downtrodden with your blood, and I said to you, 'With your blood, live,' and I said to you, 'With your blood, live.'" The Navi seems to be telling us that the two types of blood (blood of Korban Pesach and blood of Bris Milah) enabled the Bnei Yisroel to live and not be killed when the Egyptian firstborns were killed. With regard to redemption, the next Posuk in Sefer Yechezkel (16:7) says, "but you were naked and bare," followed by the subsequent Posuk saying, "And I passed by you and saw you, and behold your time was the time of love, and I spread My skirt over you, and I covered your nakedness." These Pesukim imply that although the Bnei Yisroel were naked of Mitzvos since the time of redemption promised to Avrohom had come, Hashem redeemed us, in the merit of our forefathers. This is all opposite from what "Rabi Masyah used to say" and would not give us an answer as to why the Korban Pesach had to be designated four days before it was slaughtered.

Bo

The Mechilta is of the opinion that the question of why the Korban Pesach had to be designated four days before it was slaughtered forced Rabi Masyah to explain the Pesukim in Sefer Yechezkel differently so that we would have an answer to this question. It is much better for the Bnei Yisroel if they are redeemed because of their own merits as opposed to just the merits of our forefathers. The Alshich presents a moshul to explain this concept. A King once had a very good friend who passed away, leaving over a son who was poorly behaved, even to the King. The King told the son that because his father had been such a good friend, the King would do good things for the son. However, the poorly behaved son got even worse and started doing illegal activities. Eventually, the King stopped doing good things for the son. If the son, however, had been a well-behaved member of the Kingdom, the King would have told the son that because his father was such a good friend and had left over such an outstanding well-behaved son, he would do good things for him. In this case, the King would likely continue to reward the son forever. The Alshich says that Rabi Masyah is of the opinion that the Pesukim in Yechezkel are said from the perspective that it would be advantageous if the Bnei Yisroel had their own merits to be redeemed. Therefore, Hashem gave the Bnei Yisroel the two Mitzvos, Korban Pesach and Bris Milah as Sefer Yechezkel (16:6) tells us when it says, "And I passed by you and saw you downtrodden with your blood, and I said to you, 'With your blood, live,' and I said to you, 'With your blood, live.'" The "living" the Navi is referring to, says the Alshich, is a life of freedom/redemption. The next Pesukim explain that the reason Hashem gave the Bnei Yisroel these two Mitzvos was because the time of redemption had arrived and the Bnei Yisroel as, Sefer Yechezkel (16:7) says, "were naked and bare." He concludes that the Mechilta points out how Rabi Masyah knew to take the Pesukim in this manner as opposed to the simple manner outlined above. Sefer Zechariah (9:11) says, "You, also-with the blood of your covenant; I have freed your prisoners from a pit in which there was no water." The Eben Ezra explains that the "blood of the covenant" being discussed is the blood of Korban Pesach and Bris Milah, which gave the merit that the Bnei Yisroel were freed from a "pit in which there was no water." A "pit in which there was no water," says the Alshich, is referring to the exile in Egypt. Therefore, Rabi Masyah had proof from a Posuk in Navi to his way of understanding the Pesukim in Sefer Yechezkel.

Parenthetically the Mechilta also presents the opinion of Rabi Elazar HaKapor. He says that indeed the Bnei Yisroel had four Mitzvos that they kept in Egypt: (1) they did not do immoral acts, (2) they did not speak Loshon Horah, (3) they did not change their Hebrew names, and (4) they did not change their language from Hebrew. Rabi Masyah says that these four Mitzvos, even though they were great, weren't action Mitzvos and were only prohibitions the Bnei Yisroel kept from doing. Reward in this world is only given for action Mitzvos. For non-action (not doing wrong) Mitzvos, explains the Shach, the reward is that one is saved from punishments in this world. Only by doing action Mitzvos do we show that we are serving Hashem, since otherwise, we would not do these Mitzvos, like offering a Korban Pesach or doing a Bris Milah, whereas one would need to read the mind of a person to understand why he is refraining from doing something.

2) The Daas Zekanim and Tosfos in Shabbos 87b answer our question similarly. When the Bnei Yisroel took or purchased the Korban Pesach, the Egyptians asked why they were doing it, the Egyptians being especially concerned because it was their idol. The Bnei Yisroel answered that four

Bo

days from now, all firstborns would die except Hashem will skip over the houses of those that do the Korban Pesach. Hearing this, the Egyptian firstborns went to Pharaoh and demanded that he send out the Bnei Yisroel immediately, since otherwise, he would cause all the firstborns to die. Pharaoh refused to give in to their demands, and the firstborns started a war with Pharaoh's army killing many Egyptians. This is what Dovid HaMelech means in Hallel HaGodol in Tehillim (136:10) (which we say in the Shabbos Davening) when he says, לְמַכֵּה מִצְרַיִם בִּבְכוֹרֵיהֶם (To Him (Hashem) who smote the Egyptians with their firstborn).

3) The Daas Zekanim, quoting Rav Yitzchak Aviro, the Alshich, and the Maskil LeDovid, answer our question similarly. We have mentioned in the first answer that Rashi is of the opinion the Mitzvah of Bris Milah was only given to be done on the night the Bnei Yisroel slaughtered the Korban Pesach and not four days before. Our answer is of the opinion the Mitzvah of Bris Milah was given to be done when the Bnei Yisroel were commanded to acquire the Koran Pesach five days before they left Egypt. In this way, the Bnei Yisroel could be fully recovered from the Bris Milah when they needed to travel to leave Egypt. In addition, says the Maskil LeDovid, when one converts, one also needs to immerse oneself in a Mikveh after having a Bris Milah. We paskin that one only immerses oneself after one has fully recovered from the Bris Milah, which takes three days. Having a Bris Milah when they were acquiring the Korban Pesach four days before they needed to slaughter it allowed them to immerse themselves and fully complete the conversion process before slaughtering the Korban Pesach. The Alshich explains the connection between acquiring the Korban Pesach and Bris Milah. Shemos (12:21) says מִשְׁכוּ וּקְחוּ לָכֶם צֹאן לְמִשְׁפְּחֹתֵיכֶם וְשַׁחֲטוּ הַפָּסַח (Draw forth and acquire for yourselves sheep for your families and slaughter the Korban Pesach). The Mechilta ponders why the seemingly superfluous word מִשְׁכוּ (draw forth) was needed. It says the Bnei Yisroel served idols, and before they could take the Korban Pesach, they needed to draw their hand away from serving idols and only serve Hashem. By immediately following the act of acquiring the Korban Pesach with a Bris Milah, the Bnei Yisroel not only abandoned worshipping idols but also entered into a covenant with Hashem to serve Him.

In practice, the Shemos Raba (19:5) says that though some agreed, many of the Bnei Yisroel refused to have a Bris Milah. Hashem then told Moshe to slaughter and roast his Korban Pesach. Hashem had the winds gather up some of the air of Gan Eden and combined it with the smell of that Korban Pesach. The smell so overwhelmed the Bnei Yisroel that they all came running to Moshe, requesting they have a piece of Moshe's Korban Pesach. Moshe told the people Hashem had commanded that only people with a Bris Milah are allowed to eat from the Korban Pesach. The people were so overcome with the smell and desire to eat the Korban Pesach that they all agreed to have a Bris Milah. The blood of their Bris Milah intermingled with that of the blood of the Korban Pesach as Sefer Yechezkel (16:6) says, וָאֶעֱבֹר עָלַיִךְ וָאֶרְאֵךְ מִתְבּוֹסֶסֶת בְּדָמָיִךְ וָאֹמַר לָךְ בְּדָמַיִךְ חֲיִי וָאֹמַר לָךְ בְּדָמַיִךְ חֲיִי (And I passed by you and saw you downtrodden with your blood, and I said to you, "With your blood, live," and I said to you, "With your blood, live."). The two types of blood intermingling are why the Novi mentions blood twice. The Navi talks about two types of blood because one was the blood of Bris Milah and the other the blood of the Korban Pesach, the two merits the Bnei Yisroel had to go out of Egypt.

Bo

A Korban Pesach can only be eaten by those who were designated to eat from it before the Korban Pesach was slaughtered. That being the case, the Maskil LeDovid ponders the question of how the Bnei Yisroel could eat from Moshe's Korban Pesach after it had already been slaughtered. Moreover, since they had not had a Bris Milah, they were prohibited from eating the Korban Pesach and therefore could not be designated for Moshe's Korban Pesach. He presents various answers. One answer he says is that the Mitzvah of needing to be designated before slaughtering was swept aside by the great Mitzvah of making a Korban Pesach. Only in subsequent years after leaving Egypt and after being given the opportunity to offer the Korban Pesach a month later (Pesach Sheni) would the Mitzvah of needing to be designated before slaughtering prevent one from eating from the Korban Pesach. The reason being that one could instead bring the Korban Pesach on Pesach Sheni. He also says that the Bris Milah took place just a little while before nightfall since one does not do a Bris Milah at night.

4) The Ralbag also presents an answer to our question. We can probably more appreciate what he says if we examine the Midrash Tanchuma in Vayerah (22), which, when analyzing the Akeidah, asks, "why did Hashem make Avrohom wait until the third day after commanding him to do the Akeidah until He showed Avrohom the place to do the Akeidah?" It answers that if Hashem immediately showed Avrohom the mountain, then the naysayers amongst the nations would say the only reason Avrohom carried out Hashem's commandment was that he was too overwhelmed and shocked by Hashem's commandment to use logic and reason. Rather Hashem gave Avrohom plenty of time to think over whether to go forth and do the Akeidah. Similarly, the Ralbag says that Hashem wanted to give the Bnei Yisroel four days to think about the fact that they were going to slaughter the main idol of the Egyptians, which they had also served. In this way, when the Bnei Yisroel slaughter the Korban Pesach, we can be sure they were doing it with their own free will and not just because they were overwhelmed with Hashem's Mitzvah to slaughter it.

5) The Midrash Lekach Tov, Rabeinu Yona, the Shach, and the Oznayim LeTorah answer our question similarly. They say the Bnei Yisroel had to undergo a process to believe in Hashem and not to be afraid of the Egyptian's reaction to what they were doing. Before this, as slaves, the Bnei Yisroel were always afraid, especially since it occurred many times that the Egyptians would take severe retribution against them if they had issues with their actions. For example, when Moshe first came to Pharaoh and asked him to let the Bnei Yisroel go to serve Hashem for three days, Pharaoh took retribution for such a request by increasing their workload to an impossible level by withholding straw for bricks. The first step occurred by having the Bnei Yisroel acquire and designate a lamb (the main idol of the Egyptians). During those four days, when the Egyptians either saw or heard the lamb and asked the Bnei Yisroel what their plans were, they were to answer the Egyptians that they were going to slaughter it, in four days' time. Even though the Egyptians had plenty of time to react and even to gather together to take revenge for what the Bnei Yisroel were planning to do to their idol, Hashem dulled the Egyptians teeth, and they said and did nothing. This was a major step in convincing the Bnei Yisroel they could believe in Hashem's protection and not be afraid of the Egyptian's reaction to what they were doing. As the Oznayim LeTorah says, they could hear the lamb bound up and crying for help for four days and saw no one came to help it, despite it being the Egyptian's deity. In addition, seeing no one help also helped erase the thought

Bo

from the minds of the many Bnei Yisroel who had also served the lamb that it was a deity. This process continued after the slaughtering of the lamb, by Hashem having the Bnei Yisroel publicly roast the lamb outdoors over a fire and by putting the blood on the doorposts, both of which were in full view of the Egyptians. Rabeinu Yona adds that Hashem commanding the Bnei Yisroel not to leave their houses the entire night when the Egyptian firstborns were being killed was also part of the process. Shemos (12:30) says, "And Pharaoh arose at night, he and all his servants and all the Egyptians, and there was a great outcry in Egypt, for there was no house in which no one was dead." Despite this outcry, the Bnei Yisroel did nothing to either help or console the Egyptians in their time of need and did not worry that the Egyptians would take revenge against them for doing nothing, despite the Egyptian's great anguish. The Shach quotes the Yalkut Shimoni 195 about what happened when Moshe told the Bnei Yisroel to acquire and designate the Korban Pesach four days before slaughtering it. It says that the Bnei Yisroel responded to Moshe similarly to how Moshe had responded to Pharaoh when Pharaoh suggested the Bnei Yisroel serve Hashem in Egypt instead of going to the desert. The Midrash Lekach Tov also says that this was the Bnei Yisroel's initial reaction. Moshe tells Pharaoh in Shemos (8:22), "Will we sacrifice the deity of the Egyptians before their eyes, and they will not stone us?" Despite this initial reaction, Hashem ingrained in the Bnei Yisroel that he would protect them, and they had nothing to worry about in the Egyptian's reaction to what they did.

6) The Midrash Lekach Tov and Oznayim LeTorah answer our question similarly. They say that in the merit of doing this Mitzvah, the Bnei Yisroel would merit the Jordan River splitting on the same day (the 10th of Nisan) and allow the Bnei Yisroel to travel into Eretz Yisroel to conquer it as it says in Sefer Yehoshua (4:19), "And the people came up out of the Jordan on the tenth day of the first month (Nisan).

7) The Kli Yakor also presents an answer to our question. We have mentioned previously that the Bnei Yisroel needed to be saved from the wrath of the Egyptians, as Moshe tells Pharaoh in Shemos (8:22): "Will we sacrifice the deity of the Egyptians before their eyes, and they will not stone us?" The Gemorah in Sotah 21a quotes Rav Yosef, who says that in the time one is involved in performing a Mitzvah, it protects one from punishment, and it saves one from sinning. Therefore, says the Kli Yakor, Hashem gave the Bnei Yisroel a constant Mitzvah to watch the Korban Pesach from getting a blemish for four days prior to slaughtering it, to protect them from being attacked by the Egyptians. This is also the reason the four Mitzvos the Bnei Yisroel kept from doing in Egypt were not enough to protect them since they needed a Mitzvah they were constantly doing.

8) The Shach presents another answer to our question. He notes that our Posuk begins with the phrase: וְהָיָה לָכֶם לְמִשְׁמֶרֶת (And you shall keep it for inspection (literally watching). He says that just like we were commanded to watch the lamb, so it does not get any blemishes, doing this Mitzvah will also cause us to be watched and protected by Hashem, so the Egyptians do not harm us. He finds a hint to this concept by the fact that the word וְהָיָה contains all the letters of Hashem's name (albeit in a different order with the letter yud and vov switching places). The four days are the four letters of Hashem's name, rendering the Egyptians powerless to harm us. He also points out that the Hebrew word for lamb is also mentioned four times in this topic.

Bo

9) The Zohar in Shemos 39b also ponders our question. It says the Bnei Yisroel were put under the dominion of the lamb idol for 400 years, corresponding to the fact that they were to be slaves in Egypt for 400 years. Even though Hashem shortened the 400 years down to only 210 years, since the original plan was for 400 years and we were ready to remain in Egypt for 400 years, it is considered as if it was 400 years. Symmetrically, the lamb was put under our dominion for four days as retribution for us being under its dominion for 400 years.

Since Killing the Firstborn Was Done by Hashem Why Did the Bnei Yisroel Have to Worry About the Destroying Angel?

וְעָבַרְתִּי בְאֶרֶץ מִצְרַיִם בַּלַּיְלָה הַזֶּה וְהִכֵּיתִי כָל בְּכוֹר בְּאֶרֶץ מִצְרַיִם מֵאָדָם וְעַד בְּהֵמָה וּבְכָל אֱלֹהֵי מִצְרַיִם אֶעֱשֶׂה שְׁפָטִים אֲנִי ה'. וְהָיָה הַדָּם לָכֶם לְאֹת עַל הַבָּתִּים אֲשֶׁר אַתֶּם שָׁם וְרָאִיתִי אֶת הַדָּם וּפָסַחְתִּי עֲלֵכֶם וְלֹא יִהְיֶה בָכֶם נֶגֶף לְמַשְׁחִית בְּהַכֹּתִי בְּאֶרֶץ מִצְרָיִם. (יב:יב-יג) Shemos (12:12-13) I (Hashem) will pass through the land of Egypt on this night, and I will smite every firstborn in the land of Egypt, both man and beast, and upon all the gods of Egypt will I wreak judgments I, Hashem. And the blood will be for you for a sign upon the houses where you will be, and I will see the blood and skip over you, and there will be no destroying angel to destroy you when I smite the people of the land of Egypt.

If the plague of the killing of the firstborn was done by Hashem himself, why did the Bnei Yisroel have to worry about being destroyed by a destroying angel?

Introduction
We say in the Hagadah וְעָבַרְתִּי בְאֶרֶץ מִצְרַיִם בַּלַּיְלָה הַזֶּה - אֲנִי וְלֹא מַלְאָךְ וְהִכֵּיתִי כָל בְּכוֹר בְּאֶרֶץ מִצְרַיִם - אֲנִי וְלֹא שָׂרָף וּבְכָל אֱלֹהֵי מִצְרַיִם אֶעֱשֶׂה שְׁפָטִים - אֲנִי וְלֹא הַשָּׁלִיחַ אֲנִי ה' - אֲנִי הוּא וְלֹא אַחֵר "I will pass through the land of Egypt," I and not an angel; "And I will smite every firstborn in the land of Egypt," I and not a Seraph angel; "And I will carry out judgments against all the gods of Egypt," I and not a messenger; "I- Hashem," it is I, and none other! From this passage of the Hagadah, we see very clearly that the killing of the firstborns was done by Hashem himself.

The Ramban and Mizrachi have a difference of opinion over exactly how we derive that the plague was done by Hashem himself from our Posuk. The Ramban says we derive it from the fact that our Posuk uses the first person to describe what will happen by saying, for example: "I will smite every firstborn in the land of Egypt." The Mizrachi says that we do find cases where the first person is used to describe what will happen in a plague, and yet the plague is done by an angel. An example of this is when Sancherev is besieging Yerushalayim, and Sefer Melachim II (19:34) says, "And I will protect this city to save it, for My sake and for the sake of My servant Dovid." Yet the next Posuk says, "And it came to pass on that night that an angel of Hashem went out and slew one hundred eighty-five thousand of the camp of Assyria. And they arose in the morning, and behold; they were all dead corpses." The Ramban would be of the opinion that when the Posuk explicitly clarifies the plague was done by an angel, there is no problem in using the first person to describe what will happen. We also find examples in the Torah where the Torah says that Hashem did something where really an angel did the something. For example, Shemos (4:24) says, וַיְהִי בַדֶּרֶךְ

Bo

בַּמָּלוֹן וַיִּפְגְּשֵׁהוּ ה' וַיְבַקֵּשׁ הֲמִיתוֹ (Now he (Moshe) was on the way, in an inn, that Hashem met him and sought to put him to death). The Gemorah in Nedorim 32a says that it was not Hashem but rather his angel, the Satan, that met Moshe and wanted to kill Moshe.

Rabeinu Bechay says the reason Hashem had to perform the miracle by himself without angels is that angels can only judge and punish according to the letter of the law and not show any mercy. According to the letter of the law, the Bnei Yisroel were not deserving of being saved. Therefore, Hashem himself, who can also judge with mercy and not strictly according to the letter of the law, had to perform the plague so that He could show mercy to the Bnei Yisroel and save them. We can understand what the Rabeinu Bechay is saying a bit deeper if we also consider what the Nisivos Shalom says in his essay explaining Beraishis (50:25). The Gemorah in Sanhedrin 98a when discussing when the final redemption will occur, explains the phrase of Sefer Yeshayahu (60:22) which says, אֲנִי ה' בְּעִתָּהּ אֲחִישֶׁנָּה (I am Hashem, in its time I will hasten it). The phrase seems self-contradictory since if the final redemption will come in its time, then how will Hashem make it come quicker (hasten it), and if Hashem makes it come quicker, then it will come before its time. Rav Yehoshua ben Levi explains if the Bnei Yisroel are deserving, then Hashem will hasten the redemption, but if the Bnei Yisroel are not deserving, then it will come in its preordained time. The Nisivos Shalom says that the redemption from Egypt worked the same way. However, there was a problem with redeeming the Bnei Yisroel from Egypt. Chazal tell us that the Bnei Yisroel were on the 49th and last level of Tumah in Egypt, and if they had stayed in Egypt any longer, they would have fallen to the 50th level of Tumah for which there would be no hope of redemption. Parenthetically the Shach on Shemos (12:7) says the redemption from Egypt is mentioned 49 times in the Torah. This number of times is to hint to us that the Bnei Yisroel were only redeemed from Egypt since they did not fall to the 50th level of Tumah. Therefore, even though neither the Bnei Yisroel were deserving of redemption nor had the preordained time of 400 years been reached, the Bnei Yisroel had to be redeemed anyway even though the letter of the law said the Bnei Yisroel had no right to be redeemed. Only Hashem, who can also judge with mercy and not strictly according to the letter of the law, had to perform the plague so that Hashem could show mercy to the Bnei Yisroel, save them from the plague, and redeem them.

The Beis HaLevi has a different approach as to why Hashem had to perform the plague himself. The Zohar in Terumah 150b says that the fire of Gehenom comes from the heat of the desires of wicked people to follow their Yetzer Horah. It explains that there was a time in history when the fire in Gehenom was extinguished and did not burn at all. To understand when this occurred, we examine Nechemia (9:4), which says when the Bnei Yisroel returned to Eretz Yisroel with Ezra and Nechemia to rebuild the Beis Hamikdosh, "they cried out in a huge voice to Hashem." The Gemorah in Yuma 69b and Sanhedrin 64a explain that they cried out, "Woe, Woe, it is he who has destroyed the Beis Hamikdosh, burnt the sanctuary, killed all the righteous people, driven all Bnei Yisroel into exile, and is still dancing around among us! Hashem has surely given him to us so that we may receive reward through him. We want neither him nor any reward through him! Rashi explains that they were talking about the Yetzer Horah that entices one to worship idolatry. A tablet fell down from Heaven for them, upon which the word Emes (truth) was written. Rashi explains that this was a sign from Heaven that Hashem agrees with their request. They fasted for three days and three

Bo

nights, and Heaven gave him (the Yetzer Horah of idolatry) to them. He came out from the Holy of Holies like a fiery young lion. The Toras Chaim ponders what the Yetzer Horah is doing in the Holy of Holies. He answers that each person encompasses a small world similar to the physical world that we live in. Just like the Yetzer Horah is found inside the essence of every person, he is also found inside the essence of the world, which is where Hashem's Shechinah rests in the Holy of Holies.

The Prophet (Zechariah) said to them, "This is the Yetzer Horah of idolatry. As they captured the Yetzer Horah of idolatry, a hair of his beard fell out, and he raised his voice, and it was heard to a distance of 400 parsas. Parenthetically for calibration of how big a parsa is, Tosfos in Baba Metzia 28a says Eretz Yisroel is 400 parsas by 400 parsas. After hearing this tremendous noise, they said: "How should we act? Perhaps, Chas VeShalom, they might have mercy on him in Heaven!" The prophet said to them: "Put him into a leaden pot, close its opening with lead, because lead absorbs sound well." They said: "Since this is a time of mercy, let us pray for mercy for the Yetzer Horah of sin (immorality)." They davened for mercy, and he was handed over to them. He said to them; you should realize that if you kill him (me), the world will no longer continue to exist. They put him in prison for three days, then looked in the whole land of Eretz Yisroel for a fresh egg and could not find one. Rashi says that even those eggs which had already started to form stopped continuing to form since the warm environment in the reproductive organs of the chickens cooled off. They said: "What should we do now? Should we kill him? The world would then no longer exist. We can't beg for half mercy since in Heaven they do not grant halves." Rashi on these Gemorahs says that by "half mercy," they meant that the Yetzer Horah of immorality would not arouse a person to sin but would allow a person to reproduce. They put out his (the Yetzer Horah of immorality) eyes and let him go. Putting out his eyes helped so that he at least no longer entices men to commit incest. However, Rashi explains that the Yetzer Horah still entices a person to sin with a married woman. Obviously, all the details in the above are not to be taken completely literally.

The Zohar says that during the time the Yetzer Horah was in the leaden pot, the fires of Gehenom were extinguished since even the wicked people had no fiery desire to serve the Yetzer Horah. When the Yetzer Horah was let out, the fires of Gehenom returned, since now the wicked people again had the heat of the fiery desire to serve the Yetzer Horah. In the spiritual world of Gehenom, it is not fire that burns but rather desires that burn. Given that wicked people are full of desires, all that needs to be done is transfer wicked people to Gehenom, and they will be burned by their own desires, which they were completely consumed within this world. Based on this Zohar, the Beis HaLevi says in the spiritual world, since the desires do the burning, the force of fire in the spiritual world does not burn and destroy, and it has a completely different function.

Using this concept, the Beis HaLevi explains how Hashem performs most miracles in this world. For example, the Beraishis Raba (38:13) and Rashi on Beraishis (11:28) write that the gigantic oven that they needed to make the bricks for the tower of Bavel in Parshas Noach served a dual purpose. They threatened that anyone who did not want to heed the legislation to serve idols would be burnt alive by being put into this gigantic furnace. The Beraishis Raba tells us that Avrohom's father, Terach owned a store that sold idols. One day Terach took a vacation and put Avrohom in charge of

Bo

the store. The first customer came in and asked to buy an idol. Avrohom asked the customer how old he was, and he answered that he was 60 years old. Avrohom asked the customer, "how is it that a 60-year-old man wants to buy an idol that was just made a few days ago?" The customer was embarrassed and left the store. A woman customer came in carrying a large tray of flour, which she left with Avrohom and asked him to use it as an offering for the idols in the store. With this Avrohom, came up with a plan to end all this nonsense. Avrohom took a sledgehammer and broke all the idols except for the biggest one. Avrohom then took the hammer and put it in the hand of the biggest idol. When Terach returned and saw all the destruction, he asked Avrohom for an explanation. Avrohom told Terach that a woman came in with a large tray of flour to give as an offering to the idols. When he put down the tray near the idols, the idols began quarreling with each other over who should get the offering. Finally, said Avrohom, the biggest idol, grabbed a hammer and smashed all the smaller idols so that it could get the offering.

Terach looked at Avrohom and said, "why are you insulting my intelligence?" "Do you really think that idols can speak and quarrel with each other, not to mention, have feelings and intelligence?" asked Terach. Avrohom answered Terach, "Don't you hear what you are saying about your idols and what lack of power they really have?" Terach was not assuaged, and he reported what his son had done to Nimrod the King. After some debate, Nimrod ordered Avrohom to be thrown into the fiery furnace. Hashem made a miracle, and Avrohom was saved from this fiery furnace.

The Gemorah in Pesachim 118a relates that seeing Avrohom thrown into the fiery furnace Gavriel volunteered his services to Hashem to go down and cool the fire so that the righteous Avrohom would be saved. However, Hashem told Gavriel that since both Hashem and Avrohom are singularly unique in their worlds, being that Hashem is the one true Deity and Avrohom is the only one in the physical world to forsake idolatry and practice monotheism, it is fitting that Hashem himself should save Avrohom. Nevertheless, Hashem promised Gavriel that there would come a time when Avrohom's three descendants will also need to be saved from a fiery furnace, and then Hashem will allow Gavriel to save them. Years later, Nevuchadnetzar threw Chananyah, Mishael, and Azariah into a fiery furnace. Gavriel, who was the ministering angel of fire, was chosen to go down and make the fire cold on the inside of the furnace to save them while making it hot on the outside. The Rashbam explains the need to make the fire hotter on the outside was so that the people who threw Chananyah, Mishael, and Azariah into the fiery furnace should be burnt as Sefer Doniel (3:22) relates. The Beis HaLevi explains the way Gavriel saved Chananyah, Mishael, and Azariah was by coming down into the physical world and transforming the fire which burned in the furnace into its properties in the spiritual world. In the spiritual world, the desires of the wicked men who threw them into the furnace caused them to become burnt, while the force of fire turned spiritual no longer had the property of burning Chananyah, Mishael, and Azariah. Therefore, the miracle of their saving was only a miracle in the physical world, while in the spiritual world, everything proceeded as to the norm in the spiritual world. Such a miracle can be done by an angel.

In Egypt, the Bnei Yisroel became so spiritually contaminated by the Egyptians that even in the spiritual world, no miracle could be done for them which could redeem them from Egypt. We can see how bad the Bnei Yisroel got in Egypt if we consider what happened when the Bnei Yisroel

Bo

were at the Red Sea. The Zohar in Parshas Terumah 170b says when the Bnei Yisroel came to the Red Sea, Hashem wanted to split the Sea. The angel who is in charge of Egypt, called Rahav, came and asked for justice. Rahav said, Master of the World, why do you want to punish the Egyptians and split the Sea for the Bnei Yisroel. Both the Egyptians and the Bnei Yisroel are wicked, and Hashem's ways are of justice and truth. The Egyptians serve idols, and the Bnei Yisroel serve idols. The Egyptians are immoral, and the Bnei Yisroel are immoral. The Egyptians are murderers, and the Bnei Yisroel are murderers. Rahav was correct, and therefore Hashem had to take into account the merits of our forefathers to split the Sea. Because of the bad spiritual state of the Bnei Yisroel, says the Beis HaLevi, even in the spiritual world of the angels, the Bnei Yisroel did not deserve to be redeemed. Therefore, it would not be possible for the Bnei Yisroel to be redeemed through an angel, and rather Hashem himself had to redeem the Bnei Yisroel. Similarly, at the splitting of the Red Sea, the angels and especially Rahav were dumbfounded that the Bnei Yisroel were being saved, and therefore that miracle also had to be done by Hashem himself.

The Shach presents another reason why Hashem had to come by himself during the plague of the killing of the firstborn. The Shemos Raba (19:5) says that besides the tribe of Levi, all Bnei Yisroel stopped giving their son's a Bris Milah. Hashem wanted to redeem them, but the Bnei Yisroel did not have any merits. Therefore, Hashem told Moshe to give the Bnei Yisroel a Bris Milah to give them some merits. Though some agreed, many of the Bnei Yisroel refused to have a Bris Milah. Hashem then told Moshe to slaughter and roast his Korban Pesach. Hashem had the winds gather up some of the air of Gan Eden and combined it with the smell of that Korban Pesach. The smell so overwhelmed the Bnei Yisroel that they all came running to Moshe, requesting that they have a piece of Moshe's Korban Pesach. Moshe told the people Hashem had commanded that only people with a Bris Milah are allowed to eat from the Korban Pesach. The people were so overcome with the smell and desire to eat the Korban Pesach that they all agreed to have a Bris Milah. The blood of their Bris Milah intermingled with that of the blood of the Korban Pesach as Sefer Yechezkel (16:6) says, וָאֶעֱבֹר עָלַיִךְ וָאֶרְאֵךְ מִתְבּוֹסֶסֶת בְּדָמָיִךְ וָאֹמַר לָךְ בְּדָמַיִךְ חֲיִי וָאֹמַר לָךְ בְּדָמַיִךְ חֲיִי (And I passed by you and saw you downtrodden with your blood, and I said to you, "With your blood, live," and I said to you, "With your blood, live."). The reason the Navi talks about two types of blood is that one was the blood of Bris Milah and the other the blood of the Korban Pesach, the two merits the Bnei Yisroel had to go out of Egypt. In the beginning of Parshas Vayerah, Hashem visits Avrohom to cure Avrohom of the pain of his Bris Milah. Immediately after Hashem visits, Avrohom is cured and able to run after his guests to invite them in and prepare a meal for them. The Bnei Yisroel had to leave Egypt the next morning after their Bris Milah and travel into the desert. The Shach says Hashem came at midnight not only to kill the Egyptian firstborns but also to cure all the Bnei Yisroel from just having a Bris Milah so that they would be able to travel the next day, pain-free and with the utmost of joy that they had been redeemed from Egypt.

The Alshich ponders the question of why Hashem could not have sent the destroying angel with the instructions to skip over any house which had blood on the doorposts instead of having to come himself. The Shemos Raba (18:2) says that those Egyptians who were afraid that Moshe's prophesy of the killing of the firstborn would take place brought their firstborn to stay in the house of a Jew and forced the Jews to let the firstborn stay. Therefore, there were many houses with blood on their

Bo

doorpost which had Egyptian firstborns inside, making giving such simplified instructions to the destroying angel impossible. The reality of the firstborn Egyptians being and dying in many Jewish homes gives new meaning to the phrase "I will see the blood and skip over you." In fact, the Sifsei Tzadik says that "skipping over" just means that in the houses of the Bnei Yisroel, there was no panic and terror as there was in the house of the Egyptians. Shemos (12:30) says, "And Pharaoh arose at night, he and all his servants and all the Egyptians, and there was a great outcry in Egypt, for there was no house in which no one was dead." Rashi on the Posuk says that if there was no firstborn in the house, the oldest family member died. It is interesting to note that someone who brought their firstborn to a Jewish house had not only the firstborn in the Jewish house die but also the next oldest child who they thought was safe in the Egyptian house also died. In addition, other Egyptians died from the plague of the destroying angel, causing much fear and panic as the Torah relates: "there was a great outcry in Egypt." The Bnei Yisroel knew in advance that the firstborn Egyptians in their house would die, so they did not panic while the Egyptians were not prepared for the plague to kill so many people, leading to their great outcry.

Our Posuk says, וּבְכָל אֱלֹהֵי מִצְרַיִם אֶעֱשֶׂה שְׁפָטִים אֲנִי ה'. (and upon all the gods of Egypt will I wreak judgments I, Hashem). The Mishna in Avodah Zora 54b records a question that the Gentile philosophers asked the Jewish Sages in Rome: "If Hashem does not want idols, why doesn't Hashem get rid of the idol." The sages answered, "If idol worshippers would only worship something that the world has no need for, Hashem would get rid of the idols. However, they worship the sun, moon, stars, and constellations. Should Hashem destroy the world because of these fools?" The Gentile philosophers replied, "Let Hashem then destroy every idol which is not necessary for the world and leave all idols which are necessary for the world to exist." The sages answered, "This would then strengthen the belief in these idols since their worshippers would say the proof they are true deities can be seen by the fact that as opposed to the other idols which Hashem got rid of, these idols are not being destroyed." The Meiri points out that the Sages just answered the philosophers' foolish question with an answer that answered the question. In addition, he points out that part of the reason for recording this story is to strengthen the belief of those Jews who might question why Hashem allows idols to exist for so many years. Following the teachings of this Mishna, the Alshich comments on why it was necessary to add the words אֲנִי ה' (I am Hashem) to the phrase in our Posuk telling us that Hashem destroyed the gods of Egypt. He says that otherwise, one might think the non-Egyptian idols which were not destroyed were true deities. To reinforce that this is not true, Hashem added on a reminder that He is the only deity when the Posuk adds on the words אֲנִי ה' (I am Hashem). We should also mention the Toras Chaim on this Gemorah says that it seems absurd that Hashem would make a miracle almost every day and destroy all the idols that idol worshippers are foolish enough to make. Rather the idols being discussed are those idols which, through deep knowledge of the power of Tumah by their craftsman, were able to speak intelligently. The question being asked is why Hashem does not block off this power so no one would ever be able to create such an idol.

Shemos (12:29) describes the plague being carried out when it says, "It came to pass at midnight, and Hashem smote every firstborn in the land of Egypt, from the firstborn of Pharaoh who sits on his throne to the firstborn of the captive who is in the dungeon, and every firstborn animal."

Bo

Rabeinu Bechay ponders the question of why the Torah doesn't mention that the gods of the Egyptians were also destroyed, as was foretold in our Posuk. Destroying the gods of the Egyptians was quite a miracle; as the Mechilta describes it, all their wooden and stone idols rotted, and all the metal idols melted, so it would seem appropriate to mention this miracle. He says the Egyptians did not find out about their gods until the next day when they went to worship their idols. Therefore, the Torah only describes the plague they knew about immediately, which was the death of the firstborns. Parenthetically, the Tzedah LeDerech says the reason Hashem destroyed all the Egyptian idols was so that they couldn't ascribe the plague of the firstborn to any of their idols.

The Rosh, as quoted by the Ksav VeHakabola, does not consider Rabeinu Bechay's reason for not ascribing the plague of the firstborn to any Egyptian idols as enough reason to perform such a gigantic miracle of having all the idols decay or melt. Rather he says that the main Egyptian idol was the lamb and that any human born when the sun begins to enter the constellation of the lamb was considered a holy or super-human person. Along with killing the firstborns, Hashem also killed every one whom the Egyptians thought were holy or super-human in the plague of killing the firstborn.

The Tzedah LeDerech ponders the question of why the firstborn animals were killed. He says the Egyptians served all firstborn animals as deities. He explains that since the main idol of the Egyptians was the lamb which is the first of all constellations, they extended their idols to include any first, like a firstborn.

1) The Alshich presents an answer to our question. According to him, our question does not begin since he says that there was no destroying angel, and the entire plague was done by Hashem. When our Posuk says, וְלֹא יִהְיֶה בָכֶם נֶגֶף לְמַשְׁחִית בְּהַכֹּתִי בְּאֶרֶץ מִצְרָיִם (and there will be no plague done by the destroying angel to destroy you when I smite the people of the land of Egypt) it means that there will be no destroying angel and only Hashem was doing the plague so that the plague does not affect the Bnei Yisroel.

2) The Sforno and Mizrachi answer our question similarly. Tehillim (78:49) when speaking about the ten plagues says, יְשַׁלַּח בָּם חֲרוֹן אַפּוֹ עֶבְרָה וָזַעַם וְצָרָה מִשְׁלַחַת מַלְאֲכֵי רָעִים (He dispatched against them the kindling of His anger-wrath, fury, and trouble, a delegation of evil angels). In the Hagadah, we say: "Rabi Akiva says, 'From where can we derive that every plague that the Holy One, blessed be He, brought upon the Egyptians in Egypt was composed of five plagues? As it says in Tehillim (78:49): 'He sent upon them the fierceness of His anger, wrath, and fury, and trouble, a delegation of evil angels.' 'The fierceness of His anger' corresponds to one; 'wrath' two; 'and fury' three; 'and trouble' four; 'a delegation of evil angels' five. You can say from here that in Egypt, they were struck with fifty plagues and at the Sea, they were struck with two hundred and fifty plagues." The Sforno and Mizrachi say that along with the plague of killing the Egyptian firstborn and saving the Jewish firstborn which Hashem did, there was also these other plagues including "a delegation of evil angels," which was done by the angels. In fact, the Targum Yonason ben Uziel says that Hashem took with him 90,000 times 10,000 angels or 900,000,000 angels. The blood on the doorposts was necessary to save the Bnei Yisroel from the angel of destruction, who was another

Bo

component of this and the other nine plagues. It is not clear to me why they would be of the opinion that the blood was necessary for this plague and not the other nine plagues. Presumably, the reason is that the accompanying other parts of each plague had some aspect of the plague. Since this plague was about killing the firstborns, the accompanying other parts of the plague were also killing. It was this that the blood prevented happening to the Bnei Yisroel, despite the fact that we will soon see, the Bnei Yisroel may have deserved it.

In his Sefer Mayan Beis HaShoaivah, Rav Schwab says the plague of "upon all the gods of Egypt will I wreak judgments" mentioned in our Posuk was done by the angels that accompanied Hashem when he was killing the Egyptian firstborns. Shemos (12:21) says מִשְׁכוּ וּקְחוּ לָכֶם צֹאן לְמִשְׁפְּחֹתֵיכֶם וְשַׁחֲטוּ הַפָּסַח (Draw forth and buy for yourselves sheep for your families and slaughter the Korban Pesach). The Mechilta ponders why the seemingly superfluous word מִשְׁכוּ (draw forth) was needed. It says that the Bnei Yisroel served idols, and before they could take the Korban Pesach, they needed to draw their hand away from serving idols and only serve Hashem. Since the idols the angels were destroying were also served by the Bnei Yisroel, the angel destroying the Egyptian idols could also start a plague against the Bnei Yisroel since they also sinned in serving idols. However, by putting the blood of the Korban Pesach on the doors of their houses, the Bnei Yisroel showed that they slaughtered the Korban Pesach, which they were only able to do if they drew their hand away from idols and stopped serving them. Therefore, the blood would show the angel that the Bnei Yisroel were no longer serving idols, and consequently, the angel would withhold his plague from those houses which had blood on the doors.

As another proof of how steeped the Bnei Yisroel were in worshipping idols, Rav Schwab references a Bach on Tur, Orach Chaim 430. The Tur ponders why the Shabbos before Pesach is called Shabbos HaGodol (The Great Shabbos). He says that on this day, the teeth of the Egyptians were dulled (similar to a dog that can no longer bite because its teeth are completely dull). This occurred when upon asking the Bnei Yisroel why they had taken a lamb for a Korban Pesach and being told that they were going to slaughter the god of the Egyptians for Hashem, the Egyptians were unable to say or do anything to stop them. Based on the Mechilta we have quoted, the Bach explains that the Bnei Yisroel had also served this god of the Egyptians. The Egyptians were paralyzed with the thought that their very idol, which the Bnei Yisroel had also served, was going to be suddenly denigrated and slaughtered in the service of Hashem. The fact the Egyptians could not say or do anything to stop this on the day of Shabbos HaGodol is why this Shabbos is referred to as the "Great Shabbos."

3) The Abarbanel also ponders our question and says that the destroying angel refers to the Egyptians. In the merit of putting blood from the Korban Pesach on their doorpost, Hashem will protect the Bnei Yisroel from being attacked by the Egyptians who, in their bitter predicament of losing their firstborns, would look for revenge against the Bnei Yisroel. Parenthetically he also says that one of the reasons for the command in Shemos (12:22) "and you shall not go out, any man from the entrance of his house until morning" was to prevent the Egyptians in their agitated state from seeing the Bnei Yisroel and attacking them.

Bo

4) The Nisivos, in his Sefer Emes LeYaakov, also presents an answer to our question. In addition to our question, he ponders the question of how the plague of killing the firstborn differed from all the other plagues where Hashem caused the plague to only affect the Egyptians and not the Bnei Yisroel. Shemos (12:37) says, "The Bnei Yisroel journeyed from Ramsais to Succos, about six hundred thousand on foot, the men, besides the young children." The Nisivos says that with such a large number of people, especially when we also include the women and children, it would be natural for at least one and perhaps a number of people to die of natural causes that night. Rather, the miracle was, as Shemos (12:30) says, "there was a great outcry in Egypt" but not in the house of the Bnei Yisroel since no Jew died that night nor even got sick that night so that the Bnei Yisroel went out of Egypt in complete happiness. He is of the opinion that the "destroying angel" was none other than the "angel of death." This aspect of the plague of firstborns was unique to this plague and not the first nine plagues

5) The Chasam Sofer, in the section of his Sefer dealing with the topic of Pesach, also ponders our question. He says that the Egyptian firstborns did not immediately die at midnight, but rather they were mortally wounded and were killed at the first time of daylight by the destroying angel. In a Teshuva to his father-in-law Rabi Akiva Eiger in Yoreh Deah (346), he explains this answer a bit more. He quotes the introduction to Meseches Smochos, which says explicitly that Hashem mortally wounded the Egyptian firstborns at midnight and that they only died in the morning. The Braisah in Meseches Semochos explains the reason for this with a Moshul to someone who gives food to a child and is told to make the child's mother aware of this. In a similar way, says the Braisah, Hashem wanted to inform the Bnei Yisroel that he had killed the Egyptian firstborn. Therefore, Hashem waited till morning when it was light, not to mention when the Bnei Yisroel were no longer under the prohibition of Shemos (12:22) "and you shall not go out, any man from the entrance of his house until morning," for the firstborns to die and for the Egyptians to begin burying them. The Nachalas Yaakov, in his explanation of this Braisah, makes an interesting point about why Hashem only mortally wounded the Egyptian firstborns at midnight. In Sanhedrin 39a, a heretic asked Rav Abahu how Hashem could have become Tahor (spiritually clean) after burying Moshe. The heretic also was of the opinion that Hashem is a Kohen since Hashem said in Shemos (25:2) at the beginning of Parshas Terumah: וְיִקְחוּ לִי תְּרוּמָה (take for me Terumah (donation for the Mishkan)) and Terumah goes only to a Kohen. The heretic continued that Hashem cannot immerse himself in water to become Tahor since the heretic quoted Sefer Yeshayahu (40:12) that all the water of the world only covers the fist of Hashem. Though it was a heretical question, Rav Abahu answered and said that Hashem used fire to become Tahor. Tosfos on this Gemorah ponders why the heretic didn't ask how Hashem could become Tameh (spiritually impure) since the Bnei Yisroel, and hence Moshe, are the sons of Hashem and a Kohen can become Tameh to his child. The Nachalas Yaakov says that Tosfos' answer would not answer a better question the heretic could have asked, which is how Hashem killed the Egyptian firstborns and consequentially became Tameh even though Egyptians are not the sons of Hashem. The Nachalas Yaakov says that this Braisah provided the answer to this question since Hashem indeed did not kill the Egyptian firstborns but merely mortally wounded them so that Hashem did not become Tameh. The Chasam Sofer in the Teshuva to Rabi Akiva Eiger also offers proof that the Egyptian firstborns died in the daytime. Bamidbar (8:17) says, כִּי לִי כָל בְּכוֹר בִּבְנֵי יִשְׂרָאֵל בָּאָדָם וּבַבְּהֵמָה בְּיוֹם הַכֹּתִי כָל בְּכוֹר בְּאֶרֶץ מִצְרַיִם הִקְדַּשְׁתִּי אֹתָם לִי

Bo

(For all the firstborn among the Bnei Yisroel are Mine, both man and beast; on **the day** that I smote all the firstborn in the land of Egypt I sanctified them for Myself.). Since that Posuk uses the term "day" and not "night," implies that the Egyptian firstborns were killed during the day.

Parenthetically we also learn a lesson from the introduction of the Chasam Sofer's Teshuva to Rabi Akiva Eiger. Rabi Akiva Eiger sent his son-in-law, the Poseik (Halachic arbitrator) of the generation, a Halachic question about the laws of mourning. The Chasam Sofer says that when he received the letter with the question, he was very hesitant about delving into the sources to answer the question. However, since the question came from his father-in-law, who was the scholar of that generation, he felt that he nonetheless, despite his hesitation, needed to research and answer the question. He writes that upon beginning to research the answer, he got the news that his mother had been Niftar. The reason he had been hesitant to research the laws of mourning was that he felt that learning the laws of mourning was not a good omen for someone who was not in mourning, and in fact, what he had been hesitant about did indeed occur. It is also interesting to note that historically his father was Niftar before his mother, so he had already been involved in the laws of mourning. In light of what had happened to him, he writes to his father-in-law when he should read his reply. The Chasam Sofer, who wrote his reply a couple of weeks before Pesach, wrote that Rabi Akiva Eiger could read his reply on Tisha Be'Av (almost four months later), which came out that year on Shabbos since the day is a day of mourning. Alternatively, given the possibility that Moshiach could come before Tisha Be'Av, it would not be a problem to read his reply if Moshiach came since, with the coming of Moshiach, no more death would be known in this world. As a third possibility, he noted that he was a person who was very afraid of bad omens, and it is possible that his father-in-law, who was not so fearful, would not be affected by reading the reply. The third possibility would seem to be in keeping with what the Gemorah in Pesachim110b concludes about the danger of doing pairs of things. The Gemorah says that the general rule is that someone who is overly worried about doing things in pairs will be likely harmed if he is negligent and does something in pairs. On the other hand, someone who is not overly worried about doing things in pairs will be much less likely to be harmed if he is negligent and does something in pairs. However, although one should not be excessively cautious about doing things in pairs, one should exercise some caution with doing things in pairs. This introduction to this Teshuva shows that one should exercise some caution in not delving into the laws of mourning, especially when one's parents are alive, since it could be a bad omen.

6) The Beis HaLevi also presents an answer to our question. He says that the actual killing of the firstborns was done by Hashem, Himself. With all the dead bodies, much disease was spread throughout Egypt. This happens even in modern times when there is a large loss of life, and as can be expected, especially in olden times, causing many other people who were not firstborns to be affected by the disease and contamination and consequently also die. This secondary plague is what Dovid HaMelech means in Hallel HaGodol in Tehillim (136:10) (which we say in the Shabbos Davening) when he says, לְמַכֵּה מִצְרַיִם בִּבְכוֹרֵיהֶם (To Him (Hashem) who smote the Egyptians with their firstborn). That is, the rest of the Egyptians were smitten from a plague caused by the (death of) the firstborns. This plague was led by the destroying angel (מַשְׁחִית), and in our Posuk the Bnei Yisroel are promised that if they put the blood of the Korban Pesach on their houses, "there will be

Bo

no plague to destroy you." The Beis HaLevi says that this is why the tenth plague is called מַכַּת בְּכוֹרוֹת (literally, the smiting of the firstborns) instead of הריגת בכורות (killing of the firstborns), since not only were the firstborns killed but their killing also killed other Egyptians. With this explanation, we can also understand Shemos (12:27) which says, וַאֲמַרְתֶּם זֶבַח פֶּסַח הוּא לַה' אֲשֶׁר פָּסַח עַל בָּתֵּי בְנֵי יִשְׂרָאֵל בְּמִצְרַיִם בְּנָגְפּוֹ אֶת מִצְרַיִם וְאֶת בָּתֵּינוּ הִצִּיל וַיִּקֹּד הָעָם וַיִּשְׁתַּחֲווּ (you shall say, It is a Korban Pesach to Hashem, for He passed over the houses of the Bnei Yisroel in Egypt when He smote the Egyptians, and He saved our houses. And the people kneeled and prostrated themselves). This Posuk seems to be repetitive when it says first that "He passed over the houses of the Bnei Yisroel" and then "He saved our houses." The second part, "He saved our houses," is referring to Hashem saving us from the plague of the destroying angel.

7) The Nitziv presents a somewhat esoteric answer to our question, which is difficult to understand. He gives a Moshul to a state or territory that has rebelled against a King. The King wants to come and take retribution from those that have rebelled, but he wants to do it in such a way that he kills the ones who have rebelled and not those who played no part in the rebellion. If the King just sends in his army, they have no way of knowing who did and who did not take part in the rebellion. The King comes up with a plan to sort this out. The King announces that he will be personally visiting the city. Afraid that the King will take offense and retribution if they do not come out to honor him, all the rebelling leaders come out to greet the King in the hope that their honoring of the King will be taken into account if the King finds out they were part of the people who rebelled. The King then sends in his army to kill all who have come. In a similar way, Hashem went to Egypt, and because of that, all the important spiritual forces come out to greet Hashem. The Nitziv says that firstborns have a much stronger spiritual force than a non-firstborn, and therefore the spiritual force or angel of the firstborn went out to greet Hashem. In Sefer Shoftim (13:22), after seeing an angel, Shimshon's father Monoach says to his wife, "We shall surely die because we have seen God (the angel)." In general, anyone who sees an angel dies unless either they have prepared themselves spiritually for this encounter or (2) Hashem saves them from dying. The Egyptian firstborns met their spiritual force or angel who had come, and this caused the firstborns to die. The Jewish firstborns would have also died had Hashem not saved them in the merit that they put blood on their doorposts.

Why Does One Posuk Mention Putting the Blood on the Lintel and Then on the Doorposts While Another Says to Do the Opposite?

Shemos וּלְקַחְתֶּם אֲגֻדַּת אֵזוֹב וּטְבַלְתֶּם בַּדָּם אֲשֶׁר בַּסַּף וְהִגַּעְתֶּם אֶל הַמַּשְׁקוֹף וְאֶל שְׁתֵּי הַמְּזוּזֹת מִן הַדָּם אֲשֶׁר בַּסָּף (יב:כב) (12:22) And you shall take a bunch of hyssop and immerse it in the blood that is in the basin, and you shall extend to the lintel and to the two doorposts the blood that is in the basin.

Previously Shemos (12:7) had said, וְלָקְחוּ מִן הַדָּם וְנָתְנוּ עַל שְׁתֵּי הַמְּזוּזֹת וְעַל הַמַּשְׁקוֹף עַל הַבָּתִּים אֲשֶׁר יֹאכְלוּ אֹתוֹ בָּהֶם (And they shall take some of the blood and put it on the two doorposts and on the lintel, on the houses in which they will eat it.). Our Posuk is prefaced by the previous Posuk saying: "Moshe summoned all the elders of Yisroel and said to them." Shemos (12:7) is prefaced by Shemos (12:1), which says, "Hashem spoke to Moshe and to Aharon in the land of Egypt, saying."

332

Bo

Why does our Posuk, said by Moshe, first mention putting the blood on the lintel and then on the doorposts while the previous Posuk, said by Hashem, first mentions putting the blood on the two doorposts and then on the lintel?

Introduction
The Chizkuni says that the blood sprinkled on the lintel and doorposts spells out the Hebrew letter ח. The Chizkuni says that ח stands for חַיִּים (life), meaning that those in the house with the blood on the lintel and doorposts should live.

1) The Mechilta on Shemos (12:7) presents an answer to our question. We will follow the Malbim's explanation of the Mechilta. Typically, when the Torah tells us to do a Mitzvah involving two or more items, the order of the items must be followed. Therefore, when Shemos (12:7) says, "take some of the blood and put it on the two doorposts and on the lintel," the order of first putting blood on the two doorposts before putting blood on the lintel must be followed. However, this rule is only applicable in cases where the Torah elsewhere keeps this same order of items. If the Torah switches the order elsewhere, this indicates that one can fulfill the Mitzvah by doing the items in any order. Since the Torah does indeed switch the order of putting the blood on the doorposts and lintel in our Posuk, we know that one can fulfill the Mitzvah in either order. We note that the Malbim points out that, like any other Mitzvah, when multiple items are used, it is preferable to first use the item that is closest to him. In Shulchan Aruch, Orach Chaim (473:4), the Pesach Seder plate is discussed. The Rema says that the items on the Pesach Seder Plate should be ordered so that the items needed first during the Seder are closest to him.

The Nitziv ponders the question of how this answer fully answers our question since it seems like two classes of people are being addressed. Even though one can fulfill the Mitzvah in either order, it seems that to the class of people addressed in Shemos (12:7), it is preferable if they first put the blood on the doorposts and then on the lintel. To the class of people addressed, in our Posuk, it is preferable if they first put the blood on the lintel and then on the doorposts.

2) The Kli Yakor also presents an answer to our question. He says that we must realize that our Posuk is quoting how Moshe told over the details of the commandment about the Korban Pesach to the Bnei Yisroel, which the previous Posuk in Shemos (12:7) is quoting how Hashem told over the commandment to Moshe. Malachi (3:7) says, לְמִימֵי אֲבֹתֵיכֶם סַרְתֶּם מֵחֻקַּי וְלֹא שְׁמַרְתֶּם שׁוּבוּ אֵלַי וְאָשׁוּבָה אֲלֵיכֶם אָמַר ה' צְבָקוֹת (From the days of your fathers you have departed from My laws and have not kept them. 'Return to Me, and I will return to you,' said Hashem of the Lord of Hosts). The Kli Yakor says that the מַשְׁקוֹף (lintel), the top most part of a doorway, is symbolic of Hashem who is above all. As proof of this Tehillim (102:20) says, כִּי הִשְׁקִיף מִמְּרוֹם קָדְשׁוֹ ה' מִשָּׁמַיִם אֶל אֶרֶץ הִבִּיט (For He has looked down from His holy height; Hashem looked from heaven to earth). The word for looking down in this Posuk is the same word as מַשְׁקוֹף (lintel). The two doorposts are symbolic of our forefathers and foremothers in whose merit we all are dependent. Hashem wanted to give honor to our forefathers and foremothers, and that is why the first Posuk in Shemos (12:7), which is quoting Hashem commanding Moshe how to do the sprinkling, begins with sprinkling the blood on the doorpost (symbolic of forefathers and foremothers) and subsequently commands to sprinkle

Bo

blood on the lintel (symbolic of Hashem). The Tzror HaMor, as quoted by the Tzedah LeDerech, answers similarly to the Kli Yakor, except that he says the two doorposts are symbolic of Moshe and Aharon. Hashem wanted to give honor to Moshe and Aharon as the primary causes of the redemption from Egypt, while Moshe properly gave honor to Hashem as the primary cause of the redemption from Egypt.

This concept of the Kli Yakor is similar to something the Kedushas Levi says. The Sefer has a section with explanations of the Zechiros (remembrances) that the Torah tells us to remember. In the Zechira of going out of Egypt, he ponders the question of why we call the holiday of Pesach, Pesach, while the Torah, in general, refers to it as the Chag HaMatzos (Holiday of Matzos). For example, Shemos (23:15) says, אֶת חַג הַמַּצּוֹת תִּשְׁמֹר (You shall observe the festival of Matzos). Vayikra (23:5-6) says, בַּחֹדֶשׁ הָרִאשׁוֹן בְּאַרְבָּעָה עָשָׂר לַחֹדֶשׁ בֵּין הָעַרְבָּיִם פֶּסַח לַה'. וּבַחֲמִשָּׁה עָשָׂר יוֹם לַחֹדֶשׁ הַזֶּה חַג הַמַּצּוֹת לַה' שִׁבְעַת יָמִים מַצּוֹת תֹּאכֵלוּ (In the first month, on the fourteenth of the month, in the afternoon, you shall sacrifice the Korban Pesach to Hashem. And on the fifteenth day of that month is the Festival of Matzos to Hashem; you shall eat Matzos for a seven-day period.). Even when the Torah does mention the word Pesach, it is mentioned in reference to the Korban Pesach.

The Kedushas Levi explains that Pesach refers to the miracle Hashem did for the Bnei Yisroel to redeem us from Egypt. Shemos (12:23) describes this when it says, "Hashem will pass to smite the Egyptians, and He will see the blood on the lintel and on the two doorposts, and Hashem will pass over the entrance, and He will not permit the destroyer to enter your houses to smite you." Chag HaMatzos refers to what the Bnei Yisroel did as Shemos (12:39) says, "They (Bnei Yisroel) baked the dough that they had taken out of Egypt as unleavened cakes, for it had not leavened, for they were driven out of Egypt, and they could not tarry, and also, they had not made provisions for themselves." Sefer Yirmiyahu (2:2) underscore how Hashem appreciated the Bnei Yisroel going out of Egypt to the desert without any provisions when Yirmiyahu prophesizes: "Go and call out in the ears of Yerushalayim, saying: so said Hashem: I remember to you the lovingkindness of your youth, the love of your nuptials, your following Me in the desert, in a land not sown." Therefore, we refer to Pesach as Pesach to recognize the great miracle Hashem did for us when Hashem took us out of Egypt, while Hashem refers to Pesach as Chag HaMatzos to recognize the great faith we had in Hashem when Hashem took us out of Egypt. We also see with the Tefillin of Hashem how Hashem praises himself with the Bnei Yisroel. The Gemorah in Brochos 6a tells us that in Hashem's Tefillin are Pesukim which praise the Bnei Yisroel. An example of one Posuk is Divrei HaYomim I (17:21) which says, וּמִי כְּעַמְּךָ יִשְׂרָאֵל גּוֹי אֶחָד בָּאָרֶץ אֲשֶׁר הָלַךְ הָאֱלֹקִים לִפְדּוֹת לוֹ עָם לָשׂוּם לְךָ שֵׁם גְּדֻלּוֹת וְנֹרָאוֹת לְגָרֵשׁ מִפְּנֵי עַמְּךָ אֲשֶׁר פָּדִיתָ מִמִּצְרַיִם גּוֹיִם (And who is like Your people Yisroel, one nation in the world, whom G-d went to redeem for Himself as a people, to make You a name of great and fearful things, to drive nations from before Your people, whom You redeemed from Egypt). Another example is Devorim (26:19) which says, "and to make you (Bnei Yisroel) supreme, above all the nations that He made, so that you will have praise, a distinguished name, and glory; and so that you will be a holy people to Hashem, your G-d, as He spoke.

3) The Kli Yakor presents another answer to our question. Rashi on Shir HaShirim (7:2) points out that from the Pesukim in Shir HaShirim, we see the Bnei Yisroel praise Hashem from the top of the

Bo

"body" to the bottom while Hashem praises us from the bottom of the body to the top. Shir HaShirim (5:11-15), in describing Hashem say, "His head is as the finest gold; his locks are curled, they are as black as a raven. His eyes are like doves beside rivulets of water, bathing in milk, fitly set. His jaws are like a bed of spice, growths of aromatic plants; his lips are like roses, dripping with flowing myrrh. His hands are like wheels of gold, set with beryl; his abdomen is as a block of ivory, overlaid with sapphires. His legs are as pillars of marble, founded upon sockets of fine gold; his appearance is like the Lebanon, chosen as the cedars." Shir HaShirim (7:2-6), in describing the Bnei Yisroel say, "How fair are your feet in sandals, O daughter of nobles! The curves of your thighs are like jewels, the handiwork of a craftsman. Your navel is like a round basin, where no mixed wine is lacking; your belly is like a stack of wheat, fenced in with roses. Your two breasts are like two fawns, the twins of a gazelle. Your neck is like an ivory tower; your eyes are like pools in Cheshbon, by the gate of Bas-Rabbim; your face is as the tower of Lebanon, facing towards Damascus. Your head upon you is like Carmel, and the braided locks of your head are like purple; the king is bound in the tresses." Rashi explains that the reason for this difference in description is that we want to draw Hashem down to us while Hashem wants to draw us up to Hashem.

Following the observation presented in Rashi, the Kli Yakor says that when Hashem is describing what the Bnei Yisroel should do, Hashem starts from the bottom (doorposts) and goes to the top (lintel) so that we will be drawn up to Hashem. In our Posuk, when Moshe is describing how we should serve Hashem, Moshe starts the description from the top (lintel) and goes downward to the doorposts so that we will try and draw Hashem down to us.

4) The Alshich also ponders our question. He makes the observation that in our Posuk, we are told how to sprinkle the blood when the Torah says, "And you shall take a bunch of hyssop." In the previous Shemos (12:7), no mention at all is made about using a "bunch of hyssop" or anything else to sprinkle the blood. Rashi quoting the Gemorah in Sukkah 13a, says that because the Torah describes the hyssop as a bunch, it means that there should be three hyssop stalks tied together. We have previously mentioned that the Shemos Raba (17:3) says the reason for putting blood on the lintel was to invoke the merit of Avrohom, while the blood on the two doorposts was to invoke the merits of Yitzchak and Yaakov. The Alshich says that Moshe calculated that the reason why in Shemos (12:7), Hashem said to first put the blood on the doorposts and then on the lintel was because the Bnei Yisroel did not have sufficient merit they had to gradually go from bottom to top. That being the case, Moshe devised a way, and Hashem agreed with it, for the Bnei Yisroel to reach having our all three forefathers together by taking three hyssop branches tied together. Using the hyssop branches, Moshe told the Bnei Yisroel that they could immediately sprinkle on the lintel since they already had the merit of all three forefathers.

5) The grandson of the Nodeh BeYehuda, in his Sefer Yad HaMelech, and quoted in the Nodeh BeYehuda on the Torah, also ponders our question. He points out that there is another difference between our Posuk and Shemos (12:7). Our Posuk says that when taking the blood, "you shall extend or reach it to the lintel and to the two doorposts." Shemos (12:7) says to, "put it on the two doorposts and on the lintel."

Bo

Shulchan Aruch, Orach Chaim (42:1) paskins that it is forbidden to change either the Tefillin themselves or the Retzuos (straps) of the head Tefillin to that of the hand Tefillin. The Shulchan Aruch writes the reason for this is because the head Tefillin has a higher degree of holiness than the hand Tefillin and it is forbidden to change something used for a higher degree of holiness to a lower degree of holiness. The Shulchan Aruch quoting the opinion of Rashi, says that the head Tefillin is holier because it contains both the Shin and Daled of Hashem's name Shakai while the hand Tefillin only contains the Yud. The Yad HaMelech quotes Tosfos in Megilah 26b, who says that the head Tefillin is holier since they are on top of the head and visible to everyone while the hand Tefillin (at least its box) is not visible to everyone. The reason it matters in holiness whether the Tefillin is visible to everyone is that Tefillin are called a sign by the Torah. The Yad LeMelech extends this concept of Tosfos to say that when one has two objects which are a sign for something, the higher one has more holiness.

We have previously mentioned that Shemos (12:13) says, "And the blood will be for you for a sign upon the houses where you will be, and I will see the blood and skip over you." The Yad HaMelech says that since it is a sign, similar to what Tefillin are, the rule that the higher object has more holiness would apply. Therefore, the lintel would have more holiness than the doorposts. Since Hashem said the blood should be applied by putting, one would be forced to first put the blood on the doorposts before putting the blood on the lintel. If one put the blood on the lintel, the finger or hyssop grass that applied the blood would have a bit of blood on it that touched the lintel and went back on the finger or hyssop. Since this blood had touched the holier lintel, it would be improper for the bit of blood to be applied to the less holy doorposts. Therefore. Hashem said to first put the blood on the less holy doorposts and then on the more hold lintel. It is permitted to apply the blood by either putting or sprinkling it. Moshe told this to the Bnei Yisroel, but the part that the Torah quotes is Moshe telling the Bnei Yisroel one can sprinkle the blood. When one sprinkles blood, the hyssop is at a distance from the object being sprinkled, and the blood is flung at the object. That being the case, one should first sprinkle the holier lintel since when one next sprinkles the doorposts, none of the blood in the second sprinkle would have first touched the lintel.

6) The Meshech Chochmah presents an answer to our question. Shemos (12:13) says, וְהָיָה הַדָּם לָכֶם לְאֹת עַל הַבָּתִּים אֲשֶׁר אַתֶּם שָׁם וְרָאִיתִי אֶת הַדָּם וּפָסַחְתִּי עֲלֵכֶם (And the blood will be for you for a sign upon the houses where you will be, and I will see the blood and skip over you). He points out that the Targum Yonason ben Uziel translates this Posuk as "the blood of the Korban Pesach and the blood of the Bris Milah mixed together should be for you a sign upon the houses where you will be, and I will see the blood which will be a merit for you and skip over you." The Targum Yonason ben Uziel on our Posuk says that the blood was put into an earthenware vessel. The Meshech Chochmah says that using a bunch of hyssop and an earthenware vessel to put blood on a house is similar to the procedure done on a house with leprosy when it meets the condition to be purified from its leprosy as outlined in Vayikra (14:48-53). Purifying a house from leprosy is the same as purifying a house from idol worship. Two Pesukim previous to our Posuk, Shemos (12:21) says, מִשְׁכוּ וּקְחוּ לָכֶם צֹאן לְמִשְׁפְּחֹתֵיכֶם וְשַׁחֲטוּ הַפָּסַח (Draw forth and acquire for yourselves sheep for your families and slaughter the Korban Pesach). The Mechilta ponders why the seemingly superfluous word מִשְׁכוּ (draw forth) was needed. It says the Bnei Yisroel served idols, and before they could take the Korban Pesach,

Bo

they needed to draw their hand away from serving idols and only serve Hashem. Purification from idol worship is why the house in Egypt needed blood put on its lintel and doorposts. We note that the Zohar in Shemos (35b) also says that the reason for the blood was to purify the houses from idol worship.

In addition to having been idol worshippers, the Bnei Yisroel had also stopped giving themselves a Bris Milah. The Yalkut Shimoni (268) at the end of Parshas Beshalach tells us the Bnei Yisroel had one main Mitzvah, doing a Bris Milah, which they kept in Egypt being that it had been given to and handed down from Avrohom. The Egyptians, seeing it was their main Mitzvah, went to the Bnei Yisroel and told them to give up the Mitzvah of Bris Milah, thereby becoming similar to the Egyptians, and as a reward, the Egyptians promised to make the slavery work lighter. Over time the Bnei Yisroel, except for the tribe of Levi, stopped giving their sons a Bris Milah.

The Shemos Raba (17:3) says the reason for putting blood on the lintel was to invoke the merit of Avrohom, while the blood on the two doorposts was to invoke the merits of Yitzchak and Yaakov. The Shemos Raba (1:35) says that the lintel invoked Avrohom because our forefathers Avrohom was the greatest in converts and because Avrohom was the greatest of the forefathers. The Eitz Yosef explains that Avrohom was the first and greatest to convert to Judaism. The Bnei Yisroel in Egypt were similar to a Convert as they were repenting from serving idols and were returning to Judaism. The lintel as the highest part of the doorway, therefore, invoked the merit of Avrohom. The Yedei Moshe says the doorposts invoked the merit of Yitzchak and Yaakov since Yitzchak and Yaakov did not move even a small amount from Hashem, similar to the doorposts which don't move from the door.

Since the Bnei Yisroel had just done their Bris Milah and had just done Teshuva from worshipping idols, the merit of Avrohom, who was the first to get the Mitzvah of Bris Milah and was the epitome of someone who gave up serving idols to serve Hashem, was the main merit that these Bnei Yisroel invoked. Therefore, says the Meshech Chochmah, they first put the blood on the lintel, which we have shown above invoked the merit of Avrohom.

The introduction to Shemos (12:7), which commanded the Bnei Yisroel to first put blood on the doorposts and then on the lintel is found in Shemos (12:3) which says, דַּבְּרוּ אֶל כָּל עֲדַת יִשְׂרָאֵל לֵאמֹר (speak to all the congregation of Yisroel saying). The Mechilta on this Posuk, as explained by the Malbim, says that this was said to the Sanhedrin (Supreme Court) of Elders of the Bnei Yisroel. The Midrash Tanchuma on Vaera (6) says that the tribe of Levi was exempt from the very hard work in Egypt. Based on this, it stands to reason that this Sanhedrim was mainly composed of the tribe of Levi who were not part of the slavery in Egypt and therefore had time to study the Torah. The Sifrei on Devorim (33:9) says that the tribe of Levi kept serving Hashem and did not serve idols in Egypt. We have also mentioned above that the tribe of Levi continued to do the Mitzvah of Bris Milah in Egypt. For them, it was appropriate to first put the blood on the two doorposts, which invoked the merit of Yitzchak and Yaakov, who did not move even a small amount from Hashem similar to the doorposts which don't move from the door.

Bo

7) We can infer an answer to our question from what the Ponim Yofos says. He says the two doorposts are symbolic of the two Beis Hamikdosh, while the lintel is symbolic of the third Beis Hamikdosh, which we pray will speedily be built in our days. The Ohr HaChaim on Bamidbar (20:8) (and in other places in his commentary), which is speaking about Moshe hitting the rock to get water from it, explains why Moshe and Aharon could not live and go into Eretz Yisroel. Had Moshe gone into Eretz Yisroel, he would have built the one and only Beis Hamikdosh, which could never be destroyed. However, Hashem saw the Bnei Yisroel would in the future greatly sin, and it would be to their advantage for Hashem's anger to be taken out on the wood and stone of the Beis Hamikdosh by destroying it as opposed to, Chas VeShalom, destroying the Bnei Yisroel. This explanation explains what Moshe means in Devorim (1:37) when he says, "Hashem was also angry with me because of you, saying, 'Neither will you go there (to Eretz Yisroel).'" Using this Ohr HaChaim, we can explain that by putting the blood first on the two doorposts (first two Beis Hamikdosh) and then on the lintel (third Beis Hamikdosh), Hashem was showing us that we had to purify ourselves by living through the times of the building and destruction of the Beis Hamikdosh to merit having the final Beis Hamikdosh. Moshe and the Bnei Yisroel, at that point, expected to ideally go straight into Eretz Yisroel and build the final Beis Hamikdosh, and therefore Moshe commanded the Bnei Yisroel to first sprinkle the blood on the lintel. Only if this first-choice way would fail would Moshe and the Bnei Yisroel consider the second choice of having a temporary first and second Beis Hamikdosh.

8) The Nitziv also presents an answer to our question. We will choose to slightly modify his answer. We have mentioned previously that the Shemos Raba (17:3) says the reason for putting blood on the lintel was to invoke the merit of Avrohom, while the blood on the two doorposts was to invoke the merits of Yitzchak and Yaakov. The Mishna in Pirkei Avos (1:2) says that the world stands on three pillars: Torah, service of Hashem, and doing kind deeds with one's fellow man. The Mayanah Shel Torah on Beraishis (12:2) quotes the Ohel Torah, who says that each of our forefathers excelled in one of these pillars. The Yalkut Shimoni on Tehillim, Chapter 37, says that when Avrohom met Shem, he asked him what the merit was that Shem and his family were allowed to leave the ark. Shem answered that they did a righteous act by not sleeping at all since they gave each animal its food at the proper time for each. Avrohom was extremely impressed that even doing righteousness for animals was a great merit. He reasoned how much more so is it important to do righteous acts with fellow human beings who are created in the likeness of Hashem. At that point, Avrohom decided to build an Aishel, an inn where people could get food, drink, and rest, so that he could do righteous acts to humans. Thus, Avrohom excelled in doing kind deeds with one's fellow man. Yitzchak excelled in the service of Hashem. Though Yitzchak was 37 years old at the time of the Akeidah, after being told that Hashem wanted him to be a sacrifice, Yitzchak had no issues with giving up his life for the service of Hashem. Beraishis (25:27) describes Yaakov as one who "abided in tents." Rashi quoting from Beraishis Raba (63:10), says that Yaakov spent all day in the study tents. Thus, Yaakov excelled in the pillar of the Torah.

Our Posuk, says the Nitziv, was mainly directed at the elders of the Bnei Yisroel as the previous Posuk to ours says, "Moshe summoned all the elders of Yisroel and said to them." Because Moshe was addressing the elders who had the responsibility to take care of the Bnei Yisroel, Moshe said to

Bo

first put the blood on the lintel to invoke Avrohom's merit. A community leader must be ready to get involved in all types of kind deeds to help and aid their community. Shemos (12:7) addressed the common person. The common person is typically more involved in the Torah and service of Hashem. That is why in Shemos (12:7), the two doorposts (Yitzchak and Yaakov) are to have blood put on them first.

9) Rav Sternbuch, in his Sefer Taam V'Daas, also ponders our question. The Gemorah in Nidah 31a says that there are three partners in the creation of every person, one's mother and father, who supply the body while Hashem supplies the soul, along with eyesight, hearing, facial features, the power of speech, mobility, and intellectual insight. Rav Sternbuch explains that the two doorposts are symbolic of the father and mother of each individual, while the lintel is symbolic of Hashem. He says that especially on Pesach, where we focus on giving Chinuch to the younger generation, it is important to stress that the younger generation must be amenable to getting instruction and guidelines from their three partners. From the perspective of the parents, they must know that they need to do everything in their power, which is symbolized by (giving their) blood, to give Chinuch to the younger generator while not forgetting that they must also serve Hashem and do His Mitzvos. Hashem, in his humility, stressed first putting the blood on the doorposts, meaning to first worry about the Chinuch of one's children and only subsequently worrying about the lintel (serving Hashem). Moshe stressed to first worry about putting the blood on the lintel (serving Hashem) and then worry about giving Chinuch to one's children. He decries those who sent their children to Yeshivos and Kollel without worry about their own Torah learning needs. It is always more effective for the children to see how hard the parents are toiling in their own learning and thereby provide the children with a role model to follow.

10) The Hegyona Shel Torah also presents an answer to our question. He says that the sprinkling of blood served two purposes. The first purpose was to save the inhabitants of the house from dying in the plague of the killing of the firstborn. The second purpose was to remind the inhabitants of the house that it was forbidden for them to leave the house until morning as the end of our Shemos (12:22) Posuk says, "and you shall not go out, any man from the entrance of his house until morning." If the person absent-mindedly tried to walk out the door, the person would see the blood as a reminder. The blood on the doorposts was a reminder for the person walking out of the house. The Gemorah in Kidushin 31a says that a person is forbidden to walk four cubits (Amos) with an erect posture since Sefer Yeshayahu (6:3) (which we say in Kedusha) says, מְלֹא כָל הָאָרֶץ כְּבוֹדוֹ (the whole earth is full of His (Hashem's) glory). The Maharsha explains that walking in such a manner would be a direct contradiction to this Posuk. The person would be figuratively saying that Hashem is not in the four cubits that the person walked, otherwise the person would not show the arrogance to walk with an erect posture in Hashem's presence. Blood on the lintel was the sign to Hashem to save the inhabitants of the house from dying in the plague of the killing of the firstborn. The Gemorah says in Sukkah 5a that Hashem's Shechinah does not descend to below ten hand-breaths from the earth. Since the Gemorah in Yuma 11b says that the minimum dimensions of an entrance are at least ten hand-breaths high and four hand-breaths wide, the lintel will always be higher than ten hand-breaths and in the domain that Hashem's Shechinah rests. Similar to the concept that we have mentioned previously from the Kedushas Levi, the Hegyona Shel Torah says the reason

Bo

Hashem mentioned first putting the blood on the doorposts was to give honor to the Bnei Yisroel by mentioning their sign first. Similarly, Moshe mentioned the sign of the blood on the lintel first to give honor to Hashem.

The Hegyona Shel Torah ponders why a Mezuzah is only placed on one doorpost and not on both doorposts and, for that matter, not on the lintel. Regarding why a Mezuzah is not placed on the lintel, he says that it is a similar reason as to why the blood was placed on the doorposts in Egypt. That is, it is the doorposts and not the lintel where signs are placed for people to see and remember since it is always clearly in their field of vision. In Shulchan Aruch, Yoreh Deah (287:2), the Rema comments that everyone who has a fear of heaven should put a Mezuzah on all one's doors as opposed to only putting a Mezuzah on the main door. The Taz on the Rema's comment says that the Mezuzah protects from bad spiritual winds entering into one's home. With regard to why a Mezuzah is not placed on both doorposts, the Hegyona Shel Torah says that both doorposts signify that a person should not leave the house. It is not recommended and hardy feasible for a person to remain in one's house forever. The Mezuzah is reminding us that when we venture out of our houses to the world at large we must be careful not to bring spiritually damaging winds back into our houses. Shulchan Aruch, Yoreh Deah (286:3) paskins that a Shul, which does not have a place inside it for the Shamash (caretaker) to live in, does not require a Mezuzah. Though most Shuls in our times do have a Mezuzah, this is because the Shuls are not just used for davening but also are used for eating when, for example, a Kiddush is made. The Gemorah says in Kidushin 30b that the strategy to combat the Yetzer Horah is to go to the Shul or Beis Midrash, where the Yetzer Horah stays away from. Therefore, no bad spiritual winds will enter the Shul since the Yetzer Horah says away from the Shul, and hence a Shul does not need a Mezuzah.

11) We can derive another answer to our question from what Rav Yitzchak Sorotzkin says in his Sefer Gevuras Yitzchak. He points out that there were two reasons and, in fact, two placings of blood on the doorposts and lintel. The Mechilta on Shemos (12:7) says that there were three Altars for the blood, the two doorposts and the lintel. That is, the Korban Pesach had a similar Halacha to the Korban Pesach, which was in the future offered every Pesach, in that it was a Korban whose blood was sprinkled on the Mizbeach in the Beis Hamikdosh. In addition, the Pirkei D'Rabi Eliezer (29) says that the Bnei Yisroel took the blood from the Korban Pesach and mixed it with the blood from their Bris Milah, and put this mixture of blood on the lintel. It continues and says that this mixture of blood was a sign for Hashem to have pity and spare the people in that house from dying in the plague of the killing of the firstborn. The first blood, which they used as a Korban whose blood was sprinkled on the Mizbeach, had to be only from the Korban Pesach itself, and the mixture of the two types of blood could not be used for this purpose.

We can apply the above to answer our question since, according to Rav Sorotzkin, there were two separate types of blood placed on the doorpost and lintel. We can say that Shemos (12:7) is referring to the blood of the Korban, and for that blood, it was preferable to sprinkle it first on the doorposts and then on the lintel. The second blood placement, which was from a mixture of blood, was mainly for the lintel, as the Pirkei D'Rabi Eliezer says. That being the case, our Posuk says to first put that blood on the lintel and subsequently on the doorposts.

Bo

Why Does the Torah Add the Words כֵּן עָשׂוּ (So They Did), a Seemingly Superfluous Phrase?

וַיֵּלְכוּ וַיַּעֲשׂוּ בְּנֵי יִשְׂרָאֵל כַּאֲשֶׁר צִוָּה ה' אֶת מֹשֶׁה וְאַהֲרֹן כֵּן עָשׂוּ (יב:כח) Shemos (12:28) So the Bnei Yisroel went and did; as Hashem commanded Moshe and Aharon, so they did.

Why does the Torah add the words כֵּן עָשׂוּ (so they did)?

Introduction
Rashi on our Posuk says that our Posuk is describing what happened on Rosh Chodesh Nisan. Given that it was still ten days before the Bnei Yisroel had to actually begin doing this Mitzvah of bringing a Korban Pesach, it is strange that our Posuk says, "So the Bnei Yisroel went and did," when they hadn't yet done the Mitzvah. Rashi quoting the Mechilta on our Posuk, says that the Bnei Yisroel immediately decided on Rosh Chodesh Nisan that they would do the Mitzvah in its proper time, and with this acceptance, Hashem already considered it as if they had already done the Mitzvah. The Midrash Lekach Tov quotes a Posuk from Daniyel to prove this concept. Daniyel (10:12) says, "for, since the first day that you (Daniyel) set your heart to contemplate and to fast before your G-d, your words were heard, and I (the angel saying the prophecy) have come because of your words." Rav Simcha Zissel Ziv from Kelm, in his Sefer Ohr Rav Simcha Zissel, points out that once they accepted to do the Mitzvah, they received a reward every second for doing the Mitzvah of Korban Pesach. This adds up to many times the reward they also received when they actually did the Mitzvah. We can apply this rule to doing all Mitzvos, meaning that once we accept and prepare ourselves to do a Mitzvah, we can get many times the reward that one gets for just doing a Mitzvah.

The Maskil LeDovid points out that at the end of our topic Shemos (12:50) the Torah says, וַיַּעֲשׂוּ כָּל בְּנֵי יִשְׂרָאֵל כַּאֲשֶׁר צִוָּה ה' אֶת מֹשֶׁה וְאֶת אַהֲרֹן כֵּן עָשׂוּ (All the Bnei Yisroel did; as Hashem had commanded Moshe and Aharon, so they did.). This is almost a complete repetition of our Posuk. The Maskil LeDovid says that since that Posuk is at the end of the topic, it is speaking about the actual doing of the Korban Pesach while our Posuk is speaking about when the Bnei Yisroel heard about and accepted to do the Mitzvah. Parenthetically the Nitziv points out that Shemos (12:50) says, "All the Bnei Yisroel did," while out Posuk says, "The Bnei Yisroel did." Since a whole group of people could get together and eat one Korban Pesach, it implies not every single person had to be involved with all the preparations of the Korban Pesach. However, when it came to eating, every person had to eat, so that Shemos (12:50), which is speaking about the actual doing, tells us that at least with respect to eating "All the Bnei Yisroel" ate the Korban Pesach.

The Oznayim LeTorah says that even on Rosh Chodesh Nisan, the Bnei Yisroel did something. A few Pesukim earlier, Shemos (12:21) says מִשְׁכוּ וּקְחוּ לָכֶם צֹאן לְמִשְׁפְּחֹתֵיכֶם וְשַׁחֲטוּ הַפָּסַח (Draw forth and take for yourselves sheep for your families and slaughter the Passover sacrifice). The Mechilta quotes Rav Yossi HaGlili, who says that "drawing forth" means to draw forth themselves from serving idols and instead start clinging to Mitzvos. The Zohar in Parshas Terumah 170b says that when the Bnei Yisroel came to the Red Sea, Hashem wanted to split the sea. The angel who is in charge of Egypt, called Rahav, came and asked for justice. Rahav said, "Master of the World, why

Bo

do you want to punish the Egyptians and split the sea for the Bnei Yisroel." Among the arguments Rahav made was just like the Egyptians serve idols; also, the Bnei Yisroel serve idols. Based on the above, the Oznayim LeTorah says that the Bnei Yisroel indeed did do something on Rosh Chodesh Nisan, and that was they did Teshuva from serving idols. We note that not all Meforshim agree that our Posuk is describing what occurred on Rosh Chodesh Nisan. The Eben Ezra and Ramban both say that our Posuk is describing what occurred on the tenth of Nisan.

Rashi also quotes the Mechilta, which says our Posuk says that the Bnei Yisroel "went and did" because the Bnei Yisroel were given reward for all the walking needed to do for the Mitzvah in addition to the reward for doing the Mitzvah. The Malbim on the first Posuk and Sifrah in Vayikra explains that normally when the Torah describes two actions taken by one person or group, the Torah puts the person or group's name between the two actions. For example, Beraishis (12:7) says וַיֵּרָא ה' אֶל אַבְרָם וַיֹּאמֶר (And Hashem appeared to Avram, and Hashem said). Beraishis (18:23) says, וַיִּגַּשׁ אַבְרָהָם וַיֹּאמַר (And Avraham approached and he said). Beraishis (21:8) says, וַיִּגְדַּל הַיֶּלֶד וַיִּגָּמַל (And the child (Yitzchak) grew and was weaned). Beraishis (29:32) says, וַתַּהַר לֵאָה וַתֵּלֶד בֵּן (And Leah conceived and bore a son). The Malbim says there are many more examples. According to this general rule, our Posuk should have said וַיֵּלְכוּ בְּנֵי יִשְׂרָאֵל וַיַּעֲשׂוּ instead of וַיֵּלְכוּ וַיַּעֲשׂוּ בְּנֵי יִשְׂרָאֵל. Our Posuk uses this strange phraseology to compare the "going and doing" and derive that they both came with a reward. The Meam Loez explains that the payment of a reward for going, which is termed the "reward of steps," is true for all Mitzvos. He says that one cannot compare the reward one receives for doing a Mitzvah in the comfort of one's home to someone who has to travel long distances in difficult conditions to do a Mitzvah.

1) It is unclear from the Posuk whether the words כֵּן עָשׂוּ (so they did) is referring to the Bnei Yisroel or is referring to Moshe and Aharon. We will first consider the answers to our question if כֵּן עָשׂוּ (so they did) refers to the Bnei Yisroel. The Mechilta, which is the source for both Rashi and the Ramban's answer to our question, says that by adding the words כֵּן עָשׂוּ, the Torah is praising the Bnei Yisroel for doing all the details that Moshe and Aharon had commanded them to do for this Mitzvah. The Ramban explains that in general, when the Torah adds the words כֵּן עָשׂוּ (so they did), it means that they did everything they were commanded to do. Examples of this are found in Beraishis (6:22) which says, וַיַּעַשׂ נֹחַ כְּכֹל אֲשֶׁר צִוָּה אֹתוֹ אֱלֹקִים כֵּן עָשָׂה (And Noah did; according to all that G-d had commanded him, so he did.) and in Shemos (39:43) וַיַּרְא מֹשֶׁה אֶת כָּל הַמְּלָאכָה וְהִנֵּה עָשׂוּ אֹתָהּ כַּאֲשֶׁר צִוָּה ה' כֵּן עָשׂוּ (Moshe saw the entire work, and lo! they had done it as Hashem had commanded, so had they done.).

Rav Chavel, in his commentary on the Ramban, and the Ksav Sofer, explain why the Bnei Yisroel are praised for doing all the details of this Mitzvah. We have explained in the introduction that the Bnei Yisroel were serving idols in Egypt. Therefore, they say it is extremely praiseworthy that even though the Bnei Yisroel served idols and despite the fact that it was hard for the Bnei Yisroel to give up serving idols, nonetheless, the Bnei Yisroel immediately listened and accepted to slaughter the sheep, which was their main idol. Moreover, says the Ksav Sofer, the Bnei Yisroel accepted to do this Mitzvah with a full heart and complete happiness with no longer any thoughts entering their minds about serving idols.

Bo

2) The Baal HaTurim also presents an answer to our question. The Yalkut Shimoni (268) at the end of Parshas Beshalach tells us that the Bnei Yisroel had one main Mitzvah, doing a Bris Milah, which they kept in Egypt being that it had been given to and handed down from Avrohom. The Egyptians, seeing that it was their main Mitzvah, went to the Bnei Yisroel and told them to give up the Mitzvah of Bris Milah, thereby becoming similar to the Egyptians, and as a reward, the Egyptians promised to make the slavery work lighter. Over time the Bnei Yisroel, except for the tribe of Levi, stopped giving their sons a Bris Milah. The Baal HaTurim says that the extra words כֵּן עָשׂוּ (so they did) is added in, to hint to us about another Mitzvah the Bnei Yisroel did. Not only did they do the Mitzvah of Korban Pesach, but they also did the Mitzvah of Bris Milah, especially since only those who had a Bris Milah were allowed to eat from the Korban Pesach.

The Shach says that there is a connection between the Mitzvah of Korban Peach and Bris Milah. If one spells out the Hebrew letters into the words that make up their pronunciation, the Hebrew word for Pesach (פסח) is פה סמך חת whose numerical value adds up to 613. 613 is the number of Mitzvos in the Torah which alludes to the fact that one who does the Mitzvah of Korban Pesach properly is considered as if he had done all 613 Mitzvos of the Torah. The Gemorah in Nedorim 32a says that the Mitzvah of Bris Milah is as important as all the rest of the Mitzvos. The Kli Yakor, in his Sefer Ollelos Ephraim (Section 3-Parshas Mishpotim), writes a beautiful hint to this statement of the Gemorah. Bris Milah is many times shortened to one word Bris since it is the main Bris (covenant) between Hashem and the Jewish people. The numerical value of Bris (ברית) is 612. Since there are in total 613 Mitzvos, the one Mitzvah of Bris (Milah) is equal to the other 612 Mitzvos.

3) The Abarbanel also ponders our question. He points out that a few Pesukim earlier, Shemos (12:21) tells us, וַיִּקְרָא מֹשֶׁה לְכָל זִקְנֵי יִשְׂרָאֵל וַיֹּאמֶר אֲלֵהֶם מִשְׁכוּ וּקְחוּ לָכֶם צֹאן לְמִשְׁפְּחֹתֵיכֶם וְשַׁחֲטוּ הַפָּסַח (Moshe summoned all the elders of Yisroel and said to them, "Draw forth and take for yourselves sheep for your families and slaughter the Korban Pesach."). The Abarbanel ponders why Moshe called only the elders of the Bnei Yisroel and not all the Bnei Yisroel. He explains that Moshe felt that the Mitzvah of Korban Pesach, where the Bnei Yisroel slaughtered the idol of the Egyptians which the Bnei Yisroel had also been serving, would be difficult for the Bnei Yisroel to do. In addition, Moshe felt the Bnei Yisroel would be afraid of the reaction of the Egyptians when they saw them taking their idols for slaughter. Therefore, Moshe called the elders and told them to serve as examples for the Bnei Yisroel by being the first to start making the preparations for slaughtering the Korban Pesach on the tenth of Nisan. Seeing that the elders had been called, the Bnei Yisroel also came and overheard Moshe telling this to the elders. Like the Eben Ezra and Ramban we have mentioned in the introduction, the Abarbanel also is of the opinion that our Posuk described what happened on the tenth of Nisan. Our Posuk, when it adds in the words כֵּן עָשׂוּ (so they did), tells us that the Bnei Yisroel did not wait for the elders to serve as examples, but they immediately went and also started the preparations for doing the Korban Pesach.

4) The Ksav Sofer also presents an answer to our question. He points out that this was the first Mitzvah which the Bnei Yisroel had ever received from Moshe and Aharon for them to do. That being the case, the Bnei Yisroel had to first believe the Mitzvah Moshe and Aharon had told them

Bo

was from Hashem, actually came from Hashem and was not, Chas VeShalom, invented by Moshe and Aharon. The words in our Posuk, "as Hashem commanded Moshe and Aharon, so they did" means the Bnei Yisroel first accepted that the words came from Hashem and continued to accept this from Rosh Chodesh Nisan until it was time to start preparing the Korban Pesach without any second thoughts on the matter. More specifically, the words כֵּן עָשׂוּ (so they did) implies that they continuously accepted the Mitzvah came from Hashem during this entire time period from hearing the Mitzvah until doing it.

5) The Ksav Sofer presents another answer to our question. He says the Bnei Yisroel were so excited to do the Mitzvah that each reminded his friend to do the Mitzvah. The phrase in our Posuk, which says, "as Hashem commanded Moshe and Aharon, so they did," means the Bnei Yisroel took on the role of Moshe and Aharon, whose jobs it was to remind the Bnei Yisroel, by reminding each other to do the Mitzvah.

6) The Oznayim LeTorah also presents an answer to our question. He says the Bnei Yisroel could have done this Mitzvah of bringing a Korban Pesach because it would lead to their redemption from Egypt, a selfish and self-centered reason. However, our Posuk tells us the Bnei Yisroel did the Mitzvah of Korban Pesach altruistically only because "Hashem commanded Moshe and Aharon." The Ohr HaChaim also says the Bnei Yisroel did this Mitzvah completely altruistically.

7) The Mechilta on our Posuk also tells us that the phrase כֵּן עָשׂוּ (so they did) can be referring to Moshe and Aharon. If we accept this opinion, we must answer the question of why one would think Moshe and Aharon would not fulfill the Mitzvah. The Meam Loez, Malbim, and Rav Shavel on the Ramban all explain the reason for doing the Mitzvah of Korban Pesach was to erase all thoughts of idol worship from the hearts of the Bnei Yisroel, who we have mentioned previously were ingrained in serving idols. Taking the main Egyptian idol, the sheep, and using it instead for serving HaKodosh Baruch Hu, involved risking their lives to do so since it could be expected the Egyptians would vigorously protest. Taking this risk was the reason for Korban Pesach. Given that Moshe and Aharon had never, Chas VeShalom, served idols, at first glance, it would seem that they had no need to do the Mitzvah of Korban Pesach. Nonetheless, Moshe and Aharon did the Mitzvah of Korban Pesach to at least allow themselves to take part in sanctifying Hashem in front of the Egyptians by risking their lives in bringing the Korban Pesach. In addition, says Rav Chavel, Moshe and Aharon did the Mitzvah solely because they wanted to do the Mitzvah of Hashem without any reason.

8) The Taz, in his Sefer Divrei Dovid, and the Torah Temimah answer our question similarly. The Midrash Tanchuma on Vaera (6) says that the tribe of Levi was exempt from the very hard work in Egypt. Since Moshe and Aharon were members of the tribe of Levi, they were not enslaved, and they did not need to be redeemed from Egypt. Nonetheless, since Korban Pesach was a Mitzvah from Hashem, Moshe and Aharon did the Mitzvah with the intention of fulfilling a Mitzvah of Hashem. The Nachalas Yaakov is not happy with this explanation since it would equally apply to all of the tribe of Levi, being that they also did not need to be redeemed from Egypt. Therefore, if

Bo

this answer was correct, says the Nachalas Yaakov, the Torah should have said even all the members of the tribe of Levi did this Mitzvah.

9) The Mizrachi, Maharal in Gur Aryeh, and the Maskil LeDovid answer our question similarly. They say that the purpose of doing the Mitzvah of Korban Pesach was to give the Bnei Yisroel the merit to be redeemed from Egypt. Having been chosen as redeemers points out the Maharal; obviously, Moshe and Aharon had the merit to be redeemed from Egypt. In addition, says the Maskil LeDovid, Moshe and Aharon had many Mitzvos since they got all the Mitzvos of helping others do Mitzvos, like this Mitzvah, to their credit. Nonetheless, since Korban Pesach was a Mitzvah from Hashem, Moshe and Aharon did the Mitzvah with the pure intention of fulfilling a Mitzvah of Hashem.

The Nachalas Yaakov answers our question in a similar way. The Mechilta on Shemos (12:6) is the source of Rashi's explanation as to why the Bnei Yisroel in Egypt had to take the Korban Pesach on the tenth of Nisan, four days before slaughtering it on the 14th of Nisan. The Mechilta quotes Sefer Yechezkel (16:8) which says, וָאֶעֱבֹר עָלַיִךְ וָאֶרְאֵךְ וְהִנֵּה עִתֵּךְ עֵת דֹּדִים וָאֶפְרֹשׂ כְּנָפִי עָלַיִךְ וָאֲכַסֶּה עֶרְוָתֵךְ (And I passed by you and saw you, and behold your time was the time of love, and I spread My wings over you, and I covered your nakedness). The Mechilta explains the time had come to fulfill the oath which Hashem swore to Avrohom to redeem his children. However, the previous Posuk says וְאַתְּ עֵרֹם וְעֶרְיָה (you were naked and bare), which means that we were naked and bare of Mitzvos and merits. Therefore, Hashem gave us two Mitzvos which involved blood (the blood of Korban Pesach and the blood of Bris Milah). In addition, Hashem gave us the Mitzvah of taking the Korban Pesach four days earlier, on the tenth of Nisan, so that we could have the extra Mitzvah of protecting the Korban Pesach from getting a blemish for these four days. The Nachalas Yaakov says that I would have thought that since Moshe and Aharon had other Mitzvos to their credit, they would not need the Mitzvah of watching the Korban Pesach for these four days. Nonetheless, since all aspects of the Mitzvah of Korban Pesach was a Mitzvah from Hashem, Moshe and Aharon did all facets of the Mitzvah. The Chasam Sofer take this idea a step further. He says that it was an embarrassment for Moshe and Aharon to take the Korban Pesach on the tenth of the month since, unlike the Bnei Yisroel, they were not bereft of Mitzvos. By our Posuk saying כֵּן עָשׂוּ (so they did), we are told that despite the perceived embarrassment, Moshe and Aharon also took their Korban Pesach on the tenth of the month. To explain why Moshe and Aharon did this, he quotes Ezra (10:2) which says, וַיַּעַן שְׁכַנְיָה בֶן יְחִיאֵל מִבְּנֵי עֵילָם וַיֹּאמֶר לְעֶזְרָא אֲנַחְנוּ מָעַלְנוּ בֵאלֹקֵינוּ וַנֹּשֶׁב נָשִׁים נָכְרִיּוֹת מֵעַמֵּי הָאָרֶץ (And Shechaniah, the son of Yechiel, of the sons of Eylam, raised his voice and said to Ezra, "We have betrayed our G-d, and we have taken in foreign wives of the peoples of the land). The Malbim on the Posuk explains that relative to the total amount of people, the number of people who had taken foreign (non-Jewish) wives was very small. However, since they had taken foreign wives publicly without the protest of the leaders, the sin was considered a community sin. In a similar way, Moshe and Aharon included themselves in the lack of merits of the people of their generation, and therefore they also took the Korban Pesach from the tenth of the month.

10) The Chasam Sofer also presents another answer to our question. He quotes Tehillim (119:14) which says, בְּדֶרֶךְ עֵדְוֹתֶיךָ שַׂשְׂתִּי כְּעַל כָּל הוֹן (With the way of Your testimonies I rejoiced as over all

Bo

riches). The Chasam Sofer explains that with Mitzvos, which are testimony to the miracles Hashem performed for us, like eating the Korban Pesach, eating Matzah, etc., one is happy when one does them since it reminds us Hashem did these miracles for us. Therefore, the Bnei Yisroel accepted and did the Mitzvah of Korban Pesach with much joy and enthusiasm. Moshe and Aharon realized that they would never merit to do the Mitzvah of Korban Pesach nor any other Mitzvah whose main time to perform it would only occur after the Bnei Yisroel entered Eretz Yisroel. One would never think that Moshe and Aharon would not do the Mitzvah of Korban Pesach, but one might think that their enthusiasm for this Mitzvah would not be as great as the rest of the Bnei Yisroel. Therefore our Posuk says כֵּן עָשׂוּ (so they did) to tell us that Moshe and Aharon accepted and did this Mitzvah with the same enthusiasm and happiness as all the rest of the Bnei Yisroel.

11) The Ksav Sofer and Nitziv answer our question similarly. The Ksav Sofer says that obviously eating the Korban Pesach is not something another person can do, but buying the sheep from the marketplace and all the preparations can be done by someone else. From the perspective of Moshe and Aharon as leaders, one could have thought that they might have gotten one of their servants to do all the preparations. As the Nitziv says, we might have thought they might have held themselves as too dignified to do the preparations themselves. However, our Posuk tells us that Moshe and Aharon did all the preparations and buying themselves so that they could participate in all facets of the Mitzvah. In general, one must remember for all Mitzvos that cleaning out the Menorah each day was a Mitzvah, and one should not cavalierly think that it is below one's dignity to do this. This was the lesson Moshe and Aharon taught us at the first Mitzvah of Korban Pesach.

12) The Ksav Sofer presents another answer to the question of what our Posuk is teaching us by saying that כֵּן עָשׂוּ (so they did) refers to Moshe and Aharon. The Mishna in Pirkei Avos (5:18) says מֹשֶׁה זָכָה וְזִכָּה אֶת הָרַבִּים זְכוּת הָרַבִּים תָּלוּי בּוֹ (Moshe was meritorious and caused the community to be meritorious, so the community's merit is attributed to him). By the Mitzvah of Korban Pesach, Moshe and Aharon caused the entire Bnei Yisroel to be meritorious and do the Mitzvah of Korban Pesach. Therefore, says the Ksav Sofer, כֵּן עָשׂוּ (so they did) referring to Moshe and Aharon means Moshe and Aharon got merit as if they did all the Korban Pesachim of each of the Bnei Yisroel.

13) The Maor VaShemesh also ponders the question of how כֵּן עָשׂוּ (so they did) refers to Moshe and Aharon. Shemos (12:23) says, "Hashem will pass to smite the Egyptians, and He will see the blood on the lintel and on the two doorposts, and Hashem will pass over the entrance, and He will not permit the destroyer to enter your houses to smite you." This very much sounds like the Torah telling us the purpose of bringing the Korban Pesach is as protection from the destroyer. One might have thought Moshe and Aharon did not need this protection and therefore did not do the Mitzvah of Korban Pesach. Rather כֵּן עָשׂוּ (so they did) tells us that Moshe and Aharon did the Mitzvah for the only reason of it being a Mitzvah from Hashem and did not consider the selfish reason of protection from the destroyer.

14) Rav Sternbuch, in his Sefer Taam V'Daas, also presents an answer to our question. He says the main purpose of the Mitzvah of Korban Pesach was to implant faith in Hashem that Hashem would make a miracle and prevent the Egyptians from protesting against the Bnei Yisroel slaughtering their

Bo

idol, the sheep. Moshe and Aharon were on such a lofty level that they saw Hashem's miraculous hand in everything happening in nature and this belief was already firmly implanted in them. Therefore, one would have thought that Moshe and Aharon would not need to do the Mitzvah of Korban Pesach. Rather כֵּן עָשׂוּ (so they did) tells us that Moshe and Aharon did the Mitzvah since they wanted to do a Mitzvah of Hashem, irrespective of the reason for the Mitzvah. Rav Moshe Feinstein, in his Sefer Dorash Moshe, says a similar answer to that of Rav Sternbuch.

15) Rav Chaim Kanievsky, in his Sefer Taamah D'Krah, also offers an answer to our question. The Gemorah in Pesachim 91a says that we do not shecht a Korban Pesach for only old people because we are afraid that they will be too weak to eat the Korban Pesach and it will be under the prohibition of Nosar (leftover after the valid time to eat it). Our Posuk tells us that Moshe and Aharon made their own Korban Pesach despite the fact that they were 83 and 80 years old, respectively. They weren't afraid because both of them were prophets and the Gemorah in Nedorim 38a says that Hashem only rests his prophetic spirit on someone who is mighty, wealthy, wise, and humble. A might person does not have to worry about this issue. Though Moshe's wife and sons were still in Midyan, I am not sure, according to this answer, why Aharon did not include his four sons and his wife on the Korban Pesach.

Why Is the Donkey the Only Non-Kosher Animal That Needs to Be Redeemed?

וְכָל פֶּטֶר חֲמֹר תִּפְדֶּה בְשֶׂה וְאִם לֹא תִפְדֶּה וַעֲרַפְתּוֹ (יג:יג) Shemos (13:13) And every firstborn donkey you shall redeem with a lamb, and if you do not redeem it, you shall decapitate it

Why is the donkey the only non-kosher animal that needs to be redeemed?

Introduction
The Gemorah in Bechoros 11a says that if one has a firstborn donkey but does not have a lamb to redeem it with, one can redeem it with its value in money or by an item worth the value of the donkey. The Gemorah further says that the Torah told us to redeem a donkey with a lamb to make it easier for the owner. If one uses a lamb, one can use even a lamb of minimal worth to redeem even a donkey of great worth. The Shulchan Aruch in Yoreh Deah (321:5) Paskins like this Gemorah. The Ksav VeHakabola writes that had our Posuk written בְשֶׂה תִּפְדֶּה instead of תִּפְדֶּה בְשֶׂה then only a lamb could be used for the redemption and nothing else. Our Posuk when it writes תִּפְדֶּה בְשֶׂה, means to redeem it preferably with a lamb.

Shemos (12:5) speaking about the Korban Pesach says, שֶׂה תָמִים זָכָר בֶּן שָׁנָה יִהְיֶה לָכֶם מִן הַכְּבָשִׂים וּמִן הָעִזִּים תִּקָּחוּ (You shall have a perfect male lamb in its first year; you may take it either from the sheep or from the goats.). Similar to Korban Pesach, the שֶׂה (lamb) in our Posuk can be either a sheep or a goat, since both are called a שֶׂה (lamb).

The Midrash Lekach Tov says the firstborn donkey is decapitated if it is not redeemed is because by not redeeming his donkey with a lamb and giving the lamb to the Kohen, the owner caused the

Bo

Kohen to lose out on getting a lamb. As a measure for measure punishment of causing monetary damage to the Kohen, the owner loses the value of his donkey, especially since after the donkey is decapitated, no benefit is halachically allowed to be derived from the donkey.

Bamidbar (18:15) says, "Every first issue of the womb of any creature, which they (the Bnei Yisroel) present to Hashem, whether of man or beast, shall be yours (the Kohanim). However, you shall redeem the firstborn of man, and the firstborn of unclean animals you shall redeem." The Gemorah in Bechoros 4b presents a difference of opinion between Rav Yochanon and Resh Lakish about when the Halachos of redemption of the firstborn went into effect. Rav Yochanon is of the opinion that the Halachos of redemption of the firstborn went into effect while the Bnei Yisroel were in the desert since our Posuk was told to the Bnei Yisroel while they were still in Egypt, implying that from that point and forward, the Halachos were in effect. Resh Lakish is of the opinion that the Halachos of redemption of the firstborns was not applied in the desert since the Halachos of firstborn are introduced in Shemos (13:11) with "And it will come to pass when Hashem will bring you into the land of the Canaanites, as He swore to you and to your forefathers, and He has given it to you." Rav Yochanon is of the opinion that Shemos (13:11) talking about entering the land of Canaan is written to tell us that the reward of keeping the Mitzvah of redemption of the firstborn in the desert will be getting the land of the Canaanites. The Gemorah questions the opinion of Resh Lakish with a Mishnah in Zevachim 112b, which says that until the Mishkan was put up in the desert, one could offer Korbanos on Bomos (high places), and the firstborns offered the Korbanos. Therefore, we see that firstborns were sanctified in the desert. The Gemorah clarifies the opinion of Resh Lakish to mean that the Mishnah in Zevachim 112b is speaking about firstborns who were born in Egypt before the Halachos of our Posuk were given. Since they were born before the Halachos were given, the Halachos of redemption of firstborns did not apply to them. When the Mishkan was put up in the desert, Kohanim now offered Korbanos because the firstborns sinned when the Golden Calf was made. Given that the Mishkan was put up on Rosh Chodesh Nisan slightly less than a year after the Bnei Yisroel left Egypt, and that firstborns born after the Bnei Yisroel left Egypt would have been less than a year old, they would not have yet been capable or eligible to bring Korbanos.

The Meshech Chochmah is of the opinion that Rav Yochanon is correct and the Halachos of redeeming the firstborns applied immediately when the Bnei Yisroel left Egypt. Given that Kohanim were not designated until the Mishkan was put up, he ponders how they could redeem the firstborns before the Mishkan was put up and the Kohanim designated. Applied practically to the case of a donkey, what did one do with a lamb that one redeemed for a firstborn donkey? He says that since there were no Kohanim designated to receive the lamb, the owner redeemed the donkey for a lamb and then slaughtered and ate the lamb himself. He derives his opinion from the fourth Mishna in the first Perek of Bechoros. The Mishnah speaks of a case where two donkeys, one who had previous children and one who did not have previous children, gave birth. One of the donkeys gave birth to a male donkey and the other to a female donkey, and the baby donkeys got mixed up, so we don't know which gave birth to which. Since if the baby boy donkey was given birth to by the mother who had previous children, the boy donkey would not need to be redeemed; there is no proof that the owner has to redeem the boy donkey. On the other hand, it would need to be

Bo

redeemed if it was born to the donkey that didn't have previous children. In this case, the Mishna says the owner redeems the baby boy donkey with a lamb and can then slaughter and eat the lamb himself.

Parenthetically, the Ramban is of the opinion that we follow the opinion of Resh Lakish, which means that there never was a case of needing to redeem a firstborn before the Kohanim were designated. He points out that the firstborns leaving Egypt were sanctified, and later when the Mishkan was put up, they, along with any newly born firstborns, were redeemed for Leviyim in Bamidbar, chapter 3.

1) The Gemorah in Bechoros 5b and the Mechilta in Parshas Beshalach on Shemos (17:8) ponder our question. The Gemorah and Mechilta say that Rav Chanina related how he asked this very question to Rav Elazar in the great study hall. According to the Gemorah, Rav Elazar answered that it is a Gezayras HaKosuv (literally, a decree of the Posuk, meaning a decree of Hashem), while according to the Mechilta Rav Elazar answered that it is a Gezayras HaMelech (decree of the king (Hashem)). By definition, a Gezayras HaKosuv or a Gezayras HaMelech need not have a reason that we can comprehend. The classic case of a Gezayras HaKosuv or Gezayras HaMelech is Porah Adumah (the red heifer) in Bamidbar chapter 19. Rashi on Bamidbar (19:1), quoting the Midrash Tanchuma in Chukkas (8), says that Porah Adumah is a decree that Hashem decreed and therefore we have no right to challenge it.

2) Rashi on our Posuk quotes the Gemorah in Bechoros 5b that the fact a donkey is the only non-kosher animal that needs to be redeemed is a Gezayras HaKosuv. In addition to quoting the Gemorah, Rashi says that the reason for the decree is because the firstborn of the Egyptians are compared to donkeys. The Nachalas Yaakov explains that Rashi is giving this reason on his own as a logical way of explaining the reason for the decree, but that at its base, it is possible that we cannot fully comprehend its reason. The Maharsha on the Gemorah in Bechoros 5b is also perplexed as to why Rashi says it is a Gezayras HaKosuv and then says the reason for the decree is because the firstborn of the Egyptians are compared to donkeys. The Maharsha explains that Rashi is saying it is a Gezayras HaKosuv and without a logical humanly understandable reason that firstborn non-kosher animals should have the sanctity of being termed firstborns. Once non-kosher animals have this distinction, there is a reason why donkeys were chosen for this special distinction, and that is because the firstborn of the Egyptians are compared to donkeys.

The Midrash Lekach Tov, Rabeinu Bechay, and Mizrachi explain that Egyptians are compared to donkeys in Sefer Yechezkel (23:19-20) which says, "And she increased her harlotries, to remember the days of her youth, when she played the harlot in the land of Egypt. And she lusted for their concubines, those whose flesh is the flesh of donkeys, and whose issue is the issue of horses." The Maskil LeDovid explains why Rashi had to preface his reason by saying that it is a Gezayras HaKosuv. Had Rashi's reason been the complete reason, we would be perplexed by the fact that Rashi emphasizes the fact that the Posuk in Yechezkel compares the Egyptians to donkeys while ignoring the fact that the same Posuk also compares them to horses. According to Rashi's reason, we would then be left bereft of an explanation as to why a firstborn horse does not need to be

Bo

redeemed. In Beraishis (22:5), at the Akeidah, Avrohom tells his two servants (Eliezer and Yishmael), "Stay here with the donkey, and I and the lad will go yonder, and we will prostrate ourselves and return to you." The Yalkut Shimoni in Beraishis 99 says that on this day, Avrohom saw a cloud wrapping around the mountain ahead of them and surmised that this must be the mountain Hashem had told them to go to and do the Akeidah. Avrohom then asked Yitzchak if he saw anything, and he told Avrohom that he also saw this cloud. Avrohom next asked his two servants if they saw anything, and they said that they didn't see anything. The Yalkut says that this prompted Avrohom to tell his servants to remain with the donkey since neither you nor the donkey sees anything. Chazal derive from this Posuk that there are certain Halachos where Gentiles and especially Gentile servants have a similar Halacha to a donkey. However, both this Midrash and the Gemoros compare all Gentiles and not just Egyptians to donkeys, so it is not proof to Rashi's statement that Egyptians are compared to donkeys.

3) The Gemorah in Bechoros 5b and the Mechilta in Parshas Beshalach on Shemos (17:8) also present a second reason as to why donkeys are the only non-kosher animal to require redemption. They say that donkeys helped the Bnei Yisroel when they went out of Egypt since there was not one Yisroel who did not take 90 donkeys (the Gemorah says that these donkeys were the best donkeys which could carry more than an average donkey) laden with the gold and silver of Egypt. Making the donkey special and requiring the donkey to be redeemed is a reward for its exemplary behavior. Rashi also quotes this reason. The Maskil LeDovid says the reason Rashi did not present this reason as the simple explanation of why the donkey is unique in this Mitzvah is because the Torah tells us that "if you do not redeem it, you shall decapitate it." Decapitating the donkey does not seem to be fitting as part of a reward for helping the Bnei Yisroel carry their burdens when they went out of Egypt. Therefore, Rashi also presents the reason we have quoted in the previous answer.

The Bechor Shor says that since both kosher and non-kosher firstborn animals were killed at the time of the plague of the firstborn, it was necessary to commemorate this by requiring non-kosher animals to be redeemed. Otherwise, we would think that non-kosher animals were not affected by the plague. On the other hand, non-kosher animals are disgusting, and requiring them to be redeemed would not be appetizing. Therefore, Hashem chose only one non-kosher animal to need redemption. Hashem specifically chose the donkey since they were so instrumental in helping us carry our burdens when we left Egypt.

The Ben Yehoyoda on this Gemorah ponders the significance of the number 90, as in the number of donkeys that carried out the riches from Egypt. The Ben Yehoyoda says that the Gematria (numerical value) of the Hebrew word for water (מַיִם) is also 90. The number 90 signifies the victory over the Egyptians who wanted to destroy the Bnei Yisroel by throwing their firstborn babies into the water. The Eyun Yaakov presents another reason for the significance of the number 90. Hashem told Avrohom in the Bris Bain HaBesorim (Beraishis (15:13) that the Bnei Yisroel would be enslaved and afflicted in a strange land. Hashem also promised in Beraishis (15:14) "afterwards they (Bnei Yisroel) will leave the land with a great amount of riches." The Gemorah in Brochos says the reason Hashem commanded the Bnei Yisroel to borrow so much gold and silver from the Egyptians was so the Tzadik Avrohom should not be able to say that Hashem fulfilled the

Bo

promise of enslaving and afflicting the Bnei Yisroel and not the promise of leaving with great riches. Without this commandment, the Bnei Yisroel would have been very happy to just finally leave Egypt. The Anaf Yosef says that at the splitting of the Red Sea, the Bnei Yisroel got even more riches than when they left Egypt. The great riches at the Red Sea would have fulfilled Hashem's promise of leaving Egypt with great riches; however, Hashem, as an extra measure, wanted Avrohom to see the promise fulfilled immediately on stepping outside of the land of Egypt. The Eyun Yaakov says that since the riches now were for Avrohom, who is termed the Tzadik in this Gemorah, the 90 donkeys represented the numerical value of the letter Tzadik.

The Ben Yehoyoda ponders the fact that if each of the 600,000 grown men who left Egypt went out with 90 donkeys, the total amount of donkeys would be 54 million donkeys, an astronomical number that is difficult to believe at face value. The Ben Yehoyoda says the Gemorah does not mean that each person physically had 90 donkeys, but rather the value of all the riches which the Bnei Yisroel carried out was that of a load of 90 donkeys. This meant that they took out much precious gold and silver to be worth this much. Alternatively, only the head of every family went out with 90 donkeys, reducing greatly the total amount of donkeys that went out of Egypt. In his notes on this Gemorah, Rav Yaakov Emden answers similarly that only every head of family or very important person went out with 90 donkeys. The Eyun Yaakov says that it is interesting to note that when Rashi in Chumash quotes this reason, Rashi says that everyone had many donkeys without explicitly saying 90 as the Gemorah says.

Rav Simcha Zissel, in his Sefer Ohr Rav Simcha Zissel, observes the fact that donkeys are rewarded for helping the Bnei Yisroel fulfill the Mitzvah detailed in Shemos (11:2) "Please, speak into the ears of the people, and let them borrow, each man from his friend and each woman from her friend, silver vessels and golden vessels." If donkeys, who have no free will or intention to help the Bnei Yisroel, fulfill a Mitzvah and are rewarded, how much more so is a person with free will rewarded for helping someone else do a Mitzvah.

4) The Sforno also presents an answer to our question. He points out that the Posuk following ours says וְהָיָה כִּי יִשְׁאָלְךָ בִנְךָ מָחָר לֵאמֹר מַה זֹּאת וְאָמַרְתָּ אֵלָיו בְּחֹזֶק יָד הוֹצִיאָנוּ ה' מִמִּצְרַיִם מִבֵּית עֲבָדִים (And it will come to pass if your son asks you in the future, saying, "What is this?" you shall say to him, "With a mighty hand did Hashem take us out of Egypt, out of the house of bondage."). In the Hagadah, this is known as the question of the simple son. The Sforno says the question being asked here is why a non-kosher animal, which can never be made holy by itself or by being brought as a sacrifice, needs to be redeemed. Moreover, the simple son is asking why it must be decapitated if it is not redeemed. The answer is that the mighty hand of Hashem caused the Egyptians to exert great pressure on the Bnei Yisroel to leave. Because of this pressure, we did not have time to obtain and use wagons to carry our possessions out of Egypt but instead had to use donkeys which miraculously, in an extremely short amount of time, were able to fit and carry all these possessions. This answers the question of why the donkey needs to be redeemed since the donkey commemorates what happened when we left Egypt.

Bo

The Sforno says the next Posuk answers the question of why the donkey must be decapitated if it is not redeemed. It says, וַיְהִי כִּי הִקְשָׁה פַרְעֹה לְשַׁלְּחֵנוּ וַיַּהֲרֹג ה' כָּל בְּכוֹר בְּאֶרֶץ מִצְרָיִם (And it came to pass when Pharaoh was too stubborn to let us out, Hashem slew every firstborn in the land of Egypt). We have explained previously that the Egyptians, and especially their leader Pharaoh, are compared to a donkey. The Bnei Yisroel are compared to a lamb as Sefer Yirmiyahu (50:17) says, שֶׂה פְזוּרָה יִשְׂרָאֵל אֲרָיוֹת הִדִּיחוּ (Yisroel is a scattered lamb, the lions (other nations) have driven him (Yisroel) away). Pharaoh could have redeemed himself and his nation by allowing the Bnei Yisroel to leave Egypt. He (Pharaoh, the donkey) chose not to allow the lamb (Bnei Yisroel) to be redeemed, and therefore Pharaoh was decapitated by having his head (firstborn) killed. That is why the donkey must be decapitated if he is not redeemed.

Parenthetically, the Sforno says the Bnei Yisroel firstborns were also fit to die when the firstborns of the Egyptians were killed. When the angels come to Sodom to save Lot, they say to him in Beraishis (19:15), "Get up, take your wife and your two daughters who are here, lest you perish because of the sins of the city." On Shemos (12:13), he explains that, in essence, the plague of the killing of the firstborn contained two major components. Hashem himself did the actual killing of the firstborn as it says in Shemos (12:12), which is also quoted in the Hagadah, "I will pass through the land of Egypt on this night, and I will smite every firstborn in the land of Egypt, both man and beast, and upon all the gods of Egypt will I wreak judgments I, Hashem." Since Hashem did this part himself, it was not necessary for the Bnei Yisroel to put blood on their doorposts from the Korban Pesach since Hashem knows all and does not need the blood as a sign. The next Posuk describes why the blood was needed when it says, "And the blood will be for you for a sign upon the houses where you will be, and I will see the blood and skip over you, and there will be no plague against you for the destroying angel when I smite the people of the land of Egypt." For this second part of the plague, without the blood, the Bnei Yisroel would have also been affected by the destroying angel like Lot, had he not left, would have been affected when the destroying angel was destroying Sodom. As the Gemorah in Baba Kama 60a writes in explaining why Shemos (12:22) says, "you shall not go out, any man from the entrance of his house until morning," once the angel of destruction has been given the authority to damage it will not distinguish between the righteous and the wicked. In such a situation, the only ones who are not affected by the destroying angel are the totally righteous people, which the vast majority of the Bnei Yisroel were not. On our Posuk, the Sforno says that the firstborn Jews were in an even more precarious situation, being that the plague directly affected the Egyptian firstborns. The rest of the Bnei Yisroel and even the blood on their doorposts would not have fully protected them from the destroying angel. The same argument caused the firstborn animals to also be in a similarly precarious situation. To combat this, Hashem designated the Jewish firstborns and also the firstborn animals as holy. Now that they were holy, they would not be affected by the destroying angel, similar to how the angel does not affect totally righteous people. According to the Sforno, this explains why the Torah at this point discusses how to redeem firstborn people, kosher animals, and the non-kosher donkey.

5) The Bechor Shor also ponders our question. He says donkeys were chosen to be redeemed since they were instrumental, right at the beginning of the redemption, when they helped Moshe travel to Egypt. Shemos (4:20) says, "So Moshe took his wife and his sons, mounted them upon the donkey,

Bo

and he returned to the land of Egypt, and Moshe took the staff of G-d in his hand." Making the donkey special and requiring the donkey to be redeemed is a reward for its exemplary behavior in taking Moshe and his family to Egypt.

6) The Midrash Lekach Tov, Chinuch, and Abarbanel answer our question similarly. As we have explained previously, they are of the opinion that the Egyptians are compared to a donkey. They say that the reason for decapitating the donkey is to commemorate Hashem's killing of the firstborn Egyptians. The Midrash Lekach Tov says that the Hebrew word for donkey חֲמוֹר is written in our Posuk חֲמֹר (missing the Hebrew letter Vav). This is because the numerical value of the way donkey is written in our Posuk is 248, which is the number of limbs in a human body. This signifies that the donkey in our Posuk is commemorating a human body. The Oznayim LeTorah explains that really all firstborn donkeys should have been decapitated for this commemoration. However, Hashem is concerned about the loss of money that would be incurred by the Bnei Yisroel if all the firstborn donkeys were decapitated. Therefore, Hashem allowed the firstborn donkeys to be redeemed with a lamb. As we have explained in the introduction, the lamb was typically worth a lot less than the donkey it was redeemed for. If the owner chooses not to redeem it and is ostensibly not concerned for his money, then the default action is performed that of decapitating it to commemorate the firstborn Egyptians being killed.

7) The Meshech Chochmah also ponders our question. He says that donkeys were used when Yosef's brothers first went down to Egypt to get food and are mentioned many times when the brothers come down to Yosef. For example, Beraishis (42:26) says, "And they (the brothers) loaded their grain upon their donkeys, and they went away from there (Egypt). Beraishis (43:18) says, "On account of the money that came back in our sacks at first, we are brought, to roll upon us and to fall upon us and to take us as slaves and our donkeys as well." Beraishis (44:3) says, "The morning became light, and the men were sent on their way they and their donkeys." By designating firstborn donkeys, as well as firstborn people and firstborn kosher animals as intrinsically holy and needing redemption, Hashem showed that the Bnei Yisroel were intrinsically holy and were under divine supervision of all their activities during the entire exile in Egypt. The intrinsic holiness was granted to the Bnei Yisroel because of the merits of our forefathers. Even the first details, the donkeys the brothers brought with them to Egypt, were divinely orchestrated for a reason.

8) Rav Hirsch also presents an answer to our question. Beraishis (49:11) speaks about Moshiach and says, "He binds his donkey to a vine, and to a vine branch he binds his young donkey." He ponders why Moshiach will ride on a donkey as opposed to a horse, which is the more typical animal used for riding. He says a donkey is an animal of peace since it carries its rider at a leisurely pace and bears the rider's packs and baggage for him. A horse runs quickly and is used to represent military might. This idea also explains the description of Moshiach's coming in Zechariah (9:9) "Be exceedingly happy, O daughter of Tzion; Shout, O daughter of Yerushalayim. Behold! Your king shall come to you. He is just and victorious; humble, and riding a donkey and a young donkey, the offspring of she-donkeys." Parenthetically, he explains the reason the Posuk in Zechariah adds the phrase "the offspring of she-donkeys" is to point out that the donkey Moshiach is riding comes from a large collection of donkeys which Moshiach has since his stables are filled with donkeys and not

Bo

horses. The specific items the Torah designates as needing redemption were chosen to show that our bodies (redemption of our children), our food (Kosher animals), and our possessions (donkeys) all belong to Hashem. There is a Mitzvah detailed at the beginning of Parshas Ki Sovo called Bekurim, which obligates one to bring the first fruits which are harvested to Hashem. After toiling many days and hours in the field to grow his crops, a farmer has a strong desire to finally taste the first fruits of his labors; he must instead bring them to Hashem to show that the field and the crops which grow on it belong to Hashem. In a similar way by redeeming the firstborn children, food, and possessions show that they all belong to Hashem. The Halacha of decapitating a donkey that has not been redeemed shows that if one wants to be self-centered and not acknowledge that his possession comes from Hashem, he has sentenced himself to the destruction of his property.

Why Is Tefillin Put on the Weaker Arm?

Shemos (13:16) וְהָיָה לְאוֹת עַל יָדְכָה וּלְטוֹטָפֹת בֵּין עֵינֶיךָ כִּי בְּחֹזֶק יָד הוֹצִיאָנוּ ה' מִמִּצְרָיִם (יג:טז) And it shall be for a sign upon your hand and for ornaments between your eyes, for with a mighty hand did Hashem take us out of Egypt.

Why is Tefillin put on the weaker arm?

Introduction
The Gemorah in Menochos 37a cites several opinions as to how we know that Tefillin must be put on the weaker arm. Rav Ashi's opinion is that it is derived from the unusual spelling of the Hebrew word "your hand" which is spelled as יָדְכָה instead of the typical way of יָדְךָ as it is spelled in Shemos (13:9). The reason for the unusual spelling of יָדְכָה is to allude to the fact that Tefillin must be put on יד כהה (weaker hand). יָדְכָה is a contraction of the two words יד כהה being that the last ה of the word כהה is silent.

The Gemorah in Menochos 36b-37a also presents the opinion of the Rabonon who say that whenever the Tanach says the Hebrew word hand (יָד) without specifying which hand, it refers to the left hand. For example, Sefer Shoftim (5:26) says, יָדָהּ לַיָּתֵד תִּשְׁלַחְנָה וִימִינָהּ לְהַלְמוּת עֲמֵלִים (She (Yoel) put forth her hand to the pin, and her right hand to strike the weary (Sisra)). Similarly. Tehillim (74:11) says, לָמָּה תָשִׁיב יָדְךָ וִימִינֶךָ מִקֶּרֶב חֵיקְךָ כַלֵּה (Why do You withdraw Your hand, even Your right hand? Draw it out from within Your bosom). In both these Pesukim, mentioning the right hand after mentioning the word hand without any adjective of right or left implies that the first mention of hand without any adjective is the left hand. Beraishis (48:17) says, וַיַּרְא יוֹסֵף כִּי יָשִׁית אָבִיו יַד יְמִינוֹ עַל רֹאשׁ אֶפְרַיִם וַיֵּרַע בְּעֵינָיו (And Yosef saw that his father (Yaakov) was placing his right hand on Ephraim's head, and it displeased him). In this Posuk, it must say right hand instead of just hand, since if the Torah had just said hand, it would be referring to his left hand. The Chizkuni on our Posuk says that this rule, mentioning hand without an adjective of right or left means that it is the left hand, is true in most cases but not in all cases.

In addition, the Gemorah in Menochos 37a presents the opinion of Rav Noson. He quotes two Pesukim in Kriyas Shema, which are juxtaposed together. Devorim (6:8-9) say, וּקְשַׁרְתָּם לְאוֹת עַל יָדֶךָ

Bo

וְהָיוּ לְטֹטָפֹת בֵּין עֵינֶיךָ. וּכְתַבְתָּם עַל מְזֻזוֹת בֵּיתֶךָ וּבִשְׁעָרֶיךָ. (And you shall bind them (Tefillin) for a sign upon your hand, and they shall be for ornaments between your eyes. And you shall write them (Mezuzah) upon the doorposts of your house and upon your gates.). Rav Noson says that similar to Mezuzah, which is written by most people with the right hand (if they are right-handed), Tefillin should also be bound with the right hand (if one is right-handed). One can only bind one's Tefillin using the right hand if one binds them on his left arm.

The Ohr HaChaim points out that at first glance, it would seem more appropriate to put Tefillin on our right arm since it is the more powerful and important arm.

Rabeinu Bechay presents what he calls the simple explanation for the unusual spelling of יָדְכָה in our Posuk. The numerical value (Gematria) of the extra Hebrew letter "Heh" is five. "Heh" informs us that there are five compartments where the written sections of the Torah are placed in the Tefillin. There are four sections of the Torah placed in the Tefillin: (1) the section called קַדֵּשׁ (Shemos (13:1-10), (2) the section called וְהָיָה כִּי יְבִאֲךָ (Shemos (13:11-16), (3) the first paragraph of Kriyas Shema, and (4) the second paragraph of Kriyas Shema. The Tefillin put on the head contains four compartments, one for each of these four Torah sections, while the Tefillin put on the arm contains one compartment where all four Torah sections written on one piece of parchment is placed.

Our Posuk says that the reason for wearing Tefillin is because Hashem took us out of Egypt with a mighty hand. The Chizkuni says that this is the reason we wear the hand Tefillin. He says that the reason we wear Tefillin on our heads is a remembrance of the signs and wonders Hashem performed when Hashem took us out of Egypt.

A left-handed person wears his hand Tefillin on his right (weaker) arm. We will see below that some of the answers are not consistent with a left-handed person wearing Tefillin on his right (weaker) arm. According to these answers, we are forced to say that the Torah made the general rule for a person to wear Tefillin on their weaker hand since for the majority of people who are right-handed, the reason for wearing hand Tefillin on the left hand applies. We note that in previous generations, the vast majority of children tending to be left-handed were trained to become right-handed, and therefore the vast majority of the people were right-handed.

1) The Ramban and Ralbag present an answer to our question. By putting the hand Tefillin on our left arm, we place it opposite our heart on the left side of our bodies. We find many times that the heart is called the seat of wisdom and thoughts. For example, Shemos (35:10) says, וְכָל חֲכַם לֵב בָּכֶם (And every wise-hearted man among you). We mention in davening every day Mishlay (19:21) which says, רַבּוֹת מַחֲשָׁבוֹת בְּלֶב אִישׁ (There are many thoughts in a man's heart). Similarly, Beraishis (6:5) says, וְכָל יֵצֶר מַחְשְׁבֹת לִבּוֹ רַק רַע כָּל הַיּוֹם (and every product of the thoughts of his heart was only evil all the time). When Shlomo asks Hashem for wisdom, Sefer Melachim I (3:9) says, "Give Your servant an understanding heart to judge Your people, that I may discern between good and bad; for who is able to judge this Your great people?" We put these sections of the Torah, which speak about Hashem taking us out of Egypt on our heads, the part of the body which contains our memory and thoughts, and opposite our hearts, which contains our wisdom and thoughts. Thereby, we are

Bo

always to remember and think about the fact that Hashem redeemed us from Egypt. The Ramban takes this concept a step further since if we remember that Hashem took us out of Egypt, then we are forced to acknowledge and remember that Hashem is our master. Once we realize Hashem is our master, we will do his positive Mitzvos and watch ourselves from doing his negative Mitzvos.

In the second paragraph of Kriyas Shema, we mention Devorim (11:18) which says, וְשַׂמְתֶּם אֶת דְּבָרַי אֵלֶּה עַל לְבַבְכֶם וְעַל נַפְשְׁכֶם וּקְשַׁרְתֶּם אֹתָם לְאוֹת עַל יֶדְכֶם וְהָיוּ לְטוֹטָפֹת בֵּין עֵינֵיכֶם (And you shall set these words of Mine upon your heart and upon your soul, and bind them for a sign upon your hand and they shall be for ornaments between your eyes.). The Gemorah in Brochos 13b quotes Rav Yitzchak, who derives from this Posuk that the hand Tefillin must be placed opposite the heart. We can imply from here, similar to what the Ramban and Ralbag say, that the requirement for putting Tefillin on the left arm is to facilitate the Tefillin being opposite the heart.

Tefillin are always to remember and think about the fact that Hashem redeemed us from Egypt. The Nitziv says that when a person tells his son a major concept that he wants the son to keep, the father first tells his son in great detail about the concept, and then every day, the father briefly mentions the concept as a reminder. Similarly, on Pesach, we delve into great depth about how Hashem took us out of Egypt, and putting on Tefillin is the brief daily reminder of Hashem taking us out of Egypt.

The only problem with the Ramban and Ralbag's answer is that it does not address why a left-handed person puts the Tefillin on his right arm, which is obviously not opposite his heart. We have dealt with this issue in the introduction. We note that in the LeShem Yichud prayer said before putting on Tefillin, both right- and left-handed people say: "Hashem has commanded us to put Tefillin on the arm to recall the outstretched arm of the Egyptian redemption and that it be opposite the heart thereby to subjugate the desires and thoughts of our heart to Hashem's service." Even though a left-handed person does not put the hand Tefillin on opposite the heart, he says this prayer.

We have previously said that the Ramban writes that Tefillin remind us that Hashem is our master. Once we realize Hashem is our master, we will do his positive Mitzvos and watch ourselves from doing his negative Mitzvos. The Shulchan Aruch, Orach Chaim (38:11) Paskins that it is forbidden to take off one's Tefillin in front of his Rebbe. Rather one should turn to one's side and in this manner not take the Tefillin off in front of his Rebbe. We note that the Mishnah Berurah says that his Rebbe, in this case, is referring to a Rebbe from whom one has learned the majority of his Torah knowledge. Rav Simcha Zissel, in his Sefer Ohr Rav Simcha Zissel, says that for a long time, he had not known the reason for this Din (law). He writes that he saw in Rav Yaakov Emden's siddur that one should not even take off one's Tefillin in front of Seforim. He finally found out the reason when he obtained a Vilna Gaon Siddur. The Vilna Gaon says that one should not take off one's Tefillin in a shul or a Beis HaMidrash, so it should not appear that one is doing away with the fear of Hashem; in His own "house." Preferably, one should go to one's house and take off one's Tefillin there. Failing that, one should not take off one's Tefillin in front of the Holy Ark in the shul or Beis Midrash. Wearing Tefillin is akin to accepting the yoke of heaven and the doing of all of Hashem's Mitzvos. Taking off one's Tefillin in front of one's Rebbe would be an affront to his Rebbe from whom he has learned so much of Hashem's Mitzvos. Parenthetically, we should

Bo

mention that some people do put on and take off their Tefillin either at home or in a room adjoining the shul.

2) The Chizkuni and Ralbag answer our question similarly. They say that the Mitzvah of Tefillin is to bind the arm. Therefore, the right arm, which is the more important arm, performs the Mitzvah by binding the left arm. We find the right hand is in general used to perform Mitzvos. Shulchan Aruch, Orach Chaim (206:4) says that any item which one wants to make a Brocha on to eat or smell should be held in the person's right hand when the person is saying the Brocha. This answer answers the question of why a left-handed person puts his hand Tefillin on his right (weaker) arm.

3) The Chizkuni and Shach present another answer to our question. For a right-handed person, the right hand is typically used to reach, feel, and grab all sorts of things, and therefore, it is used much more often than the left hand. Because the right hand is used to help one satisfy all one's physical desires, it is not appropriate that Hashem's name mentioned many times in the paragraphs of the Tefillin should rest on the right arm. This answer answers the question of why a left-handed person puts his hand Tefillin on his right (weaker) arm.

4) The Ohr HaChaim also ponders our question. He says that Hashem's hand is sometimes referred to as a mighty hand, as in our Posuk, or as a great hand as Shemos (14:31) says, וַיַּרְא יִשְׂרָאֵל אֶת הַיָּד הַגְּדֹלָה (And Yisroel saw the great hand). The great hand of Hashem is used for kindness and good (the right hand), while the mighty hand (the left hand) is used to punish those who do evil. Since, in general, taking us out of Egypt was done with the mighty hand (left hand), we are to remember this left hand by putting Tefillin on it. This answer does not answer the question of why a left-handed person puts his hand Tefillin on his right (weaker) arm.

5) The Kli Yakor also presents an answer to our question. He says that physicality acts against the attainment of spirituality and understanding and vice versa. The Gemorah in Baba Metzia 87a says that until Avrohom's time, there was no such thing as growing old. Avrohom davened that people should grow old, and starting from him; people grew old. The Maharal, in his explanation of the Gemorah in Baba Metzia 87a, and the Nisivos, in Nachalas Yaakov, similarly explain the reason for the change that Avrohom davened for. From the time a person is born, his Neshama can grow and become more powerful by doing Mitzvos and good deeds. As we grow older, our physical capabilities become weaker. However, with regard to knowledge capabilities, the last Mishna in Meseches Kinim says that people unlearned in Torah, the older they get, the less capable their knowledge capability gets. However, for those learned in Torah, the older they get, the more their knowledge becomes keener. They explain that the weaker the physical body gets, the more ability the spiritual Neshama has to grow stronger. Since the Kli Yakor was the Maharal's handpicked successor when the Maharal was approaching one hundred years of age and could no longer lead the city of Prague, it is not at all surprising that he uses this same concept as the Maharal. The Kli Yakor also says that one of the reasons for the slavery in Egypt was so our physical bodies' power would be diminished, thereby enabling us to obtain greater spirituality and understanding.

Bo

The Kli Yakor says that one's weaker hand is the left, and therefore it is situated next to the heart, which contains the seat of understanding. One's physically strong right hand is the seat of physical strength. That being the case, the appropriate place for Tefillin is on the left side, which is the side of spirituality and understanding appropriate for the service of Hashem. The Kli Yakor doesn't explain this, but at first blush, this concept may seem in contradiction to what we explained in the introduction that we find the right hand is in general used to perform Mitzvos. For example, we have previously mentioned that Shulchan Aruch, Orach Chaim (206:4) says that any item which one wants to make a Brocha on to eat or smell should be held in the person's right hand when the person is saying the Brocha. It would seem that the reason for using the right hand is that we want to train it to take physical things like eating and smelling and by making a Brocha on them transform them into a spiritual thing. Putting on Tefillin is not a physical thing but rather a spiritual thing, and that is why, according to the Kli Yakor, we identify it with the left hand. This answer does not answer the question of why a left-handed person puts his hand Tefillin on his right (weaker) arm.

6) The Kli Yakor also presents another answer to our question. A person must remember that it is not through his own physical strength that a person is victorious, but rather it is due to Hashem. Devorim (8:17) says that a person may mistakenly say: "My strength and the might of my hand has accumulated this wealth for me." Rather says the next Posuk, "But you must remember Hashem your G-d, for it is He that gives you strength to make wealth, in order to establish His covenant which He swore to your forefathers, as it is this day." The Kli Yakor says that this is what Dovid HaMelech means in Tehillim (16:8-9) which says, שִׁוִּיתִי ה' לְנֶגְדִּי תָמִיד כִּי מִימִינִי בַּל אֶמּוֹט. לָכֵן שָׂמַח לִבִּי וַיָּגֶל כְּבוֹדִי אַף בְּשָׂרִי יִשְׁכֹּן לָבֶטַח. (I have placed Hashem before me constantly; because He is at my right hand, I will not falter. Therefore, my heart rejoiced, and my soul was glad; even my flesh shall dwell in safety.). He explains that Dovid HaMelech was troubled by the fact that the heart is on the left side of the body, and the liver is on the right side of the body. He also explains that the liver is the seat of one's physical desires. Therefore, Dovid thought that the liver (physical desires) on the dominant right side of the body was more important than the heart (wisdom and thoughts) on the left subservient side of the body. Dovid soon realized that he hadn't considered our need to constantly remember that Hashem is opposite us. That being the case, Hashem's right hand is opposite our left, and Hashem's left hand is opposite our right. Since our liver, even though it is on our dominant side, faces Hashem, we need not fear that we will not be able to control it since Hashem will help us. That is why Dovid concludes, "because He is at my right hand, I will not falter. Therefore, my heart rejoiced, and my soul was glad; even my flesh shall dwell in safety."

The Kli Yakor says that if we place Hashem before us constantly, our left side will be the more dominant side since it will reflect the fact that Hashem's right side is opposite it, meaning that it is dominant. Tefillin, on the left hand, will remind us that no actions or results are obtained by a person's own actions without Hashem's help making the action happen. This answer does not answer the question of why a left-handed person puts his hand Tefillin on his right (weaker) arm.

7) The Mor Dror, as quoted by the Meorah Shel Torah, also presents an answer to our question. When Hashem was redeeming us from Egypt, Pharaoh stubbornly refused to let the Bnei Yisroel leave Egypt, even for just a period of three days, and he did everything he could to fight Hashem's

will. Instead of the arrogance of Pharaoh, we must act with humility. By putting Tefillin on our weaker hand, we emphasize that we must act this way with respect to Hashem. This answer does answer the question of why a left-handed person puts his hand Tefillin on his right (weaker) arm.

8) The Nitziv also ponders our question. In the third paragraph of Kriyas Shema, Bamidbar (15:39) says, וְהָיָה לָכֶם לְצִיצִת וּרְאִיתֶם אֹתוֹ וּזְכַרְתֶּם אֶת כָּל מִצְוֹת ה' וַעֲשִׂיתֶם אֹתָם וְלֹא תָתוּרוּ אַחֲרֵי לְבַבְכֶם וְאַחֲרֵי עֵינֵיכֶם אֲשֶׁר אַתֶּם זֹנִים אַחֲרֵיהֶם (This shall be Tzitzis for you, and when you see it, you will remember all the commandments of Hashem to perform them, and you shall not wander after your hearts and after your eyes after which you are going astray.). The eyes and the heart are the two things that lead a person astray since the eye sees something physical which the heart desires. The two boxes of Tefillin, says the Nitziv, correspond to the two Torahs, the Written Torah and the Oral Torah, which are our spiritual armor to protect us. The Written Torah corresponds to the head Tefillin which is visible for everyone to see since this Torah is written and visible to all.

The Gemorah in Menochos 35b says that when Devorim (28:10) says, וְרָאוּ כָּל עַמֵּי הָאָרֶץ כִּי שֵׁם ה' נִקְרָא עָלֶיךָ וְיָרְאוּ מִמֶּךָ (Then all the peoples of the earth will see that the name of Hashem is called upon you, and they will fear you.) it refers to the head Tefillin which the eye of other people see when one is wearing it. Therefore, the head Tefillin protects us from what our eyes see. The Oral Torah corresponds to the hand Tefillin, which is worn opposite the heart. The Oral Torah originally was transmitted "by heart" without it being written down, and therefore the hand Tefillin corresponds to protecting us from the desires of the heart. Consequently, the hand Tefillin must be put on the weaker hand so that it will be next to the heart and protect us from the heart's desires leading us astray. The Ksav VeHakabola also answers similarly to the Nitziv. This answer does not answer the question of why a left-handed person puts his hand Tefillin on his right (weaker) arm.

Made in the USA
Columbia, SC
25 November 2024

62fe6574-5f08-42d6-b687-007f8a8372ecR01